English Learner's Guide
to
Homophones
and
Heteronyms

homophone /ˈhoʊmᵊfoʊn/
n : Words are homophones if they are pronounced the same but differ in spelling and meaning; e.g., "*Ewes use yews* for shade."

heteronym /ˈhɛtᵊɹoʊnɪm/
n : Words are heteronyms if they are spelled the same but differ in pronunciation; e.g., *bow*.

Compiled by S. J. Lieberman

ISBN: 978-1-79482-396-9

CONTENTS

INTRODUCTION

*This book is **not** a linguistically perfect pronunciation reference.* Its purpose is a guide for speakers whose first language is not American English. International Pronunciation Alphabet (IPA) pronunciations herein represent what they **most likely** will hear informally spoken by native English speakers in the United States; many of these are judgment calls. Regional mannerisms as spoken in New England (/pɑk//ðə//kɑ/ for *Park the car.*), the New York City area (/ʤit//ʤɛt/ for *Did you eat yet?*) and southern states (/hɑ//ˈðɛɪə/ for *Hi there!*) are not included here.

Spelling and pronunciation are difficult for English learners because the language does not have a reasonably consistent letter-pronunciation relationship as enjoyed by many other languages. The language transition from Middle English to Modern English was generally accomplished during the 15th century. Word contributions from many other languages (German, Latin, French, Nordic, etc.) resulted in many spelling and pronunciation variations. Consequently, there are several ways to write similar sounds. Furthermore, there are sounds that are linguistically different, yet non-native speakers cannot differentiate among them; hence, this is the reason there are so many homophones. This book contains over 2,500 words in more than 1,100 groups. Granted, some of them are archaic and others are not commonly used; they are included if they appear in a major abridged dictionary. But for a few exceptions, proper names of people and places are not included.

The definitions include many synonyms to show various meanings for the words. This is useful to provide language variation and subtlety.

Different forms of the same verbs and nouns are not listed unless there is another word in the group that sounds like the variations. For example, *altar, alter* are listed, but not *altars, alters*. However, *waive, wave* and *waiver, waver* are listed because the former pair are verbs and the latter are nouns. Words of repetition such as *resew, resow* are also excluded because *sew, sow* are defined elsewhere. However, *recede, reseed* appear because *recede* is not a repeated version of *cede,* which is a homophone of *seed.* Negated words are also excluded if their meanings are mere opposites of the positive homophones (*unreal* and *unreel*). Another example is *C, sea, see* and *C's, seas, sees, seize*; although the first three words in each group are different forms of the same corresponding words, the second group contains the unrelated word *seize.*

Spelling variations are not considered to be homophones when they have the same meaning (*tatoo, tattoo* and *socks, sox*).

Words that sound clearly different to native English speakers, but not to non-native speakers, are near homophones. (Sometimes even native speakers can't tell the difference.) These words are shown italicized such as *finally, finely* (the former has three syllables and the latter has two); each word is displayed with has its own IPA pronunciation. For non-native speakers, these **are** true homophones. To appreciate this difficulty, many native English speakers cannot differentiate between the Spanish *r* and *rr: pero* (but) and *perro* (dog); *ahora* (now) and *ahorra* (save). These two examples are near homophones to native Spanish speakers, but homophones to many Spanish learners.

Words that sound exactly the same (or so similarly that even many native English speakers cannot tell the difference) are considered true homophones in this book. These are shown with a common IPA pronunciation such as **ewe, yew, you** /ju/.

Word pronunciation differences that are clear to native English speakers, but may sound the same to non-native speakers, are considered *almost* homophones. These word groups are *italisized* . Each word within these groups is shown with its own IPA pronunciation.

Word groups that include *wh* words (e.g., *watt, what*) are included as true homophones because many non-native English speakers cannot hear the difference, even when the soft /h/ sound that starts the *wh* word is exaggerated. Therefore, these are included as true homophones. In fact, some current dictionaries use /w/ as an alternate pronunciation for /hw/ because of regional variations in the U.S.A.

Heteronyms are included because, for all intents and purposes, many of them may as well be near homophones to non-native English speakers.

You will also find many homographs within the definitions. These are words with different meanings but are spelled and pronounced identically; e.g., *bear* and *fair*.

Definitions herein were derived from several sources including the lexical reference system developed by the Cognitive Science Laboratory at Princeton University. The purpose is twofold: to produce a combination of dictionary and thesaurus that is more intuitively usable. As a result, many synonyms are provided for most definitions.

PARTS OF SPEECH

These abbreviated terms are used herein to identify the part of speech for each word.

1st pers plu	first person plural
2nd pers sing	second person singular
3rd pers sing	third person singular
abbr	abbreviation
adj	adjective
adv	adverb
alt	alternate
ant	antonym
compar	comparative
conj	conjunction
contr	contraction
interj	interjection
n	noun
past part	past participle
plu	plural
prep	preposition
pron	pronoun
sing	singular
syn	synonym
v	verb
var	variation

PRONUNCIATION SYMBOLS

International Phonetic Alphabet (IPA) symbols define word pronunciations in this book. Examples are used here with commonly known words. The underlined letters represent each phoneme's pronunciation.

IPA	VOWELS Example	IPA	CONSONENTS Example
ɑ	hot, what	b	bad, cab
æ	cat, black	d	did, lady
aɪ	time, eye	ð	then, either, mother
aʊ	now, out	dʒ	just, large, garage
ɔ	call, four	ʃ	crash, she
ɔɪ	boy, join	f	tough, for, phase, stiff
ɛ	bed, met	g	give, flag, garage
ʌ	cup, luck, but, the	h	hello, how
ə	away, cinema	j	yellow, yes
ɛə	air, where	k	cat, back
ɛɪ	eight, say	l	leg, little
ɪ	hit, sit	m	man, lemon
i	be, heat, see, happy	n	no, ten, know
oʊ	go, home	ŋ	hang, singer
ʊ	could, wood, put	p	map, pet
u	blue, food	ɹ	red, try
ju	beauty, pure, queue	s	sing, miss, ceiling
ᵊd	dated, aided NOTE 1	t	take, setting
ᵊl	auricle NOTE 1	tʃ	check, church
ᵊm	handsome NOTE 1	v	five, voice
ᵊn	straighten NOTE 1	w	wet, window
ᵊɹ	better NOTE 1	z	buzz, lazy
ᵊs	surplus NOTE 1	ʒ	pleasure, vision
		θ	both, think

NOTE 1: /ə/ and /ᵊ/ are pronounced as in *further* /'fəɹðᵊɹ/. That is, /ᵊ/ is a much shorter vowel than /ə/.

NOTE 2: In many instances /t/ sounds like /d/ when spoken informally. For example, *latter* should sound like /'lætᵊɹ/; but is usually heard as /'lædᵊɹ/. Therefore, *ladder* and *latter* are considered to be homophones. (See definition for *sandhi*.)

NOTE 3: The phonemes /æ/ and /ɛə/ are sometimes used interchangeably depending upon regional usage. Therefore, judgments were made using (arguably) the most commonly heard American sound.

NOTE 4: The phonemes /ə/ and /ɑ/ (as in *aloud* /ə'laʊd/ or /ɑ'laʊd/) are used interchangeably depending upon regional usage. Therefore, judgments were made here too.

HOMOPHONES

The homophones and *near homophones* defined in this book.

a, ay, eh
absence, absents
acanthous,
acanthus
accede, axseed, exceed
accept, except
accidence, accidents
acclamation, acclimation
acts, ax
ad, add
addition, edition
adds, ads, adz
adduce, educe
ade, aid, aide
adherence, adherents
adolescence, adolescents
adventuress, adventurous
aerie, airy
affect, effect
affluence, affluents
ai, aye, eye, I
ail, ale
air, are, e'er, ere, err, eyre, heir
aisle, I'll, isle
ait, ate, eight
alimentary, elementary
all, awl
allowed, aloud
allude, elude
allusion, elusion, illusion
allusive, elusive, illusive
altar, alter
analyst, annalist
anger, angor
ant, aunt
ante, anti, auntie
antecedence, antecedents
apatite, appetite
apprise, apprize
arc, ark
are, R
arrant, errant
ascendance, ascendents
ascent, assent
asperate, aspirate
assistance, assistants
astringence, astringents
attar, odder, otter
attendance, attendants
auger, augur

aught, ought
aural, oral
aureole, oriole
auricle, oracle
autograft, autographed
away, aweigh
awful, offal
axel, axil, axle
axes, axis
ayed, eyed, I'd
B, be, bee
bach, batch
bad, bade
bael, bel, bell, belle
bai, bi, buy, by, bye
bail, bale
bailee, bailey, bailie
bailer, bailor, baler
bait, bate
baited, bated
baize, bays, beys
bald, balled, bawled
ball, bawl
balm, bomb
band, banned
bands, banns, bans
bang, bhang
bard, barred
bare, bear
bark, barque
baron, barren
baroness, barrenness
barrel, beryl
base, bass
basal, basil
based, baste
bask, basque
bat, batt
bay, bey
bazaar, bizarre
beach, beech
beat, beet
beau, bow
beaut, butte
been, bin
beer, bier
bees, bise
beetle, betel
belligerence, belligerents
benzene, benzine

HOMOPHONES

berg, burg, burgh
Berghal, burgle
berry, bury
berth, birth
better, bettor
bight, bite, byte
billed, build
bird, burred
birl, burl
birr, burr
bit, bitt
blend, blende
blew, blue
bloc, block
boar, bore
board, bored
boarder, border
bobbin, bobbing
bocks, box
bode, bowed
bold, bowled
bolder, boulder
bole, boll, bowl
boos, booze
bootie, booty
born, borne, bourne
borough, burro, burrow
bough, bow
boughs, bouse, bows
bouillon, bullion
boy, buoy
brae, bray
braes, braise, brays, braze
braid, brayed
brail, braille
brain, brane
brake, break
breach, breech
bread, bred
breadth, breath
bream, brim
brewed, brood
brews, brewis, bruise
bridal, bridle
broach, brooch
broom, brougham
brows, browse
brr, bur, burr
bruit, brut, brute
buccal, buckle
burger, burgher
bus, buss

bused, bussed, bust
but, butt
byre, buyer
C, cee, sea, see
C's, cees, seas, sees, seize
cache, cash
cachou, cashew
calculous, calculus
calendar, calender, colander
calix, calyx
calk, caulk
call, caul
callous, callus
calques, calx
canapé, canopy
cannon, canon
cant, can't
canter, cantor
canvas, canvass
capital, capitol
carat, caret, carrot, karat
caries, carries
carol, carrel
carpal, carpel
cart, carte, kart
cask, casque
cast, caste
caster, castor
catch, ketch
caudal, caudle
cause, caws
cay, key, quay
cedar, seeder
cede, seed
ceil, seal, seel
ceiling, sealing
cel, cell, sell
cellar, seller
censer, censor, sensor
census, senses
cent, scent, sent
cense, cents, scents, sense
cerate, serrate
cere, sear, seer, sere
cereal, serial
cerous, cirrus, serous
cession, session
cetaceous, setaceous
chaise, shays
champagne, champaign
chance, chants
chard, charred

HOMOPHONES

chary, cherry
chased, chaste
chauffeur, shofar
cheap, cheep
chews, choose
chic, sheik
chili, chilly
choir, quire
choler, collar
choral, coral
chorale, corral
chord, cord, cored
chordate, cordate
chough, chuff
chute, shoot
cinque, sink, sync
cite, sight, site
clack, claque
clairvoyance, clairvoyants
clause, claws
clew, clue
click, clique, klick
climb, clime
close, clothes, cloze
coal, cole, kohl
coaled, cold
coaming, combing
coarse, corse, course
coat, cote
coax, cokes
cocks, cox
coddling, codling
coffer, cougher
coif, quaff
coiffeur, coiffure
coign, coin, quoin
coir, coyer
collard, collared
colonel, kernel
color, culler
come, cum
comedy, comity
complacence, complaisance
complacent, complaisant
complement, compliment
complementary, complimentary
con, conn
conceded, conceited
conch conk
concord, conquered
conker, conquer
consonance, consonants

continence, continents
coo, coup
coolie, coolly, coulee
coop, coupe
cops, copse
coquet, coquette
core, corps
correspondence, correspondents
cosign, cosine
council, counsel
councilor, counselor
courier, currier
courtesy, curtesy
cousin, cozen
coward, cowered, cowherd
craft, kraft
crape, crepe
creak, creek
cream, crème
crew, krewe
crewed, crude
crewel, cruel
crews, cruise, cruse, krewes
cubical, cubicle
cubit, qubit
cue, Q, queue
currant, current
curser, cursor
cygnet, signet
cymbal, symbol
dam, damn
day, dey
days, daze, deys
deader, debtor
dean, dene
dear, deer
deasil, diesel
decadence, decadents
deem, deme
demean, demesne
dense, dents
dental, dentil
dependence, dependents
depose, depots
depositary, depository
depravation, deprivation
descent, dissent
desert, dessert
deterrence, deterrents
deviance, deviants
deviser, devisor, divisor
deuce, douce

HOMOPHONES

dew, do, due
dewed, dude
dhol, dhole, dol, dole
dhow, tao
dial, diel
diarist, direst
die, dye
died, dyed
dine, dyne
dinghy, dingy
dire, dyer
disburse, disperse
discreet, discrete
discussed, disgust
dissidence, dissidents
djinn, gin
do, doe, dough
doc, dock
docks, docs, dox
docile, dossal
doer, dour
does, dos, doughs, doze
done, dun
donjon, dungeon
dos, dues
dost, dust
dour, dower
dowager, dowitcher
draft, draught
drier, dryer
droop, drupe
dual, duel
ducked, duct
ducks, ducts
dyeing, dying
E's, ease
earn, erne, urn
eave, eve
edition (see addition)
educe (see adduce)
eek, eke
effect (see affect)
effluence, effluents
eight (see ate)
el, ell, L
elation, illation
elementary (see alimentary)
elicit, illicit
elision, elysian
elusive, illusive
emerge, immerge
eminent, immanent, imminent

ends, ens
enrapt, enwrapped
ensure, insure
entrance, entrants
epic, epoch
equivalence, equivalents
e're (see air)
ere (see air)
err (see air)
errant (see arrant)
erupt, irrupt
eruption, irruption
evaporate, evaporite
ewe, *hue, U, yew, you*
ewer, you're
ewes, *hues, U's, use, yews*
exceed (see accede)
except (see accept)
exercise, exorcise
expansive, expensive
extant, extent
expedience, expedients
eye (see aye)
eyed (see ayed)
eyelet, islet
eyre (see air)
facts, fax
faerie, fairy, ferry
faille, file, phial, phyle
fain, fane, feign
faint, feint
fair, fare
faker, fakir
farci, farcy
faro, farrow, pharaoh
fate, fete
faun, fawn
faux, foe
fay, fey
fays, faze, phase
fear, fere
feat, feet
feeder, fetor
felloe, fellow
feral, ferule, ferrule
fern, firn
feted, fetid
feudal, futile
few, phew
fiancé, fiancee
fiche, fish
filar, filer

I-4

HOMOPHONES

file (see faille)
filter, philter
finally, finely
find, fined
fir, fur
firs, furs, furze
fisher, fissure
fizz, phiz
flacks, flax
flair, flare
flea, flee
fleche, flesh
flecks, flex
flew, flu, flue
flocks, phlox
floe, flow
florescence, fluorescence
flour, flower
foaled, fold
for, fore, four
forego, forgo
formally, formerly
fort, forte
forth, fourth
forward, foreword
foul, fowl
fraise, frays, phrase
franc, frank
frayed, 'fraid
frees, freeze, frieze
friar, fryer
fuehrer, furor
fungous, fungus
furs, furze
g, gee
gaff, gaffe
gage, gauge
gait, gate
gaiter, gator
gamble, gambol
gamin, gammon
gang, gangue
gantlet, gauntlet
garret, garrote
garrulous, garrulus
gays, gaze
gel, jell
gene, jean
genet, jennet
gest, jest
ghat, got
gibe, jibe

gild, gilled, guild
gilder, guilder
gilt, guilt
gin (see djinn)
giro, gyro
glair, glare
glands, glans
gloom, glume
glows, gloze
glutenous, glutinous
gneiss, nice
gnu, knew, new, nu
gnus, news, nus
gored, gourd
gorgeous, gorges
gorilla, guerrilla
grade, grayed
grader, grater, greater
graft, graphed
grate, great
grays, graze
greaves, grieves
greisen, grison
grill, grille
grip, grippe
grisly, gristly, grizzly
groan, grown
grocer, grosser
guarantee, guaranty
guessed, guest
guide, guyed
guise, guys
hail, hale
hair, hare
hairier, harrier
hairy, harry
hall, haul
hallo, hallow, hello, hollow
halve, have
handmade, handmaid
handsome, hansom
hangar, hanger
hardy, hearty
hart, heart
haws, hawse
hay, hey
haze, heys
heal, heel, he'll
hear, here
heard, herd
hears, here's
he'd, heed

HOMOPHONES

heir (see air)
heroin, heroine
hertz, hurts
hew, hue, whew
hi, hie, high
hide, hied
higher, hire
him, hymn
ho, hoe
hoar, whore
hoard, horde, whored
hoarse, horse
hoes, hose
hold, holed
hole, whole
holey, holy, wholly
holm, home
hoop, whoop
horsed, horst
hostel, hostile
hour, our
house, how's
humerus, humorous
hurdle, hurtle
I (see aye)
I'd (see ayed)
idle, idol, idyll
ileum, ilium
I'll (see aisle)
illation (see elation)
illuminance, illuminants
illusive (see elusive)
immanent (see eminent)
immerge (see emerge)
imminent (see eminent)
impassable, impassible
impatience, impatiens
in, inn
incidence, incidents
incite, insight
incompetence, incompetents
independence, independents
indict, indite
indicter, inditer
indigence, indigents
indiscreet, indiscrete
influence, influents
inequity, iniquity
innocence, innocents
insolate, insulate
instance, instants
insure (see ensure)

intense, intents
intension, intention
invade, inveighed
irrupt (see erupt)
irruption (see eruption)
isle (see aisle)
islet (see eyelet)
its, it's
J, jay
jalousie, jealousy
jam, jamb
jean (see gene)
jell (see gel)
jennet (see genet)
jewel, joule
Jewry, jury
jinks, jinx
kain (see cain)
kernal (see colonel)
ketch (see catch)
key (see cay)
kill, kiln
klick (see click)
knap, nap
knave, nave
knead, kneed, need
knew (see gnu)
knickers, nickers
knight, night
knit, nit
knob, nob
knobble, nobble
knock, nock
knot, not
know, no
knows, noes, nose
kohl (see coal)
kraft (see craft)
krewe (see crew)
krewes (see crews)
L (see el)
laager, lager, logger
label, labile
lac, lack
lacks, lax
ladder, latter
lade, laid
lai, lay, lea,lei, ley
lain, lane
lair, layer
lais, lase, lays, laze, leas, leis, leys
lam, lamb

HOMOPHONES

lama, llama

laps, lapse

laser, lazar

lea, lee, li

leach, leech

lead, led

leader, lieder, liter

leaf, lief

leak, leek

lean, lien

lear, leer, lehr

leased, least

lends, lens

less, loess

lessen, lesson

lesser, lessor

let us, lettuce

lets, let's

levee, levy

lewdest, lutist

liable, libel

liar, lyre

lichen, liken

licker, liquor

lickerish, licorice

lie, lye

lieu, loo

lightening, lightning

limb, limn

linch, lynch

links, lynx

literal, littoral

lo, low

load, lode, lowed

loan, lone

loath, loathe

lo-cal, locale

loch, lock, lough

lochs, locks, lox

loon, lune

loop, loupe

loos, lose

lore, lower

loot, lute

loyalest, loyalist

maar, mar

Mach, mock

macs, max

madam, madame

madder, matter

made, maid

magnate, magnet

mail, male

main, mane

maize, mays, maze

mall, maul

manakin, mannequin, manikin

mandrel, mandrill

manner, manor

mantel, mantle

marc, mark, marque

mare, mayor

marquee, marquis

marshal, martial

marten, martin

maser, mazer

mask, masque

massed, mast

massif, massive

mat, matte

material, materiel

me, mi

mead, meed

mean, mesne, mien

meat, meet, mete

meatier, meteor

medal, meddle

meddler, medlar

meddlesome, mettlesome

meeter, meter

meets, metes

men's, mends

metal, mettle

mew, mu

mewl, mule

mews, mus, muse

mho, mow

micks, mix

middy, midi

might, mite

mil, mill

millenary, millinery

mince, mints

mind, mined

minds, mines

miner, minor

minion, minyan

minks, minx

missal, missile

missed, mist

misses, missus

moan, mown

moat, mote

mode, mowed

I-7

HOMOPHONES

mood, mooed
moor, more
moose, mousse
moral, morale, morel
mordant, mordent
morn, mourn
morning, mourning
mucous, mucus
murre, myrrh
muscat, musket
muscle, mussel
mussed, must
mustard, mustered
nap (see knap)
naught, nought
naval, navel
nave (see knave)
nay, nee, neigh
need (see knead)
new (see gnu)
news (see gnus)
nick (see knick)
nickers (see knickers)
nicks, nix
night (see knight)
nit (see knit)
no (see know)
nob (see knob)
nobble (see knobble)
nock (see knock)
noes (see knows)
none, nun
nose (see knows)
not (see knot)
nu (see gnu)
nus (see gnus)
O, oh, owe
oar, o'er, or, ore
odder (see attar)
ode, owed
offal (see awful)
oleo, olio
once, wants, wonts
one, won
oracle (see auricle)
oral (see aural)
ordinance, ordnance
oriel, oriole
otter (see attar)
ought (see aught)
our (see hour)
outcast, outcaste

overate, overrate
overdo, overdue
overseas, oversees
ox-eyed, oxide
P, pea, pee
paced, paste
packed, pact
packs, pax
paddy, patty
paean, peon
paid, payed
pail, pale
pain, pane
pair, pare, payer, pear
paired, pared
palate, palet, palette,
   pallet, pellet
pall, pawl
par, parr
parish, perish
parity, parody
par, parr
passable, passible
passed, past
pâte, pot
patience, patients
pause, paws
pea, pee
peace, piece
peachy, pichi
peak, peek, pique
peal, peel
pealing, peeling
pearl, perle, purl
pearlite, perlite
pecten, pectin
pedal, peddle
peer, pier
pekoe, picot
pelisse, police
penal, penile
penance, pennants
pendant, pendent
penitence, penitents
people, pipal
per, purr
pervade, purveyed
petit, petty
petrel, petrol
pharaoh (see faro)
phase (see fays)
phew (see few)

I-8

HOMOPHONES

phial (see faille)
philter (see filter)
phiz (see fizz)
phlox (see flocks)
phosphorous, phosphorus
phrase (see fraise)
pi, pie
pica, pika
picks, pix
picnic, pyknic
pidgin, pigeon
pinion, pinon
pistil, pistol
place, plaice
plain, plane
plaintiff, plaintive
plait, plate
plantar, planter
platan, platen
pleas, please
pleural, plural
pliers, plyers
plough, plow
plum, plumb
pocks, pox
poem, pome
polar, poler, poller
pole, poll
politic, politick
ponds, pons
poof, pouf
poor, pore, pour
populace, populous
praise, prays, preys
prau, prow
pray, prey
precedence, precedents, presidents
precedent, president
premier, premiere
presence, presents
presser, pressor
pride, pried
prier, prior
pries, prize
primer, primmer
prince, prints
principal, principle
profit, prophet
pros, prose
protean, protein
Psalter, salter
pseud, sued

psi, sigh, xi
psis, sighs, size, xis
psychosis, sycosis
pupal, pupil
puts, putz
puttee, putty
Q (see cue)
quaff (see coif)
quarts, quartz
quay (see key)
qubit (see cubit)
quean, queen
queue (see cue)
quietest, quietist
quince, quints
quire (see choir)
quitter, quittor
quoin (see coign)
R (see are)
rabbet, rabbit
rack, wrack
racket, racquet
radical, radicle
raid, rayed
rail, rale
rain, reign, rein
raise, rays, raze
raiser, razer, razor
rancor, ranker
rap, wrap
rapped, rapt, wrapped
rational, rationale
ray, re
reactance, reactants
read, red, redd
read, rede, reed
real, reel
rebait, rebate
recede, reseed
receipt, reseat
recite, resite
reck, wreck
reek, wreak
reference, referents
remark, remarque
rends, wrens
residence, residents
rest, wrest
retch, wretch
review, revue
rex, wrecks
rheum, room

I-9

HOMOPHONES

rheumy, roomie, roomy
rho, roe, row
rhos, roes, rose, rows
rhumb, rum
rhyme, rime
rigger, rigor
right, rite, wright, write
righting, writing
rime, rhyme
ring, wring
rise, ryes
ritz, writs
road, rode, rowed
roan, rown
roc, rock
roil, royal
role, roll
rood, rude, rued
roomer, rumor
root, route
rote, wrote
rough, ruff
rouse, rows
rout, route
roux, rue
rues, ruse
rung, wrong, wrung
rye, wry
sac, sack
saccharin, saccharine
sachet, sashay
sacs, sacks, sacques, sax
sail, sale
sailer, sailor
salter (see Psalter)
salver, salvor
sandhi, sandy
sane, seine
sari, sorry
satiric, satyric
sault, sue
saurel, sorrel
saver, savor
scalar, scaler
scoot, scute
scend, send
scene, seen
scent (see cent)
scents (see cense)
scion, sion
scissile, sisal
scull, skull

sea (see C)
seal (see ceil)
sealing (see ceiling)
seam, seem
seamen, semen
sear (see cere)
seas (see C's)
season, seisin
sects, sex
see (see C)
seed (see cede)
seel (see ceil)
seeder (see cedar)
seer (see cere)
sees (see C's)
seidel, sidle
seize (see C's)
sell (see cel)
seller (see cellar)
senate, sennet, sennit
sense (see cense)
senses (see census)
sensor (see censer)
sent (see cent)
seraph, serif
sere (see cere)
serene, serine
serial (see cereal)
serf, surf
serge, surge
serous (see cerous)
serrate (see cerate)
session (see cession)
set, sett
setaceous (see cetaceous)
settler, settlor
sew, so, sow
sewer, sower
sewer, suer
sewn, sown
shake, sheik
shays (see chaise)
shear, sheer
sheik (see chic)
shew, shoe, shoo
shier, shire
shoed, shooed
shone, shown
shoot (see chute)
sic, sick
sics, six
side, sighed

I-10

HOMOPHONES

sigh (see psi)
sigher, sire
sighs (see psis)
sight (see cite)
sign, sine
signet (see cygnet)
silicon, silicone
sink (see cinque)
site (see cite)
size (see psis)
slay, sleigh
sleave, sleeve
sleight, slight
slew, slough, slue
sloe, slough, slow
soar, sore
soared, sword
sol, sole, soul
sold, soled, souled
some, sum
son, sun
sonny, sunny
sordid, sorted
sough, sow
spade, spayed
spec, speck
spier, spire
spinner, spinor
stabile, stable
staff, staph
staid, stayed
stair, stare
stake, steak
statice, status
stationary, stationery
steal, steel, stele
step, steppe
stile, style
stolen, stolon
stoop, stoup
straight, strait
straighten, straiten
strider, stridor
subtler, sutler
succor, sucker
suede, swayed
suite, sweet
summary, summery
sundae, Sunday
surplice, surplus
swat, swot
sycosis (see psychosis)

symbol (see cymbal)
sync (see cinque)
T, tea, tee, ti
Ts, teas, tease, tees, tis
tacet, tacit
tachs, tacks, tax
tacked, tact
tael, tail, tale
talesman, talisman
tao (see dhow)
taper, tapir
tare, tear
taro, tarot
tarry, terry
tartar, tarter
taught, taut
taupe, tope
team, teem
tear, tier
tearer, terror
tec, tech
tends, tens
tenner, tenor
tense, tents
tenser, tensor
teras, terrace
tern, terne, turn
ternary, ternery, turnery
terse, tierce
testees, testes
than, then
the, thee
their, there, they're
theirs, there's
therefor, therefore
threw, through
throes, throws
throne, thrown
thyme, time
tic, tick
tide, tied
tier, tire
tighten, titan
tighter, titer
'til, till
timber, timbre
to, too, two
toad, toed, towed
toady, tody
tocsin, toxin
toe, tow
toke, toque

HOMOPHONES

told, tolled

tole, toll

ton, tonne, tun

tongue, tung

tool, tulle

toon, tune

tooter, tutor

topee, topi

tor, tore, torr

tort, torte

tough, tuff

toughed, tuft

tracked, tract

trader, traitor

tray, trey

trews, trues

triptik, triptych

troche, trochee

troop, troupe

trooper, trouper

trussed, trust

truster, trustor

tucks, tux

twill, 'twill

U (see ewe)

udder, utter

undo, undue

urn (see earn)

U's (see ewes)

use (see ewes)

vail, vale, veil

vain, vane, vein

valance, valence

valiance, valiants

variance, variants

vary, very

vellum, velum

veracious, voracious

verdure, verger

verses, versus

vial, vile, viol

vice, vise

villain, villein

viscous, viscus

wack, Wac, whack

wacks, WACS, wax, whacks

waddle, wattle, what'll

wade, weighed

wail, wale, whale

wailer, whaler

wain, wane

waist, waste

wait, weight

waive, wave

waiver, waver

walk, wok

wand, wanned

want, wont

wants (see once)

war, wore

ward, warred

ware, wear, weir, where

warn, worn

wart, wort

wary, wherry

watt, what, wot

wattle, what'll

watts, what's

way, weigh, whey

we, wee, whee

weak, week

weal, we'll, wheal, wheel

weald, wheeled, wield

wean, ween

weather, wether, whether

weave, we've

we'd, weed

wedding, wetting, whetting

wees, wheeze

weir, we're

weld, welled

wen, when

wends, wens, when's

we're, weir

were, whir

wet, whet

whew (see hew)

which, witch

Whig, wig

while, wile

whiled, wild

whin, win

whine, wine

whined, wind, wined, wynd

whines, winds, wines

whirl, whorl

whirled, whorled, world

whirred, word

whish, wish

whist, wist

whit, wit

white, wight, wite

whither, wither

whoa, woe

HOMOPHONES

whole (see hole)
wholly (see holey)
whoop (see hoop)
whore (see hoar)
whored (see hoard)
who's, whose
why, wye, Y
whys, wise
windlass, windless
winds, wins, winze
won (see one)
wonts (see once)
wood, would
worst, wurst
wrap (see rap)
wrapped (see rapped)
wreak (see reek)
wreck (see reck)
wrecks (see rex)
wrens (see rends)
wrest (see rest)
wretch (see retch)
wright (see right)
wring (see ring)
write (see right)
writing (see righting)
writs (see ritz)
wrong (see rung)
wrote (see rote)
wrung (see rung)
wry (see rye)
xenia, zinnia
xi (see psi)
xis (see psis)
yew (see ewe)
yews (see ewes)
yoke, yolk
yore, your, you're
you (see ewe)
you'll, Yule
you're (see ewer)
zinnia (see xenia)

HOMOPHONES

-A-

A, ay, eh /ɛɪ/

A

n 1: the blood group whose red cells carry the A antigen [syn: type.A, group A] 2: a metric unit of length equal to one ten billionth of a.meter (or 0.0001 micron); used to specify wavelengths of.electromagnetic radiation [syn: angstrom, angstrom unit] 3: any of several fat-soluble vitamins essential for normal vision; prevents night blindness or inflammation or dryness of the eyes [syn: vitamin A, antiophthalmic factor, axerophthol] 4: one of the four nucleotides used in building DNA; all four nucleotides have a common phosphate group and a sugar (ribose) [syn: deoxyadenosine monophosphate] 5: (biochemistry) purine base found in DNA and RNA; pairs with thymine in DNA and with uracil in RNA [syn: adenine] 6: the basic unit of electric current adopted under the Systeme International d'Unites; "a typical household circuit carries 15 to 50 amps" [syn: ampere, amp] 7: the 1st letter of the Roman alphabet 8: indefinite article; "What a nice day!"

ay

inter: expression of sorrow or regret

eh

inter: expression of inquiry or surprise

absence, absents /'æbsɛnts/

absence

n 1: the state of being absent; "he was surprised by the absence of any explanation" [ant: presence] 2: failure to be present [ant: presence] 3: the time interval during which something or somebody is away; "he visited during my absence" 4: epilepsy characterized by paroxysmal attacks of brief clouding of consciousness (a possible other abnormalities) [syn: petit mal epilepsy]

absents

v: (3rd pers sing) to keep (oneself) away "He absents himself from church."

acanthous, acanthus /'əkɛənθəs/

acanthous

adj : shaped like a spine or thorn [syn: acanthoid, spinous]

acanthus

n : any plant of the genus Acanthus having large spiny leaves and spikes or white or purplish flowers; native to Mediterranean region but widely cultivated [also: acanthi (pl)]

accede, axseed, exceed

accede /æk'sid/

v 1: submit or yield to another's wish or opinion; "The government acceded to the military pressure" [syn: submit, bow, defer, give in] 2: be compatible or in accordance with; "You must adhere to the rules" [syn: adhere] 3: to agree or express agreement; "Yes, the Maestro assented." [syn: assent, acquiesce] [ant: dissent]

axseed /'æksid/

n : European herb resembling vetch; naturalized in the eastern United States; having umbels of pink-and-white flowers and sharp-angled pods [syn: crown vetch, Coronilla varia]

exceed /ɛk'sid/

v 1: go beyond; "Their loyalty exceeds their national bonds" [syn: transcend, surpass] 2: go beyond; "She exceeded our expectations"; "She topped her performance of last year" [syn: transcend, overstep, pass, go past, top] 3: be or do something to a greater degree; "her performance surpasses that of any other student I know"; "She outdoes all other athletes"; "This exceeds all my expectations" [syn: surpass, outstrip, outmatch, outgo, outdo, surmount]

accept, except

accept /æk'sɛpt/

v 1: consider or hold as true; "I cannot accept the dogma of this church"; "accept an argument" [ant: reject] 2: receive willingly something given or offered; "The only girl who would have him was the miller's daughter"; "I won't have this dog in my house!"; "Please accept my present" [syn: take, have] [ant: refuse] 3: give an affirmative reply to; respond favorably to: "I cannot accept your invitation"; "I go for this resolution" [syn: consent, go for] [ant: refuse] 4: react favorably to; consider right and proper; "People did not accept atonal music at that time"; "We accept the idea of universal health care" 5: admit into a group or community; "accept students for graduate study"; "We'll have to vote on whether or not to admit a new member" [syn: admit, take, take on] 6: take on as one's own the expenses or debts of another person; "I'll accept the charges"; "She agreed to bear the responsibility" [syn: bear, take over, assume] 7: tolerate or accommodate oneself to; "I shall have to accept these unpleasant working conditions"; "I swallowed the insult"; "She has learned to live with her husband's little idiosyncrasies" [syn: live with, swallow] 8: be designed to hold or take; "This surface will not take the dye" [syn: take] 9: of a deliberative body: receive (a report) officially, as from a committee 10:

make use of or accept for some purpose; "take a risk"; "take an opportunity" [syn: take] 11: be sexually responsive to, used of a female domesticated mammal; "The cow accepted the bull"

except /ɛk'sɛpt/

v 1: take exception to [syn: demur] 2: prevent from being included or considered or accepted; "The bad results were excluded from the report"; "Leave off the top piece" [syn: exclude, leave out, leave off, omit, take out] [ant: include]

accidence, accidents

/'æksɪdɛnts/

accidence

n : the part of grammar that deals with the inflections of words [syn: inflectional morphology]

accidents

n : (plu of accident) 1: mishaps; especially ones causing injury or death 2: anything that happens by chance without an apparent cause [syn: fortuities, chance events]

acclamation, acclimation

/'æklɪmeɪʃɪn/

acclamation

n : enthusiastic approval; "the book met with modest acclaim"; "he acknowledged the acclamation of the crowd"; "they gave him more éclat than he really deserved" [syn: acclaim, plaudits, plaudit, éclat]

acclimation

n : adaptation to a new climate (a new temperature or altitude or environment) [syn: acclimatization,]

acts, ax

acts /ækts/

n : (plu of act) 1: legal documents codifying the results of deliberations of a committee or society or legislative body [syn: enactments] 2: things that people do or cause to happen [syn: human actions, human activities] 3: subdivisions of a play or opera or ballet 4: short theatrical performances that are part of a longer program; "he did his acts three times every evening"; "she had catchy little routines"; "they were some of the best numbers he ever did" [syn: routines, numbers, turns, bits] 5: manifestations of insincerity; "he put on quite some acts for her benefit" 6: the performances of some composite cognitive activity; operations that affect mental contents; "the processes of thinking"; "the acts of remembering" [syn: processes, cognitive processes, operations, cognitive operations]

v : (3rd pers sing of act) 1: performs an action; "think before you act"; "He acts quickly" [syn: moves] [ant: refrains] 2: behaves in a certain manner; shows a certain behavior; conducts or comports oneself; "You should act like an adult"; "Don't behave like a fool"; "What makes her do this way?"; "She played the servant her husband's master" [syn: behaves, does] 3: play a role or part; "Gielgud played Hamlet"; "She wants to act Lady Macbeth, but she is too young for the role" [syn: plays, represents] 4: discharges one's duties; "She acts as the chair"; "In what capacity are you acting?" 5: pretends to have certain qualities or state of mind; "He acts the idiot"; "She plays deaf when the news are bad" [syn: plays, acts as] 6: is suitable for theatrical performance: "This scene acts well" 7: has an effect or outcome; often the one desired or expected; "The voting process doesn't work as well as people thought"; "How does your idea work in practice?"; "This method doesn't work"; "The brakes of my new car act quickly"; "The medicine works only if you take it with a lot of water" [syn: works] 8: engages in an activity, often for no particular purpose other than pleasure 9: behaves unnaturally or affectedly; "She's just acting" [syn: dissembles, pretends] 10: performs on a stage or theater; "She acts in this play"; "He acted in "Julius Caesar"; "I played in "A Christmas Carol" [syn: plays, role-plays, playacts]

axe /æks/

n : an edge tool with a heavy bladed head mounted across a handle [syn: ax]

v 1: chop or split with an ax, as of wood [syn: ax] 2: terminate, as of a project or a program; "The NSF will axe the research program and stop funding it" [syn: ax]

ad, add /ɛəd/

ad

n 1: public promotion of products or services [syn: advertisement]

add

v 1: make an addition (to); join with others; increase by another or several; "She will add a personal note to her letter"; "Add insult to injury" [ant: take away] 2: state or say further; " `It doesn't matter,' " he says" [syn: append, supply] 3: of a quality, as in: "The music will add a lot to the play"; "You bring a special atmosphere to our meetings"; "This adds a light note to the program" [syn: lend, impart, bestow, contribute, bring] 4: make an addition by combining numbers; "Add 27 and 49, please!" [syn: add together] [ant: subtract] 5: determine the sum of; "Add all the people in this town to those of the neighboring town" [syn: total, sum, sum up, summate, tote up, add together, tally, add up] 6: constitute an addition; "This paper adds to her reputation"

HOMOPHONES

addition, edition

addition /'ædɪʃɪn/

n 1: a component that is added to something to improve it; "the addition of a bathroom was a major improvement"; "the addition of cinnamon improved the flavor" [syn: improver] 2: the act of adding one thing to another; "the addition of flowers created a pleasing effect"; "the addition of a leap day every four years" [ant: subtraction] 3: something added to what you have already; "the librarian shelved the new accessions"; "he was a new addition to the staff" [syn: accession] 4: a quantity that is added; "there was an addition to property taxes this year"; "they recorded the cattle's gain in weight over a period of weeks" [syn: increase, gain] 5: a suburban area laid out in streets and lots for a future residential area 6: the arithmetic operation of summing; calculating the sum of two or more numbers; "the summation of four and three gives seven"; "four plus three equals seven" [syn: summation, plus]

edition /'edɪʃɪn/

n 1: the form in which a text (especially a printed book) is published 2: all of the identical copies of something offered to the public at the same time; "the first edition appeared in 1920" or "it was too late for the morning edition" or "they issued a limited edition of Bach recordings" 3: an issue of a newspaper; "he read it in yesterday's edition of the Times"

adds, ads, adz /ædz/

adds

v 1: (3rd pers. sing. to add) (see ad)

ads

n 1: (plu. of ad) (see ad)

adz

n : an edge tool used to cut and shape wood [syn: adze]

adduce, educe

adduce /æ'dus/

v : advance evidence for [syn: abduce, cite]

educe /ɛ'dus/

v 1: deduce (a principle) or construe (a meaning); "We will educe some interesting linguistic data from the native informant" [syn: evoke, elicit, extract, draw out] 2: develop or evolve, especially from a latent or potential state [syn: derive]

ade, aid, aide /eɪd/

ade

n : a sweetened beverage of diluted fruit juice [syn: fruit drink]

aid

n 1: a resource: "visual aids in teaching"; "economic assistance to depressed areas" [syn: assistance, help] 2: the activity of contributing to the fulfillment of a need or furtherance of an effort or purpose: "he gave me an assist with the housework";

"could not walk without assistance"; "rescue party went to their aid"; "offered his help in unloading" [syn: assist, assistance, help] 3: a gift of money to support a worthy person or cause [syn: economic aid] 4: the work of caring for or attending to someone or something; "no medical care was required"; "the old car needed constant attention" [syn: care, attention, tending]

v 1: give help or assistance; be of service; "Everyone aided during the earthquake"; "Can you help me carry this table?" "She never helps around the house" [syn: help, assist] 2: improve the condition of; "These pills will aid the patient" [syn: help]

aide

n 1: an officer who acts as military assistant to a more senior officer [syn: adjutant, aide-de-camp] 2: someone who acts as assistant [syn: auxiliary]

adherence, adherents / əd'hiɪɛnts/

adherence

n 1: faithful support for a religion or cause or political party [syn: attachment] 2: the property of sticking together (as of glue and wood) or the joining of surfaces of different composition [syn: adhesiveness, adhesion, bond]

adherents

n : (plu. adherent) individuals who believe and help to spread the doctrine of another [syn: disciples]

adolescence, adolescents /'ædoulesɛnts/

adolescence

n 1: the time period between the beginning of puberty and adulthood 2: in the state that someone is in between puberty and adulthood

adolescents

n : (plu. adolescent) juveniles between the onset of puberty and maturity [syn: striplings, teenagers]

adventuress, adventurous /æd'vɛntʃɹᵊs/

adventuress

n : a woman adventurer

adventurous

adj : willing to undertake or seeking out new and daring enterprises; "adventurous pioneers"; "the risks and gains of an adventuresome economy" [syn: adventuresome] [ant: unadventurous]

aerie, airy /'ɛəɹi/

aerie

n 1: the lofty nest of a bird of prey (such as a hawk or eagle) 2: any habitation at a high altitude

airy

adj 1: open to or abounding in fresh air; "airy rooms" [syn: aired] 2: not practical or realizable; speculative; "airy theories about socioeconomic improvement"; "visionary schemes for getting rich" [syn: impractical, visionary] 3: having little or no perceptible weight; so light as to resemble air; "airy gauze curtains" 4: characterized by lightness and insubstantiality; as impalpable or intangible as air; "aerial fancies"; "an airy apparition"; "physical rather than ethereal forms" [syn: aerial, ethereal]

affect, effect

affect /ˈəfɛkt/

n : the conscious subjective aspect of feeling or emotion

v 1: have an effect upon; "Will the new rules affect me?" [syn: impact, bear upon, bear on, touch on, touch] 2: act physically on; have an effect upon 3: connect closely and often incriminatingly; "This new ruling affects your business" [syn: involve, regard]

effect /ˈɪfɛkt/

n 1: a phenomenon that follows and is caused by some previous phenomenon; "the magnetic effect was greater when the rod was lengthwise" [syn: consequence, outcome, result, event, issue, upshot] 2: an outward appearance; "he made a good impression"; "I wanted to create an impression of success"; "she retained that bold effect in her reproductions of the original painting" [syn: impression] 3: (of a law) having legal validity; "the law is still in effect" [syn: force] 4: a symptom caused by an illness or a drug; "the effects of sleep loss"; "the effect of the anesthetic" 5: an impression (especially one that is artificial or contrived); "he just did it for effect" 6: the central meaning or theme of a speech or literary work [syn: essence, burden, core, gist]

v 1: cause to happen or occur; "The scientists set up a shockwave" [syn: effectuate, bring about, set up] 2: act so as to bring about; "effect a change"

affluence, affluents
/ˈæfluɛnts/

affluence

n : abundant wealth [syn: richness]

affluents

n 1: affluent persons; persons who financially well off; "the so-called emerging affluents" 2: river or stream branches that flow into the main stream [syn: feeder, tributary] [ant: distributary]

ai, aye, eye, I /aɪ/

ai

n : a sloth that has three long claws on each forefoot [syn: three-toed sloth, Bradypus tridactylus]

aye

n : an affirmative vote or voter "the ayes

have it"

v : to vote in the affirmative

eye

n 1: the organ of sight (`peeper' is an informal term for `eye') [syn: oculus, optic, peeper] 2: good discernment (either with the eyes or as if with the eyes); "she has an eye for fresh talent"; "he has an artist's eye" 3: attention to what is seen; "he tried to catch her eye" 4: an area that is approximately central within some larger region; "it is in the center of town"; "they ran forward into the heart of the struggle"; "they were in the eye of the storm" [syn: center, middle, heart] 5: a small hole or loop (as in a needle); "the thread wouldn't go through the eye"

v : look at [syn: eyeball]

I

pron : the first person; the one who is doing an action "I am happy."

adj : used of a single unit or thing; not two or more; [syn: one, 1]

n 1: a nonmetallic element belonging to the halogens; used especially in medicine and photography and in dyes; occurs naturally only in combination in small quantities (as in sea water or rocks) [syn: iodine, atomic number 53] 2: the smallest whole number or a numeral representing that number; "he has the one but will need a two and three to go with it"; "they had lunch at one" [syn: one, 1, ace, single, unity] 3: the 9th letter of the Roman alphabet.

ail, ale /ɛɪl/

ail

n : aromatic bulb used as seasoning [syn: garlic]

v 1: be unwell, ill, or ill disposed 2: cause bodily suffering to [syn: afflict, trouble, pain]

ale

n : fermented alcoholic beverage similar to but heavier than beer

air, are, e'er, ere, err, eyre, heir /ɛəɹ/

air

adj : relating to or characteristic of or occurring in the air; "air war"; "air safety"; "air travel" [ant: land, sea]

n 1: a mixture of gases (especially oxygen) required for breathing; the stuff that the wind consists of; "air pollution"; "a smell of chemicals in the air"; "open a window and let in some air"; "I need some fresh air" 2: travel via aircraft; "air travel involves too much waiting in airports"; "if you've time to spare go by air" [syn: air travel, aviation] 3: the region above the ground; "her hand stopped in mid air"; "he threw the ball into the air" 4: a distinctive but intangible quality surrounding a person or thing: "an air of mystery"; "the house had

HOMOPHONES

a neglected air"; "an atmosphere of defeat pervaded the candidate's headquarters"; "the place had an aura of romance" [syn: aura, atmosphere] 5: medium for radio and television broadcasting; "the program was on the air from 9 til midnight"; "the president used the airwaves to take his message to the people" [syn: airwave] 6: a slight wind (usually refreshing); "the breeze was cooled by the lake"; "as he waited he could feel the air on his neck" [syn: breeze, zephyr, gentle wind] 7: a succession of notes forming a distinctive sequence; "she was humming an air from Beethoven" [syn: tune, melody, strain, melodic line, line, melodic phrase] 8: (archaic) once thought to be one of four elements composing the universe (Empedocles)

v 1: expose to fresh air, as of old clothing; "aerate your old sneakers" [syn: air out, aerate] 2: be broadcast; "This show will air Saturdays at 2 P.M." 3: broadcast over the airwaves, as in radio or television; "We cannot air this X-rated song" [syn: send, broadcast, beam, transmit] 4: make public; "She aired her opinions on welfare" [syn: publicize, bare] 5: expose to warm or heated air, so as to dry; "Air linen" 6: expose to cool or cold air so as to cool or freshen; "air the old winter clothes"; "air out the smoke-filled rooms" [syn: vent, ventilate, air out]

are

n: a unit of surface area equal to 100 square meters

e'er

adv : (contr : ever) at all times; all the time and on every occasion; "I will always be there to help you"; "always arrives on time"; "there is always some pollution in the air"; "ever hoping to strike it rich"; "ever busy" [syn: always, ever] [ant: never]

ere

prep : previous to; before.
conj : rather than; before

err

v 1: to make a mistake or be incorrect "To err is human."; [syn: mistake, slip] 2: wander from a direct course or at random; "The child strayed from the path and her parents lost sight of her"; "don't drift from the set course" [syn: stray, drift]

eyre

n : a circuit traveled by an itinerant justice in medieval England or the court he presided over

heir

n 1: a person who is entitled by law or by the terms of a will to inherit the estate of another [syn: inheritor, heritor] 2: a person who inherits some title or office [syn:

successor]

aisle, I'll, isle /aɪl/

aisle

n 1: a long narrow passage (as in a cave or woods) 2: passageway between seating areas as in an auditorium or passenger vehicle or between areas of shelves of goods as in stores [syn: gangway] 3: part of a church divided laterally from the nave proper by rows of pillars or columns

I'll

contr : I will

isle

n : a small island [syn: islet]

alimentary, elementary

alimentary /æˈlɪmentˀɹi/

adj : providing nourishment; "good nourishing food" [syn: nourishing, nutrient, nutritious, nutritive]

elementary /ɛˈlɪmentˀɹi/

adj 1: easy and not involved or complicated; "an elementary problem in statistics"; "elementary, my dear Watson"; "a simple game"; "found an uncomplicated solution to the problem" [syn: simple, uncomplicated, unproblematic] 2: of or being the essential or basic part; "an elementary need for love and nurturing" [syn: primary]

all, awl /ɔl/

all

adj 1: quantifier; used with either mass or count nouns to indicate the whole number or amount of or every one of a class; "we sat up all night"; "ate all the food"; "all men are mortal"; "all parties are welcome" [syn: all of] [ant: some, none] 2: completely given to or absorbed by; "became all attention"

adv : to a complete degree or to the full or entire extent; "he was wholly convinced"; "entirely satisfied with the meal"; "it was completely different from what we expected"; "was completely at fault"; "a totally new situation"; "the directions were all wrong"; "It was not altogether her fault"; "an altogether new approach"; ('whole' is often used informally for 'wholly' as in "a whole new idea") [syn: wholly, entirely, completely, totally, altogether, whole] [ant: partly]

awl

n : a pointed tool for marking surfaces or for punching small holes

allowed, aloud /əˈlaʊd/

allowed

v (past of allow) 1: made it possible through a specific action or lack of action for something to happen; "This allowed the water to rush in [syn: let, permitted] [ant: prevented, inhibited] 2: gave permission; "She allowed her son to visit her estranged husband [syn: permitted, let,

HOMOPHONES

countenanced] [ant: forbid] 3: let have; "grant permission"; "Mandela was allowed few visitors in prison" [syn: granted] [ant: denied] 4: give or assign a share of money or time to a particular person or cause; "I earmarked this money for your research" [syn: appropriated, earmarked, set aside, reserved] 5: made a possibility or provided opportunity for; permitted to be attainable or caused to remain; "This left no room for improvement"; "The evidence allowed only one conclusion"; "allowed for mistakes"; "left lots of time for the trip" [syn: left, allowed for, provided for] 6: allowed or planned for a certain possibility; conceded the truth or validity of something; "I allowed for this possibility"; "The seamstress planned for 5% shrinkage after the first wash" [syn: took into account] 7: afforded possibility: "This problem admitted of no solution"; "This short story allowed of several different interpretations" [syn: admitted] 8: allowed the other team to score; "give up a run", in baseball [syn: gave up] 9: granted as a discount or in exchange; "The camera store owner allowed me $50 on my old camera" 10: allowed the presence of; "Dogs are not allowed here"; "Children are not permitted beyond this point" [syn: permitted]

aloud
adv 1: using the voice; not silently; "please read the passage aloud"; "he laughed out loud" [syn: out loud] 2: with relatively high volume; "the band played loudly"; "she spoke loudly and angrily"; "he spoke loud enough for those at the back of the room to hear him"; "cried aloud for help" [syn: loudly, loud] [ant: softly]

allude, elude
allude /əˈlud/
v : make a more or less disguised reference to; "He alluded to the problem but did not mention it" [syn: touch, advert]

elude /ɛˈlud/
v 1: escape, either physically or mentally; "The thief eluded the police"; "This difficult idea seems to evade her"; "The event evades explanation" [syn: evade, bilk] 2: be incomprehensible to; escape understanding by; "What you are seeing in him eludes me" [syn: escape] 3: avoid or try to avoid fulfilling, answering, or performing (duties, questions, or issues); "He dodged the issue"; "she skirted the problem"; "They tend to elude their responsibilities"; "he evaded the questions skillfully" [syn: hedge, fudge, evade, put off, circumvent, parry, skirt, dodge, duck, sidestep]

allusion, elusion, illusion
allusion /əˈluʒⁿn/
n : passing reference or indirect mention

elusion /ɛˈluʒⁿn/
n : the act of avoiding capture (especially by cunning) [syn: slip, eluding]

illusion /ɪˈluʒⁿn/
n 1: an erroneous mental representation [syn: semblance] 2: something many people believe that is false; "they have the illusion that I am very wealthy" [syn: fantasy, fancy] 3: the act of deluding; deception by creating illusory ideas [syn: delusion, head game] 4: an illusory feat; considered magical by naive observers [syn: magic trick, conjuring trick, trick, magic, legerdemain, conjuration, deception]

allusive, elusive, illusive
allusive /əˈlusɪv/
adj : characterized by indirect references; "allusive speech is characterized by allusions"

elusive /ɛˈlusɪv/
adj 1:difficult to describe; "a haunting elusive odor" 2: skillful at eluding capture; "a cabal of conspirators, each more elusive than the archterrorist"- David Kline [syn: evasive] 3: be difficult to detect or grasp by the mind; "his whole attitude had undergone a subtle change"; "a subtle difference"; "that elusive thing the soul" [syn:subtle]

illusive /ɪˈlusɪv/
n 1: an erroneous mental representation [syn: semblance] 2: something many people believe that is false; "they have the illusion that I am very wealthy" [syn: fantasy, fancy] 3: the act of deluding; deception by creating illusory ideas [syn: delusion, head game] 4: an illusory feat; considered magical by naive observers [syn: magic trick, conjuring trick, trick, magic, legerdemain, conjuration, deception]

altar, alter /ˈɔltəʳ/
altar
n 1: the table in Christian churches where communion is given [syn: communion table, Lord's table] 2: a raised structure on which gifts or sacrifices to a god are made

alter
v 1: cause to change; make different; cause a transformation; "The discussion will alter my thinking about the issue" [syn: change] 2: make or become different in some particular way, without permanently losing one's or its former characteristics or essence; "The supermarket's selection of vegetables will alter according to the season" [syn: change, vary] 3: make an alteration to; "This dress needs to be altered" 4: insert words into texts [syn:

interpolate, falsify] 5: castrate, used with animals; "Will you neuter your dog?" [syn: spay, neuter]

analyst, annalist /'ænəlɪst/

analyst

n 1: someone who is skilled at analyzing data 2: an expert who studies financial data (on credit or securities or sales or financial patterns etc.) and recommends appropriate business actions 3: a licensed practitioner of psychoanalysis [syn: psychoanalyst]

annalist

n : a historian who writes annals

anger, angor /'ɛɪŋgʰɹ/

anger

n 1: a strong emotion; a feeling that is oriented toward some real or supposed grievance [syn: choler, ire] 2: the state of being angry [syn: angriness] 3: belligerence aroused by a real or supposed wrong (personified as one of the deadly sins) [syn: wrath, ire]
v 1: make angry; "The news angered him" 2: become angry; "He angers easily" [syn: see red]

angor

n : (medical) extreme distress or mental anguish, usually of physical origin

ant, aunt /ɛænt/

ant

n : social insect living in organized colonies; characteristically the males and fertile queen have wings during breeding season; wingless sterile females are the workers [syn: pismire]

aunt (also /ɑnt/)

n : the sister of your father or mother; the wife of your uncle [syn: auntie, aunty] [ant: uncle]

ante, anti, auntie /'ɛænti/

ante

adj 1: (prefix) in front of or before in space; "'ante' is a prefix in the word 'anteroom'" 2: (prefix) prior to or before in time; "'ante' is a prefix in the word 'antenatal'"
n : (in poker) the initial contribution that each player makes to the pot
v : place one's stake, in a poker game

anti

adj 1: (prefix) opposite or opposing or neutralizing; "'ant' is a prefix in 'antacid'"; "'anti' is a prefix in 'antihistamine' and 'antifreeze'" [syn: ant] 2: not in favor of (an action or proposal etc.) [ant: pro]

auntie (also /ɑnti/ or /ɔnti/)

n 1: the sister of your father or mother; the wife of your uncle [syn: aunt, aunty] [ant: uncle] 2: an endearment form for aunt

antecedence, antecedents /æn'tɪsɪd°nts/

antecedence

n : preceding in time [syn: priority, antecedency, anteriority, precedence,

precedency] [ant: posteriority]

antecedents

n 1: someone from whom you are descended (but usually more remote than a grandparent) [syn: ancestor, ascendant, ascendent, root] [ant: descendant] 2: a preceding occurrence or cause or event 3: anything that precedes something similar in time; "phrenology was an antecedent of modern neuroscience" [syn: forerunner] 4: the referent of an anaphor; a phrase or clause that is referred to by an anaphoric pronoun

apatite, appetite /'æpʰtaɪt/

apatite

n : a common complex mineral consisting of calcium fluoride phosphate or calcium chloride phosphate; a source of phosphorus

appetite

n : a feeling of craving something; "an appetite for life" [syn: appetency, appetence]

apprise, apprize /ə'pɹaɪz/

apprise

v : give notice, inform, tell; "they were apprised of his decision"

apprize

v : value, appreciate, prize; "he apprized their work"

arc, ark /ɑɹk/

arc

n 1: electrical conduction through a gas in an applied electric field [syn: discharge, spark, electric arc, electric, discharge] 2: a continuous portion of a circle 3: something curved in shape [syn: bow]
v : form an arch [syn: arch, curve]

ark

n 1: (Judaism) sacred chest where the ancient Hebrews kept the two tablets containing the Ten Commandments [syn: ark of the covenant] 2: a boat built by Noah to save his family and animals from the Flood

are, R /ɑɹ/

are

v: 2ⁿᵈ person present of be

R

n 1: a unit of radiation exposure; the dose of ionizing radiation that will produce 1 electrostatic unit of electricity in 1 cc of dry air [syn: roentgen] 2: (physics) the universal constant in the gas equation: pressure times volume = R times temperature; equal to 8.3143 joules per Kelvin per mole [syn: gas constant, universal gas constant] 3: the 18th letter of the Roman alphabet; 4: the length of a line segment between the center and circumference of a circle or sphere [syn: radius, r]

HOMOPHONES

arrant, errant

arrant /'æɹᵊnt/

adj : without qualification; used informally as (often pejorative) intensifiers; "an arrant fool"; "a complete coward"; "a consummate fool"; "a double-dyed villain"; "gross negligence"; "a perfect idiot"; "pure folly"; "what a sodding mess"; "stark staring mad"; "a thoroughgoing villain"; "utter nonsense" [syn: complete, consummate, double-dyed, everlasting, gross, perfect, pure, sodding, stark, staring, thoroughgoing, utter]

errant /'ɛɹᵊnt/

adj : capable of making an error; "all men are error-prone" [syn: erring, error-prone]

ascendance, ascendants

/ə'sɛndents/

ascendance

n : the state that exists when one person or group has power over another; "her apparent dominance of her husband was really her attempt to make him pay attention to her" [syn: dominance, ascendence, ascendancy, ascendency, control]

ascendants

n 1: positions or states of being dominant or in control [syn: ascendent] 2: persons from whom you are descended (but usually more remote than grandparents) [syn: ancestors, antecedents, roots] [ant: descendants]

ascent, assent /'æsɛnt/

ascent

n 1: an upward slope or grade (as in a road); "In its ascent, the car couldn't make the grade" [syn: acclivity, rise, raise, climb, upgrade] [ant: descent] 2: a movement upward; "they cheered the rise of the hot-air balloon" [syn: rise, rising, ascension] [ant: fall] 3: the act of changing location in an upward direction [syn: rise, ascension, ascending]

assent

n : agreement with a statement or proposal to do something; "he gave his assent eagerly"; "a murmur of acquiescence from the assembly" [syn: acquiescence]

v : to agree or express agreement: "Yes, I will assent.." [syn: accede, acquiesce] [ant: dissent]

asperate, aspirate /'æspɹ ɹɛɪt/

asperate

v : to make uneven; roughen

aspirate

n : a consonant pronounced with aspiration

v 1: remove as if by suction; "draw in air" [syn: draw in, suck in] 2: pronounce with aspiration; of stop sounds 3: suck in air

assistance, assistants

/ə'sɪstᵊnts/

assistance

n 1: the activity of contributing to the fulfillment of a need or furtherance of an effort or purpose: "he gave me an assist with the housework"; "could not walk without assistance"; "rescue party went to their aid"; "offered his help in unloading" [syn: aid, assist, help] 2: a resource: "visual aids in teaching"; "economic assistance to depressed areas" [syn: aid, help]

assistants

n : (plu. assistant) people who contribute to the fulfillment of a need or furtherance of an effort or purpose; "my invaluable assistants"; "they hired additional help to finish the work" [syn: helpers, help, supporters]

ate, ait, eight /ɛɪt/

ate

v : (past of to eat) "He ate his food."

ait

n : (British) a small island

eight

adj : being one more than seven [syn: 8, viii]

n : the cardinal number that is the sum of seven and one [syn: 8, VIII, eighter, eighter from Decatur, octet]

astringence, astringents

/ə'stɹɪndʒɛnts/

astringence

n : a sharp astringent taste; the taste experience when a substance causes the mouth to pucker [syn: astringency]

astringents

n : a drug that causes contraction of body tissues and canals [syn: astringent drug, styptic]

attar, odder, otter

attar /'atᵊɹ/

n : essential oil or perfume obtained from flowers [syn: atar, athar, ottar]

odder /'adᵊɹ/

adj (compar of odd): beyond or deviating more from the usual or expected; "they speak with an odder dialect than the people in the North [syn: more curious, funnier, more peculiar, queerer]

otter /'atᵊɹ/

n 1: the fur of an otter 2: freshwater carnivorous mammal having webbed and clawed feet and dark brown fur

attendance, attendants

/ə'tɛndɛnts/

attendance

n : the act of being present (at a meeting or event etc.) [syn: attending] [ant: nonattendance]

attendants

n 1: (plu. of attendant) people who wait on or tend to or attend to the needs of another

HOMOPHONES

[syn: tender] 2: a person who participates in a meeting; "he was a regular attender at department meetings"; "the gathering satisfied both organizers and attendees" [syn: attendee]

auger, augur /'ɔgɹ/

auger

n 1: a long flexible steel coil for dislodging stoppages in curved pipes [syn: plumber's snake] 2: hand tool for boring holes [syn: gimlet, screw auger, wimble]

augur

n : (in ancient Rome) a religious official who interpreted omens to guide public policy

v 1: indicate by signs; "These signs bode bad news" [syn: bode, portend, auspicate, prognosticate, omen, presage, betoken, foreshadow, foretell, prefigure, forecast, predict] 2: predict from an omen

aught, ought /ɔt/

aught

n : a quantity of no importance; "it looked like nothing I had ever seen before"; "reduced to nil all the work we had done"; "we racked up a pathetic goose egg"; "it was all for naught"; "I didn't hear zilch about it" [syn: nothing, nil, nix, nada, null, cipher, goose egg, naught, zero, zilch, zip]

ought

v 1: expresses an emotional, practical, or other reason for doing something: "You had better put on warm clothes"; "You should call your mother-in-law"; "The State ought to repair the bridges" [syn: should, had better] 2: be logically necessary [syn: should, must, need]

aural, oral /'ɔɹəl/

aural

adj 1: of or pertaining to hearing or the ear; "an animal with a very sensitive aural apparatus" 2: relating to or characterized by an aura; "various aural effects that precede a migraine headache"

oral

adj 1: using speech rather than writing; "an oral tradition"; "an oral agreement [syn: unwritten] 2: of or relating to or affecting or for use in the mouth; "oral hygiene"; "an oral thermometer"; "an oral vaccine" 3: (anatomy) of or involving the mouth or mouth region or the surface on which the mouth is located; "the oral cavity"; "the oral mucous membrane"; "the oral surface of a starfish" [ant: aboral] 4: (psychoanalysis) a stage in psychosexual development when the child's interest is concentrated in the mouth; fixation at this stage is said to result in dependence, selfishness, and aggression [ant: anal]

n : an examination conducted by word of mouth [syn: oral exam, oral examination, viva voce]

aureole, oriole /'ɔɹiɪl/

aureole

n 1: the outermost region of the sun's atmosphere; visible as a white halo during a solar eclipse [syn: corona] 2: an indication of radiant light drawn around the head of a saint [syn: aura, halo, nimbus, glory, gloriole]

oriole

n 1: mostly tropical songbird; the male is usually bright orange and black [syn: Old World oriole] 2: American songbird; male is black and orange or yellow [syn: New World oriole, American oriole]

auricle, oracle /'ɔɹɪkəl/

auricle

n 1: a small conical pouch projecting from the upper anterior part of each atrium of the heart [syn: atrial auricle] 2: the externally visible cartilaginous structure of the external ear [syn: ear]

oracle

n 1: an authoritative person who divines the future [syn: prophet, seer, vaticinator] 2: a prophecy (usually obscure or allegorical) revealed by a priest or priestess; believed to be infallible 3: a shrine where an oracular god is consulted

autograft, autographed /'ɔtougɹæft/

autograft

n : tissue that is taken from one site and grafted to another site on the same person; "skin from his thigh replaced the burned skin on his arms" [syn: autoplasty]

autographed

adj : bearing an autograph; "an autographed copy of his latest book"

away, aweigh /ə'wɛɪ/ or /ɑ'wɛɪ/

away

adj 1: distant in either space or time; "the town is a mile away"; "a country far away"; "the game is a week away" 2: away from home or business; "he didn't leave an away phone number" 3: not present; having left; "he's away right now"; "you must not allow a stranger into the house when your mother is away"; "everyone is gone now"; "the departed guests" [syn: gone, departed] 4: (sport) used of an opponent's ground; "an away game" [ant: home] 5: (of a baseball pitch) on the far side of home plate from the batter; "the pitch was away (or wide)"; "an outside pitch" [syn: outside]

adv 1: from a particular thing or place or position; "ran away from the lion"; " wanted to get away from there"; "sent the children away to boarding school"; "the teacher waved the children away from the dead animal"; "went off to school"; "they drove off"; ('forth' is obsolete as in "go forth and preach") [syn: off, forth] 2: from one's possession; "he gave out money to the poor"; "gave away the tickets" [syn: out] 3: out of the way (especially away from one's thoughts); "brush the objections aside"; "pushed all doubts away" [syn: aside] 4: out of existence; "the music faded away"; "tried to explain away the affair of the letter"- H.E.Scudder; "idled the hours away"; "her fingernails were worn away" 5: at a distance in space or time; "the boat was 5 miles off (or away)"; "the party is still 2 weeks off (or away)"; "away back in the 18th century" [syn: off] 6: indicating continuing action, continuously or steadily; "he worked away at the project for more than a year"; "the child kept hammering away as if his life depended on it" 7: so as to be removed or gotten rid of; "cleared the mess away"; "the rotted wood had to be cut away" 8: freely or at will; "fire away! 9: in or into a proper place (especially for storage or safekeeping); "put the toys away; "her jewels are locked away in a safe"; "filed the letter away" 10: in a different direction; "turn aside"; "turn away one's face"; "glanced away" [syn: aside] 11: in reserve; not for immediate use; "started setting aside money to buy a car"; "put something by for her old age"; "has a nest egg tucked away for a rainy day" [syn: aside, by]**aweigh**

adj 1: (used of an anchor) hanging clear of the bottom; "anchors aweigh" 2: (nautical) of an anchor; just clear of the bottom

awful, offal /'ɔfəl/

awful

adj 1: exceptionally bad or displeasing; "atrocious taste"; "abominable workmanship"; "an awful voice"; "dreadful manners"; "a painful performance"; "terrible handwriting"; "an unspeakable odor came sweeping into the room" [syn: atrocious, abominable, dreadful, painful, terrible, unspeakable] 2: causing fear or dread or terror; "the awful war"; "an awful risk"; "dire news"; "a career or vengeance so direful that London was shocked"; "the dread presence of the headmaster"; "polio is no longer the dreaded disease it once was"; "a dreadful storm"; "a fearful howling"; "horrendous explosions shook the city"; "a terrible curse" [syn: dire, direful, dreaded, dreadful, fearful, fearsome, frightening, horrendous, horrific, terrible] 3: offensive or even (of persons) malicious; "in a nasty mood"; "a nasty accident"; "a nasty shock"; "a nasty smell"; "a nasty trick to pull"; "Will he say nasty things at my funeral?"- Ezra Pound [syn: nasty] [ant: nice] 4: inspired by a feeling of fearful wonderment or reverence; "awed by the silence"; "awful worshippers with bowed heads" [syn: awed] 5: inspiring awe or admiration or wonder; "New York is an amazing city"; "the Grand Canyon is an awe-inspiring sight"; "the awesome complexity of the universe"; "this sea, whose gently awful stirrings seem to speak of some hidden soul beneath"- Melville; "Westminster Hall's awing majesty, so vast, so high, so silent" [syn: amazing, awe-inspiring, awesome, awing]

adv : (informal) used as intensifiers, as in "terribly interesting"; "I'm awful sorry" [syn: terribly, awfully, frightfully]

offal

n : viscera and trimmings of a butchered animal often considered inedible by humans

axel, axil, axle /'æksəl/

axel

n : a jump in figure skating from the outer forward edge of one skate with 1 1/2 turns taken in the air and a return to the outer backward edge of the other skate

axil

n : the upper angle between an axis and an offshoot such as a branch or leafstalk

axle

n : a shaft on which a wheel rotates

axes, axis /'æksɪs/

axes

n : (plu. of axe) (see acts)

v : (3rd pers sing of axe) (see acts)

axis

n 1: a straight line through a body or figure that satisfies certain conditions 2: the center around which something rotates [syn: axis of rotation] 3: the main stem or central part about which plant organs or plant parts such as branches are arranged 4: a group of countries in special alliance [syn: bloc] 5: the 2nd cervical vertebra; serves as a pivot for turning the head [syn: axis vertebra]

ayed, eyed, I'd /aɪd/

ayed

v : (past of aye) : voted affirmatively; "They all ayed the change."

eyed

adj : having one or more eyes

v : (past of eye) : "He was eyed with suspicion."

I'd

contr : I would; "I'd have come sooner if it didn't rain."

-B-

B, be, bee /bi/

B

n 1: the blood group whose red cells carry the B antigen [syn: type B, group B] 2: aerobic rod-shaped spore-producing bacterium; often occurring in chainlike formations [syn: bacillus, bacilli, 3: originally thought to be a single vitamin but now separated into several B vitamins [syn:[B-complex vitamin, complex, vitamin B complex, vitamin B, B vitamin] 4: a trivalent metalloid element; occurs both in a hard black crystal and in the form of a yellow or brown powder [syn: boron, atomic number 5] 5: a logarithmic unit of sound intensity equal to 10 decibels [syn: bel] 6: (atomic or nuclear physics) a unit of nuclear cross section; the effective circular area that one particle presents to another as a target for an encounter [syn: barn] 7: the 2nd letter of the Roman alphabet

be

n : a light strong brittle gray toxic bivalent metallic element [syn: beryllium, Be, atomic number 4]

v 1: have the quality of existance; "I am, you are, he is, we are, they are", 2: be identical to; be someone or something, as in "The president of the company is John Smith"; "This is my house" 3: occupy a certain position or area; be somewhere; "Where is my umbrella?" "The tool shed is in the back"; also for abstract situations and relations: "What is behind this behavior?" 4: have an existence, be extant; "Is there a God?" [syn: exist] 5: happen, occur, take place; ""I lost my wallet; this was during the visit to my parents' house"; "There were two hundred people at his funeral"; "There was a lot of noise in the kitchen" 6: be identical or equivalent to: "One dollar equals 1,000 rubles these days!" [syn: equal] [ant: differ] 7: form or compose; "This money is my only income"; "The stone wall was the backdrop for the performance", "These constitute my entire belonging"; "The children made up the chorus"; "This sum represents my entire income for a year"; "These few men comprise his entire army" [syn: constitute, represent, make up, comprise] 8: work in a specific place, with a specific subject, or in a specific function; "He is a herpetologist; "She is our resident philosopher" [syn: follow] 9: represent, as of a character on stage; "Derek Jacobi was Hamlet" [syn: embody, personify] 10: spend or use time: "I may be an hour" 11: have life, be alive; "Our great leader is no more"; "My grandfather lived until the end of war" [syn: live] 12: to remain unmolested, undisturbed, or uninterrupted -- used only in infinitive form; "let her be" 13: be priced at; "These shoes cost $100" [syn: cost]

bee

n 1: any of numerous hairy-bodied insects including social and solitary species 2: a social gathering to carry out some communal task or to hold competitions

bach, batch /bætʃ/

bach

v : lead a bachelor's existence; "He wants to bach it after his divorce." [syn: bachelor]

batch

n 1: all the loaves of bread baked at the same time 2: (often followed by `of") a large number or amount or extent; "a batch of letters"; "a deal of trouble"; "a lot of money"; "he made a mint on the stock market"; "it must have cost plenty" [syn: deal, flock, good deal, great deal, hatful, heap, lot, mass, mess, mickle, mint, muckle, peck, pile, plenty, pot, quite a little, raft, sight, slew, spate, stack, tidy sum, wad, whole lot, whole slew] 3: a collection of things or persons to be handled together [syn: clutch]

v : batch together; assemble or process as a batch

bad, bade /bɛəd/ or /bæd/

bad

adj 1: having undesirable or negative qualities; "a bad report card"; "his sloppy appearance made a bad impression"; "a bad little boy"; "clothes in bad shape"; "a bad cut"; "bad luck"; "the news was very bad"; "the reviews were bad"; "the pay is bad"; "it was a bad light for reading"; "the movie was a bad choice" [ant: good] 2: very intense; "a bad headache"; "in a big rage"; "had a big (or bad) shock"; "a bad earthquake"; "a bad storm" [syn: big] 3: feeling physical discomfort or pain; "my throat feels bad"; "she felt bad all over"; ('tough' is occasionally used colloquially for `bad' as in "he was feeling tough after a restless night") [syn: tough] 4: (of foodstuffs) not in an edible or usable condition; "bad meat"; "a refrigerator full of spoilt food" [syn: spoiled, spoilt] 5: not capable of being collected; "a bad (or uncollectible) debt" [syn: uncollectible] 6: below average in quality or performance; "a bad chess player"; "a bad recital" 7: (linguistics; informal) "so-called bad grammar" 8: not financially safe or secure; "a bad investment"; "high risk investments"; "anything that promises to pay too much can't help being risky"; "speculative business enterprises" [syn: insecure, risky, high-risk, speculative]

HOMOPHONES

9: physically unsound or diseased; "has a bad back"; "a bad heart"; "bad teeth"; "an unsound limb"; "unsound teeth" [syn: unfit, unsound] 10: capable of harming; "bad habits"; "bad air"; "smoking is bad for you" 11: keenly sorry or regretful; "felt bad about letting the team down"; "was sorry that she had treated him so badly"; "felt bad about breaking the vase" [syn: sorry] 12: characterized by wickedness or immorality; "led a very bad life" [syn: immoral] 13: reproduced fraudulently; "like a bad penny..."; "a forged twenty dollar bill" [syn: forged] 14: not working properly; "a bad telephone connection"; "a defective appliance" [syn: defective]
n : that which is below standard or expectations as of ethics or decency: "take the bad with the good" [syn: badness] [ant: good]
adv 1: with great intensity; "the injury hurt badly"; "the buildings were badly shaken"; (`bad' is a nonstandard variant for `badly' as in "it hurts bad" or "we need water bad") [syn: badly] 2: very much; strongly; "I wanted it badly enough to work hard for it"; "the cables had sagged badly"; "they were badly in need of help"; "he wants a bicycle so bad he can taste it" [syn: badly]

bade
v alternate form of bid

bael, bel, bell, belle /bɛl/
bael
n: a spiney Indian citrus tree; the fruit thereof

bel
n 1: a logarithmic unit of sound intensity equal to 10 decibels [syn: **B**] 2: Babylonian god of the earth; one of the supreme triad including Anu and Ea; earlier identified with En-lil

bell
n 1: a hollow device made of metal that makes a ringing sound when struck 2: a push button at an outer door that gives a ringing or buzzing signal when pushed [syn: doorbell, buzzer] 3: the sound of a bell: "saved by the bell" 4: (nautical) each of the eight half-hour units of nautical time signaled by strokes of a ship's bell; eight bells signals 4:00, 8:00, or 12:00 o'clock, either a.m. or p.m. [syn: ship's bell] 5: the shape of a bell [syn: bell shape, campana] 6: American inventor of the telephone (1847-1922) [syn: Bell, Alexander Bell, Alexander Graham Bell] 7: a percussion instrument consisting of vertical metal tubes of different lengths that are struck with a hammer [syn: chime, gong] 8: the flared opening of a tubular device
v : attach a bell to; "bell cows"

belle
n : a young woman who is the most charming and beautiful of several rivals; "she was the belle of the ball"

bai, bi, buy, by, bye /baɪ/
bai
n : a seasonal yellow mist in Japan and eastern China due to dust storms in China's interior

bi
adj 1: bisexual 2: (prefix for two of something); biweekly is twice a week; biannual is twice a year; etc.

buy
n : an advantageous purchase; "she got a bargain at the auction"; "the stock was a real buy at that price" [syn: bargain, steal]
v 1: obtain by purchase; acquire by means of a financial transaction: "The family purchased a new car"; "The conglomerate acquired a new company"; "She buys for the big department store" [syn: purchase] [ant: sell] 2: make illegal payments to in exchange for favors or influence; "This judge can be bought" [syn: bribe, corrupt] 3: acquire by trade or sacrifice or exchange; "She wanted to buy his love with her dedication to him and his work" 4: accept as true: "I can't buy this story" 5: be worth or be capable of buying; "This sum will buy you a ride on the train"

by
adj : minor or subordinate; `by' is often used in combination; "a side interest"; "a by (or bye) effect"; "only a by comment"; "by-election"; "bye-election"; "a by-product"; "by-play" [syn: side, bye]
adv 1: so as to pass a given point; "every hour a train goes past" [syn: past] 2: in reserve; not for immediate use; "started setting aside money to buy a car"; "put something by for her old age"; "has a nest egg tucked away for a rainy day" [syn: aside, away]

bye
adj : minor or subordinate; `by' is often used in combination; "a side interest"; "a by (or bye) effect"; "only a by comment"; "by-election"; "bye-election"; "a by-product"; "by-play" [syn: side, by]
n 1: you advance to the next round in a tournament without playing an opponent; "he had a bye in the first round" [syn: pass] 2: a farewell remark; "they said their good-byes" [syn: adieu, adios, arrivederci, auf wiedersehen, au revoir, bye-bye, cheerio, good-by, good-bye, goodbye, good day, sayonara, so long]

bail, bale /beɪl/
bail
n 1: (criminal law) money that must be forfeited by the bondsman if an accused person fails to appear in court for trial; "the judge set bail at $10,000"; "a $10,000 bond was furnished by an alderman" [syn:

bail bond, bond] 2: the legal system that allows an accused person to be temporarily released from custody (usually on condition that a sum of money guarantees their appearance at trial); "he is out on bail"

v 1: release after a security has been paid 2: deliver something in trust to somebody for a special purpose and for a limited period 3: secure the release of (someone) by providing security 4: empty (a vessel) by bailing 5: remove (water) from a vessel with a container

bale

n : a large bundle bound for storage or transport

v : make into a bale; "bale hay"

bailee, bailey, bailie /ˈbeɪli/

bailee

n : the agent to whom property involved in a bailment is delivered

bailey

n 1: : the outer courtyard of a castle 2: the outer defensive wall that surrounds the outer courtyard of a castle

bailie

n : a Scottish municipal magistrate corresponding to an English alderman

bailer, bailor, baler /ˈbeɪlʲɹ/

bailer

n : a bucket used for bailing water

bailor

n : a person who delivers personal property to another in trust

baler

n : 1: a person who makes or forms bundles or packages 2: a group of turtles

bait, bate /beɪt/

bait

n 1: anything that serves as an enticement [syn: come-on, hook, lure, sweetener] 2: something used to lure victims into danger [syn: decoy, lure]

v 1: harass with persistent criticism or carping; "Did they bait the freshmen?"; "The children teased the new teacher"; "Don't ride me so hard over my failure"; "His fellow workers razzed him when he wore a jacket and tie" [syn: tease, razz, rag, cod, tantalize, taunt, twit, rally, ride] 2: lure, entice, or entrap with bait 3: attack with dogs or set dogs upon

bate

v 1: moderate or restrain; lessen the force of; "He will bate his breath when talking about this affair"; "capable of bating his enthusiasm" 2: flap the wings wildly or frantically; used of falcons 3: soak in a special solution to soften and remove chemicals used in previous treatments; "bate hides and skins"

baited, bated /ˈbeɪtɪd/

baited

v : (past tense of "bait")

bated

v : (past tense of "bate")

baize, bays, beys /beɪz/

baize

n : a bright green fabric napped to resemble felt; used to cover gaming tables

bays

n 1: (plu. of bay) (see bay)

beys

n : (plu of bey) (see bey)

bald, balled, bawled /bɔld/

bald

adj 1: with no effort to conceal; "a barefaced lie" [syn: barefaced] 2: without the natural or usual covering; "a bald spot on the lawn"; "bare hills" [syn: bare, denuded, denudate] 3: lacking hair on all or most of the scalp; "a bald pate"; "a bald-headed gentleman" [syn: bald-headed, bald-pated]

v : grow bald; lose hair on one's head; "He is balding already"

balled

adj : formed or gathered into a ball; "balled cotton"

bawled

v : (past tense of "bawl"); "She bawled at the funeral."

ball, bawl /bɔl/

ball

n 1: round object that is hit or thrown or kicked in games; "the ball traveled 90 mph on his serve"; "the mayor threw out the first ball" 2: a solid projectile shot by a musket; "they had to carry a ramrod as well as powder and ball" [syn: musket ball] 3: any object with a spherical shape; "a ball of fire" [syn: globe, orb] 4: a lavish formal dance; "she was the loveliest girl at the ball" 5: one of the two male reproductive glands that produce spermatozoa and secrete androgens; "she kicked him in the balls and got away" [syn: testis, testicle, nut, egg] 6: a spherical object used as a plaything; "he played with his rubber ball in the bathtub" 7: a compact mass; "a ball of mud caught him on the shoulder" [syn: clod, glob, lump, clump, chunk] 8: a more or less rounded anatomical body or mass; ball of the human foot or ball at the base of the thumb; "he stood on the balls of his feet" 9: a ball game played with a bat and ball between two teams of 9 players; teams take turns at bat trying to score run; "he played baseball in high school"; "there was a baseball game on every empty lot"; "there was a desire for National League ball in the area"; "play ball!" [syn: baseball, baseball game] 10: a pitch that is not in the strike zone; "he threw nine

HOMOPHONES

straight balls before the manager yanked him"

v : form into a ball by winding, rolling, etc.; ball wool, for example

bawl

v 1: shout loudly and without restraint [syn: bellow] 2: make a raucous noise [syn: yawp] 3: cry loudly; "She will bawl during that movie."

balm, bomb /bam/

balm

n 1: any of various aromatic resinous substances used for healing and soothing 2: semisolid preparation (usually containing a medicine) applied externally as a remedy or for soothing an irritation [syn: ointment, unction, unguent, salve]

bomb

n 1: an explosive device fused to denote under specific conditions 2: strong sealed vessel for measuring heat of combustion [syn: bomb calorimeter] 3: an event that fails badly or is totally ineffectual; "the first experiment was a real turkey"; "the meeting was a dud as far as new business was concerned" [syn: turkey, dud]

v 1: throw bombs at or attack with bombs; "The Americans bombed Baghdad." [syn: bombard] 2: fail to get a passing grade; "She studied hard but failed nevertheless"; "Did I fail the test? Yes, you bombed!" [syn: fail, flunk, flush it] [ant: pass]

band, banned /bɛənd/

band

n 1: an unofficial association of people or groups; "the smart set goes there"; "they were an angry lot" [syn: set, circle, lot] 2: instrumentalists not including string players 3: a stripe of contrasting color; "chromosomes exhibit characteristic bands" [syn: striation] 4: a strip or stripe of a contrasting color or material [syn: banding, stripe] 5: a group of musicians playing popular music for dancing [syn: dance band, dance orchestra] 6: a range of frequencies between two limits 7: something elongated that is worn around the body or one of the limbs 8: jewelry consisting of a circular band of a precious metal worn on the finger; "she had rings on every finger" [syn: ring] 9: put around something to hold it together

v : bind or tie together, as with a band

banned

adj : forbidden by law [syn: prohibited]

bands, banns, bans /bɛənz/

bands

n : (plu of band) 1: unofficial associations of people or groups; "the smart set goes there"; "they were an angry lot" [syn: sets, circles, lot] 2: instrumentalists not including string players 3: stripes of contrasting color; "chromosomes exhibit

characteristic bands" [syn: striations] 4: strips or stripes of contrasting colors or material [syn: bandings, stripes] 5: groups of musicians playing popular music for dancing [syn: dance bands, dance orchestras] 6: ranges of frequencies between two limits 7: things elongated that are worn around the body or the limbs 8: jewelry consisting of a circular band of a precious metal worn on the finger; "she had rings on every finger" [syn: rings] 9: bindings put around other things to hold them together

v : (3rd pers sing of band) : bind or tie together, as with a band

banns

n : a public announcement (in church) of a proposed marriage

bans

n : (plu of ban) 1: a decree that prohibits something [syn: prohibition, interdiction, proscription] 2: an official prohibition or edict against something [syn: banning, forbiddance, forbidding]

v : (3rd pers sing of ban) 1: prohibit esp. by legal means or social pressure; "Smoking is banned in this building" 2: forbid the public distribution of; as of movies or newspapers [syn: censor] 3: ban from a place of residence, as for punishment [syn: banish] 4: expel from a community or group [syn: banish, ostracize, shun, cast out, blackball]

bang, bhang /bɛɪŋ/

bang

n 1: a vigorous blow; "the sudden knock floored him"; "he took a bash right in his face"; "he got a bang on the head" [syn: knock, bash, smash, belt] 2: a sudden very loud noise [syn: blowup, clap, eruption, blast, loud noise] 3: a fringe of banged hair (cut short squarely across the forehead) 4: the swift release of a store of affective force; "they got a great bang out of it"; "what a rush!"; "he does it for kicks" [syn: boot, charge, rush, flush, thrill, kick] 5: a conspicuous success; "that song was his first hit and marked the beginning of his career" [syn: hit, smash, strike]

adv : (informal) directly; "he ran bang into the pole"; "ran slap into her" [syn: slap, slapdash, smack, bolt]

v 1: strike violently [syn: slam] 2: to produce a sharp often metallic explosive or percussive sound: "One of them banged the sash of the window nearest my bed" 3: close violently; "He slammed the door shut" [syn: slam] 4: move noisily; "The window banged shut"; "The old man banged around the house" 5: have sexual intercourse with; "This student sleeps with everyone in her dorm"; "Adam knew Eve" (know is archaic); "Were you ever intimate

HOMOPHONES

with this man?" [syn: love, make out, make love, sleep with, get laid, have sex, know, do it, be intimate, have intercourse, have it away, have it off, screw, fuck, jazz, eff, hump, lie with, bed, have a go at it, get it on, bonk, do]

bhang

n : a preparation of the leaves and flowers of the hemp plant; much used in India

bard, barred /baɹd/

bard

n 1: a lyric poet 2: an ornamental caparison for a horse

v : put a caparison on; of horses [syn: caparison, dress up]

barred

adj 1: firmly fastened or secured against opening; "windows and doors were all fast"; "a locked closet"; "left the house properly secured" [syn: bolted, fast, latched, locked, secured] 2: preventing entry or exit or a course of action; "a barricaded street"; "barred doors"; "the blockaded harbor" [syn: barricaded, blockaded]

bare, bear /bɛəɹ/

bare

adj 1: denuded of leaves; "the bare branches of winter" 2: completely unclothed; "bare bodies"; "naked from the waste up"; "a nude model" [syn: au natural, naked, nude] 3: lacking in amplitude or quantity; "a bare livelihood"; "a scanty harvest"; "a spare diet" [syn: scanty, spare] 4: without the natural or usual covering; "a bald spot on the lawn"; "bare hills" [syn: bald, denuded, denudate] 5: not having a protective covering; "unsheathed cables"; "a bare blade" [syn: unsheathed] [ant: sheathed] 6: just barely adequate or within a lower limit; "a bare majority"; "a marginal victory" [syn: marginal] 7: apart from anything else; without additions or modifications; "only the bare facts"; "shocked by the mere idea"; "the simple passage of time was enough"; "the simple truth" [syn: mere, simple] 8: lacking a surface finish such as paint; "bare wood"; "unfinished furniture" [syn: unfinished] 9: providing no shelter or sustenance; "bare rocky hills"; "barren lands"; "the bleak treeless regions of the high Andes"; "the desolate surface of the moon"; "a stark landscape" [syn: barren, bleak, desolate, stark] 10: having extraneous everything removed including contents; "the bare walls"; "the cupboard was bare" [syn: stripped] 11: showing ground without the usual covering of grass; "a carefully swept bare yard around the house"

v 1: lay bare; "bare your breasts"; "bare your feelings" 2: make public; "She aired her opinions on welfare" [syn: publicize,

air] 3: lay bare; "denude a forest" [syn: denude, denudate, strip]

bear

n 1: massive carnivorous or omnivorous mammals with long shaggy coats and strong claws 2: an investor with a pessimistic market outlook [ant: bull]

v 1: have: "bear a resemblance"; "bear a signature" 2: give birth (to a newborn); "My wife had twins yesterday!" [syn: give birth, deliver, birth, have] 3: put up with something or somebody unpleasant; "I cannot bear his constant criticism"; "The new secretary had to endure a lot of unprofessional remarks"; "he learned to tolerate the heat" [syn: endure, stomach, stand, tolerate, support, brook, abide, suffer, put up] 4: move while holding up or supporting; "Bear gifts"; "bear a heavy load"; also with communication nouns: "bear news"; "bearing orders" 5: bring forth, "The apple tree bore delicious apples this year"; "The unidentified plant bore gorgeous flowers" [syn: turn out] 6: take on as one's own the expenses or debts of another person; "I'll accept the charges"; "She agreed to bear the responsibility" [syn: take over, accept, assume] 7: contain or hold; have within: "The jar carries wine"; "The canteen holds fresh water"; "This can contains water" [syn: hold, carry, contain] 8: bring in; as of investments; "interest-bearing accounts"; "How much does this savings certificate pay annually?" [syn: yield, pay] 9: have on one's person; "He wore a red ribbon"; "bear a scar" [syn: wear] 10: behave in a certain manner; "She carried herself well"; "he bore himself with dignity"; "They conducted themselves well during these difficult times" [syn: behave, acquit, deport, conduct, comport, carry] 11: have rightfully; of rights, titles, and offices; "She bears the title of Duchess"; "He held the governorship for almost a decade" [syn: hold] 12: support or hold in a certain manner; "She holds her head high"; "He carried himself upright" [syn: hold, carry] 13: be pregnant with; "She is bearing his child"; "The are expecting another child in January"; "I am carrying his child" [syn: carry, gestate, expect]

bark, barque /baɹk/

bark

n 1: tough protective covering of the woody stems and roots of trees and other woody plants 2: a noise resembling the bark of a dog 3: a sailing ship with 3 (or more) masts [syn: barque] 4: the sound made by a dog

v 1: speak in an unfriendly tone; "She barked into the telephone." 2: cover with bark 3: remove the bark of a tree [syn:

skin] 4: make barking sounds; "The dogs barked at the stranger" 5: tan (a skin) with bark tannins

barque

n : a sailing ship with 3 (or more) masts [syn: bark]

baron, barren /'bæɹɪn/

baron

n 1: a nobleman (in various countries) of varying rank [syn: Baron] 2: a British peer of the lowest rank [syn: Baron] 3: a very wealthy or powerful businessman; "an oil baron" [syn: big businessman, business leader, king, magnate, mogul, power, top executive, tycoon]

barren

adj 1: without offspring; "in some societies a barren woman is rejected by her tribesmen" [syn: childless] 2: not fertile or productive; "a barren tree"; "soil too infertile to sustain real pasture" [syn: infertile] 3: providing no shelter or sustenance; "bare rocky hills"; "barren lands"; "the bleak treeless regions of the high Andes"; "the desolate surface of the moon"; "a stark landscape" [syn: bare, bleak, desolate, stark] 4: not bearing offspring; "a barren woman"; "learned early in his marriage that he was sterile" [syn: sterile] 5: incapable of sustaining life; "the dead and barren Moon"

n : an uninhabited wilderness that is worthless for cultivation; "the barrens of central Africa"; "the trackless wastes of the desert" [syn: waste, wasteland]

baroness, barrenness
/'bæɹənəs/

baroness

n : a noblewoman who holds the rank of baron or who is the wife or widow of a baron

barrenness

n 1: the state (usually of a woman) of having no children or being unable to have children 2: a condition yielding nothing of value [syn: fruitlessness, aridity] [ant: fruitfulness]

barrel, beryl /'bæɹɪl/

barrel

n 1: a tube through which a bullet travels when a gun is fired [syn: gun barrel] 2: a cylindrical container that holds liquids [syn: cask] 3: a bulging cylindrical shape; hollow with flat ends [syn: drum] 4: the quantity that a barrel (of any size) will hold [syn: barrelful] 5: any of various units of capacity; "a barrel of beer is 31 gallons and a barrel of oil is 42 gallons" [syn: bbl]

v : put in barrels

beryl

n : a mineral which is the chief source of beryllium; colored transparent varieties are valued as gems

base, bass /beIs/

base

adj 1: serving as or forming a base; "the painter applied a base coat followed by two finishing coats" [syn: basal] 2: (used of metals) consisting of or alloyed with inferior metal; "base coins of aluminum"; "a base metal" 3: of low birth or station (`base' is archaic in this sense); "baseborn wretches with dirty faces"; "of humble (or lowly) birth" [syn: baseborn, humble, lowly] 4: not adhering to ethical or moral principles; "base and unpatriotic motives"; "a base, degrading way of life"; "cheating is dishonorable"; "they considered colonialism immoral"; "unethical practices in handling public funds" [syn: dishonorable, immoral, unethical] 5: having or showing an ignoble lack of honor or morality; "that liberal obedience without which your army would be a base rabble"- Edmund Burke; "taking a mean advantage"; "chok'd with ambition of the meaner sort"- Shakespeare; "something essentially vulgar and mean spirited in politics" [syn: mean, mean spirited] 6: (archaic) illegitimate [syn: baseborn] 7: debased; not genuine; "an attempt to eliminate the base coinage"

n 1: any of various water-soluble compounds capable of turning litmus blue and reacting with an acid to form a salt and water; "bases include oxides and hydroxides of metals and ammonia" [syn: alkali] 2: installation from which a military force initiates operations; "the attack wiped out our forward bases" [syn: base of operations] 3: lowest support of a structure; "it was built on a base of solid rock"; "he stood at the foot of the tower" [syn: foundation, fundament, foot, groundwork, substructure, understructure] 4: place that runner must touch before scoring; "he scrambled to get back to the bag" [syn: bag] 5: (in a digital numeration system) the positive integer that is equivalent to one in the next higher counting place; "10 is the radix of the decimal system" [syn: radix] 6: the bottom or lowest part; "the base of the mountain" 7: (anatomy) the part of an organ nearest its point of attachment; "the base of the skull" 8: a lower limit; "the government established a wage floor" [syn: floor] 9: the fundamental assumptions underlying an explanation; "the whole argument rested on a basis of conjecture" [syn: basis, foundation, fundament, groundwork, cornerstone] 10: a support or foundation; "the base of the lamp" [syn: pedestal, stand] 11: the bottom side of a geometric figure from which the altitude can be constructed; "the base of the triangle" 12:

HOMOPHONES

the place where you are stationed and from which missions start and end [syn: home] 13: (linguistics) the form of a word after all affixes are removed; "thematic vowels are part of the stem" [syn: root, root word, stem, theme, radical] 14: the stock of basic facilities and capital equipment needed for the functioning of a country or area; "the industrial base of Japan" [syn: infrastructure] 15: the principal ingredient of a mixture; "glycerinated gelatin is used as a base for many ointments"; "he told the painter that he wanted a yellow base with just a hint of green"; "everything she cooked seemed to have rice as the base" 16: a flat bottom on which something is intended to sit; "a tub should sit on its own base" 17: (electronics) the part of a transistor that separates the emitter from the collector

v 1: use as a basis for; found on; "base a claim on some observation" [syn: establish, ground, found] 2: use (purified cocaine) by burning it and inhaling the fumes [syn: free-base] 3: assign to a station [syn: station, post, send, place]

bass

adj : having or denoting a low vocal or instrumental range; "a deep voice"; "a bass voice is lower than a baritone voice"; "a bass clarinet" [syn: deep]

n 1: the lowest part of the musical range 2: the lowest part in polyphonic music [syn: bass part] 3: an adult male singer with the lowest voice [syn: basso 4: the lowest adult male singing voice [syn: bass voice, basso] 5: the member with the lowest range of a family of musical instruments

basal, basil /ˈbeɪzɪl/

basal (also /ˈbeɪsɪl/)

adj 1: especially of leaves; located at the base of a plant or stem; especially arising directly from the root or rootstock or a root-like stem; "basal placentation"; "radical leaves" [syn: radical] [ant: cauline] 2: serving as or forming a base; "the painter applied a base coat followed by two finishing coats" [syn: base] 3: of primary importance; "basic truths" [syn: basic, primary]

basil

n 1: any of several Old World tropical aromatic annual or perennial herbs of the genus Ocimum 2: leaves or the common basil; used fresh or dried [syn: sweet basil]

based, baste /beɪst/

based

adj 1: being derived from; usually followed by "on" or "upon": "a film based on a best-selling novel" 2: having a base; "firmly based ice" 3: having a basis; often used as combining terms; "a soundly based argument"; "well-founded suspicions"

[syn: founded] 4: having a base of operations; "a company based in Atlanta"

baste

n : loose temporary stitches [syn: basting, tacking]

v 1: cover with liquid before cooking; "baste a roast" 2: strike violently and repeatedly; "She clobbered the man who tried to attack her" [syn: clobber, batter] 3: sew together loosely, with large stitches; "baste a hem"

bask, basque /bɛæsk/

bask

v 1: derive or receive pleasure from; get enjoyment from; take pleasure in; "She relished her fame and basked in her glory" [syn: enjoy, relish, savor] 2: be exposed; "The seals were basking in the sun"

basque

n 1: a woman's close-fitting bodice

bat, batt /bæt/

bat

n 1: nocturnal mouse-like mammal with forelimbs modified to form membranous wings and anatomical adaptations for echolocation by which they navigate [syn: chiropteran] 2: (baseball) a turn batting; "he was at bat when it happened"; "he got 4 hits in 4 at-bats" [syn: at-bat] 3: a small racket with a long handle used for playing squash [syn: squash racket, squash racquet] 4: a bat used in playing cricket [syn: cricket bat] 5: a club used for hitting a ball in various games

v 1: strike with, or as if with a baseball bat; "bat the ball" 2: wink briefly; "bat one's eyelids" [syn: flutter] 3: have a turn at bat; "Jones bats first, followed by Martinez" 4: use a bat; "Who's batting?"

batt

n : sheet of material as for insulation or felt [syn: batting]

bay, bey /beɪ/

bay

adj : (used of animals especially a horse) of a moderate reddish-brown color

n 1: an indentation of a shoreline larger than a cove but smaller than an gulf 2: the sound of a hound on the scent 3: small Mediterranean evergreen tree with small blackish berries and glossy aromatic leaves used for flavoring in cooking; also used by ancient Greeks to crown victors [syn: true laurel, bay laurel, bay tree] 4: a compartment on a ship between decks; often used as a hospital; "they put him in the sick bay" 5: a compartment in an aircraft used for some specific purpose; "he opened the bomb bay" 6: a small recess opening off a larger room [syn: alcove] 7: a horse of a moderate reddish-brown color

v 1: utter in deep prolonged tones 2: bark

with prolonged noises, of dogs [syn: quest]

bey

n 1: provincial governor in the Ottoman Empire 2: former native ruler of Tunisia 3: courtesy title in Turkey and Egypt

bazaar, bizarre /bɪ'zɑɹ/

bazaar

n 1: a shop where a variety of goods are sold 2: a street of small shops (especially in Orient) 3: a sale of miscellany; often for charity; "the church bazaar" [syn: fair]

bizarre

adj : conspicuously or grossly unconventional or unusual; "restaurants of bizarre design--one like a hat, another like a rabbit"; "famed for his eccentric spelling"; "a freakish combination of styles"; "the outlandish clothes of teenagers"; "outré and affected stage antics" [syn: eccentric, freakish, freaky, flaky, outlandish, outré]

beach, beech /bitʃ/

beach

n : an area of sand sloping down to the water of a sea or lake
v : land on a beach, as of watercraft

beech

n 1: any of several large deciduous trees with rounded spreading crowns and smooth gray bark and small sweet edible triangular nuts enclosed in burs; north temperate regions [syn: beech tree] 2: wood of any of various beech trees; used for flooring and containers and plywood and tool handles [syn: beech wood]

beat, beet /bit/

beat

adj : (informal) very tired; "was all in at the end of the day"; "so beat I could flop down and go to sleep anywhere"; "bushed after all that exercise"; "I'm dead after that long trip" [syn: all in, bushed, dead]
n 1: a regular route for a sentry or policeman; "in the old days a policeman walked a beat and knew all his people by name" [syn: round] 2: the rhythmic contraction and expansion of the arteries with each beat of the heart; "he could feel the beat of her heart" [syn: pulse, pulsation, heartbeat] 3: the basic rhythmic unit in a piece of music; "the piece has a fast rhythm"; "the conductor set the beat" [syn: rhythm, musical rhythm] 4: a single pulsation of an oscillation produced by adding two waves of different frequencies; has a frequency equal to the difference between the two oscillations 5: a member of the beat generation; a nonconformist in dress and behavior [syn: beatnik] 6: the sound of stroke or blow; "he heard the beat of a drum" 7: (prosody) the accent in a metrical foot of verse [syn: meter, measure, cadence] 8: a regular rate of repetition; "the coxswain raised the beat"

9: a stroke or blow; "the signal was two beats on the steam pipe" 10: the act of beating to windward; sailing as close as possible to the direction from which the wind is blowing
v 1: come out better in a competition, race, or conflict; "Agassi beat Becker in the tennis championship"; "We beat the competition"; "Harvard defeated Yale in the last football game" [syn: beat out, crush, trounce, vanquish] 2: give a beating to; subject to a beating, either as a punishment or as an act of aggression; "Thugs beat him up when he walked down the street late at night"; "The teacher used to beat the students" [syn: beat up] 3: hit repeatedly; "beat on the door"; "beat the table with his shoe" 4: move rhythmically; "Her heart was beating fast" [syn: pound, thump] 5: shape by beating; "beat swords into ploughshares" 6: make a rhythmic sound: "Rain drummed against the windshield"; "The drums beat all night" [syn: drum, thrum] 7: glare or strike with great intensity; "The sun was beating down on us" 8: move with a thrashing motion; "The bird flapped its wings"; "The eagle beat its wings and soared high into the sky" [syn: flap] 9: sail with much tacking or with difficulty; "The boat beat in the strong wind" 10: stir vigorously; "beat the egg whites"; "beat the cream" [syn: scramble] 11: strike (a part of one's own body) repeatedly, as in great emotion or in accompaniment to music; "beat one's breast"; "beat one's foot rhythmically" 12: be superior: "Reading beats watching television"; "This sure beats work!" 13: deprive somebody of something by deceit; "The con-man beat me out of $50"; "This salesman ripped us off!"; "we were cheated by their clever-sounding scheme"; "They chiseled me out of my money" [syn: cheat, rip off, chisel] 14: make a sound like a clock or a timer; "the clocks were ticking"; "the grandfather clock beat midnight" [syn: tick, tick tock, ticktack] 15: move with a flapping motion; "The bird's wings were flapping" [syn: flap] 16: indicate by beating; as with the fingers or drumsticks; "Beat the rhythm" 17: make by pounding or trampling; "beat a path through the forest" 18: produce a rhythm by striking repeatedly; "beat the drum" 19: strike (water or bushes) repeatedly to rouse animals for hunting 20: beat through cleverness and wit; "I beat the traffic"; "She outfoxed her competitors" [syn: outwit, overreach, outsmart, outfox, circumvent] 21: be a mystery or bewildering to: "This beats me!" "Got me--I don't know the answer!" [syn: perplex, get, puzzle, mystify, baffle,

HOMOPHONES

bewilder, flummox, stupefy, nonplus, gravel, amaze, dumbfound] 22: wear out completely; "This kind of work exhausts me"; "I'm beat"; "He was all washed up after the exam" [syn: exhaust, wash up, tucker, tucker out]

beet

n 1: biennial Eurasian plant usually having a swollen edible root; widely cultivated as a food crop [syn: common beet] 2: round red root vegetable [syn: beetroot]

beau, bow /boʊ/

beau

n 1: a man who is the lover of a girl or young woman; "if I'd known he was her boyfriend I wouldn't have asked" [syn: boyfriend, fellow, swain, young man] 2: a man who is much concerned with his dress and appearance [syn: dandy, dude, fop, gallant, sheik, swell, fashion plate, clotheshorse]

bow

n 1: a knot with two loops and loose ends; used to tie shoelaces [syn: bowknot] 2: a slightly curved piece of resilient wood with taut horsehair strands, used in playing certain stringed instrument 3: curved piece of resilient wood with taut cord to propel arrows 4: something curved in shape [syn: arc] 5: a decorative interlacing of ribbons 6: a stroke with a curved piece of wood with taut horsehair strands that is used in playing stringed instruments

v : play on a string instrument

beaut, butte /bʊət/

beaut

n : an outstanding example of its kind; "his roses were beauties"; "when I make a mistake it's a beaut" [syn: beauty]

butte

n : a hill that rises abruptly from the surrounding region; has a flat top and sloping sides

been, bin /bɪn/

been

v : (past of be) "I had been at school."

bin

n 1: a container; usually has a lid 2: the quantity contained in a bin [syn: binful] 3: an identification number consisting of a two-part code assigned to banks and savings associations; the first part shows the location and the second identifies the bank itself [syn: bank identification number, BIN, ABA transit number]

v : store in bins

beer, bier /bɪɹ/

beer

n : fermented alcoholic beverage brewed from malt and hops [syn: suds]

bier

n 1: a coffin along with its stand; "we followed the bier to the graveyard" 2: a

stand to support a corpse or a coffin prior to burial

bees, bise /biz/

bees

n 1: any of numerous hairy-bodied insects including social and solitary species 2: social gatherings to carry out some communal task or to hold competitions; "quilting bees"

bise

n : a dry cold north wind in southeastern France [syn: bize]

beetle, betel /ˈbitᵊl/

beetle

adj : jutting or overhanging; "beetle brows" [syn: beetling]

n 1: insect having biting mouthparts and front wings modified to form horny covers overlying the membranous rear wings 2: a tool resembling a hammer but with a large head (usually wooden); used to drive wedges or ram down paving stones or for crushing or beating or flattening or smoothing [syn: mallet]

v 1: be suspended over or hang over [syn: overhang] 2: beat with a beetle **betel**

n : Asian pepper plant whose dried leaves are chewed with betel nut (seed of the betel palm) by southeast Asians [syn: betel pepper, Piper betel]

belligerence, belligerents /bəˈlɪdʒɹɛnts/

belligerence

n 1: hostile or warlike attitude or nature [syn: belligerency] 2: a disposition to fight [syn: aggressiveness, contentiousness, pugnacity, quarrelsomeness]

belligerents

n : (plu. of belligerent) people who fight (or are fighting) [syn: combatants, battlers, fighters, scrappers]

benzene, benzine /ˈbɛnzin/

benzene

n : a colorless liquid hydrocarbon used as a solvent or motor fuel; highly inflammable; carcinogenic [syn: benzine, benzol]

benzine

n : var benzene)

berg, burg, burgh /bɝg/

berg

n : a large mass of ice floating at sea; usually broken off of a polar glacier [syn: iceberg]

burg

n : colloquial American term for a town; "I've lived in this burg all my life"

burgh

n : a borough in Scotland

berghal, burgle /ˈbɝgᵊl/

berghal

adj : (archaic) belonging to a berg

burgle

v : commit a burglary; enter and rob a

HOMOPHONES

dwelling [syn: burglarize, heist]

berry, bury /'bɛɹi/

berry

n 1: any of numerous small edible pulpy fruits either simple (grape; blueberry) or aggregate (blackberry; raspberry) 2: a pulpy and usually edible small fruit having any of various structures: e.g. strawberry or raspberry or blueberry

v : pick or gather berries; "We went berrying in the summer"

bury

v 1: cover from sight 2: place in a grave or tomb; "Stalin was buried behind the Kremlin wall on Red Square"; "The pharaohs were entombed in the pyramids"; "My grandfather was laid to rest last Sunday" [syn: entomb, inter, lay to rest] 3: place in the earth and cover with soil; "They buried the stolen goods" 4: enclose or envelop completely, as if by swallowing; "The huge waves swallowed the small boat and it sank shortly thereafter" [syn: immerse, engross, swallow, swallow up, eat up] 5: embed deeply; "She sank her fingers into the soft sand"; "He buried his head in her lap" [syn: sink] 6: dismiss from the mind; stop remembering; "I tried to bury these unpleasant memories" [syn: forget] [ant: remember]

berth, birth /bɜɹθ/

berth

n 1: a job in an organization; "he occupied a post in the treasury" [syn: position, post, office, spot, place, situation] 2: a place where a craft can be made fast [syn: mooring, moorage, slip] 3: a bed on a ship or train; usually in tiers [syn: bunk, built in bed]

v 1: provide with a berth 2: secure in or as if in a berth or dock; "tie up the boat" [syn: moor, tie up] 3: come into or dock at a wharf; "the big ship wharfed in the evening" [syn: moor, wharf]

birth

n 1: the time when something begins (especially life); "they divorced after the birth of the child" or "his election signaled the birth of a new age" [ant: death] 2: the event of being born; "they celebrated the birth of their first child" [syn: nativity, nascence] [ant: death] 3: the process of giving birth [syn: parturition, giving birth, birthing] 4: the kinship relation of an offspring to the parents [syn: parentage]

v : give birth (to a newborn); "My wife had twins yesterday!" [syn: give birth, deliver, bear, have]

better, bettor /'bɛtəɹ/

better

adj 1: (compar of good) superior to another (of the same class or set or kind) in excellence or quality or desirability or suitability; more highly skilled than another; "You're a better man than I am, Gunga Din"; "a better coat"; "a better type of car"; "a suit with a better fit"; "a better chance of success"; "produced a better mousetrap"; "she's better in math than in history" [ant: worse] 2: changed for the better in health or fitness; "her health is better now"; "I feel better" [ant: worse] 3: wiser or more advantageous and hence advisable; "it would be better to speak to him"; 4: more than half; "argued for the better part of an hour"

n 1: one having claim to precedence; a superior; "the common man has been kept in his place by his betters" 2: something better; "I expected better of him" 3: someone who bets [syn: bettor, wagerer, punter] 4: the superior one of two alternatives; "chose the better of the two"

adv : (compar of good) 1: in a better or more excellent manner or more advantageously or attractively or to a greater degree etc.; "She had never sung better"; "a deed better left undone"; "better suited to the job" 2: from a position of superiority or authority; "I know better."

v 1: surpass in excellence; "She bettered her own record"; "break a record" [syn: break] 2: to make better; "The editor improved the manuscript with his changes" [syn: improve, amend, ameliorate, meliorate] [ant: worsen] 3: get better; "The weather improved toward evening." [syn: improve, ameliorate, meliorate] [ant: worsen]

bettor

n : someone who bets [syn: better, wagerer, punter]

bight, bite, byte /baɪt/

bight

n 1: a loop in a rope 2: a bend or curve (especially in a coastline) 3: a broad bay formed by an indentation (a bight) in the shoreline; "the Bight of Benin" 4: the middle part of a slack rope (as distinguished from its ends)

v : fasten with a bight

bite

n 1: a wound resulting from biting 2: a small amount of solid food; a mouthful; "all they had left was a bit of bread" [syn: morsel, bit] 3: a painful wound caused by the thrust of a stinger into skin [syn: sting, insect bite] 4: a light informal meal [syn: collation, snack, nosh] 5: a sharp bitter taste property [syn: pungency, sharpness] 6: the act of gripping or chewing off with the teeth and jaws [syn: chomp]

v 1: to grip, cut off, or tear with or as if with the teeth or jaws; "Gunny invariably tried to bite her" [syn: seize with teeth] 2: cause a sharp of stinging pain or discomfort; "The sun burned his face"

HOMOPHONES

[syn: sting, burn] 3: penetrate or cut, as with a knife; "The fork bit into the surface" 4: of insects, scorpions, or other animals; "A bee stung my arm yesterday." [syn: sting, prick]

byte

n : a sequence of 8 bits (enough to represent one character of alphanumeric data) processed as a single unit of information

billed, build /bɪld/

billed

adj (combining form) having a beak or bill as specified; "a thick-billed bird"; "a long-billed cap"

v : (past of bill) to charge a fee, The mechanic billed me $200 for car repairs

build

n 1: constitution of the human body [syn: physique, body-build,]   2: alternative names for the body of a human being; "Leonardo studied the human body"; "he has a strong physique"; "the spirit is willing but the flesh is weak" [syn: human body, physical body, material body, soma, figure, physique, anatomy, shape, bod, chassis, frame, form, flesh]

v 1: make by combining materials and parts: "this little pig made his house out of straw"; "Some eccentric constructed an electric brassiere warmer" [syn: construct, make]   2: form steadily; "Resistance to the manager's plan built up quickly" [syn: build up, work up, progress]   3: build or establish something abstract; "build a reputation" [syn: establish]   4: improve the cleansing action of; build detergents   5: order, supervise, or finance the construction of; "The government is building new schools in this state"   6: give form to, according to a plan; "build a modern nation"; "build a million-dollar business"   7: be engaged in building; "These architects build in interesting and new styles"   8: found or ground; "build a defense on nothing but the accused person's reputation"   9: increase or strengthen gradually; "This investment is building interest"; "We worked up courage" [syn: build up, work up]   10: develop and grow; "Suspense was building right from the beginning of the opera"

bird, burred /bɜɹd/

bird

n 1: warm-blooded egg-laying vertebrates characterized by feathers and forelimbs modified as wings   2: the flesh of a bird or fowl (wild or domestic) used as food [syn: fowl]   3: informal terms for a (young) woman [syn: dame, doll, wench, skirt, chick]   4: a cry or noise made to express displeasure or contempt [syn: boo, hoot, Bronx cheer, hiss, raspberry, razzing, snort]   5: an offensive physical expression

by raising the middle finger of a closed fist "He gave him the bird."   6: badminton equipment consisting of a ball of cork or rubber with a crown of feathers [syn: shuttlecock, birdie, shuttle]

v : watch and study birds in their natural habitat [syn: bird watch]

burred

adj : having or covered with protective barbs or quills or spines or thorns etc.; "a horse with a short bristly mane"; "bristly shrubs"; "burred fruits" [syn: barbed, briary, briery, bristled, bristly, burry, prickly, spiny, thorny]

birl, burl /bɜɹl/

birl

v 1: cause a floating log to rotate by treading [syn: birle]   2: cause to spin; "spin a coin" [syn: whirl, spin, twirl]

burl

n 1: the wood cut from a tree burl or outgrowth; often used decoratively in veneer   2: a large rounded outgrowth on the trunk or branch of a tree   3: soft lump or unevenness in a yarn; either an imperfection or created by design [syn: slub, knot]

v : remove the burls from cloth

birr, brr, burr /bɜɹ/

birr

n 1: the basic unit of money in Ethiopia; equal to 100 cents   2: sound of something in rapid motion; "whir of a bird's wings"; "the whir of the propellers" [syn: whir, whirr, whirring]

v : make a soft swishing sound; "the motor whirred"; "the car engine purred" [syn: whizz, whiz, whirr, whir, purr]

brr

n : an expression to demonstrate being in a cold or chilly condition

burr (alt /bʌɹ/)

n 1: seed vessel having hooks or prickles [syn: bur]   2: rough projection left on a workpiece after drilling or cutting   3: rotary file for smoothing rough edges left on a workpiece   4: small bit used in dentistry or surgery [syn: bur]

v : remove the burrs from [syn: bur]

bit, bitt /bɪt/

bit

n 1: a small quantity; "a spot of tea"; "a bit of paper" [syn: spot]   2: a small fragment of something broken off from the whole; "a bit of rock caught him in the eye" [syn: chip, flake, fleck, scrap]   3: an indefinitely short time; "wait just a moment"; "it only takes a minute"; "in just a bit" [syn: moment, minute, second]   4: an instance of some kind; "it was a nice piece of work"; "he had a bit of good luck" [syn: piece]   5: piece of metal held in horse's mouth by reins and used to control the horse while

HOMOPHONES

riding; "the horse was not accustomed to a bit" 6: a unit of measurement of information (from Binary + digIT); the amount of information in a system having two equiprobable states; "there are 8 bits in a byte" 7: a small amount of solid food; a mouthful; "all they had left was a bit of bread" [syn: morsel, bite] 8: a small fragment; "overheard snatches of their conversation" [syn: snatch] 9: a short theatrical performance that is part of a longer program; "he did his act three times every evening"; "she had a catchy little routine"; "it was one of the best numbers he ever did" [syn: act, routine, number, turn] 10: the cutting part of a drill; usually pointed and threaded and is replaceable in a brace or bitstock or drill press; "he looked around for the right size bit"

v : (past of bite)

bitt

n : a strong post (as on a wharf or quay or ship for attaching mooring lines); "the ship lines were secured with bitts" [syn: bollard]

v : secure with a bitt; "bitt the ship line"

blend, blende /blɛnd/

blend

n 1: an occurrence of thorough mixing 2: a new word formed by joining two others and combining their meanings; "'smog' is a blend of 'smoke' and 'fog'"; "'motel' is a portmanteau word made by combining 'motor' and 'hotel'"; "'brunch' is a well-known portmanteau of 'breakfast' and 'lunch'" [syn: portmanteau word, portmanteau] 3: the act of blending components together thoroughly [syn: blending]

v 1: combine into one; "blend the nuts and raisins together"; "he blends in with the crowd"; "We don't intermingle much" [syn: intermix, immingle, intermingle] 2: blend or harmonize; "This flavor will blend with those in your dish"; "This sofa won't go with the chairs" [syn: go, blend in] 3: mix together different elements; "The colors blend well" [syn: flux, mix, conflate, commingle, immix, fuse, coalesce, meld, combine, merge]

blende

n : an ore that is the chief source of zinc; consists largely of zinc sulfide in crystalline form [syn: zinc blende, sphalerite]

blew, blue /blu/

blew

v (past of blow) 1: exhale hard; "blow on the soup to cool it down" 2: be blowing or storming; "The wind blew from the West." 3: free of obstruction by blowing air through: "blow one's nose" 4: be in motion due to some air or water current; "The leaves were blowing in the wind";

"the boat drifted on the lake"; "The sailboat was adrift on the open sea"; "the shipwrecked boat drifted away from the shore" [syn: floated, drifted, been adrift] 5: make a sound as if blown; "The whistle blew" 6: shape by blowing; "Blow a glass vase" 7: make a mess of, destroy or ruin [syn: botched, bumbled, fumbled, botched up, muffed, flubbed, screwed up, balled up, spoiled, mucked up, bungled, fluffed, bollixed, bollixed up, bobbled, mishandled, loused up, fouled up, messed up, fucked up] 8: spend thoughtlessly; throw away; "He wasted his inheritance on his insincere friends" [syn: wasted, squandered] [ant: conserved] 9: spend lavishly or wastefully on; "He blew a lot of money on his new home theater" [syn: squandered] [ant: saved] 10: sound by having air expelled through a tube; "The trumpets blew" 11: play or sound a wind instrument; "She blew the horn" 12: provide sexual gratification through oral stimulation [syn: fellated, went down on] 13: cause air to go in, on, or through: "Blow my hair dry" 14: cause to move by means of an air current; "The wind blew the leaves around in the yard" 15: spout moist air from the blowhole, as of some marine mammals; "The whales blew" 16: leave; informal or rude: "shove off!"; "The children shoved along"; "Blow now!" [syn: shoved off, shoved along] 17: lay eggs; of certain insects 18: cause to be revealed and jeopardized; "The story blew their cover"; "The double agent was blown by the other side" 19: show off [syn: boasted, touted, swashed, shot a line, bragged, gassed, blustered, vaunted, gasconade] 20: allow to regain its breath; "blow a horse" 21: melt, break, or become otherwise unusable; "The light bulbs blew out"; "The fuse blew" [syn: blew out, burned out] 22: burst suddenly; "The tire blew"; "We blew a tire"

blue

adj 1: having a color similar to that of a clear unclouded sky; "October's bright blue weather"- Helen Hunt Jackson; "a blue flame"; "blue haze of tobacco smoke" [syn: bluish, light-blue, dark-blue] 2: used to signify the Union forces in the Civil War (who wore blue uniforms); "a ragged blue line" 3: wearing blue; "the painting is called `the blue boy'"; "the blue team" 4: low in spirits; "lonely and blue in a strange city"; "depressed by the loss of his job"; "a dispirited and resigned expression on her face"; "downcast after his defeat"; "feeling discouraged and downhearted" [syn: depressed, dispirited, down, downcast, downhearted, down in the mouth, low, low-spirited] 5: characterized by profanity or cursing; "foul-mouthed and blasphemous"; "blue language"; "profane words" [syn: blasphemous, profane] 6: suggestive of sexual impropriety; "a blue movie"; "blue jokes"; "he skips asterisks and gives you the gamy details"; "a juicy scandal"; "a naughty wink"; "naughty words"; "racy anecdotes"; "a risqué story"; "spicy gossip" [syn: gamy, juicy, naughty, racy, risqué, spicy] 7: belonging to or characteristic of the nobility or aristocracy; "an aristocratic family"; "aristocratic Bostonians"; "aristocratic government"; "a blue family"; "blue blood"; "the blue-blooded aristocracy"; "of gentle blood"; "patrician landholders of the American South"; "aristocratic bearing"; "aristocratic features"; "patrician tastes" [syn: aristocratic, blue-blooded, gentle, patrician] 8: morally rigorous and strict; "blue laws"; "the puritan work ethic"; "puritanical distaste for alcohol"; "she was anything but puritanical in her behavior" [syn: puritan, puritanical] 9: tinged with blue or purple from cold or contusion; "the children's lips are blue from cold"; "a blue bruise" [syn: bluish] 10: characterized by or marked with a bluish color; "a blue fox"; "the great blue whale"; "a blue spruce" 11: causing dejection; "a blue day"; "the dark days of the war"; "a week of rainy depressing weather"; "a disconsolate winter landscape"; "the first dismal dispiriting days of November"; "a dark gloomy day"; "grim rainy weather" [syn: dark, depressing, disconsolate, dismal, dispiriting, gloomy, grim]

n 1: the color of the clear sky in the daytime; "he had eyes of bright blue" [syn: blueness] 2: blue clothing; "she was wearing blue" 3: any organization or party whose uniforms or badges are blue; "the Union army was a vast blue" 4: the sky as viewed during daylight; "he shot an arrow into the blue" [syn: blue sky, blue air, wild blue yonder] 5: used to whiten laundry or hair or give it a bluish tinge [syn: bluing] 6: the sodium salt of amobarbital that is used as a barbiturate; used as a sedative and a hypnotic [syn: amobarbital sodium, blue angel, Amytal] 7: any of numerous small chiefly blue butterflies of the family Lycaenidae 7: a sudden, inspirational thought "His suggestion came out of the blue!"

v : turn blue

bloc, block /blak/

bloc

n : a group of countries in special alliance [syn: axis]

block

n 1: a solid piece of something (usually having flat rectangular sides); "the pyramids were built with large stone blocks" 2: a rectangular area in a city surrounded by streets and usually containing several buildings; "he lives in the next block" [syn: city block] 3: a three-dimensional shape with six square or rectangular sides [syn: cube] 4: a number or quantity of related things dealt with as a unit; "he reserved a large block of seats"; "he held a large block of the company's stock" 5: housing in a large building that is divided into separate units; "there is a block of classrooms in the west wing" 6: (computer science) a sector or group of sectors that function as the smallest data unit permitted; "since blocks are often defined as a single sector, the terms `block' and `sector' are sometimes used interchangeably" 7: an inability to remember or think of something you normally can do; often caused by emotional tension; "I knew his name perfectly well but I had a temporary block" [syn: mental block] 8: a simple machine consisting of a wheel with a groove in which a rope can run to change the direction or point of application of a force applied to the rope [syn: pulley, pulley-block] 9: a metal casting containing the cylinders and cooling ducts of an engine; "the engine had to be replaced because the block was cracked" [syn: engine block, cylinder block] 10: an obstruction in a pipe or tube; "we had to call a plumber to clear out the blockage in the drainpipe" [syn: blockage, closure, occlusion, stop, stoppage] 11: a platform from which an auctioneer sells; "they put their paintings on the block" [syn: auction block] 12: the act of blocking someone's path with your body (as in football); "he threw a rolling block into the line backer" [syn: blocking, interference]

v 1: render unsuitable for passage; "block the way"; "barricade the streets" [syn: barricade, blockade, block off, block up, bar] 2: hinder or prevent the progress or accomplishment of; "His brother blocked him at every turn" [syn: obstruct, blockade, hinder, stymie, embarrass] 3: stop from happening or developing; "Block his election"; "Halt the process" [syn: stop, halt, kibosh] 4: interfere with or prevent the reception of signals; "Jam the Voice of America"; "block the signals emitted by this station" [syn: jam] 5: run on a block system; "block trains" 6: interrupt the normal function of by means of anesthesia; "block a nerve"; "block a muscle" 7: shut out from view; "The thick curtain blocked the action on the stage" 8: stamp or emboss a title or design on a book with a block; "block the book cover" 9:

obstruct, as of a passage; "My nose is all stuffed"; "Her arteries are blocked" [syn: stuff, lug, choke up] [ant: unstuff] 10: block passage through; "obstruct the path" [syn: obstruct, impede, occlude, jam, close up] [ant: free] 11: support, secure, or raise with a block; "block a plate for printing"; "block the wheels of a car" 12: impede the movement of (an opponent or a ball), as in sports or fights; "block an attack" [syn: parry, deflect] 13: be unable to remember; "I'm drawing a blank"; "You are blocking the name of your first wife!" [syn: forget, blank out, draw a blank] [ant: remember] 14: shape by using a block: "Block a hat"; "block a garment" 15: shape into a block or blocks; "block the graphs so one can see the results clearly" 16: prohibit the conversion or use of (assets); "Blocked funds"; "Freeze the assets of this hostile government" [syn: freeze, immobilize [ant: unblock, unblock]

boar, bore /bɔɹ/
boar
n 1: Old World wild swine having a narrow body and prominent tusks from which most domestic swine come; introduced in United States [syn: wild boar, Sus scrofa] 2: an uncastrated male hog

bore
n 1: a person who evokes boredom [syn: dullard] 2: a high wave (often dangerous) caused by tidal flow (as by colliding tidal currents or in a narrow estuary) [syn: tidal bore, eager] 3: diameter of a tube or gun barrel [syn: caliber] 4: (mining terms) a hole or passage made by a drill; usually made for exploratory purposes [syn: bore-hole, drill hole]
v 1: cause to be bored [syn: tire] [ant: interest] 2: drill a hole into [syn: drill] 3: (past of bear)

board, bored /bɔɹd/
board
n 1: a committee having supervisory powers; "the board has seven members" 2: a flat piece of material designed for a special purpose; "he nailed boards across the windows" 3: a stout length of sawn timber; made in a wide variety of sizes and used for many purposes [syn: plank] 4: a board on which information can be displayed to public view [syn: display panel, display board] 5: a flat portable surface (usually rectangular) designed for board games; "he got out the board and set up the pieces" [syn: game board] 6: food or meals in general; "she sets a fine table"; "room and board" [syn: table] 7: electrical device consisting of an insulated panel containing switches and dials and meters for controlling other electrical devices; "he checked the instrument panel"; "suddenly

the board lit up like a Christmas tree" [syn: control panel, instrument panel, control board, panel] 8: a printed circuit that can be inserted into expansion slots in a computer to increase the computer's capabilities [syn: circuit board, circuit card, card] 9: a table at which meals are served; "he helped her clear the dining table"; "a feast was spread upon the board" [syn: dining table]
v 1: get on board of (trains, buses, ships, aircraft, etc.) [syn: get on] [ant: get off] 2: live and take one's meals (in a certain place) [syn: room] 3: lodge and take meals (at) 4: provide food and lodging (for)

bored
adj 1: tired of the world; "bored with life"; "strolled through the museum with a bored air" [syn: world-weary] 2: uninterested because of frequent exposure or indulgence; "his blasé indifference"; "a petulant blasé air"; "the bored gaze of the successful film star" [syn: blasé]

boarder, border /ˈbɔɹdɚ/
boarder
n 1: a tenant in someone's house [syn: lodger, roomer] 2: someone who forces their way aboard ship; "stand by to repel boarders" 3: a pupil who lives at school during term time

border
n 1: a line that indicates a boundary [syn: boundary line, borderline, delimitation] 2: the boundary line or the area immediately inside the boundary [syn: margin, perimeter] 3: the boundary of a surface [syn: edge] 4: a decorative recessed or relieved surface on an edge [syn: molding] 5: a strip forming the outer edge of something: "the rug had a wide blue border"
v 1: extend on all sides of simultaneously; encircle; "The forest borders my property" [syn: surround, skirt] 2: form the boundary of; be contiguous to [syn: bound] 3: enclose in or as if in a frame; "frame a picture" [syn: frame, frame in] 4: provide with a border or edge; "edge the tablecloth with embroidery" [syn: edge] 5: lie adjacent to another; "Canada adjoins the U.S." [syn: adjoin, edge, abut, butt, butt against, butt on]

bobbin, bobbing /ˈbɑbɪn/
bobbin
n : a winder around which thread or tape or film or other flexible materials can be wound [syn: spool, reel]

bobbing (also /ˈbɑbɪŋ/)
v : (progressive of bob)1: move up and down repeatedly; "When the red, red robin goes bobbin' along."; "They're bobbing for apples." 2: ride a bobsled; "The boys bobbed down the hill screaming with

HOMOPHONES

pleasure" [syn: bobsledding] 3: remove or shorten the tail of an animal [syn: docking, tailing] 4: make a curtsy; usually done only by girls and women; as a sign of respect; "She curtsied when she shook the Queen's hand" [syn: curtsying] 5: cut hair in the style of a bob; "Bernice bobs her hair these days!"

bocks, box /baks/
bocks
n : (plu. of bock) strong dark beers brewed in the fall and aged through the winter for spring consumption [syn: bock beers]

box
n 1: a (usually rectangular) container; may have a lid; "he rummaged through a box of spare parts" 2: private area in a theater or grandstand where a small group can watch the performance; "the royal box was empty" [syn: loge] 3: the quantity contained in a box; "he gave her a box of chocolates" [syn: boxful] 4: a predicament from which a skillful or graceful escape is impossible; "his lying got him into a tight corner" [syn: corner] 5: a rectangular drawing; "the flowchart contained many boxes" 6: evergreen shrubs or small trees [syn: boxwood] 7: any one of several designated areas on a ball field where the batter or catcher or coaches are positioned; "the umpire warned the batter to stay in the batter's box" 8: the driver's seat on a coach; "an armed guard sat in the box with the driver" [syn: box seat] 9: separate partitioned area in a public place for a few people; "the sentry stayed in his box to avoid the cold" 10: a blow with the hand (usually on the ear); "I gave him a good box on the ear"
v 1: put into a box; "box the gift, please" [syn: package] [ant: unbox] 2: hit with the fist; "I'll box your ears!" 3: engage in a boxing match; in sport

bode, bowed /boud/
bode
v : indicate by signs; "These signs bode bad news" [syn: portend, auspicate, prognosticate, omen, presage, betoken, foreshadow, augur, foretell, prefigure, forecast, predict]

bowed
adj 1: used especially of the head or upper back; "a bent head and sloping shoulders" [syn: bent, inclined] 2: (music) of a stringed instrument; sounded by stroking with a bow [ant: plucked] 3: (architecture) forming or resembling an arch; "an arched ceiling" [syn: arced, arched, arching] 4: have legs that curve outward at the knees [syn: bandy, bandy-legged, bowleg, bowlegged]

bold, bowled /bould/
bold
adj 1: fearless and daring; "bold settlers on some foreign shore"; "a bold speech"; "a bold adventure" [ant: timid] 2: clear and distinct; "bold handwriting"; "a figure carved in bold relief"; "a bold design" 3: very steep; having a prominent and almost vertical front; "a bluff headland"; "where the bold chalk cliffs of England rise"; "a sheer descent of rock" [syn: bluff, sheer]
n : a typeface with thick heavy lines [syn: boldface, bold face]

bowled
adj : having the shape of a bowl
v : (past of "bowl"); "She bowled a good game."

bolder, boulder /'bouldɹ/
bolder
adj (compar of bold); "He made a bolder statement than the teacher."

boulder
n 1: a large smooth mass of rock detached from its place of origin

bole, boll, bowl /boul/
bole
n 1: a soft oily clay used as a pigment (especially a reddish brown pigment) 2: the main stem of a tree; usually covered with bark; the bole is usually the part that is commercially useful for lumber [syn: trunk, tree trunk]

boll
n : the rounded seed-bearing capsule of a cotton or flax plant

bowl
n 1: a round vessel that is open at the top; used for holding fruit or liquids or for serving food 2: a concave shape with an open top [syn: trough] 3: a dish that is round and open at the top for serving foods 4: the quantity contained in a bowl [syn: bowlful] 5: a large structure for open-air sports or entertainments [syn: stadium, arena] 6: a wooden ball (with flattened sides) used in the game of bowls 7: a small round container that is open at the top for holding tobacco [syn: pipe bowl]
v 1: roll (a ball), as in bowling 2: go bowling

boos, booze /buz/
boos
n : (plu. of boo) cries or noises made to express displeasure or contempt [syn: hoots, Bronx cheers, hisses, raspberries, razzings, snorts, birds]
v : (3rd pers sing of boo) shows displeasure, as after a performance or speech [syn: hisses] [ant: applauds]

booze
n : distilled rather than fermented [syn: liquor, spirits, hard drink, hard liquor, John Barleycorn, strong drink]

HOMOPHONES

v : consume alcohol; "We were up drinking all night" [syn: drink, fuddle]

bootie, booty /'buti/

bootie

n : a slipper that is soft and wool (usu. for babies) [syn: bootee]

booty

n 1: goods or money obtained illegally [syn: loot, pillage, plunder, prize, swag] 2: (slang) derriere

born, borne /bɔɹn/

born

adj 1: brought into existence; "he was a child born of adultery" [ant: unborn] 2: being talented through inherited qualities; "a natural leader"; "a born musician"; "an innate talent" [syn: natural,, innate]

borne

v : (past of bear); "He had borne guilt for twenty years."

bourne

n : a small stream; a brook

borough, burro, burrow /'bʌɹou/

borough

n 1: one of the administrative divisions of a large city "New York City has five boroughs." 2: an English town that forms the constituency of a member of Parliament

burro

n : small donkey used as a pack animal

burrow

n : a hole in the ground made by an animal for shelter [syn: tunnel]

v : move through by or as by digging; "burrow through the forest" [syn: tunnel]

bough, bow /baʊ/

bough

n : any of the larger branches of a tree

bow

adj : pertaining to the forward part of a vessel

n 1: front part of a vessel or aircraft; "he pointed the bow of the boat toward the finish line" [syn: fore, prow, stem] 2: an appearance by actors or performers at the end of the concert or play in order to acknowledge the applause of the audience [syn: curtain call]

v 1: bend one's knee or body, or lower one's head; "He bowed before the King"; "She bowed her head in shame" [syn: bow down] 2: submit or yield to another's wish or opinion; "The government bowed to the military pressure" [syn: submit, defer, accede, give in] 3: bend the head or the upper part of the body in a gesture of respect or greeting; "He bowed before the King" 4: bend one's back forward from the waist on down; "he crouched down"; "She bowed before the Queen"; "The young man stooped to pick up the girl's

purse" [syn: crouch, stoop, bend]

boughs, bouse, bows /baʊz/

boughs

n : (plu of bough)

bouse

v : haul with a tackle [syn: bowse]

bows

v : (3ʳᵈ pers sing of bow); "he bows before the king"

bouillon, bullion /'buljɪn/

bouillon

n : a clear seasoned broth

bullion

n 1: a mass of precious metal (usually in the form of bars or ingots) 2: gold or silver in bars or ingots

boy, buoy /bɔɪ/

boy

n 1: a youthful male person; "the baby was a boy"; "she made the boy brush his teeth every night"; "most soldiers are only boys in uniform" [syn: male child] [ant: girl, female child]

2: a friendly informal reference to a grown man; "he likes to play golf with the boys" 3: a male human offspring; "their son became a famous judge"; "his boy is taller than he is" [syn: son] [ant: daughter] 4: offensive term for Black man; "get out of my way boy"

buoy (also 'bu: i:

n : bright-colored; a float attached by rope to the seabed to mark channels in a harbor or underwater hazards

v 1: float on the surface of water 2: keep afloat: "The life vest buoyed him up" [syn: buoy up] 3: mark with a buoy

brae, bray /bɹeɪ/

brae

n : (Scotland) a slope or hillside

bray

n : the cry of an ass

v 1: braying characteristic of donkeys [syn: hee-haw] 2: reduce to small pieces or particles by pounding or abrading; "grind the spices in a mortar"; "mash the garlic" [syn: grind, mash, crunch, comminute] 3: laugh loudly and harshly

braid, brayed /bɹeɪd/

braid

n 1: a hairdo formed by interweaving three or more strands [syn: plait, tress, twist] 2: trimming used to decorate clothes or curtains [syn: gold braid, braiding]

v 1: make by braiding [syn: lace, plait] 2: decorate with braids or ribbons; "braid a collar" 3: form or weave into a braid or braids; "braid hair" [ant: unbraid]

brayed

v : (past of bray) "The donkey brayed all day."

HOMOPHONES

brail, braille /bɹeɪl/

brail

n 1: a rope for hauling a sail 2: a dip net for hauling fish

v 1: take in a sail with a brail 2: haul fish aboard with brails

braille

n: a point system of writing in which patterns of raised dots represent letters and numerals [syn: Braille]

v: transcribe in Braille

braes, braise, brays, braze / bɹɛɪz/

braes

n : a hillside or slope in Scotland or northern England

braise

v : cook in a small amount of liquid; "braise beef"

brays

v : (3rd pers sing) 1: braying characteristic of donkeys [syn: hee-haws] 2: reduces to small pieces or particles by pounding or abrading; "grinds the spices in a mortar"; "mashes the garlic" [syn: grinds, mashes, crunches, comminutes] 3: laughs loudly and harshly

braze

v : solder together by using hard solder with a high melting point

brain, brane /bɹeɪn/

brain

n 1: that part of the central nervous system that includes all the higher nervous centers; enclosed within the skull; continuous with the spinal cord; [syn: encephalon] 2: mental ability; "he's got plenty of brains but no common sense") [syn: brainpower, learning ability, mental capacity, mentality, wit] 3: that which is responsible for one's thoughts and feelings; the seat of the faculty of reason; "his mind wandered"; "I couldn't get his words out of my head") [syn: mind, head, psyche, nous] 4: someone who has exceptional intellectual ability and originality; "Mozart was a child genius"; "he's smart but he's no Einstein" [syn: genius, mastermind, brainiac, Einstein] 5: the brain of certain animals used as meat

v 1: hit on the head 2: kill by smashing someone's skull

brane

n: (theoretical physics) space and region that defines the observable universe as dictated by string theory. [syn: membrane]

brake, break /bɹeɪk/

brake

n 1: a restraint used to slow or stop a vehicle 2: any of various ferns of the genus Pteris having pinnately compound leaves and including several popular houseplants 3: large coarse fern often several feet high; essentially weed ferns; cosmopolitan [syn: bracken, pasture brake, Pteridium aquilinum] 4: an area thickly overgrown usually with one kind of plant

v 1: stop traveling by applying a brake; "We had to brake suddenly when a chicken crossed the road" 2: cause to stop by applying the brakes

break

n 1: some abrupt occurrence that interrupts; "the telephone is an annoying interruption"; "there was a break in the action when a player was hurt" [syn: interruption] 2: an unexpected piece of good luck; "he finally got his big break" [syn: good luck, happy chance] 3: (geology) a crack in the earth's crust resulting from the displacement of one side with respect to the other; "they built it right over a geological fault" [syn: fault, geological fault, shift, fracture] 4: a personal or social separation (as between opposing factions); "they hoped to avoid a break in relations" [syn: rupture, breach, severance, rift, falling out] 5: a pause from doing something (as work); "we took a 10-minute break"; "he took time out to recuperate" [syn: respite, recess, time out] 6: the act of breaking something; "the breakage was unavoidable" [syn: breakage, breaking] 7: a time interval during which there is a temporary cessation of something [syn: pause, intermission, interruption, suspension] 8: breaking of hard tissue such as bone; "it was a nasty fracture"; "the break seems to have been caused by a fall" [syn: fracture] 9: the occurrence of breaking; "the break in the dam threatened the valley" 10: the opening shot that scatters the balls in billiards or pool 11: (tennis) a score consisting of winning a game when your opponent was serving; "he was up two breaks in the second set" [syn: break of serve] 12: an act of delaying or interrupting the continuity; "it was presented without commercial breaks" [syn: interruption, disruption, gap] 13: a sudden dash; "he made a break for the open door" 14: any frame in which a bowler fails to make a strike or spare; "the break in the eighth frame cost him the match" [syn: open frame] 15: an escape from jail; "the breakout was carefully planned" [syn: breakout, jailbreak, prison break, prison-breaking]

v 1: end prematurely; "She interrupted her pregnancy"; "break a lucky streak" [syn: interrupt] 2: become separated into pieces or fragments; "The figurine broke"; "The freshly baked loaf fell apart" [syn: separate, split up, fall apart, come apart] 3: destroy the integrity of; usually by force; cause to separate into pieces or fragments; "He broke the glass plate"; "She broke the

HOMOPHONES

match" 4: render inoperable or ineffective; "You broke the alarm clock when you took it apart!" 5: ruin completely; "He busted my radio!" [syn: bust] [ant: repair] 6: act in disregard of laws and rules; "offend all laws of humanity"; "violate the basic laws or human civilization"; "break a law" [syn: transgress, offend, infract, violate, go against, breach] 7: move away or escape suddenly; "The horses broke from the stable"; "Three inmates broke jail" [syn: break out, break away] 8: scatter or part; "The clouds broke after the heavy downpour" 9: force out or release suddenly and often violently something pent up; "break into tears"; "erupt in anger" [syn: burst, erupt] 10: prevent completion; "stop the project"; "break the silence" [syn: break off, discontinue, stop] 11: enter someone's property in an unauthorized manner, usually with the intent to steal or commit a violent act; "Someone broke in while I was on vacation"; "They broke into my car and stole my radio!" [syn: break in] 12: make submissive, obedient, or useful, as of wild animals or new items: "The horse was tough to break"; used metaphorically for people [syn: break in] 13: fail to agree with; be in violation of; as of rules or patterns; "He violated the agreement to stay away from his ex-wife"; "You are breaking the law!" [syn: violate, go against] [ant: conform to] 14: surpass in excellence; "She bettered her own record"; "break a record" [syn: better] 15: make known to the public information that was previously known only to a few people or that was meant to be kept a secret; "The auction house would not disclose the price at which the van Gogh had sold"; "The actress won't reveal how old she is"; "bring out the truth"; "he broke the news to her" [syn: disclose, let on, bring out, reveal, discover, expose, declare, divulge, impart, give away, let out] 16: come into being; "light broke over the horizon"; "Voices broke in the air" 17: stop operating or functioning; "The engine finally went"; "The car died on the road"; "The bus we traveled in broke down on the way to town"; "The coffee maker broke"; "The engine failed on the way to town"; "her eyesight went after the accident" [syn: fail, go bad, give way, die, give out, conk out, go, break down] 18: interrupt a continued activity; "She had broken with the traditional patterns" [syn: break away] 19: make a rupture in the ranks of the enemy or one's own by quitting or fleeing (military usage); "The ranks broke" 20: curl over and fall apart in surf or foam, of waves; "The surf broke" 21: lessen in force or effect; "soften a shock"; "break a

fall" [syn: dampen, damp, soften, weaken] 22: be broken in; "If the new teacher won't break, we'll add some stress" 23: come to an end; "The heat wave finally broke yesterday" 24: vary or interrupt a uniformity or continuity; "The flat plain was broken by sharply mesas" 25: cause to give up a habit; "She finally broke herself of smoking cigarettes" 26: give up: "break cigarette smoking" 27: come forth or begin from a state of latency; "The first winter storm broke over New York" 28: happen or take place; "Things have been breaking pretty well for us in the past few months" (informal) 29: cause the failure or ruin of; "His peccadilloes finally broke his marriage"; "This play will either make or break the playwright" [ant: make] 30: invalidate by judicial action; "The will was broken" 31: stop or interrupt; "He broke the engagement"; "We had to break our plans for a trip to China" 32: divide into pieces, as by bending or cutting; "break the loaf of bread"; "break the crackers" 33: discontinue an association or relation; go different ways; "The business partners broke over a tax question"; "The couple separated after 25 years of marriage"; "My friend and I split up" [syn: separate, part, split up, split, break up] 34: assign to a lower position; reduce in rank; "She was demoted because she always speaks up" [syn: demote, bump, relegate, kick downstairs] [ant: promote] 35: reduce to bankruptcy; "My daughter's fancy wedding is going to break me!" [syn: bankrupt, ruin] 36: change directions suddenly 37: emerge from the surface, as of fish in water; "The whales broke" 38: break down, literally or metaphorically; "The wall collapsed"; "The business collapsed"; "The dam broke"; "The roof collapsed"; "The wall gave in"; "The roof finally gave under the weight of the ice" [syn: collapse, fall in, cave in, give, give way, founder] 39: do a break dance; "Kids were break-dancing at the street corner" [syn: break dance, break-dance] 40: exchange for smaller units of money; "I had to break a $100 bill just to buy the candy" 41: destroy the completeness of a set of related items; "The book dealer would not break the set" [syn: break up] 42: make the opening shot that scatters the balls, in billiards or pool 43: separate from a clinch, in boxing; "The referee broke the boxers" 44: go to pieces; "The lawn mower finally broke"; "The gears wore out"; "The old chair finally fell apart completely" [syn: wear, wear out, bust, fall apart] 45: break a piece from a whole; "break a branch from a tree" [syn: break off, snap off] 46: pierce the surface of;

HOMOPHONES

"The fish broke the water" 47: become punctured or penetrated: "The skin broke" 48: pierce or penetrate; "The blade broke her skin" 49: be released or become known; of news; "News of her death broke in the morning" [syn: get out, get around] 50: cease an action temporarily; "We pause for station identification"; "let's break for lunch" [syn: pause, intermit] 51: interrupt the flow of current in; "break a circuit" 52: undergo breaking; "The simple vowels broke in many Germanic languages" 53: find a flaw in: "break an alibi" 54: find the solution or key to; "break the code" 55: change suddenly from one tone quality or register to another; "Her voice broke to a whisper when she started to talk about her children" 56: stop and wait, as if awaiting further instructions or developments; "Hold on a moment!"; "We broke at noon" [syn: hold on, stop] 57: happen, as of an event; "Report the news as it develops"; "These political movements recrudesce from time to time" [syn: recrudesce, develop] 58: become fractured; break or crack on the surface only; "The glass cracked when it was heated" [syn: crack, check] 59: of the male voice in puberty; "his voice is breaking--he should no longer sing in the choir" 60: fall sharply; "stock prices broke" 61: fracture a bone of: "I broke my foot while playing hockey" [syn: fracture] 62: diminish or discontinue abruptly; "The patient's fever broke last night" 63: weaken or destroy in spirit or body; "For a hero loves the world till it breaks him"--Yeats

breach, breech /bɹitʃ/
breach
n 1: a failure to perform some promised act or obligation 2: an opening (especially a gap in a dike or fortification) 3: a personal or social separation (as between opposing factions); "they hoped to avoid a break in relations" [syn: rupture, break, severance, rift, falling out]
v 1: act in disregard of laws and rules; "offend all laws of humanity"; "violate the basic laws or human civilization"; "break a law" [syn: transgress, offend, infract, violate, go against, break] 2: make an opening or gap in [syn: gap]
breech
n : opening in the rear of the barrel of a gun where bullets can be loaded [syn: rear of barrel, rear of tube]

bread, bred /bɹɛd/
bread
n 1: food made from dough of flour or meal and usually raised with yeast or baking powder and then baked [syn: breadstuff, staff of life] 2: informal terms for money [syn: shekels, gelt, dough, dinero, lucre,

loot, pelf, moolah, cabbage, kale]
v : cover with bread crumbs, as of pork chops
bred
v (past of breed) 1: call forth [syn: engendered, spawned] 2: copulate with a female, used esp. of horses; "The horse covered the mare" 3: of plants or animals; "She bred dogs" 4: had young; used of animals; derogatory when used for people [syn: multiplied]

bream, brim /bɹɪm/
bream (also /bɹim/)
n 1: flesh of various freshwater fishes of North America or of Europe [syn: freshwater bream] 2: flesh of any of various saltwater fishes of the family Sparidae or the family Bramidae [syn: sea bream] 3: any of numerous marine percoid fishes especially (but not exclusively) of the family Sparidae [syn: sea bream] 4: any of various usually edible freshwater percoid fishes having compressed bodies and shiny scales; especially (but not exclusively) of the genus Lepomis [syn: freshwater bream]
v : clean (a ship's bottom) with heat
brim
n 1: the top edge of a vessel [syn: rim, lip] 2: a circular projection that sticks outward from the crown of a hat
v 1: be completely full; "His eyes brimmed with tears" 2: fill as much as possible; "brim a cup to good fellowship" [also: brimming, brimmed]

breadth, breath_
breadth /bɹɛdθ/
n 1: the capacity to understand a broad range of topics; "a teacher must have a breadth of knowledge of the subject"; "a man distinguished by the largeness and scope of his views" 2: extent of something from side to side
breath /bɹɛθ/
n 1: the process of taking in and expelling air during breathing; "he took a deep breath and dived into the pool"; "he was fighting to his last breath" 2: the air that is inhaled and exhaled in respiration; "his sour breath offended her" 3: a short respite 4: an indirect suggestion; "not a breath of scandal ever touched her" 5: a slight movement of the air; "there wasn't a breath of air in the room"

brewed, brood /bɹud/
brewed
adj having been prepared by brewing; having set in boiling water to extract the flavor; "the tea is brewed" [syn: steeped, infused]
brood
adj : good at incubating eggs especially a

fowl kept for that purpose; "a brood hen" [syn: brooding, hatching]

n : the young of an animal cared for at one time

v 1: think moodily or anxiously about something [syn: worry, dwell] 2: hang over, as of something threatening, dark, or menacing; "The terrible vision brooded over her all day long" [syn: hover, loom, bulk large] 3: be in a huff [syn: sulk, pout] 4: be in a huff; be silent or sullen [syn: sulk, grizzle, stew] 5: sit on (eggs); "Birds brood"; "The female covers the eggs" [syn: hatch, cover, incubate].

brews, brewis, bruise /bɹuz/
brews

n : drinks made by steeping and boiling and fermenting rather than distilling [syn: brewages]

v 1: prepare by brewing; of alcoholic beverages 2: sit or let sit in boiling water to extract the flavor; "She brews tea everyday." [syn: steeps, infuses]

brewis

n : bread soaked in broth, drippings of roast meat, milk, or water and butter.

bruise

n : an injury that doesn't break the skin but results in some discoloration [syn: contusion]

v 1: injure the underlying soft tissue of bone of; "I bruised my knee" [syn: contuse] 2: hurt the feelings of; "She hurt me when she did not include me among her guests"; "This remark really bruised me ego" [syn: hurt, wound, injure, offend, spite] 3: break up into small pieces, as in food preparation; "bruise the berries with a wooden spoon and strain them" 4: damage (plant tissue) by abrasion of pressure; "The customer bruised the strawberries by squeezing them"

bridal, bridle /bɹaɪdᵊl/
bridal

adj 1: of or relating to a wedding; "bridal procession"; "nuptial day"; "spousal rites"; "wedding cake"; "marriage vows" [syn: nuptial, spousal] 2: designed for a bride; "bridal gown"

n : archaic terms for a wedding or wedding feast [syn: espousal]

bridle

n 1: headgear for a horse; includes a headstall and bit and reins to give the rider or driver control 2: the act of restraining power or action or limiting excess; "his common sense is a bridle to his quick temper" [syn: check, curb]

v 1: put a bridle on; "bridle horses" 2: respond to the reins, as of horses

broach, brooch /bɹoʊtʃ/
broach

n : a decorative pin worn by women [syn: brooch, breastpin]

v : bring up a topic for discussion [syn: initiate]

brooch

n : a decorative pin worn by women [syn: broach, breastpin]

v : fasten with or as if with a brooch [syn: clasp]

broom, brougham /bɹum/
broom

n 1: a cleaning implement for sweeping; bundle of straws or twigs attached to a long handle 2: any of various shrubs of the genera Cytisus or Genista or Spartium having long slender branches and racemes of yellow flowers 3: common Old World heath represented by many varieties; low evergreen grown widely in the northern hemisphere [syn: heather, ling, Scots heather, Calluna vulgaris]

v 1: sweep with a broom or as if with a broom; "Sweep the crumbs off the table"; "Sweep under the bed" [syn: sweep] 2: finish with a broom

brougham

n 1: light carriage; pulled by a single horse 2: a sedan that has no roof over the driver's seat

brows, browse /bɹaʊz/
brows

n 1: (plu of brow) the part of the face above the eyes [syn: foreheads] 2: the arch of hair above each eye [syn: eyebrows, supercilia] 3: the peak of a hill; "the sun set behind the brow of distant hills" [syn: hilltops]

browse

n 1: reading superficially or at random [syn: browsing] 2: the act of feeding by continual nibbling [syn: browsing]..3: tender shoots, twigs and leaves fit for cattle food

v 1: shop around; not necessarily buying; "I don't need help, I'm just browsing" [syn: shop] 2: feed as in a meadow or pasture; "the herd was grazing" [syn: crop, graze, range, pasture] 3: look around casually and randomly, without seeking anything in particular; "browse a computer directory"; "surf the internet or the world wide web" [syn: surf] 4: eat lightly, try different dishes; "There was so much food at the party that we quickly got sated just by browsing" [syn: graze]

bruit, brut, brute /bɹut/
bruit

v : tell or spread rumors; "It was rumored that the next president would be a woman" [syn: rumor]

brut

adj : (of champagne) extremely dry

brute

adj : resembling a beast; showing lack of human sensibility; "beastly desires";

HOMOPHONES

"a bestial nature"; "brute force"; "a dull and brutish man"; "bestial treatment of prisoners" [syn: beastly, bestial, brutish]

n 1: a cruelly rapacious person [syn: beast, wolf, savage, wildcat] 2: a living organism characterized by voluntary movement [syn: animal, animate being, beast, creature, fauna]

buccal, buckle /'bʌkəl/

buccal

adj 1: of or relating to or toward the cheek 2: lying within the mouth; "a buccal gland" 3: toward the inside of the cheek; "the buccal aspect of the gum" [syn: cheek]

buckle

n 1: fastener that fastens together two ends of a belt or strap; often has loose prong 2: a shape distorted by twisting or folding [syn: warp]

v 1: fasten with a buckle or buckles [syn: clasp] [ant: unbuckle] 2: fold or collapse; "His knees buckled" [syn: crumple] 3: bend out of shape, as under pressure or from heat; "The highway buckled during the heat wave" [syn: heave, warp]

burger, burgher /'bɜːrɡər/

burger

n : var hamburger

burgher

n 1: a citizen of an English borough [syn: burgess] 2: a member of the middle class [syn: bourgeois]

bus, buss /bʌs/

bus

n 1: a vehicle carrying many passengers; used for public transport; "he always rode the bus to work" [syn: autobus, coach, double-decker, jitney, motorbus, motor coach, omnibus] 2: an electrical conductor that makes a common connection between several circuits; "the bus in this computer can transmit data either way between any two components of the system" 3: a car that is old and unreliable; "the fenders had fallen off that old bus" [syn: jalopy, heap]

v 1: send or move around by bus; "The children were bussed to school" 2: ride in a bus 3: remove used dishes from the table, in restaurants

buss

n : a caress with the lips [syn: kiss, osculation]

v : touch with the lips or press the lips (against someone's mouth or other body part) as an expression of love, greeting, etc.; "The newly married couple kissed"; "She kissed her grandfather on the forehead when she entered the room" [syn: kiss, osculate]

bused, bussed, bust /bʌst/

bused

v : (past bus) "The children are bused to school."

bussed

v : (past bussed) "He bussed his girlfriend.) [syn: kissed]

bust

adj : lacking funds; [syn: broke, stone-broke]

n 1: a complete failure; "the play was a dismal flop" [syn: flop] 2: a sculpture of the head and shoulders of a person 3: an occasion for excessive eating or drinking; "they went on a bust that lasted three days" [syn: tear, binge, bout] 4: an arrest by police

v 1: ruin completely; "He busted my radio!" [syn: break] [ant: repair] 2: search without warning, make a sudden surprise attack on; "The police raided the crack house" [syn: raid] 3: separate or cause to separate abruptly; "The rope snapped"; "tear the paper" [syn: tear, rupture, snap] 4: go to pieces; "The lawn mower finally broke"; "The gears wore out"; "The old chair finally fell apart completely" [syn: break, wear, wear out, fall apart] 5: break open or apart suddenly and forcefully; "The dam burst" [syn: burst]

but, butt /bʌt/

but

conj : and nothing more; "But, I was merely asking"; "but it is simply a matter of time"; " but just a scratch"; "but he was only a child"; "hopes that last but a moment" [syn: merely, simply, just, only]

butt

n 1: thick end of the handle [syn: butt end] 2: a victim of ridicule or pranks [syn: goat, laughingstock, stooge] 3: the fleshy part of the human body that you sit on [syn: buttocks, nates, arse, backside, bum, buns, can, fundament, hindquarters, hind end, keister, posterior, prat, rear, rear end, rump, stern, seat, tail, tail end, tushie, tush, bottom, behind, derriere, fanny, ass, booty] 4: sports equipment consisting of an object set up for a marksman or archer to aim at [syn: target] 5: finely ground tobacco wrapped in paper; for smoking [syn: cigarette, cigarette, coffin nail, fag] 6: a joint made by fastening ends together without overlapping [syn: butt joint] 7: a large cask (especially one holding a volume equivalent to 2 hogsheads or 126 gallons) 8: the small unused part of something (especially the end of a cigarette that is left after smoking) [syn: stub]

v 1: lie adjacent to another; "Canada adjoins the U.S." [syn: border, adjoin, edge, abut, butt against, butt on] 2: to strike, thrust or shove against, often with head or horns: "He butted his sister out of the way." [syn: bunt] 3: place end to end without overlapping; "The frames must be butted at the joints"

I-44

HOMOPHONES

byre, buyer /baɪɹ/
byre
n : a cow barn
buyer (also /'baɪjᵊɹ/)
n : a person who buys [syn: purchaser, emptor, vendee]

-C-

c, cee, sea, see /si/
c
adj 1: of a temperature scale that registers the freezing point of water as 0 degrees C and the boiling point as 100 degrees C under normal atmospheric pressure [syn: Celsius, centigrade] 2: being ten more than ninety [syn: hundred, a hundred, one hundred, 100]
n 1: a degree on the Centigrade scale of temperature [syn: degree Centigrade, degree Celsius, C] 2: the speed at which light travels in a vacuum; the constancy and universality of the speed of light is recognized by defining it to be exactly 299,792,458 meters per second [syn: speed of light, light speed] 3: ten 10s [syn: hundred, 100, C, century, one C] 4: a general-purpose programming language closely associated with the UNIX operating system [syn: C] 4: the 3rd letter of the Roman alphabet [syn: C] 5: a narcotic (alkaloid) extracted from coca leaves; used as a surface anesthetic or taken for pleasure; can become addictive [syn: cocaine, coke, snow, C] 6: an abundant nonmetallic tetravalent element occurring in three allotropic forms: amorphous carbon and graphite and diamond; occurs in all organic compounds [syn: carbon, C, atomic number 6]
cee
n : the letter C
sea
adj : relating to or characteristic of or occurring on the sea or ships; "sea stories"; "sea smells"; "sea traffic" [ant: air, land]
n 1: a division of an ocean or a large body of salt water partially enclosed by land 2: anything apparently limitless in quantity or volume [syn: ocean] 3: turbulent water with swells of considerable size; "heavy seas"
see
n : the seat within a bishop's diocese where his cathedral is located
adv : compare (used in texts to point the reader to another location in the text) [syn: cf., confer, see also]
v 1: perceive by sight or have the power to perceive by sight; "You have to be a good observer to see all the details"; "Can you see the bird in that tree?" "He is blind--he cannot see" 2: perceive mentally, as of an idea; "Now I see!"; "I just can't see your point"; "Does she realize how important this decision is?"; "I don't understand the idea" [syn: understand, realize] 3: perceive with any or all of one's senses; "We found

HOMOPHONES

Republicans winning the offices"; "You'll see a lot of cheating in this school"; give rise to or be characterized by; "The 1960 saw the rebellion of the younger generation against established traditions"; "I want to see results" [syn: witness, find] 4: imagine; conceive of; see in one's mind; "I can't see him on horseback!" "I can see what will happen"; "I can see a risk in this strategy" [syn: visualize, envision, project, fancy, figure, picture, image] 5: consider or deem to be; regard; "She views this quite differently from me"; "I consider her to be shallow"; "I don't see the situation quite as negatively as you do" [syn: consider, reckon, view, regard] 6: get to know or become aware of, usually accidentally; "I learned that she has two grown-up children"; "I see that you have been promoted" [syn: learn, hear, get word, get wind, pick up, find out, get a line, discover] 7: see or watch; "view a show on television"; "This program will be seen all over the world"; "view an exhibition"; "Catch a show on Broadway"; "see a movie" [syn: watch, view, catch, take in] 8: find out, learn, or determine with certainty, usually by making an inquiry or other effort; "I want to see whether she speaks French"; "See whether it works"; "find out if he speaks Russian"; "Check whether the train leaves on time" [syn: determine, check, find out, ascertain, watch, learn] 9: come together; "I'll probably see you at the meeting"; "How nice to see you again!" [syn: meet, ran into, encounter, run across, come across] 10: be careful or certain to do something; make certain of something; "He verified that the valves were closed"; "See that the curtains are closed"; "control the quality of the product" [syn: check, insure, see to it, ensure, control, ascertain, assure] 11: go to see for professional or business reasons; "You should see a lawyer"; "We had to see a psychiatrist" 12: go to see for a social visit; "I went to see my friend Mary the other day" 13: visit a place, as for entertainment; "We went to see the Eiffel Tower in the morning" [syn: visit] 14: take charge of or deal with; "Could you see about lunch?"; "I must attend to this matter"; "She took care of this business" [syn: attend, take care, look] 15: receive as a specified guest; "the doctor will see you now"; "The minister doesn't see anybody before noon" 16: date regularly; have a steady relationship with; "Did you know that she is seeing an older man?" "He is dating his former wife again!" [syn: go steady, go out, date] 17: see and understand, have a good eye; "The artist must first learn to see" 18:

deliberate or decide; "See whether you can come tomorrow"; "let's see--which movie should we see tonight?" 19: observe as if with an eye; "The camera saw the burglary and recorded it" 20: observe, check out, and look over carefully or inspect; "The customs agent examined the baggage"; "I must see your passport before you can enter the country" [syn: examine] 21: go or live through; "We had many trials to go through"; "he saw action in Viet Nam" [syn: experience, undergo, go through] 22: accompany or escort: "I'll see you to the door" [syn: escort] 23: match or meet in card games; "I saw the bet of one of my fellow players" 24: make sense of; assign a meaning to; "What message do you see in this letter?" "How do you interpret his behavior?" [syn: interpret, construe]

C's, cees, seas, sees, seize
/siz/

C's
n : (plu of C): (see C); "The exam grades were low; many C's and D's."

cees
n : more than one letter C

seas
n : (plu of sea): (see C); "The seas were rough."

sees
v : (3rd pers sing of see): (see C); "He sees on weekends."

seize
v 1: take hold of; grab; "The salesclerk quickly seized the money on the counter"; "She clutched her purse"; "The mother seized her child by the arm"; "Birds of prey often seize small mammals" [syn: apprehend, clutch] 2: take or capture by force; "The terrorists seized the politicians"; "The rebels threaten to seize civilian hostages" 3: take possession of without permission or take with force, as after a conquest or invasion; "the invaders seized the land and property of the inhabitants"; "The army seized the town"; "The militia captured the castle" [syn: appropriate, capture, conquer, take over] 4: take by legal authority; "The FBI seized the drugs"; "The customs agents impounded the illegal shipment"; "The police confiscated the stolen artwork" [syn: impound, attach, sequester, confiscate] 5: take control of; take as one's right or possession; "He assumed to himself the right to fill all positions in the town"; "he usurped my rights"; "She seized control of the throne after her husband died" [syn: assume, usurp, take over, arrogate] 6: hook by a pull on the line; "strike a fish" 7: affect; "Fear seized the prisoners"; "The patient was seized with unbearable pains"; "He was seized with a dreadful disease"

HOMOPHONES

[syn: clutch, get hold of] 8: capture the attention or imagination of; "This story will grab you"; "The movie seized my imagination" [syn: grab]

cache, cash /kæʃ/
cache
n 1: a hidden storage space (for money or provisions or weapons) 2: a secret store of valuables or money [syn: hoard, stash] 3: (computer science) RAM memory that is set aside as a specialized buffer storage that is continually updated; used to optimize data transfers between system elements with different characteristics [syn: memory cache]
v : save up as for future use [syn: hoard, stash, lay away, hive up, squirrel away]

cash
n 1: money in the form of bills or coins [syn: hard cash, hard currency] 2: prompt payment for goods or services in currency or by check [syn: immediate payment] [ant: credit]
v : exchange for cash [syn: cash in]

cachou, cashew /'kæʃu/
cachou
n : a scented lozenge used to sweeten the breath (e.g. to conceal the odor of tobacco)

cashew
n 1: tropical American evergreen tree bearing kidney-shaped nuts that are edible only when roasted [syn: cashew tree, Anacardium occidental] 2: kidney-shaped nut edible only when roasted [syn: cashew nut]

cain, cane, kain /kɛɪn/
cain
n : a percentage of the crop paid as rent in ireland or Scotland

cane
n 1: a stick that people can lean on to help them walk 2: a strong slender often flexible stem as of bamboos, reeds, rattans, or sugar cane 3: a stiff switch used to hit students as punishment
v : beat with a cane [syn: flog, lambast]

kain
n : a sarong; grass skirt

calculous, calculus
/'kælkuəlˢs/
calculous
adj : relating to or caused by or having a calculus or calculi

calculus
n 1: a hard lump produced by the concretion of mineral salts; found in hollow organs or ducts of the body; "renal calculi can be very painful" [syn: concretion] 2: an incrustation that forms on the teeth and gums [syn: tartar, tophus] 3: the branch of mathematics that is concerned with limits and with the differentiation and integration of functions [syn: the calculus,

infinitesimal calculus]

calendar, calender, colander
calendar /'kælendˢ.ɹ/
n 1: a system of timekeeping that defines the beginning and length and divisions of the year 2: a list or register of events (appointments or social events or court cases etc); "I have you on my calendar for next Monday" 3: a tabular array of the days (usually for one year)
v : enter into a calendar

calender /'kælendˢ.ɹ/
n : a machine that smoothes or glazes paper or cloth by pressing it between plates or passing it through rollers
v : press between rollers or plates so as to smooth, glaze, or thin into sheets; as of paper or cloth

colander /'kolendˢ.ɹ/
n : bowl-shaped strainer; used to wash or drain foods

calix, calyx /'kɛɪlɪks/
calix
n 1: chalice; 2: cup

calyx
n : the sepals of a flower collectively forming the outer floral envelope or layer of the perianth enclosing a developing bud; usually green

calk, caulk /kɔk/
calk
n : a metal cleat on the bottom front of a horseshoe to prevent slipping
v 1: provide with calks; "calk horse shoes" 2: injure with a calk

caulk
v : seal with caulking; "caulk the window"

call, caul /kɔl/
call
n 1: a telephone connection; "she reported several anonymous calls"; "he placed a phone call to London"; "he heard the phone ringing but didn't want to take the call" [syn: phone call, telephone call] 2: a special disposition (as if from a divine source) to pursue a particular course; "he was disappointed that he had not heard the Call" 3: a loud utterance; often in protest or opposition; "the speaker was interrupted by loud cries from the rear of the audience" [syn: cry, outcry, yell, shout, vociferation] 4: a demand especially in the phrase "the call of duty" [syn: claim] 5: the characteristic sound produced by a bird; "a bird will not learn its song unless it hears it at an early age" [syn: birdcall, birdsong, song] 6: a brief social visit: "senior professors' wives no longer make afternoon calls on newcomers" 7: a demand by a broker that a customer deposit enough to bring his margin up to the minimum requirement [syn: margin call] 8: a demand for a show of hands

in a card game; "after two raises there was a call" 9: a request; "many calls for Christmas stories"; "not many calls for buggy whips" 10: an instruction that interrupts the program being executed; "Visual Basic performs calls by simply giving the name of the routine to be executed" 11: brief visit in an official or professional capacity: "the pastor's visits to his parishioners"; "a visit to a dentist"; "the salesman's call on a customer" 12: (sports) the decision made by an umpire or referee; "he was ejected for protesting the call" 13: the option to buy a given stock (or stock index or commodity future) at a given price before a given date [syn: call option] [ant: put option]

v 1: assign a specified, proper name to; "They named their son David"; "The new school was named after the famous Civil Rights leader" [syn: name] 2: get or try to get into communication (with someone) by telephone; "I tried to call you all night"; "Take two aspirin and call me in the morning" [syn: telephone, call up, phone, ring] 3: ascribe a quality to or give a name of a common noun that reflects a quality; "He called me a bastard"; "She called her children lazy and ungrateful" 4: order, request, or command to come; "She was called into the director's office"; "Call the police!" [syn: send for] 5: utter a sudden loud cry; "she cried with pain when the doctor inserted the needle"; "I yelled to her from the window but she couldn't hear me" [syn: shout, shout out, cry, yell, scream, holler, squall] 6: pay a brief visit; "The mayor likes to call on some of the prominent citizens" [syn: visit, call in] 7: call a meeting; invite or command to meet; "The Wannsee Conference was called to discuss the 'Final Solution'; "The new dean calls meetings every week" 8: order or request or give a command for; "The unions called a general strike for Sunday" 9: order, summon, or request for a specific duty or activity, work, role; "He was already called 4 times for jury duty"; "They called him to active military duty" 10: indicate a decision in regard to (sports): "call balls and strikes behind the plate" 11: stop or postpone because of adverse conditions, such as bad weather; "call a football game" 12: read aloud to check for omissions or absentees; "Call roll" 13: send a message or attempt to reach someone by radio, phone, etc.; make a signal to in order to transmit a message; "Hawaii is calling!"; "A transmitter in Samoa was heard calling" 14: declare in the capacity of an umpire or referee; "call a runner out" 15: utter a characteristic note or cry; "blue jays called to one another"

16: utter in a loud voice or announce; "He called my name"; "The auctioneer called the bids" 17: make a prediction about; tell in advance; "Call the outcome of an election" [syn: predict, foretell, prognosticate, forebode, anticipate, promise] 18: challenge (somebody) to make good on a statement; charge with or censure for an offense; "He deserves to be called on that" 19: consider or regard as being; "I would not call her beautiful" 20: demand payment of, as of a loan; "Call a loan" [syn: call in] 21: give the calls (to the dancers) for a square dance [syn: call off] 22: greet, as with a prescribed form, title, or name; "He always addresses me with `Sir'"; "Call me Mister"; "She calls him by first name" [syn: address] 23: make a stop in a harbor; "The ship will call in Honolulu tomorrow" 24: make a demand in card games, as for a card or a suit or a show of hands; "He called his trump" [syn: bid] 25: require the presentation of for redemption before maturation; "Call a bond" 26: lure by imitating the characteristic call of an animal; "Call ducks" 27: challenge the sincerity or truthfulness of; "call the speaker on a question of fact" 28: rouse somebody from sleep with a call; "I was called at 5 A.M. this morning"

caul

n 1: part of the peritoneum attached to the stomach and to the colon and covering the intestines [syn: greater omentum, gastro colic omentum] 2: the inner embryonic membrane of higher vertebrates (especially when covering the head at birth) [syn: veil, embryonic membrane]

callous, callus /'kæl°s/
callous

adj : emotionally hardened; "a callous indifference to suffering"; "cold-blooded and indurate to public opinion" [syn: thick-skinned, indurate, pachydermatous]

v : make insensitive or callous

callus

n 1: an area of skin that is thick or hard from continual pressure or friction (as the sole of the foot) [syn: callosity] 2: bony tissue formed during the healing of a fractured bone 3: (botany) an isolated thickening of tissue, especially a stiff protuberance on the lip of an orchid

v 1: cause a callus to form on; "The long march had callused his feet" 2: form a callus or calluses; "His foot callused"

calques, calx /kælks/
calques

n : expressions introduced into one language by translating it from another language [syn: loan translations]

calx

n : a white crystalline oxide used in the

production of calcium hydroxide [syn: calcium oxide, quicklime, lime, calcined lime, fluxing lime, unslaked lime, burnt lime]

canapé, canopy

canapé /ˈkænəpɛɪ/

n : an appetizer consisting usually of a thin slice of bread or toast spread with caviar or cheese or other savory food

canopy /ˈkænəpi/

n 1: the transparent covering of an aircraft cockpit 2: the umbrella-like part of a parachute that fills with air 3: a covering (usually of cloth) that serves as a roof to shelter an area from the weather

v : cover with a canopy

cannon, canon /ˈkænɪn/

cannon

n 1: a large artillery gun that is usually on wheels 2: (medieval) a cylindrical piece of armor plate to protect the arm 3: heavy automatic gun fired from an airplane 4: lower part of the leg extending from the hock to the fetlock in hoofed mammals [syn: shank] 5: a shot in billiards in which the cue ball contacts one object ball and then the other [syn: carom]

v 1: make a cannon, in billiards 2: fire a cannon

canon

n 1: a rule or especially body of rules or principles generally established as valid and fundamental in a field or art or philosophy: "the neoclassical canon"; "canons of polite society" 2: a priest who is a member of a cathedral chapter 3: a contrapuntal piece of music in which a melody in one part is imitated exactly in other parts 4: a complete list of saints that have been recognized by the Roman Catholic Church 5: a collection of books accepted as holy scripture especially the books of the Bible recognized by any Christian church as genuine and inspired

cant, can't /kɛənt/

cant

adj : having the slant of a bevel; "a bevel edge"; "a cant buttress" [syn: bevel, beveled]

n 1: stock phrases that have become nonsense through endless repetition [syn: buzzword] 2: a slope in the turn of a road or track; the outside is higher than the inside in order to reduce the effects of centrifugal force [syn: bank, camber] 3: a characteristic language of a particular group (as among thieves); "they don't speak our lingo" [syn: jargon, slang, lingo, argot, patois, vernacular] 4: insincere talk about religion or morals [syn: pious platitude] 5: two surfaces meeting at an angle different from 90 degrees [syn: bevel, chamfer]

v : heel over [syn: cant over, tilt, slant, pitch]

can't

v : (contraction) cannot

canter, cantor /ˈkɛəntʰɹ/

canter

n : a smooth 3-beat gait; between a trot and a gallop [syn: lope]

v 1: ride at a canter; "The men cantered away" 2: go at a canter, of horses 3: ride at a cantering pace; "He cantered the horse across the meadow"

cantor

n 1: the musical director of a choir [syn: choirmaster, precentor] 2: the official of a synagogue who conducts the liturgical part of the service and sings or chants the prayers intended to be performed as solos [syn: hazan]

canvas, canvass /ˈkɛənvɪs/

canvas

n 1: heavy closely woven fabric (used for clothing or chairs or sails or tents) 2: an oil painting on canvas 3: the setting for a narrative or fictional or dramatic account; "the crowded canvas of history;" "the movie demanded a dramatic canvas of sound" 4: a tent made of canvas [syn: canvas tent] 5: a large piece of fabric (as canvas) by means of which wind is used to propel a sailing vessel [syn: sail, sheet] 6: the mat that forms the floor of the ring in which boxers or professional wrestlers compete; "the boxer picked himself up off the canvas"

canvass

v 1: get the opinions of people, for example [syn: poll] 2: solicit votes from potential voters in an electoral campaign 3: consider in detail and subject to an analysis in order to discover essential features or meaning; "analyze a sonnet by Shakespeare"; "analyze the evidence in a criminal trial"; "analyze your real motives" [syn: analyze, study, examine]

capital, capitol /ˈkæpɪtʰl/

capital

adj 1: (British) first-rate; "a capital fellow"; "a capital idea" 2: punishable by death; "a capital offense" 3: of primary important; "our capital concern was to avoid defeat" 4: uppercase; "capital A"; "great A"; "many medieval manuscripts are in majuscule script" [syn: great, majuscule]

n 1: assets available for use in the production of further assets [syn: working capital] 2: wealth in the form of money or property owned by a person or business and human resources of economic value 3: a seat of government 4: one of the large alphabetic characters used as the first letter in proper names and sometimes for emphasis; (printers once kept type for

HOMOPHONES

capitals and small letters in separate cases; capitals were kept in the upper half of the type case and so became known as upper-case letters) [syn: upper case, upper-case letter] [ant: small letter 5: the upper part of a column that supports the entablature [syn: chapiter, cap]

capitol
n 1: a building where a state legislative body meets 2: the government building in Washington where the United States Senate and the House of Representatives meet [syn: Capitol, Capitol Building]

carat, caret, carrot, karat /'kæɹɪt/

carat
n 1: a unit of weight for precious stones = 200 mg 2: the unit of measurement for the proportion of gold in an alloy; 18-karat gold is 75% gold; 24-karat gold is pure gold [syn: karat]

caret
n : a mark used by an author or editor to indicate where something is to be inserted into a text

carrot
n 1: deep orange edible root of the cultivated carrot plant 2: perennial plant widely cultivated as an annual in many varieties for its long conical deep-orange edible roots; temperate and tropical regions [syn: cultivated carrot, Daucus carota sativa] 3: orange root; important source of carotene 4: promise of reward as in "carrot and stick"; "used the carrot of subsidized housing for the workers to get their vote"

karat
n : var carat

caries, carries /'kɛəɹiz/

caries
n : soft decayed area in a tooth; progressive decay can lead to the death of a tooth [syn: cavity, dental caries, tooth decay]

carries
v : (3rd person sing of carry; "He carries a heavy burden."

carol, carrel /'kæɹɪl/

carol
n 1: joyful religious song celebrating the birth of Christ [syn: Christmas carol] 2: a joyful song (usually celebrating the birth of Christ)
v : sing carols; "They went caroling on Christmas Day"

carrel
n : small individual study area in a library [syn: cubicle, stall]

carpal, carpel /'kaɹpəl/

carpal
adj : of or relating to the wrist; "Carpal tunnel syndrome"
n : any of the eight small bones of the wrist

[syn: carpal bone, wrist bone]

carpel
n : a simple pistil or one element of a compound pistil

cart, carte, kart /kaɹt/

cart
n 1: a heavy open wagon usually having two wheels and drawn by an animal 2: wheeled vehicle that can be pushed by a person; may have one or two or four wheels; "he used a handcart to carry the rocks away"; "their pushcart was piled high with groceries" [syn: handcart, pushcart, go-cart]
v 1: draw slowly or heavily; "haul stones"; "haul nets" [syn: haul, hale, drag] 2: transport something in a cart [syn: haul]

carte
n : a list of dishes available at a restaurant; "the menu was in French" [syn: menu, bill of fare, card, carte du jour]

kart
n : a miniature racing motorcar

cask, casque /kɛəsk/

cask
n 1: the quantity a cask will hold [syn: caskful] 2: a cylindrical container that holds liquids [syn: barrel]

casque
n : (15-16th century) any armor for the head; usually ornate without a visor

cast, caste /kɛəst/

cast
adj : (of molten metal or glass) formed by pouring or pressing into a mold
n 1: the actors in a play [syn: cast of characters, dramatis personae] 2: container into which liquid is poured to create a given shape when it hardens [syn: mold, mould] 3: the distinctive form in which a thing is made; "pottery of this cast was found throughout the region" [syn: mold, stamp] 4: the visual appearance of something or someone; "the delicate cast of his features" [syn: form, shape] 5: bandage consisting of a firm covering (often made of plaster of Paris) that immobilizes broken bones while they heal [syn: plaster cast, plaster bandage] 6: object formed by a mold [syn: casting] 7: the act of throwing dice [syn: roll] 8: the act of throwing a fishing line out over the water by means of a rod and reel [syn: casting] 9: a violent throw [syn: hurl]
v 1: put or send forth; "She threw the flashlight beam into the corner"; "The setting sun threw long shadows"; "cast a spell"; "cast a warm light" [syn: project, contrive, throw] 2: deposit; "cast a vote"; "cast a ballot" 3: select to play, sing, or dance a part in a play, movie, musical, opera, or ballet; "He cast a young woman in the role of Desdemona"

4: throw forcefully [syn: hurl, hurtle] 5: assign the roles of (a movie or a play) to actors; "Who cast this beautiful movie?" 6: move about aimlessly or without any destination, often in search of food or employment; "The gypsies roamed the woods"; "roving vagabonds"; "the wandering Jew"; "The cattle roam across the prairie"; "the laborers drift from one town to the next" [syn: wander, swan, stray, tramp, roam, ramble, rove, range, drift, vagabond] 7: form by pouring (e.g., wax or hot metal) into a cast or mold; "cast a bronze sculpture" [syn: mold, mould] 8: get rid of; "he shed his image as a pushy boss" [syn: shed, cast off, shake off, throw, throw off, throw away, drop] 9: choose at random; "draw a card"; "cast lots" [syn: draw] 10: formulate in a particular style or language; "I wouldn't put it that way"; "She cast her request in very polite language" [syn: frame, redact, put, couch] 11: eject the contents of the stomach through the mouth; "After drinking too much, the students vomited" [syn: vomit, vomit up, sick, cat, regurgitate, be sick, disgorge, retch, puke, barf, spew, chuck, upchuck, honk, throw up] [ant: keep down]

caste
n 1: social status or position conferred by a system based on class: "lose caste by doing work beneath one's station" 2: (Hindu) a hereditary social class stratified according to ritual purity 3: a social class separated from others by distinctions of hereditary rank or profession or wealth

caster, castor /ˈkæstəɹ/
caster
n 1: a worker who casts molten metal into finished products 2: a pivoting roller attached to the bottom of furniture or trucks or portable machines to make them movable [syn: castor]
castor
n 1: a multiple star with 6 components; second brightest in Gemini; close to Pollux [syn: Castor, Alpha Geminorum] 2: a pivoting roller attached to the bottom of furniture or trucks or portable machines to make them movable [syn: caster] 3: a hat made of beaver fur or similar material [syn: beaver] 4: type genus of the Castoridae: beavers [syn: Castor, genus Castor]

catch, ketch
catch /kætʃ/
n 1: a hidden drawback; "it sounds good but what's the catch?" 2: the quantity that was caught; "the catch was only 10 fish" [syn: haul] 3: a person regarded as a good matrimonial prospect [syn: match] 4: anything that is caught (especially if it is worth catching); "he shared his catch with the others" 5: a break or check in the

voice (usually a sign of strong emotion) 6: a restraint that checks the motion of something; "he used a book as a stop to hold the door open" [syn: stop] 7: a fastener that fastens or locks a door or window 8: a cooperative game in which a ball is passed back and forth; "he played catch with his son in the backyard" 9: the act of catching an object with the hands; "Mays made the catch with his back to the plate"; "he made a grab for the ball before it landed"; "Martin's snatch at the bridle failed and the horse raced away"; "the infielder's snap and throw was a single motion" [syn: grab, snatch, snap] 10: the act of apprehending (especially apprehending a criminal); "the policeman on the beat got credit for the collar" [syn: apprehension, arrest, collar, pinch, taking into custody]

v 1: discover or come upon accidentally, suddenly, or unexpectedly; catch somebody doing something or in a certain state; "She caught her son eating candy"; "She was caught shoplifting" 2: perceive with the senses quickly, suddenly, or momentarily; "I caught the aroma of coffee"; "He caught the allusion in her glance"; "ears open to catch every sound"; "The dog picked up the scent"; "Catch a glimpse" [syn: pick up] 3: reach with a blow or hit in a particular spot; "the rock caught her in the back of the head"; "The blow got him in the back"; "The punch caught him in the stomach" [syn: get] 4: take hold of so as to seize or restrain or stop the motion of; "Catch the ball!"; "Grab the elevator door!" [syn: grab, take hold of] 5: succeed in catching or seizing, especially after a chase; "We finally got the suspect"; "Did you catch the thief?" [syn: get, capture] 6: to hook or entangle; "One foot caught in the stirrup" [syn: hitch] [ant: unhitch] 7: attract and fix; "His look caught her"; "She caught his eye"; "Catch the attention of the waiter" [syn: arrest, get] 8: capture as if by hunting, snaring, or trapping; "I caught a rabbit in the trap toady" [syn: capture] 9: reach in time; "I have to catch a train at 7 o'clock" 10: get or regain something necessary, usually quickly or briefly; "Catch some sleep"; "catch one's breath" 11: catch up with and possibly overtake; "The Rolls Royce caught us near the exit ramp" [syn: overtake, catch up with] 12: be struck or affected by; "catch fire"; "catch the mood" 13: check oneself during an action; "She managed to catch herself before telling her boss what was on her mind" 14: hear, usually without the knowledge of the speakers; "We overheard the conversation at the next table" [syn: take in, overhear] 15:

HOMOPHONES

see or watch; "view a show on television"; "This program will be seen all over the world"; "view an exhibition"; "Catch a show on Broadway"; "see a movie" [syn: watch, view, see, take in] 16: cause to become accidentally or suddenly caught, ensnared, or entangled; "I caught the hem of my dress in the brambles"; "I caught the hem of my dress in the brambles" 17: detect a blunder or misstep; "The reporter tripped up the senator" [syn: trip up] 18: grasp with the mind or develop an understanding of; "did you catch that allusion?"; "We caught something of his theory in the lecture"; "don't catch your meaning"; "did you get it?"; "She didn't get the joke"; "I just don't get him" [syn: get] 19: contract; "did you catch a cold?" 20: start burning; "The fire caught" 21: perceive by hearing; "I didn't catch your name"; "She didn't get his name when they met the first time" [syn: get] 22: suffer from the receipt of; "She will catch hell for this behavior!" [syn: get] 23: attract; cause to be enamored; "She captured all the men's hearts" [syn: capture, enamour, trance, becharm, enamor, captivate, beguile, charm, fascinate, bewitch, entrance, enchant] 24: apprehend and reproduce accurately; "She really caught the spirit of the place in her drawings"; "She got the mood just right in her photographs" [syn: get] 25: take in and retain; "We have a big barrel to catch the rainwater" 26: spread or be communicated; "The fashion did not catch" 27: be the catcher; "Who is catching?" 28: become aware of; "he caught her staring out the window" 29: delay or hold up; prevent from proceeding on schedule or as planned; "I was caught in traffic and missed the meeting"

ketch /ketʃ/

n : a sailing vessel with two masts; the mizzen is forward of the rudderpost

caudal, caudle /ˈkɔdəl/

caudal

adj 1: constituting or relating to a tail; "caudal appendage" [ant: cephalic] 2: resembling a tail [syn: tail like] 3: (of quadrupeds) situated in or directed toward the part of the body from which the tail arises; "caudal fins"; "the caudal end of the body"

adv : toward the posterior end of the body [syn: caudally]

caudle

n : a drink made of wine or warm ale mixed with bread or gruel, eggs, sugar and spices; usually given to the ill

cause, caws /kɔz/

cause

n 1: events that provide the generative force that is the origin of something; "they are trying to determine the cause of the

crash" 2: a justification for something existing or happening; "he had no cause to complain"; "they had good reason to rejoice" [syn: reason, grounds] 3: a series of actions advancing a principle or tending toward a particular end; "he supported populist campaigns"; "they worked in the cause of world peace"; "the team was ready for a drive toward the pennant"; "the movement to end slavery"; "contributed to the war effort" [syn: campaign, crusade, drive, movement, effort] 4: any entity that causes events to happen [syn: causal agent, causal agency] 5: (law) a comprehensive term for any proceeding in a court of law whereby an individual seeks a legal remedy; "the family brought suit against the landlord" [syn: lawsuit, suit, case]

v 1: give rise to; cause to happen or occur, not always intentionally; "cause a commotion"; "make a stir"; "cause an accident" [syn: do, make] 2: cause to do; cause to act in a specified manner: "The ads induced me to buy a VCR"; "My children finally got me to buy a computer"; "My wife made me buy a new sofa" [syn: induce, stimulate, have, get, make]

caws

n : (plu caw) the sounds made by corvine birds

v : utter a cry, characteristic of crows, rooks, or ravens; "That crow caws all day."

cay, key, quay /ki/

cay

n : a coral reef or shoal off the southern coast of Florida [syn: key, Florida keys]

key

adj 1: serving as an essential component; "a cardinal rule"; "the central cause of the problem"; "an example that was fundamental to the argument"; "computers are fundamental to modern industrial structure" [syn: cardinal, central, fundamental, primal] 2: effective; producing a desired effect; "the operative word" [syn: operative]

n 1: metal device shaped in such a way that when it is inserted into the appropriate lock the lock's mechanism can be rotated 2: something crucial for explaining; "the key to development is economic integration" 3: pitch of the voice; "he spoke in a low key" 4: any of 24 major or minor diatonic scales that provide the tonal framework for a piece of music [syn: tonality] [ant: atonality] 5: one thousand grams; the basic unit of mass adopted under the System International d'Unites; "a kilogram is approximately 2.2 pounds"; "they were carrying two keys of heroin" [syn: kilogram, kg, kilo] 6: a coral reef off the southern coast of Florida [syn: cay, Florida keys] 7: a list of

HOMOPHONES

words or phrases that explain symbols or abbreviations 8: mechanical device used to wind another device that is driven by a spring (as a clock) [syn: winder] 9: a lever that actuates a mechanism when depressed v 1: as in botany or biology, for example [syn: identify, discover, key out, distinguish, describe, name] 2: provide with a key; "We were keyed after the locks were changed in the building" 3: vandalize a car by scratching the sides with a key" 4: regulate the musical pitch of 5: harmonize with or adjust to; "key one's actions to the voters' prevailing attitude"

quay

n : wharf usually built parallel to the shoreline

cedar, seeder /ˈsidəɹ/

cedar

n 1: any of numerous trees of the family Cupressaceae that resemble cedars [syn: cedar tree] 2: durable aromatic wood of any of numerous cedar trees; especially wood of the red cedar often used for cedar chests [syn: cedar wood] 3: any cedar of the genus Cedrus [syn: cedar tree, true cedar]

seeder

n 1: a person who seeds clouds [syn: cloud seeder] 2: a mechanical device that sows grass seed or grain evenly over the ground 3: a kitchen utensil that removes seeds from fruit

cede, seed /sid/

cede

v 1: give over; surrender or relinquish to the physical control of another [syn: concede, yield, grant] 2: relinquish possession or control over; "The squatters had to surrender the building after the police moved in" [syn: surrender, deliver, give up]

seed

n 1: a small hard fruit 2: a mature fertilized plant ovule consisting of an embryo and its food source and having a protective coat or testa 3: one of the outstanding players in a tournament [syn: seeded player] 4: anything that provides inspiration for later work [syn: source, germ] 5: the thick white fluid containing spermatozoa that is ejaculated by the male genital tract [syn: semen, seminal fluid, ejaculate, cum] v 1: go to seed; shed seeds; "The dandelions went to seed" 2: help (an enterprise) in its early stages of development by providing seed money 3: bear seeds 4: place (seeds) in the ground for future growth; "She sowed sunflower seeds" [syn: sow, sough] 5: distribute (players or teams) so that outstanding teams or players will not meet in the early rounds; as of a tennis or golf player 6: sprinkle with silver iodide

particles to disperse and cause rain; "seed clouds" 7: inoculate with microorganisms 8: remove the seeds form, as of grapes

ceil, seal, seel /sil/

ceil

v : 1: to provide a ship with a lining 2:to provide with a ceiling

seal

n 1: fastener consisting of a resinous composition that is plastic when warm; used for sealing documents and parcels and letters [syn: sealing wax] 2: a device incised to make an impression; used to secure a closing or to authenticate documents [syn: stamp] 3: the pelt or fur (especially the under fur) of a seal; "a coat of seal" [syn: sealskin] 4: a stamp affixed to a document (as to attest to its authenticity or to seal it); "the warrant bore the sheriff's seal" 5: an indication of approved or superior status [syn: cachet, seal of approval] 6: a finishing coat applied to exclude moisture 7: fastener that provides a tight and perfect closure 8: any of numerous marine mammals that come on shore to breed; chiefly of cold regions v 1: close with or as if with a seal; "She sealed the letter with hot wax" [ant: unseal] 2: make tight; secure against leakage; "seal the windows" [syn: seal off] 3: decide irrevocably; "sealing dooms" 4: affix a seal to 5: cover with varnish [syn: varnish] 6: hunt seals

seel

v : sew up the eyelids of hawks and falcons

ceiling, sealing /ˈsiliŋ/

ceiling

n 1: the overhead upper surface of a room; "he hated painting the ceiling" 2: (meteorology) altitude of the lowest layer of clouds 3: an upper limit on what is allowed: "they established a cap for prices" [syn: cap] 4: maximum altitude at which a plane can fly (under specified conditions)

sealing

n : the act of treating something to make it repel water [syn: waterproofing]

cel, cell, sell /sɛl/

cel

n : a transparent sheet of celluloid on which objects are drawn or painted in the making of animated cartoons

cell

n 1: any small compartment; "the cells of a honeycomb" 2: the basic structural and functional unit of all organisms; cells may exist as independent units of life (as in monads) or may form colonies or tissues as in higher plants and animals 3: a device that delivers an electric current as the result of a chemical reaction [syn: electric cell] 4: a small unit serving as the nucleus of a larger political movement [syn: cadre] 5: small room is which a monk or nun lives [syn: cubicle] 6: a room where a prisoner is kept [syn: jail cell, prison cell]

sell

n : the activity of persuading someone to buy; "it was a hard sell"

v 1: exchange or deliver for money or its equivalent; "He sold his house in January"; "She sells her body to survive and support her drug habit" [ant: buy] 2: be sold at a certain price or in a certain way: "These books sell like hot cakes" 3: do business; offer for sale as for one's livelihood; "She deals in gold"; "The brothers sell shoes" [syn: deal, trade] 4: persuade somebody to accept something; "The French try to sell us their image as great lovers" 5: give up for a price or reward: "She sold her principles for a successful career" 6: deliver to an enemy by treachery; "Judas sold Jesus"; "The spy betrayed his country" [syn: betray] 7: be approved of or gain acceptance; "The new idea sold well in certain circles" 8: be responsible for the sale of; "All her publicity sold the products"

cellar, seller /'sɛlʲɹ/

cellar

n 1: the lowermost portion of a structure partly or wholly below ground level; often used for storage [syn: basement] 2: an excavation where root vegetables are stored [syn: root cellar] 3: storage space where wines are stored [syn: wine cellar]

seller

n : someone who promotes or exchanges goods or services for money [syn: marketer, vender, vendor, trafficker]

cense, cents, scents, sense

cense /sɛns/

v : perfume especially with a censer [syn: incense, thurify]

cents /sɛnts/

n : (plu of sent) "The apple costs fifty cents."

scents /sɛnts/

n : (plu of scent) "There are several scents in this room."

v : (3rd pers sing of scent) "She scents the room with air fresheners."

sense /sɛns/

n 1: a general conscious awareness; "a sense of security"; "a sense of happiness"; "a sense of danger"; "a sense of self" 2: the meaning of a word or expression; the way in which a word or expression or situation can be interpreted; "the dictionary gave several senses for the word"; "in the best sense charity is really a duty"; "the signifier is linked to the signified" [syn: signified] 3: the faculty through which the external world is apprehended [syn: sensation, sentience, sentiency, sensory faculty] 4: sound practical judgment; "I can't see the sense in doing it now"; "he hasn't got the sense God gave little green apples"; "fortunately she had the sense to run away" [syn: common sense, good sense, gumption, horse sense, mother wit] 5: a natural appreciation or ability; "a keen musical sense"; "a good sense of timing"

v : perceive by a physical sensation, e.g., coming from the skin or muscles; "I sense the wind"; "She felt an object brushing her arm"; "He felt his flesh crawl"; "She sensed the heat when she got out of the car" [syn: feel]

censer, censor, sensor /'sɛnsʲɹ/

censer

n : a container for burning incense (especially one that is swung on a chain in a religious ritual) [syn: thurible]

censor

n : a person who is authorized to read publications or correspondence or to watch theatrical performances and suppress in whole or in part anything considered obscene or politically unacceptable

v 1: forbid the public distribution of; as of movies or newspapers [syn: ban] 2: subject to political, religious, or moral censorship; "This magazine is censored by the government"

sensor

n : any device that receives a signal or stimulus (as heat or pressure or light or motion etc.) and responds to it [syn: detector, sensing element]

census, senses /'sɛnsɪs/

census

n : a period count of the population [syn: nose count]

v : conduct a census; "They censused the deer in the forest"

senses

n : (plu of sense) "We have five senses... sight, touch, taste, smell and hearing."

v : (3rd pers sing of sense) "He senses danger."

cent, scent, sent /sɛnt/

cent

n 1: a fractional monetary unit of several countries 2: a coin worth one-hundredth of the value of the basic unit [syn: penny, centime]

scent

n 1: a distinctive odor that is pleasant [syn: aroma, fragrance, perfume] 2: an odor left in passing by which a person or animal can be traced 3: any property detected by the olfactory system [syn: olfactory property, smell, aroma, odor]

v 1: cause to smell or be smelly [syn:

HOMOPHONES

odorize] [ant: deodorize] 2: catch the scent of; get wind of; "The dog nosed out the drugs" [syn: nose, wind] 3: apply perfume to; "She perfumes herself every day" [syn: perfume]

sent
adj : caused or enabled to go or be conveyed or transmitted [ant: unsent]
v : (past of send) "She sent the package last week."

cerate, serrate /'sɛɹɛɪt/
cerate
n : a hard medicated paste made of lard or oil mixed with wax or resin

serrate
adj : notched like a saw with teeth pointing toward the apex [syn: serrated, saw-toothed, toothed, notched]

cere, sear, seer, sere /siɹ/
cere
v : wrap in a cerecloth, as of a corpse

sear
adj : (used especially of vegetation) having lost all moisture; "dried-up grass"; "the desert was edged with sere vegetation"; "shrivelled leaves on the unwatered seedlings"; "withered vines" [syn: dried-up, sere, shriveled, withered]
v 1: make very hot; "searing heat" [syn: scorch] 2: cause to wither or parch from exposure to heat; "The sun parched the earth" [syn: parch, scorch]

seer
n 1: a person with unusual powers of foresight [syn: visionary, illusionist] 2: an observer who perceives visually; "an incurable seer of movies" 3: an authoritative person who divines the future [syn: prophet, oracle, vaticinator]

sere
adj : (var of sear)
n :a series of ecological communities that succeed one another in the biotic development of an area or formation

cereal, serial /'siɹɪl/
cereal
adj : made of grain or relating to grain or the plants that produce it; "a cereal beverage"; "cereal grasses"
n 1: grass whose starchy grains are used as food: wheat; rice; rye; oats; maize; buckwheat; millet [syn: cereal grass] 2: cereal grain suitable as food for human beings [syn: grain, food grain] 3: a breakfast food prepared from grain

serial
adj 1: in regular succession without gaps; "serial concerts" [syn: consecutive, sequent, sequential, successive] 2: (music) pertaining to or composed in serial technique; "serial music" 3: pertaining to or occurring in or producing a series; "serial monogamy" or "serial killing"; "a serial killer" 4: (computer science) of or relating to the sequential performance of multiple operations; "serial processing" [syn: in series, nonparallel]
n 1: a serialized set of programs; "a comedy series"; "the Masterworks concert series" [syn: series] 2: a periodical that appears at scheduled times [syn: series, serial publication]

cerous, cirrus, serous /'siɹəs/
cerous
adj : of or relating to or containing cerium with valence 3

cirrus
n 1: usually coiled 2: a wispy white cloud (usually of fine ice crystals) at a high altitude (4 to 8 miles) [syn: cirrus cloud] 3: a slender flexible animal appendage as on barnacles or crinoids or many insects; often tactile

serous
adj : of or producing or containing serum; "a serous exudate"

cession, session /'sɛʃɪn/
cession
n : the act of ceding [syn: ceding]

session
n 1: a meeting for execution of a group's functions; "it was the opening session of the legislature" 2: the time during which a school holds classes; "they had to shorten the school term" [syn: school term, academic term, academic session] 3: a meeting devoted to a particular activity; "a filming session"; "a gossip session" 4: a meeting of spiritualists; "the séance was held in the medium's parlor" [syn: séance, sitting]

cetaceous, setaceous /sɪ'teɪʃəs/
cetaceous
adj : of or relating to whales and dolphins etc [syn: cetacean]

setaceous
adj 1: having or consisting of bristles; bristly "a setaceous moth" 2: resembling bristles or a bristle "setaceous whiskers"

chaise, shays /ʃeɪz/
chaise
n 1: a long chair; for reclining [syn: chaise lounge, daybed]

shays
n : carriages consisting of two wheels and a calash top; drawn by a single horse

champagne, champaign /ʃæm'peɪn/
champagne
n : a white sparkling wine either produced in Champagne (France) or resembling that produced there [syn: bubbly]

champaign
n 1: extensive tract of level open land; "they emerged from the woods onto a vast

open plain"; "he longed for the fields of his youth" [syn: plain, field]

chance, chants /tʃɛənts/

chance

adj : occurring or appearing or singled out by chance; "their accidental meeting led to a renewal of their friendship"; "seek help from casual passers-by"; "a casual meeting"; "a chance occurrence" [syn: accidental, casual]

n 1: a possibility due to a favorable combination of circumstances; "the holiday gave us the opportunity to visit Washington"; "now is your chance" [syn: opportunity] 2: an unknown and unpredictable phenomenon that causes an event to result one way rather than another; "bad luck caused his downfall"; "we ran into each other by pure chance" [syn: luck, fortune, hazard] 3: a risk involving danger; "you take a chance when you let her drive" 4: a measure of how likely it is that some event will occur; "what is the probability of rain?"; "we have a good chance of winning" [syn: probability]

v 1: be the case by chance; "I chanced to meet my old friend in the street" 2: take a risk in the hope of a favorable outcome; "When you buy these stocks you are gambling" [syn: gamble, risk, hazard, take chances, adventure, run a risk, take a chance] 3: come upon, as if by accident; meet with; "We find this idea in Plato"; "I happened upon the most wonderful bakery not very far from here"; "She chanced upon an interesting book in the bookstore the other day" [syn: find, happen, bump, encounter]

chants

n : (plu of chant) : a repetitive songs in which as many syllables as necessary are assigned to a single tone

v : (3rd pers sing of chant) 1: recite with musical intonation; recite as a chant; "The rabbi chants a prayer every evening." [syn: intones, intonates, cantillates] 2: utter monotonously and repetitively and rhythmically; "The students chanted the same slogan over and over again" [syn: intones]

chard, charred /tʃɑɹd/

chard

n 1: beet lacking swollen root; grown as a vegetable for its edible leaves and stalks [syn: Swiss chard, spinach beet, leaf beet, chard plant, Beta vulgaris cicla] 2: long succulent whitish stalks with large green leaves [syn: Swiss chard, spinach beet, leaf beet]

charred

adj : to be scorched; "The fire caused the trees to be charred.";[syn: scorched, burnt, burned]

v : (past of char) "The fire charred the trees." [syn: scorched, burnt, burned]

chary, cherry /'tʃɛɹi/

chary (alt /'tʃæɹi/)

adj : characterized by great cautious and wariness; "a cagey avoidance of a definite answer"; "chary of the risks involved"; "a chary investor" [syn: cagey]

cherry

adj : having any of numerous bright or strong colors reminiscent of the color of blood or cherries or tomatoes or rubies [syn: red, reddish, ruddy, blood-red, carmine, cerise, cherry-red, crimson, ruby, ruby-red, scarlet]

n 1: wood of any of various cherry trees especially the black cherry 2: any of numerous trees and shrubs producing a small fleshy round fruit with a single hard stone; many also produce a valuable hardwood [syn: cherry tree] 3: fruit with a single hard stone 4: a red the color of ripe cherries [syn: cerise, cherry red]

chased, chaste /tʃeɪst/

chased

n : a person who is being chased; "the film jumped back and forth from the chaser to the chased" (or "...from the pursuer to the pursued") [syn: pursued]

v : (past of chase) "He chased her into the building." [syn: pursued]

chaste

adj 1: morally pure especially not having experienced sexual intercourse; "a holy woman innocent and chaste" [ant: unchaste] 2: pure and simple in design or style; "a chaste border of conventionalized flowers" 3: abstaining from unlawful sexual intercourse

chauffeur, shofar /'ʃoufɚ/

chauffeur

n : a man paid to drive a privately owned car

v : drive someone in a vehicle [syn: drive around]

shofar

n : an ancient musical horn made from the horn of a ram; used in ancient times by the Israelites to sound a warning or a summons; used in synagogues today on solemn occasions

cheap, cheep /tʃip/

cheap

adj 1: relatively low in price or charging low prices; "it would have been cheap at twice the price"; "inexpensive family restaurants" [syn: inexpensive] [ant: expensive] 2: tastelessly showy; "a flash car"; "a flashy ring"; "garish colors"; "a gaudy costume"; "loud sport shirts"; "a meretricious yet stylish book"; "tawdry ornaments" [syn: brassy, flash, flashy, garish, gaudy, gimcrack, loud, meretricious, tacky, tatty, tawdry, trashy] 3: (informal) of very poor quality [syn: bum, cheesy, chintzy, crummy, punk, sleazy, tinny] 4: embarrassingly stingy [syn: chintzy]

cheep
cheep

n : the short weak cry of a young bird [syn: peep]

v : make high-pitched sounds; of birds [syn: twirp, chirp, chirrup]

chews, choose /tʃuz/
chews

n : (plu of chew) 1: wads of something chewable as tobacco [syn: chaws, cud, quid, plugs, wads]

v : (3rd pers sing of chew) : chew (food); "He chews his bubble gum"; "Chew your food and don't swallow it!"; "The cows were masticating the grass" [syn: masticate, jaw]

choose

v 1: pick out, select, or choose from a number of alternatives; "Take any one of these cards"; "Choose a good husband for your daughter"; "She selected a pair of shoes from among the dozen the salesgirl had shown her" [syn: take, select, pick out] 2: select as an alternative; choose instead; prefer as an alternative; "I always choose the fish over the meat courses in this restaurant"; "She opted for the job on the East coast" [syn: prefer, opt] 3: see fit or proper to act in a certain way; decide to act in a certain way; "She chose not to attend classes and now she failed the exam"

chic, sheik /ʃik/
chic

adj : elegant and stylish; "chic elegance"; "a smart new dress"; "a suit of voguish cut" [syn: smart, voguish]

n : elegance by virtue of being fashionable [syn: chicness, modishness, smartness, stylishness, swank, last word]

sheik

n 1: the leader of an Arab village or family [syn: sheikh, Arab chief] 2: a man who is much concerned with his dress and appearance [syn: dandy, dude, fop, gallant, beau, swell, fashion plate, clotheshorse]

chili, chilly /tʃɪli/
chili

n 1: (Mexican) ground beef and chili peppers or chili powder often with tomatoes and kidney beans [syn: chili con carne] 2: very hot and finely tapering pepper of special pungency [syn: chili pepper, chilly]

chilly

adj 1: uncomfortably cool; "a chill wind"; "chilly weather" [syn: chill] 2: not characterized by emotion; "a female form in marble--a chilly but ideal medium for depicting abstract virtues"-

C.W.Cunningham 3: lacking warmth of feeling; "a chilly greeting"; "an unfriendly manner" [syn: unfriendly]

choir, quire /kwaɪʊ/
choir

n 1: a chorus that sings as part of a religious ceremony 2: a family of similar musical instrument playing together [syn: consort] 3: the area occupied by singers; the part of the chancel between sanctuary and nave

v : sing in a choir [syn: chorus]

quire

n : a quantity of paper; 24 or 25 sheets

choler, collar /'kɑlᵊɹ/
choler

n 1: an irritable petulant feeling [syn: irritability, crossness, fretfulness, fussiness, peevishness, petulance] 2: a strong emotion; a feeling that is oriented toward some real or supposed grievance [syn: anger, ire] 3: a humor that was once believed to be secreted by the liver and to cause irritability and anger [syn: yellow bile]

collar

n 1: a band that fits around the neck and is usually folded over [syn: neckband] 2: a band of leather or rope that is placed around an animal's neck as a harness or to identify it 3: necklace that fits tightly around a woman's neck [syn: choker, dog collar, choker] 4: a figurative restraint; "a collar on program trading in the stock market" 5: the act of apprehending (especially apprehending a criminal); "the policeman on the beat got credit for the collar" [syn: apprehension, arrest, catch, pinch, taking into custody]

v 1: take into custody, as of suspected criminals, by the police [syn: nail, apprehend, arrest, pick up, nab, cop] 2: seize by the neck or collar 3: furnish with a collar; "collar the dog"

choral, coral /'kɔɹɪl/
choral

adj : related to or written for or performed by a chorus or choir; "choral composition"; "choral ensemble"

n : a stately Protestant (especially Lutheran) hymn tune

coral

adj : of a strong pink to yellowish-pink color

n 1: a variable color averaging a deep pink 2: the hard stony skeleton of a Mediterranean coral that has a delicate red or pink color and is used for jewelry [syn: red coral, precious coral] 3: unfertilized lobster roe; reddens in cooking; used as garnish or to color sauces 4: marine colonial polyp characterized by a calcareous skeleton; masses in a variety of shapes often forming reefs

HOMOPHONES

chorale, corral /kɔˈɹæl/
chorale
n : a stately Protestant (especially Lutheran) hymn tune
corral
n : a pen for cattle [syn: cow pen, cattle pen]
v 1: enclose in a corral; "corral the horses" 2: arrange wagons so that they form a corral 3: collect or gather; "corralling votes for an election"

chord, cord, cored /kɔɹd/
chord
n 1: a straight line connecting two points on a curve 2: a combination of three or more notes that blend harmoniously when sounded together
v 1: play chords on, as of string instruments 2: bring into consonance, harmony, or accord while making music or singing [syn: harmonize]
cord
n 1: a line made of twisted fibers or threads; "the bundle was tied with a cord" 2: a unit of amount of wood cut for burning; 128 cubic feet 3: a light insulated conductor for household use [syn: electric cord] 4: a cut pile fabric with vertical ribs; usually made of cotton [syn: corduroy]
v 1: stack in cords, of wood 2: bind or tie with a cord
cored
adj : having a core removed
v : (past of core) "He cored the apple."; [syn: removed the core]

chordate, cordate /ˈkɔɹdeɪt/
chordate
adj : of or relating to or characteristic of the Chordata
n : any animal of the phylum Chordata having a notochord or spinal column
cordate
adj : of a leaf shape [syn: heart-shaped]

chough, chuff /tʃʌf/
chough
n : a European corvine bird of small or medium size with red legs and glossy black plumage
chuff
v : blow hard and loudly [syn: puff, huff]

chute, shoot /ʃut/
chute
n 1: rescue equipment consisting of a device that fills with air and retards your fall [syn: parachute] 2: sloping channel through which things can descend [syn: slide, slideway, sloping trough]
shoot
n 1: a new branch 2: the act of shooting at targets; "they hold a shoot every weekend during the summer" 3: a photographing session; "the fashion model was hired for a shoot."
v 1: hit with a missile from a weapon [syn: hit, pip] 2: kill by firing a missile [syn: pip] 3: fire a shot 4: make a film or photograph of something; "take a scene"; "shoot a movie" [syn: film, take] 5: send forth suddenly, intensely, swiftly; "shoot a glance" 6: run or move very quickly or hastily; "She dashed into the yard" [syn: dart, dash, scoot, scud, flash] 7: move quickly and violently; "The car tore down the street"; "He came charging into my office" [syn: tear, shoot down, charge, buck] 8: play a shot; hit a ball; as in games involving a ball such as golf, hockey, etc. 9: record on photographic film "I photographed the scene of the accident" [syn: photograph, snap] 10: emit (as light, flame, or fumes) suddenly and forcefully; "The dragon shot fumes and flames out of its mouth." 11: cause a shooting pain 12: force or drive (a fluid or gas) into by piercing; "inject hydrogen into the balloon" [syn: inject] 13: spend frivolously and unwisely; "Fritter away one's inheritance" [syn: fritter, frivol away, dissipate, fritter away, fool, fool away] 14: produce buds, branches, or germinate; of plants [syn: spud, germinate, pullulate, bourgeon, burgeon forth, sprout] 15: give an injection to; "We injected the glucose into the patient's vein" [syn: inject]

cinque, sink, sync /sɪŋk/
cinque
n : the cardinal number that is the sum of four and one [syn: five, 5, V, quint, quintet, fivesome, quintuplet, pentad, fin, Phoebe, Little Phoebe]
sink
n 1: plumbing fixture consisting of a water basin fixed to a wall or floor and having a drainpipe and a faucet 2: a covered cistern; waste water and sewage flow into it [syn: cesspool, cesspit, sump]
v 1: fall or drop to a lower place or level; "He sank to his knees." [syn: drop, drop down] [ant: rise] 2: cause to sink; "The Japanese sank American ships in Pearl Harbour" 3: pass into a specified state or condition: "He sank into Nirvana" [syn: pass, lapse] 4: go under, "The raft sank and its occupants drowned" [syn: settle, go down, go under] [ant: float] 5: descend into or as if into some soft substance or place; "He sank into bed"; "She subsided into the chair" [syn: subside] 6: appear to move downward; "The sun dipped below the horizon"; "The setting sun sank below the tree line" [syn: dip] 7: fall heavily or suddenly; decline markedly; "The real estate market fell off" [syn: slump, fall off] 8: fall or sink heavily; "He slumped onto the couch"; "My spirits sank" [syn: slump, slide down] 9: embed deeply; "She sank

her fingers into the soft sand"; "He buried his head in her lap" [syn: bury]

sync

v : make synchronous and adjust in time or manner; "Let's synchronize our efforts" [syn: synchronize] [ant: unsynchronized]

cite, sight, site /saɪt/

cite

v 1: make reference to: "His name was mentioned in connection with the invention" [syn: mention, advert, bring up, name, refer] 2: cite, as for an outstanding achievement [syn: mention, acknowledge] 3: refer to [syn: reference] 4: repeat a passage from; "He quoted the Bible to her [syn: quote] 5: advance evidence for [syn: adduce] 6: call in an official matter, such as to attend court [syn: summon, summons]

sight

n 1: an instance of visual perception; "the sight of his wife brought him back to reality"; "the train was an unexpected sight" 2: anything that is seen; "he was a familiar sight on the television" or "they went to Paris to see the sights" 3: the ability to see; the faculty of vision [syn: vision, visual sense, visual modality] 4: a optical instrument for aiding the eye in aiming, as on a firearm or surveying instrument 5: a range of mental vision; "in his sight he could do no wrong" 6: the range of vision; "out of sight of land" [syn: ken] 7: the act of looking or seeing or observing; "he tried to get a better view of it"; "his survey of the battlefield was limited" [syn: view, survey] 8: (often followed by `of') a large number or amount or extent: "a batch of letters"; "a deal of trouble"; "a lot of money"; "he made a mint on the stock market"; "it must have cost plenty" [syn: batch, deal, flock, good deal, great deal, hatful, heap, lot, mass, mess, mint, peck, pile, plenty, pot, quite a little, raft, slew, spate, stack, tidy sum, wad, whole lot, whole slew]

v : catch sight of; to perceive with the eyes: "caught sight of the kings men coming over the ridge."

site

n 1: the piece of land on which something is located (or is to be located): "a good site for the school" [syn: land site] 2: physical position in relation to the surroundings [syn: situation] 3: a computer connected to the internet that maintains a series of web pages on the World Wide Web; "the Israeli web site was damaged by hostile hackers" [syn: web site, internet site]

v : assign a location to; "The company located some of their agents in Los Angeles" [syn: locate, place]

clack, claque /klæk/

clack

n 1: a sharp abrupt noise as if two objects hit together; may be repeated [syn: clap] 2: a simple valve with a hinge on one side; allows fluid to flow in only one direction [syn: clack valve, clapper valve]

v 1: make a rattling sound [syn: clatter, brattle] 2: make a clucking sounds, characteristic of hens [syn: cluck, click] 3: speak (about unimportant matters) rapidly and incessantly [syn: chatter, piffle, palaver, prate, tittle-tattle, twaddle, maunder, prattle, blab, gibber, tattle, blabber, gabble]

claque

n : a group of followers hired to applaud at a performance

clairvoyance, clairvoyants /klɛəˈvɔɪjənts/

clairvoyance

n : apparent power to perceive things that are not present to the senses [syn: second sight, extrasensory perception, E.S.P., ESP]

clairvoyants

n : persons who have the power of clairvoyance

clause, claws /klɔz/

clause

n 1: (grammar) an expression including a subject and predicate but not constituting a complete sentence 2: a separate section of a legal document (as a statute or contract or will) [syn: article]

claws

n : (plu of claw) 1: sharp curved horny process on the toe of a bird or some mammals or reptiles 2: a mechanical device that is curved or bent to suspend or hold or pull something [syn: hooks] 3: a structure like a pincer on the limb of a crustacean or other arthropods [syn: nippers, pincers] 4: a bird's foot that has claws

v : (3rd pers sing of claw) 1: move as if by clawing, seizing, or digging; "They clawed their way to the top of the mountain" 2: clutch as if in panic: "She claws the doorknob" 3: scratch, scrape, pull, or dig with claws or nails 4: attacks as if with claws; "The politician clawed his rival"

clew, clue /klu/

clew

n 1: a ball of yarn or cord or thread
v : roll into a ball

clue

n 1: a slight indication [syn: hint] 2: evidence that helps to solve a problem

click, clique, klick /klɪk/

click

n 1: a short light metallic sound [syn: chink, clink] 2: depression of a button on

HOMOPHONES

a computer mouse: "a click on the right button for example" [syn: mouse click] 3: a stop consonant made by the suction of air into the mouth (as in Bantu) [syn: suction stop] 4: a hinged catch that fits into a notch of a ratchet to move a wheel forward or prevent it from moving backward [syn: pawl, detent, dog]

v 1: move or strike with a click; "then the brightness as he clicked on the light." [syn: snap] 2: make a clicking or ticking sound; "The clock ticked away" [syn: tick] 3: click repeatedly or uncontrollably, as of teeth [syn: chatter] 4: cause to make a snapping sound; of fingers [syn: snap, flick] 5: produce a click; "Xhosa speakers click" 6: make a clucking sounds, characteristic of hens [syn: cluck, clack] 7: become clear suddenly; "It dawned on him that she had betrayed him" [syn: get through, dawn, come home, get across, sink in, penetrate, fall into place]

clique

n : an exclusive circle of people with a common purpose [syn: coterie, in group, inner circle, pack, camp]

klick

n : a metric unit of length equal to 1000 meters (or 621.371 miles) [syn: kilometer, km]

climb, clime /klaɪm/
climb

n 1: an upward slope or grade (as in a road); "the car couldn't make the grade" [syn: ascent, acclivity, rise, raise, upgrade] [ant: descent] 2: an event that involves rising to a higher point (as in altitude or temperature or intensity etc.) [syn: climbing, mounting] 3: the act of climbing something [syn: mount]

v 1: go upward with gradual or continuous progress; "Did you ever climb up the hill behind your house?" [syn: climb up, mount, go up] 2: move with difficulty, by grasping 3: go up or advance; "Sales were climbing after prices were lowered" [syn: wax, mount, rise] [ant: wane] 4: slope upward: "The path climbed all the way to the top of the hill" 5: improve one's social status; "This young man knows how to climb the social ladder" 6: increase in value or to a higher point; "prices climbed steeply"; "the value of our house rose sharply last year" [syn: rise, go up]

clime

n : the weather in some location averaged over some long period of time [syn: climate]

close, clothes, cloze /kloʊz/
close

n 1: the temporal end; the concluding time; "the stopping point of each round was signaled by a bell"; "the market was

up at the finish"; "they were playing better at the close of the season" [syn: stopping point, finale, finis, finish, last, conclusion] 2: the last section of a communication; "in conclusion I want to say..." [syn: conclusion, end, closing, ending] 3: the concluding part of any performance [syn: finale, closing curtain, finis]

v 1: cease to operate or cause to cease operating; "The owners decided to move and to close the factory"; "My business closes every night at 8 P.M. [syn: fold, shut down, close down] [ant: open] 2: complete a business deal, negotiation, or an agreement; "We will close on the house on Friday"; "They closed the deal on the building" 3: move so that an opening or passage is obstructed; make shut; "Close the door"; "shut the window" [syn: shut] [ant: open] 4: bar access to; "Due to the accident, the road had to be closed for several hours" 5: finish or terminate; of meetings, speeches, etc. "The meeting was closed with a charge by the chairman of the board" [ant: open] 6: draw near: "The probe closed with the space station" 7: come to a close; "The concert closed with a nocturne by Chopin" 8: become closed; "The windows closed with a loud bang" [syn: shut] [ant: open] 9: come together, as if in an embrace; "Her arms closed around her long lost relative" [syn: come together] 10: unite or bring into contact or bring together the edges of; "close the circuit"; "close a wound" 11: bring together all the elements or parts of: "Management closed ranks" 12: engage at close quarters; "close with the enemy" 13: cause a window or an application to disappear on a computer desktop [ant: open] 14: fill or stop up; "Can you close the cracks with caulking?" [syn: fill, fill up]

clothes

n : covering designed to be worn on a person's body [syn: clothing, apparel, vesture, wearing apparel, wear, article of clothing]

cloze

adj : based on or being a test of reading skill using the cloze procedure

coal, cole, kohl /koʊl/
coal

n 1: fossil fuel consisting of carbonized vegetable matter deposited in the Carboniferous period 2: a hot glowing or smoldering fragment of wood or coal left from a fire [syn: ember]

v 1: burn to charcoal; "Without a drenching rain, the forest fire will char everything." [syn: char] 2: supply with coal 3: take in coal, as of a ship

cole

n 1: a hardy cabbage with coarse curly

leaves that do not form a head [syn: kale, borecole] 2: coarse curly-leafed cabbage [syn: kale]

kohl

n : a cosmetic preparation used by women in Egypt and Arabia to darken the edges of their eyelids

coaled, cold /koʊld/

coaled

v : (past of coal) 1: burned to coal 2: supplied with coal 3: took in coal

cold

adj 1: used of physical coldness; having a low or inadequate temperature or feeling a sensation of coldness or having been made cold by e.g. ice or refrigeration; "a cold climate"; "a cold room"; "dinner has gotten cold"; "cold fingers"; "if you are cold, turn up the heat"; "a cold beer" [ant: hot] 2: extended meanings; especially of psychological coldness; without human warmth or emotion; "a cold unfriendly nod"; "a cold and unaffectionate person"; "a cold impersonal manner"; "cold logic"; "the concert left me cold" [ant: hot] 3: having lost freshness through passage of time; "a cold trail"; "dogs attempting to catch a cold scent" 4: (color) giving no sensation of warmth; "a cold bluish gray" 5: marked by errorless familiarity; "had her lines cold before rehearsals started" 6: no longer new; uninteresting; "cold (or stale) news" [syn: stale] 7: so intense as to be almost uncontrollable; "cold fury gripped him" 8: sexually unresponsive; "was cold to his advances"; "a frigid woman" [syn: frigid] 9: without compunction or human feeling; "in cold blood"; "cold-blooded killing"; "insensate destruction" [syn: cold-blooded, inhuman, insensate] 10: feeling or showing no enthusiasm; "a cold audience"; "a cold response to the new play" 11: unconscious from a blow or shock or intoxication; "the boxer was out cold"; "pass out cold" 12: of a seeker; far from the object sought 13: lacking the warmth of life; "cold in his grave"

n 1: a mild viral infection involving the nose and respiratory passages (but not the lungs); "will they never find a cure for the common cold?" [syn: common cold] 2: the absence of heat; "the coldness made our breath visible"; "come in out of the cold"; "cold is a vasoconstrictor" [syn: coldness, low temperature] [ant: hotness] 3: the sensation produced by low temperatures; "he shivered from the cold"; "the cold helped clear his head" [syn: coldness]

coaming, combing /'koʊmɪŋ/

coaming

n : a raised framework around a hatchway on a ship to keep water out

combing

n : the act of drawing a comb through hair; "his hair needed a comb" [syn: comb]

v : (progressive of comb); "She's combing her hair."

coarse, corse, course /kɔɹs/

coarse

adj 1: of texture; large-grained or rough to the touch; "coarse meal"; "coarse sand"; "a coarse weave" [ant: fine] 2: lacking refinement or cultivation or taste; "he had coarse manners but a first-rate mind"; "behavior that branded him as common"; "an untutored and uncouth human being"; "an uncouth soldier--a real tough guy"; "appealing to the vulgar taste for violence"; "the vulgar display of the newly rich" [syn: common, uncouth, vulgar] 3: of low or inferior quality or value; "of what coarse metal ye are molded"- Shakespeare; "produced...the common cloths used by the poorer population" [syn: common] 4: conspicuously and tastelessly indecent; "coarse language"; "a crude joke"; "crude behavior"; "an earthy sense of humor"; "a revoltingly gross expletive"; "a vulgar gesture"; "full of language so vulgar it should have been edited" [syn: crude, earthy, gross, vulgar]

corse

n : (archaic) corpse

course

n 1: education imparted in a series of lessons or class meetings; "he took a course in basket weaving"; "flirting is not unknown in college classes" [syn: course of study, course of instruction, class] 2: a connected series of events or actions or developments; "the government took a firm course"; "historians can only point out those lines for which evidence is available" [syn: line] 3: facility consisting of a circumscribed area of land or water laid out for a sport; "the course had only nine holes"; "the course was less than a mile" 4: a mode of action; "if you persist in that course you will surely fail" [syn: course of action] 5: a line or route along which something travels or moves: "the hurricane demolished houses in its path"; "the track of an animal"; "the course of the river" [syn: path, track] 6: general line of orientation: "the river takes a southern course"; "the northeastern trend of the coast" [syn: trend] 7: part of a meal served at one time; "she prepared a three course meal" 8: a layer of masonry; "a course of bricks" [syn: row]

adv : as might be expected; "naturally, the lawyer sent us a huge bill" [syn: naturally, of course] [ant: unnaturally]

v 1: move along, of liquids; "Water flowed into the cave" [syn: run, flow] 2: hunt

HOMOPHONES

(game) with hounds; "He often courses hares"

coat, cote /kout/

coat

n 1: an outer garment that has sleeves and covers the body from shoulder down; worn outdoors 2: a thin layer covering something; "a second coat of paint" [syn: coating] 3: growth of hair or wool or fur covering the body of an animal [syn: pelage]

v 1: put a coat on; cover the surface of; furnish with a surface; "coat the cake with chocolate" [syn: surface] 2: cover or provide with a coat 3: form a coat over; "Dirt had coated her face" [syn: cake]

cote

n : a small shelter for domestic animals (as sheep or pigeons)

coax, cokes /kouks/

coax

v : influence or urge by gentle urging, caressing, or flattering; "He palavered her into going along" [syn: wheedle, cajole, palaver, blarney, sweet-talk, inveigle]

cokes

v : (3rd pers sing of coke) become coke; "petroleum oil cokes after distillation"

cocks, cox /kaks/

cocks

n : (plu of cock) 1: obscene terms for penis [syn: pricks, dicks, shafts, peckers, peters, tools, one-eyed snakes] 2: faucet consisting of a rotating device for regulating flow of a liquid [syn: stopcocks, turncocks] 3: adult male chicken [syn: roosters] 4: adult male bird

v : (3rd pers sing of cock) 1: tilt or slant to one side; "cock one's head" 2: set the trigger of a firearm back for firing 3: to walk with a lofty proud gait, often in an attempt to impress others: "He strut around like a rooster in a hen house." [syn: swaggers, ruffles, prances, struts, sashays]

cox

n 1: either of two related enzymes that control the production of prostaglandin and are blocked by aspirin [syn: cyclooxygenase, Cox] 2: the helmsman of a ship's boat or a racing crew [syn: coxswain]

v : act as the coxswain, in a boat race

coir, coyer /kɔɪjˈɹ/

coir

n : stiff coarse fiber from the outer husk of a coconut

coyer

adj (compar of coy) 1: affectedly modest or shy especially in a playful or provocative way [syn: more demure, more overmodest] 2: showing marked and often playful or irritating evasiveness or reluctance to make a definite or committing statement;

"a politician coy about his intentions" 3: modestly or warily rejecting approaches or overtures; "like a wild young colt, very inquisitive but very coy and not to be easily cajoled"

coddling, codling /'kadliŋ/

coddling

v 1: cook in water just below the boiling point "coddle eggs" 2: treat indulgently [syn: pamper, baby]

codling

n : young codfish

coffer, cougher /'kɔfɹ/

coffer

n 1: an ornamental sunken panel in a ceiling or dome [syn: caisson, lacuna] 2: a chest especially for storing valuables

cougher

n : a person who coughs

coif, quaff /kwaf/

coif

n : a skullcap worn by nuns under a veil or by soldiers under a hood of mail or formerly by British sergeants-at-law

v 1: cover with a coif 2: arrange attractively; "dress my hair for the wedding" [syn: dress, arrange, set, do, coiffure]

quaff

n : a hearty draft

v : to swallow hurriedly or greedily or in one draught: "My car gulped 20 gallons without even wiping its mouth." [syn: gulp, swig]

coiffeur, coiffure /kwɑ'fuɹ/

coiffeur

n : a man hairdresser

coiffure

n : the arrangement of the hair (especially a woman's hair) [syn: hairdo, hair style]

v : arrange attractively; "dress my hair for the wedding" [syn: dress, arrange, set, do, coif, coiffe]

coign, coin, quoin /kɔɪn/

coign

n 1: expandable metal or wooden wedge used by printers to lock up a form within a chase [syn: quoin] 2: the keystone of an arch [syn: quoin]

coin

n : a metal piece (usually a disc) used as money

v 1: of phrases or words 2: form by stamping, punching, or printing; "strike coins"; "strike a medal" [syn: mint, strike]

quoin

n 1: the keystone of an arch [syn: coign] 2: (architecture) solid exterior angle of a building; especially one formed by a cornerstone [syn: corner]

collard, collared /'kaləɹd/

collard

n : variety of kale having smooth leaves

I-62

HOMOPHONES

collared
adj : the state of wearing a collar; "The dog is collared."

v : having a collar applied; "The dog is being collared."

colonel, kernel /'kɜⁱnɪl/
colonel
n : a commissioned military officer in the United States Army or Air Force or Marines who ranks above a lieutenant colonel and below a brigadier general

kernel
n 1: the inner and usually edible part of a seed or grain or nut or fruit stone: "black walnut kernels are difficult to get out of the shell" [syn: meat] 2: a single whole grain of a cereal: "a kernel of corn" 3: the choicest or most essential or most vital part of some idea or experience: "the gist of the prosecutor's argument"; "the heart and soul of the Republican Party"; "the nub of the story" [syn: substance, core, center, essence, gist, heart, heart and soul, inwardness, marrow, meat, nub, pith, sum, nitty-gritty]

color, culler /kʌlⁱʳ/
color
adj : (photography) "color film"; "he rented a color television"; "in glorious color"; "marvelous color illustrations" [ant: black-and-white]

n 1: a visual attribute of things that results from the light they emit or transmit or reflect; "white is made up of many different wavelengths of light" [syn: coloring] [ant: colorlessness] 2: interest and variety and intensity: "the Puritan Period was lacking in color" [syn: vividness] 3: the timbre of a musical sound; "the recording fails to capture the true color of the original music" 4: a race with skin pigmentation different from the white race (especially Blacks) [syn: people of color] 5: outward or token appearance or form; "he tried to give his actions a semblance of authenticity"; "the situation soon took on a different color" [syn: semblance] 6: any material used for its color [syn: coloring material] 7: (high energy physics) the characteristic of quarks that determines their role in the strong interaction; each flavor of quarks comes in three colors 8: the appearance of objects (or light sources) described in terms of a person's perception of their hue and lightness (or brightness) and saturation v 1: add color to; "The child colored the drawings"; "Fall colored the trees"; "colorize black and white film" [syn: colorize, color in] [ant: discolor] 2: distort; "My personal feelings color my judgment in this case" [syn: distort] 3: modify or bias; "His political ideas color his lectures" 4: decorate with colors; "color

the walls with paint in warm tones" [syn: emblazon] 5: gloss or excuse; "color a lie" [syn: gloss] 6: change color, often in an undesired manner; "The shirts discolored" [syn: discolor]

culler
n : someone who culls, picks out [syn: selector, gatherer, collector]

come, cum /kʌm/
come
v 1: move toward, travel toward something or somebody or approach something or somebody; "He came singing down the road"; "Come with me to the Casbah"; "come down here!"; "come out of the closet!"; "come into the room" [syn: come up] [ant: go] 2: reach a destination; arrive by movement or by making progress; "She arrived home at 7 o'clock"; "He got into college"; "She didn't get to Chicago until after midnight" [syn: arrive, get] [ant: leave] 3: come to pass; arrive, as in due course; "The first success came three days later"; "It came as a shock"; "Dawn comes early in June" 4: reach a state, relation, or condition; "The water came to a boil"; "We came to understand the true meaning of life"; "Their anger came to a boil"; " I came to realize the true meaning of life" 5: to be the product or result; "Melons come from a vine"; "Understanding comes from experience" [syn: follow] 6: enter or assume a condition, relation, use, or position; "He came into contact with a terrorist group"; "The shoes came untied"; "I came to see his point of view"; "her face went red with anger"; "The knot came loose"; "Your wish will come true" 7: be found or available; "These shoes come in three colors; The furniture comes unassembled" 8: come forth; "A scream came from the woman's mouth"; "His breath came hard" [syn: issue forth] 9: be a native of; "She hails from Kalamazoo" [syn: hail] 10: extend or reach; "The water came up to my waist"; "The sleeves come to your knuckles" 11: exist or occur in a certain point in a series; "Next came the student from France" 12: come from; be connected by a relationship of blood, for example; "She was descended from an old Italian noble family"; "he comes from humble origins" [syn: derive, descend] 13: cover a certain distance: "She came a long way" 14: come under, be classified or included; "fall into a category"; "This comes under a new heading" [syn: fall] 15: happen as a result; "Nothing good will come of this" 16: add up in number or quantity; "The bills amounted to $2,000"; "The bill came to $2,000" [syn: total, number, add up, amount] 17: develop into; "This idea will never amount to anything";

HOMOPHONES

"nothing came of his grandiose plans" [syn: add up, amount] 18: be received, as of news on the radio or television; "News came in of the massacre in Rwanda" [syn: come in] 19: come to one's mind; suggest itself; "It occurred to me that we should hire another secretary"; "A great idea then came to her" [syn: occur] 20: proceed or get along; "How is she doing in her new job?" "How are you making out in graduate school?" "He's come a long way" [syn: do, fare, make out, get along] 21: experience orgasm; "she could not come because she was too upset" 22: have a certain priority; "My family comes first"

cum
n : the thick white fluid containing spermatozoa that is ejaculated by the male genital tract [syn: semen, seed, seminal fluid, ejaculate]

comedy, comity

comedy /ˈkɑmɛdi/
n 1: light and humorous drama with a happy ending [ant: tragedy] 2: a comic incident or series of incidents [syn: drollery, clowning, funniness]

comity /ˈkɑmɪti/
n : a state or atmosphere of harmony or mutual civility and respect

complacence, omplaisance
/kʌmˈpleɪsɪnts/

complacence
n : the feeling you have when you are satisfied with yourself; "his complacency was absolutely disgusting" [syn: complacency, self-complacency, self-satisfaction]

complaisance
n : a disposition or tendency to yield to the will of others [syn: compliance, compliancy, obligingness, deference]

complacent, complaisant
/kʌmˈpleɪsɪnt/

complacent
adj : contented to a fault; "he had become complacent after years of success"; "his self-satisfied dignity" [syn: self-satisfied]

complaisant
adj : showing a cheerful willingness to do favors for others; "to close one's eyes like a complaisant husband whose wife was taken a lover"; "the obliging waiter was in no hurry for us to leave" [syn: obliging]

complement, compliment

complement /ˈkɑmpləmənt/
n 1: a word or phrase used to complete a grammatical construction 2: a complete number or quantity: "a full complement" 3: number needed to make up whole force: "a full complement of workers" [syn: full complement] 4: something added to complete or make perfect: "a fine wine is a perfect complement to the dinner" 5: one

of a series of enzymes in the blood serum that are part of the immune response 6: either of two parts that mutually complete each other
v : make complementary to; "I need some pepper to complement the sweet touch in the soup"

compliment /ˈkɑmplɪmɛnt/
n : a remark (or act) expressing praise and admiration
v 1: pay a compliment to [syn: congratulate] 2: express respect or esteem for

complementary, complimentary

complementary /kɑmˈplɛmɛntəɹi/
adj 1: acting as or providing a complement (something that completes the whole) [syn: completing] 2: of words so related that each is the negation of the other; "'male' and 'female' are complementary terms" 3: of or relating to or suggestive of complementation; "interchangeable electric outlets" [syn: interchangeable]
n : either one of two chromatic colors that when mixed together give white (in the case of lights) or gray (in the case of pigments); "yellow and blue are complementaries" [syn: complementary color]

complimentary /kɑmˈplɪmɛntəɹi/
adj 1: conveying or resembling a compliment; "a complimentary remark" [ant: uncomplimentary] 2: costing nothing; "complimentary tickets" [syn: costless, free, gratis, gratuitous] 3: obsequiously complimentary; "they listened with flattering interest" [syn: adulatory]

con, conn /kɑn/

con
n 1: an argument opposed to a proposal [ant: pro] 2: a person serving a sentence in a jail or prison [syn: convict, inmate, jailbird] 3: a swindle in which you cheat at gambling or persuade a person to buy worthless property [syn: bunco, bunco game, , confidence trick, confidence game, con game, gyp, hustle, sting, flimflam]
adv : on the negative side; "much was written pro and con" [syn: in opposition] [ant: pro]
v 1: deprive of by deceit; "He conned me out of my inheritance"; "She defrauded the customers who trusted her"; "the cashier gypped me when he gave me too little change" [syn: victimize, swindle, rook, goldbrick, nobble, diddle, bunco, defraud, scam, mulct, gyp] 2: commit to memory; learn by heart; "Have you memorized your lines for the play yet?" [syn: memorize, learn]

conn
v : conduct or direct the steering of a ship or plane

HOMOPHONES

conceded, conceited

conceded /kən'sidɪd/

adj : owned up to; "his admitted doubts"; "the conceded error"; "a confessed murderer"; "a self-confessed plagiarist" [syn: admitted, conceded, confessed, self-confessed]

v : (past of concede); "He conceded his error."; [syn: granted]; [ant: denied]

conceited /kən'sitɪd/

adj : characteristic of false pride; having an exaggerated sense of self-importance; "a conceited fool"; "an attitude of self-conceited arrogance"; "an egotistical disregard of others"; "so swollen by victory that he was unfit for normal duty"; "growing ever more swollen-headed and arbitrary"; "vain about her clothes" [syn: egotistic, egotistical, self-conceited, swollen, swollen-headed, vain]

conch, conk /kaŋk/

conch

n : any of various edible tropical marine gastropods of the genus Strombus having a brightly-colored spiral shell with large outer lip

conk

n : (British) informal term for the nose

v 1: come to a stop; "The car stalled in the driveway" [syn: stall] 2: hit, esp. on the head; "The stranger conked him and he fainted" 3: die (colloquial); "The old man finally kicked the bucket" [syn: kick the bucket, buy the farm, drop dead, pop off, choke, croak, snuff it] 4: pass out from weakness, physical or emotional distress due to a loss of blood supply to the brain [syn: faint, swoon, pass out]

concord, conquered

concord /'kaŋkɔɪd/ or /kan'kɔɪd/)

n 1: a harmonious state of things and their properties (as of colors and sounds); congruity of parts with one another and with the whole [syn: harmony, accord, concordance] 2: the determination of grammatical inflection on the basis of word relations [syn: agreement] 3: agreement of opinions [syn: harmony, concordance]

v 1: go together; "The colors don't harmonize"; "Their ideas concorded" [syn: harmonize, consort, accord, fit in, agree] 2: arrange by concord or agreement; "Concord the conditions for the marriage of the Prince of Wales with a commoner" 3: arrange the words of a text so as to create a concordance; "The team concorded several thousand nouns, verbs, and adjectives" 4: be in accord; be in agreement; "We agreed on the terms of the settlement"; "I can't agree with you"; "I hold with those you say life is sacred"; "Both philosophers concord on this point" [syn: agree, hold, concur] [ant: disagree]

conquered /'kaŋkəɪd/

adj : decisively defeated in combat [syn: beaten, overcome, overthrown, overwhelmed, routed, vanquished]

v : (past of conquer); "The U.S. conquered Japan,"

conker, conquer /'kaŋkəɪ/

conker

n 1: the inedible nutlike seed of the horse chestnut [syn: buckeye, horse chestnut] 2: someone who hits, esp. on the head

conquer

v : to defeat in combat; "When did the U.S. conquer Japan?"

consonance, consonants /'kansənɛnts/

consonance

n 1: the repetition of consonants (or consonant patterns) especially at the ends of words [syn: consonant rhyme] 2: the property of sounding harmonious [syn: harmoniousness]

consonants

adj 1: involving or characterized by harmony [syn: harmonic, harmonical, harmonized,, in harmony] 2: in keeping; "salaries agreeable with current trends"; "plans conformable with your wishes"; "expressed views concordant with his background" [syn: accordant, agreeable, conformable, in accord, in agreement, concordant]

n 1: a speech sound that is not a vowel [ant: vowel] 2: a letter of the alphabet standing for a spoken consonant

continence, continents /'kantɪnɛnts/

continence

n 1: the exercise of self constraint in sexual matters [syn: continency] 2: voluntary control over urinary and fecal discharge

continents

n : the large landmasses of the earth; "there are seven continents; Africa, Antarctica, Asia, Australia, Europe, North America and South America "; "pioneers had to cross the continent on foot"

coo, coup /ku/

coo

n : the sound made by a pigeon

v 1: speak softly or lovingly; "The mother who held her baby was cooing softly" 2: cry softly, as of pigeons

coup

n 1: a sudden and decisive change of government illegally or by force [syn: coup d'etat, putsch, takeover] 2: a brilliant and notable success

coolie, coolly, coulee /'kuli/

coolie

n : an offensive name for an unskilled Asian laborer

coolly

adv : in a composed and unconcerned manner; "without more ado Barker borrowed a knife from his brigade Major and honed it on a carborundum stone as coolly as a butcher" [syn: nervelessly, nonchalantly]

coulee

n 1: a small stream 2: a dry stream bed 3: a small or shallow ravine [syn. gully] 4: a thick sheet or stream of lava

coop, coupe /kup/

coop

n 1: a farm building for housing poultry [syn: chicken coop, hencoop, henhouse] 2: an enclosure made or wire or metal bars in which birds or animals are kept [syn: cage]

coupe

n : a car with two doors and front seats and a luggage compartment

cops, copse /kaps/

cops

n : (plu for cop); informal term for policemen
v : (3rd pers sing for cop) 1: take by theft; "Someone snitched my wallet!" [syn: hooks, snitches, thieves, knocks off, gloms, steals, robs] 2: take into custody, as of suspected criminals, by the police [syn: collars, nails, apprehends, arrests, picks up, nabs]; 3: to plea bargain; "cops a plea"

copse

n : a dense growth of bushes [syn: brush, brushwood, coppice, thicket]

coquet, coquette /kou'kɛt/

coquet

v : talk or behave amorously, without serious intentions; "The guys always try to chat up the new secretaries"; "My husband never flirts with other women" [syn: chat up, flirt, dally, butterfly, coquette, romance, philander, mash]

coquette

n : a seductive woman who uses her sex appeal to exploit men [syn: flirt, vamp, minx, tease, prickteaser, cockteaser]

core, corps /kɔɹ/

core

n 1: the center of an object; "do not eat the apple core" 2: a small group of indispensable persons or things; "five periodicals make up the core of their publishing program" [syn: nucleus, core group] 3: the central part of the earth 4: the choicest or most essential or most vital part of some idea or experience: "the gist of the prosecutor's argument"; "the heart and soul of the Republican Party"; "the nub of the story" [syn: kernel, substance, center, essence, gist, heart, heart and soul, inwardness, marrow, meat, nub, pith, sum, nitty-gritty] 5: a cylindrical sample of soil or rock obtained with a hollow drill 6: the

central meaning or theme of a speech or literary work [syn: effect, essence, burden, gist] 7: the chamber of a nuclear reactor containing the fissile material where the reaction takes place 8: a bar of magnetic material (as soft iron) that passes through a coil and serves to increase the inductance of the coil
v : remove the core or center from; "core an apple"

corps

n 1: an army unit usually consisting of two or more divisions 2: a body of people associated together; "diplomatic corps"

correspondence, correspondents /'kɔɹɛspandɛnts/

correspondence

n 1: communication by the exchange of letters 2: compatibility of observations; "there was no agreement between theory and measurement"; "the results of two tests were in correspondence" [syn: agreement] 3: the relation of correspondence in degree or size or amount [syn: commensurateness, proportionality] 4: a function such that for every element of one set there is a unique element of another set [syn: mapping, map] 5: communication by exchange of letters 6: (mathematics) an attribute of a shape; exact correspondence of form on opposite sides of a dividing line or plane [syn: symmetry, balance] [ant: asymmetry] 7: similarity by virtue of correspondence [syn: parallelism]

correspondents

n : (plu of correspondent); 1: people who communicate by means of letters [syn: letter writers] 2: journalists employed to provide news stories for newspapers or broadcast media [syn: newspapermen, newspaperwomen, news writers, pressmen]

cosign, cosine /'kousaɪn/

cosign

v 1: sign jointly; "Husband and wife co-signed the lease" [syn: co-sign] 2: sign and endorse (another person's signature), as for a loan [syn: co-sign]

cosine

n : trigonometric function; ratio of the adjacent side to the hypotenuse [syn: cos]

council, counsel /'kaunsɪl/

council

n 1: a body serving in an administrative capacity; "student council" 2: a meeting of people for consultation; "emergency council"

counsel

n 1: a lawyer who pleads cases in court [syn: advocate, counselor, counselor-at-law, pleader] 2: direction or advice as to a decision or course of action [syn:

HOMOPHONES

guidance, counseling, direction]
v : give advice to [syn: advise]

councilor, counselor
/'kaʊnsɪlɹ/

councilor
n : a member of a council [syn: council member, councillor]

counselor
n 1: some who gives advice about problems [syn: counsellor] 2: someone who has supervisory duties at a summer camp [syn: counsellor] 3: a lawyer who pleads cases in court [syn: advocate, counsel, counselor, counselor-at-law, pleader]

courier, currier /'kʌriɹ/

courier (alt /'kuɹiɹ/)
n : a person who carries a message [syn: messenger]

currier
n: a craftsman who prepares leather for use

courtesy, curtesy /'kʌtɪsi/

courtesy
n 1: a courteous or respectful or considerate act 2: a courteous or respectful or considerate remark 3: a courteous manner [syn: good manners] [ant: discourtesy]

curtesy
n : a husband's interest upon the death of his wife in the real property of an estate that she either solely owned or inherited provided they bore a child capable of inheriting the estate

cousin, cozen /'kʌzɪn/

cousin
n : the child of your aunt or uncle [syn: first cousin, full cousin]

cozen
v 1: be false to; be dishonest with [syn: deceive, lead on, delude] 2: act with artful deceit 3: cheat or trick; "He cozened the money out of the old man"

coward, cowered, cowherd

coward /'kaʊwɘɹd/
adj : lacking courage; ignobly timid and faint-hearted; "cowardly dogs, ye will not aid me then"- P.B.Shelley [syn: cowardly, fearful] [ant: brave]
n 1: a person who shows fear or timidity

cowered /'kaʊwɘɹd/
v : (past of cower) 1: crouch or curl up [syn: huddle] 2: show submission or fear; "The faculty cowered during the autocratic president's presentation." [syn: fawn, crawl, creep, cringe, grovel]

cowherd /'kaʊhɘɹd/
n : a hired hand who tends cattle and performs other duties on horseback [syn: cowboy, cowpuncher, puncher, cowman, cattleman, cowpoke, cowhand]

craft, kraft /kɹɛəft/

craft
n 1: the skilled practice of a practical occupation; "he learned his craft as an apprentice" [syn: trade] 2: a vehicle designed for navigation in or on water or air or through outer space 3: people who perform a particular kind of skilled work; "he represented the craft of brewers"; "as they say in the trade" [syn: trade] 4: skill in an occupation or trade [syn: craftsmanship, workmanship] 5: shrewdness as demonstrated by being skilled in deception [syn: craftiness, cunning, foxiness, guile, slyness, wiliness]
v : make by hand and with much skill; "The artisan crafted a complicated tool"

kraft
n : strong wrapping paper made from pulp processed with a sulfur solution [syn: kraft paper]

crape, crepe /kɹeɪp/

crape
n : a soft thin light fabric with a crinkled surface [syn: crepe]
v 1: cover with crape 2: curl tightly, of hair [syn: crimp, frizzle, frizz, kink up, kink]

crepe
n 1: paper with a crinkled texture; usually colored and used for decorations [syn: crepe paper] 2: small very thin pancake [syn: crepe, French pancake]

creak, creek /kɹik/

creak
n : a squeaking sound; "the creak of the floorboards gave him away" [syn: creaking]
v : make a high-pitched, screeching noise, as of a door [syn: squeak, screech]

creek
n 1: a natural stream of water smaller than a river (and often a tributary of a river); "the creek dried up every summer" [syn: brook]

cream, crème /kɹim/

cream
n 1: the best people or things in a group; "the cream of England's young men were killed in the Great War" [syn: pick] 2: the part of milk containing the butterfat 3: toiletry consisting of any of various substances resembling cream that have a soothing and moisturizing effect when applied to the skin [syn: ointment, emollient]
v 1: make creamy by beating; "Cream the butter" 2: put on cream, as on one's face or body; "She creams her face every night" 3: remove from the surface; "skim cream from the surface of milk" [syn: skim, skim off, cream off] 4: add cream to one's coffee 5: soundly defeat an opponent (slang) ; "The visiting team was creamed."

crème
n : a sweet liqueur

HOMOPHONES

crew, cru, krewe /kɹu/

crew
n 1: the men who man a ship or aircraft 2: an organized group of workmen [syn: gang, work party] 3: an informal body of friends; "he still hangs out with the same crowd" [syn: crowd, gang, bunch] 4: the team of men manning a racing shell
v : serve as a crew member on

cru
n 1: a vineyard or wine-producing region in France. 2: a grade or class of wine

krewe
n : a New Orleans social group whose members organize and participate as costumed paraders in the annual Mardi Gras carnival

crewed, crude /kɹud/

crewed
v : serve as a crew member on

crude
adj 1: not carefully or expertly made; "managed to make a crude splint"; "a crude cabin of logs with bark still on them"; "rough carpentry" [syn: rough] 2: conspicuously and tastelessly indecent; "coarse language"; "a crude joke"; "crude behavior"; "an earthy sense of humor"; "a revoltingly gross expletive"; "a vulgar gesture"; "full of language so vulgar it should have been edited" [syn: coarse, earthy, gross, vulgar] 3: not refined or processed; "unrefined ore"; "crude oil" [syn: unrefined, unprocessed] [ant: refined] 4: belonging to an early stage of technical development; characterized by simplicity and (often) crudeness; "the crude weapons and rude agricultural implements of early man"; "primitive movies of the 1890s"; "primitive living conditions in the Appalachian mountains" [syn: primitive, rude] 5: devoid of any qualifications or disguise or adornment; "the blunt truth"; "the crude facts"; "facing the stark reality of the deadline" [syn: blunt, crude, stark] 6: not processed or subjected to analysis; "raw data"; "the raw cost of production"; "only the crude vital statistics" [syn: raw]
n : a dark oil consisting mainly of hydrocarbons [syn: petroleum, crude oil, coal oil, rock oil, fossil oil]

crewel, cruel /'kɹuɛl/

crewel
n : slackly twisted yarn used for embroidery

cruel
adj 1: lacking or showing kindness or compassion or mercy [syn: unkind] 2: (of persons or their actions) able or disposed to inflict pain or suffering; "a barbarous crime"; "brutal beatings"; "cruel tortures"; "Stalin's roughshod treatment of the kulaks"; "a savage slap"; "vicious kicks" [syn: barbarous, brutal, fell, roughshod, savage, vicious] 3: (of weapons or instruments) causing suffering and pain; "brutal instruments of torture"; "cruel weapons of war" [syn: brutal] 4: (of circumstances; especially weather) causing suffering; "brutal weather"; "northern winters can be cruel"; "a cruel world"; "a harsh climate; "a rigorous climate"; "unkind winters" [syn: brutal, harsh, rigorous, unkind]

crews, cruise, crus, cruse, krewes /kɹuz/

crews
n : (plu of crew) 1: the men who man a ship or aircraft 2: an organized group of workmen [syn: gangs, work parties] 3: an informal body of friends; "he still hangs out with the same crowd" [syn: crowds, gangs, bunches] 4: the team of men manning a racing shell
v : (3rd pers sing of crew) : serve as a crew member on

cruise
n : an ocean trip taken for pleasure [syn: sail]
v 1: drive around aimlessly but ostentatiously and at leisure; "She cruised the neighborhood in her new convertible" 2: travel at a moderate speed; of vessels or airplanes 3: look for a sexual partner in a public place; "The men were cruising the park" 4: go on a cruise

crus
n : (plu of cru) (see crew)

cruse
n : small jar; holds liquid (oil or water)

krewes
n : (plu of krewe) (see crew)

cubical, cubicle /'kuəbɪkəl/

cubical
adj : shaped like a cube [syn: cube-shaped]

cubicle
n 1: small room is which a monk or nun lives [syn: cell] 2: small individual study area in a library [syn: carrel, stall] 3: small area set off by walls for special use [syn: booth, stall, kiosk]

cubit, qubit /'kuəbɪt/

cubit
n : an ancient unit of length based on the length of the forearm

qubit
n : A quantum bit

cue, Q, queue /kuə/

cue
n 1: an actor's line that immediately precedes and serves as a reminder for some action or speech 2: evidence that helps to solve a problem [syn: clue, clew] 3: a stimulus that provides information about what to do [syn: discriminative stimulus] 4: sports implement consisting

HOMOPHONES

of a tapering rod used to strike a cue ball in pool or billiards [syn: cue stick, pool cue, pool stick]

v : assist (somebody acting or reciting) by suggesting the next words of something forgotten or imperfectly learned [syn: prompt, remind]

Q

n : the 17th letter of the Roman alphabet [syn: q]

queue

n 1: a line of people or vehicles waiting for something [syn: waiting line]   2: (information processing) an ordered list of tasks to be performed or messages to be transmitted 3: a braid of hair at the back of the head

v : form a queue, form a line, stand in line [syn: line up, queue up]

currant, current /'kʌɹɪnt/
currant

n 1: any of several tart red or black berries used primarily for jellies and jams 2: any of various deciduous shrubs of the genus Ribes bearing currants [syn: currant bush] 3: small dried seedless raisin grown in the Mediterranean region and California; used in cooking

current

adj : occurring in or belonging to the present time; "current events"; "the current topic"; "current negotiations"; "current psychoanalytic theories"; "the ship's current position"

n 1: a flow of electricity through a conductor; "the current was measured in amperes" [syn: electric current] 2: a steady flow (usually from natural causes); "the raft floated downstream on the current"; "he felt a stream of air" [syn: stream] 3: dominant course (suggestive of running water) of successive events or ideas: "two streams of development run through American history"; "stream of consciousness"; "the flow of thought"; "the current of history" [syn: stream, flow]

curser, cursor /'kɜɹsəɹ/
curser

n : a person who curses

cursor

n : (computer science) indicator consisting of a movable spot of light (an icon) on a visual display; moving the cursor allows the user to point to commands or screen positions [syn; pointer]

cygnet, signet /'sɪgnɛt/
cygnet

n : a young swan

signet

n : a seal (especially one used to mark documents officially)

cymbal, symbol /'sɪmbᵊl/
cymbal

n : a percussion instrument consisting of a concave brass disk; makes a loud crashing sound when hit with a drumstick or when two are struck together

symbol

n 1: an arbitrary sign (written or printed) that has acquired a conventional significance

2: something visible that by association or convention represents something else that is invisible; "the eagle is a symbol of the United States" [syn: symbolization, symbolic representation]

HOMOPHONES

-D-

dam, damn /dæm/

dam

n 1: a barrier constructed to contain the flow or water or to keep out the sea [syn: dike, dyke, levee] 2: a metric unit of length equal to ten meters [syn: decameter] 3: female parent of an animal especially domestic livestock

v : obstruct with, or as if with, a dam [syn: dam up]

damn

adj 1: used as expletives; "oh, damn (or goddamn)!" [syn: goddamn] 2: expletives used informally as intensifiers; "he's a blasted idiot"; "it's a blamed shame"; "a blame cold winter"; "not a blessed dime"; "I'll be damned (or blessed or darned or goddamned) if I'll do any such thing"; "he's a damn (or goddamn or goddamned) fool"; "a deuced idiot"; "tired or his everlasting whimpering"; "an infernal nuisance" [syn: blasted, blame, blamed, blessed, damned, darned, deuced, everlasting, goddamn, goddamned, infernal]

n : something of little value; "it is not worth a damn"; "not worth shucks" [syn: darn, hoot, shit, shucks, tinker's damn, tinker's dam]

adv : (intensifier) "you are bloody right"; "Why are you so all-fired aggressive?" [syn: bloody, all-fired]

v : wish harm upon; put a curse on; "The bad witch cursed the child" [syn: curse, imprecate, maledict] [ant: bless]

day, dey /deɪ/

day

n 1: time for Earth to make a complete rotation on its axis; "two days later they left"; "they put on two performances every day"; "there are 30,000 passengers per day" [syn: twenty-four hours, solar day, mean solar day] 2: some point or period in time; "it should arrive any day now"; "after that day she never trusted him again"; "those were the days"; "these days it is not unusual" 3: the time after sunrise and before sunset while it is light outside; "the dawn turned night into day"; "it is easier to make the repairs in the daytime" [syn: daytime, daylight] [ant: night] 4: a day assigned to a particular purpose or observance; "Mother's Day" 5: the recurring hours when you are not sleeping (especially those when you are working); "my day began early this morning"; "it was a busy day on the stock exchange"; "she called it a day and went to bed" 6: an era of existence or influence; "in the day of the dinosaurs"; "in the days of the Roman Empire"; "in the days of sailing ships"; "he was a successful pianist in his day" 7: a period of opportunity; "he deserves his day in court"; "every dog has his day" 8: the period of time taken by a particular planet (e.g. Mars) to make a complete rotation on its axis; "how long is a day on Jupiter?" 9: the time for one complete rotation of the earth relative to a particular star, about 4 minutes shorter than a mean solar day [syn: sidereal day]

dey

n 1: used formerly as the title of the governor of Algiers before the French conquest in 1830 2: used formerly as the title for rulers of the states of Tunis and Tripoli.

days, daze, deys /deɪz/

days

n : (plu of day) (see day); "There are seven days in a week."

daze

n 1: the feeling of distress and disbelief that you have when something bad happens accidentally; "his mother's death left him in a daze"; "he was numb with shock" [syn: shock, stupor] 2: confusion characterized by lack of clarity [syn: fog, haze]

v 1: to cause someone to lose clear vision, esp. from intense light; "She was dazzled by the bright headlights" [syn: dazzle, bedazzle] 2: overcome esp. with astonishment or disbelief; "The news stunned her" [syn: stun]

deys

n : ruling officials of the Ottoman Empire in northern Africa

deader, debtor /'dɛdəɹ/

deader

adj : more deprived of life; (one cannot be more dead than dead, therefore this form is used colloquially to describe failure – "His career is deader than a doornail")

debtor (also /'dɛtəɹ/)

n : a person who owes a creditor; someone who has the obligation of paying a debt [ant: creditor]

n, dene /din/

dean

n 1: an administrator in charge of a division of a university or college 2: a man who is the senior member of a group; "he is the dean of foreign correspondents" [syn: doyen] 3: (Roman Catholic) the head of the College of Cardinals

dene

n : (British); valley

dear, deer /diɹ/

dear

adj 1: dearly loved [syn: beloved, darling] 2: with or in a close or intimate relationship; "a good friend"; "my sisters and brothers are near and dear" [syn: good, near] 3: earnest; "one's dearest wish"; "devout wishes for their success"; "heartfelt condolences" [syn: devout, earnest, heartfelt] 4: having a high price; "costly jewelry"; "high-priced merchandise"; "much too dear for my pocketbook"; "a pricey restaurant" [syn: costly, high-priced, pricey]

n 1: a beloved person; used as terms of endearment [syn: beloved, dearest, loved one, honey, love] 2: a sweet innocent mild-mannered person (especially a child) [syn: lamb]

adv 1: with affection; "she loved him dearly"; "he treats her affectionately" [syn: dearly, affectionately] 2: at a great cost; "he paid dearly for the food"; "this cost him dear" [syn: dearly]

deer

n : large woodland mammal (like those that pull Santa's sleigh) distinguished from Bovidae by the male's having solid deciduous antlers [syn: cervid]

deasil, diesel /ˈdizəl/

deasil

adj : clockwise, right-handwise

diesel

n : an internal-combustion engine that burns heavy oil [syn: diesel engine, diesel motor]

decadence,   decadents /ˈdɛkɪdɛnts/

decadence

n : the state of being degenerate in mental or moral qualities [syn: degeneracy, degeneration, decadency]

decadents

n : persons who have fallen into a decadent state (morally or artistically)

deem, deme /dim/

deem

v : keep in mind or convey as a conviction or view; "take for granted"; "view as important"; "hold these truths to be self-evident"; "I hold him personally responsible" [syn: hold, view as, take for]

deme

n 1: a local population of closely related organisms [syn: gamodeme] 2: a unit of local government in ancient Attica

demean, demesne /ˈdemin/

demean

v : reduce in worth, character, etc.; disgrace; dishonor [syn: degrade, disgrace, put down]

demesne

n 1: extensive landed property (especially in the country) retained by the owner for his own use; "the family owned a large estate on Long Island" [syn: estate, land, landed estate, acres] 2: territory over which rule or control is exercised; "his

domain extended into Europe"; "he made it the law of the land" [syn: domain, land]

dense, dents /dɛnts/

dense

adj 1: permitting little if any light to pass through because of denseness of matter; "dense smoke"; "heavy fog"; "impenetrable gloom" [syn: heavy, impenetrable] 2: closely crowded together; "a compact shopping center"; "a dense population"; "thick crowds" [syn: compact, thick] 3: hard to pass through because of dense growth; "dense vegetation"; "thick woods" [syn: thick] 4: having high relative density or specific gravity; "dense as lead" 5: slow to learn or understand; lacking intellectual acuity; "so dense he never understands anything I say to him"; "never met anyone quite so dim"; "although dull at classical learning, at mathematics he was uncommonly quick"- Thackeray; "dumb officials make some really dumb decisions"; "he was either normally stupid or being deliberately obtuse"; "worked with the slow students" [syn: dim, dull, dumb, obtuse, slow]

dents

n : (plu of dent) 1: an appreciable consequence (especially a lessening); "it made a dent in my bank account" 2: depressions scratched or carved into a surface [syn: incisions, scratches, pricks, slit] 3: an impression in a surface (as made by a blow) [syn: gouge, nick]

v : (3rd pers sing of dent) : make a dent into [syn: indents]

dental, dentil /ˈdɛntl/

dental

adj 1: of or relating to the teeth; "dental floss" 2: of or relating to dentistry; "dental student"

dentil

n : one of a series of small projecting rectangular blocks under a cornice

dependence, dependents /dɪˈpɛndɛnts/

dependence

n 1: lack of independence or self-sufficiency dependency 2: being abnormally dependent on something that is psychologically or physically habit-forming (especially alcohol or narcotic drugs) [syn: addiction, dependency]

dependents

n : people who rely on other people for support (especially financial support)

depose, depots

depose /dɪˈpouz/

v 1: force to leave (an office) [syn: force out] 2: make a deposition; declare under oath [syn: swear, depone]

depots /ˈdipouz/

n 1: stations where transport vehicles

load or unload passengers or goods [syn: terminals]   2: a depository for goods; "storehouses were built close to the docks" [syn: storehouses, storages, stores]

depositary, depository

depositary /dɪ'pazɪtəɹi/

n : a person entrusted with something for preservation or safekeeping [syn: trustee]

depository /dɪ'pazɪtɔɹi/

n : a facility where things can be deposited for safekeeping [syn: deposit, repository]

depravation, deprivation

/'dɛpɹɪveɪʃ°n/

depravation

n: a state of being debased, especially morally [syn: corrupted]

deprivation

n 1: a state of extreme poverty [syn: privation, want]   2: the disadvantage that results from losing something; "his loss of credibility led to his resignation" or "losing him is no great deprivation" [syn: loss]   3: act of depriving [syn: privation]

descent, dissent

descent /dɪ'sɛnt/

n 1: a movement downward 2: properties attributable to your ancestry; "he comes from good origins" [syn: origin, extraction]   3: the act of changing your location in a downward direction   4: the kinship relation between an individual and the individual's progenitors [syn: line of descent, lineage, filiation]   5: a downward slope [syn: declivity, fall, decline, declension, downslope] [ant: ascent]   6: the descendants of one individual; "his entire lineage has been warriors" [syn: lineage, line, line of descent, bloodline, blood line, blood, pedigree, ancestry, origin, parentage, stock]

dissent /dɪ'sɛnt/

n 1: (law) the difference of one judge's opinion from that of the majority; "he expressed his dissent in a contrary opinion"   2: a difference of opinion   3: the act of protesting; a public (often organized) manifestation of dissent [syn: protest, objection]

v 1: withhold assent; "Several Republicans dissented" [ant: assent]   2: fight back, also metaphorically: "His body protested against the harsh training" [syn: protest, resist]   3: be of different opinions; "I beg to differ!"; "She disagrees with her husband on many questions" [syn: disagree, differ, take issue]   [ant: agree]

desert, dessert /dɪ'zɜɹt/

desert

v 1: leave someone who needs or counts on you; leave in the lurch; "The mother deserted her children" [syn: abandon, forsake]   2: desert (a cause, a country or an army), often in order to join the opposing

cause, country, or army; "If soldiers deserted Hitler's army, they were shot" [syn: defect]

dessert

n : a sweet served as the last course of a meal [syn: sweet]

deterrence, deterrents

/'dɪtəɹɪnts/

deterrence

n 1: a negative motivational influence [syn: disincentive] [ant: incentive]   2: communication that makes you afraid to try something [syn: determent, intimidation]   3: the act or process of discouraging actions or preventing occurrences by instilling fear or doubt or anxiety

deterrents

n : immaterial things that interfere with or delay action or progress [syn: hindrance, impediment, balk, baulk, check, handicap]

deviance, deviants /'diviɛnts/

deviance

n 1: an aberrant state or condition [syn: aberrance, aberrancy, aberration]   2: deviate behavior [syn: deviation]

deviants

n : (plu of deviant) : a people whose behavior deviates from what is acceptable especially in sexual behavior [syn: perverts, deviates, degenerates]

deviser, devisor, divisor /dɪ'vaɪzəɹ/

deviser

n : a person who makes plans [syn: planner, contriver]

deviser

n : someone who disposes real property in a will

divisor

n 1: one of two or more integers that can be exactly divided into another integer; "what are the 4 factors of 6?" [syn: factor]   2: the number by which a dividend is divided

deuce, douce /dus/

deuce

n 1: a tie in tennis or table tennis that requires winning two successive points to win the game   2: the cardinal number that is the sum of one and one or a numeral representing this number [syn: two, 2, II]   3: a word used in exclamations of confusion; "what the devil"; "the deuce with it"; "the dickens you say" [syn: devil, dickens]   4: one of the four playing cards in a deck that have two spots

douce

adj : soft (music), sweet, smooth

dew, do, due /du/

dew

n : water that has condensed on a cool surface overnight from water vapor in the air; "in the morning the grass was wet with dew"

HOMOPHONES

<u>do</u>
n 1: an uproarious party [syn: bash, brawl]
v 1: engage in: "make love, not war";
"make an effort"; "do research"; "do
nothing"; "make revolution" [syn: make]
2: to act or perform an action; "John did
the painting, the weeding, and he cleaned
out the gutters" [syn: perform, execute]
3: get (something) done; "I did my job"
[syn: perform] 4: proceed or get along;
"How is she doing in her new job?" "How
are you making out in graduate school?"
"He's come a long way" [syn: fare,
make out, come, get along] 5: give rise
to; cause to happen or occur, not always
intentionally; "cause a commotion";
"make a stir"; "cause an accident" [syn:
cause, make] 6: carry out or practice; as
of jobs and professions: "practice law"
[syn: practice, exercise] 7: be sufficient;
be adequate, either in quality or quantity;
"A few words would answer"; "This car
suits my purpose well"; "Will $100 do?";
"A "B" grade doesn't suffice to get me into
medical school"; "Nothing else will serve"
[syn: suffice, answer, serve] 8: create or
design, often in a certain way; "Do my
room in blue"; "I did this piece in wood
to express my love for the forest" [syn:
make] [ant: unmake] 9: behave in a certain
manner; show a certain behavior; conduct
or comport oneself; "You should act like
an adult"; "Don't behave like a fool";
"What makes her do this way?"; "She
played the servant her husband's master"
[syn: act, behave] 10: spend time in prison
or in a labor camp; "He did six years for
embezzlement" [syn: serve] 11: carry
on or manage; "We could do with a little
more help around here" [syn: manage] 12:
arrange attractively; "dress my hair for the
wedding" [syn: dress, arrange, set, coif,
coiffure] 13: travel or traverse (a distance)
"This car does 150 miles per hour"; "We
did 6 miles on our hike every day"
<u>due</u>
adj 1: owed and payable immediately or
on demand; "payment is due" [syn: owed]
[ant: undue] 2: proper and appropriate;
fitting; "richly deserved punishment";
"due esteem" [syn: deserved] 3:
scheduled to arrive; "the train is due in
15 minutes" 4: suitable to or expected
in the circumstances; "all due respect";
"due cause to honor them"; "a long due
promotion"; "in due course" [ant: undue]
5: reasonable in the circumstances;
"gave my comments due consideration";
"exercising due care"
n 1: that which is deserved or owed: "give
the devil his due" 2: a payment that is due
(e.g., as the price of membership); "the
society dropped him for non-payment of

dues"
adv : directly or exactly; straight; "went
due North"
dewed, dude /dud/
<u>dewed</u>
adj : having been covered with dew
<u>dude</u>
n 1: friendly term for a man; 2: (old usage)
a man who is much concerned with his
dress and appearance [syn: dandy, fop,
gallant, sheik, beau, swell, fashion plate,
clotheshorse]
dhol, dhole, dol, dole /doʊl/
<u>dhol</u>
n : double-sided barrel Indian drum
<u>dhole</u>
n : fierce wild dog of the forests of central
and southeast Asia that hunts in packs
[syn: Cuon alpinus]
<u>dol</u>
n 1: a unit of pain intensity
<u>dole</u>
n 1: a share of money or food or clothing
that has been charitably given 2: money
received from the state [syn: pogy, pogey]
dhow, tao /daʊ/
<u>dhow</u>
n : a lateen-rigged sailing vessel used by
Arabs
<u>tao</u>
n 1: an adherent of any branch of Taoism
[syn: Taoist] 2: the ultimate principle of
the universe
dial, diel /'daɪəl/ (alt /daɪl/)
<u>dial</u>
n 1: the face of a timepiece; graduated to
show the hours 2: the control on a radio
or television set that is used for tuning 3:
the circular graduated indicator on various
measuring instruments 4: (archaic) a
disc on a telephone that is rotated a fixed
distance for each number called [syn:
telephone dial]
v 1: (archaic) operate a dial to select a
telephone number; "You must take the
receiver off the hook before you dial" 2:
(archaic) choose by means of a dial; "dial a
telephone number"
<u>diel</u>
adj : lasting 24 hours or having a 24-hour
period;"diel fluctuations in temperature"
n : a period of 24 hours
diarist, direst /'daɪərɪst/
<u>diarist</u>
n : someone who keeps a diary or journal
[syn: diary keeper, journalist]
<u>direst</u>
adj 1: (superlative of dire) most fraught
with extreme danger; most hopeless
die, dye /daɪ/
<u>die</u>
n 1: small cubes with 1 to 6 spots on the
faces; used to generate random numbers

HOMOPHONES

[syn: dice]   2: a device used for shaping metal   3: a cutting tool that is fitted into a diestock and used for cutting male (external) screw threads on screws or bolts or pipes or rods

v 1: pass from physical life and lose all bodily attributes and functions necessary to sustain life; "She died from cancer"; "They children perished in the fire"; "The patient went peacefully" [syn: decease, perish, go, exit, pass away, expire, pass] [ant: be born]   2: suffer or face the pain of death; "Martyrs may die every day for their faith"   3: be brought to or as if to the point of death by an intense emotion such as embarrassment, amusement, or shame; "I was dying with embarrassment when my little lie was discovered"; "We almost died laughing during the show"   4: stop operating or functioning; "The engine finally went"; "The car died on the road"; "The bus we traveled in broke down on the way to town"; "The coffee maker broke"; "The engine failed on the way to town"; "her eyesight went after the accident" [syn: fail, go bad, give way, give out, conk out, go, break, break down]   5: feel indifferent towards; "She died to worldly things and eventually entered a monastery"   6: languish as with love or desire; "She dying for a cigarette";/ "Those shoes are to die for" "I was dying to leave"   7: cut or shape with a die; "Die out leather for belts" [syn: die out]   8: to be on base at the end of an inning, of a baseball player   9: lose sparkle or bouquet, of wine or beer; "pall" is an obsolete word [syn: pall, become flat]   10: disappear or come to an end; "Their anger died"; "My secret will die with me!"   11: suffer spiritual death; be damned (in the religious sense); "Whosoever believes in me shall never die"

dye

n : a usually soluble substance for staining or coloring e.g. fabrics or hair [syn: dyestuff]

v : color with dye; "Please dye these shoes"

died, dyed   /daɪd/
died

v : (past of die) (see die)

dyed

adj 1: colored or impregnated with dye [syn: tinted]   2: (used of color) artificially produced; not natural; "a bleached blonde" [syn: bleached, colored]

dine, dyne   /daɪn/
dine

v 1: have supper; eat dinner; "We often dine with friends in this restaurant"   2: give dinner to; host for dinner; "I'm wining and dining my friends"

dyne

n : a unit of force equal to the force that

imparts an acceleration of 1 cm/sec/sec to a mass of 1 gram

dinghy, dingy   /'dɪŋi/
dinghy

n : a small boat of shallow draft with cross thwarts for seats and rowlocks for oars with which it is propelled [syn: dory, rowboat]

dingy

adj : (slang) crazy, insane

dire, dyer   /'daɪjɚ/
dire

adj 1: fraught with extreme danger; nearly hopeless; "a desperate illness"; "on all fronts the Allies were in a desperate situation due to lack of materiel"- G.C.Marshall; "a dire emergency" [syn: desperate]   2: causing fear or dread or terror; "the awful war"; "an awful risk"; "dire news"; "a career or vengeance so direful that London was shocked"; "the dread presence of the headmaster"; "polio is no longer the dreaded disease it once was"; "a dreadful storm"; "a fearful howling"; "horrendous explosions shook the city"; "a terrible curse" [syn: awful, direful, dreaded, dreadful, fearful, fearsome, frightening, horrendous, horrific, terrible]

dyer

n : someone whose job is to dye cloth

disburse, disperse
disburse   /dɪs'bɚs/

v : pay out; "they disburse bonus checks"

disperse   /dɪs'pɚs/

v 1: distribute loosely; "He scattered gun powder under the wagon." [syn: scatter, sprinkle, dot, dust]   2: to cause to separate and go in different directions, of crowds, for example; "She waved her hand and scattered the crows." [syn: dissipate, dispel, break up, scatter]   3: move away from each other; "The crowds dispersed"; "The children scattered in all directions when the teacher approached"; [syn: dissipate, scatter, spread out]   4: cause to separate; "break up kidney stones"; "disperse particles" [syn: break up, scatter]   5: cause to become widely known; "spread information"; "circulate a rumor"; "broadcast the news" [syn: circulate, circularize, distribute, disseminate, propagate, broadcast, spread, diffuse, pass around]

discreet, discrete   /dɪs'kɹit/
discreet

adj 1: marked by prudence or modesty and wise self-restraint; "his trusted discreet aide"; "a discreet, finely wrought gold necklace [ant: indiscreet]   2: unobtrusively perceptive and sympathetic; "a discerning editor"; "a discreet silence" [syn: discerning]   3: heedful of potential

HOMOPHONES

consequences; "circumspect actions"; "physicians are now more circumspect about recommending its use"; "a discreet investor" [syn: circumspect]

discrete

adj : constituting a separate entity or part; "a government with three discrete divisions"; "on two distinct occasions" [syn: distinct]

discussed, disgust /dɪsˈgʌst/

discussed

v : (past of discuss) : "We discussed the subject for two hours."

disgust

n : strong feelings of dislike

v 1: fill with distaste; "This foul language disgusts me" [syn: revolt, repel] 2: cause aversion in; offend the moral sense of [syn: revolt, nauseate, sicken, churn up]

dissidence, dissidents /ˈdɪsɪdənts/

dissidence

n : disagreement; especially disagreement with the government

dissidents

n : (plu of dissident) : people who dissent from some established policy [syn: dissentesr, protesters, objectors, contestants]

djinn, gin /dʒɪn/

djinn

n : (plu of djinni) : spirits believed by Muslims to inhabit the earth and influence mankind by appearing in the form of humans or animals [syn: genies, jinn]

gin

n 1: strong liquor flavored with juniper berries 2: a trap for birds or small mammals; often has a noose [syn: snare, noose] 3: a machine that separates the seeds from raw cotton fibers [syn: cotton gin] 4: a form of rummy in which a player can go out if the cards remaining in their hand total less than 10 points [syn: gin rummy, knock rummy]

v 1: separate the seeds from (cotton) with a cotton gin 2: trap with a gin; "gin game"

do, doe, dough /doʊ/

do

n: the syllable naming the first (tonic) note of any major scale in solmization "do re me fa so la ti do"

doe

n : mature female of mammals of which the male is called `buck' [syn: female deer]

dough

n 1: a flour mixture stiff enough to knead or roll 2: informal terms for money [syn: shekels, gelt, bread, dinero, lucre, loot, pelf, moolah, cabbage, kale]

doc, dock /dak/

doc

n 1: a licensed medical practitioner; "I felt so bad I went to see my doctor" [syn: doctor, physician, MD, Dr., medico]

dock

n 1: an enclosure in a court of law where the defendant sits during the trial 2: any of certain coarse weedy plants with long taproots, sometimes used as table greens or in folk medicine [syn: sorrel, sour grass] 3: a platform built out from the shore into the water and supported by piles; provides access to ships and boats [syn: pier, wharf, wharfage] 4: a platform where trucks or trains can be loaded or unloaded [syn: loading dock] 5: landing in a harbor next to a pier where ships are loaded and unloaded or repaired; may have gates to let water in or out; "the ship arrived at the dock more than a day late" [syn: dockage, docking facility] 6: the solid bony part of the tail of an animal as distinguished from the hair 7: a short or shortened tail of certain animals [syn: bobtail, bob]

v 1: come into dock; "the ship docked" [ant: undock] 2: deprive someone of benefits, as a penalty 3: deduct from someone's wages 4: remove or shorten the tail of an animal [syn: tail, bob] 5: haul into a dock; "dock the ships" [ant: undock

docks, docs, dox /daks/

docks (plu of dock) (see dock)

docs (plu of doctors) (see doc)

dox (also doxx)

v: to publish the private personal information of (another person) or reveal the identity of (an online poster) without the consent of that individual; "the professor was doxed by a bitter student who failed her class"

docile, dossal /ˈdasəl/

docile

adj 1: willing to be taught or led or supervised or directed; "the docile masses of an enslaved nation" [ant: stubborn] 2: ready and willing to be taught; "docile pupils eager for instruction"; "teachable youngsters" [syn: teachable] 3: easily handled or managed; "a gentle old horse, docile and obedient" [syn: gentle]

dossal

n : An ornamental hanging of rich fabric, as behind an altar.

doer, dour /ˈduər/

doer

n : a person who takes an active part

dour (also /ˈdaʊər/)

adj 1: stubbornly unyielding; "dogged persistence"; "dour determination" [syn: bulldog, dogged, pertinacious, tenacious, unyielding] 2: harshly uninviting or formidable in manner or appearance; "a dour, self-sacrificing life"; "a forbidding scowl" [syn: forbidding, grim] 3: showing a brooding ill humor; "a dark scowl";

HOMOPHONES

"the proverbially dour New England Puritan"; "a glum, hopeless shrug"; "he sat in moody silence"; "a morose and unsociable manner"; "a sour temper"; "a sullen crowd" [syn: dark, glowering, glum, moody, morose, saturnine, sour, sullen]

does, dos, doughs, doze / doʊz /

does
n : (plu of doe) : "The does were grazing in the meadow."

dos
n : (plu of do) (see do)

doughs
n : (plu of dough) (see do)

doze
n : a light fitful sleep [syn: drowse]
v : sleep lightly or for a short period of time [syn: snooze, drowse]

done, dun / dʌn /

done
adj 1: having finished or arrived at completion; "certain to make history before he's done"; "it's a done deed"; "after the treatment, the patient is through except for follow-up"; "almost through with his studies" [syn: through, through with] 2: cooked until ready to serve

dun
adj : of a dull grayish brown to brownish gray color; "the dun and dreary prairie"
n 1: horse of a dull brownish gray color 2: a color varying around light grayish brown; "she wore a dun raincoat" [syn: grayish brown, fawn]
v 1: annoy constantly [syn: nag, torment, rag, bedevil, crucify, frustrate]   2: persistently ask for overdue payment; "The grocer dunned his customers every day by telephone" 3: cure by salting; "dun codfish" 4: make a dun color

donjon, dungeon / 'dʌndʒɪn /

donjon
n : the main tower within the walls of a medieval castle or fortress [syn: keep]

dungeon
n: a dark cell (usually underground) where prisoners can be confined

dos, dues / duz /

dos
n : used in expression "...dos and don'ts..."

dues
n : periodic membership fee paid by members of an organization

dost, dust / dʌst /

dost
v : (archaic form of do) : "The lady dost complain!"

dust
n 1: fine powdery material such as dry earth or pollen that can be blown about in the air; "the furniture was covered with dust" 2: the remains of something that has been destroyed or broken up [syn: debris, junk, rubble, detritus] 3: free microscopic particles of solid material; "astronomers say that the empty space between planets actually contains measurable amounts of dust"
v 1: remove the dust from, as of furniture 2: rub the dust over a surface so as to blur the outlines of a shape; "The artist dusted the charcoal drawing down to a faint image" 3: cover with a light dusting of a substance; "dust the bread with flour" 4: distribute loosely; "He scattered gun powder under the wagon." [syn: scatter, sprinkle, dot, disperse]

dour, dower / 'daʊəɹ /

dour
adj 1: stubbornly unyielding; "dogged persistence"; "dour determination"; "the most vocal and pertinacious of all the critics; "men tenacious of opinion" [syn: bulldog, dogged, pertinacious, tenacious, unyielding]   2: harshly uninviting or formidable in manner or appearance; "a dour, self-sacrificing life"; "a forbidding scowl"; "a grim man loving duty more than humanity" [syn: forbidding, grim] 3: showing a brooding ill humor; "a dark scowl"; "the proverbially dour New England Puritan"; "a glum, hopeless shrug"; "he sat in moody silence"; "a morose and unsociable manner"; "a sullen crowd" [syn: dark, glowering, glum, moody, morose, saturnine, sour, sullen]

dower
n 1: money or property brought by a woman to her husband at marriage [syn: dowry, dowery] 2: a life estate to which a wife is entitled on the death of her husband
v : furnish with an endowment; "When she got married, she got dowered" [syn: endow]

dowager, dowitcher

dowager / 'daʊwɪdʒɹ /
n : a widow holding property received from her deceased husband

dowitcher / 'daʊwɪtʃəɹ /
n : shorebird of the sandpiper family that resembles a snipe

drier, dryer / 'dɹaɪəɹ /

drier
n 1: a substance that promotes drying (e.g., calcium oxide absorbs water and is used to remove moisture) [syn: desiccant, drying agent] 2: an appliance that removes moisture [syn: dryer]
adj : (compar of dry)

dryer
n : an appliance that removes moisture [syn: drier]

HOMOPHONES

droop, drupe /dɹup/

droop

n : a shape that sags; "there was a sag in the chair seat" [syn: sag]
v 1: droop, sink, or settle from or as if from pressure or loss of tautness [syn: sag, swag, flag] 2: hang loosely or laxly; "His tongue lolled" [syn: loll] 3: become limp; "The flowers wilted" [syn: wilt]

drupe

n : fleshy indehiscent fruit with a single seed: e.g. almond; peach; plum; cherry; elderberry; olive; jujube [syn: stone fruit]

dual, duel /ˈduəl/

dual

adj 1: consisting of or involving two parts or components usually in pairs; "an egg with a double yolk"; "a double (binary) star"; "double doors"; "dual controls for pilot and copilot"; "duple (or double) time consists of two (or a multiple of two) beats to a measure" [syn: double, duple] 2: having more than one decidedly dissimilar aspects or qualities; "a double (or dual) role for an actor"; "the office of a clergyman is twofold; public preaching and private influence"- R.W.Emerson [syn: double, twofold] 3: a grammatical number category referring to two items or units (as opposed to one item (singular) or more than one item (plural)); "ancient Greek had the dual form but it has merged with the plural form in modern Greek"

duel

n 1: a prearranged fight with deadly weapons by two people (accompanied by seconds) in order to settle a quarrel over a point of honor 2: any struggle between two skillful opponents (individuals or groups)
v : fight a duel, as over one's honor or a woman; "In the 19th century, men often dueled over small matters"

ducked, duct /dʌkt/

ducked

v : (past of duck) 1: to move (the head or body) quickly downwards or away: "Before he could duck, another stone struck him." 2: submerge or plunge suddenly 3: dip into a liquid: "He dipped into the pool" [syn: dip, douse] 4: avoid or try to avoid, as of duties, questions and issues; "He ducked the issue" [syn: hedged, fudged, evaded, put off, circumvented, parried, eluded, skirted, dodged, sidestepped]

duct

n 1: a bodily passage or tube conveying a secretion or other substance [syn: canal, channel] 2: a continuous tube formed by a row of elongated cells lacking intervening end walls 3: an enclosed conduit for a fluid

ducks, ducts /dʌks/

ducks

n 1: small wild or domesticated web-footed broad-billed swimming birds usually having a depressed body and short legs 2: heavy cotton fabrics of plain weave; used for clothing and tents
v : (3rd pers sing of duck) 1: to move (the head or body) quickly downwards or away; "He ducks before another stone could strike him" 2: submerges or plunges suddenly 3: dips in a liquid; "He dips into the pool" [syn: dips, douses] 4: avoids or tries to avoid fulfilling, answering, or performing (duties, questions, or issues); "He dodges the issue"; "she skirts the problem"; "He tends to evade their responsibilities"; "he evades the questions skillfully" [syn: hedges, fudges, evades, puts off, circumvents, parries, eludes, skirts, dodges, sidesteps]

ducts (also /dʌkts/)

n 1: a bodily passage or tube lined with epithelial cells and conveying a secretion or other substance; "the tear duct was obstructed"; "the alimentary canal"; "poison is released through a duct in the snake's fangs" [syn: epithelial duct, canal, channel] 2: a continuous tube formed by a row of elongated cells lacking intervening end walls 3: an enclosed conduit for a fluid

dyeing, dying /ˈdaɪɪŋ/

dyeing

n : the use of dye to change the color of something permanently

dying

adj 1: in or associated with the process of passing from life or ceasing to be; "a dying man"; "his dying wish"; "a dying fire"; "a dying civilization" 2: (colloquial) eagerly desirous; "anxious to see the new show at the museum"; "dying to hear who won"
n : the time when something ends; "it was the death of all his plans"; "a dying of old hopes" [syn: death, demise] [ant: birth]

HOMOPHONES

-E-

E's, ease /iz/

E's

n : (plu of E) : [syn: e's]

ease

n 1: freedom from difficulty or hardship or effort: "he rose through the ranks with apparent ease"; "they put it into containers for ease of transportation" [syn: easiness, simplicity] [ant: difficulty] 2: a freedom from financial difficulty that promotes a comfortable state: "a life of luxury and ease"; "he had all the material comforts of this world" [syn: comfort] 3: the condition of being comfortable or relieved (especially after being relieved of distress); "he enjoyed his relief from responsibility"; "getting it off his conscience gave him some ease" [syn: relief] 4: freedom from constraint or embarrassment; "I am never at ease with strangers" [syn: informality] 5: freedom from activity (work or strain or responsibility); "took his repose by the swimming pool" [syn: rest, repose, relaxation]

v 1: move gently or carefully; "He eased himself into the chair" 2: ease physically [syn: comfort] 3: make easier; "you could facilitate the process by sharing your knowledge" [syn: facilitate, alleviate] 4: lessen the intensity of; calm; as of of anxieties and fears [syn: still, allay, relieve]

earn, erne, urn /ən/

earn

v 1: acquire or deserve by one's efforts or actions [syn: garner] 2: earn on some commercial or business transaction; earn as salary or wages; "How much do you make a month in your new job?" "She earns a lot in her new job"; "this merger brought in lots of money"; "He clears $5,000 each month" [syn: gain, take in, clear, make, realize, pull in, bring in]

erne

n : bulky grayish-brown eagle with a short wedge-shaped white tail; of Europe and Greenland [syn: ern, gray sea eagle, European sea eagle, white-tailed sea eagle, Haliatus albicilla]

urn

n 1: a large vase that usually has a pedestal or feet 2: a large pot for making coffee or tea

eave, eve /iv/

eave

n : the overhang at the lower edge of a roof

eve

n : 1 evening (poetic) "Winter oft, at eve resumes the breeze."--Thomson. 2. the evening before a holiday "He had to work on Christmas eve." 3: the period immediately preceding some important event "the eve of independence"

edition (see addition)

educe (see adduce)

eek, eke /ik/

eek

inter : an expression of fright or delight

eke

v : to obtain with great difficulty; usually used with out ; "You'll eke out a living as a poet"

effect (see affect)

effluence, effluents /'ɛfluənts/

effluence

n : the process of flowing out [syn: outflow, efflux] [ant: inflow, inflow]

effluents

n : waters mixed with waste matter; "Different effluents are discharged from that complex"[syn: wastewaters, sewer waters]

eight (see ate)

el, ell, L /ɛl/

el

n 1: angular distance above the horizon (especially of a celestial object) [syn: elevation, altitude] 2: an electric elevated railway [syn: elevated railway, elevated railroad, overhead railway] 3: 12th letter of the Roman alphabet

ell

n : an extension at the end and at right angles to the main building

L

n : 12th letter of the Roman alphabet; [syn: el]

elation, illation

elation /i'leɪʃən/

n 1: an exhilarating psychological state of pride and optimism; an absence of depression [ant: depression] 2: a feeling of joy and pride [syn: high spirits]

illation /ɪ'leɪʃən/

illation

n : the reasoning involved in drawing a conclusion or making a logical judgment on the basis of circumstantial evidence and prior conclusions rather than on the basis of direct observation [syn: inference]

elementary (see alimentary)

elicit, illicit

elicit /ɛ'lɪsɪt/

v 1: call forth; of emotions, feelings, and responses; "arouse pity"; "raise a smile"; "evoke sympathy" [syn: arouse, enkindle, kindle, evoke, fire, raise, provoke] 2: deduce (a principle) or construe (a meaning); "We drew out some interesting linguistic data from the native informant" [syn: educe, evoke, extract, draw out] 3: derive by reason; "elicit a solution"

HOMOPHONES

illicit /ɪ'lɪsɪt/
adj 1: contrary to accepted morality (especially sexual morality) or convention; "an illicit association with his secretary" [ant: licit] 2: contrary to or forbidden by law; "an illegitimate seizure of power"; "illicit trade"; "an outlaw strike"; "unlawful measures" [syn: illegitimate, outlawed, unlawful]

elision, elysian /ɛ'liʒɪn/
elision
n 1: omission of a sound between two words (usually a vowel and the end of one word or the beginning of the next) 2: a deliberate act of omission; "with the exception of the children, everyone was told the news" [syn: exception, exclusion]

elysian
adj 1: relating to the Elysian Fields 2: resembling paradise; causing happiness; "elysian peace"; "a paradisal place without work or struggle"; "paradisial isles"; "an age of paradisiacal happiness" [syn: paradisiacal, paradisiac, paradisaic, paradisal, paradisial] 3: of such surpassing excellence as to suggest divine inspiration; "her pies were simply divine"; "the divine Shakespeare"; "an elysian meal"; "an inspired performance" [syn: divine, inspired]

elusive, illusive /ɪ'lusɪv/
elusive
adj 1: difficult to describe; "a haunting elusive odor" 2: skillful at eluding capture; [syn: evasive] 3: be difficult to detect or grasp by the mind; "his whole attitude had undergone a subtle change"; "a subtle difference"; "that elusive thing the soul" [syn: subtle]

illusive
adj : based on or having the nature of an illusion; "illusive hopes of finding a better job"; "Secret activities offer presidents the alluring but often illusory promise that they can achieve foreign policy goals without the bothersome debate and open decision that are staples of democracy" [syn: illusory]

emerge, immerge
emerge /i'məɹdʒ/
v 1: come out into view, as from concealment; "Suddenly, the proprietor emerged from his office" 2: come out of; "Water issued from the hole in the wall"; "The words seemed to come out by themselves" [syn: issue, come out, come forth, go forth, egress] 3: become known or apparent; "Some nice results emerged from the study" 4: come up to the surface of or rise, as from water; also used metaphorically: "He felt new emotions emerge" 5: happen or occur as a result of something [syn: come forth]

immerge /ɪ'məɹdʒ/
v : to plunge into or immerse oneself in something

eminent, immanent, imminent
eminent /'ɛmɪnɛnt/
adj 1: (used of persons) standing above others in character or attainment or reputation; "our distinguished professor"; "an eminent scholar"; "a great statesman" [syn: distinguished, great] 2: standing above others in quality or position; "people in high places"; "the high priest"; "eminent members of the community" [syn: high] 3: having achieved eminence; "an eminent physician" 4: of imposing height; especially standing out above others; "an eminent peak"; "lofty mountains"; "the soaring spires of the cathedral"; "towering icebergs" [syn: lofty, soaring, towering]

immanent /'ɪmanɛnt/
adj : (philosophy) of a mental act; occurring entirely within the mind [syn: subjective]

imminent /'ɪmɪnɛnt/
adj : close in time; about to occur; "retribution is at hand"; "some people believe the day of judgment is close at hand"; "in imminent danger"; "his impending retirement" [syn: at hand, close at hand, impending]

ends, ens /ɛndz/
ends
n : (plu of end) 1: extremities of things that have length; "the ends of the pole"; "she knotted the ends of the thread" 2: the states of affairs that plans are intended to achieve and that (when achieved) terminates behaviors intended to achieve them; "the ends justify the means" [syn: goals] 3: the surfaces at either extremity of a three-dimensional object; "the ends of the box are marked `This side up'" 4: (football) the persons who play at both ends of the line of scrimmage 5: two places from which people are communicating to each other; "both ends wrote at the same time"
v : (3ʳᵈ pers sing of end) 1: have an end, in a temporal, spatial, or quantitative sense; either spatial or metaphorical; "the bronchiole ends in a capillary bed"; "Your rights stop where you infringe upon the rights of other"; "My property ends by the bushes"; "The symphony ends in a pianissimo" [syn: stops, finishes, terminates, ceases] [ant: begins] 2: brings to an end or halt; "She ends their friendship when she finds out that he had once been convicted of a crime"; "The attack on Poland terminates the relatively peaceful period after WWI" [syn: terminates] [ant: begins, gets down] 3: put an end to; "The terrible news ends our hopes that he had

survived"

ens
n : (plu of en): half the width of an em; "place ens in the text where necessary"

enrapt, enwrapped /ɛn'ɹæpt/

enrapt
adj : wholly absorbed with rapture

enwrapped
adj 1: wrapped up or enclosed within a covering; "the little packet enwrapped in a faded yellow envelope" 2: enclosed or enveloped in something immaterial; "she sat enwrapped in sullen defiance"; "a sleeping town enwrapped in silence" 3: wholly absorbed as in thought; "deep in thought"; "that engrossed look or rapt delight"; "the book had her totally engrossed"; "enwrapped in dreams"; "rapt with wonder"; "wrapped in thought" [syn: absorbed, engrossed, intent, rapt, wrapped]

ensure, insure

ensure /ɛn'ʃuɹ/
v 1: make certain of; "This nest egg will ensure a nice retirement for us"; "Preparation will guarantee success!" [syn: guarantee, insure, assure, secure] 2: be careful or certain to do something; make certain of something; "He verified that the valves were closed"; "See that the curtains are closed"; "control the quality of the product" [syn: see, check, insure, see to it, control, ascertain, assure]

insure /ɪn'ʃuɹ/
v 1: protect by insurance; "The insurance won't cover this" [syn: cover, underwrite] 2: take out insurance for

entrance, entrants /'ɛntɹənts/

entrance
n 1: something that provides access (entry or exit); "they waited at the entrance to the garden"; "beggars waited just outside the entryway to the cathedral" [syn: entranceway, entryway, entry, entree] 2: a movement into or inward [syn: incoming] 3: the act of entering; "she made a grand entrance" [syn: entering, entry, ingress, incoming]

entrants
n 1: commodities that enter competition with established merchandise; " well publicized entrants are digital cameras" 2: any new participants in some activity [syn: newcomers, fledglings, starters, neophytes, freshmen, newbies] 3: people who enter; "new entrants to the country must go though immigration procedures" 4: people who enter a competition

epic, epoch /'ɛpɪk/

epic
adj 1: surpassing the ordinary especially in size or scale; "an epic voyage"; "of heroic proportions"; "heroic sculpture" [syn: heroic, larger-than-life] 2: constituting

or having to do with or suggestive of a literary epic; "epic tradition" [syn: epical]
n : a long narrative poem telling of a hero's deeds [syn: epic poem, epos]

epoch
n 1: a period marked by distinctive character or reckoned from a fixed point or event [syn: era] 2: (astronomy) the precise date that is the point of reference for which information (as coordinates of a celestial body) is referred [syn: date of reference] 3: a unit of geological time

equivalence, equivalents
/i'kwɪvɪlɛnts/

equivalence
n 1: a state of being essentially equal or equivalent: "on a par with the best" [syn: equality, par] 2: essential equality and interchangeability [ant: nonequivalence] 3: qualities that are comparable; "no comparison between the two books"; "beyond compare" [syn: comparison, compare, comparability]

equivalents
n : (plu of equivalent) 1: persons or things equal to another in value or measure or force or effect or significance etc: "send two dollars or equivalents in stamps

e're (see air)

ere (see air)

err (see air)

errant (see arrant)

erupt, irrupt

erupt /i'ɹʌpt/
v 1: start abruptly; "After 1989, peace broke out in the former East Bloc" [syn: break out] 2: erupt or intensify suddenly; "Unrest erupted in the country"; "Tempers flared at the meeting" [syn: flare up, flare, break open, burst out] 3: start to burn; "Marsh gases ignited suddenly." [syn: ignite, catch fire, take fire] 4: as of teeth, for example; "The tooth erupted and had to be extracted" [syn: come out, break through, push through] 5: become active and spew forth lava and rocks; of volcanoes; "Vesuvius erupts once in a while" [syn: belch] 6: become suddenly excited or angry; "She flares up easily" [syn: flare, flare up] 7: force out or release suddenly and often violently something pent up; "break into tears"; "erupt in anger" [syn: break, burst] 8: become raw or open; as of skin eruptions; "He broke out in hives"; "My skin breaks out when I eat strawberries"; "Such boils tend to recrudesce" [syn: recrudesce, break out]

irrupt /ɪ'ɹʌpt/
v 1: enter uninvited; "They intruded on our dinner party" [syn: intrude] 2: intrude on uninvited: "The nosy couple broke in on our conversation"; "She irrupted into our sitting room" [syn: break in]

HOMOPHONES

eruption, irruption

eruption /ɪˈrʌpʃɪn/

n 1: the sudden occurrence of a violent discharge of steam and volcanic material [syn: volcanic eruption] 2: symptom consisting of a breaking out and becoming visible 3: (of volcanoes) pouring out fumes or lava [syn: eructation] 4: a sudden very loud noise [syn: bang, blowup, clap, blast, loud noise] 5: the emergence of a tooth as it breaks through the gum

irruption /ɪˈrʌpʃɪn/

n : a sudden violent entrance; a bursting in; "the recent irruption of bad manners"

evaporate, evaporite

evaporate /ɪˈvæpəɹeɪt/

v : lose or cause to lose liquid by vaporization leaving a more concentrated residue; "evaporate milk" [syn: vaporize]

evaporite /ɪˈvæpəɹaɪt/

n : the sediment that is left after the evaporation of seawater

ewe, hue, U, yew, you

ewe /ʊə/)

n : female sheep

hue /hʊə/

n: the quality of a color as determined by its dominant wavelength [syn: chromacity] v 1: take on color or become colored; "In highlights it hued to a dull silver-grey" 2: suffuse with color [syn: imbue]

U /ʊə/

n 1: the 21st letter of the Roman alphabet [syn: letter u] 2: a base containing nitrogen that is found in RNA (but not in DNA) and derived from pyrimidine; pairs with adenine [syn: uracil] 3: a heavy toxic silvery-white radioactive metallic element; occurs in many isotopes; used for nuclear fuels and nuclear weapons [uranium, atomic number 92]

yew /ʊə/

n 1: wood of a yew; especially the durable fine-grained light brown or red wood of the English yew valued for cabinetwork and archery bows 2: any of numerous evergreen trees or shrubs having red cup-shaped berries and flattened needlelike leaves

you /ʊə/

pronoun : (2nd pers) "You are very beautiful"

ewer, you're /ʊəɹ/

ewer

n : an open vessel with a handle and a spout for pouring [syn: pitcher]

you're

contr : you are (also /jɔɹ/)

ewes, hues, U's, use, yews

ewes /ʊəz/

n : (plu of ewe) : "Ewes use yews for shade."

hues /hʊəz/

n : (plu of hue) : "Rainbows have many hues."

U's /ʊəz/

n : more than one letter U

use /ʊəz/

v 1: put into service; make work or employ (something) for a particular purpose or for its inherent or natural purpose: "use your head!"; "we only use Spanish at home"; "I can't make use of this tool"; "Apply a magnetic field here"; "This thinking was applied to many projects"; "How do you utilize this tool?"; "I apply this rule to get good results"; "use the plastic bags to store the food"; "He doesn't know how to use a computer" [syn: utilize, apply, employ] 2: take or consume (regularly); "She uses drugs rarely" 3: seek or achieve an end by using to one's advantage; "She uses her influential friends to get jobs"; "The president's wife used her good connections" 4: use up, consume fully; " The legislature expended its time on school questions." [syn: expend] 5: avail oneself to; "apply a principle"; "practice a religion"; "use care when going down the stairs"; "use your common sense"; "practice non-violent resistance" [syn: practice, apply] 6: habitually do something (use only in the past tense); "She used to call her mother every week but now she calls only occasionally"; "I used to get sick when I ate in that dining hall"; "They used to vacation in the Bahamas"

yews /ʊəz/

n : (plu of yew) : "The ewes use yews for shade."

exceed (see accede)

except (see accept)

exercise, exorcise /ˈɛksˀɹsaɪz/

exercise

n 1: the activity of exerting your muscles in various ways to keep fit; "the doctor recommended regular exercise"; "he did some exercising"; "the physical exertion required by his work kept him fit" [syn: exercising, physical exercise, physical exertion, workout] 2: the act of using; "the steps were worn from years of use" [syn: use, usage, utilization, employment] 3: systematic training by multiple repetitions; "practice makes perfect" [syn: practice, drill, practice session] 4: a task performed or problem solved in order to develop skill or understanding; "you must work the examples at the end of each chapter in the textbook" [syn: example] 5: (usually plural) a ceremony that involves processions and speeches; "academic exercises"

v 1: put to use; "exert one's power or influence" [syn: exert] 2: carry out or

HOMOPHONES

practice; as of jobs and professions: "practice law" [syn: practice, do] 3: give a work-out to: "Some parents exercise their infants"; "My personal trainer works me hard"; "work one's muscles" [syn: work, work out] 4: do physical exercise; "She works out in the gym every day" [syn: work out] 5: learn by repetition [syn: drill, practice]

exorcise

v : expel through adjuration or prayers; of evil spirits; in certain religions [syn: exorcize]

extant, extent

extant /'ɛkstɛənt/

adj : still in existence; not extinct or destroyed or lost; "extant manuscripts"; "specimens of graphic art found among extant barbaric folk" [ant: extinct]

extent /ɛk'stɛnt/

n 1: the point or degree to which something extends; "the extent of the damage"; "the full extent of the law"; "to a certain extent she was right" 2: the distance over which something extends

expansive, expensive

expansive /ɛk'spɛənsɪv/

adj 1: able or tending to expand or characterized by expansion; "Expansive materials"; "the expansive force of fire" 2: of behavior that is impressive and ambitious in scale or scope; "an expansive lifestyle"; "in the grand manner"; "collecting on a grand scale"; "heroic undertakings" [syn: grand, heroic] 3: marked by exaggerated feelings of euphoria and delusions of grandeur 4: expansive, friendly and open and willing to talk; "wine made the guest expansive" [syn: talkative]

expensive /ɛk'spɛnsɪv/

adj : high in price or charging high prices; "expensive clothes"; "an expensive shop"

expedience, expedients / ɛk'spidiɛnts/

expedience

n 1: the quality of being suited to the end in view [syn: expediency] [ant: inexpedience, inexpedience] 2: taking advantage of opportunities without regard for the consequences for others [syn: opportunism, self-interest, self-seeking]

expedients

n : means to an end; not necessarily principled or ethical ones

eye (see aye)

eyed, I'd /aɪd/

eyed

adj : having an eye or eyes or eyelike feature especially as specified; often used in combination; "an eyed hook"; "a peacock's eyed feathers"; "red-eyed" [ant: eyeless]

v : "He eyed him with suspicion." [syn: looked at]

I'd

contr : I would

eyed (see ayed)

eyelet, islet /'aɪlɛt/

eyelet

n 1: a small hole (usually round and finished around the edges) in cloth or leather for the passage of a cord 2: fastener consisting of a metal ring for lining a small hole to permit the attachment of cords or lines [syn: cringle, loop, grommet, grummet]

islet

n : a small island [syn: isle]

eyre (see air)

HOMOPHONES

-F-

facts, fax

facts /fækts/

n : (plu of fact) 1: pieces of information about circumstances that exist or events that have occurred; "first you must collect all the facts of the case" 2: statements or assertions of verified information about something that is the case or has happened; "he supported his argument with an impressive array of facts" 3: events known to have happened or some things known to have existed; "your fears have no basis in fact"; "how much of the story is fact and how much fiction is hard to tell" 4: concepts whose truth can be proved; "scientific hypotheses are not facts"

fax /fæks/

n : duplicator that transmits the copy by wire or radio [syn: facsimile, facsimile machine]

v : send something via a facsimile machine; "Can you fax me the report right away?"

faerie, fairy, ferry

faerie /ˈfɛəɹi/

n 1: small, human in form, playful, having magical powers [syn: fairy, faery, sprite] 2: the enchanted realm of fairies [syn: fairyland, faery]

fairy /ˈfɛəɹi/

adj : or pertaining to or resembling (especially in delicacy) a fairy or fairies [syn: faery, faerie]

n 1: small, human in form, playful, having magical powers [syn: faery, faerie, sprite] 2: offensive terms for an openly homosexual man [syn: fagot, faggot, fag, nancy, pansy, queen, queer, poof, pouf]

ferry /ˈfɛɹi/

n 1: a boat that transports people or vehicles across a body of water and operates on a regular schedule [syn: ferryboat] 2: transport by boat or aircraft [syn: ferrying]

v 1: transport from one place to another 2: transport by ferry 3: travel by ferry

faille, file, phial, phyle /faɪl/

faille

n : a ribbed woven fabric of silk or rayon or cotton

file

n 1: a set of related records (either written or electronic) kept together [syn: data file] 2: a line of persons or things ranged one behind the other [syn: single file, Indian file] 3: office furniture consisting of a container for keeping papers in order [syn: file cabinet, filing cabinet] 4: a steel hand tool with small sharp teeth on some or all of its surfaces; used for smoothing wood or metal

v 1: register in a public office or in a court of law; "file for divorce"; "file a complaint" [syn: register] 2: smooth with a file; "file one's fingernails" 3: proceed in file 4: file a formal charge against; "The suspect was charged with murdering his wife" [syn: charge, lodge] 5: place in a file [syn: file away]

phial

n : a small bottle that contains a drug (especially a sealed sterile container for injection by needle) [syn: vial, ampule]

phyle

n : a tribe of ancient Athenians

fain, fane, feign /feɪn/

fain

adj : having made preparations; "prepared to take risks" [syn: disposed, inclined, prepared]

adv : in a willing manner; "this was gladly agreed to"; "I would fain do it" [syn: gladly]

fane

n : temple, church

feign

v 1: make believe; "He feigned that he was ill"; "He shammed a headache" [syn: sham, pretend, affect, dissemble] 2: make a pretence of; "She assumed indifference, even though she was seething with anger"; "he feigned sleep" [syn: simulate, assume, sham]

faint, feint /feɪnt/

faint

adj 1: barely perceptible; lacking clarity or brightness or loudness etc; "a faint outline"; "the wan sun cast faint shadows"; "the faint light of a distant candle"; "faint colors"; "a faint hissing sound"; "a faint aroma" 2: lacking clarity or distinctness; "a dim figure in the distance"; "only a faint recollection"; "shadowy figures in the gloom"; "saw a vague outline of a building through the fog"; "a few wispy memories of childhood" [syn: dim, shadowy, vague, wispy] 3: lacking strength or vigor; "damning with faint praise"; "faint resistance"; "feeble efforts"; "a feeble voice" [syn: feeble] 4: weak and likely to lose consciousness; "suddenly felt faint from the pain"; "was sick and faint from hunger"; "felt light in the head"; "a swooning fit"; "light-headed with wine"; "light-headed from lack of sleep" [syn: light, swooning, light-headed, lightheaded] 5: indistinctly understood or felt or perceived; "a faint clue to the origin of the mystery"; "haven't the faintest idea" 6: lacking conviction or boldness or courage; "faint heart ne'er won fair lady" [syn: fainthearted, timid]

n : a spontaneous loss of consciousness caused by insufficient blood to the brain

HOMOPHONES

"She felt a faint coming on upon hearing the bad news."[syn: swoon, syncope]

v : pass out from weakness, physical or emotional distress due to a loss of blood supply to the brain [syn: conk, swoon, pass out]

feint

n : any distracting maneuver (as a mock attack)

v : deceive with a feint

fair, fare /ˈfɛəɹ/

fair

adj 1: free from favoritism or self-interest or bias or deception; or conforming with established standards or rules; "a fair referee"; "fair deal"; "on a fair footing"; "a fair fight"; "by fair means or foul" [syn: just] [ant: unfair] 2: showing lack of favoritism; "the cold neutrality of an impartial judge" [syn: impartial] [ant: partial] 3: more than adequate in quality; "fair work" 4: not excessive or extreme; "a fairish income"; "reasonable prices" [syn: fairish, reasonable] 5: visually appealing; "our fair city" [syn: sightly] 6: very pleasing to the eye; "my bonny lass"; "there's a bonny bay beyond"; "a comely face"; "young fair maidens" [syn: bonny, bonnie, comely] 7: (of a baseball) hit between the foul lines; "he hit a fair ball over the third base bag" [ant: foul] 8: of no exceptional quality or ability; "a novel of average merit"; "only a fair performance of the sonata"; "in fair health"; "the caliber of the students has gone from mediocre to above average"; "the performance was middling at best" [syn: average, mediocre, middling] 9: attractively feminine (especially in the phrase "the fair sex") [syn: fair] 10: (of a manuscript) having few alterations or corrections; "fair copy"; "a clean manuscript" [syn: clean] 11: free of clouds or rain; "today will be fair and warm" 12: (used of hair or skin) pale or light-colored; "a fair complexion"; [syn: fairish]

n 1: a traveling show; having sideshows and rides and games of skill etc. [syn: carnival, funfair] 2: gathering of producers to promote business: "world fair"; "trade fair"; "book fair" 3: a competitive exhibition of farm products; "she won a blue ribbon for her baking at the county fair" 4: a sale of miscellany; often for charity; "the church bazaar" [syn: bazaar]

v : join so that the external surfaces blend smoothly

fare

n 1: an agenda of things to do; "they worked rapidly down the menu of reports" [syn: menu] 2: the sum charged for riding in a public conveyance 3: a paying (taxi) passenger 4: the food and drink that are regularly consumed

v 1: proceed or get along; "You will fare well in your new job." "How is she doing in her new job?" "How are you making out in graduate school?" "He's come a long way" [syn: do, make out, come, get along] 2: eat well

faker, fakir /ˈfeɪkəɹ/

faker

n : a person who makes deceitful pretenses [syn: imposter, imposter, pretender, fake, fraud, sham, shammer, pseudo, role player]

fakir

n : a Muslim or Hindu mendicant monk who is regarded as a holy man

farci, farcy /ˈfɑɹsi/

farci

adj : stuffed with forcemeat "oysters farci" [syn: farcie]

farcy

n : a chronic and fatal disease of cattle and horses [syn: glanders]

faro, farrow, pharaoh /ˈfɛəɹoʊ/

faro

n : a card game in which players bet against the dealer on the cards he will draw from a dealing box

farrow

n : the production of a litter of pigs [syn: farrowing]

v : give birth; "sows farrow" [syn: pig]

pharaoh

n : the title of the ancient Egyptian kings

fate, fete /feɪt/

fate

n 1: an event (or course of events) that will inevitably happen in the future [syn: destiny] 2: the ultimate agency that predetermines the course of events (often personified as a woman); "we are helpless in the face of Destiny" [syn: Destiny, Fate] 3: your overall circumstances or condition in life (including everything that happens to you): "whatever my fortune may be"; "deserved a better fate"; "has a happy lot"; "the luck of the Irish"; "a victim of circumstances"; "success that was her portion" [syn: fortune, destiny, luck, lot, circumstances, portion]

v : decree or designate beforehand; "She was destined to become a great pianist" [syn: destine, doom, designate]

fete

n 1: an elaborate party (often outdoors) [syn: feast, fiesta] 2: an organized series of acts and performances (usually in one place); "a drama festival" [syn: festival]

v : have a celebration; "They were feting the patriarch of the family"; "After the exam, the students were celebrating" [syn: celebrate]

HOMOPHONES

faun, fawn /fɔn/
faun
n : ancient Italian deity in human shape, with horns, pointed ears and a goat's tail; equivalent to Greek satyr

fawn
n 1: a color varying around light grayish brown; "she wore a dun raincoat" [syn: dun, grayish brown, grayish brown] 2: young deer
v 1: show submission or fear [syn: crawl, creep, cringe, cower, grovel] 2: try to gain favor by cringing or flattering; "He is always kowtowing to his boss" [syn: toady, truckle, bootlick, kowtow, suck up] 3: have fawns, of deer

faux, foe /foʊ/
faux
adj : not genuine or real; being an imitation of the genuine article; "it isn't fake anything; it's real synthetic fur"; "faux pearls"; "false teeth"; "decorated with imitation palm leaves"; "a purse of simulated alligator hide" [syn: fake, false, imitation, simulated]

foe
n 1: an armed adversary (especially a member of an opposing military force); "a soldier must be prepared to kill his enemies" [syn: enemy, foeman, opposition, opponent] 2: a personal enemy; "they had been political foes for years" [syn: enemy] [ant: ally]

fay, fey /feɪ/
fay
v : to fit or join closely or tightly
n : fairy, elf
adj : resembling an elf

fey
adj 1: slightly insane [syn: touched] 2: suggestive of an elf in strangeness and otherworldliness; "thunderbolts quivered with elfin flares of heat lightning"; "the fey quality was there, the ability to see the moon at midday"- John Mason Brown [syn: elfin]

fays, faze, phase /feɪz/
fays
n : (plu of fay) [syn: fairies, elves]

faze
v : disturb the composure of [syn: unnerve, enervate, unsettle]phase
n 1: (physical chemistry) a distinct state of matter in a system; matter that is identical in chemical composition and physical state and separated from other material by the phase boundary: "the reaction occurs in the liquid phase of the system" [syn: form] 2: any distinct time period in a sequence of events; "we are in a transitional stage in which many former ideas must be revised or rejected" [syn: stage] 3: a particular point in the time of a cycle; measured from some arbitrary zero and expressed as an angle [syn: phase angle] 4: (astronomy) the particular appearance of a body's state of illumination (especially one of the recurring shapes of the part of Earth's moon that is illuminated by the sun); "the full phase of the moon"
v 1: arrange in phases or stages: "phase a withdrawal" 2: adjust so as to be in a synchronized condition; "he phased the intake with the output of the machine"

fear, fere /fiɹ/
fear
n 1: an emotion experienced in anticipation of some specific pain or danger (usually accompanied by a desire to flee or fight) [syn: fearfulness, fright] [ant: fearlessness] 2: an anxious feeling; "care had aged him"; "they hushed it up out of fear of public reaction" [syn: concern, care]
v 1: be afraid or feel anxious or apprehensive about a possible or probable situation or event; "I fear she might get aggressive" 2: be afraid or scared of; be frightened of; "I fear the winters in Moscow"; "We should not fear the Communists!" [syn: dread] 3: be sorry; used to introduce an unpleasant statement: "I fear I won't make it to your wedding party" 4: be uneasy or apprehensive about; "I fear the results of the final exams" 5: be in awe of; "Fear God as your father" [syn: reverence, revere, venerate]

fere
n : (archaic) : friend, companion, spouse

feat, feet /fit/
feat
n : a notable achievement: "climbing Mt. Everest was a great feat" "he performed a great deed"; "the book was her finest effort" [syn: deed, effort, exploit]

feet
n : (plu of foot) 1: a linear unit of length equal to 12 inches or a third of a yard; "he is six feet tall" [syn: ft] 2: the feet of a human being; "his bare feet projected from his trousers"; "armored from head to foot" [syn: human feet,] 3: the feet of a vertebrate other than a human being [syn: animal feet] 4: a support resembling a pedal extremity; "two feet of the chair were on the carpet" 5: any of various organs of locomotion or attachment in invertebrates [syn: invertebrate feet]

feeder, fetor /'fidɚ/
feeder
n 1: an animal being fattened or suitable for fattening 2: someone who consumes food for nourishment [syn: eater] 3: a branch that flows into the main stream [syn: tributary, affluent] [ant: distributary] 4: a machine that automatically provides a supply of some material; "the feeder

HOMOPHONES

discharged feed into a trough for the livestock" [syn: self-feeder]

fetor
n : a distinctive odor that is offensively unpleasant [syn: malodor, stench, stink, reek, mephitis]

felloe, fellow /ˈfɛloʊ/
felloe
n : rim (or part of the rim) into which spokes are inserted [syn: felly]

fellow
adj : being associated as a companion or associate; "fellow traveler"; "brother workers"; "sister ship" [syn: brother, sister]
n 1: a boy or man; "that chap is your host"; "there's a fellow at the door"; "he's a likable cuss" [syn: chap, feller, lad, gent, fella, blighter, cuss] 2: a person who is frequently in the company of another; "drinking companions"; "comrades in arms" [syn: companion, comrade, familiar, associate] 3: a person who is member of your class or profession; "the surgeon consulted his colleagues"; "he sent e-mail to his fellow hackers" [syn: colleague, confrere] 4: an informal form of address for a man; "Say, fellow, what are you doing?"; "Hey buster, what's up?" [syn: buster] 5: a man who is the lover of a girl or young woman; "if I'd known he was her boyfriend I wouldn't have asked" [syn: boyfriend, beau, swain, young man]

feral, ferule, ferrule /ˈfɛɹɪl/
feral
adj : wild and menacing; "a feral cat" [syn: ferine, savage]

ferule
n : a switch (a stick or cane or flat paddle) used to punish children

ferrule
n : a metal cap or band placed on a wooden pole to prevent splitting [syn: collet]

fern, firn /ˈfəɹn/
fern
n : any of numerous flowerless and seedless vascular plants having true roots from a rhizome and fronds that uncurl upward; reproduce by spores

firn
n : partially compacted snow that forms the surface part of the upper part of a glacier [syn: névé]

feted, fetid /ˈfɛtɪd/
feted
v : (past of fete) (var fêted) 1: celebrated or honored with a festival, a feast, or an elaborate entertainment 2: paid honor to

fetid
adj : offensively malodorous; "a putrid smell" [syn: foul, foul-smelling, funky, noisome, smelly, putrid, stinking]

feudal, futile
feudal /ˈfuədᵊl/
adj : of or relating to or characteristic of feudalism [syn: feudalistic]

futile /ˈfuətɪl/
adj 1: producing no result or effect; "a futile effort"; "the therapy was ineffectual"; "an otiose undertaking"; "an unavailing attempt" [syn: ineffectual, otiose, unavailing] 2: unproductive of success; "a fruitless search"; "futile years after her artistic peak"; "a sleeveless errand"; "a vain attempt" [syn: bootless, fruitless, sleeveless, vain]

few, phew /fʊə/
few
adj : (quantifier used with count nouns, often preceded by `a') a small number; "a few weeks ago"; "a few more wagons than usual"; "an invalid's pleasures are few and far between"; "few roses were still blooming"; "few women have led troops in battle" [ant: many]
n 1: an indefinite but relatively small number; "they bought a case of beer and drank a few" 2: a small elite group; "it was designed for the discriminating few"

phew
interj : used to express relief, fatigue, surprise, or disgust

fiancé, fiancée /fiˈɑnsɛɪ/
fiancé
n : a man who is engaged to be married [syn: groom-to-be]

fiancee
n : a woman who is engaged to be married [syn: bride-to-be]

fiche, fish /fɪʃ/
fiche
n : small sheet of microfilm on which many pages of material have been photographed; a magnification system is used to read the material [syn: microfiche]

fish
n 1: any of various mostly cold-blooded aquatic vertebrates usually having scales and breathing through gills 2: the flesh of fish used as food
v 1: seek indirectly; "fish for compliments" [syn: angle] 2: catch or try to catch fish or shellfish; "I like to go fishing on weekends"

filar, filer /ˈfaɪlᵊɹ/
filar
adj : related to or having filaments especially across a field of view; "a filar eyepiece"

filer
n 1: a party who files a notice with a law court 2: a clerk who is employed to maintain the files of an organization [syn: file clerk, filing clerk]

HOMOPHONES

file (see faille)

filter, philter /ˈfɪltᵊɹ/

filter

n 1: device that removes something from whatever passes through it 2: n electrical device that alters the frequency spectrum of signals passing through it

v 1: remove by passing through a filter; "filter out the impurities" [syn: filtrate, strain, separate out, filter out] 2: pass through; "Water permeates sand easily" [syn: percolate, sink in, permeate] 3: run or flow slowly, or in an unsteady stream: "reports began to dribble in." [syn: trickle, dribble]

philter

n : a drink credited with magical power; can make the one who takes it love the one who gave it [syn: philtre, love-potion, love-philter, love-philtre]

finally, finely

finally /ˈfaɪnəli/

adv 1: after a long period of time or an especially long delay; "at length they arrived" [syn: eventually, at length] 2: the item at the end; "last, I'll discuss family values" [syn: last, lastly, in conclusion] 3: as the end result of a succession or process; "ultimately he had to give in"; "at long last the winter was over" [syn: ultimately, in the end, at last, at long last]

finely /ˈfaɪnli/

adv 1: in tiny pieces; "the surfaces were finely granular" [ant: coarsely] 2: in an elegant manner; "finely costumed actors" 3: in a superior and skilled manner; "the soldiers were fighting finely" [syn: fine] 4: in a delicate manner; "finely shaped features"; "her fine drawn body" [syn: fine, delicately, exquisitely]

find, fined /faɪnd/

find

n 1: a productive insight [syn: discovery, breakthrough] 2: the act of discovering something [syn: discovery, uncovering]

v 1: come upon, as if by accident; meet with; "We find this idea in Plato"; "I happened upon the most wonderful bakery not very far from here"; "She chanced upon an interesting book in the bookstore the other day" [syn: happen, chance, bump, encounter] 2: discover or determine the existence, presence, or fact of; "She detected high levels of lead in her drinking water"; "We found traces of lead in the paint" [syn: detect, observe, discover, notice] 3: come upon after searching; find the location of something that was missed or lost; "Did you find your glasses?" "I cannot find my gloves!" [syn: regain] [ant: lose] 4: after a calculation, investigation, experiment, survey, or study; "find the product of two numbers"; "The physicist

who found the elusive particle won the Nobel Prize" [syn: determine, find out, ascertain] 5: come to believe on the basis of emotion, intuitions, or indefinite grounds: "I feel that he doesn't like me"; "I find him to be obnoxious"; "I found the movie rather entertaining" [syn: feel] 6: perceive with any or all of one's senses; "We found Republicans winning the offices"; "You'll see a lot of cheating in this school"; give rise to or be characterized by; "The 1960 saw the rebellion of the younger generation against established traditions"; "I want to see results" [syn: witness, see] 7: get something or somebody for a specific purpose; "I found this gadget that will serve as a bottle opener"; "I got hold of these tools to fix our plumbing"; "The chairman got hold of a secretary on Friday night to type the urgent letter" [syn: line up, get hold, come up] 8: make a discovery, make a new finding; "Roentgen discovered X-rays"; "Physicists believe they found a new elementary particle" [syn: discover] 9: make a discovery; "She found that he had lied to her"; "The story is false, so far as I can discover" [syn: discover] 10: obtain through effort or management; "She found the time and energy to take care of her aging parents"; "We found the money to send our sons to college" 11: decide on and make a declaration about; "find someone guilty" [syn: rule] 12: receive a specified treatment (abstract); "These aspects of civilization do not find expression or receive an interpretation"; "His movie received a good review"; "I got nothing but trouble for my good intentions" [syn: receive, get, obtain, incur] 13: perceive oneself to be in a certain condition or place; "I found myself in a difficult situation"; "When he woke up, he found himself in a hospital room" 14: get or find back; recover the use of; "She regained control of herself"; "She found her voice and replied quickly" [syn: recover, retrieve, regain] 15: succeed in reaching; arrive at; "The arrow found its mark" 16: accept and make use of one's personality, abilities, and situation; "My son went to Berkeley to find himself" [syn: find oneself]

fined

adj : punished by the imposition of a penalty [syn: penalized]

v : (past of fine) "He was fined $200 for speeding."

fir, fur /fʌ/

fir

n 1: nonresinous wood of a fir tree 2: any of various evergreen trees of the genus Abies; chiefly of upland areas [syn: fir tree, true fir]

HOMOPHONES

fur
n 1: the dressed hairy coat of a mammal [syn: pelt] 2: dense coat of fine silky hairs on an mammals e.g. cat or seal or weasel 3: a garment made of fur

firs, furs, furze /fʌɹz/

firs
n : (plu of fir)

furs
n : (plu of furs)

furze
n : very spiny and dense evergreen shrub with fragrant golden-yellow flowers; common throughout western Europe [syn: gorse, whin, Irish gorse, Ulex europaeus]

fisher, fissure /ˈfɪʃəɹ/

fisher
n 1: someone whose occupation is catching fish [syn: fisherman] 2: large dark brown North American arboreal carnivorous mammal [syn: pekan, fisher cat, black cat, Martes pennanti]

fissure
n 1: a long narrow depression in a surface [syn: crevice, cranny, crack, chap] 2: a long narrow opening [syn: crack, cleft, crevice] 3: (anatomy) a long narrow slit or groove that divides an organ into lobes
v : break into fissures or fine cracks

fizz, phiz /fɪz/

fizz
n : an effervescent beverage (usually alcoholic)
v : of liquids; "The ice cream soda was fizzing" [syn: foam, froth, effervesce, sparkle]

phiz
n: the human face (`kisser' and `smiler' and `mug' are informal terms for `face'; `phiz' is British) [syn: countenance, physiognomy, visage, kisser, smiler, mug]

flacks, flax /flæks/

flacks
n : (plu of flack) slick spokespersons who can turn any criticism to the advantage of their employer [syn: flak catchers, flaks, flack catchers]

flax
n 1: fiber of the flax plant that is made into thread and woven into linen fabric 2: plant of the genus Linum that is cultivated for its seeds and for the fibers of its stem

flair, flare /flɛəɹ/

flair
n 1: a natural talent; "he has a flair for mathematics"; "he has a genius for interior decorating" [syn: genius] 2: distinctive and stylish elegance; "he wooed her with the confident dash of a cavalry officer" [syn: dash, elan, panache, style]

flare
n 1: a shape that spreads outward; "the skirt had a wide flare" 2: a sudden burst of flame 3: a burst of light used to communicate or illuminate [syn: flash] 4: reddening of the skin spreading outward from a focus of infection or irritation 5: a sudden eruption of intense high-energy radiation from the sun's surface; associated with sunspots and radio interference [syn: solar flare]
v 1: burn brightly; "Every star seemed to flare with new intensity." [syn: flame up, blaze up, burn up] 2: become suddenly excited or angry; "She flares up easily" [syn: flare up, erupt] 3: become flared and widen, usually at one end; "The bellbottom pants flare out" [syn: flare out] 4: shine with a sudden light; "The night sky flared with the massive bombardment." [syn: flame] 5: erupt or intensify suddenly; "Unrest erupted in the country"; "Tempers flared at the meeting" [syn: erupt, flare up, break open, burst out]

flea, flee /fli/

flea
n : any wingless blood-sucking parasitic insect noted for ability to leap

flee
v : to run away: "He threw down his gun and fled." [syn: fly, take flight]

flèche, flesh /flɛʃ/

flèche
n : a slender spire above the intersection of the nave and transepts of a church [syn: spire]

flesh
n 1: the soft tissue of the body of a vertebrate: mainly muscle tissue and fat 2: alternative names for the body of a human being; "Leonardo studied the human body"; "he has a strong physique"; "the spirit is willing but the flesh is weak" [syn: human body, physical body, material body, soma, build, figure, physique, anatomy, shape, bod, chassis, frame, form] 3: a soft moist part of a fruit [syn: pulp]

flecks, flex /flɛks/

flecks
n : (plu of fleck) 1: small fragments of something broken off from the whole; " bits of rock caught him in the eye" [syn: bits, chips, flakes, scraps] 2: small contrasting parts of something; "bald spots"; "a leopard's spots"; "patches of thin ice": "flecks of red" [syn: spots, speckles, dapples, patches]
v : (3rd pers sing of fleck): makes a spot or mark onto; "The wine spots the tablecloth" [syn: spots, blobs, blots]

flew, flu, flue /flu/

flew
v : (past of fly) : "Birds flew south for the winter."

flu
n : an acute febrile highly contagious viral disease [syn: influenza, grippe]

HOMOPHONES

flue

n 1: flat blade-like projection on the arm of an anchor [syn: fluke] 2: organ pipe whose tone is produced by air passing across the sharp edge of a fissure or lip [syn: flue pipe, labial pipe] 3: a conduit to carry off smoke

flocks, phlox /flɑks/
flocks

n : (plu of flock) 1: church congregations guided by pastors 2: a groups of birds 3: (often followed by `of') a large number or amount or extent: "a batches of letters"; "deals of trouble"; " lots of money"; "he made a mint on the stock market"; "it must have cost plenty" [syn: batches, deals, good deals, great deals, hatfuls, heaps, lots, masses, messes, mints, piles, plenty, pots, quite a little, rafts, sights, slews, spates, stacks, tidy sums, wads, whole lots, whole slews] 4: an orderly crowd; "a troop of children" [syn: troops] 5: groups of sheep or goats

v : (3rd pers sing of flock) 1: move as a crowd or in a group; "The tourist group flocks to the shrine where the statue was said to have shed tears" 2: come together as in a cluster or flock; "The poets constellate in this town every summer" [syn: clusters, constellates, clumps]

phlox

n : any polemoniaceous plant of the genus Phlox; chiefly North American; cultivated for their clusters of flowers

floe, flow /floʊ/
floe

n : a flat mass of ice (smaller than an ice field) floating at sea [syn: ice floe]

flow

n 1: the motion characteristic of fluids (liquids or gases) [syn: flowing] 2: the amount of fluid that flows in a given time [syn: flow rate, rate of flow] 3: the act of flowing or streaming; continuous progression [syn: stream] 4: any uninterrupted stream or discharge 5: something that resembles a flowing stream in moving continuously; "a stream of people emptied from the terminal"; "the museum had planned carefully for the flow of visitors" [syn: stream] 6: dominant course (suggestive of running water) of successive events or ideas: "two streams of development run through American history"; "stream of consciousness"; "the flow of thought"; "the current of history" [syn: stream, current] 7: the monthly discharge of blood from the uterus of nonpregnant women from puberty to menopause; "the women were sickly and subject to excessive menstruation" [syn: menstruation, menses, period]

v 1: move or progress freely as if in a stream; "The crowd flowed out of the stadium" [syn: flux] 2: move along, of liquids; "Water flowed into the cave" [syn: run, course] 3: cause to flow; "The artist flowed the washes on the paper" 4: be abundantly present; "The champagne flowed at the wedding" 5: fall or flow in a certain way; "This dress hangs well"; "Her long black hair flowed down her back" [syn: hang, fall] 6: cover or swamp with water 7: undergo menstruation; "She started menstruating at the age of 11" [syn: menstruate]

florescence, fluorescence /flɔˈɹɛsɛnts/
florescence

n : the time and process of budding and unfolding of blossoms [syn: blossoming, flowering, inflorescence, anthesis, efflorescence]

fluorescence

fluorescence

n : light emitted during absorption of radiation of some other (invisible) wavelength

flour, flower /ˈflaʊəɹ/
flour

n : fine powdery foodstuff obtained by grinding and sifting the meal of a cereal grain

v 1: cover with flour, as of fish or meat, in cooking 2: convert grain into flour

flower

n 1: a plant cultivated for its blooms or blossoms 2: reproductive organ of angiosperm plants especially one having showy or colorful parts [syn: bloom, blossom] 3: the period of greatest prosperity or productivity "She is enjoying the flower of her youth." [syn: prime, peak, heyday, bloom, blossom, efflorescence, flush]

v : produce or yield flowers; "The cherry tree bloomed" [syn: bloom, blossom]

foaled, fold /foʊld/
foaled

adj : (used of a horse or related animal) born

fold

adj : (used in combination) multiplied by a specified number; "'fold' is a combing form in expressions like 'a fifty-fold increase'"

n 1: an angular shape made by folding [syn: crease, flexure, crimp, bend] 2: a group of people who adhere to a common faith and habitually attend a given church [syn: congregation, faithful] 3: a folded part (as a fold of skin or muscle) 4: a pen for sheep [syn: sheepfold, sheep pen, sheepcote] 5: the act of folding; "he gave the napkins a double fold" [syn: folding]

v 1: bend or lay so that one part covers the

HOMOPHONES

other; "fold up the newspaper"; "turn up your collar" [syn: fold up, turn up] [ant: unfold] 2: intertwine; "fold one's hands, arms, or legs" 3: incorporate a food ingredient into a mixture by repeatedly turning it over without stirring or beating; "Fold the egg whites into the batter" 4: cease to operate or cause to cease operating; "The owners decided to move and to close the factory"; "My business closes every night at 8 P.M. [syn: close, shut down, close down] [ant: open] 5: confine in a fold, like sheep [syn: pen up] 6: become folded or folded up; "The bed folds in a jiffy" [syn: fold up]

for, fore, four /fɔɹ/
for

prep : 1: Used to indicate the object, aim, or purpose of an action or activity: "trained for the ministry"; "put the house up for sale"; "plans to run for senator" 2: Used to indicate the object of a desire, intention, or perception: "had a nose for news"; "eager for success" 3: Used to indicate the recipient or beneficiary of an action: "prepared lunch for us" 4: On behalf of: "spoke for all the members" 5: In favor of: "Were they for or against the proposal?" 6: In place of: "a substitute for eggs" 7: Used to indicate equivalence or equality: "paid ten dollars for a ticket"; "repeated the conversation word for word" 8 Used to indicate correlation or correspondence: "took two steps back for every step forward" 9 Used to indicate amount, extent, or duration: "a bill for five dollars"; "walked for miles"; "stood in line for an hour" 10 Used to indicate a specific time: "had an appointment for two o'clock" 11 Used to indicate a number of attempts: "shot three for four from the foul line" 12 As being: take for granted; "mistook me for the librarian" 13 Used to indicate an actual or implied listing or choosing: "For one thing, we can't afford it." 14 As a result of; because of: "jumped for joy" 15 Used to indicate appropriateness or suitability: "It will be for the judge to decide." 16 Notwithstanding; despite: "For all the problems, it was a valuable experience." 17 As regards; concerning: "a stickler for neatness" 18 Considering the nature or usual character of: "was spry for his advanced age" 19 In honor of: "named for her grandmother"
conj. : Because; since.

fore

adj 1: (nautical) situated at or toward the bow of a vessel [ant: aft] 2: located anteriorly [syn: front]

n : front part of a vessel or aircraft; "he pointed the bow of the boat toward the finish line" [syn: bow, prow, stem]

adv : near or toward the bow of a ship or cockpit of a plane; "the captain went fore (or forward) to check the instruments" [syn: forward] [ant: aft]

four

adj : being one more than three [syn: 4, iv]
n : the cardinal number that is the sum of three and one [syn: 4, IV, tetrad, quatern, quaternion, quaternary, quaternity, quartet, quadruplet, foursome, Little Joe]

forego, forgo /fɔɹ'gou/
forego

v : be earlier in time; go back further [syn: predate, precede, antecede, antedate] [ant: postdate]

forgo

v 1: do without; "We are dispensing with formalities" [syn: waive, relinquish, foreswear, dispense with] 2: lose or lose the right to by some error, offense, or crime [syn: forfeit, give up, throw overboard, waive] [ant: claim] 3: refrain from consuming; "You will have to forgo alcohol" [syn: give up]

formally, formerly
formally /'fɔɹməli/

adv 1: with official authorization; "the club will be formally recognized" [syn: officially] 2: in a formal manner; "he was dressed rather formally" [syn: with formality] [ant: informally]

formerly /'fɔɹmˠli/

adv : at a previous time; "he formally loved her"; "her erstwhile writing" [syn: once, at one time, erstwhile]

fort, forte /fɔɹt/
fort

n 1: a fortified military post where troops are stationed [syn: garrison] 2: a fortified defensive structure [syn: fortress]
v 1: gather in, or as if in, a fort, as for protection or defense [syn: fort up] 2: enclose by or as if by a fortification [syn: fortify] 3: station in a fort, as of troops

forte (alt fo:r 'tei)

adj : used chiefly as a direction or description in music; "the forte passages in the composition" [syn: loud] [ant: piano]
n 1: an asset of special worth or utility; "cooking is his forte" [syn: strong suit, long suit, metier, specialty, strong point, strength] [ant: weak point] 2: (music) with great loudness [syn: fortissimo] 3: the stronger part of a sword blade between the hilt and the foible
adv : used as a direction in music; to be played relatively loudly [syn: loudly] [ant: piano]

forth, fourth /fɔɹθ/
forth

adv 1: from a particular thing or place or position; "ran away from the lion"; " wanted to get away from there"; "sent the children away to boarding school"; "the teacher waved the children away from the dead animal"; "went off to school"; "they drove off"; ('forth' is obsolete as in "go forth and preach") [syn: away, off] 2: forward in time or order or degree; "from that time forth"; "from the sixth century onward" [syn: forward, onward] 3: out into view; "came forth from the crowd"; "put my ideas forth"

fourth

adj : coming next after the third and just before the fifth in position or time or degree or magnitude; "the fourth period of geologic time extends from the end of the third period to the present" [syn: 4th, quaternary]

n 1: following the third position; number four in a countable series 2: one of four equal parts; "a quarter of a pound" [syn: one-fourth, quarter, fourth part, twenty-five percent] 3: the musical interval between one note and another four notes away from it

adv : in the fourth place; "fourthly, you must pay the rent on the first of the month" [syn: fourthly]

forward, foreword /'brɛwɾd/

forward (also /'fɔɪɪd/ and /'fɔɹɪd/)

adj 1: at or near or directed toward the front; "the forward section of the aircraft"; "a forward plunge down the stairs"; "forward motion" [ant: backward] 2: situated at or toward the front; "the fore cabins"; "the forward part of the ship" 3: situated in the front; "the forward section of the aircraft" 4: moving toward a position ahead; "forward motion"; "the onward course of events" [syn: onward] 5: used of temperament or behavior; lacking restraint or modesty; "a forward child badly in need of discipline" [ant: backward] 6: of the transmission gear causing forward movement in a motor vehicle; "in a forward gear" [ant: reverse] 7: moving forward [syn: advancing, forward-moving]

n 1: the person who plays the position of forward on a basketball team 2: a position on a basketball team

adv 1: at or to or toward the front; "he faced forward"; "step forward"; "she practiced sewing backward as well as frontward on her new sewing machine"; [syn: forwards, frontward, frontward] [ant: back] 2: forward in time or order or degree; "from that time forth"; "from the sixth century onward" [syn: forth, onward] 3: toward the future; forward in time; "I like to look ahead in imagination to what the future may bring"; "I look forward to seeing you" [syn: ahead] [ant: back, back] 4: in a forward direction; "go ahead"; "the train

moved ahead slowly"; "the boat lurched ahead"; "moved onward into the forest"; "they went slowly forward in the mud" [syn: ahead, onward, onwards, forwards] 5: near or toward the bow of a ship or cockpit of a plane; "the captain went fore (or forward) to check the instruments" [syn: fore] [ant: aft]

v : send or ship onward from an intermediate post or station in transit; "forward my mail" [syn: send on]

foreword

n : a short introductory essay preceding the text of a book [syn: preface, prolusion]

foul, fowl /faʊl/

foul

adj 1: highly offensive; arousing aversion or disgust; "a disgusting smell"; "distasteful language"; "a loathsome disease"; "the idea of eating meat is repellent to me"; "revolting food"; "a wicked stench" [syn: disgusting, disgustful, distasteful, loathly, loathsome, repellent, repellant, repelling, revolting, wicked, yucky] 2: offensively malodorous; "a putrid smell" [syn: fetid, foul-smelling, funky, noisome, smelly, putrid, stinking] 3: violating accepted standards or rules; "a dirty fighter"; "used foul means to gain power"; "a nasty unsporting serve"; "fined for unsportsmanlike behavior" [syn: cheating, dirty, unsporting, unsportsmanlike] 4: (of a baseball) not hit between the foul lines [ant: fair] 5: (of a manuscript) defaced with changes; "foul (or dirty) copy" [syn: dirty, marked-up] 6: (informal) thoroughly unpleasant; "filthy (or foul or nasty or vile) weather we're having" [syn: filthy, nasty, vile] 7: characterized by obscenity; "had a filthy mouth"; "foul language"; "smutty jokes" [syn: filthy, nasty, smutty] 8: disgustingly dirty; filled or smeared with offensive matter; "as filthy as a pigsty"; "a foul pond"; "a nasty pigsty of a room" [syn: filthy, nasty] 9: especially of a ship's lines etc; "with its sails afoul"; "a foul anchor" [syn: afoul, fouled]

n : (sports) an act that violates of the rules of the sport

v 1: hit a foul ball, in baseball 2: make impure; "The industrial wastes polluted the lake" [syn: pollute, contaminate] 3: become or cause to become obstructed; "The leaves clog our drains in the Fall"; "The water pipe is backed up" [syn: clog, choke off, clog up, back up, congest, choke] [ant: unclog] 4: commit a foul; break the rules 5: spot, stain, or pollute; "The townspeople defiled the river by emptying raw sewage into it" [syn: befoul, defile, maculate] 6: make foul; "foul the water" 7: become foul or dirty

HOMOPHONES

fowl

n 1: a domesticated gallinaceous bird though to be descended from the red jungle fowl [syn: domestic fowl, poultry] 2: the flesh of a bird or fowl (wild or domestic) used as food [syn: bird]
v 1: hunt fowl 2: hunt fowl, as in the forest

franc, frank /fɹɛŋk/

franc

n : the basic monetary unit in many countries; equal to 100 centimes

frank

adj 1: characterized by disconcerting directness in manner or speech; without subtlety or evasion; "blunt talking and straight shooting"; "a blunt New England farmer"; "I gave them my candid opinion"; "forthright criticism"; "a forthright approach to the problem"; "tell me what you think--and you may just as well be frank"; "it is possible to be outspoken without being rude"; "plainspoken and to the point"; "a point-blank accusation" [syn: blunt, candid, forthright, free-spoken, outspoken, plainspoken, point-blank] 2: clearly manifest; evident; "frank enjoyment"
n 1: a member of the ancient Germanic peoples who spread from the Rhine into the Roman Empire in the 4th century [syn: Frank] 2: a smooth-textured sausage of minced beef or pork usually smoked; often served on a bread roll [syn: frankfurter, hotdog, hot dog, wiener, wienerwurst, weenie]
v 1: stamp with a postmark to indicate date and time of mailing [syn: postmark] 2: exempt by means of an official pass or letter, as from customs or other checks

frayed, 'fraid /fɹeɪd/

frayed

adj : worn away or tattered along the edges; "frayed cuffs"
v : (past of fray) :"He frayed the rope by rubbing it along the edge of the pier."

'fraid

adj : a dialectic form of afraid

fraise, frays, phrase /fɹeɪz/

fraise

n 1: a ruff for the neck worn in the 16th century 2: sloping or horizontal rampart of pointed stakes

frays

n : (plu of fray): noisy fights [syn: affrays, disturbances, ruffles]
v : (3rd pers sing of fray) 1: wears away by rubbing; "The friction frays the sleeve" [syn: frazzles] 2: causes friction; "my sweater scratches" [syn: rubs, frets, chafes, scratches]

phrase

n 1: an expression forming a grammatical constituent of a sentence but not containing a finite verb 2: a short musical passage two to four measures long [syn: musical phrase] 3: an expression whose meanings cannot be inferred from the meanings of the words that make it up [syn: idiom, idiomatic expression, phrasal idiom, set phrase]
v : put into words or an expression; "He formulated his concerns to the board of trustees" [syn: formulate, word, articulate]

frees, freeze, frieze /fɹiz/

frees

v : (3rd pers sing of free) 1: grants freedom to; frees from confinement [syn: liberates, releases, unloosens, loosens] [ant: confines] 2: relieves from; "Rids the house of pests" [syn: rids, disembarrasses] 3: removes or forcse out from a position; "The dentist dislodged the piece of food that had been stuck under my gums"; "He finally could free the legs of the earthquake victim who was buried in the rubble" [syn: dislodges] [ant: lodges] 4: grants relief or an exemption from a rule or requirement to; "She exempted me from the exam" [syn: exempts, relieves] [ant: enforces] 5: makes available or frees for sale or publication [syn: releases] 6: frees from obligations or duties [syn: discharges] 7: frees or removes obstruction from [syn: disengages] [ant: obstructs] 8: lets off the hook; "I absolve you from this responsibility" [syn: absolves, justifies] [ant: blames] 9: parts with [syn: releases, relinquishes, gives up] 10: makes available, as of assets; or frees for sale or publication [syn: unblocks, unfreezes, releases] [ant: freezes]

freeze

n 1: the withdrawal of heat to change something from a liquid to a solid [syn: freezing] 2: weather cold enough to cause freezing [syn: frost] 3: an interruption or temporary suspension of progress or movement: "a halt in the arms race"; "a nuclear freeze" [syn: halt] 4: fixing (of prices or wages etc) at a particular level: "a freeze on hiring"
v 1: change to ice; "The water in the bowl froze" [ant: boil] 2: stop moving or become immobilized; "When he saw the police car he froze" [syn: stop dead] 3: be cold; "I could freeze to death in this office when the air conditioning is turned on" 4: cause to freeze; "Freeze the leftover food" 5: stop a process or a habit by imposing a freeze on it; "Suspend the aid to the war-torn country" [syn: suspend] 6: be very cold, below the freezing point; "It is freezing in Kalamazoo." 7: change from a liquid to a solid when cold; "Water freezes at 32 degrees Fahrenheit" [syn: freeze out, freeze down] 8: prohibit the conversion or

HOMOPHONES

use of (assets); "Blocked funds"; "Freeze the assets of this hostile government" [syn: block, immobilize,] [ant: unblock, unblock] 9: anesthetize by cold, as for certain surgical procedures 10: suddenly behave coldly and formally; "She froze when she saw her ex-husband"

frieze
n 1: an architectural ornament consisting of a horizontal sculptured band between the architrave and the cornice 2: a heavy woolen fabric with a long nap

friar, fryer /fɹaɪjəɹ/

friar
n : a male religious of an order of mendicant preachers of the gospel [syn: mendicant]

fryer
n : 1: flesh of a medium-sized young chicken suitable for frying [syn: pullet, frier] 2: a deep utensil for frying foods [syn: frier]

fuehrer, furor /ˈfʊəɹəɹ/

fuehrer
n : person in authority, leader; [syn: tyrant]

furor
n 1: an interest followed with exaggerated zeal; "he always follows the latest fads"; "it was all the rage that season" [syn: fad, craze, cult, rage] 2: a sudden outburst (as of protest)

fungous, fungus /ˈfʌngɪs/

fungous
adj : of or relating to fungi [syn: fungal]

fungus
n : a parasitic plant lacking chlorophyll and leaves and true stems and roots and reproducing by spores

furs, furze /fʌɹz/

furs
n : (plu of fur) : "That coat is made of several furs."

furze
n : very spiny and dense evergreen shrub with fragrant golden-yellow flowers; common throughout western Europe [syn: gorse, whin, Irish gorse, Ulex europaeus]

-G-

g, gee /dʒi/

g
n 1: a metric unit of weight equal to one thousandth of a kilogram [syn: gram, gm] 3: a unit of force equal to the force exerted by gravity; used to indicate the force to which a body is subjected when it is accelerated [syn: gee] 3: a unit of information equal to one billion (1,000,000,000) bytes or one thousand megabytes [syn: gigabyte, Gigabyte, G, GB] 4: (physics) the universal constant relating force to mass and distance in Newton's law of gravitation [syn: gravitational constant, universal gravitational constant, constant of gravitation] 5: the 7th letter of the Roman alphabet [syn: G]

gee
n : a unit of force equal to the force exerted by gravity; used to indicate the force to which a body is subjected when it is accelerated [syn: g]
v 1: turn to the right side, as of horses or draft animals 2: as to a horse

gaff, gaffe /gɛəf/

gaff
n 1: a spar rising aft from a mast to support the head of a quadrilateral fore-and-aft sail 2: an iron hook with a handle; used for landing large fish 3: a sharp metal spur or spike fastened to the leg of a gamecock. 4: A climbing hook used by telephone and electric line workers. 5: slang a trick or gimmick, especially one used in a swindle or to rig a game 6: slang harshness of treatment; abuse
v 1: to hook or land (a fish) using a gaff 2: to equip (a gamecock) with a gaff 3: slang to take in or defraud; swindle 4: slang to rig or fix in order to cheat: knew that the carnival games had been gaffed

gaffe
n : a socially awkward or tactless act [syn: faux pas, solecism, slip, gaucherie]

gage, gauge /gɛɪdʒ/

gage
n 1: a measuring instrument for measuring and indicating a quantity or for testing conformity with a standard [syn: gauge] 2: a strong-smelling plant from whose dried leaves a number of euphoriant and hallucinogenic drugs are prepared [syn: marijuana, marihuana, ganja, pot, grass, dope, weed, sess, sens, skunk, Mary-Jane, Cannabis sativa]
v : place a bet on; "Which horse are you backing?" "I'm betting on the new horse" [syn: bet on, back, stake, game, punt]

HOMOPHONES

gauge

n : (var of gage) a measuring instrument (see gage 1:)

v : form an opinion about; judge tentatively; form an estimate of, esp. quantities or time; "I estimate this chicken to weigh at three pounds" [syn: estimate, approximate, guess, judge]

gait, gate /geɪt/

gait

n 1: the rate of moving (especially walking or running) [syn: pace] 2: a horse's manner of moving 3: a person's manner of walking

gate

n 1: a door-like movable barrier in a fence or wall 2: a computer circuit with several inputs but only one output that can be activated by particular combinations of inputs [syn: logic gate] 3: total admission receipts at a sports event 4: passageway (as in an air terminal) where passengers can embark or disembark

v 1: supply with a gate: "The house was gated" 2: control with a valve or other device that functions like a gate 3: restrict movement to the dormitory or campus, of British schoolboys, as a means of punishment

gaiter, gator /geɪtᵊɹ/

gaiter

n 1: a cloth covering (a legging) that provides covering for the instep and ankles [syn: spat, spats] 2: a shoe covering the ankle with elastic gores in the sides 3: legging consisting of a cloth or leather covering for the leg from the knee to the ankle

gator

n : either of two amphibious reptiles related to crocodiles but with shorter broader snouts [syn: alligator]

gamble, gambol /ˈgæmbᵊl/

gamble

n 1: money that is risked for possible monetary gain 2: a risky act or venture

v 1: take a risk in the hope of a favorable outcome; "You gamble when you buy these stocks." [syn: chance, risk, hazard, take chances, adventure, run a risk, take a chance] 2: play games for money

gambol

n : gay or light-hearted recreational activity for diversion or amusement; "it was all done in play"; "their frolic in the surf threatened to become ugly" [syn: play, frolic, romp, caper]

v : play boisterously; "The children frolicked in the garden"; "the gamboling lambs in the meadows"; "The toddlers romped in the playroom" [syn: frolic, lark, rollick, skylark, disport, sport, cavort, frisk, romp, run around, lark about]

gamin, gammon /ˈgæmɪn/

gamin

n : a homeless child who has been abandoned and roams the streets [syn: street arab, throwaway]

gammon

n 1: meat cut from the thigh of a hog (usually smoked) [syn: ham, jambon] 2: hind portion of a side of bacon

gang, gangue /gɛɪŋ/

gang

n 1: an association of criminals; "police tried to break up the gang"; "a pack of thieves" [syn: pack, ring, mob] 2: an informal body of friends; "he still hangs out with the same crowd" [syn: crowd, crew, bunch] 3: an organized group of workmen [syn: crew, work party] 4: tool consisting of a combination of implements arranged to work together

v : act as a gang [syn: gang up]

gangue

n : worthless rock in which valuable metals or minerals occur

gantlet, gauntlet /ˈgɑntlɛt/

gantlet

n : the convergence of two parallel railroad tracks in a narrow place; the inner rails cross and run parallel and then diverge so a train remains on its own tracks at all times

gauntlet (also /ˈgɔntlɛt/)

n 1: a glove of armored leather; protects the hand [syn: metal glove] 2: a glove with long sleeve 3: a form of punishment or torture in which people armed with sticks or other weapons arrange themselves in two lines facing each other and beat the person forced to run between them. 4: lines of people so arranged in a gauntlet 5: an onslaught or attack from all sides: "The hostages ran the gauntlet of insult on their way to the airport" 6: a severe trial; an ordeal

garret, garrote /ˈgæɹɪt/

garret

n : floor consisting of open space at the top of a house just below roof; often used for storage [syn: loft, attic]

garrote

n : an instrument of execution for execution by strangulation [syn: iron collar]

v : strangle with an iron collar; "people were garrotted during the Inquisition in Spain" [syn: scrag]

garrulous, garrulus /ˈgæɹʊlˈs/

garrulous (also /ˈgæɹʊəlˈs/)

adj : full of trivial conversation; "kept from her housework by gabby neighbors" [syn: chatty, gabby, loquacious, talkative, talky]

garrulus

n : type genus of the Garrulinae: Old World jays [syn: genus Garrulus]

HOMOPHONES

gays, gaze /gɛɪz/
gays
n : (plu of gay): people who practice homosexuality [syn: homosexuals, homos]
gaze
n : a long fixed look; "he fixed his paternal gaze on me" [syn: regard]
v : look at with fixed eyes; "The students gazed at the teacher with amazement" [syn: stare]

gel, jell /dʒɛl/
gel
n : a colloid in a more solid form than a sol [syn: colloidal gel]
v 1: become a gel; "The solid, when heated, gelled" 2: apply mousse to; of hair [syn: mousse]
jell
v : become gelatinous; "the liquid jelled after we added the enzyme" [syn: set, congeal]

gene, jean /dʒin/
gene
n : a self-replicating protein molecule that occupies a fixed place on a chromosome; a unit of heredity
jean
n 1: close-fitting pants of heavy denim for casual wear (usually in the plural) [syn: blue jean, denim] 2: a coarse durable twill-weave cotton fabric [syn: denim, dungaree]

genet, jennet /'dʒɛnɛt/
genet
n : agile Old World viverrine having a spotted coat and long ringed tail [syn: Genetta genetta]
jennet
n : female donkey [syn: jenny, jenny ass]

ghat, got /gɑt/
ghat
n : stairway in India leading down to a landing on the water
got
v : (past of get); he got nothing for all his work"

gibe, jibe /dʒɑɪb/
gibe
n : an aggressive remark directed at a person like a missile and intended to have a telling effect; "his parting shot was `drop dead'"; "she threw shafts of sarcasm"; "she takes a dig at me every chance she gets" [syn: shot, shaft, slam, dig, barb, jibe]
v 1: be compatible, similar or consistent; coincide in their characteristics; "The two stories don't jibe in many details"; "The handwriting checks with the signature on the check"; "The suspect's fingerprints don't match those on the gun" [syn: match, fit, correspond, check, jibe, tally, agree] [ant: disagree] 2: laugh or scoff

at; "The crowd jeered at the speaker" [syn: jeer, scoff, flout, barrack]
jibe
n : (var of gibe)
v 1: shift from one side of the ship to the other; "The sail jibed wildly" [syn: gybe, jib, change course]

gild, gilled, guild /gɪld/
gild
n : (var of guild)
v : decorate with, or as if with, gold leaf or liquid gold
gilled
adj : provided with gills; "a gilled tadpole" [syn: branchiate]
guild
n : a formal association of people with similar interests; "trades people formed guilds in the middle ages"; "he joined a golf club"; "they formed a small lunch society"; "men from the fraternal order will staff the soup kitchen today" [syn: club, society, gild, lodge, order]

gilder, guilder /'gɪldɚ/
gilder
n : someone whose occupation is apply an overlay of gold or gilt
guilder
n : the basic unit of money in the Netherlands and Suriname; equal to 100 cents [syn: gulden, florin]

gilt, guilt /gɪlt/
gilt
adj : having the deep slightly brownish color of gold; "long aureate (or golden) hair"; "a gold carpet" [syn: aureate, gilded, gold, golden]
n : a coating of gold or of something that looks like gold [syn: gilding]
guilt
n 1: the state of having committed an offense [syn: guiltiness] [ant: innocence] 2: remorse cause by feeling responsible for some offence [syn: guilty conscience, guilt feelings, guilt trip]

gin (see djinn)

giro, gyro /'dʒɑɪɹoʊ/
giro
1: a check given by the British government to someone who is unemployed; it can be cashed either at a bank or at the post office [syn: giro cheque] 2: a British financial system in which a bank or a post office transfers money from one account to another when they receive authorization to do so
gyro
n 1: a Greek sandwich: sliced roast lamb with onion and tomato stuffed into pita bread 2: rotating mechanism in the form of a universally mounted spinning wheel that offers resistance to turns in any direction [syn: gyroscope]

HOMOPHONES

glair, glare /glɛər/
glair
n : a sizing liquid made from egg white

glare
n 1: great brightness; "a glare of sunlight"; "the flowers were a blaze of color" [syn: blaze, brilliance] 2: an angry stare [syn: glower]
v 1: look with a fixed gaze: "The girl glared at the man who tried to make a pass at her" [syn: glower] 2: be sharply reflected; "The moon glared back at itself from the lake's surface." 3: shine with a harsh, uncomfortably brilliant light; "Not even the sea can glare like the sun." 4: shine intensely; "The sun glared down on us"

glands, glans /glɛənz/
glands
n : organs that synthesize substances needed by the body and release it through ducts or directly into the bloodstream [syn: secretory organ, secretor]

glans
n : a small rounded gland-like structure; especially that at the end of the penis or clitoris

gloom, glume /glum/
gloom
n 1: a state of partial or total darkness; "he struck a match to dispel the gloom" [syn: somberness] 2: a feeling of melancholy apprehension [syn: gloominess, somberness] 3: an atmosphere of depression and melancholy; "gloom pervaded the office" [syn: gloominess, glumness]

glume
n : small dry membranous bract found in inflorescences of Gramineae and Cyperaceae grass

glows, gloze /glouz/
glows
v : (3rd pers sing of glow) 1: emits a steady even light without flames; "The firefly glows and flies about in the garden" 2: especially of the complexion: shows a strong bright color, such as red or pink; "Her face glows when she comes out of the sauna" [syn: beams, radiates, shines] 3: shines intensely, as if with heat; "The fire burns" [syn: burns] 4: be exuberant or high-spirited; "My heart glows" 5: experiences a feeling of well-being or happiness, as from good health or an intense emotion; "She beams with joy"; "Her face radiates with happiness" [syn: beams, radiates, shines]

gloze
v : to gloss or flatter

glutenous, glutinous
/ˈglutɪnəs/
glutenous
adj : having the cohesiveness of wheat-flour dough

glutinous
adj : having the properties of glue [syn: gluey, gummy, mucilaginous, pasty, sticky, viscid, viscous]

gneiss, nice /naɪs/
gneiss
n : a laminated metamorphic rock similar to granite

nice
adj 1: pleasant or pleasing or agreeable in nature or appearance; "what a nice fellow you are and we all thought you so nasty"- George Meredith; "nice manners"; "a nice dress"; "a nice face"; "a nice day"; "had a nice time at the party"; "the corn and tomatoes are nice today" [ant: nasty] 2: socially or conventionally correct; refined or virtuous; "from a decent family"; "a nice girl" [syn: decent] 3: done with delicacy and skill; "a nice bit of craft"; "a job requiring nice measurements with a micrometer"; "a nice shot" [syn: skillful] 4: excessively fastidious and easily disgusted; "too nice about his food to take to camp cooking"; "so squeamish he would only touch the toilet handle with his elbow" [syn: dainty, overnice, prissy, squeamish] 5: noting distinctions with nicety; "a discriminating interior designer"; "a nice sense of color"; "a nice point in the argument" [syn: discriminate] 6: exhibiting courtesy and politeness; "a nice gesture" [syn: courteous, gracious]

gnu, knew, new, nu /nu/
gnu
n : large African antelope having a head with horns like an ox and a long tufted tail [syn: wildebeest]

knew
v : (past of know)

new
adj 1: not of long duration; having just (or relatively recently) come into being or been made or acquired or discovered; "a new law"; "new cars"; "a new comet"; "a new friend"; "a new year"; "the New World" [ant: old] 2: other than the former one(s); different; "they now have a new leaders"; "my new car is four years old but has only 15,000 miles on it"; "ready to take a new direction" 3: having no previous example or precedent or parallel; "a time of unexampled prosperity" [syn: unexampled] 4: of a kind not seen before; "the computer produced a completely novel proof of a well-known theorem" [syn: fresh, novel] 5: lacking training or experience; "the new men were eager to

fight"; "raw recruits"; "he was still wet behind the ears when he shipped as a hand on a merchant vessel" [syn: raw, wet behind the ears] 6: of a new (often outrageous) kind or fashion [syn: newfangled] 7: (often followed by 'to') unfamiliar; "new experiences"; "experiences new to him"; "errors of someone new to the job" [syn: new to] 8: (of crops) harvested at an early stage of development; before complete maturity; "baby carrots"; "new potatoes"; "young corn" [syn: baby, young] 9: unaffected by use or exposure; "it looks like new" 10: (linguistics) in use after Medieval times; "New Egyptian was the language of the 18th to 21st dynasties" [syn: New] 11: (linguistics) used of a living language; being the current stage in its development; "Modern English"; "New Hebrew is Israeli Hebrew" [syn: Modern, New]

adv : very recently; "grass new washed by the rain"; "they are newly married"; "newly raised objections"; "a newly arranged hairdo"; "a freshly cleaned floor"; "we are fresh out of tomatoes" [syn: recently, newly, freshly, fresh

nu

n : the 13th letter of the Greek alphabet

gnus, news, nus /nuz/

gnus

n : (plu of gnu)

news

n 1: new information about specific and timely events; "they awaited news of the outcome" [syn: intelligence, tidings, word] 2: new information of any kind; "it was news to me" 3: a program devoted to news; "we watch the 7 o'clock news every night" [syn: news program, news show] 4: information reported in a newspaper or news magazine; "the news of my death was greatly exaggerated" 5: the quality of being sufficiently interesting to be reported in news bulletins; "the judge conceded the newsworthiness of the trial"; "he is no longer news in the fashion world" [syn: newsworthiness]

nus

n : (plu of nu)

gored, gourd /gɔɹd/

gored

v : (past of gore) : "The bull's horn gored the bullfighter."

adj : having a pierced wound caused by a horn or tusk "The bullfighter is gored!"

gourd

n 1: bottle made from the dried shell of a bottle gourd [syn: calabash] 2: any of numerous inedible fruits with hard rinds 3: any vine of the family Cucurbitaceae that bears fruits with hard rinds [syn: gourd vine]

gorgeous, gorges

gorgeous /ˈgɔɹdʒɪs/

adj : dazzlingly beautiful; "a gorgeous Victorian gown"

gorges /ˈgɔɹdʒɪz/

n : (plu of gorge) 1: a deep ravine (usually with a river running through it) 2: a narrow pass (especially one between mountains)

v : (3rd pers sing of gorge) : overeats or eats immodestly; makes a pig of oneself "He's fat because he always gorges himself at the buffet." [syn: ingurgitates, overindulges, gluts, stuffs, engorges, overeats, gormandizes, gourmandizes, binges, pig outs, satiates, scarfs out] [ant: nibbles]

gorilla, guerilla /gəˈɹɪlə/

gorilla

n : largest anthropoid ape; terrestrial and vegetarian; of forests of central west Africa

guerrilla (alt guerilla)

adj : used of independent armed resistance forces; "guerrilla warfare"; "partisan forces" [syn: underground, irregular]

n : a member of an irregular armed force that fights a stronger force by sabotage and harassment [syn: irregular, insurgent]

grade, grayed /gɹeɪd/

grade

adj 1: at surface level; "a grade crossing" [syn: ground-level] 2: (of domestic animals) improved by selective breeding

n 1: a body of students who are taught together; "early morning classes are always sleepy" [syn: class, form] 2: a relative position or degree of value in a graded group: "lumber of the highest grade" [syn: level, tier] 3: the gradient of a slope or road or other surface: "the road had a steep grade" 4: one-hundredth of a right angle [syn: grad] 5: a number or letter indicating quality (especially of a student's performance); "she made good marks in algebra"; "grade A milk"; "what was your score on your homework?" [syn: mark, score] 6: the height of the ground on which something stands: "the base of the tower was below grade" [syn: ground level] 7: a position on a scale of intensity or amount or quality: "a moderate degree of intelligence"; "a high level of care is required"; "it is all a matter of degree" [syn: degree, level] 8: the property possessed by a line or surface that departs from the horizontal; "a five-degree grade" [syn: gradient, slope]

v 1: assign a rank or rating to; "how would you rank these students?" [syn: rate, rank, range, order, place] 2: level to the right gradient 3: assign a grade or rank to, according to one's evaluation; "grade tests"; "score the SAT essays"; "mark homework" [syn: score, mark] 4: determine the grade of or assign a grade to

HOMOPHONES

grayed

adj : deprived of color; "colors dulled by too much sun"; "grayed with the dust of the road" [syn: dulled]

v : (past of gray) : "The sun grayed the building." [syn: became gray]

grader, grater, greater
/ˈgɹeɪtəʳɹ/

grader

n 1: a judge who assigns grades to something 2: a machine for leveling earth

grater (also /ˈgɹeɪtəʳɹ/)

n : utensil with sharp perforations for shredding foods (as vegetables or cheese)

greater (also /ˈgɹeɪtʳəʔ/ɹ/)

adj (comparative of great) : greater in size or importance or degree; "for the greater good of the community"; "the greater Antilles" [syn: more] [ant: lesser]

graft, graphed (gr@ft)

graft

n 1: (surgery) tissue or organ transplanted from a donor to a recipient; in some cases the patient can be both donor and recipient [syn: transplant] 2: the practice of offering something (usually money) in order to gain an illicit advantage [syn: bribery] 3: the act of grafting something onto something else [syn: grafting]

v 1: cause to grow together parts from different plants; "graft the cherry tree branch onto the plum tree" [syn: engraft] 2: place the organ of a donor into the body of a recipient [syn: transplant]

graphed

adj 1: represented by a graph 2: plotted on a graph

grate, great /gɹeɪt/

grate

n 1: a frame of iron bars to hold a fire [syn: grating] 2: a harsh rasping sound made by scraping something 3: a barrier that has parallel or crossed bars blocking a passage but admitting air [syn: grating]

v 1: furnish with a grate; "a grated fireplace" 2: gnaw into; make resentful or angry; "The injustice grated her" [syn: eat into, fret, rankle] 3: reduce to small shreds or pulverize by rubbing against a rough or sharp perforated surface; "grate carrots and onions"; "grate nutmeg" [syn: grind] 5: scratch repeatedly; "The cat scraped at the armchair" [syn: scrape]

great

adj 1: relatively large in size or number or extent; larger than others of its kind; "a great juicy steak"; "a great multitude"; "the great auk"; "a great old oak"; "a great ocean liner"; "a great delay" 2: more than usual; "great expectations"; "great worry" 3: (used of persons) standing above others in character or attainment or reputation; "our distinguished professor"; "an eminent scholar"; "a great statesman" [syn: distinguished, eminent] 4: of major significance or importance; "a great work of art"; "Einstein was one of the outstanding figures of the 20th century" [syn: outstanding] 5: remarkable or out of the ordinary in degree or magnitude or effect; "a great crisis"; "had a great stake in the outcome" 6: (informal) very good; "a bully pulpit"; "a neat sports car"; "had a great time at the party"; "you look simply smashing" [syn: bang-up, bully, corking, cracking, dandy, groovy, keen, neat, nifty, not bad, peachy, slap-up, swell, smashing] 7: uppercase; "capital A"; "great A"; "many medieval manuscripts are in majuscule script" [syn: capital, majuscule] 8: marked by active interest and enthusiasm; "an avid sports fan"; "a great walker"; "an eager beaver" [syn: avid, eager, zealous] 9: in an advanced stage of pregnancy; "was big with child"; "was great with child" [syn: big, enceinte, expectant, gravid, large, heavy, with child]

grays, graze /gɹeɪz/

grays

n (plu of gray) : "The ships are painted with various grays." [syn: shades of gray]

graze

n 1: a superficial abrasion 2: the act of grazing [syn: grazing]

v 1: feed as in a meadow or pasture; "the herd was grazing" [syn: crop, browse, range, pasture] 2: break the skin (of a body part) by scraping; "She was grazed by the stray bullet" 3: let (animals) feed in a field or pasture or meadow [syn: crop, pasture] 4: scrape gently [syn: crease, rake] 5: eat lightly, try different dishes; "There was so much food at the party that we quickly got sated just by browsing" [syn: browse]

greaves, grieves /gɹivz/

greaves

n : armor plate that protects legs below the knee [syn: greave, jambeau]

grieves

v : (3rd pers sing of grieve) 1: feel grief; eat one's heart out [syn: sorrow] 2: break the heart of; cause to feel sorrow [syn: aggrieve]

greisen, grison /ˈgɹaɪsəʳn/

greisen

n : a granitic rock composed of quartz and mica

grison

n : carnivore of Central America and South America resembling a weasel with a grayish-white back and dark underparts [syn: Grison vittatus, Galictis vittatus]

HOMOPHONES

grill, grille /ɡɹɪl/

grill

n 1: a restaurant where food is cooked on a grill 2: a framework of metal bars used as a partition or a grate; "he cooked hamburgers on the grill" [syn: grille, grillwork]

v : cook over a grill; "grill the sausages"

grille

n 1: small opening (like a window in a door) through which business can be transacted [syn: wicket, lattice] 2: grating that admits cooling air to car's radiator [syn: radiator grille] 3: (var of grill)

grip, grippe /ɡɹɪp/

grip

n 1: the act of grasping; "he released his clasp on my arm"; "he has a strong grip for an old man"; "she kept a firm hold on the railing" [syn: clasp, clench, clutch, clutches, grasp, hold] 2: the appendage to an object that is designed to be held in order to use or move it [syn: handle, handgrip, hold] 3: a portable rectangular traveling bag for carrying clothes; "he carried his small bag onto the plane with him" [syn: bag, traveling bag, suitcase] 4: the friction between a body and the surface on which it moves (as between an automobile tire and the road) [syn: traction, adhesive friction] 5: worker who moves the camera around while a film or television show is being made 6: a firm controlling influence; "he was in the grip of a powerful emotion" or "a terrible power had her its grasp" [syn: grasp] 7: a flat wire hairpin whose prongs press tightly together; used to hold bobbed hair in place; "in England they call a bobby pin a grip" [syn: bobby pin, hairgrip]

v 1: hold fast or firmly; "He gripped the steering wheel" 2: to grip or seize, as in a wrestling match; "the two men grappled with each other for several minutes" [syn: grapple] 3: to render motionless, as with a fixed stare or by arousing terror or awe: "The eye of the Ancient Mariner fascinated the wedding guest." Burton; "The serpent fascinates its prey the power of his eyes." Todd & Bowman [syn: fascinate, transfix, spellbind] 4: hold firmly [syn: grasp, hold on]

grippe

n : an acute febrile highly contagious viral disease [syn: influenza, flu]

grisly, gristly, grizzly

grisly /ˈɡɹɪzli/

adj : shockingly repellent; inspiring horror; "ghastly wounds"; "the grim aftermath of the bombing"; "the grim task of burying the victims"; "a grisly murder"; "gruesome evidence of human sacrifice"; "macabre tales of war and plague in the Middle ages"; "macabre tortures conceived by madmen" [syn: ghastly, grim, gruesome, macabre]

gristly /ˈɡɹɪstli/

adj : difficult to chew [syn: cartilaginous, rubbery]

grizzly /ˈɡɹɪzli/

n : powerful brownish-yellow bear of the uplands of western North America [syn: grizzly bear, silvertip, Ursus horribilis, Ursus arctos horribilis]

groan, grown /ɡɹoʊn/

groan

n : an utterance expressing pain or disapproval [syn: moan]

v : indicate pain, discomfort, or displeasure; "The students groaned when the professor got out the exam booklets"; "The ancient door soughed when opened" [syn: moan, sough]

grown

adj : (of animals) fully developed; "an adult animal"; "a grown woman" [syn: adult, big, full-grown, fully grown, grownup]

grocer, grosser /ˈɡɹoʊsər/

grocer

n : a retail merchant who sells foodstuffs (and some household supplies)

grosser

adj (compar of gross) : conspicuously and tastelessly indecent; "coarser language"; "a cruder joke"; "cruder behavior"; "an earthier sense of humor"; "a revoltingly grosser expletive"; "a more vulgar gesture"; "full of language so vulgar it should have been edited" [syn: coarser, cruder, earthier, more vulgar]

guarantee, guaranty /ˈɡæɹənti/

guarantee

n 1: a written assurance that some product or service will be provided or will meet certain specifications [syn: warrant, warranty] 2: a pledge that something will happen or that something is true; "there is no guarantee that they are not lying" 3: (alt guaranty)

v 1: give surety or assume responsibility; "I vouch for the quality of my products" [syn: vouch] 2: make certain of; "This nest egg will ensure a nice retirement for us"; "Preparation will guarantee success!" [syn: ensure, insure, assure, secure] 3: promise or guarantee [syn: undertake] 4: stand behind [syn: warrant]

guaranty

n : a collateral agreement to answer for the debt of another in case that person defaults [syn: guarantee]

guessed, guest /ɡɛst/

guessed

v : (past of guess) 1: expected, believed, or supposed; "I imagined she earned a

HOMOPHONES

lot of money with her new novel"; "I thought to find her in a bad state"; "he didn't think to find her in the kitchen"; "I guessed she was angry at me for standing her up" [syn: thought, opined, supposed, imagined, reckoned] 2: put forward, of a guess; "I am guessing that the price of real estate will rise again" [syn: ventured, hazarded] 3: form an opinion about; judge tentatively; form an estimate of, esp. quantities or time; "I estimate this chicken to weigh at three pounds" [syn: estimated, gauged, approximated, judged] 4: guess correctly; solve by guessing; "He guessed the right number of beans in the jar and won the prize" [syn: inferred]

guest

adj : staying temporarily; "a visiting foreigner"; "guest conductor" [syn: visiting, guest]
n 1: a visitor to whom hospitality is extended [syn: invitee] 2: a customer of a hotel or restaurant etc. 3: (computer science) any computer that is hooked up to a computer network [syn: node, client]

guide, guyed /gaɪd/

guide

n 1: someone employed to conduct others [syn: usher] 2: someone who shows the way by leading or advising 3: something that offers basic information or instruction [syn: guidebook] 4: a model or standard for making comparisons [syn: template] 5: someone who can find paths through unexplored territory [syn: scout, pathfinder]
v 1: direct the course; determine the direction of traveling [syn: steer, maneuver, direct, point, head] 2: take somebody somewhere; "We lead him to our chief"; "can you take me to the main entrance?"; "He conducted us to the palace" [syn: lead, take, direct, conduct] 3: be a guiding force, as with directions or advice; "The teacher steered the gifted students towards the more challenging courses" [syn: steer] 4: use as a guide; "They had the lights to guide on" [syn: guide on] 5: guide or pass over something; "He ran his eyes over her body"; "She ran her fingers along the carved figurine"; "He drew her hair through his fingers" [syn: run, draw, pass]

guyed

adj : to be steadied with cables or ropes ; "The Italians guyed the Tower of Pisa to prevent it from collapsing"
v : (past of guy) 1: subjected to laughter or ridicule: "The students poked fun at the inexperienced teacher" [syn: ridiculed, blackguarded, laughed at, jested at, ribbed, made fun, poked fun] 2: steadied with a guy "The tower was guyed with cables."

guise, guys /gaɪz/

guise

n : an artful or simulated semblance; "under the guise of friendship he betrayed them" [syn: pretense, pretext]

guys

n (plu of guy) 1: an informal term for a youth or man; "nice guys"; "guys only do it for their dolls" [syn: cats, hombres, bozos] 2: a rope or cable that is used to brace something (especially a tent) [syn: guy cable, guy rope]
v 1: (3rd pers sing) for guy : steadies or reinforces with a guy 2: subjects to laughter or ridicule; [syn: ridicules, roasts, blackguards, laughs at, jests at, ribs, makes fun, pokes fun]

HOMOPHONES

-H-

hail, hale /hɛɪl/
hail
n 1: precipitation of ice pellets when there are strong rising air currents 2: enthusiastic greeting

v 1: praise vociferously [syn: acclaim, herald] 2: be a native of; "She hails from Kalamazoo" [syn: come] 3: call for, as of cabs 4: greet enthusiastically or joyfully [syn: herald] 5: precipitate as small ice particles; "It hailed for an hour."

hale
adj : exhibiting or restored to vigorous good health; "hale and hearty"; "whole in mind and body"; "a whole person again" [syn: whole]

v 1: to cause to do through pressure or necessity, by physical, moral or intellectual means :"She haled him to take a job in the city" [syn: coerce, pressure, force] 2: draw slowly or heavily; "haul stones"; "haul nets" [syn: haul, cart, drag]

hair, hare /hɛəɹ/
hair
n 1: dense growth of hairs covering the body or parts of it (as on the human head); helps prevent heat loss; "he combed his hair" 2: a very small distance or space; "they escaped by a hair's-breadth"; "they lost by a hair" [syn: hair's-breadth, hairbreadth] 3: filamentous hairlike growth on a plant; "peach fuzz" [syn: fuzz] 4: any of the cylindrical filaments characteristically growing from the epidermis of a mammal; "there is a hair in my soup" 5: cloth woven from horsehair or camelhair; used for upholstery or stiffening in garments [syn: haircloth] 6: a filamentous projection or process on an organism

hare
n 1: swift timid long-eared mammal larger than a rabbit having a divided upper lip and long hind legs; young born furred and with open eyes 2: flesh of any of various rabbits or hares (wild or domesticated) eaten as food [syn: rabbit]

v : run quickly; "He hared down the hill"

hairier, harrier /ˈhɛəɹiəɹ/
hairier
adj : (compar of hairy) 1: having or covered with more hair; "Jacob was hairier than his father 2: hazardous and frightening; "we had hairier moments in the mountains"

harrier
n 1: a persistent attacker; "the harassers were not members of the regular army" [syn: harasser] 2: a hound that resembles a foxhound but is smaller; used to hunt rabbits 3: hawks that hunt over meadows and marshes and prey on small terrestrial animals

hairy, harry /ˈhɛəɹi/
hairy
adj 1: having or covered with hair; "Jacob was a hairy man"; "a hairy caterpillar" [syn: hirsute] [ant: hairless] 2: hazardous and frightening; "hairy moments in the mountains"

harry
v 1: annoy continually or chronically; "He is known to harry his staff when he is overworked" [syn: harass, hassle, chivy, chivvy, beset, plague, molest, provoke] 2: make a pillaging or destructive raid on (a place), as in wartimes [syn: ravage]

hall, haul /hɔl/
hall
n 1: an interior passage or corridor onto which rooms open; "the elevators were at the end of the hall" [syn: hallway] 2: a large entrance or reception room or area [syn: anteroom, antechamber, entrance hall, foyer, lobby, vestibule] 3: a large room for gatherings or entertainment; "lecture hall"; "pool hall" 4: living quarters at a college or university where students live [syn: dormitory, dorm, residence hall, student residence] 5: the large room of a manor or castle [syn: manor hall] 6: a large and imposing house [syn: mansion, mansion house, manse, residence] 7: a large building used by a college or university for teaching or research; "halls of learning" 8: a large building for meetings or entertainment

haul
n 1: the act of drawing or hauling something; "the haul up the hill went very slowly" [syn: draw, haulage] 2: the quantity that was caught; "the catch was only 10 fish" [syn: catch]

v 1: draw slowly or heavily; "haul stones"; "haul nets" [syn: hale, cart, drag] 2: transport, as in a truck 3: transport something in a cart [syn: cart]

hallo, hallow, hello, hollow
hallo /ˈhalou/
n : a very loud utterance (like the sound of an animal); "his bellow filled the hallway" [syn: bellow, bellowing, holler, hollering, hollo, roar, roaring, yowl]

v 1: encourage somebody by crying hollo 2: cry hollo 3: utter a sudden loud cry; "she cried with pain when the doctor inserted the needle"; "I yelled to her from the window but she couldn't hear me" [syn: shout, shout out, cry, call, yell, scream, holler, squall]

hallow /ˈhælou/
v : render holy by means of religious rites [syn: consecrate, bless, sanctify] [ant:

HOMOPHONES

desecrate]

hello /ˈhɛloʊ/ or /həˈloʊ/ or /hʌˈloʊ/

n : an expression of greeting; "every morning they exchanged polite hellos" [syn: hullo, hi, howdy, how-do-you-do]

hollow /ˈhɑloʊ/

adj 1: not solid; having a space or gap or cavity; "a hollow wall"; "a hollow tree"; "hollow cheeks"; "his face became gaunter and more hollow with each year" [ant: solid] 2: deliberately deceptive; "hollow (or false) promises"; "false pretenses" [syn: false] 3: as if echoing in a hollow space; "the hollow sound of footsteps in the empty ballroom" 4: devoid of significance or point; "empty promises"; "a hollow victory"; "vacuous comments" [syn: empty, vacuous]

n 1: a cavity or space in something; "hunger had caused the hollows in their cheeks" 2: a small valley between mountains; "he built himself a cabin in a hollow high up in the Appalachians" [syn: holler] 3: a depression hollowed out of solid matter [syn: hole]

v 1: remove the inner part or the core of; "the mining company wants to excavate the hillside" [syn: excavate, dig] 2: remove the interior of; "hollow out a tree trunk" [syn: hollow out, core out]

halve, have /hæv/

halve

v : divide by two. divide into halves; "Halve the cake"

have

n : a person who possesses great material wealth [syn: rich person, wealthy person]

v 1: have or possess, either in a concrete or an abstract sense: "I have $1,000 in the bank"; "I have got two beautiful daughters"; "I hold a Master's degree from Harvard" [syn: have got, hold] 2: have as a feature; "They have the most famous chefs in France" [syn: feature] [ant: miss] 3: of mental or physical states or experiences: "have an idea"; "experience vertigo"; "get nauseous"; "undergo a strange sensation"; "The chemical undergoes a sudden change"; "The fluid undergoes shear"; "receive injuries"; "have a feeling" [syn: experience, receive, get, undergo] 4: have ownership or possession of; "He has three houses in Florida"; "How many cars does she have?" [syn: own, possess] 5: be obliged, required, or forced to; "You have to get her driver's license" [syn: must, have got, need] 6: cause to move; cause to be in a certain position or condition: "You have your squad on the ball"; "This let me in for a big surprise"; "He got a girl into trouble" [syn: get, let] 7: serve oneself to, or consume regularly; "Have another bowl of chicken soup!" "I don't take sugar in my coffee" [syn: consume, ingest, take in, take] 8: have a personal or business relationship with someone; "have an assistant"; "have a lover" 9: organize or be responsible for; "hold a reception," "have, throw, or make a party", "give a course", etc. [syn: hold, throw, make, give] 10: have left; "I have two years left"; "I don't have any money left" "They have two more years before they retire" 11: be confronted with: "What do we have here?"; "Now we have a fine mess" 12: undergo; "The stocks had a fast run-up" [syn: experience] 13: suffer from; be ill with; "She has arthritis" 14: cause to do; cause to act in a specified manner: "The ads induced me to buy a VCR"; "My children finally got me to buy a computer"; "My wife made me buy a new sofa" [syn: induce, stimulate, cause, get, make] 15: receive willingly something given or offered; "The only girl who would have him was the miller's daughter"; "I won't have this dog in my house!"; "Please accept my present" [syn: accept, take] [ant: refuse] 16: get something; come into possession of; "receive payment"; "receive a gift"; "receive letters from the front" [syn: receive] 17: undergo (as of injuries and illnesses); "She suffered a fracture in the accident"; "You will have an insulin shock after eating three candy bars"; "She got a bruise on her leg"; "He got his arm broken in the scuffle" [syn: suffer, sustain, get] 18: achieve a point or goal, as in a sport; "Nicklaus had a 70"; "The Brazilian team got 4 goals"; "She made 29 points that day" [syn: get, make] 19: give birth (to a newborn); "My wife had twins yesterday!" [syn: give birth, deliver, bear, birth] 20: have sex with; archaic use; "He had taken this woman when she was most vulnerable" [syn: take] 21: be likely or probable; "They have to be kidding" [syn: must]

handmade, handmaid /ˈhɛəndmeɪd/

handmade

adj : made by hand or a hand process; "delicate handmade baby dresses" [syn: hand-crafted] [ant: machine-made]

handmaid

n 1: in a subordinate position; "theology should be the handmaiden of ethics"; "the state cannot be a servant of the church" [syn: handmaiden, servant] 2: a personal maid or female attendant [syn: handmaiden]

handsome, hansom /ˈhɛənsəm/

handsome

adj 1: pleasing in appearance especially

by reason of conformity to ideals of form and proportion; "a fine-looking woman"; "a good-looking man"; "better-looking than her sister"; [syn: fine-looking, good-looking, better-looking, well-favored] 2: given or giving freely; "was a handsome tipper"; "the bounteous goodness of God"; "bountiful compliments"; "a freehanded host"; "a handsome allowance"; "Saturday's child is loving and giving"; "a liberal backer of the arts"; "a munificent gift"; "her fond and openhanded grandfather" [syn: big, bighearted, bounteous, bountiful, freehanded, giving, liberal, openhanded]

hansom
n : a two-wheeled horse-drawn covered carriage with the driver's seat above and behind the passengers [syn: hansom cab]

hangar, hanger /ˈhɛɪŋɡ⸱ɹ/
hangar
n : a large building at an airport where aircraft can be stored and maintained [syn: airdock, repair shed]

hanger
n 1: a worker who hangs something 2: anything from which something can be hung

hardy, hearty /ˈhɑɹdi/
hardy
adj 1: having rugged physical strength; inured to fatigue or hardships; "hardy explorers of northern Canada"; "proud of her tall stalwart son"; "stout seamen"; "sturdy young athletes" [syn: stalwart, stout, sturdy] 2: resolute and without fear [syn: doughty, fearless] 3: able to survive under unfavorable conditions; "strawberries are hardy and easy to grow"; "camels are tough and hardy creatures"

hearty
adj 1: showing warm and heartfelt friendliness; "gave us a cordial reception"; "a hearty welcome" [syn: cordial] 2: providing abundant nourishment; "a hearty meal"; "good solid food"; "ate a substantial breakfast" [syn: satisfying, solid, substantial] 3: endowed with or exhibiting great bodily or mental health; "a hearty glow of health" [syn: full-blooded, lusty, red-blooded] 4: consuming abundantly and with gusto; "a hearty (or healthy) appetite" 5: without reservation; "hearty support"

hart, heart /hɑɹt/
hart
n : male red deer [syn: stag]

heart
n 1: the locus of feelings and intuitions; "in your heart you know it is true"; "her story would melt your bosom" [syn: bosom] 2: the hollow muscular organ located behind the sternum and between the lungs;

its rhythmic contractions pump blood through the body; "he stood still, his heart thumping wildly" [syn: pump, ticker] 3: the courage to carry on: "he kept fighting on pure spunk"; "you haven't got the heart for baseball" [syn: mettle, nerve, spunk] 4: an area that is approximately central within some larger region; "it is in the center of town"; "they ran forward into the heart of the struggle"; "they were in the eye of the storm" [syn: center, middle, eye] 5: the choicest or most essential or most vital part of some idea or experience: "the gist of the prosecutor's argument"; "the heart and soul of the Republican Party"; "the nub of the story" [syn: kernel, substance, core, center, essence, gist, heart and soul, inwardness, marrow, meat, nub, pith, sum, nitty-gritty] 6: an inclination or tendency of a certain kind; "he had a change of heart" [syn: spirit] 7: a plane figure with rounded sides curving inward at the top and intersecting at the bottom; conventionally used on playing cards and valentines; "he drew a heart and called it a valentine" 8: a firm rather dry variety meat (usually beef or veal); "a five-pound beef heart will serve six" 9: a positive feeling of liking; "he had trouble expressing the affection he felt"; "the child won everyone's heart" [syn: affection, fondness, tenderness, warmheartedness] 10: a playing card in the major suit of hearts; "he led the queen of hearts"

haws, hawse /hɔz/
haws
n 1: spring-flowering shrubs or small trees of the genus Crataegus [syn: hawthorn] 2: the nictitating membranes of a horse : commands to a team of animals to turn left [ant: gee]
v : utterances of speech hesitation "he hemmed and hawed"

hawse
n : the hole that an anchor rope passes through [syn: awsehole, hawsepipe]

hay, hey /hɛɪ/
hay
n : grass mowed and cured for use as fodder

hey
interj : a call for attention or to express a greeting, exultation, surprise or interrogation

haze, heys /hɛɪz/
haze
n 1: atmospheric moisture or dust or smoke that causes reduced visibility 2: confusion characterized by lack of clarity [syn: daze, fog]
v 1: become hazy, dull, or cloudy 2: harass by imposing humiliating or painful tasks, as in military institutions

HOMOPHONES

heys
interj : calls for attention or to express interrogation, surprise, or exultation

heal, heel, he'll /hil/
heal
v 1: get healthy again; "The wound is healing slowly" 2: heal or recover; "My broken leg is mending" [syn: mend] 3: provide a cure for, make healthy again [syn: cure]

heel
n 1: the back part of a shoe or boot that touches the ground 2: the back part of the human foot 3: someone who is morally reprehensible; "you dirty dog" [syn: cad, bounder, blackguard, dog, hound] 4: the piece of leather that fits the heel [syn: counter]
v 1: follow at the heels of a person 2: perform with the heels, of a dance 3: strike with the heel of the club, of golf balls 4: put a new heel on; "heel shoes" [syn: reheel]

he'll
contr : he will

hear, here /hiɹ/
hear
v 1: perceive sound; perceive by the auditory sense 2: get to know or become aware of, usually accidentally; "I hear that she has two grown-up children"; "I hear that you have been promoted" [syn: learn, get word, get wind, pick up, find out, get a line, discover, see] 3: examine or hear (evidence or a case) by judicial process; "The jury had heard all the evidence"; "The case will be tried in California" [syn: try] 4: receive a communication from someone: "We heard nothing from our son for five years" 5: listen and pay attention; "Listen to your father"; "We must hear the expert before we make a decision" [syn: listen, take heed]

here
adj : being here now; "is everyone here?"; "present company excepted"
n 1: the present location; this place; "where do we go from here?" [ant: there]
adv 1: in or at this place; where the speaker or writer is; "I work here"; "turn here"; "radio waves received here on Earth" [ant: there] 2: in this circumstance or respect or on this point or detail; "what do we have here?"; "here I must disagree" 3: to this place (especially toward the speaker); "come here, please" [syn: hither] [ant: there] 4: at this time; now; "we'll adjourn here for lunch and discuss the remaining issues this afternoon"

heard, herd /həɹd/
heard
v : (past of hear) : "I heard the good news!"

herd
n 1: a group of cattle or sheep or other domestic mammals all of the same kind that are grouped together by humans 2: a group of wild animals of one species that remain together: antelope or elephants or seals or whales or zebra 3: a crowd especially of ordinary or undistinguished persons or things; "his brilliance raised him above the ruck"; "the children resembled a fairy herd" [syn: ruck]
v 1: cause to herd, drive, or crowd together; "We herded the children into a spare classroom" [syn: crowd] 2: move together, like a herd 3: keep, move, or drive animals; "Who will herd the cattle when the cowboy dies?"

hears, here's /hiɹz/
hears
v : (3rd pers sing of hear) : "He hears every word you say."

here's
contr : here is; "Here's the book I promised to bring."

he'd, heed /hid/
he'd
contr : he would

heed
n : paying particular notice (as to children or helpless people); "his attentiveness to her wishes"; "he spends without heed to the consequences" [syn: attentiveness, regard, paying attention] [ant: inattentiveness]
v : pay close attention to; give heed to; "Heed the advice of the old men" [syn: mind, listen]

heir (see air)

heroin, heroine /ˈhɛɹoʊɪn/
heroin
n : a narcotic that is considered a hard drug; a highly addictive morphine derivative [syn: diacetylmorphine, H, horse, junk, scag, shit, smack]

heroine
n 1: the main good female character in a work of fiction 2: a woman possessing heroic qualities

hertz, hurts /həɹts/
hertz
n 1: the unit of frequency; one Hertz has a periodic interval of one second [syn: Hertz, Hz, cycle per second, cycles/second, cps, cycle]

hurts
v : (3rd pers sing of hurt) 1: be the source of pain [syn: aches, smarts] 2: give trouble or pain to; "Tell me if this exercise hurts your back" 3: cause anguish;, make miserable [syn: pains, anguishes] 4: cause damage or affect negatively; "The new competition hurts our business." [syn: injures] 5: hurt the feelings of; "She hurts me when she does not include me among her guests";

"This remark really bruises my ego" [syn: wounds, injures, bruises, offends, spites] 6: feel physical pain; "Were you hurting after the accident?" [syn: aches, suffers] 7: feel pain or be in pain [syn: suffers] [ant: be well]

hew, hue, whew /hʊə/

hew

v 1: make or shape as with an axe; "hew out a path in the rock" [syn: hew out] 2: strike with an axe; cut down, strike; "hew an oak"

hue

n : the quality of a color as determined by its dominant wavelength [syn: chromaticity]

v 1: take on color or become colored; "In highlights it hued to a dull silver-gray" 2: suffuse with color [syn: imbue, tinge]

whew

interj 1: expression of amazement, discomfort, or relief 2: a whistling sound or a sound like a half-formed whistle uttered as an exclamation; "He gave a long whew when he realized the size of the job."

hi, hie, high /haɪ/

hi

n 1: an expression of greeting; "every morning they exchanged polite hellos" [syn: hello, hullo, howdy, how-do-you-do]

hie

v : step on it; "They hie down the hall to receive their guests"; "The cars race down the street" [syn: rush, hotfoot, hasten, speed, race, pelt along, rush along, cannonball along, bucket along, belt along] [ant: linger]

high

adj 1: greater than normal in degree or intensity or amount; "a high temperature"; "a high price"; "the high point of his career"; "high risks"; "has high hopes"; "the river is high"; "he has a high opinion of himself" [ant: low] 2: (literal meanings) being at or having a relatively great or specific elevation or upward extension; "a high mountain"; "high ceilings"; "high buildings"; "a high forehead"; "a high incline"; "a foot high"; sometimes used in combination; "knee-high grass" [ant: low] 3: standing above others in quality or position; "people in high places"; "the high priest"; "eminent members of the community" [syn: eminent] 4: used of sounds and voices; high in pitch or frequency [syn: high-pitched] [ant: low] 5: happy and excited and energetic [syn: in high spirits] 6: used of the smell of game beginning to taint [syn: gamy] 7: slightly and pleasantly intoxicated from alcohol or a drug (especially marijuana) [syn: mellow]

n 1: a lofty level or position or degree: "summer temperatures reached an all-time high" [ant: low] 2: an air mass of higher than normal pressure; "the east coast benefits from a Bermuda high" [syn: high pressure] 3: a state of sustained elation; "I'm on a permanent high these days" [ant: low spirits] 4: a state of altered consciousness induced by alcohol or narcotics; "they took drugs to get a high on" 5: a high place; "they stood on high and observed the countryside" or "he doesn't like heights" [syn: heights] 6: a public secondary school usually including grades 9 through 12; "he goes to the neighborhood high school" [syn: senior high school, senior high, high school, high school] 7: a forward gear with a gear ratio giving high vehicle velocity for a given engine speed [syn: high gear]

adv 1: at a great altitude; "he climbed high on the ladder" [syn: high up] 2: in or to a high position, amount, or degree; "prices have gone up far too high" 3: in a rich manner; "he lives high" [syn: richly, luxuriously] 4: far up toward the source; "he lives high up the river"

hide, hied /haɪd/

hide

n 1: the dressed skin of an animal (especially a large animal) [syn: fell] 2: body covering of a living animal [syn: pelt, skin]

v 1: prevent from being seen or discovered; "Muslim women hide their faces" [syn: conceal] [ant: show] 2: be or go into hiding; keep out of sight, as for protection and safety: "Probably their horses would be close to where they was hide"; "They hide out in a cabin in Montana" [syn: hide out] 3: go into hiding or conceal oneself; "Where does your little brother hide?" 4: cover as if with a shroud; "The origins of this civilization are shrouded in mystery" [syn: shroud, enshroud, cover] 5: make undecipherable or imperceptible by obscuring or concealing [syn: obscure, blot out, obliterate]

hied

v : (past of hie) : "He hied to the airport to meet his family." [syn: rushed, hurried]

higher, hire /ˈhaɪjəɹ/

higher

adj (compar of high) : a greater height "He flew higher than anyone else."

hire

v 1: engage for work; "I need to hire two new secretaries for the department"; "How many people has she employed?" [syn: engage, employ] [ant: fire] 2: hold under a lease or rental agreement; of goods and services [syn: rent, charter, lease] 3: engage in a commercial transaction; "We

HOMOPHONES

took an apartment on a quiet street"; "Let's rent a car"; "Shall we take a guide in Rome?" [syn: lease, rent, charter, engage, take]

him, hymn /hɪm/
him
pron : referring to a masculine object "Give the book to him."

hymn
n : a song of praise (to God or to a saint or to a nation) [syn: anthem]
v 1: sing a hymn 2: praise by singing a hymn: "They will hymn their love of God"

ho, hoe /hoʊ/
ho
interj : used to attract attention to something "The watch shouted 'Land ho'."
n : (slang) whore

hoe
n : a tool with a flat blade attached at right angles to a long handle
v : dig with a hoe

hoar, whore /hɔr/
hoar
adj : showing characteristics of age, especially having gray or white hair; "whose beard with age is hoar"-Coleridge; "nodded his hoary head" [syn: gray, gray-haired, gray-headed, hoary, white-haired]
n : ice crystals forming a white deposit (especially on objects outside) [syn: frost, hoarfrost, rime]

whore
n : a woman who engages in sexual intercourse for money [syn: prostitute, cocotte, harlot, trollop, bawd, tart, fancy woman, working girl, sporting lady, lady of pleasure, woman of the street]
v 1: corrupt by lewd intercourse 2: have unlawful sex with a whore

hoard, horde, whored /hɔrd/
hoard
n : a secret store of valuables or money [syn: cache, stash]
v 1: save up as for future use [syn: stash, cache, lay away, hive up, squirrel away] 2: get together [syn: collect, accumulate, pile up, amass, compile]

horde
n 1: a vast multitude [syn: host, legion] 2: a nomadic community 3: a moving crowd [syn: drove, swarm]

whored
v : (past of whore) "The sailors whored all night during shore leave."

hoarse, horse /hɔrs/
hoarse
adj : deep and harsh sounding as if from shouting or illness or emotion; "gruff voices"; "the dog's gruff barking"; "hoarse cries"; "His voice was hoarse from coughing so much." [syn: gruff, husky]

horse
n 1: solid-hoofed herbivorous quadruped domesticated since prehistoric times [syn: Equus caballus] 2: a padded gymnastic apparatus on legs 3: troops trained to fight on horseback: "500 horse led the attack" [syn: cavalry, horse cavalry] 4: a framework for holding wood that is being sawed [syn: sawhorse, sawbuck, buck] 5: a chessman in the shape of a horse's head; can move two squares horizontally and one vertically (or vice versa) [syn: knight] 6: a narcotic that is considered a hard drug; a highly addictive morphine derivative [syn: heroin, diacetylmorphine, H, junk, scag, shit, smack]
v : provide with a horse or horses

hoes, hose /hoʊz/
hoes
n : (plu of hoe)

hose
n 1: socks and stockings and tights collectively (the British include underwear as hosiery) [syn: hosiery] 2: man's garment of the 16th and 17th centuries; worn with a doublet [syn: tights] 3: a flexible pipe for conveying a liquid or gas [syn: hosepipe]
v : water with a hose; "hose the lawn" [syn: hose down]

hold, holed /hoʊld/
hold
n 1: the act of grasping; "he released his clasp on my arm"; "he has a strong grip for an old man"; "she kept a firm hold on the railing" [syn: clasp, clench, clutch, clutches, grasp, grip] 2: understanding of the nature or meaning or quality or magnitude of something; "he has a good grasp of accounting practices" [syn: appreciation, grasp] 3: power by which something or someone is affected or dominated: "he has a hold over them" 4: time during which some action is awaited; "instant replay caused too long a delay"; "he ordered a hold in the action" [syn: delay, time lag, postponement, wait] 5: a state of being confined (usually for a short time); "his detention was politically motivated"; "the prisoner is on hold"; "he is in the custody of police" [syn: detention, custody] 6: (archaic) a stronghold 7: a cell in a jail or prison [syn: keep] 8: the appendage to an object that is designed to be held in order to use or move it [syn: handle, grip, handgrip] 9: the space in a ship or aircraft for storing cargo [syn: cargo area, cargo deck, cargo hold, storage area]
v 1: organize or be responsible for; "hold a reception," "have, throw, or make a party", "give a course", etc. [syn: throw, have, make, give] 2: keep in a certain state,

HOMOPHONES

position, or activity; e.g., "keep clean"; "hold in place"; "She always held herself as a lady"; "The students keep me on my toes" [syn: keep, maintain] 3: have or hold in one's hands; "Hold this bowl for a moment, please"; also metaphorically: "A crazy idea took hold of him" [syn: take hold] [ant: let go of] 4: to close within bounds, limit or hold back from movement; "This holds the local until the express passengers change trains"; "About a dozen animals were held inside the stockade"; "The illegal immigrants were held at a detention center"; "The terrorists held the journalists for ransom" [syn: restrain, confine] 5: have rightfully; of rights, titles, and offices; "She bears the title of Duchess"; "He held the governorship for almost a decade" [syn: bear] 6: have or possess, either in a concrete or an abstract sense: "She has $1,000 in the bank"; "He has got two beautiful daughters"; "She holds a Master's degree from Harvard" [syn: have, have got] 7: keep in mind or convey as a conviction or view; "take for granted"; "view as important"; "hold these truths to be self-evident"; "I hold him personally responsible" [syn: deem, view as, take for] 8: contain or hold; have within: "The jar carries wine"; "The canteen holds fresh water"; "This can contains water" [syn: bear, carry, contain] 9: lessen the intensity of; temper; hold in restraint; hold or keep within limits; "moderate your alcohol intake" "hold your tongue"; "hold your temper"; "control your anger" [syn: control, hold in, contain, check, curb, moderate] 10: remain in a certain state, position, or condition; "The weather held"; "They held on the road and kept marching" 11: maintain; as of a theory, thoughts, or feelings; "bear a grudge"; "hold a grudge" [syn: harbor, entertain, nurse] 12: hold on to [syn: reserve, retain] 13: assert or affirm; "Rousseau's philosophy holds that people are inherently good" 14: remain committed to; "I hold to these ideas" 15: keep in one's possession [syn: retain, keep back, hold back] 16: be the physical support of; carry the weight of; "The beam holds up the roof"; "He supported me with one hand while I balanced on the beam"; "What's holding that mirror?" [syn: support, sustain, hold up] 17: hold the attention of; "The soprano held the audience"; "This story held our interest"; "She can hold an audience spellbound" 18: keep from exhaling or expelling; "hold your breath" 19: support or hold in a certain manner; "She holds her head high"; "He carried himself upright" [syn: carry, bear] 20: have room for; hold without crowding; "This hotel can accommodate 250 guests";

"The theater admits 300 people"; "The auditorium can't hold more than 500 people" [syn: accommodate, admit] 21: be capable of holding or containing; "This box won't take all the items"; "The flask holds one gallon" [syn: contain, take] 22: be valid, applicable, or true; "This theory still holds" [syn: prevail, obtain] 23: take and maintain control over, often by violent means; "The dissatisfied students held the President's office for almost a week" 24: protect against a challenge or attack: "Hold that position behind the trees!" "Hold the bridge against the enemy's attacks" [syn: defend, guard] 25: declare to be; "She was declared incompetent"; " judge held that the defendant was innocent" [syn: declare, adjudge] 26: have as a major characteristic; "The novel holds many surprises"; "The book holds in store much valuable advise" 27: cause to stop; "Halt the engines"; "Arrest the progress"; "halt the presses" [syn: halt, arrest] 28: bind by an obligation; cause to be indebted; "He's held by a contract' "I'll hold you by your promise" [syn: oblige, bind] 29: cover as for protection against noise or smell; "She held her ears when the jackhammer started to operate"; "hold one's nose" 30: drink alcohol without showing ill effects; "He can hold his liquor"; "he had drunk more than he could carry" [syn: carry] 31: be pertinent or relevant or applicable; "The same laws apply to you!" "This theory holds for all irrational numbers"; "The same rules go for everyone" [syn: apply, go for] 32: arrange for and reserve in advance; "reserve a seat on a flight"; "We booked tickets to the show"; "please hold a table at Maxim's" [syn: reserve, book] 33: resist or confront with resistance; "The politician defied public opinion"; "The new material withstands even the greatest wear and tear"; "The bridge held" [syn: defy, withstand, hold up] 34: keep from departing; "Hold the taxi"; "Hold the horse" 35: stop dealing with; "hold all calls to the President's office while he is in a meeting" 36: aim, point, or direct: "Hold the fire extinguisher directly on the flames" 37: be in accord; be in agreement; "We agreed on the terms of the settlement"; "I can't agree with you!"; "I hold with those you say life is sacred"; "Both philosophers concord on this point" [syn: agree, concur, concord] [ant: disagree]

holed

v : (past of hole) "They holed a new tunnel in the mountain." [syn: made a hole]

hole, whole /houl/
hole

n 1: an opening into or through something 2: an opening deliberately made in or through something 3: one playing period (from tee to green) on a golf course; "he played 18 holes [syn: golf hole] 4: an unoccupied space 5: a depression hollowed out of solid matter [syn: hollow] 6: a fault; "he shot holes in my argument" 7: informal terms for a difficult situation; "his decision got the company into a hole"; "he made a muddle of his marriage" [syn: fix, jam, mess, muddle, pickle, kettle of fish] 8: informal terms for the mouth [syn: trap, maw, yap, gob]

v 1: in golf: hit the ball into the hole [syn: hole out] 2: make holes in

whole

adj 1: including all components without exception; being one unit or constituting the full amount or extent or duration; complete; "gave his whole attention"; "a whole wardrobe for the tropics"; "the whole hog"; "a whole week"; "the baby cried the whole trip home"; "a whole loaf of bread" [ant: fractional] 2: (of siblings) having the same parents; "whole brothers and sisters" [ant: half] 3: exhibiting or restored to vigorous good health; "hale and hearty"; "whole in mind and body"; "a whole person again" [syn: hale]

n 1: all of something including all its component elements or parts; "Europe as a whole"; "the whole of American literature" 2: an assemblage of parts that is regarded as a single entity; "how big is that part compared to the whole?"; "the repairman simply replaced the unit" [syn: whole thing, unit]

adv : to a complete degree or to the full or entire extent; "he was wholly convinced"; "entirely satisfied with the meal"; "it was completely different from what we expected"; "was completely at fault"; "a totally new situation"; "the directions were all wrong"; "It was not altogether her fault"; "an altogether new approach"; ('whole' is often used informally for `wholly' as in "a whole new idea") [syn: wholly, entirely, completely, totally, all, altogether] [ant: partly]

holey, holy, wholly /'houli/
holey

adj : being full of holes; allowing passage in and out; "our unfenced and largely unpoliced border inevitably has been very porous" [syn: porous]

holy

adj : belonging to or derived from or associated with a divine power [ant: unholy]

n : a sacred place of pilgrimage [syn: holy place, sanctum]

wholly

adv : to a complete degree or to the full or entire extent; "he was wholly convinced";

"entirely satisfied with the meal"; "it was completely different from what we expected"; "was completely at fault"; "a totally new situation"; "the directions were all wrong"; "It was not altogether her fault"; "an altogether new approach"; ('whole' is often used informally for `wholly' as in "a whole new idea") [syn: entirely, completely, totally, all, altogether] [ant: partly]

holm, home /houm/
holm

n : (British) an island in a river

home

adj 1: (sport) used of your own ground; "a home game" [ant: away] 2: relating to or being where one lives or where one's roots are; "my home town" 3: having controlling authority; where important decisions are made; "home base"; "home office" 4: relating to or taking place in a home or house or household; "home cooking"; "home furnishings"; "home care for the elderly" 5: inside the country; "the British Home Office has broader responsibilities than the United States Department of the Interior" "the nation's internal politics" [syn: interior, internal, national]

n 1: where you live; "deliver the package to my home"; "he doesn't have a home to go to"; "your place or mine?" [syn: place] 2: housing that someone is living in; "he built a modest dwelling near the pond"; "they raise money to provide homes for the homeless" [syn: dwelling, domicile, abode, habitation, dwelling house] 3: the country or state or city where you live; "Canadian tariffs enabled United States lumber companies to raise prices at home"; "his home is New Jersey" 4: an environment offering affection and security; "home is where the heart is"; "he grew up in a good Christian home"; "there's no place like home" 5: an institution where people are cared for; "a home for the elderly" [syn: nursing home, rest home] 6: the place where you are stationed and from which missions start and end [syn: base] 7: a social unit living together; "he moved his family to Virginia"; "It was a good Christian household"; "I waited until the whole house was asleep"; "the teacher asked how many people made up his home" [syn: family, household, house, ménage] 8: (baseball) base consisting of a rubber slab where the batter stands; it must be touched by a base runner in order to score; "he ruled that the runner failed to touch home" [syn: home plate, plate] 9: place where something began and flourished; "the United States is the home of basketball"

adv 1: at or to or in the direction of one's

HOMOPHONES

home or family; "He stays home on weekends"; "after the game the children brought friends home for supper"; "I'll be home tomorrow"; "came riding home in style"; "I hope you will come home for Christmas"; "I'll take her home"; "don't forget to write home" 2: on or to the point aimed at; "the arrow struck home" 3: to the fullest extent; to the heart; "drove the nail home"; "drove his point home"; "his comments hit home"

v 1: provide with, or send to, a home 2: return home accurately from a long distance, as of some birds; "homing pigeons"

hoop, whoop /hup/

hoop

n 1: a light curved skeleton to spread out a skirt 2: a rigid circular band of metal or wood or other material used for holding or fastening or hanging or pulling; "there was still a rusty iron hoop for tying a horse" [syn: ring] 3: a small arch used as croquet equipment [syn: wicket] 4: horizontal hoop with a net through which players try to throw the basketball [syn: basket, basketball hoop]

v : bind or fasten with a hoop; "hoop vats"

whoop

n : a loud hooting cry of exultation or excitement

v 1: shout, as if with joy or enthusiasm; "The children whooped when they were led to the picnic table" 2: cough spasmodically; "The patient with emphysema is hacking all day" [syn: hack]

horsed, horst /hɔɹst/

horsed

adj : provided with a horse

v : (past of horse) : played or handled roughly; "The boys horsed around."

horst

n : a ridge of the earth's crust that has been forced upward between two faults and so is higher than the surrounding land

hostel, hostile /'hɑstəl/

hostel

n 1: a hotel providing overnight lodging for travelers [syn: hostelry, inn, lodge] 2: inexpensive supervised lodging (especially for youths on bicycling trips) [syn: youth hostel, student lodging]

hostile

adj 1: characterized by enmity or ill will; "a hostile nation"; "a hostile remark"; "hostile actions" [ant: amicable] 2: not belonging to your own country's forces or those of an ally; "hostile naval and air forces" [ant: friendly] 3: very unfriendly; "a hostile attitude" 4: impossible to bring into friendly accord; "hostile factions" 5: very unfavorable to life or growth; "a hostile climate"; "an uncongenial atmosphere";

"an uncongenial soil"; "the unfriendly environment at high altitudes" [syn: uncongenial, unfriendly] 6: marked by features that oppose constructive treatment or development; "not able to accomplish much in such a hostile environment" 7: (business) used of attempts to buy or take control of a business; "hostile takeover"; "hostile tender offer"

hour, our /auɹ/

hour

n 1: a period of time equal to 1/24th of a day; "the job will take more than an hour" [syn: hr, 60 minutes] 2: clock time; "the hour is getting late" [syn: time of day] 3: a special and memorable period; "it was their finest hour" 4: distance measured by the time taken to cover it; "we live an hour from the airport"

our

pron (1st pers plu): having possession by more than one person; "Come visit our new house."

house, how's /hauz/

house

v 1: contain or cover; "Where will we house all these people?" 2: provide housing for [syn: put up]

how's

contr : how is; "How's the project coming along?"

humerus, humorous /'hjuəməɹəs/

humerus

n : bone extending from the shoulder to the elbow

humorous

adj : full of or characterized by humor; "humorous stories"; "humorous cartoons"; "in a humorous vein" [syn: funny] [ant: humorless]

hurdle, hurtle

hurdle /'həɹdəl/

n 1: a light movable barrier that competitors must leap over in certain races 2: an obstacle that you are expected to overcome; "the last hurdle before graduation" 3: the act of vaulting [syn: vault]

v : jump a hurdle

hurtle /'həɹtəl/

v 1: move with or as if with a rushing sound; "The cars hurtled by" 2: make a thrusting forward movement [syn: lunge, hurl, thrust] 3: throw forcefully [syn: hurl, cast]

HOMOPHONES

-I-

I (see aye)
I'd (see eyed)
idle, idol, idyll /'aɪdªl/
idle
adj 1: not in action or at work; "an idle laborer"; "idle drifters"; "the idle rich"; "an idle mind" [ant: busy] 2: without a basis in reason or fact; "baseless gossip"; "the allegations proved groundless"; "idle talk"; "unfounded suspicions"; "unwarranted jealousy" [syn: baseless, groundless, unfounded, unwarranted] 3: not in active use; "the machinery sat idle during the strike"; "idle hands" [syn: unused] 4: silly or trivial; "idle pleasure"; "light banter"; "light idle chatter" [syn: light] 5: lacking a sense of restraint or responsibility; "idle tongue"; "a loose tongue" [syn: loose] 6: not yielding a return; "dead capital"; "idle funds" [syn: dead] 7: not having a job; "idle carpenters"; "jobless transients"; "many people in the area were out of work" [syn: jobless, out of work]
v 1: run disconnected or idle; "the engine is idling" [ant: run] 2: be idle; exist in a changeless situation; "The old man sat and stagnated on his porch"; "He slugged in bed all morning" [syn: laze, slug, stagnate] [ant: work]
idol
n 1: a material effigy that is worshipped as a god; "thou shalt not make unto thee any graven image"; "money was his god" [syn: graven image, god] 2: someone who is adored blindly and excessively [syn: matinee idol] 3: an ideal instance; a perfect embodiment of a concept [syn: paragon, perfection, beau ideal]
idyll
n 1: an episode of such pastoral or romantic charm as to qualify as the subject of a poetic idyll [syn: idyl] 2: a musical composition that evokes rural life [syn: pastoral] 3: a short descriptive poem of rural or pastoral life [syn: eclogue, bucolic]
I'll (see aisle)
illation (see elation)
illuminance, illuminants /ɪ'lumɪnɪnts/
illuminance
n : the luminous flux incident on a unit area [syn: illumination]
illuminants
n : things that can serve as light sources
illusive (see elusive)
immanent (see eminent)
immerge (see emerge)
imminent (see eminent)
ileum, ilium /'ɪliªm/

ileum
n : the part of the small intestine between the jejunum and the cecum
ilium
n : the upper and widest of the three bones making up the hipbone
impassable, impassible /ɪm'pæsɪbªl/
impassable
adj : impossible to pass [syn: unpassable] [ant: passable]
impassible
adj : 1: Incapable of suffering; inaccessible to harm or pain 2: not to be touched or moved to passion or sympathy 3 unfeeling, or not showing feeling 4: without sensation. [syn: impassive]
impatience, impatiens
impatience /ɪm'peɪʃnts/
n 1: a lack of patience; irritation with anything that causes delay [syn: restlessness] 2: a restless desire for change and excitement 3: a dislike of anything that causes delay [ant: patience]
impatiens /ɪm'peɪʃªnz/
n : a type of flowering plant [syn: touch-me-not, jewelweed, snapweed, I. Balsamina, lady's slipper, common garden balsam]
in, inn /ɪn/
in
adj 1: not out; "it's ten o'clock and the children are in"; "the tide is in" [ant: out] 2: inside e.g. an organization; used as a combining form; "an in-house editor"; "in-home nursing programs" 3: holding office; "the in party" 4: directed or bound inward; "took the in bus"; "the in basket" 5: (informal) "the in thing to do"; "large shoulder pads are in"
adv 1: to or toward the inside of; "come in"; "smash in the door" [syn: inwards, inward] 2: inside an enclosed space [ant: out]
inn
n : a hotel providing overnight lodging for travelers [syn: hostel, hostelry, lodge]
incidence, incidents /'ɪnsɪdɛnts/
incidence
n 1: the relative frequency of occurrence of something [syn: relative incidence] 2: the striking of a light beam on a surface; "he measured the angle of incidence of the reflected light"
incidents
n 1: (plu of incident) more than one single distinct event 2: public disturbances: "the police investigated several robbery incidents at the mall"
incite, insight
incite /ɪn'saɪt/
v 1: give an incentive; "This moved me

to sacrifice my career" [syn: motivate, propel, move, prompt] 2: provoke or stir up; "incite a riot"; "set off great unrest among the people" [syn: instigate, set off, stir up] 3: urge on; cause to act [syn: prod, egg on]

insight /'ɪnsaɪt/
n 1: clear or deep perception of a situation [syn: penetration] 2: a feeling of understanding [syn: perceptiveness, perceptivity] 3: the clear (and often sudden) understanding of a complex situation [syn: brainstorm, brainwave] 4: grasping the inner nature of things intuitively [syn: sixth sense]

incompetence, incompetents /ɪn'kɑmpɪtɛnts/
incompetence
n 1: lack of physical or intellectual ability or qualifications [syn: incompetency] [ant: competence] 2: inability of a part or organ to function properly
incompetents
n : persons who are not competent to take effective action [syn: incompetent persons]

independence, independents /ɪndɪ'pɛndənts/
independence
n 1: freedom from control or influence of another or others [syn: independency] 2: the successful ending of the American Revolution; "they maintained close relations with England even after independence"
independents
n : (plu of independent)1: neutral or uncommitted persons (especially in politics) 2: writers or artists who sell services to different employers without a long-term contract with any of them [syn: freelancers, self-employed persons]

indict, indite /ɪn'daɪt/
indict
v : accuse formally of a crime
indite
v : produce a literary work; He likes to indite short stories." "She composed a poem."; "He wrote four novels" [syn: write, compose, pen]

indicter, inditer /ɪn'daɪtəʳ/
indicter
n: a person who indicts (see indict)
inditer
n : a person who indites (see indite)

indigence, indigents /'ɪndɪdʒɪnts/
indigence
n : a state of extreme poverty or destitution; "their indigence appalled him"; "a general state of need exists among the homeless" [syn: need, penury, beggary, pauperism]

indigents
n : (plu of indigent) : persons suffering from indigence [syn: beggars, paupers]

indiscreet, indiscrete /'ɪndɪskiɪt/
indiscreet
adj : lacking discretion; injudicious; "her behavior was indiscreet at the very best" [ant: discreet]
indiscrete
adj : not divided or divisible into parts; "layers that were fused into an indiscrete mass"

influence, influents /'ɪnfluɛnts/
influence
n 1: a power to affect persons or events especially power based on prestige etc; "used her parents' influence to get the job" 2: causing something without any direct or apparent effort 3: a cognitive factor that tends to have an effect on what you do; "her wishes had a great influence on his thinking" 4: the effect of one thing (or person) on another; "the influence of mechanical action" 5: one having power to influence another; "she was the most important influence in my life"; "he was a bad influence on the children"
v 1: have and exert influence or effect; "The artist's work influenced the young painter"; "She worked on her friends to support the political candidate" [syn: act upon, work] 2: shape or influence; give direction to; "experience often determines ability"; "mold public opinion" [syn: determine, shape, mold, regulate] 3: induce into action by using one's charm; "She charmed him into giving her all his money" [syn: charm, tempt]
influents
1 : inflows such as a tributary or stream 2: fluid inputs to a reservoir or process 3: factors such as particular animals that modify the balance and stability of an ecological community

inequity, iniquity /ɪn'ɛkwɪti/
inequity
n 1: partiality that is not fair or equitable [syn: unfairness] [ant: fairness] 2: injustice by virtue of not being equitable [syn: unfairness] [ant: fairness, fairness]
iniquity /ɪn'ɪkwɪti/
n 1: absence of moral or spiritual values; "Their deed shall forever live in iniquity."" [syn: wickedness, darkness, dark] 2: morally objectionable behavior [syn: evil, immorality, wickedness] 3: an unjust act [syn: injustice, unfairness]

innocence, innocents /'ɪnəsɪnts/
innocence
n 1: the quality of innocent naiveté [syn: artlessness, ingenuousness, naturalness]

2: the state of being free from sin or moral wrong; lacking a knowledge of evil [syn: purity, sinlessness] 3: a state or condition of being innocent of a specific crime or offense; "the trial established his innocence" [ant: guilt]

innocents

n : (plu of innocent) : people who lacks knowledge of evil "Children are the innocents of war." [syn: inexperienced person]

insolate, insulate

insolate /'ɪnsoʊleɪt/

v : expose to the rays of the sun or affect by exposure to the sun; "insolating paper may turn it yellow and cause it to crumble"; "These herbs suffer when sunned" [syn: sun, solarize]

insulate /'ɪnsʌleɪt/

v 1: protect from heat, cold, noise, etc. by surrounding with insulating material; "We had his bedroom insulated before winter came" 2: place or set apart; "They isolated the political prisoners from the other inmates" [syn: isolate]

instance, instants /'ɪnstɪnts/

instance

n 1: an occurrence of something; "it was a case of bad judgment"; "another instance occurred yesterday"; "but there is always the famous example of the Smiths" [syn: case, example] 2: a single item of information that is representative of a type; "this patient provides a typical example of the syndrome"; "there is a good example on page 10" [syn: example, illustration, representative]

v : clarify by giving an example of [syn: exemplify, illustrate]

instants

n : (plu of instant): a particular point in time; "There were several instants when he fell asleep during the job." [syn: moments, times]

insure (see ensure)

intense, intents /ɪn'tɛnts/

intense

adj 1: in an extreme degree; "intense heat"; "intense anxiety,"; "intense desire"; "intense emotion"; "the skunk's intense acrid odor"; "intense pain"; "enemy fire was intense" [ant: mild] 2: extremely sharp or intense; "acute pain"; "felt acute annoyance"; "intense itching and burning" [syn: acute] 3: (of color) having the highest saturation; "vivid green"; "intense blue" [syn: vivid]

intents

n : (plu of intent) : anticipated outcomes that are intended or that guide your planned actions; "his intents were to provide a new translation and a new format"; "good intentions are not enough";

"they were created with the conscious aims of answering immediate needs"; "he made no secret of his designs" [syn: purposes, intentions, aims, designs]

intension, intention / ɪn'tɛnʃɪn/

intension

n 1: what you must know in order to determine the reference of an expression [syn: connotation] 2: state or quality of being intense; intensity 3: The state or quality of being intense; intensity. 4: The act of becoming intense or more intense; intensification. 5: (logic) the sum of the attributes contained in a term

intention

n 1: an anticipated outcome that is intended or that guides your planned actions; "his intent was to provide a new translation"; "good intentions are not enough"; "it was created with the conscious aim of answering immediate needs"; "he made no secret of his designs" [syn: purpose, intent, aim, design] 2: (usually plural) the goal with respect to a marriage proposal; "his intentions are entirely honorable" 3: an act of intending; a volition that you intend to carry out; "my intention changed once I saw her"

invade, inveighed /ɪn'veɪd/

invade

v 1: march aggressively into another's territory by military force for the purposes of conquest and occupation; "Hitler invaded Poland on September 1, 1939" [syn: occupy] 2: to intrude upon, infringe, encroach on, violate; This new colleague invades my territory"; "The neighbors intrude on your privacy" [syn: intrude on, obtrude upon, encroach upon] 3: occupy in large numbers or live on a host; "cockroaches invaded my kitchen"; "Ants overran the picnic table"; "the Kudzu plant infests much of the South" [syn: overrun, infest] 4: penetrate or assault, in a harmful or injurious way; "The cancer had invaded her lungs"

inveighed

v : (past of inveigh) : complained bitterly; gave vent to angry disapproval; protested vehemently [syn: railed]

irrupt (see erupt)

irruption (see eruption)

isle (see aisle)

islet (see eyelet)

its, it's /ɪts/

its

pron (3rd pers sing): having possession by a single entity (not a person); "The house needs its outside painted."; "The cat ate all its food."

it's

contr : it is

HOMOPHONES

-J-

J, jay /dʒeɪ/
J
n: the 10th letter of the Roman alphabet [syn: j]
jay
ŋ: crested largely blue bird

jalousie, jealousy
jalousie /'dʒæləsi/
n 1: a window with glass louvers [syn: louvered window] 2: a shutter made of angled slats
jealousy /'dʒɛləsi/
n 1: a feeling of jealous envy (especially of a rival) [syn: green-eyed monster] 2: zealous vigilance: "cherish their official political freedom with fierce jealousy"

jam, jamb /dʒæm/
jam
n 1: preserve of crushed fruit 2: informal terms for a difficult situation; "he got into a terrible jam"; "he made a muddle of his marriage" [syn: fix, hole, mess, muddle, pickle, kettle of fish] 3: a dense crowd of people [syn: crush, press] 4: deliberate radiation or reflection of electromagnetic energy for the purpose of disrupting enemy use of electronic devices or systems [syn: jamming, electronic jamming]
v 1: press tightly together or cram; "The crowd packed the auditorium" [syn: throng, mob, pack, pile] 2: push forcibly, as of brakes: "The driver jammed the brake pedal to the floor" 3: crush or bruise; "jam a toe" [syn: crush] 4: interfere with or prevent the reception of signals; "Jam the Voice of America"; "block the signals emitted by this station" [syn: block] 5: get stuck and immobilized; "the mechanism jammed" 6: crowd or pack to capacity; "the theater was jam-packed" [syn: jam pack, ram, chock up, cram, wad, pack] 7: block passage through; "obstruct the path" [syn: obstruct, impede, occlude, block, close up] [ant: free] 8: eat until one is sated; "He filled up on turkey" [syn: fill up, fill, stuff, cram]
jamb
n : upright consisting of a vertical side member of a door or window frame

jean (see gene)
jell (see gel)
jennet (see genet)
jewel, joule /dʒul/
jewel (also /'dʒuɛl/)
n 1: a precious or semiprecious stone incorporated into a piece of jewelry [syn: gem, precious stone] 2: a person who possesses extraordinarily desirable characteristics [syn: gem]
v : adorn or decorate with precious stones; "jeweled dresses" [syn: bejewel]
joule
n 1: a unit of electrical energy equal to the work done when a current of one ampere passes through a resistance of one ohm for one second [syn: J, watt second]

Jewry, jury /'dʒuɹi/
Jewry
n : Jews collectively
jury
n 1: a body of citizens sworn to give a true verdict according to the evidence presented in a court of law 2: a committee appointed to judge a competition [syn: panel]

jinks, jinx /dʒɪnks/
jinks
n : noisy and mischievous merrymaking [syn: high jinks]
jinx
n 1: a person believed to bring bad luck to those around him [syn: jonah] 2: an evil spell; "a witch put a curse on his whole family" [syn: hex, curse]
v 1: cast a spell over someone or something; put a hex on someone or something [syn: hex, bewitch, glamour, witch, enchant] 2: foredoom to failure; "This project is jinxed!"

HOMOPHONES

-K-

kain (see cain)
kernal (see colonel)
ketch (see ketch)
key (see cay)
kill, kiln /kɪl/
kill

n 1: the act of terminating a life [syn: killing, putting to death] 2: the destruction of an enemy plane or ship or tank or missile; "the pilot reported two kills during the mission"

v 1: cause to die; put to death, usually intentionally or knowingly; "This man killed several people when he tried to rob a bank"; "The farmer killed a pig for the holidays"; "kill a motion" [syn: defeat, vote down, vote out] 3: cause the death of, without intention; "She was killed in the collision of three cars" 4: end or extinguish by forceful means; "Stamp out poverty!" [syn: stamp out] 5: be fatal; "cigarettes kill"; "drunken driving kills" 6: be the source of great pain for; "These new shoes are killing me!" 7: overwhelm with hilarity, pleasure, or admiration; "The comedian was so funny, he was killing me!" 8: hit with so much force as to make a return impossible, in racket games; "She killed the ball" 9: hit with great force, in sports; "He killed the ball" 10: deprive of life; "AIDS has killed thousands in Africa" 11: drink down entirely; "He downed three martinis before dinner"; "She killed a bottle of brandy that night" [syn: toss off, bolt down, belt down, pour down, down, drink down] 12: mark for deletion, rub off, or erase, as of writings; "kill these lines in the President's speech" [syn: obliterate, wipe out] 13: tire out completely; "The daily stress of her work is killing her" 14: cause to cease operating; "kill the engine" 15: destroy a vitally essential quality of or in; "Eating artichokes kills the taste of all other foods"

kiln (also /kɪlnʒ/)

n : a large oven for firing or burning or drying such things as porcelain or bricks

klick (see click)
knap, nap /næp/
knap

n : crest of a hill

v 1: strike sharply; "rap him on the knuckles" [syn: rap] 2: break a small piece off from; "chip the glass"; "chip a tooth" [syn: chip, cut off, break off]

nap

n 1: a period of time spent sleeping; "he felt better after a little sleep"; "a brief nap" [syn: sleep] 2: a soft or fuzzy surface

texture 3: a short sleep (usually not in bed) [syn: catnap, cat sleep, forty winks, short sleep, snooze]

v : take a siesta; "She naps everyday after lunch for an hour" [syn: catnap, catch a wink]

knave, nave /neɪv/
knave

n 1: a deceitful and unreliable scoundrel [syn: rogue, rascal, rapscallion, scalawag, scallywag, varlet] 2: one of four face cards in a deck bearing a picture of a young prince [syn: jack]

nave

n : the central area of a church

knead, kneed, need /nid/
knead

v 1: make uniform; "knead dough"; "work the clay until it is soft" [syn: work] 2: usually for medicinal or relaxation purposes [syn: massage, rub down]

kneed

v: (past of knee) : strike with the knee "She kneed her attacker in the groin."

need

n 1: a condition requiring relief; "she satisfied his need for affection"; "God has no need of men to accomplish His work"; "there is a demand for jobs" [syn: demand] 2: anything that is necessary but lacking; "he had sufficient means to meet his simple needs"; "I tried to supply his wants" [syn: want] 3: the psychological feature that arouses an organism to action; the reason for the action; "we did not understand his motivation"; "he acted with the best of motives" [syn: motivation, motive] 4: a state of extreme poverty or destitution; "their indigence appalled him"; "a general state of need exists among the homeless" [syn: indigence, penury, beggary, pauperism]

v 1: require as useful, just, or proper; "It takes nerve to do what she did"; "success usually requires hard work"; "This job asks a lot of patience and skill"; "This position demands a lot of personal sacrifice"; "This dinner needs a spectacular dessert" [syn: necessitate, ask, require, take, involve, call for, demand] 2: have need of: "This piano will need the attention of a competent tuner" [syn: want, require] 3: be obliged, required, or forced to; "She needs to get her driver's license" [syn: must, have, have got] 4: be in want of 5: be logically necessary [syn: should, ought, must] 6: have or feel a need for: "always needing friends and money"

knew (see gnu)
knickers, nickers /'nɪkˈɹz/
knickers

n 1: trousers ending above the knee [syn: breeches, knee breeches, knee pants,

HOMOPHONES

knickerbockers] 2: (usually in the plural) underpants worn by women; "she was afraid that her bloomers might have been showing" [syn: bloomers, pants, drawers]

nickers

n : (plu of nicker) : the sounds made by horses [syn: neighs, whickers, whinnies]

v : (3rd pers sing of nicker) : characteristic of horses [syn; neighs, whickers, whinnies]

knight, night /naɪt/

knight

n 1: originally a person of noble birth trained to arms and chivalry; today in Great Britain a person honored by the sovereign for personal merit 2: a chessman in the shape of a horse's head; can move two squares horizontally and one vertically (or vice versa) [syn: horse]

v 1: raise (someone) to knighthood; "The Beatles were knighted" 2: invest with knighthood; make knight of [syn: dub]

night

n 1: the time after sunset and before sunrise while it is dark outside [syn: nighttime, dark] [ant: day] 2: the time between sunset and midnight; "he watched television every night" 3: the period spent sleeping; "I had a restless night" 4: the dark part of the diurnal cycle considered a time unit; "three nights later he collapsed" 5: darkness; "it vanished into the night" 6: a shortening of nightfall; "they worked from morning to night" 7: a period of ignorance or backwardness or gloom

knit, nit /nɪt/

knit

n 1: a fabric made by knitting [syn: knitted fabric] 2: a basic knitting stitch [syn: knit stitch, plain, plain stitch] 3: needlework created by interlacing yarn in a series of connected loops using straight eyeless needles or by machine [syn: knitting]

v 1: make (textiles) by knitting; "knit a scarf" 2: tie or link together [syn: entwine] 3: to gather something into small wrinkles or folds; "She puckered her lips" [syn: pucker, rumple, cockle, crumple]

nit

n 1: a luminance unit equal to 1 candle per square meter measured perpendicular to the rays from the source 2: egg or young of an insect parasitic on mammals especially a sucking louse; often attached to a hair or item of clothing

knob, nob /nab/

knob

n 1: a rounded projection or protuberance 2: a round handle 3: any thickened enlargement [syn: node, thickening] 4: an ornament in the shape of a ball on the hilt of a sword or dagger [syn: pommel]

nob

n : an elegantly dressed man (often with affected manners)

knobble, nobble /'nabᵊl/

knobble

n : a small knob

nobble

v 1: deprive of by deceit; "He swindled me out of my inheritance"; "She defrauded the customers who trusted her"; "the cashier gypped me when he gave me too little change" [syn: swindle, rook, goldbrick, diddle, bunco, defraud, scam, mulct, gyp, con] 2: make off with belongings of others [syn: pilfer, cabbage, purloin, pinch, abstract, snarf, swipe, hook, sneak, filch, lift] 3: of people [syn: kidnap, abduct, snatch] 4: disable by drugging, as of a race horse

knock, nock /nak/

knock

n 1: the sound of knocking (as on a door or in an engine or bearing); "the knocking grew louder" [syn: knocking] 2: negative criticism [syn: roast] 3: a vigorous blow; "the sudden knock floored him"; "he took a bash right in his face"; "he got a bang on the head" [syn: bash, bang, smash, belt] 4: a bad experience; "the school of hard knocks" 5: the act of hitting vigorously; "he gave the table a whack" [syn: belt, rap, whack, whang]

v 1: deliver a sharp blow or push :"He knocked the glass clear across the room." [syn: strike hard] 2: rap with the knuckles; "knock on the door" 3: knock against with force or violence; "My car bumped into the tree" [syn: bump] 4: make light, repeated taps on a surface; "he was tapping his fingers on the table impatiently" [syn: tap, rap, pink] 5: of car engines, when firing too early [syn: ping]

nock

n : part of an arrow having a notch for the bowstring

v : make small marks into the surface of; "score the clay before firing it" [syn: score, mark]

knot, not /nat/

knot

n 1: a tight cluster of people or things; "a small knot of women listened to his sermon" 2: any of various fastenings formed by looping and tying a rope (or cord) upon itself or to another rope or to another object 3: a hard cross-grained round piece of wood in a board where a branch emerged; "the saw buckled when it hit a knot" 4: something twisted and tight and swollen; "their muscles stood out in knots"; "the old man's fists were two great gnarls"; "his stomach was in knots" [syn: gnarl] 5: a unit of length used in navigation; equivalent to the distance spanned by one minute of arc in latitude;

HOMOPHONES

1,852 meters [syn: nautical mile, mile, mi, naut mi, international nautical mile, air mile] 6: soft lump or unevenness in a yarn; either an imperfection or created by design [syn: slub, burl] 7: sandpiper that breeds in the arctic and winters in the S hemisphere [syn: grayback, Calidris canutus]

v 1: make into knots; make knots out of 2: tie or fasten into a knot 3: tangle or complicate; "a raveled story" [syn: ravel, tangle] [ant: unravel, unravel]

not
adv : negation of a word or group of words; "he does not speak French"; "she is not going"; "they are not friends"; "not many"; "not much"; "not at all"

know, no /noʊ/
know
v 1: be cognizant or aware of a fact or a specific piece of information; possess knowledge or information about; "I know that the President lied to the people"; "I want to know who is winning the game!"; "I know it's time" [syn: cognize] [ant: ignore] 2: know how to do or perform something; "She knows how to knit"; "Does your husband know how to cook?" 3: be aware of the truth of something; have a belief or faith in something; regard as true beyond any doubt; "I know that I left the key on the table"; "Galileo knew that the earth moves around the sun" 4: be familiar or acquainted with a person or an object; "She doesn't know this composer"; "Do you know my sister?" "We know this movie"; "I know him under a different name"; "This flower is known as a Peruvian Lily" 5: have firsthand knowledge of states, situations, emotions, or sensations; "I know the feeling!" "have you ever known hunger?"; "I have lived a kind of hell when I was a drug addict"; "The holocaust survivors have lived a nightmare"; "I lived through two divorces" [syn: experience, live] 6: discern; "His greed knew no limits" [syn: acknowledge, recognize] 7: have fixed in the mind; "I know Latin"; "This student knows her irregular verbs"; "Do you know the poem well enough to recite it?" 8: have sexual intercourse with; "This student sleeps with everyone in her dorm"; "Adam knew Eve" (know is archaic) [syn: sleep] 9: know the nature or character of; "we all knew her as a big show-off" 10: be able to distinguish. recognize as being different; "The child knows right from wrong" 11: perceive as familiar; "I know this voice!"

no
adj : quantifier; used with either mass nouns or plural count nouns for indicating a complete or almost complete lack or zero quantity of; "we have no bananas";

"no eggs left and no money to buy any"; "have you no decency?"; "did it with no help"; "I'll get you there in no time" [ant: all, some]

n 1: a negative; "his no was loud and clear" [ant: yes]

adv 1: referring to the degree to which a certain quality is present; "he was no heavier than a child" [syn: no more] 2: not in any degree or manner; not at all; "he is no better today" 3: used to express refusal or denial or disagreement etc or especially to emphasize a negative statement; "no, you are wrong"

knows, noes, nose /noʊz/
knows
v : (3rd pers sing of know) : "She knows how to play the violin."

noes
n : (plu of no) : "He answered the question with a bunch of noes." [syn: nos]

nose
n 1: the organ of smell and entrance to the respiratory tract; the prominent part of the face of man or other mammals; "he has a cold in the nose" [syn: olfactory organ] 2: a front that resembles a human nose (especially the front of an aircraft); "the nose of the rocket heated up on reentry" 3: the front or forward projection of a tool or weapon; "he ducked under the nose of the gun" 4: a small distance; "my horse lost the race by a nose" 5: the sense of smell (especially in animals); "the hound has a good nose" 6: a natural skill; "he has a nose for good deals" 7: a projecting spout from which a fluid is discharged [syn: nozzle]
v 1: search or inquire in a meddlesome way; "This guy is always nosing around the office" [syn: pry, poke] 2: advance the forward part of with caution; "She nosed the car into the left lane" 3: catch the scent of; get wind of; "The dog nosed out the drugs" [syn: scent, wind] 4: push or move with the nose 5: rub noses [syn: nuzzle] 6: defeat by a narrow margin

kohl (see coal)
kraft (see craft)
krewe (see crew)
krewes (see crews)

-L-

L (see el)

laager, lager, logger /'lagʰ.ɪ/

laager

n : (South African) a camp defended by a circular formation of wagons

lager

n : beer stored for aging

logger

n : a lumberman who cuts logs into lengths after the trees have been felled

label, labile /'lɛɪbʰl/

label

n 1 : a brief description given for purposes of identification; "the label Modern is applied to many different kinds of architecture" 2 : trade name of a company that produces musical recordings; "the artists and repertoire department of a recording label is responsible for finding new talent" [syn: recording label] 3 : a radioactive isotope that is used in a compound in order to trace the mechanism of a chemical reaction 4 : an identifying or descriptive marker that is attached to an object

v 1 : assign a label to; designate with a label; "These students were labeled `learning disabled'" 2 : attach a tag or label to; "label these bottles" [syn: tag, mark] 3 : pronounce judgment on; "They labeled him unfit to work here" [syn: pronounce, judge] 4 : distinguish (as a compound or molecule) by introducing a labeled atom 5 : distinguish (an element or atom) by using a radioactive isotope or an isotope of unusual mass for tracing through chemical reactions

labile (also /'lɛɪbaɪl/)

adj 1 : open to change; liable to change; "an emotionally labile person" 2 : (chemistry, physics, biology) readily undergoing change or breakdown

lac, lack /læk/

lac

n : resin like substance secreted by certain lac insects; used in e.g. varnishes and sealing wax

lack

n : the state of needing something that is absent or unavailable; "there is a serious lack of insight into the problem"; "water is the critical deficiency in desert regions"; "for want of a nail the shoe was lost" [syn: deficiency, want]

v 1 : be without; "You lack patience."; "There is something missing in my jewelry box!" [syn: miss] [ant: have] 2 : be without, lack; be deficient in; "want courtesy"; "want the strength to go on living"; "flood victims wanting food and shelter" [syn: want]

lacks, lax /læks/

lacks

v : (3rd pers sing for lack) : "This soup lacks salt." [syn: is missing, needs]

lax

adj 1 : lacking in rigor or strictness; "such lax and slipshod ways are no longer acceptable"; "lax in attending classes"; "slack in maintaining discipline" [syn: slack] 2 : (phonetics) pronounced with muscles relatively relaxed (e.g., the vowel sound in `bet') [ant: tense] 3 : not taut or rigid; not stretched or held tight; "a lax rope" [ant: tense] 4 : lacking in strength or firmness or resilience; "flaccid muscles"; "took his lax hand in hers"; "gave a limp handshake"; "a slack grip" [syn: flaccid, limp, slack] 5 : tolerant or lenient; "indulgent parents risk spoiling their children"; "procedures are lax and discipline is weak"; "too soft on the children" [syn: indulgent, lenient, soft] 6 : emptying easily or excessively; "loose bowels" [syn: loose]

ladder, latter /'lædʰ.ɪ/

ladder

n 1 : steps consisting of two parallel members connected by rungs; for climbing up or down 2 : a row of unraveled stitches; "she got a run in her stocking" [syn: run, ravel]

v : come unraveled or undone as if by snagging, of stockings; "Her nylons were running" [syn: run]

latter

adj 1 : referring to the second of two things or persons mentioned (or the last one or ones of several); "in the latter case" [ant: former] 2 : more advanced in time or nearer to the end in a sequence; "these latter days"; "the latter (or last) part of the book"; "latter (or later) part of the 18th century" [syn: later, last]

n : the second of two or the second mentioned of two; "Tom and Dick were both heroes but only the latter is remembered today" [ant: former]

lade, laid /lɛɪd/

lade

v 1 : remove with or as if with a ladle; of liquids [syn: ladle, laden] 2 : fill or load; "load a car" [syn: load, laden, load up]

laid

adj : set down according to a plan: "a carefully laid table with places set for four people"; "stones laid in a pattern" [syn: set]

v : (past of lie) "He laid the book on the table."

lai, lay, lea, lei, ley /lɛɪ/

lai

n : a medieval French narrative poem of

octosyllabic couplets on a romantic or adventurous theme

lay

adj 1: concerning those not members of the clergy; "set his collar in laic rather than clerical position"; "the lay ministry"; "the choir sings both sacred and secular music" [syn: laic, secular] 2: not of or from a profession; "a lay opinion as to the cause of the disease"

n 1: a narrative song with a recurrent refrain [syn: ballad] 2: a narrative poem of popular origin [syn: ballad]

v 1: put into a certain place or abstract location; "Put your things here"; "Set the tray down"; "Set the dogs on the scent of the missing children"; "Places emphasis on a certain point" [syn: put, set, place, pose, position] 2: put in a horizontal position; "lay the books on the table"; "lay the patient carefully onto the bed" [syn: put down, repose] 3: prepare or position for action or operation; "lay a fire"; "lay the foundation for a new health care plan" 4: lay eggs; of female animals; "This hen lays many eggs" 5: impose as a duty, burden, or punishment; "lay a responsibility on someone" 6: have sexual intercourse "He lays her three times a week."

lea (also /li/)

n : a field covered with grass or herbage and suitable for grazing by livestock [syn: pasture, pastureland, grazing land, lea]

lei

n : flower arrangement consisting of a circular band of foliage or flowers for ornamental purposes (esp. popular in Hawaii) [syn: wreath, garland, coronal, chaplet]

ley

n : a field covered with grass or herbage and suitable for grazing by livestock [syn: pasture, pastureland, grazing land, lea]

lain, lane /leɪn/

lain

v : (past part of lie) : "He had lain in bed all day."

lane

n 1: a narrow way or road 2: a well-defined track or path; for e.g. swimmers or lines of traffic

lair, layer /lɛəɹ/

lair

n : the habitation of wild animals [syn: den]

layer (also /'lɛɪjɚɹ/)

n 1: single thickness of usually some homogeneous substance 2: a relatively thin sheet-like expanse or region lying over or under another 3: a hen that lays eggs 4: thin structure composed of a single thickness of cells

v : make or form a layer; "layer the

different colored sands"

lam, lamb /læm/

lam

n : a rapid escape (as by criminals); "the thieves made a clean getaway"; "after the expose he had to take it on the lam" [syn: getaway]

v 1: escape or flee; take to one's heels; cut and run; "If you see this man, run!" [syn: run, scarper, turn tail, run away, bunk, break away] 2: give a thrashing to; beat hard [syn: thrash, thresh, flail]

lamb

n 1: young sheep 2: a person easily deceived or cheated (especially in financial matters) 3: a sweet innocent mild-mannered person (especially a child) [syn: dear] 4: the flesh of a young domestic sheep eaten as food

v : give birth to a lamb, of ewes

lama, llama /'lamə/

lama

n : a Tibetan or Mongolian priest of Lamaism

llama

n : wild or domesticated South American cud-chewing animal related to camels but smaller and lacking a hump

laps, lapse /læps/

laps

n : (plu of lap) 1: the upper side of the thighs of a seated person 2: an area of control or responsibility; "the job fell right in their laps" 3: flaps that lie over another part [syn: overlaps] 4: movement once around a course; "he drove several extra laps just for insurance" [syn: circles, circuits] 5: touching with the tongue [syn: licks]

v : (3rd pers sing) 1: lies partly over or alongside of something or of one another 2: passes the tongue over [syn: licks] 3: move with or make or cause to move with or make a whistling or hissing sound, as of liquids [syn: swishes] 4: takes up with the tongue; "The cat laps up the milk" [syn: laps up]

lapse

n 1: a mistake resulting from inattention [syn: oversight] 2: a break or intermission in the occurrence of something; "a lapse of three weeks between letters" 3: a failure to maintain a higher state [syn: backsliding, lapsing, relapse, relapsing, reversion, reverting]

v 1: pass into a specified state or condition; "He sank into Nirvana" [syn: sink, pass] 2: end, at least for a long time; "The correspondence lapsed" 3: drop to a lower level, as in one's morals or standards [syn: backslide] 4: go back to bad behavior; "Those who recidivate are often minor criminals" [syn: relapse, recidivate, regress, retrogress, fall back] 5: let slip; "He lapsed his membership" 6: pass by; "three years elapsed" [syn: elapse, pass, slip by, glide by, slip away, go by, slide by, go along]

lais, lase, lays, laze, leas, leis, leys
/leɪz/

lais
n : (plu of lai) (see lay)

lase
v : to print a given document via a laser printer. "OK, let's lase that sucker and see if all those graphics-macro calls did the right things."

lays
n : (plu of lay) (see lay)
v : (3rd pers sing of lay) (see lay)

laze
v : be idle; exist in a changeless situation; "The old man sat and stagnated on his porch"; "He lazed in bed all morning" [syn: idle, slug, stagnate] [ant: work]

leas (plu of lea) (see lea)

leis
n : (plu of lei) (see lei)

leys
n : (plu of ley) (see ley)

laser, lazar /ˈleɪzəɹ/

laser
n : (Light Amplification by Stimulated Emission of Radiation) optical device that produces an intense monochromatic beam of coherent light [syn: optical maser]

lazar
n : a person afflicted with leprosy [syn: leper]

lea, lee, li /li/

lea (also /leɪ/)
n 1: a unit of length of thread or yarn 2: (alt ley) (see ley)

lee
adj : towards the side away from the wind [syn: downwind]
n: the side of something that is sheltered from the wind [syn: lee side, leeward]

li
adj : being one more than fifty [syn: fifty-one, 51, LI]
n 1: a soft silver-white univalent element of the alkali metal group; the lightest metal known; occurs in several minerals [syn: Li, lithium, atomic number 3] 2: Chinese distance measure; approximately 0.5 kilometers

leach, leech /litʃ/

leach
n : the process of leaching [syn: leaching]
v 1: cause (a liquid) to leach or percolate 2: permeate; penetrate gradually; of liquids [syn: percolate] 3: remove substances from by a percolating liquid; "leach the soil" [syn: strip]

leech
n 1: carnivorous or bloodsucking aquatic or terrestrial worms typically having a sucker at each end [syn: bloodsucker, hirudinean] 2: a follower who hangs around a host (without benefit to the host) in hope of gain or advantage [syn: parasite, sponge, sponger]
v : draw blood; "In the old days, doctors routinely bled patients as part of the treatment" [syn: bleed, phlebotomize]

lead, led /lɛd/

lead
n 1: a soft heavy toxic malleable metallic element; bluish white when freshly cut but tarnishes readily to dull gray; "the children were playing with lead soldiers" [syn: Pb, atomic number 82]

led
adj : having leadership guidance
v : (past of lead) showed the way "The usher led them to their seats."

leader, lieder, liter /ˈlidɚ?/ɹ/

leader
n 1: a person who rules or guides or inspires others [ant: follower] 2: a featured article of merchandise sold at a loss in order to draw customers [syn: drawing card, loss leader]

lieder
n : German songs

liter (also ˈliː tr)
n : a metric unit of capacity equal to the volume of 1 kilogram of pure water at 4 degrees centigrade and 760 mm of mercury (or approximately 1.76 pints) [syn: l, cubic decimeter]

leaf, lief /lif/

leaf
n 1: the main organ of photosynthesis and transpiration in higher plants [syn: leafage, foliage] 2: a sheet of any written or printed material (especially in a manuscript or book) [syn: folio] 3: hinged or detachable flat section (as of a table or door)
v 1: look through a book or other written material; "He thumbed through the report"; "She leafed through the volume" [syn: flick, flip, thumb, riffle, riff] 2: turn over the pages of; "leaf a book" 3: turn over pages; "leaf through a book" 4: produce leaves, of plants

lief
adj : (archaic) very willing; "was lief to go"; "glad to help" [syn: glad]
adv : in a willing manner; "this was gladly agreed to"; "I would lief do it" [syn: gladly, fain]

leak, leek /lik/

leak
n 1: an accidental hole that allows something (fluid or light etc.) to enter or escape; "one of the tires developed a leak"

2: soft watery rot in fruits and vegetables caused by fungi 3: a euphemism for urination; "he had to take a leak" [syn: wetting, making water, passing water] 4: the unwanted discharge of a fluid from some container; "they tried to stop the escape of gas from the damaged pipe"; "he had to clean up the leak" [syn: escape, leakage, outflow] 5: unauthorized (especially deliberate) disclosure of confidential information

v 1: tell anonymously; "The news were leaked to the paper" 2: be leaked; "The news leaked out despite his secrecy" [syn: leak out] 3: enter or escape as through a hole or crack or fissure; "Water leaked out of the can into the backpack" 4: have an opening that allows light or substances to enter or go out; "The container leaks"

leek

n 1: plant having a large slender white bulb and flat overlapping dark green leaves; used in cooking[syn: scallion] 2: related to onions; white cylindrical bulb and flat dark-green leaves

lean, lien /lin/

lean

adj 1: lacking excess flesh; "you can't be too rich or too thin"; "Yon Cassius has a lean and hungry look"-Shakespeare [syn: thin] [ant: fat] 2: lacking in mineral content or combustible material; "lean ore"; "lean fuel" [ant: rich] 3: containing little excess; "a lean budget"; "a skimpy allowance" [syn: skimpy] 4: (metallurgy) low in mineral content; "a lean ore" 5: not profitable or prosperous; "a lean year"

n : the property possessed by a line or surface that departs from the vertical; "the tower had a pronounced tilt"; "the ship developed a list to starboard"; "he walked with a heavy inclination to the right" [syn: tilt, list, inclination, leaning]

v 1: to incline or bend from a vertical position; "She leaned over the banister" [syn: tilt, tip, slant, angle] 2: cause to lean or incline; "He leaned his rifle against the wall" 3: have a tendency or disposition to do or be something; be inclined; "She tends to be nervous before her lectures"; "These dresses run small"; "He inclined to corpulence" [syn: tend, be given, incline, run] 4: rely on for support; "We can lean on this man"

lien

n 1: the right to take another's property if an obligation is not discharged 2: a large dark-red oval organ on the left side of the body between the stomach and the diaphragm; produces cells involved in immune responses [syn: spleen]

lear, leer, lehr /liʌ/

lear

n : (Scottish and north England) learning; instruction

leer

n 1: a facial expression of contempt or scorn; the upper lip curls [syn: sneer] 2: a suggestive or sneering look or grin

v : look suggestively or obliquely; look or gaze with a sly, immodest, or malign expression; "The men leered at the young women on the beach"

lehr

n : an annealing oven

leased, least /list/

leased

adj : hired for exclusive temporary use; "a chartered plane"; "the chartered buses arrived on time" [syn: chartered, hired] [ant: unchartered]

v : (past of lease) "They leased the house for a month."

least

adj 1: (superlative of 'little' used with mass nouns; usually preceded by `the') quantifier meaning smallest in amount or extent or degree; "didn't care the least bit"; "he has the least talent of anyone" [ant: most] 2: minimal in magnitude; "lowest wages"; "the least amount of fat allowed"; "the smallest amount" [syn: lowest, smallest] 3: having or being distinguished by diminutive size; "the least bittern" [syn: littlest, smallest]

adv : used to form the superlative; "The garter snake is the least dangerous snake" [syn: to the lowest degree] [ant: most]

lends, lens /lɛnz/

lends (alt /lɛndz/)

v : (3rd pers sing of lend) 1: of a quality, as in: "Her presence lends a certain cachet to the company"; "The music added a lot to the play"; "She brings a special atmosphere to our meetings"; "This adds a light note to the program" [syn: imparts, bestows, contributes, adds, brings] 2: give temporarily; let have for a limited time [syn: loans] [ant: borrows] 3: have certain characteristics or qualities for something; be open to: "This story would lend itself well to serialization on television"; be vulnerable to: "The current system lends itself to great abuse"

lens

n 1: a transparent optical device used to converge or diverge transmitted light and to form images [syn: lens system] 2: genus of small erect or climbing herbs with pinnate leaves and small inconspicuous white flowers and small flattened pods: lentils [syn: Lens, genus Lens] 3: biconvex transparent body situated behind the iris in the eye; it focuses light waves on the

HOMOPHONES

retina [syn: crystalline lens] 4: electronic equipment that uses a magnetic or electric field in order to focus a beam of electrons [syn: electron lens]

less, loess /lɛs/
less
adj 1: (comparative of `little' usually used with mass nouns) a quantifier meaning not as great in amount or degree; "of less importance"; "less time to spend with the family"; "a shower uses less water"; "less than three years old" [syn: less] [ant: more] 2: (usually preceded by 'no') lower in quality; "no less than perfect" 3: (usually preceded by 'no') lower in esteem; "no less a person than the king himself" [syn: lower] 4: (nonstandard in some uses but often idiomatic with measure phrases) fewer; "less than three weeks"; "no less than 50 people attended"; "in 25 words or less"
adv 1: used to form the comparative of some adjectives and adverbs; "less interesting"; "less expensive"; "less quickly" [syn: to a lesser extent] [ant: more] 2: comparative of little; "she walks less than she should"; "he works less these days" [ant: more]

loess
n : a fine-grained unstratified accumulation of clay and silt deposited by the wind

lessen, lesson /'lɛsən/
lessen
v 1: decrease in size, extent, or range; "Lessen the amount of salt in the recipe" "The amount of homework decreased towards the end of the semester"; "The cabin pressure fell dramatically"; "her weight fall to under a hundred pounds"; "his voice fell to a whisper" [syn: decrease, diminish, fall] [ant: increase] 2: make smaller; "He decreased his staff" [syn: decrease, minify] [ant: increase] 3: wear off or die down; "The pain subsided" [syn: subside]

lesson
n 1: a unit of instruction; "he took driving lessons" 2: punishment intended as a warning to others; "they decided to make an example of him" [syn: example, deterrent example, object lesson] 3: the significance of a story or event; "the moral of the story is to love thy neighbor" [syn: moral] 4: a task assigned for individual study; "he did the lesson for today"

lesser, lessor /'lɛsəɹ/
lesser
adj 1: of less size or importance; "the lesser anteater"; "the lesser of two evils" [ant: greater] 2: smaller in size or amount or value; "the lesser powers of Europe"; "the lesser anteater"

lessor
n : someone who grants a lease [syn: lease giver]

let us, lettuce /'lɛtəs/
let us (also /'lɛtəs/)
v : (an expression which sounds like the name of a plant; (see lettuce) [syn: allow us]

lettuce
n 1: any of various plants of the genus Lactuca [syn: iceberg lettuce, romaine lettuce, bibb lettuce, etc.] 2: leaves of any of various plants of Lactuca sativa

lets, let's /lɛts/
lets
n : serves that strike the net before falling into the receiver's court; the ball must be served again [syn: net balls]
v : (3rd pers sing of let) 1: makes it possible through a specific action or lack of action for something to happen; "This permits the water to rush in"; "This sealed door won't allow the water to come into the basement"; "This will permit the rain to run off" [syn: allows, permits] [ant: prevents] 2: actively causes something to happen; "He lets it be known that he was not interested" 3: consents to, gives permission; "She permits her son to visit her estranged husband"; "I won't let the police search her basement"; "I cannot allow you to see your exam" [syn: permits, allows, countenances] [ant: forbids] 4: causes to move; causes to be in a certain position or condition; "He got his squad on the ball"; "This lets me in for a big surprise"; [syn: gets] 5: leaves unchanged; "lets it be" 6: grants use or occupation of under a term of contract; "He leases his country estate to some foreigners" [syn: leases, rents]

let's
contr : let us

levee, levy /'lɛvi/
levee
n : a barrier constructed to contain the flow or water or to keep out the sea [syn: dam, dike]

levy
n 1: a charge imposed and collected 2: the act of drafting into military service [syn: levy en masse]
v 1: impose and collect; "levy a fine" [syn: impose] 2: cause to assemble or enlist; "raise an army" [syn: recruit, raise]

lewdest, lutist /'ludɪst/
lewdest
adj (superlative of lewd) 1: suggestive of or tending to moral looseness; "lewd whisperings of a dirty old man"; "an indecent gesture"; "obscene telephone calls"; "salacious limericks" [syn: most obscene, most raunchy, most salacious]

HOMOPHONES

2: driven by lust; preoccupied with or exhibiting lustful desires; "libidinous orgies" [syn: most lascivious, most libidinous, most lustful]

lutist (also /'lutɪst/)
n : a musician who plays the lute [syn: lutenist]

liable, libel /'laɪbəl/
liable (also /'laɪəbəl/)
adj 1: at risk of or subject to experiencing something usually unpleasant; "he is apt to lose"; "she is liable to forget" [syn: apt] 2: subject to legal action; "liable to criminal charges" 3: (often followed by `to') likely to be affected with; "liable to diabetes" [syn: nonimmune, nonresistant] 4: held legally responsible; "men between the ages of 18 and 35 were liable for military service"

libel
n : a tort consisting of false and malicious publication printed for the purpose of defaming a living person
v : make slanderous statements against; "The paper was accused of libeling him"

liar, lyre /'laɪjəʳ/
liar
n : a person who has lied or who lies repeatedly [syn: untruthful person, prevaricator] [ant: square shooter]

lyre
n : a harp used by ancient civilizations for accompaniment

lichen, liken /'laɪkɪn/
lichen
n 1: any of several eruptive skin diseases characterized by hard thick lesions grouped together and resembling lichens growing on rocks 2: any thallophytic plant of the division Lichenes; occur as crusty patches or bushy growths on tree trunks or rocks or bare ground etc.

liken
v : consider or describe as similar, equal, or analogous; "We can liken the Han dynasty to the Romans"; "You cannot equate success in financial matters with greed" [syn: compare, equate]

licker, liquor /'lɪkəʳ/
licker
n : 1: a person who performs the act of licking 2: used pejoratively as "ass-licker" [syn: sycophant, brown-nose, ass kisser]

liquor
1: distilled rather than fermented [syn: spirits, booze, hard drink, hard liquor, John Barleycorn, strong drink] 2: a liquid substance that is a solution (or emulsion or suspension) used or obtained in an industrial process; "waste liquors" 3: the liquid in which vegetables or meat have be cooked [syn: pot liquor]

lickerish, licorice /'lɪkəʳɪʃ/
lickerish
adj 1: eager; craving; urged by desire; eager to taste or enjoy; greedy. "The lickerish palate of the glutton." 2. tempting the appetite; dainty "Lickerish baits, fit to ensnare a brute." --Milton. 3. lecherous; lustful

licorice
n 1: deep-rooted coarse-textured plant native to the Mediterranean region having blue flowers and pinnately compound leaves; widely cultivated in Europe for its long thick sweet roots 2: a black candy flavored with the dried root of the licorice plant

lie, lye /laɪ/
lie
n 1: a statement that deviates from or perverts the truth [syn: prevarication] 2: position or manner in which something is situated
v 1: be located or situated somewhere; occupy a certain position 2: be lying, be prostrate; be in a horizontal position; "The sick man lay in bed all day"; "the books are lying on the shelf" [ant: stand, sit] 3: originate (in); "The problems dwell in the social injustices in this country" [syn: dwell, consist, belong, lie in] 4: be and remain in a particular state or condition; "lie dormant" 5: tell an untruth; pretend with intent to deceive; "Don't lie to your parents"; "She lied when she told me she was only 29" 6: have a place in relation to something else: "The fate of Bosnia lies in the hands of the West"; "The responsibility rests with the Allies" [syn: rest] 7: assume a reclining position; "lie down on the bed until you feel better" [syn: lie down] [ant: arise]

lye
n : a strong solution of sodium or potassium hydroxide

lieu, loo /lu/
lieu
n : the function or position properly or customarily occupied or served by another: "can you go in my stead?"; "took his place"; "in lieu of" [syn: stead, position, place]

loo
n : a toilet in England [syn: water closet, closet, W.C.]

lightening, lightning /'laɪtnɪŋ/
lightening (also /'laɪtᵊnɪŋ/)
n 1: descent of the uterus into the pelvic cavity that occurs late in pregnancy; the fetus is said to have dropped 2: changing to a lighter color [syn: whitening]
v : (progressive of lighten) "He is lightening the paint color."

HOMOPHONES

lightning

n 1: abrupt electric discharge from cloud to cloud or from cloud to earth accompanied by the emission of light 2: the flash of light that accompanies an electric discharge in the atmosphere (or something resembling such a flash); can scintillate for a second or more

limb, limn /lɪm/

limb

n 1: one of the jointed appendages of an animal used for locomotion or grasping: arm; leg; wing; flipper 2: any of the main branches arising from the trunk or a bough of a tree [syn: tree branch]

limn

v 1: trace the shape of [syn: delineate, outline] 2: make a portrait of: "showing society what it looked like; portraying its ugliness and its beauties.." [syn: portray, depict]

linch, lynch /lɪntʃ/

linch

n 1: (archaic) A ledge; a right-angled projection 2: used with 'pin' as linch-pin [syn: linchpin]

lynch

v : kill without legal sanction; by a mob

links, lynx /lɪnks/

links

n : (plu of link) 1: the means of connection between things linked in series [syn: nexus] 2: a fastener that serves to join or link; "the walls are held together with metal links placed in the wet mortar during construction" [syn: linkup, tie, tie-in] 3: the state of being connected; "the connections between church and state is inescapable" [syn: connections] [ant: disjunctions] 4: connecting shapes [syn: connections] 5: units of length equal to 1/100 of a chain 6: (computing) instructions that connect parts of a program or elements on a list to other programs or lists 7: channels for communication between groups; "he provided a liaison with the guerrillas" [syn: liaison, contacts, inter-group communications] 8: two-way radio communication systems (usually microwave); parts of a more extensive telecommunication network [syn: radio links] 9: interconnecting circuits between two or more locations for the purpose of transmitting and receiving data [syn: data links] 10 : course consisting of a large landscaped area for playing golf [syn: golf course, golf links]

v : (3rd pers sing of link) 1: make a logical or causal connection; "I cannot connect these two pieces of evidence in my mind" [syn: associates, ties in, relates, links up, connects] [ant: dissociates] 2: connects, fastens, or puts together two or more

pieces; "That cable links the loudspeaker to the amplifier." "Tie the ropes together"; "Link arms" [syn: connects, ties, links up] [ant: disconnects] 3: be or become joined or united or linked; "The two streets connect to become a highway"; "Our paths joined"; "The he links up with the travelers again at the airport" [syn: connects, links up, joins, unites] 4: link with or as with a yoke; "yoke the oxen together" [syn: yokes]

lynx

n : short-tailed wildcats with usually tufted ears; valued for their fur [syn: catamount]

literal, littoral /'lɪtᵊɹɪl/

literal

adj 1: being or reflecting the essential or genuine character of something; "her actual motive"; "a genuine dilemma" [syn: actual, genuine, real] 2: without interpretation or embellishment; "a literal translation of the scene before him" 3: limited to the explicit meaning of a word or text; "a literal translation" [ant: figurative] 4: lacking stylistic embellishment; "a literal description"; "wrote good but plain prose"; "a plain unadorned account of the coronation"; "a forthright unembellished style" [syn: plain, unembellished] 5: of the clearest kind; usually used for emphasis; "it's the literal truth"; "a matter of investment, pure and simple" [syn: pure and simple] 6: (of a translation) corresponding word for word with the original; "literal translation of the article"; "an awkward word-for-word translation" [syn: word-for-word]

n : a mistake in printed matter resulting from mechanical failures of some kind [syn: misprint, erratum, typographical error, typo, literal error]

littoral

adj : relating to or situated or growing on or near a shore

n : a coastal region

lo, low /loʊ/

lo

interj : used to call attention or to express wonder or surprise "Lo, the lord is come"[syn: look, see, behold, observe]

low

adj 1: less than normal in degree or intensity or amount; "low prices"; "the reservoir is low" [ant: high] 2: literal meanings; being at or having a relatively small elevation or upward extension; "low ceilings"; "low clouds"; "low hills"; "the sun is low"; "low furniture"; "a low bow" [ant: high] 3: very low in volume; "a low murmur"; "the low-toned murmur of the surf" [syn: low-toned] 4: unrefined in character; "low comedy" 5: used of sounds and voices; low in pitch or frequency [syn:

HOMOPHONES

low-pitched] [ant: high] 6: of the most contemptible kind; "abject cowardice"; "a low stunt to pull"; "a low-down sneak"; "his miserable treatment of his family"; "You miserable skunk!"; "a scummy rabble"; "a scurvy trick" [syn: abject, low-down, miserable, scummy, scurvy] 7: low or inferior in station or quality; "a humble cottage"; "a lowly parish priest"; "a modest man of the people"; "small beginnings" [syn: humble, lowly, modest, small] 8: no longer sufficient; "supplies are low"; "our funds are depleted" [syn: depleted] 9: subdued or brought low in condition or status; "brought low"; "a broken man"; "his broken spirit" [syn: broken, crushed, humbled, humiliated] 10: low in spirits; "lonely and blue in a strange city"; "depressed by the loss of his job"; "a dispirited and resigned expression on her face"; "downcast after his defeat"; "feeling discouraged and downhearted" [syn: blue, depressed, dispirited, down, downcast, downhearted, down in the mouth, low-spirited] 11: being the gear producing the lowest drive speed; "use first gear on steep hills" [syn: first]

n 1: an air mass of lower pressure; often brings precipitation; "a low moved in over night bringing sleet and snow" [syn: low pressure, depression] 2: a low level or position or degree: "the stock market fell to a new low" [ant: high] 3: the lowest forward gear ratio in the gear box of a motor vehicle; used to start a car moving [syn: first gear, first, low gear]

adv : in a low position; near the ground; "the branches hung low"

v : make a low noise, characteristic of bovines [syn: moo]

load, lode, lowed /loʊd/

load

n 1: weight to be borne or conveyed [syn: loading, burden] 2: a quantity that can be processed or transported at one time; "the system broke down under excessive loads" [syn: loading] 3: goods carried by a large vehicle [syn: cargo, lading, freight, loading, payload, shipment, consignment] 4: (informal) an amount of alcohol sufficient to intoxicate; "he got a load on and started a brawl" 5: the power output of a generator or power plant 6: an onerous or difficult concern; "the burden of responsibility"; "that's a load off my mind" [syn: burden, encumbrance, onus] 7: a deposit of valuable ore occurring within definite boundaries separating it from surrounding rocks [syn: lode] 8: the part of a missile or torpedo that carries the explosive charge [syn: warhead, payload] 9: electrical device to which electrical power is delivered

v 1: fill or load; "load a car" [syn: lade, laden, load up] 2: provide with munitions "He loaded his gun carefully" [syn: charge] 3: fill by packing tightly; "stow the cart" [syn: stow] 4: place a load on; "Load the cart with apples" [ant: unload] 5: put (something) on a structure or conveyance; "load the bags onto the trucks"

lode

n : a deposit of valuable ore occurring within definite boundaries separating it from surrounding rocks "Wow! We hit the mother lode." [syn: load]

lowed

v : (past of low) (see low) "The cows lowed in peaceful content."

loan, lone /loʊn/

loan

n 1: the provision of money temporarily (usually at interest) 2: a word borrowed from another language; e.g. `blitz' is a German word borrowed into modern English [syn: loanword]

v : give temporarily; let have for a limited time [syn: lend] [ant: borrow]

lone

adj 1: lacking companions or companionship; "he was alone when we met him"; "she is alone much of the time"; "the lone skier on the mountain"; "a lonely fisherman stood on a tuft of gravel"; "a lonely soul"; "a solitary traveler" [syn: alone, lonely, solitary] 2: characterized by or preferring solitude in mode of life; "the eremitic element in the life of a religious colony"; "a lone wolf"; "a man of a solitary disposition" [syn: eremitic, eremitical, solitary] 3: being the only one; single and isolated from others; "the lone doctor in the entire county"; "a lonesome pine"; "an only child"; "the sole heir"; "the sole example"; "a solitary instance of cowardice"; "a solitary speck in the sky" [syn: lonesome, only, sole, solitary]

loath, loathe /loʊð/

loath

adj 1: unwillingness to do something contrary to your custom; "a reluctant smile"; "loath to admit a mistake"; "unwilling to face facts" [syn: reluctant] 2: (usually followed by `to') strongly opposed; "antipathetic to new ideas"; "averse to taking risks"; "loath to go on such short notice"; "clearly indisposed to grant their request" [syn: antipathetic, antipathetical, averse, indisposed]

loathe

v : find repugnant [syn: abhor, abominate, execrate]

lo-cal, locale /loʊ'kæl/

lo-cal

adj : food or drink low in calories

HOMOPHONES

locale
n : the scene of any event or action (especially the place of a meeting) [syn: venue, locus]

loch, lock, lough /lak/
loch
n 1: a long narrow inlet of the sea in Scotland (especially when it is nearly landlocked) 2: Scottish word for a lake

lock
n 1: fastener fitted to doors or drawers to keep them firmly closed 2: strand or cluster of hair [syn: curl, ringlet, whorl] 3: a mechanism that detonates the charge of a gun 4: enclosure consisting of a section of canal that can be closed to control the water level; used to raise or lower vessels that pass through it [syn: lock chamber] 5: a restraint incorporated into the ignition switch to prevent the use of a vehicle by persons who do not have the key [syn: ignition locks] 6: any wrestling hold in which some part of the opponent's body is twisted or pressured

v 1: fasten with a lock; "Lock the bike to the fence." [ant: unlock] 2: keep engaged; "engaged the gears" [syn: engage, mesh, operate] [ant: disengage] 3: become rigid or immoveable; of bones; "Don't lock your knees in this exercise" [ant: unlock] 4: hold in a locking position: "He locked his hands around her neck" [syn: interlock, interlace] 5: become engaged or intermeshed with one another; "They were locked in embrace" [syn: interlock] 6: hold fast (in a certain state); "He was locked in a laughing fit" 7: place in a place where something cannot be removed or someone cannot escape; "The parents locked her daughter up for the weekend"; "She locked her jewels in the safe" [syn: lock in, lock away, put away, shut up, shut away, lock up] 8: pass by means through a lock in a waterway 9: build locks in order to facilitate the navigation of vessels

lough
n 1: a long narrow (nearly landlocked) cove in Ireland 2: Irish word for a lake

lochs, locks, lox /laks/
lochs
n : (plu of loch)

locks
n : (plu of lock); "Use combination locks on the clothing lockers."
v : (3rd pers sing of lock); "This key locks the front door."

lox
n 1: a bluish transparent magnetic liquid obtained by compressing gaseous oxygen; used as an oxidizer in rocket propellants [syn: liquid oxygen, LOX] 2: brine-cured salmon

loon, lune /lun/
loon
n 1: a worthless lazy fellow 2: large somewhat primitive fish-eating diving bird of the northern hemisphere having webbed feet placed far back; related to the grebes [syn: diver] 3: a person with confused ideas; incapable of serious thought [syn: addle-head, birdbrain]

lune
n : 1. anything in the shape of a half moon. 2. a figure in the form of a crescent, bounded by two intersecting arcs of circles.

loop, loupe /lup/
loop
n 1: fastener consisting of a metal ring for lining a small hole to permit the attachment of cords or lines [syn: cringle, eyelet, grommet] 2: anything with a round or oval shape (formed by a line or cord etc.) that is closed or nearly closed 3: an inner circle of advisors "he's no longer in the loop" 4: the basic pattern of the human fingerprint 5: a computer program that performs a series of instructions repeatedly until some specified condition is satisfied 6: an intrauterine device in the shape of a loop 7: a complete electrical circuit around which current flows or a signal circulates [syn: closed circuit] [ant: open circuit] 8: a flight maneuver; aircraft flies a complete circle in the vertical plane
v 1: move in loops 2: make a loop in, as of rope or string [syn: intertwine] 3: fly loops, perform a loop, as of an airplane 4: wind around something in coils or loops [syn: coil, curl] [ant: uncoil] 5: fasten with a loop

loupe
n : small magnifying glass (usually set in an eyepiece) used by jewelers and horologists [syn: jeweler's loupe]

loos, lose /luz/
loos
n (plu of loo) : toilets in England [syn: water closets, closets, W.C.'s]

lose
v 1: fail to keep or to maintain; cease to have, either physically or in an abstract sense; "She lost her purse when she left it unattended on her seat" [ant: keep] 2: fail to win; "We lost the battle but we won the war" [ant: win] 3: suffer the loss of a person through death or removal; "She lost her husband in the war"; "The couple that wanted to adopt the child lost her when the biological parents claimed her" 4: place (something) where one cannot find it again; "I misplaced my eyeglasses" [syn: misplace, mislay] 5: miss from one's possessions; lose sight of; "I've lost my glasses again!" [ant: find] 6: allow to go out of sight; "The detective lost the man

HOMOPHONES

he was shadowing after he had to stop at a red light" 7: fail to make money in a business; make a loss or fail to profit; "I lost thousands of dollars on that bad investment!"; "The company turned a loss after the first year" [syn: turn a loss] [ant: profit, break even] 8: fail to get or obtain; "I lost the opportunity to spend a year abroad" [ant: acquire] 9: retreat [syn: fall back, drop off, fall behind, recede] [ant: gain] 10: fail to perceive or to catch with the senses or the mind; "I missed that remark"; "She missed his point"; "We lost part of what he said" [syn: miss] 11: be set at a disadvantage; "This author really suffers in translation" [syn: suffer]

lore, lower

lore /lɔɹ/

n : knowledge gained through tradition or anecdote; "early peoples passed on plant and animal lore through legend" [syn: traditional knowledge]

lower /'loʊᵊɹ/

adj 1: (usually preceded by `no') lower in esteem; "no less a person than the king himself" [syn: less] 2: inferior in rank or status; "the junior faculty"; "a lowly corporal"; "petty officialdom"; "a subordinate functionary" [syn: junior-grade, inferior, lower-ranking, lowly, petty, secondary, subaltern, subordinate] 3: the bottom one of two; "he chose the lower number" 4: of the underworld; "nether regions" [syn: chthonian, chthonic, nether]

n : the lower of two berths [syn: lower berth]

v 1: move something or somebody to a lower position; "take down the vase from the shelf" [syn: take down, let down, get down, bring down] [ant: raise] 2: set lower; "lower a rating"; "lower expectations" [syn: lour] 3: cause to drop or sink; "The lack of rain had depressed the water level in the reservoir" [syn: depress] 4: make lower or quieter; "turn down the volume of a radio" [syn: turn down, lour] 5: look angry or sullen, wrinkle one's forehead, as if to signal disapproval [syn: frown, glower, lour]

loot, lute /lut/

loot

n 1: goods or money obtained illegally [syn: booty, pillage, plunder, prize, swag] 2: informal terms for money [syn: shekels, gelt, dough, bread, dinero, lucre, pelf, moolah, cabbage, kale]

v 1: take illegally; of intellectual property: "This writer plundered from famous authors" [syn: plunder] 2: steal goods; take as spoils; "During the earthquake people looted the stores that were deserted by their owners" [syn: plunder, despoil, strip, rifle, ransack, pillage, foray]

lute

n 1: a substance for packing a joint or coating a porous surface to make it impervious to gas or liquid [syn: luting] 2: musical instrument (chordophone) consisting of a plucked instrument having a pear-shaped body, a usually bent neck, and a fretted fingerboard

loyalest, loyalist /'lɔɪjᵊlɪst/

loyalest

adj (superlative of loyal) 1: steadfast in allegiance or duty; "loyal subjects"; "loyal friends stood by him" [ant: disloyal] 2: inspired by love for your country [syn: most patriotic] [ant: most unpatriotic] 3: unwavering in devotion to friend or vow or cause; "a firm ally"; "loyal supporters"; "the true-hearted soldier...of Tippecanoe"- Campaign song for William Henry Harrison; "fast friends" [syn: most firm, most truehearted]

loyalist

n : a person who is loyal to their allegiance (especially in times of revolt) [syn: stalwart]

-M-

maar, mar /mɑɹ/

maar

n : a flat-bottomed volcanic crater that was formed by an explosion; often filled with water

mar

n 1: the month following February and preceding April [syn: March] 2: a mark or flaw that spoils the appearance of something (especially on a person's body); "a facial blemish" [syn: blemish, defect] v 1: make imperfect; "nothing marred her beauty" [syn: impair, spoil, deflower, vitiate] 2: destroy or injure severely; "mutilated bodies" [syn: mutilate]

Mach, mock /mɑk/

Mach

n : a number representing the speed of sound; "airplane flew at Mach 3 (three times the speed of sound)"

mock

adj : constituting a copy or imitation of something; "boys in mock battle"

n : the act of mocking or ridiculing; "they made a mock of him"

v 1: treat with contempt; "The new constitution mocks all democratic principles" [syn: bemock] 2: imitate with mockery and derision; "The children mocked their handicapped classmate"

macs, max /mæks/

macs

n : (plu of mac): (British) a waterproof raincoat made of rubberized fabric [syn: macintoshes, mackintoshes, macks]

max

n : (abbr for maximum) "He'll max out when he hits high C on the trumpet."

madam, madame

madam /'mædəm/

n 1: a woman of refinement; "a chauffeur opened the door of the limousine for the grand lady" [syn: dame, ma'am, lady, gentlewoman] 2: a woman who runs a house of prostitution [syn: brothel keeper]

madame /mæ'dæm/

n : a title equivalent to Mrs. for a married woman not of English-speaking nationality

madder, matter /'mædəɹ/

madder

adj (compar of mad) 1: "She became madder as the children misbehaved." [syn: angrier] 2: He became madder as his mental disease progressed." [syn: crazier]

n : Eurasian herb having small yellow flowers and red roots formerly an important source of the dye alizarin [syn: Rubia tinctorum]

v : color a moderate to strong red

matter (also /'mætəɹ/)

n 1: that which has mass and occupies space; "an atom is the smallest indivisible unit of matter" [syn: substance] 2: a vaguely specified concern; "several matters to attend to"; "it is none of your affair"; "things are going well" [syn: affair, thing] 3: some situation or event that is thought about; "he kept drifting off the topic"; "he had been thinking about the subject for several years"; "it is a matter for the police" [syn: topic, subject, issue] 4: a problem; "is anything the matter?" 5: (used with negation) having consequence; "they were friends and it was no matter who won the games" 6: written works (especially in books or magazines); "he always took some reading matter with him on the plane"

v : have weight; have import, carry weight; "It does not matter much" [syn: count, weigh]

made, maid /meɪd/

made

adj 1: produced by a manufacturing process; "bought some made goods at the local store; rope and nails" 2: (of a bed) having the sheets and blankets set in order; "a neatly made bed" [ant: unmade] 3: successful or assured of success; "now I am a made man forever"- Christopher Marlowe

v : (past of make) : "She made him a nice lunch."

maid

n 1: a female domestic [syn: maidservant, housemaid, amah] 2: an unmarried girl (especially a virgin) [syn: maiden]

magnate, magnet

magnate /'mægneɪt/

n : a very wealthy or powerful businessman: "an oil magnate" [syn: baron, big businessman, business leader, king, mogul, power, top executive, tycoon]

magnet /'mægnɪt/

n : a device that attracts iron and produces a magnetic field

mail, male /meɪl/

mail

n 1: the bags of letters and packages that are transported by the postal service 2: the system whereby messages are transmitted via the post office [syn: mail service, post, postal service] 3: a conveyance that transports mail 4: any particular collection of letters or packages that is delivered; "your mail is on the table"; "is there any post for me?"; "she was opening her post" [syn: post] 5: (medieval) flexible armor; made of interlinked metal rings [syn: chain mail, ring mail, chain armor, chain, ring armor]

v 1: send via the postal service; "I'll mail

HOMOPHONES

you the check tomorrow" [syn: get off]
2: cause to be directed or transmitted
to another place; "send me your latest
results"; "I'll mail you the paper when it's
written" [syn: post, send]

male
adj 1: (biology) being the sex (of plant
or animal) that produces gametes
(spermatozoa) that perform the fertilizing
function in generation; "a male infant";
"a male holly tree" [ant: female,
androgynous] 2: for or composed of
men or boys; "the male lead"; "masculine
attire" 3: characteristic of a man; "a deep
male voice"; "manly sports" [syn: manful,
manlike, manly, virile]
n 1: an animal that produces gametes
(spermatozoa) that can fertilize female
gametes (ova) [ant: female] 2: a person
who belongs to the sex that cannot have
babies [syn: male person] [ant: female]

main, mane /mɛɪn/
main
adj 1: most important element; "the chief
aim of living"; "the main doors were
of solid glass"; "the principal rivers of
America"; "the principal example";
"policemen were primary targets" [syn:
chief, primary, principal] 2: (grammar) of
a clause; able to stand alone syntactically
as a complete sentence; "the main (or
independent) clause in a complex sentence
has at least a subject and a verb" [syn:
independent] [ant: dependent] 3: of force;
of the greatest possible intensity; "by main
strength" [syn: main]
n 1: any very large body of (salt) water
[syn: briny] 2: a principal pipe in a system
that distributes water or gas or electricity
or that collects sewage
mane
n 1: long coarse hair growing from the
crest of the animal's neck 2: growth of
hair covering the scalp of a human being
[syn: head of hair]

maize, mays, maze /mɛɪz/
maize
n 1: tall annual cereal grass bearing
kernels on large ears: widely cultivated in
America in many varieties; the principal
cereal in Mexico and Central and South
America since pre-Columbian times [syn:
corn, Indian corn, Zea mays] 2: a strong
yellow color [syn: gamboge, lemon, lemon
yellow]
mays
n : (plu of may) 1: thorny Eurasian shrub
of small tree having dense clusters of white
to scarlet flowers followed by deep red
berries; established as an escape in eastern
North America [syn: whitethorn, English
hawthorn, Crataegus laevigata, Crataegus
oxycantha]2: (archaic) maiden

maze
n 1: complex system of paths or tunnels in
which it is easy to get lost [syn: labyrinth]
2: something jumbled or confused; "a
tangle of government regulations" [syn:
tangle, snarl]

mall, maul /mɔl/
mall
n 1: a public area set aside as a pedestrian
walk [syn: promenade] 2: mercantile
establishment consisting of a carefully
landscaped complex of shops representing
leading merchandisers; a modern version
of the traditional marketplace; "a good
plaza should have a movie house";
"they spent their weekends at the local
malls" [syn: plaza, center, shopping mall,
shopping center]
maul
n : a heavy long-handled hammer used
to drive stakes or wedges [syn: sledge,
sledgehammer]
v 1: split (wood) with a maul and wedges
2: injure badly by beating [syn: mangle]

manakin, mannequin, manikin /ˈmænəkɪn/
manakin
n: any of numerous small bright-colored
birds of Central America and South
America having short bills and elaborate
courtship behavior
mannequin
n 1: a woman who wears clothes to
display fashions; "she was too fat to be a
mannequin" [syn: fashion model, model]
2: a life-size dummy used to display
clothes [syn: form]
manikin
n 1: a person who is very small but who is
not otherwise deformed or abnormal [syn:
homunculus] 2: a small weaver bird of
Africa, Asia and Australia

mandrel, mandrill /ˈmɛəndɹɪl/
mandrel
n : any of various rotating shafts that
serve as axes for larger rotating parts [syn:
spindle, arbor]
mandrill
n : baboon of west Africa with red and blue
muzzle and hindquarters [syn: Mandrillus
sphinx]

manner, manor /ˈmænɹ/
manner
n 1: a manner of performance; "a manner
of living"; "in the characteristic New
York style"; "a way of life" [syn: mode,
style, way, fashion] 2: a way of acting
or behaving [syn: personal manner] 3: a
kind; "what manner of man are you?"
manor
n 1: the mansion of the lord of the manor
[syn: manor house] 2: the landed estate of

a lord (including the house on it)

mantel, mantle /ˈmɛəntᵊl/

mantel

n : shelf that projects from wall above fireplace; "in England they call a mantel a chimneypiece" [syn: mantelpiece, mantle, chimneypiece]

mantle

n 1: the cloak as a symbol of authority; "place the mantle of authority on younger shoulders" 2: the layer of the earth between the crust and the core 3: anything that covers; "there was a blanket of snow" [syn: blanket] 4: (zoology) a protective layer of epidermis in mollusks or brachiopods that secretes a substance forming the shell [syn: pallium] 5: (var of mantel) 6: hanging cloth used as a blind [syn: curtain, drape, drapery, pall] 7: a sleeveless garment like a cloak but shorter [syn: cape]

v 1: spread over a surface, like a mantle 2: cover like a mantle: "The ivy mantles the building"

marc, mark, marque /maɹk/

marc

n : residue of grapes or apples after pressing

mark

n 1: a number or letter indicating quality (especially of a student's performance); "she made good marks in algebra"; "grade A milk"; "what was your score on your homework?" [syn: grade, score] 2: a distinguishing symbol; "the owner's mark was on all the sheep" [syn: marker, marking] 3: a reference point to shoot at; "his arrow hit the mark" [syn: target] 4: a visible indication made on a surface; "some previous reader had covered the pages with dozens of marks" 5: the impression created by doing something unusual or extraordinary that people notice and remember; "it was in London that he made his mark"; "he left an indelible mark on the American theater" 6: a symbol of disgrace or infamy; "And the Lord set a mark upon Cain"--Genesis [syn: stigma, brand, stain] 7: a person who is gullible and easy to take advantage of [syn: chump, fool, gull, patsy, fall guy, sucker, schlemiel, soft touch, mug] 8: a written or printed symbol (as for punctuation); "his answer was just a punctuation mark" 9: a perceptible indication of something not immediately apparent (as a visible clue that something has happened); "he showed signs of strain"; "they welcomed the signs of spring" [syn: sign] 10: an indication of damage [syn: scratch, scrape, scar] 11: marking consisting of crossing lines [syn: crisscross, cross] 12: something that exactly succeeds in achieving its goal;

"the new advertising campaign was a bell ringer"; "scored a bull's eye"; "hit the mark" [syn: bell ringer, bull's eye]

v 1: attach a tag or label to; "label these bottles" [syn: tag, label] 2: designate as if by a mark; "This sign marks the border"; "He indicated where the border ended" 3: be a distinctive feature, attribute, or trait; sometimes in a very positive sense; "His modesty distinguishes him form his peers" [syn: distinguish, differentiate] 4: mark by some ceremony or observation; "We marked the anniversary of his death" [syn: commemorate] 5: make or leave a mark on; "mark the trail so that we can find our way back" 6: to accuse or condemn openly or formally; "He denounced the government action." [syn: stigmatize, brand, denounce] 7: notice or perceive; "She noted that someone was following her"; "mark my words" [syn: notice, note] [ant: ignore] 8: mark with a scar; "The skin disease scarred his face permanently" [syn: scar, pock, pit] 9: make small marks into the surface of; "score the clay before firing it" [syn: score, nock] 10: establish as the highest level or best performance: "set a record" [syn: set] 11: make underscoring marks [syn: score] 12: remove from a list; "Cross the name of the dead person off the list" [syn: cross off, cross out, strike out, strike off] 13: put a check mark on or next to; "Please check each name on the list" [syn: check, check off, mark off, tick off] 14: assign a grade or rank to, according to one's evaluation; "grade tests"; "score the SAT essays"; "mark homework" [syn: grade, score] 15: insert punctuation marks into [syn: punctuate]

marque

n : a name given to a product or service [syn: trade name, brand name, brand]

mare, mayor /mɛɹ/

mare

n 1: female equine animal [syn: female horse] 2: a dark region of considerable extent on the surface of the moon [syn: maria]

mayor (also /ˈmɛɪjᵊɹ/)

n : the head of a city government [syn: city manager]

marquee, marquis /maɹˈki/

marquee

n 1: large and often sumptuous tent [syn: pavilion] 2: permanent canopy over an entrance of a hotel etc.

marquis

n: nobleman (in various countries) ranking above a count [syn: marquess]

marshal, martial /ˈmaɹʃᵊl/

marshal

n 1: a law officer having duties similar to those of a sheriff in carrying out the

HOMOPHONES

judgments of a court of law 2: (in some countries) a military officer of highest rank
v 1: place in proper rank; of military troops 2: arrange in logical order; "marshal facts or arguments" 3: make ready for action or use; "marshal resources" [syn: mobilize, summon] 4: lead ceremoniously, as in a procession

martial

adj 1: (of persons) befitting a warrior; "a military bearing" [syn: soldierly, soldier-like, warrior-like] 2: suggesting war or military life [syn: warlike] 3: or relating to the armed forces; "martial law"

marten, martin /'mɑɹtⁿn/

marten

n : agile slender-bodied arboreal mustelids somewhat larger than weasels [syn: marten cat]

martin

n: any of various swallows with squarish or slightly forked tail and long pointed wings

maser, mazer /'meɪzⁱʳ/

maser

n : Microwave Amplification by Stimulated Emission of Radiation; amplifier that works on same principle as a laser and emits coherent microwave radiation

mazer

n : a large hardwood drinking bowl

mask, masque /mɛəsk/

mask

n 1: a covering to disguise or conceal the face 2: activity that tries to conceal something; "no mask could conceal his ignorance"; "they moved in under a mask of friendship" 3: a protective covering worn over the face
v 1: hide under a false appearance; "You mask your disappointment" [syn: dissemble, cloak] 2: put a mask on or cover with a mask; "Mask the children for Halloween" [ant: unmask] 3: cover with a sauce; "mask the meat" 4: shield from light [syn: block out]

masque

n : a party of guests wearing costumes and masks [syn: masquerade]

massed, mast /mɛəst/

massed

adj : brought together into a group or crowd; "the massed crowd in the street" "the accumulated letters in my office" [syn: accumulated, amassed, assembled, collected, congregate]
v : (past of mass) : joined together into a mass; collected or formed a mass; of crowds of people; "Crowds massed outside the palace."

mast

n 1: a vertical spar for supporting sails 2: nuts of forest trees (as beechnuts and

acorns) accumulated on the ground; used especially as food for swine 3: nuts of forest trees used as feed for swine 4: any sturdy upright pole

massif, massive

massif /'mɛəsⁱf/

n : a block of the earth's crust bounded by faults and shifted to form peaks of a mountain range

massive /mɛəsⁱv/

adj 1: imposing in size or bulk or solidity; "massive oak doors"; "Moore's massive sculptures"; "the monolithic proportions of Stalinist architecture"; "a monumental scale" [syn: monolithic, monumental] 2: being the same substance throughout; "massive silver" 3: imposing in scale or scope or degree or power; "massive retaliatory power"; "a massive increase in oil prices"; "massive changes" 4: consisting of great mass; containing a great quantity of matter; "Earth is the most massive of the terrestrial planets"

mat, matte /mæt/

mat

adj : not reflecting light; not glossy; "flat wall paint"; "a photograph with a matte finish" [syn: flat, matt, matte, matted]
n 1: a thick flat pad used as a floor covering 2: mounting consisting of a border or background for a picture [syn: matting] 3: sports equipment consisting of a piece of thick padding on the floor for gymnastic sports [syn: gym mat] 4: the property of having little or no contrast; lacking highlights or gloss [syn: flatness, lusterlessness, matt, matte] 5: table linen for an individual place setting [syn: place mat]
v 1: twist together or entwine into a confusing mass; "The child entangled the cord" [syn: entangle, tangle, snarl] [ant: disentangle, disentangle] 2: change texture so as to become matted and felt-like; "The fabric felted up after several washes" [syn: felt, felt up, mat up]

matte

adj : (var of mat)
n 1: a mixture of sulfides that forms when sulfide metal ores are smelted 2: (var of mat)

material, materiel

material /mə'tiɹiɹl/

adj 1: concerned with worldly rather than spiritual interests; "material possessions"; "material wealth"; "material comforts" 2: derived from or composed of matter; "the material universe" [ant: immaterial] 3: directly relevant to a matter especially a law case; "his support made a material difference"; "evidence material to the issue at hand"; "facts likely to influence the judgment are called material facts";

HOMOPHONES

"a material witness" [ant: immaterial] 4: concerned with or affecting physical as distinct from intellectual or psychological well-being; "material needs" 5: having material or physical form or substance [syn: corporeal] [ant: incorporeal] 6: having substance or capable of being treated as fact; not imaginary; "the substantial world"; "a mere dream, neither substantial nor practical"; "most ponderous and substantial things"- Shakespeare [syn: substantial, real] [ant: insubstantial]

n 1: the tangible substance that goes into the makeup of a physical object; "coal is a hard black material"; "wheat is the stuff they use to make bread" [syn: stuff] 2: information (data or ideas or observations) that can be used or reworked into a finished form; "the archives provided rich material for a definitive biography" 3: things needed for doing or making something; "writing materials"; "useful teaching materials" 4: artifact made by weaving or felting or knitting or crocheting natural or synthetic fibers; "the fabric in the curtains was light and semitransparent"; "woven cloth originated in Mesopotamia around 5000 BC"; "she measured off enough material for a dress" [syn: fabric, cloth, textile] 5: a person judged suitable for admission or employment; "he was university material"; "she was vice-presidential material"

materiel /mætiɹi'ɛl/
n : equipment and supplies of a military force [syn: equipage]

me, mi /mi/
me
pron : The person speaking, regarded as an object; myself; a pronoun of the first person used as the objective and dative case of the pronoun I; "he struck me" "he gave me the money" " he gave me the money to me" "he got me a hat" "he got a hat for me"

mi
n : the syllable naming the third (mediant) note of any major scale in solmization

mead, meed /mid/
mead
n: a fermented drink made of honey and water, malt, and yeast

meed
n : (archaic) a fitting reward

mean, mesne, mien /min/
mean
adj 1: (statistics) approximating the statistical norm or average or expected value; "the average income in New England is below that of the nation"; "of average height for his age"; "the mean annual rainfall" [syn: average, mean] 2: characterized by malice; "a hateful thing to do"; "in a mean mood" [syn: hateful] 3:

having or showing an ignoble lack of honor or morality; "taking a mean advantage"; "chok'd with ambition of the meaner sort"- Shakespeare; "something essentially vulgar and mean-spirited in politics" [syn: base, mean-spirited] 4: (slang) excellent; "famous for a mean backhand" 5: marked by poverty befitting a beggar; "a beggarly existence in the slums"; "a mean hut" [syn: beggarly] 6: used of persons or behavior; characterized by or indicative of lack of generosity; "a mean person"; "he left a miserly tip" [syn: miserly, tight] 7: used of sums of money; so small in amount as to deserve contempt [syn: beggarly]

n : an average of n numbers computed by adding some function of the numbers and dividing by some function of n [syn: mean value]

v 1: mean or intend to express or convey; "You never understand what I mean!" "what do his words intend?" [syn: intend] 2: have as a logical consequence; "The water shortage means that we have to stop taking long showers" [syn: entail, imply] 3: denote or connote; "'maison' means 'house' in French"; "An example sentence would show what this word means" [syn: intend, signify, stand for] 4: have in mind as a purpose; "I mean no harm"; "I only meant to help you"; "She didn't think to harm me"; "We thought to return early that night" [syn: intend, think] 5: have a specified degree of importance; "My ex-husband means nothing to me"; "Happiness means everything" 6: "I'm thinking of good food when I talk about France"; "Yes, I meant you when I complained about people who gossip!" [syn: think of, have in mind] 7: destine or designate for a certain purpose; "These flowers were meant for you"

mesne
adj : intermediate in time of occurrence or performance

mien
n : dignified manner or conduct [syn: bearing, comportment, presence]

meat, meet, mete /mit/
meat
n 1: the flesh of animals (including fishes and birds and snails) used as food 2: the inner and usually edible part of a seed or grain or nut or fruit stone: "black walnut kernels are difficult to get out of the shell" [syn: kernel] 3: the choicest or most essential or most vital part of some idea or experience: "the gist of the prosecutor's argument"; "the heart and soul of the Democratic Party"; "the nub of the story" [syn: kernel, substance, core, center, essence, gist, heart, heart and soul, inwardness, marrow, nub, pith, sum, nitty-

HOMOPHONES

gritty]

meet

adj : being precisely fitting and right [syn: fitting]

n : a meeting at which a number of athletic contests are held [syn: sports meeting]

v 1: come together; "I'll probably see you at the meeting"; "How nice to see you again!" [syn: ran into, encounter, run across, come across, see] 2: get together socially or for a specific purpose [syn: get together] 3: be adjacent or come together; "The lines converge at this point" [syn: converge] [ant: diverge, diverge] 4: fill or meet a want or need [syn: satisfy, fill, fulfill] 5: of a condition or restriction [syn: fit, conform to] 6: satisfy or fulfill; "meet a need"; "this job doesn't match my dreams" [syn: match, cope with] 7: get to know; get acquainted with; "I met this really handsome guy at a bar last night!"; "we met in Singapore" 8: collect in one place; "We assembled in the church basement"; "Let's gather in the dining room" [syn: gather, assemble, foregather] 9: meet by design; be present at the arrival of; "Can you meet me at the train station?" 10: contend against an opponent in a sport, game, or battle; "Princeton plays Yale this weekend"; "Charlie likes to play Mary" [syn: encounter, play, take on] 11: experience as a reaction; "My proposal met with much opposition" [syn: encounter, receive] 12: undergo or suffer; "meet a violent death"; "suffer a terrible fate" [syn: suffer] 13: be in direct physical contact with; make contact; "The two buildings touch"; "Their hands touched"; "The wire must not contact the metal cover"; "The surfaces contact at this point" [syn: touch, adjoin, contact]

mete

v 1: to measure 2: to allot "mete out punishment"

meatier, meteor /'mitijəɹ/

meatier

adj 1: having greater substance "Her second novel had a meatier plot than her first." 2: having more meat "My tacos are meatier than hers."

meteor

n : a streak of light in the sky at night that results when a meteoroid hits the earth's atmosphere and air friction causes the meteoroid to melt or vaporize or explode [syn: shooting star]

medal, meddle /'mɛdəl/

medal

n : an award for winning a championship or commemorating some other event [syn: decoration, laurel wreath, medallion, palm, ribbon]

meddle

v : intrude in other people's affairs or business; interfere unwantedly; "Don't meddle in my affairs!" [syn: tamper]

meddler, medlar /'mɛdləɹ/

meddler

n : an officious annoying person who interferes with others; one who meddles

medlar

n 1: small deciduous tree of southern Africa having edible fruit [syn: wild medlar, wild medlar tree, Vangueria infausta] 2: small deciduous Eurasian tree cultivated for its fruit that resemble crab apples [syn: medlar tree, Mespilus germanica] 3: South African globular fruit with brown leathery skin and sweet-acid pithy flesh 4: crabapple-like fruit used for preserves

meddlesome, mettlesome /'mɛdəlsəm/

meddlesome

adj : intrusive in a meddling or offensive manner; "an interfering old woman"; "bustling about self-importantly making an officious nuisance of himself"; "busy about other people's business" [syn: interfering, meddling, officious, busy, busybodied]

mettlesome

adj 1: having a proud and unbroken spirit 2: willing to face danger [syn: game, gamy, gritty, spirited, spunky]

meeter, meter /'mitəɹ/

meeter

n : a person who participates in a meeting; "he was a regular attender at department meetings"; "the gathering satisfied both organizers and attendees" [syn: attendant, attender, attendee]

meter

n 1: the basic unit of length adopted under the Systeme International d'Unites (approximately 1.094 yards) [syn: metre, m] 2: any of various measuring instruments for measuring a quantity 3: (prosody) the accent in a metrical foot of verse [syn: metre, measure, beat, cadence] 4: rhythm as given by division into parts of equal time [syn: metre, time]

v 1: measure with a meter; "meter the flow of water" 2: stamp with a meter indicating the postage; "meter the mail"

meets, metes /mits/

meets

n : (plu of meet)

v : (3rs pers sing of meet)

metes

n: boundary measurement "metes and bounds"

men's, mends /mɛnz/

men's

adj pertaining to or owned by men "Where's the men's locker room?"

HOMOPHONES

n : a public toilet for men [syn: men's room]

mends

v : (3rd pers sing of mend) 1: restore by replacing a part or putting together what is torn or broken; "He mends broken bones in his medical practice."; "Repair my shoes please" [syn: repairs, fixes, doctors, furbishes up, restores] [ant: breaks] 2: heals or recovers; "My broken leg is mending" [syn: heals]

metal, mettle /'mɛtˀl/

metal

adj : containing or made of or resembling or characteristic of a metal; "a metallic compound"; "metallic luster"; "the sphere has a metal surface" [syn: metallic] [ant: nonmetallic]

n 1: any of several chemical elements that are usually shiny solids that conduct heat or electricity and can be formed into sheets etc. "copper is a metal" [syn: metallic element] 2: a mixture containing two or more metallic elements or metallic and nonmetallic elements usually fused together or dissolving into each other when molten; "brass is an alloy of zinc and copper" [syn: alloy]

v : cover with metal

mettle

n : the courage to carry on: "his performance demonstrated his mettle"; "he kept fighting on pure spunk"; "you haven't got the heart for baseball" [syn: heart, nerve, spunk]

mew, mu /muə/

mew

n 1: the sound made by a cat (or any sound resembling this) [syn: meow] 2: the common gull of Eurasia and northeastern North America [syn: mew gull, sea mew, Larus canus]

v 1: cry like a cat; "the cat meowed" [syn: meow] 2: utter a high-pitched cry, as of seagulls

mu

n : the 12th letter of the Greek alphabet

mewl, mule /muəl/

mewl

v : cry weakly or softly; "she whimpered with pain" [syn: whimper]

mule

n 1: sterile offspring of a male donkey and a female horse 2: a slipper that has no fitting around the heel [syn: mules, scuff, scuffs]

mews, mus, muse /muəz/

mews

n : 1: (plu of mew) (see mew) 2: (British) street lined with building that were originally private stables but have been remodeled as dwellings; "she lives in a Chelsea mews"

v : (3rd pers sing of mew): (see mew)

mus

n : (plu of mu) (see mu)

muse

n : the source of an artist's inspiration; "Her professor was her muse"

v : reflect deeply on a subject; "I mulled over the events of the afternoon"; "philosophers have speculated on the question of God for thousands of years"; "The scientist must stop to observe and start to excogitate" [syn: chew over, think over, meditate, ponder, contemplate, reflect, mull, mull over, ruminate, speculate]

mho, mow /mou/

mho

n : a unit of conductance equal to the reciprocal of an ohm [syn: siemens, reciprocal ohm, S]

mow

n : a loft for storing hay [syn: hayloft]

v 1: cut with a blade or mower; "mow the grass" [syn: cut down] 2: make a sad face; "mop and mow" [syn: pout, mop]

micks, mix /mɪks/

micks

n : (plu of mick) : ethnic slur; persons of Irish descent

mix

n 1: a commercially prepared blend of dry ingredients [syn: premix] 2: an event that combines things in a mixture; "a gradual mixture of cultures" [syn: mixture] 3: the act of mixing; "paste made by a mix of flour and water"; "the mixing of sound channels in the recording studio" [syn: commixture, admixture, mixture, mixing]

v 1: mix together different elements; "The colors blend well" [syn: blend, flux, conflate, commingle, immix, fuse, coalesce, meld, combine, merge] 2: open (a place) to members of all races and ethnic groups; "This school is completely desegregated" [syn: desegregate, integrate] [ant: segregate] 3: to bring or combine together or with something else: "resourcefully he mingled music and dance" [syn: mingle, commix, unify, amalgamate] 4: as of electronic signals; "mixing sounds" 5: add as an additional element or part; "mix water into the drink" [syn: mix in] 6: mix so as to make a random order or arrangement; "shuffle the cards" [syn: shuffle, ruffle]

middy, midi /'mɪdi/

middy

n : blouse with a sailor collar [syn: middy blouse]

midi

adj : (of women's clothing; often used in combination) with hemline at mid-calf; "midi skirts"; "wore her dresses midi

HOMOPHONES

length" [ant: maxi, mini]
n: a standard protocol for communication between electronic musical instruments and computers [syn: musical instrument digital interface, MIDI]

might, mite /maɪt/
might
n: physical strength [syn: mightiness, power]
v 1: expresses permission; "You may leave now"; "Might I have another piece of cake?" [syn: can, may] 2: expresses possibility; "I might do it by myself" [syn: could]
mite
n 1: a small but appreciable amount; "this dish could use a touch of garlic" [syn: touch, hint, pinch, jot, speck, soupcon] 2: any of numerous very small to minute arachnids often infesting animals or plants or stored foods

mil, mill /mɪl/
mil
n 1: a unit of length equal to one thousandth of an inch; used to specify thickness (e.g., of sheets or wire) 2: a metric unit of volume equal to one thousandth of a liter [syn: milliliter, ml, cubic centimeter, cc] 3: an angular unit used in artillery; equal to 1/6400 of a complete revolution
mill
n 1: a plant consisting of buildings with facilities for manufacturing [syn: factory, manufacturing plant, manufactory] 2: machine that processes materials by grinding or crushing [syn: grinder] 3: the act of grinding [syn: grind, pulverization] v 1: move about in a confused manner [syn: mill about, mill around] 2: grind with a mill; "mill grain" 3: of the edge of a coin 4: roll out (metal) with a rolling machine

millenary, millinery /'mɪlɪnɛɹi/
millenary
adj: relating to or consisting of 1000
millinery
n 1: shop selling women's hats [syn: hat shop] 2: hats for women; the wares sold by a milliner [syn: woman's hat]

mince, mints /mɪnts/
mince
n: food chopped into small bits: "a mince of mushrooms"
v 1: make less severe or harsh; "He moderated his tone when the students burst out in tears" [syn: soften, moderate] 2: walk daintily 3: cut into small pieces; "mince the garlic"
mints
n: (plu of mint) 1 any north temperate plants of the genus Mentha with aromatic leaves and small mauve flowers 2: the leaves of a mint plant used fresh or candied

3: candies that are flavored with a mint oil [syn: mint candies] 4: plants where money is coined by authority of the government
v: (3ʳᵈ pers sing of mint): form by stamping, punching, or printing; "strikes coins"; "strikes a medal" [syn: coins, strikes]

mind, mined /maɪnd/
mind
n 1: that which is responsible for one's thoughts and feelings; the seat of the faculty of reason; what the brain does; "his mind wandered"; "I couldn't get his words out of my head" [syn: head, brain, psyche] 2: recall or remembrance; "it came to mind" 3: an opinion formed by judging something; "he was reluctant to make his judgment known"; "she changed her mind" [syn: judgment] 4: an intellectual being; "the great minds of the 17th century" [syn: thinker, creative thinker] 5: attention; "don't pay him any mind" 6: your intention; what you intend to do; "he had in mind to see his old teacher"; "the idea of the game is to capture all the pieces" [syn: idea] 7: knowledge and intellectual ability; "he reads to improve his mind"; "he has a keen intellect" [syn: intellect]
v 1: be offended or bothered by; take offense with, be bothered by: "I don't mind your behavior" 2: be concerned with or about something or somebody [syn: worry] 3: be in charge of or deal with; "She takes care of all the necessary arrangements" [syn: take care] 4: pay close attention to; give heed to; "Heed the advice of the old men" [syn: heed, listen] 5: be on one's guard; be cautious or wary about; be alert to; "Beware of telephone salesmen" [syn: beware] 6: keep in mind [syn: bear in mind] [ant: forget]
mined
adj: extracted from a source of supply as of minerals from the earth [ant: unmined]
v: (past of mine) 1: get from the earth; of ores and metals; "The mined coal from those hills." 2: lay mines; "The Vietnamese mined Cambodia"

minds, mines
minds /maɪndz/
n: (plu of mind) "Great minds developed the atomic bomb."
v: (3ʳᵈ pers sing of mind) "She minds her manners."
mines /maɪnz/
n: (plu of mine) 1: excavations in the earth from which ores and minerals are extracted 2: explosive devices that explode on contact; designed to destroy vehicles or ships or to kill or maim personnel
v: (3ʳᵈ pers sing of mine) 1: gets from the earth; of ores and metals 2: lays mines;

HOMOPHONES

"The Vietnamese mined Cambodia"
miner, minor /'maɪnⁱɹ/
miner
n : laborer who works in a mine [syn: mineworker]
minor
adj 1: of lesser importance or stature or rank; "a minor poet"; "had a minor part in the play"; "a minor official"; "many of these hardy adventurers were minor noblemen"; "minor back roads" [ant: major] 2: lesser in scope or effect; "had minor differences"; "a minor disturbance" [ant: major] 3: inferior in number or size or amount; "a minor share of the profits" [ant: major] 4: (music) of a scale or mode; "the minor keys"; "in B flat minor" [ant: major] 5: (law) not of legal age; "minor children" [syn: underage] [ant: major] 6: of lesser seriousness or danger; "suffered only minor injuries"; "some minor flooding"; "a minor tropical disturbance" [ant: major] 7: of your secondary field of academic concentration or specialization [ant: major] 8: (British) of the younger of two boys with the same family name; "Jones minor" 9: (theology) warranting only temporal punishment; "venial sin" [syn: venial] 10: limited in size or scope; "a small business"; "a newspaper with a modest circulation"; "small-scale plans"; "a pocket-size country" [syn: modest, small, small-scale, pocket-size, pocket-sized]
n : a young person of either sex (between birth and puberty); "she writes books for children"; "they're just kids"; [syn: child, kid, youngster, shaver, nipper, small fry, toddler, tike, tyke, fry, nestling]
minion, minyan /'mɪnjɪn/
minion
n : a servile or fawning dependant
minyan
n : the quorum required by Jewish law to be present for public worship (at least ten males over thirteen years of age)
minks, minx /mɪnks/
minks
n : (plu of mink) 1 fur coats made from the soft lustrous fur of minks [syn: mink coats] 2: slender-bodied semi-aquatic mammals having partially webbed feet; valued for their fur
minx
n : a seductive woman who uses her sex appeal to exploit men [syn: coquette, flirt, vamp, tease, prickteaser, cockteaser]
missal, missile /'mɪsᵊl/
missal
n : (Roman Catholic Church) a book containing all the prayers and responses needed to celebrate Mass throughout the year

missile
n 1: rocket carrying passengers or instruments or a warhead 2: a weapon that is thrown or projected [syn: projectile]
missed, mist /mɪst/
missed
adj : not caught with the senses or the mind; "words lost in the din" [syn: lost]
v : (past of miss) 1: fail to perceive or to catch with the senses or the mind; "I missed that remark"; "She missed his point"; "We lost part of what he said" [syn: lost] 2: feel or suffer from the lack of: "He misses his mother" 3: fail to attend an event or activity: "I missed the concert"; "He missed school for a week" [ant: attended] 4: leave undone or leave out; "How could I miss that typo?"; "The worker on the conveyor belt missed one out of ten" [syn: neglected, omitted, dropped, left out, overlooked] [ant: attended to] 5: fail to reach or get to: "She missed her train" 6: be without; "This soup lacks salt"; "There is something missing in my jewelry box!" [syn: lacked] [ant: had] 7: fail to reach; "The arrow missed the target" [ant: hit] 8: fail to hit the intended target [ant: hit] 9: be absent; "The child had been missing for a week" 10: fail to experience; "Fortunately, I missed the hurricane" [syn: escaped]
mist
n : a thin fog with condensation near the ground
v 1: become covered with mist; "The windshield misted over" [syn: mist over] 2: make less visible or unclear; "The stars are obscured by the clouds" [syn: obscure, befog, becloud, haze over, fog, cloud] 3: spray finely or cover with mist
misses, missus /'mɪsɪz/
misses
n : (plu of miss) 1: young women" [syn: girls, young ladies] 2: failures to hit (or meet or find etc)
v : (3rd pers sing of miss) (see missed):
missus
n : informal term of address for someone's wife [syn: Mrs., missis]
moan, mown /moʊn/
moan
n : an utterance expressing pain or disapproval [syn: groan]
v : indicate pain, discomfort, or displeasure; "The students groaned when the professor got out the exam booklets"; "The ancient door soughed when opened" [syn: groan, sough]
mown
adj : (used of grass or vegetation) having been cut down with a hand implement or machine; "the smell of new-mown hay" [syn: cut] [ant: unmown]

HOMOPHONES

moat, mote /moʊt/
moat
n : ditch dug as a fortification and usually filled with water [syn: fosse]
mote
n : (non-technical usage) a tiny piece of anything [syn: atom, molecule, particle, speck]

mode, mowed /moʊd/
mode
n 1: a manner of performance; "a manner of living"; "in the characteristic New York style"; "a way of life" [syn: manner, style, way, fashion] 2: a particular functioning condition or arrangement; "switched from keyboard to voice mode" 3: a classification of propositions on the basis of whether they claim necessity or possibility or impossibility [syn: modality] 4: verb inflections that express how the action or state is conceived by the speaker [syn: mood, modality] 5: any of various fixed orders of the various diatonic notes within an octave [syn: musical mode] 6: the most frequent value of a random variable [syn: modal value]
mowed
v : (past of mow) 1: cut with a blade or mower; "mow the grass" [syn: cut down] 2: made a sad face; "mopped and mowed" [syn: pouted, mopped] 3: kill with a weapon; "The machine gunner mowed down the enemy patrol."

mood, mooed /mud/
mood
n 1: a characteristic (habitual or relatively temporary) state of feeling; "whether he praised or cursed me depended on his temper at the time"; "he was in a bad humor" [syn: temper, humor] 2: the prevailing psychological state; "the climate of opinion"; "the national mood had changed radically since the last election" [syn: climate] 3: verb inflections that express how the action or state is conceived by the speaker [syn: mode, modality]
mooed
v : (past of moo) : made a low noise, characteristic of bovines [syn: lowed]

moor, more /mɔr/
moor (also /mʊr/)
n 1: one of the Muslim people of Africa; of mixed Arab and Berber descent; converted to Islam in the 8th century; conquerors of Spain in the 8th century [syn: Moor] 2: open land usually with peaty soil covered with heather and bracken and moss [syn: moorland]
v 1: secure in or as if in a berth or dock; "tie up the boat" [syn: berth, tie up] 2: come into or dock at a wharf; "the big ship wharfed in the evening" [syn: berth,

wharf] 3: secure with cables or ropes; "moor the boat"

more
adj 1: (compar of `much' used with mass nouns) quantifier meaning greater in size or amount or extent or degree; "more land"; "more support"; "more rain fell"; "more than a gallon" [syn: more than] [ant: less] 2: (compar of `many' used with count nouns) quantifier meaning greater in number; "a hall with more seats"; "we have no more bananas"; "more than one" [ant: fewer] 3: existing or coming by way of addition; "an additional problem"; "further information"; "there will be further delays"; "took more time" [syn: additional, further]
adv 1: used to form the comparative of some adjectives and adverbs; "more interesting"; "more beautiful"; "more quickly" [syn: to a greater extent] [ant: less] 2: compar of much; to a greater degree or extent; "he works more now"; "they eat more than they should" [ant: less]

moose, mousse /mus/
moose
n : large northern deer with enormous flattened antlers in the male; called elk in Europe and moose in North America [syn: elk, European elk, Alces alces]
mousse
n 1: a light creamy dish made from fish or meat and set with gelatin 2: a light creamy dessert set with gelatin 3: toiletry consisting of an aerosol foam used in hair styling [syn: hair mousse, hair gel]
v : apply mousse to; of hair [syn: gel]

moral, morale, morel
moral /ˈmɔrəl/
adj 1: relating to principles of right and wrong; i.e. to ethics or ethics; "moral philosophy" 2: concerned with principles of right and wrong or conforming to standards of behavior and character based on those principles; "moral sense"; "a moral scrutiny"; "a moral lesson"; "a moral quandary"; "moral convictions"; "a moral life" [ant: immoral, amoral] 3: adhering to ethical and moral principles; "it seems ethical and right"; "followed the only honorable course of action"; "had the moral courage to stand alone" [syn: ethical, honorable] 4: arising from the sense of right and wrong; "a moral obligation" 5: psychological rather than physical or tangible in effect; "a moral victory"; "moral support" 6: based on strong likelihood or firm conviction rather than actual evidence; "a moral certainty" [syn: moral]
n : the significance of a story or event; "the moral of the story is to love thy neighbor" [syn: lesson]

HOMOPHONES

morale /mɔ'ɹæl/
morale
n 1: a state of individual psychological well-being based upon a sense of confidence and usefulness and purpose 2: the spirit of a group that makes the members want the group to succeed [syn: esprit de corps, team spirit]

morel /mɔ'ɹɛl/
morel
n : any of various edible mushrooms of the genus Morchella having a brownish spongelike cap

mordant, mordent /mɔɹdɛnt/
mordant
adj : harshly ironic or sinister; "black humor"; "a grim joke"; "grim laughter"; "fun ranging from slapstick clowning... to savage mordant wit" [syn: black, grim]
n : a substance used to treat leather or other materials before dyeing; aids in dyeing process

mordent
n : a musical ornament made by a quick alteration of a principal tone with the tone usually a half step lower

morn, mourn /mɔɹn/
morn
n : (var of morning) (see morning)

mourn
v 1: fell sadness; "She is mourning her dead child" 2: observe the customs of mourning after the death of a loved one

morning, mourning /'mɔɹnɪŋ/
morning
adj : in the morning; "the morning hours"
n 1: the time period between dawn and noon; "I spent the morning running errands" [syn: morn, morning time, forenoon] 2: a conventional expression of greeting or farewell [syn: good morning] 3: the first light of day; "we got up before dawn"; "they talked until morning" [syn: dawn, dawning, aurora, first light, daybreak, break of day, break of the day, dayspring, sunrise, sunup, cockcrow] [ant: sunset] 4: the earliest period: "the dawn of civilization"; "the morning of the world" [syn: dawn]

mourning
adj : sorrowful through loss or deprivation; "bereft of hope" [syn: bereaved, bereft, grief-stricken, grieving, sorrowing]
n : state of sorrow over the death or departure of a loved one [syn: bereavement]
v : (progressive of mourn) : "She is mourning her dead child)

mucous, mucus /'mʊəkɪs/
mucous
adj : of or secreting or covered with or resembling mucus; "mucous tissue"; "mucous glands of the intestine"

mucus
n : protective secretion of the mucous membranes [syn: mucous secretion]

murre, myrrh /məɹ/
murre
n : black-and-white diving bird of northern seas

myrrh
n 1: aromatic resin used in perfume and incense [syn: gum myrrh, sweet cicely] 2: aromatic resin burned as incense and used in perfume [syn: gum myrrh]

muscat, musket /'mʌskɪt/
muscat
n 1: any of several cultivated grapevines that produce sweet white grapes [syn: muskat] 2: wine from muscat grapes [syn: muscatel, muscadel, muscadelle] 3: sweet aromatic grape used for raisins and wine [syn: muscatel, muscat grape]

musket
n : a muzzle-loading shoulder gun with a long barrel; formerly used by infantrymen

muscle, mussel /'mʌsᵊl/
muscle
n 1: one of the contractile organs of the body 2: animal tissue consisting predominantly of contractile cells [syn: muscular tissue] 3: muscular strength [syn: brawn, sinew]
v : make one's way by force: "He muscled his way into the office"

mussel
n 1: black marine bivalves usually steamed in wine 2: marine or freshwater bivalve mollusk that lives attached to rocks etc.

mussed, must /mʌst/
mussed
adj : in a state of confusion and disorderliness; "the house was mussed"
v : (past of muss) : made messy or untidy; "the child mussed up my hair" [syn: tussled]

must
adj : highly recommended; "a book that is must reading"
v 1: be obliged, required, or forced to; "She has to get her driver's license" [syn: have to, have got to, need] 2: be logically necessary [syn: should, ought, need] 3: be likely or probable; "They must be kidding." or "They have to be kidding." [syn: have to]

mustard, mustered /'mʌstᵊɹd/
mustard
n 1: any of several cruciferous plants of the genus Brassica 2: pungent powder or paste prepared from ground mustard seeds [syn: table mustard] 3: leaves eaten as cooked greens [syn: mustard greens, leaf mustard, Indian mustard]

mustered
v : (past of muster) 1: gathered or brought together; "mustered the courage to do something"; "she rallied her intellect";

HOMOPHONES

"Summoned all your courage" [syn: rallied, summoned, came up, mustered up] 2: called to duty, military service, jury duty, etc.

-N-

nap (see knap)

naught, nought /nɔt/

naught

n 1: a quantity of no importance; "it looked like nothing I had ever seen before"; "reduced to nil all the work we had done"; "we racked up a pathetic goose egg"; "it was all for naught"; "I didn't hear zilch about it" [syn: nothing, nil, nix, nada, null, aught, cipher, goose egg, zero, zilch, zip] 2: complete failure; "all my efforts led to naught"

nought

n : a mathematical element that when added to another number yields the same number [syn: zero, 0]

naval, navel /ˈneɪvəl/

naval

adj : connected with or belonging to or used in a navy; "naval history"; "naval commander"; "naval vessels"

navel

n 1: scar where the umbilical cord was attached [syn: umbilicus, bellybutton] 2: the center point or middle of something [syn: navel point]

nave (see knave)

nay, nee, neigh /neɪ/

nay

n : a negative; "the nays have it" [ant: yea]
adv : not this merely but also; not only so but; "each of us is peculiar, nay, in a sense unique"

nee

adj : (meaning literally 'born') used to indicate the maiden or family name of a married woman; "Hillary Clinton nee Rodham"

neigh

n : the sound made by a horse [syn: nicker, whicker, whinny]
v : make a sound characteristic of horses [syn: nicker, whicker, whinny]

need (see knead)

new (see gnu)

news (see gnus)

nick (see knick)

nickers (see knickers)

nicks, nix /nɪks/

nicks

n : (plu of nick) 1: impressions in a surface (as made by a blow) [syn: dent, gouge] 2: a small cut [syn: notch, snick]
v : (3rd pers sing of nick) 1: cuts slightly, with a razor; "The barber's knife nicked his cheek" [syn: snick] 2: cut a nick into [syn: chip] 3: divide or reset the tail muscles, as of horses 4: mate successfully; of livestock

HOMOPHONES

nix

n : a quantity of no importance; "it looked like nothing I had ever seen before"; "reduced to nil all the work we had done"; "we racked up a pathetic goose egg"; "it was all for naught"; "I didn't hear zilch about it" [syn: nothing, nil, nada, null, aught, cipher, goose egg, naught, zero, zilch, zip]

v : cancel; "nix the softball game because of the rain"

night (see knight)

nit (see knit)

no (see know)

nob (see knob)

nobble (see knobble)

nock (see knock)

noes (see knows)

none, nun /nʌn/

none

adv : not at all or in no way; "seemed none too pleased with his dinner"; "shirt looked none the worse for having been slept in"; "none too prosperous"; "the passage is none too clear"

nun

n 1: a woman in a religious order 2: a buoy resembling a cone [syn: conical buoy, nun buoy]

nose (see knows)

not (see knot)

nu (see gnu)

nus (see gnus)

-O-

o, oh, owe /oʊ/

o

n 1: the blood group whose red cells carry neither the A nor B antigens; "people with type O blood are universal donors" [syn: O, type O, group O] 2: the 15th letter of the Roman alphabet [syn: O]

oh

interj : an exclamation expressing various emotions, according to the tone and manner, especially surprise, pain, sorrow, anxiety, or a wish

owe

v 1: be obliged to pay or repay 2: be indebted to, in an abstract or intellectual sense; "This new theory owes much to Einstein's Relativity Theory" 3: be in debt; "She owes me $200"; "The thesis owes much to his adviser"

oar, o'er, or, ore /ɔɹ/

oar

n : an implement used to propel or steer a boat

o'er

adv : (contr for over) : throughout a period of time; "stay over the weekend" [syn: over]

or

conj : denote a a choice or alternative; "you may read or may write, -- that is, you may do one of the things at your pleasure, but not both"

ore

n : a metal-bearing mineral valuable enough to be mined

odder (see attar)

ode, owed /oʊd/

ode

n : a lyric poem with complex stanza forms

owed

adj 1: owed and payable immediately or on demand; "payment is due" [syn: due] [ant: undue] 2: owed as a debt; "outstanding bills"; "the amount still owed"; "undischarged debts" [syn: outstanding, owing, undischarged]

v : (past of owe) (see owe) : He owed me a favor."

offal (see awful)

oleo, olio /'oʊlioʊ/

oleo

n : a spread made chiefly from vegetable oils and used as a substitute for butter [syn: margarine, oleomargarine]

olio

n 1: a miscellaneous mixture [syn: hodge-podge] 2: a miscellaneous collection (as of literary or musical selections)

HOMOPHONES

once, wants, wonts /wɒnts/

once

adj : belonging to some prior time; "erstwhile friend"; "our former glory"; "the once capital of the state"; "her quondam lover" [syn: erstwhile, former, onetime, quondam, sometime]

adv 1: on one occasion; "once I ran into her" [syn: one time, in one case] 2: as soon as; "once we are home, we can rest" [syn: when] 3: at a previous time; "once he loved her"; "her erstwhile writing" [syn: formerly, at one time, erstwhile]

wants

n : (plu of want) 1: states of extreme poverty [syn: privations, deprivations] 2: the states of needing things that are absent or unavailable; "there are serious lacks of insight into the problem"; [syn: lacks, deficiencies] 3: things that are necessary but lacking; "he had sufficient means to meet his simple needs"; "I tried to supply his wants" [syn: needs] 4: specific feelings of desire; "he got his wishes"; [syn: wishes]

v : (3rd pers sing of want) 1: feels or has a desire for; wants strongly; "He wants to go home now"; "She wants her own room" [syn: desires] 2: has need of; "This piano wants the attention of a competent tuner" [syn: needs, requires] 3: wishes or demands the presence of; "He wants you here at noon!" 4: hunts or looks for; wants for a particular reason; "Uncle Sam wants you" 5: is without, lacks; is deficient in; "wants courtesy"; "wants the strength to go on living"

wonts

n : (plu of wont) 1: established customs; [syn: habits] 2: patterns of behavior acquired through frequent repetition [syn: habits, uses]

one, won /wʌn/

one

adj 1: used of a single unit or thing; not two or more; [syn: 1] 2: particular but unspecified; "early one evening" 3: being one in number--a single unit or thing; "one person is going"; "her one thought was to win"; "I'm just one player on the team"; "one day is just like the next"; "seen one horse and you've seen them all" 4: being the single appropriate individual of a kind; only; "the one horse that could win this race"; "the one person I could marry" 5: having the indivisible character of a unit; "a unitary action"; "spoke with one voice" [syn: unitary] 6: of the same kind or quality; "two animals of one species" 7: used informally as an intensifier; "that is one fine dog" 8: indefinite in time or position; "he will come one day"; "one place or another" 9:

being a single entity made by combining separate components; "three chemicals combining into one solution 10: eminent beyond or above comparison; "matchless beauty"; "the team's nonpareil center fielder"; "she's one girl in a million"; "the one and only Muhammad Ali"; "a peerless scholar"; "infamy unmatched in the Western world"; "wrote with unmatchable clarity"; "unrivaled mastery of her art" [syn: matchless, nonpareil, one and only, peerless, unmatched, unmatchable, unrivaled, unrivalled]

n 1: the smallest whole number or a numeral representing this number; "he has the one but will need a two and three to go with it"; "they had lunch at one" [syn: 1, I, ace, single, unity] 2: a single person or thing; "he is the best one"; "this is the one I ordered"

won

adj : not subject to defeat; "with that move it's a won game" [ant: lost]

v : (past of win) "We won the baseball game 3 to 1."

oracle (see auricle)

oral (see aural)

ordinance, ordnance /ˈɔːrdnɪnts/

ordinance (also /ˈɔːrdɪnrɪnts/)

n 1: an authoritative rule [syn: regulation] 2: a statute enacted by a city government 3: the act of ordaining; "the priest's family was present for his ordination" [syn: ordination]

ordnance

n 1: military supplies [syn: munitions, ordnance stores] 2: large but transportable armament [syn: artillery, heavy weapon, gun]

oriel, oriole /ˈoʊriˀəl/

oriel

n : a projecting bay window corbelled or cantilevered out from a wall [syn: oriel window]

oriole

n 1: mostly tropical songbird; the male is usually bright orange and black [syn: Old World oriole] 2: American songbird; male is black and orange or yellow [syn: New World oriole, American oriole]

otter (see attar)

ought (see aught)

our (see hour)

outcast, outcaste /ˈaʊtkɛəst/

outcast

adj : excluded from a society [syn: friendless]

n : a person who is rejected (from society or home) [syn: castaway, pariah]

outcaste

adj : not belonging to or having been expelled from a caste and thus having no place or status in society; "the foreigner was a casteless person" [syn: casteless] n : a person belonging to no caste

overate, overrate

overate /ˈoʊvˈɹɛɪt/

v : (past of overeat) : eat immodestly; make a pig of oneself [syn: gorged, ingurgitated, overindulged, glutted, stuffed, engorged, gormandized, gourmandized, binged, pigged out, satiated, scarfed out] [ant: nibbled]

overrate /ˈoʊvɹˈɹɛɪt/

v : make too high an estimate of; "He overrated his own powers" [syn: overestimate] [ant: underestimate]

overdo, overdue /ˈoʊvˈɹdu/

overdo

v : do something to an excessive degree: "Don't overdo your exercise when it's hot." [syn: exaggerate]

overdue

adj : past due; not paid at the scheduled time; "an overdue installment"; "a delinquent account" [syn: delinquent]

overseas, oversees

/ˈoʊvˈɹsiz/

overseas

adj 1: in a foreign country; "markets abroad"; "overseas markets" [syn: abroad] 2: being or passing over or across the sea; "some overseas trade in grain arose" [syn: oversea]

adv 1: beyond or across the sea; "He lived overseas for many years" [syn: oversea] 2: in a place across an ocean [syn: beyond the sea, over the sea, abroad]

oversees

v : (3rd pers sing of oversee) : watch and direct; "He personally oversees every project." [syn: supervises, superintends, manages]

ox-eyed, oxide /ˈaksaɪd/

ox-eyed

adj : having large round eyes like those of an ox; "ox-eyed Juno"

oxide

n : any compound of oxygen with another element or a radical

-P-

P, pea, pee /pi/

p

n: the 16th letter of the Roman alphabet [syn: P]

pea

n 1: seed of a pea plant 2: the fruit or seed of a pea plant 3: a leguminous plant of the genus Pisum with small white flowers and long green pods containing edible green seeds [syn: pea plant]

pee

n 1: liquid excretory product; "there was blood in his urine"; "the child had to make water" [syn: urine, piss, piddle, weewee, water] 2: informal terms for urination; "he took a pee" [syn: peeing, pissing, piss]

v : eliminate urine; "The cat likes to pee on the expensive rug" [syn: make, urinate, piddle, puddle, micturate, piss, pee-pee, make water, relieve oneself, take a leak, spend a penny, wee, wee-wee, pass water]

paced, paste /peɪst/

paced

v : (past of pace) 1: walked with slow or fast paces; "He paced up and down the hall" 2: went at a pace, as of a horse 3: measured by pacing, as of distances 4: regulated or set the pace of; "Paced your efforts"

paste

n 1: any mixture of a soft and malleable consistency 2: an adhesive made from water and flour or starch; used on paper and paperboard [syn: library paste] 3: a tasty mixture to be spread on bread or crackers [syn: spread]

v 1: join or attach with glue [syn: glue] 2: hit with the fists; "He pasted his opponent" 3: cover the surface of; "paste the wall with burlap"

packed, pact /pækt/

packed

adj 1: filled to capacity; "a suitcase jammed with dirty clothes"; "stands jam-packed with fans"; "a packed theater" [syn: jammed, jam-packed] 2: pressed together or compressed; "packed snow"

v : (past of pack) 1: arranged in a container; "packed the books into the boxes" [ant: unpacked] 2: filled to capacity; "This singer always packed the concert halls"; "The murder trial packed the court house" 3: compressed into a wad; "wadded paper into the box" [syn: bundled, wadded, compacted] 4: carried, as on one's back; "Pack your tents to the top of the mountain" 5: set up a committee or legislative body with one's own supporters so as to influence the outcome; "packed a jury" 6: had with oneself; had on one's person; "She always took an umbrella"; "I always carried money"; "She packed a gun when preparing to go into the mountains" [syn: carried, took] 7: pressed tightly together or crammed; "The crowd packed the auditorium" [syn: thronged, mobbed, piled, jammed] 8: hiked with a backpack [syn: backpacked] 9: pressed down tightly; "tamped the coffee grinds in the container to make espresso" [syn: tamped down, tamped] 10: crowded or packed to capacity; "the theater was jam-packed" [syn: jam, jam pack, ram, chock up, cram, wad] 11: sealed with packing; "packed the faucet" 12: loaded with a pack [syn: loaded down] 13: treated the body or any part of it by wrapping it, as with blankets or sheets, and applying compresses to it, or stuffed it to provide cover, containment, or therapy, or to absorb blood; "The nurse packed gauze in the wound"; "You had better pack your swollen ankle with ice"

pact

n : a written agreement between two states or sovereigns [syn: treaty, accord]

packs, pax /pæks/
packs

n : (plu of pack) 1: large indefinite numbesr; " battalions of ants"; " multitudes of TV antennas"; " pluralities of religions" [syn: battalions, large numbers, multitudes, pluralities] 2: complete collections of similar things 3: small parcels (as of cigarettes or film) 4: associations of criminals; "police tried to break up the gang"; " packs of thieves" [syn: gangs, rings, mobs] 5: exclusive circles of people with common purposes [syn: cliques, coteries, in groups, inner circles, camps] 6: groups of hunting animals 7: creams that cleanse and tone the skin [syn: face packs] 8: sheets or blankets (either dry or wet) to wrap around the body for their therapeutic effects 9: bundles (especially ones carried on the back)

v : (3rd pers sing of pack) 1: arranges in a container; "packs the books into the boxes" [ant: unpacks] 2: fills to capacity; "This singer always packs the concert halls"; "The murder trial packed the court house" 3: compresses into a wad; "wads paper into the box" [syn: bundles, wads, compacts] 4: carries, as on one's back; "Pack your tents to the top of the mountain" 5: sets up a committee or legislative body with one's own supporters so as to influence the outcome; "packs a jury" 6: has with oneself; has on one's person; "She always takes an umbrella"; "He always carries money"; "She packs a gun when she goes into the mountains" [syn: carries, takes] 7: presses tightly together or crams;

"The crowd packed the auditorium" [syn: throngs, mobs, piles, jams] 8: hikes with a backpack; "Every summer he backpacks in the Rockies" [syn: backpacks] 9: presses down tightly; "tamps the coffee grinds in the container to make espresso" [syn: tamps down, tamps] 10: seals with packing; "packs the faucet" 11: has the property of being packable or compactable or of compacting easily; "This powder compacts easily"; "Such odd-shaped items do not pack well" [syn: compacts] 12: loads with a pack [syn: loads down] 13: treats the body or any part of it by wrapping it, as with blankets or sheets, and applying compresses to it, or stuffing it to provide cover, containment, or therapy, or to absorb blood; "The nurse packs gauze in the wound"; "You had better pack your swollen ankle with ice"

pax

n 1: (Roman Catholic Church) a greeting signifying Christian love for those assisting at the Eucharist [syn: kiss of peace] 2: period characterized by absence of war

paddy, patty /'pædi/
paddy

n 1: (ethnic slur) a person of Irish descent [syn: Mick, Mickey] 2: an irrigated or flooded field where rice is grown [syn: paddy field, rice paddy] 3: rice in the husk either gathered or still in the field

patty

n 1: small flat mass of chopped food [syn: cake] 2: small pie or pasty 3: round flat candy

paean, peon /'pian/
paean

n 1: a formal expression of praise [syn: encomium, eulogy, panegyric, pean] 2: a hymn of praise (especially one sung in ancient Greece to invoke or thank a deity) [syn: pean]

peon

n : a laborer who is obliged to do menial work [syn: drudge, navvy, galley slave]

paid, payed /peɪd/
paid

adj 1: marked by the reception of pay; "paid work"; "a paid official"; "a paid announcement"; "a paid check" [ant: unpaid] 2: involving gainful employment in something often done as a hobby [syn: non-recreational] 3: yielding a fair profit [syn: gainful, paying]

v : (past of pay) 1: gave money, usually in exchange for goods or services; "I paid four dollars for this sandwich " 2: conveys, as of a compliment, regards, attention, etc.; bestows; "She paid him no mind"; "gave the orders"; "Gave him my best regards"; "pais attention" [syn: gave] 3: did or gave something to somebody in return; "Has she paid you for the work you did?" [syn: paid off, made up, compensated] 4: bore (a cost or penalty), in recompense for some action; "She paid the penalty for speaking out rashly" 5: canceled or discharged a debt [syn: paid up, anted up] [ant: defaulted] 6: brought in; "interest-bearing accounts"; "How much has this savings certificate paid annually?" [syn: yielded, bore] 7: rendered; "paid a visit" 8: "paid a call" 8: was worth it; "It paid to go through the trouble" 9: dedicated; "gave thought to"; "gave priority to"; "paid attention to" [syn: gave, devoted] 10: discharged or settled; "paid a debt"; "paid an obligation" 11: made a compensation for; "a favor that cannot be paid back"

payed

adj : (rope) slackened or allowed to run out

pail, pale /pɛɪl/
pail

n 1: a roughly cylindrical that is vessel open at the top [syn: bucket] 2: the quantity contained in a pail [syn: pailful]

pale

adj 1: very light colored; highly diluted with white; "pale green"; "pale blue eyes" 2: (of light) lacking in intensity or brightness; dim or feeble; "the pale light of a half moon"; "a pale sun"; "the late afternoon light coming through the el tracks fell in pale oblongs on the street"; "a pallid sky"; "the pale (or wan) stars"; "the wan light of dawn" [syn: pallid, wan] 3: lacking in vitality or interest or effectiveness; "a pale rendition of the aria"; "pale prose with the faint sweetness of lavender"; "a pallid performance" [syn: pallid] 4: abnormally deficient in color as suggesting physical or emotional distress; "the pallid face of the invalid"; "her wan face suddenly flushed" [syn: pallid, wan] 5: not full or rich; "high, pale, pure and lovely song"

n : a wooden strip forming part of a fence [syn: picket]

v : turn pale, as if in fear [syn: blanch, blench]

pain, pane /pɛɪn/
pain

n 1: a symptom of some physical hurt or disorder; "the patient developed severe pain and distension" [syn: hurting] 2: emotional distress; a fundamental feeling that people try to avoid; "the pain of loneliness" [syn: painfulness] [ant: pleasure] 3: a somatic sensation of acute discomfort; "as the intensity increased the sensation changed from tickle to pain" [syn: painful sensation] 4: a bothersome annoying person; "that kid is a terrible pain" [syn: pain in the neck, nuisance]

5: something or someone that causes trouble; a source of unhappiness; "a bit of a bother" [syn: annoyance, nuisance, bother, botheration, pain in the neck, pain in the ass]

v 1: cause bodily suffering to [syn: afflict, trouble, ail] 2: cause anguish;, make miserable [syn: anguish, hurt]

pane

n 1: sheet glass cut in shapes for windows or doors [syn: pane of glass, window glass] 2: a panel or section of panels in a wall or door [syn: paneling]

pair, pare, payer, pear /pɛəɹ/
pair

n 1: a set of two similar things considered as a unit [syn: brace] 2: two items of the same kind [syn: couple, doubleton, twosome, twain, brace, span, yoke, couplet, distich, duo, duet, dyad] 3: two people considered as a unit 4: a poker hand with 2 cards of the same value

v 1: form a pair or pairs; "The two old friends paired off" [syn: pair off, partner off, couple] 2: bring two objects, ideas, or people together; "This fact is coupled to the other one"; "Matchmaker, can you match my daughter with a nice young man?"; "The student was paired with a partner for collaboration on the project" [syn: match, mate, couple, twin] 3: make love; "Birds mate in the Spring" [syn: copulate, mate, couple]

pare

v 1: decrease gradually or bit by bit [syn: pare down] 2: cut small bits or pare shavings from; "whittle a piece of wood" [syn: whittle] 3: strip the skin off ("pare apples") [syn: skin, peel] 4: remove the edges from: "pare one's fingernails"; "trim the photograph" [syn: trim]

payer (also /ˈpɛɪjəɹ/)

n : a person who pays money for something [syn: remunerator]

pear

n 1: sweet juicy gritty-textured fruit available in many varieties 2: Old World tree having sweet gritty-textured juicy fruit; widely cultivated in many varieties [syn: pear tree, Pyrus communis]

paired, pared /pɛəɹd/
paired

adj 1: used of gloves, socks, etc. [syn: mated] 2: (botany) of leaves etc; growing in pairs on either side of a stem; "opposite leaves" [syn: opposite] [ant: alternate] 3: mated sexually

v : (past of pair) "She paired them up because they had mutual interests."

pared

v : (past of pare) (see pair) "They pared three bushels of potatoes."

HOMOPHONES

palate, palet, palette, pallet, pellet

palate /'pælɪt/

n : the upper surface of the mouth that separates the oral and nasal cavities [syn: roof of the mouth]

palet /'pælɪt/

n 1: interior chaff or husk of grasses; one of the chaffy scales or bractlets growing on the receptacle of many compound flowers, as the Coreopsis, the sunflower, etc. [syn: palea] 2: pendulous process of the skin on the throat of a bird, as in the turkey; a dewlap [syn: palea]

palette /'pælɪt/

n 1: the range of color characteristic of a particular artist or painting or school of art" [syn: pallet] 2: board that provides a flat surface on which artists mix paints and the range of colors used [syn: pallet] 3: one of the rounded armor plates at the armpits of a suit of armor

pallet /'pælɪt/

n 1: (var of palette) 2: a portable platform for storing or moving goods that are stacked on it 3: a hand tool with a flat blade used by potters for mixing and shaping clay 4: a mattress filled with straw or a pad made of quilts; used as a bed

pellet /'pɛlɪt/

n 1: a small sphere 2: a solid missile discharged from a firearm; "the shot buzzed past his ear" [syn: shot]

pall, pawl /pɔl/

pall

n 1: a sudden numbing dread [syn: chill] 2: burial garment in which a corpse is wrapped [syn: shroud, cerement, winding-sheet, winding-clothes] 3: hanging cloth used as a blind [syn: curtain, drape, drapery, mantle]

v 1: become less interesting or attractive [syn: dull] 2: cause to lose courage; "dashed by the refusal" [syn: daunt, dash, scare off, frighten off, scare away, frighten away, scare] 3: cover with a pall 4: cause surfeit through excess, of something that was initially pleasing: "Too much spicy food cloyed his appetite" [syn: cloy] 5: cause to become flat, of beer or wine 6: lose sparkle or bouquet, as of wine or beer; "pall" is an obsolete word [syn: die, become flat] 7: lose strength or effectiveness; become or appear boring, insipid, or tiresome (to); "the course palled on her" 8: get tired of something or somebody [syn: tire, weary, fatigue, jade]

pawl

n : a hinged catch that fits into a notch of a ratchet to move a wheel forward or prevent it from moving backward [syn: detent, click, dog]

par, parr /pɑɹ/

par

n 1: (in golf) the standard number of strokes set for each hole on a golf course, or for the entire course; "a par-5 hole"; "par for this course is 72" 2: a state of being essentially equal or equivalent: "on a par with the best" [syn: equality, equivalence]

v : make a score (on a hole) equal to par; in golf

parr

n 1: a young salmon up to 2 years old 2: the young of various fishes

parish, perish

parish /'pæɹɪʃ/

n 1: a local church community 2: the local subdivision of a diocese committed to one pastor 3: a county in Louisiana

perish /'pɛɹɪʃ/

v 1: pass from physical life and lose all bodily attributes and functions necessary to sustain life; "She died from cancer"; "They children perished in the fire"; "The patient went peacefully" [syn: die, decease, go, exit, pass away, expire, pass] [ant: be born] 2: not think about something; "Perish the thought!"

parity, parody

parity /'pæɹɪti/

n 1: (obstetrics) the number of live-born children a woman has delivered; "the parity of the mother must be considered"; "a bipara is a woman who has given birth to two children" [syn: para] 2: (mathematics) a relation between a pair of integers: if both integers are odd or both are even they have the same parity; if one is odd and the other is even they have different parity 3: (computer science) an error detection procedure in which a bit (0 or 1) added to each group of bits so that it will have either an odd number of 1's or an even number of 1's; e.g., if the parity is odd then any group of bits that arrives with an even number of 1's must contain an error [syn: parity bit] 4: (physics) parity is conserved in a universe in which the laws of physics are the same in a right-handed system of coordinates as in a left-handed system [syn: conservation of parity, space-reflection symmetry, mirror symmetry] 5: functional equality

parody /'pæɹɪdi/

n 1: a composition that imitates somebody's style in a humorous way [syn: lampoon, spoof, mockery, takeoff, burlesque, travesty, charade, pasquinade, put-on] 2: humorous or satirical mimicry [syn: mockery, takeoff]

v 1: make a spoof of; make fun of [syn: spoof] 2: make a parody of; "The students like to parody the teachers" [syn: spoof, burlesque]

HOMOPHONES

passable, passible /'pæsɪbᵊl/
passable
adj 1: able to be passed or traversed or crossed; "the road is passable" [ant: impassable] 2: about average; acceptable; "more than adequate as a secretary" [syn: adequate, fair to middling] 3: neither good nor bad; "an indifferent performance"; "a gifted painter but an indifferent actor"; "her work at the office is passable", "a so-so golfer"; "feeling only so-so"; "prepared a tolerable dinner"; "a tolerable working knowledge of French" [syn: indifferent, so-so, tolerable]
passible
adj : capable of feeling or suffering
passed, past /pɛəst/
passed
adj : being acceptable "She earned a passed grade on the exam." [syn: passing] [ant: failed, failing]
v : (past of pass) 1: went across or through; "We passed the point where the police car had parked"; "A terrible thought went through his mind" [syn: went through, went across] 2: pass by; "A black limousine passed by when she looked out the window"; "He passed his professor in the hall"; "One line of soldiers surpassed the other" [syn: traveled by, passed by, surpassed, went past, went by] 3: make laws, bills, etc.: "They passed the amendment" [syn: legislated] 4: pass by, as of time [syn: elapsed, lapsed, slipped by, glided by, slipped away, went by, slid by, went along] 5: place into the hands or custody of; "Turn the files over to me, please"; "He turned over the prisoner to his lawyers" [syn: handed, reached, passed on, turned over, gave] 6: stretch out over a distance, space, time, or scope; run or extend between two points or beyond a certain point; "Service runs all the way to Cranbury"; "His knowledge doesn't go very far"; "My memory extends back to my fourth year of life"; "The facts extend beyond a consideration of her personal assets" [syn: ran, went, led, extended] 7: travel past, as of a vehicle; "The sports car passed all the trucks" " [syn: overtook, overhauled] 8: come to pass; "What is happening?"; "The meeting took place off without an incidence"; "Nothing occurred that seemed important" [syn: happened, happed, went on, passed off, occurred, came about, took place] 9: go unchallenged; be approved; "The bill cleared the House" [syn: cleared] 10: pass in a specific way; as of time; "How are you spending your summer vacation?" [syn: spent] 11: guide or pass over something; "He ran his eyes over her body"; "She ran her fingers along the carved figurine";

"He drew her hair through his fingers" [syn: guided, ran, drew] 12: transmit information ; "Please communicate this message to all employees" [syn: communicated, passed on, put across] 13: disappear gradually; as of emotions, for example; "The pain eventually passed off" [syn: evanesced, faded, blew over, passed off, fleeted] 14: go successfully through a test or a selection process: "She passed the new Jersey Bar Exam and can practice law now" [syn: made it] [ant: failed] 15: go beyond; "She exceeded out expectations"; "She topped her performance of last year" [syn: exceeded, transcended, overstepped, went past, topped] 16: accept or judge as acceptable; "The teacher passed the student although he was weak" [ant: failed] 17: allow to go without comment or censure: "the insult passed as if unnoticed" 18: transfer to another; of rights or property; "Our house passed under his official control" 19: pass into a specified state or condition: "He sank into Nirvana" [syn: sank, lapsed] 20: be identified, regarded, accepted, or mistaken for someone or something else; as by denying one's own ancestry or background; "He could pass as his twin brother"; "She passed as a White woman even though her grandfather was Black" 21: threw (a ball) to another player; "Smith passed" 22: be inherited by; "The estate fell to my sister"; "The land returned to the family"; "The estate devolved to an heir that everybody had assumed to be dead" [syn: fell, returned, devolved] 23: cause to pass: "She passed around the plates" 24: grant authorization or clearance for; "Clear the manuscript for publication" [syn: authorized, cleared] 25: pass from physical life and lose all bodily attributes and functions necessary to sustain life; "She died from cancer"; "They children perished in the fire"; "The patient went peacefully [syn: died, deceased, perished, went, exited, passed away, expired] [ant: was born] 26: eliminate from the body; "Pass a kidney stone" [syn: excreted, eliminated]
past
adj 1: earlier than the present time; no longer current; "time past"; "his youth is past"; "this past Thursday"; "the past year" [ant: present, future] 2: of a person who has held and relinquished a position or office; "a past member of the board" [syn: past, preceding, retiring] 3: (grammar) a verb tense or other construction referring to events or states that existed at some previous time; "past participle"
n 1: the time that has elapsed; "forget the past" [syn: past times, yesteryear, yore] [ant: future] 2: a earlier period in

someone's life (especially one that they have reason to keep secret); "reporters dug into the candidate's past" 3: a verb tense that expresses actions or states in the past [syn: past tense]

adv : so as to pass a given point; "every hour a train goes past" [syn: by]

pâte, pot /pɑt/

pâte

n : plastic material for pottery

pot

n 1: metal or earthenware cooking vessel that is usually round and deep; often has a handle and lid 2: a plumbing fixture for defecation and urination [syn: toilet, can, commode, crapper, potty, stool, throne] 3: the quantity contained in a pot [syn: potful] 4: a container in which plants are cultivated [syn: flowerpot] 5: (often followed by `of') a large number or amount or extent; "a batch of letters"; "a deal of trouble"; "a pot of money"; "he made a mint on the stock market" [syn: batch, deal, flock, good deal, great deal, hatful, heap, lot, mass, mess, mickle, mint, muckle, peck, pile, plenty, quite a little, raft, sight, slew, spate, stack, tidy sum, wad, whole lot, whole slew] 6: the cumulative amount involved in a game (such as poker) [syn: jackpot, kitty] 7: slang terms for a paunch [syn: potbelly, bay window, corporation, tummy] 8: a resistor with three terminals, the third being an adjustable center terminal; used to adjust voltages in radios and TV sets [syn: potentiometer] 9: street names for marijuana [syn: grass, green goddess, dope, weed, gage, sess, sens, smoke, skunk, locoweed, Mary Jane]

v : plant in a pot; "He potted the palm"

patience, patients /'peɪʃənts/

patience

n 1: good-natured tolerance of delay or incompetence [syn: forbearance] [ant: impatience] 2: a card game played by one person [syn: solitaire]

patients

n : (plu of patient) : people who require medical care; "the number of emergency patients has grown rapidly"

pause, paws /pɔz/

pause

n 1: a time interval during which there is a temporary cessation of something [syn: intermission, break, interruption, suspension] 2: temporary inactivity

v 1: interrupt temporarily an activity before continuing; "pause to take a breath" [syn: hesitate] 2: cease an action temporarily; "We pause for station identification"; "let's break for lunch" [syn: intermit, break]

paws

n : (plu of paw) 1: clawed feet of an animal especially a quadruped 2: the (prehensile)

extremity of the superior limb; "he had the hands of a surgeon"; "he extended his mitts" [syn: hands, mitts]

v 1: scrapes with the paws; "The bear paws at the door" 2: touches clumsily; "the man paws her in his sleep"

pea, pee /pi/

pea

n 1: seed of a pea plant 2: the fruit or seed of a pea plant 3: a leguminous plant of the genus Pisum with small white flowers and long green pods containing edible green seeds [syn: pea plant]

pee

n 1: liquid excretory product; "there was blood in his urine"; "the child had to make water" [syn: urine, piss, piddle, weewee, water] 2: informal terms for urination; "he took a pee" [syn: piss]

v : eliminate urine; "Again, the cat had made on the expensive rug" [syn: make, urinate, piddle, puddle, micturate, piss, pee-pee, make water, relieve oneself, take a leak, spend a penny, wee, wee-wee, pass water, pissing, peeing]

peace, piece /pis/

peace

n 1: the state prevailing during the absence of war [ant: war] 2: harmonious relations; freedom from disputes; "the roommates lived in peace together" 3: the absence of mental stress or anxiety [syn: peacefulness, peace of mind, repose, serenity, heartsease, ataraxis] 4: the general security of public places; "he was arrested for disturbing the peace" [syn: public security] 5: a treaty to cease hostilities; "peace came on November 11th" [syn: peace treaty, pacification]

piece

n 1: a separate part of a whole: "an important piece of the evidence" 2: an item that is an instance of some type; "he designed a new piece of equipment" or "she bought a lovely piece of china" 3: a portion of a natural object; "they analyzed the river into three parts"; "he needed a piece of granite" [syn: part] 4: a musical work that has been created; "the composition is written in four movements" [syn: musical composition, opus, composition, piece of music] 5: an instance of some kind; "it was a nice piece of work"; "he had a bit of good luck" [syn: bit] 6: an artistic or literary composition; "he wrote an interesting piece on Iran"; "the children acted out a comic piece to amuse the guests" 7: a portable gun; "he wore his firearm in a shoulder holster" [syn: firearm, small-arm] 8: a serving that has been cut from a larger portion; "a piece of pie"; "a slice of bread" [syn: slice] 9: a distance; "it is down the

HOMOPHONES

road a piece" 10: an object created by a sculptor; "it was not known who created the piece" 11: a period of indeterminate length (usually short) marked by some action or condition; "he was here for a little while"; "I need to rest for a piece"; "a spell of good weather" [syn: while, spell] 12: a share of something; "a slice of the company's revenue" [syn: slice] 13: game equipment consisting of an object used in playing certain board games; "he taught me to set up the men on the chess board"; "he sacrificed a piece to get a strategic advantage" [syn: man] 14: female sexual partner [syn: piece of ass] 15: part of a collection; "She added another piece to the silverware set."

v 1: to join or unite the pieces of; "patch the skirt" [syn: patch] 2: make by putting pieces together; "She pieced a quilt" [syn: assemble, put together, set up] [ant: disassemble] 3: join during spinning, as of broken pieces of thread, slivers, or rovings 4: eat intermittently; take small bites of; "He pieced at the sandwich all morning"; "She never eats a full meal--she just picks at the food" [syn: nibble, pick] 5: repair by adding pieces; "She pieced the china cup" [syn: patch]

peachy, pichi /ˈpitʃi/
peachy
adj : very good; "he did a bully job"; "a neat sports car"; "had a great time at the party"; "you look simply smashing" [syn: bang-up, bully, corking, cracking, dandy, great, groovy, keen, neat, nifty, not bad, slap-up, swell, smashing]
pichi
n : Peruvian shrub with small pink to lavender tubular flowers; leaves yield a tonic and diuretic [syn: Fabiana imbricata]

peak, peek, pique /pik/
peak
adj 1: of a period of maximal use or demand or activity; "at peak hours the streets traffic is unbelievable" [ant: off-peak] 2: approaching or constituting a maximum; "maximal temperature"; "maximum speed"; "working at peak efficiency" [syn: highest] 3: consisting of or causing a climax; "a peak experience" [syn: climactic, peak]

n 1: the most extreme possible amount or value; "voltage peak" 2: the period of greatest prosperity or productivity [syn: flower, prime, heyday, bloom, blossom, efflorescence, flush] 3: the highest level or degree attainable: "his landscapes were deemed the acme of beauty"; "the artist's gifts are at their acme"; "at the height of her career"; "the peak of perfection"; "summer was at its peak"; "...catapulted Einstein to the pinnacle of fame"; "the summit of his

ambition"; "so many highest superlatives achieved by man"; "at the top of his profession" [syn: acme, height, elevation, pinnacle, summit, superlative, top] 4: the uppermost part of a shape; "at the peak of the pyramid" [syn: crown, summit] 5: the top point of a mountain or hill; "the view from the peak was magnificent"; "they clambered to the summit of Monadnock" [syn: crown, crest, top, tip, summit] 6: a V shape; "the cannibal's teeth were filed to sharp points" [syn: point, tip] 7: the highest point of something [syn: vertex, apex, acme] 8: a brim that projects to the front to shade the eyes; "he pulled down the bill of his cap and trudged ahead" [syn: bill, eyeshade, visor]

v : to reach the highest point; attain maximum intensity, activity: "That wild, speculative spirit peaked in 1929." [syn: reach a peak]
peek
n : a secret look [syn: peep]
v 1: look furtively [syn: peep] 2: throw a glance at; take a brief look at; "She only has time to peek at the paper"; "I only glanced--I didn't see anything interesting" [syn: glance]
pique
adj : of textiles; having parallel raised lines [syn: corded, twill, twilled]
n 1: tightly woven fabric with raised cords 2: a sudden outburst of anger; "his temper sparked like damp firewood" [syn: temper, irritation]
v : cause to feel resentment or indignation; "Her tactless remarks pique me" [syn: offend]

peal, peel /pil/
peal
n : a deep prolonged sound (as of thunder or large bells) [syn: pealing, roll, rolling]
v 1: ring recurrently; of bells [syn: toll] 2: make a ringing sound [syn: ring]
peel
n: the rind of a fruit
v 1: strip the skin off ("pare apples") [syn: skin, pare] 2: come off in flakes or thin small pieces; "The paint in my house is will peel off in this weather." [syn: peel off, flake off, flake]

pealing, peeling /ˈpilɪŋ/
pealing
n (var of peal) (see peal)
peeling
adj : having the paint loose and peeling away; "a dilapidated house with peeling paint"; "peeling row houses"
n : loss of bits of outer skin by peeling or shedding or coming off in scales [syn: desquamation, shedding]
v : (progressive of peel) (see peal); "The cooks are peeling the potatoes."

HOMOPHONES

pearl, perle, purl /pɜːl/
pearl
adj : relating to or resembling or made of or adorned with pearls or mother-of-pearl; "a pearl-handled knife"
n 1: a smooth lustrous round structure inside the shell of a clam or oyster; much valued as a jewel 2: a shade of white the color of bleached bones [syn: bone, ivory, off-white] 3: a shape that is small and round; "he studied the shapes of low-viscosity drops"; "beads of sweat on his forehead" [syn: drop, bead]
v : gather pearls, from oysters in the ocean
perle
n : a pearl-shaped medicine capsule
purl
n 1: gold or silver wire thread 2: a basic knitting stitch [syn: purl stitch]
v 1: flow in a circular current, of liquids [syn: eddy, whirlpool, swirl, whirl] 2: make a murmuring sound; "the water was purling" 3: knit with a purl stitch 4: edge or border with gold or silver embroidery 5: embroider with gold or silver thread

pearlite, perlite /ˈpɜːlaɪt/
pearlite
n : a lamellar mixture of cementite and ferrite formed during the cooling of austenite; a micro-constituent of steel and cast iron
perlite
n : volcanic glass that has a concentric shelly structure; appears as if composed of concretions; is usually grayish and sometimes spherulitic; when expanded by heat forms a lightweight aggregate used especially in concrete and plaster and as a medium for potting plants

pecten, pectin /ˈpɛktɪn/
pecten
n 1: body part that resembles a comb 2: a folded vascular pigmented membrane projecting into the vitreous humor in the eye of a bird or reptile
pectin
n : any of various water-soluble colloidal carbohydrates that occur in ripe fruit and vegetables; used in making fruit jellies and jams

pedal, peddle /ˈpɛdəl/
pedal
adj : of or relating to the feet; "the word for a pedal extremity is `foot'"
n 1: a sustained bass note [syn: pedal point] 2: a lever that is operated with the foot [syn: treadle, foot pedal, foot lever]
v 1: ride a bicycle [syn: bicycle, cycle, bike, wheel] 2: operate the pedals on a keyboard instrument
peddle
v : sell or offer for sale from place to place [syn: monger, huckster, hawk, vend, pitch]

peer, pier /pɪɹ/
peer
n 1: a person who is of equal standing with another in a group [syn: equal, match, compeer] 2: (British) a nobleman (duke or marquis or earl or viscount or baron) who is a member of the British peerage
v : look searchingly; "Peer into the back of the shop to see whether a salesman is around."
pier
n 1: a platform built out from the shore into the water and supported by piles; provides access to ships and boats [syn: wharf] 2: (architecture) a vertical supporting structure (as a portion of wall between two doors or windows) 3: a support for two adjacent bridge spans

pekoe, picot /ˈpikoʊ/
pekoe
n : a superior grade of black tea; grown in India and Sri Lanka and Java [syn: orange pekoe]
picot
n : an edging of small loops, as on lace or ribbon

pelisse, police /ˈpəlis/
pelisse
n : a sleeveless cape that is lined or trimmed with fur
police
n : the force of policemen and officers; "the law came looking for him" [syn: police force, constabulary, law]
v : maintain the security of by carrying out a control [syn: patrol]

penal, penile /ˈpinəl/
penal
adj 1: of or relating to punishment; "penal reform"; "penal code" 2: serving as or designed to impose punishment; "penal servitude"; "a penal colony" 3: subject to punishment by law; "a penal offense" [syn: punishable]
penile
adj : of or relating to the penis; "penile erection"

penance, pennants /ˈpɛnənts/
penance
n 1: remorse for your past conduct [syn: repentance, penitence] 2: a Catholic sacrament; repentance and confession and satisfaction and absolution 3: voluntary self-punishment in order to atone for some wrongdoing [syn: self-mortification, self-abasement]
pennants
n : (plu of pennant)1: the award given to the champion [syn: crown] 2: a flag longer than it is wide (and often tapering) 3: a long flag; often tapering [syn: pennon, streamer, waft]

HOMOPHONES

pendant, pendent /'pɛndᵊnt/

pendant

n 1: an adornment that hangs from a piece of jewelry (necklace or earring) 2: branched lighting fixture; often ornate; hangs from the ceiling [syn: chandelier]

pendent

adj : supported from above; "the child dabbled his dangling feet in the water"; "fuchsias in hanging pots"; "pendent bunches of grapes"; "a suspended fireplace" [syn: dangling, hanging, pendent, suspended]

penitence, penitents /'pɛnɪtɛnts/

penitence

n : remorse for past conduct [syn: repentance, penance]

penitents

n : people who repent for wrongdoing (a Roman Catholic may be admitted to penance under the direction of a confessor)

people, pipal /'pipᵊl/

people

n 1: (plural) any group of human beings (men or women or children) collectively; "old people"; "there were at least 200 people in the audience" 2: the body of citizens of a state or country; "the Spanish people" [syn: citizenry] 3: the common people generally; "separate the warriors from the mass"; "power to the people" [syn: multitude, masses, mass, hoi polloi] 4: members of a family line; "his people have been farmers for generations"; "are your people still alive?"
v 1: fill with people or supply with inhabitants; "people a room"; "The government wanted to populate the remote area of the country" [syn: populate]

pipal

n : fig tree of India noted for great size and longevity; lacks the prop roots of the banyan; regarded as sacred by Buddhists [syn: pipal tree, sacred fig, bo tree, Ficus religiosa]

per, purr /pəɹ/

per

prep : by means of; through the agency of; by; for; for each; "per annum", annually); "per capita", (by heads or according to individuals); "per curium" (by the court); per se, (by itself, of itself); "per cent" (by the hundred)

purr

n : a low vibrating sound typical of a contented cat
v 1: make a soft swishing sound, as of a motor working or wings flapping [syn: whiz, whirr, whir] 2: indicate pleasure by purring; characteristic of cats [syn: make vibrant sounds]

pervade, purveyed /pəɹ'veɪd/

pervade

v : spread or diffuse through; "An atmosphere of distrust has permeated this administration" [syn: permeate, diffuse, imbue]

purveyed

v : (past of purvey) : supplied with provisions [syn: provisioned]

petit, petty /'pɛti/

petit

adj : small; little; insignificant (obsolete except in legal language "petit larceny, etc.")

petty

adj 1: inferior in rank or status; "the junior faculty"; "a lowly corporal"; "petty officialdom"; "a subordinate functionary" [syn: junior-grade, inferior, lower, lower-ranking, lowly, secondary, subaltern, subordinate] 2: (informal terms) small and of little importance; "a petty sum of money"; "a footling gesture"; "our worries are lilliputian compared with those of countries that are at war"; "a little (or small) matter"; "Mickey Mouse regulations"; "a dispute over niggling details"; "limited to petty enterprises"; "piffling efforts"; "giving a police officer a free meal may be against the law, but it seems to be a picayune infraction" [syn: fiddling, footling, lilliputian, little, Mickey Mouse, niggling, piddling, piffling, picayune, trivial] 3: contemptibly narrow in outlook; "petty little comments"; "disgusted with their small-minded pettiness" [syn: small-minded]

petrel, petrol /'pɛtɪl/

petrel

n : relatively small long-winged tube-nosed bird that flies far from land

petrol

n : a volatile flammable mixture of hydrocarbons (hexane and heptane and octane etc.) derived from petroleum; used mainly as a fuel in internal-combustion engines [syn: gasoline, gas]

pharaoh (see faro)
phase (see fays)
phew (see few)
phial (see faille)
philter (see filter)
phiz (see fizz)
phlox (see flocks)
phosphorous, phosphorus /'fasfᵊɹəs/

phosphorous

adj : containing or characteristic of phosphorus; "phosphoric acid" [syn: phosphoric]

phosphorus

n 1: a multivalent nonmetallic element of the nitrogen family that occurs commonly

HOMOPHONES

in inorganic phosphate rocks and as organic phosphates in all living cells; is highly reactive and occurs in several allotropic forms [syn: P, atomic number 15] 2: a planet (usually Venus) seen just before sunrise in the eastern sky [syn: morning star, daystar, Phosphorus]

phrase (see fraise)

pi, pie /paɪ/
pi
n 1: the ratio of the circumference to the diameter of a circle [syn: A, 3.14159265358979323846...] 2: the 16th letter of the Greek alphabet

pie
n 1: dish baked in pastry-lined pan often with a pastry top

pica, pika /ˈpaɪkə/
pica
n 1: a linear unit (1/6 inch) used in printing [syn: em, pica em] 2: magpies [syn: Pica, genus Pica] 3: eating of earth or clay or chalk; occurs in some primitive tribes or sometimes in cases of nutritional deficiency [syn: geophagy, geophagia]

pika
n : small short-eared burrowing mammal of rocky uplands of Asia and western North America [syn: mouse hare, rock rabbit]

picks, pix /pɪks/
picks
v : (3rd pers sing of pick) 1: select carefully from a group: "She finally picked her successor"; "He picked his way carefully"; "We had to pick through a lot of data" 2: look for and gather; "pick mushrooms"; "pick flowers" [syn: plucks, culls] 3: harass with constant criticism; "Don't always pick on your little brother" [syn: blames, finds fault] 4: provoke: "pick a fight or a quarrel" 5: remove in small bits: "pick meat from a bone" 6: remove unwanted substances from, such as feathers or pits, as of chickens or fruit; "Clean the turkey" [syn: cleans] 7: pilfer or rob: "pick pockets" 8: pay for something; "pick up the tab"; "pick up the burden of high-interest mortgages" [syn: foots] 9: pull lightly but sharply with a plucking motion, as of guitar strings; "he plucked the strings of his mandolin" [syn: plucks, plunks] 10: attack with or as if with a pickaxe of ice or rocky ground, for example; "Pick open the ice" [syn: breaks up] 11: hit lightly with a picking motion [syn: pecks, beaks] 12: eat intermittently; take small bites of; "He pieced at the sandwich all morning"; "She never eats a full meal--she just picks at the food" [syn: nibbles, pieces]

pix
n 1: a chest in which coins from the mint are held to await assay [syn: pyx, pyx

chest, pix chest] 2: any receptacle in which wafers for the Eucharist are kept [syn: pyx] 3: (slang) pictures [syn: pics]

picnic, pyknic /ˈpɪknɪk/
picnic
n 1: a day devoted to an outdoor social gathering [syn: field day, outing] 2: any undertaking that is easy to do; "marketing this product will be no picnic" [syn: cinch, breeze, snap, duck soup, child's play, pushover, walkover, piece of cake] 3: any informal meal eaten outside or on an excursion
v : eat alfresco, in the open air; "We picnicked near the lake on this gorgeous Sunday"

pyknic
adj : having a squat and fleshy build; shortness of stature, broadness of girth, and powerful muscularity [syn: stocky, endomorphic] [ant: mesomorphic, ectomorphic]

pidgin, pigeon /ˈpɪdʒɪn/
pidgin
n : an artificial language used for trade between speakers of different languages

pigeon
n : wild and domesticated birds having a heavy body and short legs

pinion, pinon /ˈpɪnjən/
pinion
n 1: a gear with a small number of teeth designed to mesh with a larger wheel or rack 2: any of the larger wing or tail feathers of a bird [syn: flight feather, quill, quill feather] 3: wing of a bird [syn: pennon]
v 1: bind the arms of [syn: shackle] 2: cut the wings off (of birds)

pinon
n : any of several low-growing pines of western North America [syn: pinyon, piñon]

pistil, pistol /ˈpɪstəl/
pistil
n : the female ovule-bearing part of a flower composed of ovary and style and stigma [syn: gynoecium]

pistol
n : a firearm that is held and fired with one hand [syn: handgun, side arm, shooting iron]

place, plaice /pleɪs/
place
n 1: a point located with respect to surface features of some region; "this is a nice place for a picnic" [syn: topographic point, spot] 2: any area set aside for a particular purpose; "who owns this place?"; "the president was concerned about the property across from the White House" [syn: property] 3: an abstract mental location; "he has a special place in my thoughts"; "a

HOMOPHONES

place in my heart"; "a political system with no place for the less prominent groups" 4: a general vicinity; "He comes from a place near Chicago" 5: the function or position properly or customarily occupied or served by another: "can you go in my stead?"; "took his place"; "in lieu of" [syn: stead, position, lieu] 6: a particular situation: "If you were in my place what would you do?" [syn: shoes] 7: where you live; "deliver the package to my home"; "he doesn't have a home to go to"; "your place or mine?" [syn: home] 8: a job in an organization; "he occupied a post in the treasury" [syn: position, post, berth, office, spot, situation] 9: the particular portion of space occupied by a physical object: "he put the lamp back in its place" [syn: position] 10: proper or designated social situation: "he overstepped his place"; "the responsibilities of a man in his station"; "married above her station" [syn: station] 11: a space reserved for sitting (as in a theater or on a train or airplane); "he booked their seats in advance"; "he sat in someone else's place" [syn: seat] 12: the passage that is being read; "he lost his place on the page" 13: proper or appropriate position or location; "a woman's place is no longer in the kitchen" 14: a public square with room for pedestrians; "they met at Elm Plaza"; "Grosvenor Place" [syn: plaza, piazza] 15: an item on a list or in a sequence; "in the second place"; "moved from third to fifth position" [syn: position] 16: a blank area; "write your name in the space provided" [syn: space, blank space]
v 1: put into a certain place or abstract location; "Put your things here"; "Set the tray down"; "Set the dogs on the scent of the missing children"; "Place emphasis on a certain point" [syn: put, set, pose, position, lay] 2: place somebody in a particular situation or location: "he was placed on probation" 3: assign a rank or rating to; "how would you rank these students?" [syn: rate, rank, range, order, grade] 4: assign a location to; "The company located some of their agents in Los Angeles" [syn: locate, site] 5: to arrange for; "place a phone call", "place a bet" 6: take a place in a competition; often followed by an ordinal; "Jerry came in third in the Marathon" [syn: come in, come out] 7: intend (something) to move towards a certain goal; "He aimed his fists towards his opponent's face"; "criticism directed at her superior"; "direct your anger towards others, not towards yourself" [syn: target, aim, direct, point] 8: recognize as being; establish the identity of someone or something; "She identified the man on the 'wanted' poster" [syn: identify] 9: assign

to (a job or a home) 10: locate; "The film is set in Africa" [syn: set, localize] 11: estimate; "We put the time of arrival at 8 P.M." [syn: put, set] 12: identify the location or place of; "We localized the source of the infection" [syn: localize] 13: make an investment; "Put money into bonds" [syn: invest, put, commit] [ant: divest] 14: assign to a station [syn: station, post, base, send] 15: finish second or better in a horse or dog race; "he placed $2 on number six to place" 16: sing a note with the correct pitch

plaice
n 1: flesh of large European flatfish 2: large European food fish [syn: Pleuronectes platessa]

plaintiff, plaintive
plaintiff /ˈpleɪntɪf/
n : a person who brings an action in a court of law [syn: complainant] [ant: defendant]
plaintive /ˈpleɪntɪv/
adj : expressing sorrow [syn: mournful]

plait, plate /pleɪt/
plait
n 1: a hairdo formed by braiding or twisting the hair [syn: braid, tress, twist] 2: any of various types of fold formed by doubling fabric back upon itself and then pressing or stitching into shape [syn: pleat]
v 1: make by braiding [syn: braid, lace] 2: weave into plaits; "plait hair"

plate
n 1: a sheet of metal or wood or glass or plastic 2: (baseball) base consisting of a rubber slab where the batter stands; it must be touched by a base runner in order to score; "he ruled that the runner failed to touch home" [syn: home plate, home] 3: a full-page illustration (usually on slick paper) 4: dish on which food is served or from which food is eaten 5: the quantity contained in a plate [syn: plateful] 6: a rigid layer of the lithosphere that is believed to drift slowly 7: the thin under portion of the forequarter 8: a main course served on a plate: "a vegetable plate"; "the blue plate special" 9: any flat plate-like body structure or part 10: the positively charged electrode in a vacuum tube 11: a flat sheet of metal or glass on which a photographic image can be recorded [syn: photographic plate] 12: structural member consisting of a horizontal beam that provides bearing and anchorage 13: a shallow receptacle for collection in church [syn: collection plate] 14: a metal sheathing of uniform thickness (such as the shield attached to an artillery piece to protect the gunners) [syn: scale, shell] 15: a dental appliance that artificially replaces missing teeth [syn: denture, dental plate] 16: the position on a baseball team of the

player who is stationed behind home plate and who catches the balls that the pitcher throws; "a catcher needs a lot of protective equipment"; "he plays behind the plate" [syn: catcher]

v : coat with a layer of metal

plain, plane /pleɪn/

plain

adj 1: clearly apparent or obvious to the mind or senses; "the effects of the drought are apparent to anyone who sees the parched fields"; "evident hostility"; "manifest disapproval"; "patent advantages"; "made his meaning plain"; "it is plain that he is no reactionary"; "in plain view" [syn: apparent, evident, manifest, patent] 2: not elaborate or elaborated; simple; "plain food"; "stuck to the plain facts"; "a plain blue suit"; "a plain rectangular brick building" [ant: fancy] 3: lacking patterns especially in color [syn: unpatterned] [ant: patterned] 4: not mixed with extraneous elements; "plain water"; "sheer wine"; "not an unmixed blessing" [syn: sheer, unmingled, unmixed] 5: free from any effort to soften to disguise; "the plain and unvarnished truth"; "the unvarnished candor of old people and children" [syn: unvarnished] 6: lacking embellishment or ornamentation; "a plain hair style"; "unembellished white walls"; "functional architecture featuring stark unornamented concrete" [syn: unembellished, unornamented] 7: lacking stylistic embellishment; "a literal description"; "wrote good but plain prose"; "a plain unadorned account of the coronation"; "a forthright unembellished style" [syn: literal, unembellished] 8: comprehensible to the general public; "written for the popular press in plain non-technical language" [syn: popular] 9: lacking in physical beauty or proportion; "a homely child"; "several of the buildings were downright homely"; "a plain girl with a freckled face" [syn: homely]

n 1: extensive tract of level open land; "they emerged from the woods onto a vast open plain"; "he longed for the fields of his youth" [syn: field] 2: a basic knitting stitch [syn: knit, knit stitch, plain stitch]

adv : unmistakably; "the answer is obviously wrong"; "she was in bed and evidently in great pain"; "he was manifestly too important to leave off the guest list" [syn: field]; "it is all patently nonsense"; "she has apparently been living here for some time"; "I thought he owned the property, but apparently not"; "You are plainly wrong"; (`plain' is often used informally for `plainly' as in "he is plain stubborn") [syn: obviously, evidently, manifestly, patently, apparently, plainly]

v : express complaints, discontent, displeasure, or unhappiness; "My mother complains all day"; "She has a lot to kick about" [syn: complain, kick, sound off, kvetch] [ant: cheer]

plane

adj : having a horizontal surface in which no part is higher or lower than another; "a flat desk"; "acres of level farmland"; "a plane surface" [syn: flat, level]

n 1: an aircraft that has a fixed wing and is powered by propellers or jets; "the flight was delayed due to trouble with the airplane" [syn: airplane, aeroplane] 2: (mathematics) an unbounded two-dimensional shape; "we will refer to the plane of the graph as the X-Y plane"; "any line joining two points on a plane lies wholly on that plane" [syn: sheet] 3: a level of existence or development; "he lived on a worldly plane" 4: a power tool for smoothing or shaping wood [syn: planer, planing machine] 5: a carpenter's hand tool with an adjustable blade for smoothing or shaping wood; "the cabinetmaker used a plane for the finish work" [syn: carpenter's plane, woodworking plane]

v 1: cut slices from; "The machine shaved off fine layers from the piece of wood" [syn: shave] 2: travel on the surface of water [syn: skim]

plantar, planter /ˈplɛəntəɹ/

plantar

adj : relating to or occurring on the undersurface of the foot; "plantar warts can be very painful"

planter

n 1: the owner or manager of a plantation [syn: plantation owner] 2: a decorative pot for house plants

platan, platen /ˈplætən/

platan

n : any of several trees of the genus Platanus having thin pale bark that scales off in small plates and lobed leaves and ball-shaped heads of fruits [syn: plane tree, sycamore]

platen

n 1: work table of a machine tool 2: the flat plate of a printing press that presses the paper against the type 3: the roller on a typewriter against which the keys strike

pleas, please /pliz/

pleas

n : (plu of plea) 1: humble requests for help; "His pleas went unheeded." [syn: supplications] 2: (law) defendant's answers by a factual matter (as distinguished from demurrers) 3: answers indicating why a suit should be dismissed

please

v 1: give pleasure to; be pleasing to [syn: delight] [ant: displease] 2: be the will of or have the will (to); "he could do many things if he pleased"

pleural, plural /'pluɹəl/

pleural

adj : of or relating to the pleura or the walls of the thorax; "pleural muscles"

plural

adj : grammatical number category referring to two or more items or units [ant: singular]

n : the form of a word that is used to denote more than one [syn: plural form] [ant: singular]

pliers, plyers /'plaɪəⱼz/

pliers

n : gripping hand tools with two hinged arms and (usually) serrated jaws [syn: pair of pliers]

plyers

n : (plu of plyer): persons that work diligently or steadily (ply)

plough, plow /plaʊ/

plough

n 1: a group of seven bright stars in the constellation Ursa Major [syn: Big Dipper, Dipper, Plough] 2: a farm tool having one or more heavy blades to break the soil and cut a furrow prior to sowing [syn: plow]

v 1: move in a way resembling that of a plow cutting into or going through the soil; "The ship plowed through the water" [syn: plow] 2: to break and turn over earth esp. with a plow; "Farmer Jones plowed his east field last week"; "turn the earth in the Spring" [syn: plow, turn]

plow

n : (var of plough – this is the more common spelling)

v 1: (var of plow – this is the more common spelling) 2: deal with verbally or in some form of artistic expression; "This book deals with incest"; "The course covered all of Western Civilization"; "The new book treats the history of China" [syn: cover, treat, handle, deal, address]

plum, plumb /plʌm/

plum

n 1: any of several trees producing edible oval smooth-skinned fruit with a single hard stone [syn: plum tree] 2: any of numerous varieties of small to medium-sized round or oval smooth-skinned fruit with a single pit

adv 1: (informal) exactly; "fell plumb in the middle of the puddle" [syn: plumb] 2: (slang) completely; used as intensifiers; "clean forgot the appointment"; "I'm plumb (or plum) tuckered out" [syn: clean, plumb]

plumb

adj : exactly vertical; "the tower of Pisa is far out of plumb"

n : the metal bob of a plumb line [syn: plumb bob, plummet]

adv 1: (slang) completely; used as intensifiers; "clean forgot the appointment"; "I'm plumb (or plum) tuckered out" [syn: clean, plum] 2: conforming to the direction of a plumb line 3: (informal) exactly; "fell plumb in the middle of the puddle" [syn: plum]

v 1: measure the depth of something 2: weight with lead 3: examine thoroughly and in great depth 4: adjust with a plumb line so as to make vertical

pocks, pox /paks/

pocks

n : (plu of pock): pustules in an eruptive disease

v : (3rd pers sing for pock) : mark with a scar; "That skin disease permanently pocks a person's face." [syn: scars, marks, pits]

pox

n 1: a common venereal disease caused by the Treponema pallidum spirochete; symptoms change through progressive stages; can be congenital (transmitted through the placenta) [syn: syphilis, syph] 2: a contagious disease characterized by purulent skin eruptions that may leave pock marks

poem, pome /'poʊɛm/

poem

n : a composition written in metrical feet forming rhythmical lines [syn: verse form]

pome

n : a fleshy fruit (apple or pear or related fruits) having seed chambers and an outer fleshy part [syn: false fruit]

polar, poler, poller /'poʊləⱼ/

polar

adj 1: having a pair of equal and opposite charges 2: characterized by opposite extremes; completely opposed; "in diametric contradiction to his claims"; "diametrical (or opposite) points of view"; "opposite meanings"; "extreme and indefensible polar positions" [syn: diametric, diametrical, opposite] 3: located at or near or coming from the earth's poles; "polar diameter"; "polar zone"; "a polar air mass"; "Antarctica is the only polar continent" 4: of or existing at or near a geographical pole or within the Arctic or Antarctic Circles; "polar regions" [ant: equatorial] 5: extremely cold; "an arctic climate"; "let's get inside; I'm freezing"; "a frigid day"; "gelid waters of the North Atlantic"; "glacial winds"; "icy hands"; "polar weather" [syn: arctic, freezing, frigid, gelid, glacial, icy] 6: being of crucial importance; "a pivotal event; "the polar events of this study"; "a polar principal" [syn: pivotal]

poler

n 1: one who poles 2: a draft horse

HOMOPHONES

harnessed alongside the shaft or pole of a vehicle [syn: pole horse]

poller

n 1: person who lops or trims trees 2: person who asks questions in a poll or canvass [syn: pollster]

pole, poll /poʊl/

pole

n 1: a long (usually round) rod of wood or metal or plastic 2: a native or inhabitant of Poland [syn: Pole] 3: one of two divergent or mutually exclusive opinions; "they are at opposite poles" or "they are poles apart" 4: (British) a linear measure of 16.5 feet [syn: perch, rod] 5: a square rod of land [syn: perch, rod] 6: one of two points of intersection of the Earth's axis and the celestial sphere [syn: celestial pole] 7: one of two antipodal points where the Earth's axis of rotation intersects the Earth's surface 8: a contact on an electrical device (such as a battery) at which electric current enters or leaves [syn: terminal] 9: a long fiberglass sports implement used for pole vaulting 10: one of the two ends of a magnet where the magnetism seems to be concentrated [syn: magnetic pole]

v 1: propel with a pole; of barges on rivers, for example [syn: punt] 2: support on poles, of climbing plants, such as beans 3: deoxidize molten metals by stirring them with a wooden pole

poll

n 1: an inquiry into public opinion conducted by interviewing a random sample of people [syn: opinion poll, public opinion poll, canvass] 2: the top of the head [syn: pate, crown] 3: the part of the head between the ears 4: a tame parrot [syn: poll parrot] 5: the counting of votes (as in an election)

v 1: get the opinions of people, for example [syn: canvass, canvas] 2: vote in an election at a polling station 3: get the votes of 4: convert into a pollard, as of trees [syn: pollard]

politic, politick /ˈpɑlɪtɪk/

politic

adj 1: marked by artful prudence, expedience, and shrewdness; "it is neither polite nor politic to get into other people's quarrels"; "a politic decision"; "a politic manager"; "a politic old scoundrel"; "a shrewd and politic reply" [ant: impolitic] 2: smoothly agreeable and courteous with a degree of sophistication; "he was too politic to quarrel with so important a personage"; "the hostess averted a confrontation between two guests with a diplomatic change of subject"; "the manager pacified the customer with a smooth apology for the error"; "affable, suave, moderate men...smugly convinced of their respectability" - Ezra Pound [syn: smooth, suave]

politick

v : engage in political activities; "This colleague is always politicking"

ponds, pons /pɑnz/

ponds

n : (plu of pond) : small lakes; "the ponds were too small for sailing" [syn: pools]

pons

n : a band of nerve fibers linking the medulla oblongata and the cerebellum with the midbrain [syn: pons Varolii]

poof, pouf /pʊf/

poof

n : offensive terms for an openly homosexual man [syn: fagot, faggot, fag, fairy, nance, pansy, queen, queer]

pouf

n: thick cushion used as a seat [syn: ottoman, pouffe, hassock]

poor, pore, pour /pɔr/

poor (also /pʊr/)

adj 1: moderate to inferior in quality; "they improved the quality from mediocre to above average"; "he would make a poor spy" [syn: mediocre, second-rate] 2: deserving or inciting pity; "a hapless victim"; "miserable victims of war; "piteous appeals for help"; "pitiable homeless children"; "a pitiful fate"; "couldn't rescue the poor fellow"; "his poor distorted limbs"; "a wretched life" [syn: hapless, miserable, misfortunate, pathetic, piteous, pitiable, pitiful, wretched] 3: having little money or few possessions; "deplored the gap between rich and poor countries"; "the proverbial poor artist living in a garret" [ant: rich] 4: characterized by or indicating lack of money; "the country had a poor economy" [ant: rich, wealthy] 5: low in degree; "expectations were poor" 6: badly supplied with desirable qualities or substances; "a poor land"; "the area was poor in timber and coal"; "food poor in nutritive value" [ant: rich] 7: not sufficient to meet a need; "an inadequate income"; "a poor salary"; "money is short"; "on short rations"; "food is in short supply"; "short on experience" [syn: inadequate, short] 8: unsatisfactory; "a poor light for reading"; "poor morale" 9: yielding little by great labor; "a hardscrabble farm"; "poor soil" [syn: hardscrabble]

pore

n 1: any tiny hole admitting passage of a liquid (fluid or gas) 2: any small opening in the skin or outer surface of an animal 3: a minute epidermal pore in a leaf or stem [syn: stoma]

v : focus one's attention on something; "Please pore over your studies and not on your hobbies" [syn: concentrate, focus, center, rivet]

pour

v 1: cause to run; of liquids 2: move in large numbers; "people were pouring out of the theater" [syn: swarm, stream] 3: pour out; of wines or sherry [syn: decant, pour out] 4: flow in a spurt; of liquids 5: supply in large amounts or quantities: "We poured money into the education of our children" 6: rain heavily; "Put on your rain coat-- it's pouring outside!" [syn: pelt, stream, rain cats and dogs, rain buckets]

populace, populous /ˈpɑpuəlⁱs/

populace

n : people in general considered as a whole; "he is a hero in the eyes of the populace" [syn: public, world]

populous

adj : densely populated [syn: thickly settled]

praise, prays, preys /pɹɛɪz/

praise

n 1: an expression of approval and commendation; "he always appreciated praise for his work" [syn: congratulations, kudos] 2: offering words of homage as an act of worship; "they sang a hymn of praise to God"

v : express praise for [ant: criticize]

prays

v : (3ʳᵈ pers sing of pray) (see pray)

preys

v : (3ʳᵈ pers sing of prey) (see pray)

prau, prow /pɹaʊ/

prau

n: undecked Indonesian boat propelled by oars, paddles or oars

prow

n: front part of a vessel or aircraft; "He pointed the bow of the boat toward the finish line.") [syn: bow]

pray, prey /pɹɛɪ/

pray

v 1: address God; say a prayer 2: call upon in supplication; entreat; "I beg you to stop!" [syn: beg, implore]

prey

n 1: a person who is the victim of ridicule or exploitation by some hostile person or influence; "he fell prey to muggers"; "everyone was fair game" [syn: quarry, target, fair game] 2: animal hunted or caught for food [syn: quarry]

v 1: profit from in an exploited manner; "He feeds on her insecurity" [syn: feed] 2: prey on or hunt for [syn: raven]

precedence,   precedents, presidents

precedence /ˈpɹɛsɪdɛns/

n 1: status established in order of importance or urgency: "...its precedence

as the world's leading manufacturer of pharmaceuticals"; "national independence takes priority over class struggle" [syn: priority]   2: preceding in time [syn: priority, antecedence, anteriority] 3: the act of preceding (as in a ceremony) [syn: precession]

precedents /ˈpɹɛsɪdɛnts/

n : (plu of precedent) 1: examples that are used to justify similar occurrences at a later time [syn: cases in point] 2: (civil law) laws established by following earlier judicial decisions [syn: case law, common law]   3: subjects mentioned earlier (preceding in time)

presidents /ˈpɹɛzɪdɛnt/

n : (plu of president)

precedent, president

precedent /ˈpɹɛsɛdɛnt/

n 1: an example that is used to justify similar occurrences at a later time [syn: case in point] 2: (civil law) a law established by following earlier judicial decisions) [syn: case law, common law 3: a system of jurisprudence based on judicial precedents rather than statutory laws; "common law originated in the unwritten laws of England and was later applied in the United States" 4: a subject mentioned earlier (preceding in time

adj: preceding in time, order, or significance

president /ˈpɹɛzɪdɛnt/

n 1: an executive officer of a firm or corporation 2: President of the United States (the person who holds the office of head of state of the United States government) "the President likes to jog every morning" [syn: United States President, President, Chief Executive] 3: the chief executive of a republic 4: chairman, chairwoman, chair, chairperson (the officer who presides at the meetings of an organization; "address your remarks to the chairperson") 5: the head administrative officer of a college or university [syn: prexy]

premier, premiere /ˈpɹimjiɹ/

premier

adj 1: first in rank or degree; "an architect of premier rank"; "the prime minister" [syn: prime]   2: preceding all others in time; "the premiere showing" [syn: premiere]

n : the person who is head of state (in several countries) [syn: chancellor, prime minister]

premiere

n : the first public performance of a play or movie

v : be performed for the first time; of a play, ballet, or composition [syn: premier]

presence, presents /ˈpɹɛzɛnts/

HOMOPHONES

presence

n 1: the state of being present; current existence; "he tested for the presence of radon" [ant: absence] 2: the immediate proximity of someone or something; "she blushed in his presence"; "he sensed the presence of danger"; "he was well behaved in front of company" [syn: front] 3: an invisible spiritual being felt to be nearby 4: the impression that something is present; "he felt the presence of an evil force" 5: dignified manner or conduct [syn: bearing, comportment, mien] 6: the act of being present [ant: absence]

presents

n : (plu of present) : things given as gifts; "She received many birthday presents."

pride, pried /pɹaɪd/
pride

n 1: a feeling of self-respect and personal worth [ant: humility] 2: satisfaction with your (or another's) achievements; "he takes pride in his son's success" 3: the trait of being spurred on by a dislike of falling below your standards [ant: humility] 4: a group of lions 5: unreasonable and inordinate self-esteem (personified as one of the deadly sins)

v 1: be proud of; "He prides himself on making it into law school" [syn: plume, congratulate] 2: be proud of; "They pride themselves on their son" 3: pride or congratulate (oneself) for an achievement [syn: preen, congratulate]

pried

v : (past of pry) 1: to move or force, esp. in an effort to get something open; "The burglar jimmied the lock", "Raccoons managed to pry the lid off the garbage pail" [syn: jimmied] 2: be nosey; "Don't pry into my personal matters!" 3: search or inquire in a meddlesome way; "This guy is always nosing around the office" [syn: nosed, poked] 4: make an uninvited or presumptuous inquiry; "They pried the information out of him"

prier, prior /pɹaɪjəɹ/
prier

n : one that pries; an inquisitive person

prior

adj : earlier in time [syn: anterior]

n : the head of a religious order; in an abbey the prior is next below the abbot

pries, prize /pɹaɪz/
pries

v : (3ʳᵈ pers sing of pry) (see pried); "She pries into everyone's personal matters."; "He pries boxes open with a crowbar." [syn: prise (British)]

prize

adj : of superior grade; "choice wines"; "prime beef"; "prize carnations"; "quality paper"; "select peaches" [syn: choice,

quality, select]

n 1: something given for victory or superiority in a contest or competition; "the prize was a free trip to Europe" [syn: award] 2: goods or money obtained illegally [syn: loot, booty, pillage, plunder, swag] 3: something given as a token of victory [syn: trophy]

v 1: hold dear; "I prize these old photographs" [syn: value, treasure, appreciate] 2: regard highly; think much of [syn: respect, esteem, value] [ant: disrespect]

primer, primmer /pɹɪm˨əɹ/
primer

n : an introductory textbook

primmer

adj (compar of prim) 1: more formal and precise in manner or appearance [syn: daintier, more refined, neater, trimmer]

prince, prints /pɹɪnts/
prince

n : a male member of a royal family other than the sovereign (especially the son of a sovereign)

prints

n : (plu of print) 1: the results of the printing process [syn: black and whites] 2: pictures or designs printed from an engraving 3: fabrics with a dyed pattern pressed onto them (usually by engraved rollers) 4: printed picture produced from a photographic negative [syn: photographic prints]

v : (3ʳᵈ pers sing of print) 1: puts into print; "The newspaper prints the news of the royal couple's divorce"; "These news should not be printed" [syn: publishes] 2: writes as if with print; not cursive 3: makes into a print 4: reproduces by printing [syn: impresses]

principal, principle /pɹɪnsɪpˀl/
principal

adj : most important element; "the chief aim of living"; "the main doors were of solid glass"; "the principal rivers of America"; "the principal example"; "policemen were primary targets" [syn: chief, main, primary]

n 1: the original amount of a debt on which interest is calculated 2: the educator who has executive authority for a school; "she sent unruly pupils to see the principal" [syn: school principal, head teacher, head] 3: an actor who plays a principal role [syn: star, lead] 4: capital as contrasted with the income derived from it [syn: corpus, principal sum] 5: the major party to a financial transaction; buys and sells for his own account [syn: dealer]

principle

n 1: a basic generalization that is accepted

HOMOPHONES

as true and that can be used as a basis for reasoning or conduct; "their principles of composition characterized all their works" [syn: rule] 2: a rule or standard especially of good behavior: "a man of principle"; "he will not violate his principles" 3: a basic truth or law or assumption: "the principles of democracy" 4: a rule or law concerning a natural phenomenon or the function of a complex system: "the principle of the conservation of mass"; "the principle of jet propulsion"; "the right-hand rule for inductive fields" [syn: rule] 5: rule of personal conduct [syn: precept] 6: an explanation of the working of some device in terms of laws of nature; "the principles of internal-combustion engines" [syn: rationale]

profit, prophet /ˈpɹɑfɪt/
profit
n 1: the excess of revenues over outlays in a given period of time (including depreciation and other non-cash expenses) [syn: net income, net, net profit, lucre, profits, earnings] 2: the advantageous quality of being beneficial [syn: gain]
v 1: derive benefit from [syn: gain, benefit] 2: make a profit; gain money or materially; "The company has not profited from the merger" [ant: lose, break even]
prophet
n 1: an authoritative person who divines the future [syn: oracle, seer, vaticinator] 2: someone who speaks by divine inspiration; someone who is an interpreter of the will of God

pros, prose /pɹouz/
pros
n : (plu of pro) 1: athletes who play for pay [syn: professionals] [ant: amateurs] 2: an argument in favor of a proposal; "What are the pros and cons of this proposal?" [ant: cons]
prose
n 1: ordinary writing as distinguished from verse 2: matter of fact, commonplace, or dull expression

protean, protein /ˈpɹoutiɪn/
protean
adj : taking on different forms, displaying great diversity or variety [syn: versatile]
protein (also /ˈpɹoutin/)
n : any of a large group of nitrogenous organic compounds that are essential constituents of living cells; consist of polymers of amino acids; essential in the diet of animals for growth and for repair of tissues; can be obtained from meat, eggs, milk and legumes; "a diet high in protein"

Psalter, salter /ˈsɔltɚ/
Psalter
n : a collection of psalms for liturgical use [syn: Book of Psalms]

salter
n 1: someone who uses salt to preserve meat or fish of other foods 2: someone who makes or deals in salt [syn: salt merchant]

pseud, sued /sud/
pseud
n : a person who makes deceitful pretenses [syn: imposter, impostor, pretender, fake, faker, fraud, sham, shammer, pseudo, role player]
sued
v : (past of sue) (see sault) "The company was sued for three million dollars."

psi, sigh, xi /saɪ/
psi
n : the 23rd letter of the Greek alphabet
sigh
n 1: an often involuntary act of sighing especially when expressing an emotion or feeling (as weariness or relief) 2: the sound of gently moving or escaping air "sighs of the summer breeze"
v : 1: to take a deep audible breath (as in weariness or relief) 2: to make a sound like sighing "wind *sighing* in the branches" 3: grieve, yearn "sighing for days gone by" 4: to express by sighs 5: to utter sighs over [syn: mourn]
xi
n : the 14th letter of the Greek alphabet

psis, sighs, size, xis /saɪz/
psis
n : (plu of psi)
sighs
n : (plu of sigh)
v : (3rd pers sing of sigh)
size
adj : (used in combination) "the economy-size package"; "average-sized houses"
n 1: the physical magnitude of something (how big it is); "a wolf is about the size of a large dog" 2: the property resulting from being one of a series of graduated measurements (as of clothing); "he wears a size 13 shoe" 3: any glutinous material used to fill pores in surfaces or to stiffen fabrics; "size gives body to a fabric" [syn: sizing] 4: (informal) the actual state of affairs; "that's the size of the situation"; "she hates me, that's about the size of it" [syn: size of it] 5: a large magnitude; "he blanched when he saw the size of the bill"; "the only city of any size in that area"
v 1: cover or stiffen or glaze a porous material with size or sizing (a glutinous substance) 2: sort according to size 3: make to a size; bring to a suitable size
xis
n : (plu of xi)

HOMOPHONES

psychosis, sycosis
/sar'kousɪs/

psychosis
n : any severe mental disorder in which contact with reality is lost or highly distorted

sycosis
n : chronic inflammatory disorder of the hair follicles marked by papules, pustules, and tubercles with crusting

pupal, pupil /'pʊəpᵊl/

pupal
adj : of the insects in the chrysalis (cocoon) or post larval stage; "the pupal stage"

pupil
n 1: a learner who is enrolled in an educational institution [syn: student] 2: contractile aperture in the iris of the eye 3: a child attending school [syn: schoolchild]

puts, putz /pʊts/

puts
n : (plu of put) the option to sell a given stock (or stock index or commodity future) at a given price before a given date [syn: put options] [ant: calls, call options]

v : (3rd pers sing of put) 1: place into a certain location; "Place your things here"; "She puts the tray down"; "Set the dogs on the scent of the missing children"; "Place emphasis on a certain point" [syn: sets, places, poses, positions, lays] 2: cause to be in a certain state; cause to be in a certain relation; "That song puts me in awful good humor" 3: formulate in a particular style or language; "I wouldn't put it that way"; "She cast her request in very polite language" [syn: frames, redacts, casts, couches] 4: attributes or gives; "She puts too much emphasis on her the last statement"; "He puts all his efforts into this job"; "The teacher puts an interesting twist to the interpretation of the story" [syn: assigns] 5: makes an investment; "Puts money into bonds" [syn: invests, commits, places] [ant: divests] 6: estimates; "We put the time of arrival at 8 P.M." [syn: places, sets] 7: causes (someone) to undergo something; "He puts her to the torture" 8: adapts; "puts these words to music" 9: arranges thoughts, ideas, temporal events, etc.; "arranges my schedule"; "sets up one's life"; "He puts these memories with those of bygone times" [syn: arranges, sets up, orders]

putz
n : decoration built around a representation of the Nativity scene, creche

puttee, putty /'pʌti/

puttee
n : a strip of cloth wound around the leg to form legging; used by soldiers in World War I [syn: puttees]

putty
n : a dough-like mixture of whiting and boiled linseed oil; used especially to patch woodwork or secure panes of glass
v : apply putty in order to fix or fill, as of a window sash, for example

HOMOPHONES

-Q-

Q (see cue)
quaff (see coif)
quarts, quartz /kwɔ:ts/

quarts

n : (plu of quart) 1: a United States liquid unit equal to 32 fluid ounces; four quarts equal one gallon 2: a British imperial capacity measure (liquid or dry) equal to 2 pints or 1.136 liters 3: a United States dry unit equal to 2 pints or 67.2 cubic inches [syn: dry quarts]

quartz

n 1: colorless glass made of almost pure silica [syn: quartz glass, vitreous silica, lechatelierite, crystal] 2: a hard glossy mineral consisting of silicon dioxide in crystal form; present in most rocks (especially sandstone and granite); yellow sand is quartz with iron oxide impurities

quay (see key)
qubit (see cubit)
quean, queen /kwin/

quean

n: a disreputable woman [syn: prostitute]

queen

n 1: the only fertile female in a colony of social insects such as bees and ants and termites; its function is to lay eggs 2: a female sovereign ruler [syn: queen regnant, female monarch] [ant: king] 3: the wife or widow of a king 4: offensive terms for an openly homosexual man [syn: faggot, fag, fairy, nancy, pansy, queer, poof] 5: one of four face cards in a deck bearing a picture of a queen 6: the most powerful chess piece 7: especially large and only member of a colony of naked mole rats to bear offspring sired by only a few males 8: female cat [syn: tabby]
v 1: promote to a queen, as of a pawn in chess 2: become a queen, of a chess pawn

queue (see cue)
quietest, quietist /ˈkwaɪətɪst/

quietest

adj (superlative of quiet) 1: characterized by an absence or near absence of agitation or activity; "a quiet life"; "a quiet throng of onlookers"; "quiet peace-loving people"; "the factions remained quiet for almost 10 years" [ant: most unquiet] 2: free of noise or uproar; or making little if any sound; "a quiet audience at the concert"; "the room was dark and quiet" [ant: noisiest] 3: not showy or obtrusive; "clothes in quiet good taste" [syn: most restrained] 4: in a softened tone; "hushed voices"; "muted trumpets"; "a subdued whisper"; "a quiet reprimand" [syn: most hushed, most muted, most subdued] 5: without untoward incident or disruption;

"a placid existence"; "quiet times" [syn: most placid] 6: free from disturbance; "a ribbon of sand between the angry sea and the placid bay"; "the quiet waters of a lagoon"; "a lake of tranquil blue water reflecting a tranquil blue sky"; "a smooth channel crossing"; "scarcely a ripple on the still water"; "unruffled water" [syn: most placid, stillest, most tranquil, most unruffled] 7: (astronomy; of the sun) characterized by a low level of surface phenomena like sun spots e.g. [ant: most active]

quietist

n : a religious mystic who follows quietism
quince, quints /kwɪnts/

quince

n 1: small Asian tree with pinkish flowers and pear-shaped fruit; widely cultivated [syn: quince bush, Cydonia oblonga] 2: aromatic acid-tasting pear-shaped fruit used in preserves

quints

n 1: cardinal numbers that are the sum of four and one [syn: fives, 5s, quintets, fivesomes, quintuplets, pentads, fins, Phoebes, Little Phoebes] 2: children of group of five children born at the same time from the same pregnancy [syn: quintuplets, quins]

quire (see choir)
quitter, quittor /ˈkwɪtəɹ/

quitter

n : a person who gives up too easily

quittor

n : an infected inflammation of the feet especially of horses and donkeys
quoin (see coign)

HOMOPHONES

-R-

R (see are)

rabbet, rabbit /'ɹæbɪt/

rabbet

n : a rectangular groove made to hold two pieces together

v 1: join with a rabbet joint 2: cut a rabbet in something

rabbit

n 1: any of various burrowing animals of the family Leporidae having long ears and short tails; some domesticated and raised for pets or food [syn: coney, cony] 2: the fur of a rabbit [syn: lapin] 3: flesh of any of various rabbits or hares (wild or domesticated) eaten as food [syn: hare]

v : hunt rabbits

rack, wrack /ɹæk/

rack

n 1: framework for holding objects 2: rib section of a forequarter of veal or pork or especially lamb or mutton 3: the destruction or collapse of something; "wrack and ruin" [syn: wrack] 4: an instrument of torture that stretches or disjoints or mutilates victims [syn: wheel] 5: a support for displaying various articles; "the newspapers were arranged on a rack" [syn: stand] 6: a rapid gait of a horse in which each foot strikes the ground separately [syn: single-foot]

v 1: go at a rack, as of horses [syn: single-foot] 2: mentally search; "rack one's brains" 3: work by a rack and pinion or worm so as to extend or contract; "rack a camera" 4: obtain by coercion or intimidation; "They extorted money from the executive by threatening to reveal his past to the company boss" [syn: extort, gouge, wring] 5: go at a rack, of horses 6: run before a gale [syn: scud] 7: fly in high wind 8: draw off from the lees, as of wine 9: torment emotionally or mentally [syn: torment, torture, excruciate] 10: work on a rack, of materials such as leather 11: seize together, as of parallel ropes of a tackle in order to prevent running through the block 12: torture on the rack

wrack

n 1: dried seaweed especially that cast ashore 2: the destruction or collapse of something; "wrack and ruin" [syn: rack] 3: growth of marine vegetation especially of the large forms such as rockweeds and kelp [syn: sea wrack]

v : smash or break forcefully; "The kid busted up the car" [syn: bust up, wreck]

racket, racquet /'ɹækɪt/

racket

n 1: a loud and disturbing noise 2: an illegal enterprise (such as extortion or fraud or drug peddling or prostitution) carried on for profit [syn: fraudulent scheme, illegitimate enterprise] 3: the auditory experience of sound that lacks musical quality; sound that is a disagreeable auditory experience; "modern music is just noise to me" [syn: noise, dissonance] 4: (var racquet)

v 1: celebrate noisily; engage in uproarious festivities; "The members of the wedding party made merry all night"; "Let's whoop it up--the boss is gone!" [syn: revel, make whoopie, make merry, make happy, whoop it up, wassail] 2: make a racket 3: hit with a racket, of a ball

racquet

n : a sports implement (usually consisting of a handle and an oval frame with a tightly interlaced network of strings) used to strike a ball (or shuttlecock) in various games [syn: racket]

radical, radicle /'ɹædɪk³l/

radical

adj 1: (used of opinions and actions) far beyond the norm; "extremist political views"; "radical opinions on education"; "an ultra conservative" [syn: extremist, ultra] 2: markedly new or introducing radical change; "a revolutionary discovery"; "radical political views" [syn: revolutionary] 3: arising from or going to the root; "a radical flaw in the plan" [syn: root] 4: (linguistics) of or relating to or constituting a linguistic root; "a radical verb form" 5: (botany) especially of leaves; located at the base of a plant or stem; especially arising directly from the root or rootstock or a root-like stem; "basal placentation"; "radical leaves" [syn: basal] [ant: cauline]

n 1: (chemistry) two or more atoms bound together as a single unit and forming part of a molecule [syn: group, chemical group] 2: an atom or group of atoms with at least one unpaired electron; in the body it is usually an oxygen molecule than has lost an electron and will stabilize itself by stealing an electron from a nearby molecule; "in the body free radicals are high-energy particles that ricochet wildly and damage cells" [syn: free radical] 3: a person who has radical ideas or opinions 4: a character conveying the lexical meaning of a logogram 5: a sign placed in front of an expression to denote that a root is to be extracted [syn: radical sign] 6: (linguistics) the form of a word after all affixes are removed; "thematic vowels are part of the stem" [syn: root, root word, base, stem, theme]

radicle

n : (anatomy) a small structure resembling

HOMOPHONES

a rootlet (such as a fibril of a nerve)
raid, rayed /ɹeɪd/
raid
n 1: a sudden short attack [syn: foray, maraud] 2: an attempt by speculators to defraud investors
v 1: search without warning, make a sudden surprise attack on; "The police raided the crack house" [syn: bust] 2: enter someone else's territory [syn: foray into]
rayed
v : (past of ray) (see re)
rail, rale /ɹeɪl/
rail
n 1: a barrier consisting of a horizontal bar and supports [syn: railing] 2: short for railway; "he traveled by rail";1 "he was concerned with rail safety" 3: a bar or bars of rolled steel making a track along which vehicles can roll [syn: track, rails] 4: a horizontal bar (usually of wood) 5: any of numerous widely distributed small wading birds of the family Rallidae having short wings and very long toes for running on soft mud
v 1: complain bitterly [syn: inveigh] 2: enclose with rails; "rail in the old graves" [syn: rail in] 3: provide or enclose with rails; "The yard was railed" 4: separate with a railing; "rail off the crowds from the Presidential palace" [syn: rail off] 5: convey (goods etc.) by rails; "fresh fruit are railed from Italy to Belgium" 6: travel by rail or train; "They railed from Rome to Venice"; "She trained to Hamburg" [syn: train] 7: lay with rails; "hundreds of miles were railed out here" 8: fish with a hand-line aver the rails of a boat; "They are railing for fresh fish" 9: spread negative information about; "The Nazi propaganda vilified the Jews" [syn: vilify, revile, vituperate] 10: criticize severely; "He fulminated against the Republicans' plan to cut Medicare"; "She railed against the bad social policies [syn: fulminate]
rale
n : a rapid series of short loud sounds (as might be heard with a stethoscope in some types of respiratory disorders); "the death rattle" [syn: rattle, rattling]
rain, reign, rein /ɹeɪn/
rain
n 1: water falling in drops from vapor condensed in the atmosphere [syn: rainfall] 2: drops of fresh water that fall as precipitation from clouds [syn: rainwater] 3: anything happening rapidly or in quick successive; "a rain of bullets"; "a pelting of insults" [syn: pelting]
v : precipitate as rain; "If it rains much more, we can expect some flooding." [syn: rain down]

reign
n 1: a period during which something or somebody is dominant or powerful; "he was helpless under the reign of his egotism" 2: the period during which a monarch is sovereign; "during the reign of Henry VIII" 3: royal authority; the dominion of a monarch [syn: sovereignty]
v 1: have sovereign power; "Henry VIII reigned for a long time" 2: be larger in number, quantity, or importance; "Money reigns supreme here"; "Hispanics predominate in this neighborhood" [syn: predominate, dominate, rule, prevail]
rein
n 1: one of a pair of long straps (usually connected to the bit or the headpiece) used to control a horse 2: any means of control; "he took up the reins of government"
v 1: control and direct with or as if by reins; as of a horse [syn: harness, rein in, draw rein] 2: stop or slow up one's horse or oneself by or as if by pulling the reins; "They reined in front of the post office" [syn: rein in] 3: keep in check; "rule one's temper" [syn: rule, harness]
raise, rays, raze /ɹeɪz/
raise
n 1: the amount a salary is increased; "he got a 3% raise"; "he got a wage hike" [syn: rise, wage hike, hike, wage increase, salary increase] 2: an upward slope or grade (as in a road); "the car couldn't make the grade" [syn: ascent, acclivity, rise, climb, upgrade] [ant: descent] 3: increasing the size of a bet (as in poker); "I'll see your raise and double it" 4: the act of raising something; "he responded with a lift of his eyebrow"; "fireman learn several different raises for getting ladders up" [syn: lift, heave, elevation]
v 1: raise the level or amount of something; "raise my salary"; "raise the price of bread" 2: raise from a lower to a higher position; "Raise your hands"; "Lift a load" [syn: lift, elevate, get up, bring up] [ant: lower] 3: cause to be heard or known; express or utter; "raise a shout"; "raise a protest"; "raise a sad cry" 4: collect funds for a specific purpose; "The President raised several million dollars for his college" 5: cultivate by growing; often involves improvements by means of agricultural techniques; "The Bordeaux region produces great red wines"; "They produce good ham in Parma"; "We grow wheat here"; "We raise hogs here" [syn: grow, farm, produce] 6: bring up; "raise a family"; "bring up children" [syn: rear, bring up, nurture, parent] 7: evoke or call forth, with or as if by magic: "raise the specter of unemployment"; "he conjured wild birds in the air"; "stir a disturbance";

HOMOPHONES

"call down the spirits from the mountain" [syn: conjure, conjure up, invoke, stir, call down, arouse, bring up, put forward, call forth] 8: move upwards; "lift one's eyes" [syn: lift] 9: construct, build, or erect; "Raise a barn" [syn: erect, rear, set up, put up] [ant: level] 10: call forth; of emotions, feelings, and responses; "arouse pity"; "raise a smile"; "evoke sympathy" [syn: arouse, elicit, enkindle, kindle, evoke, fire, provoke] 11: create a disturbance, esp. by making a great noise; "raise hell"; "raise the roof"; "raise Cain" 12: raise in rank or condition: "The new law lifted many people from poverty" [syn: lift, elevate] 13: increase; "This will enhance your enjoyment"; "heighten the tension" [syn: enhance, heighten] 14: give a promotion to; "raise in rank"; assign to a higher position; "promote, upgrade, advance, kick upstairs, elevate [ant: demote] 15: cause to puff up with a leaven; of dough; "unleavened bread" [syn: leaven, prove] 16: in bridge: bid (one's partner's suit) at a higher level 17: bet more than the previous player, in poker 18: cause to assemble or enlist; "raise an army" [syn: recruit, levy] 19: put forward for consideration or discussion; "raise the question of promotions"; "bring up an unpleasant topic" [syn: bring up] 20: pronounce (vowels) by bringing the tongue closer to the roof of the mouth; "raise your `o'" 21: activate or stir up; "raise a mutiny" 22: establish radio communications with: "They managed to raise Hanoi last night" 23: multiply (a number) by itself a specified number of times: 8 is 2 raised to the power 3 24: bring (a surface, a design, etc.) into relief and cause to project; "raised edges" 25: invigorate or heighten; "lift my spirits", "lift his ego" [syn: lift] 26: put an end to, as of a siege or a blockade; "lift a ban"; "raise a siege" [syn: lift] 27: cause to become alive again; "raise from the dead"; "Slavery is already dead, and cannot be resurrected."; "Upraising ghosts" [syn: resurrect, upraise]

rays
n : (plu of ray) (see ray)
v : (3rd pers sing of ray) (see ray)

raze
v : tear down so as to make flat with the ground; "The building was leveled" [syn: level, dismantle, tear down, take down, pull down] [ant: raise]

raiser, razer, rázor /ˈɹɛɪzᵊɹ/
raiser
n 1: a bridge partner who increases the partner's bid 2: someone concerned with the science or art or business of cultivating the soil [syn: agriculturist, cultivator, grower]

razer
n : one who razes or demolishes [syn: demolisher]

razor
n : edge tool used in shaving
v : shave with a razor

rancor, ranker /ˈɹɛɪŋkᵊɹ/
rancor
n : a feeling of deep and bitter anger and ill-will [syn: resentment, bitterness, gall]

ranker
n 1: a commissioned officer who has been promoted from enlisted status 2: (British) an enlisted soldier who serves in the ranks of the armed forces

rap, wrap /ɹæp/
rap
n 1: a reproach for some lapse or misdeed; "he took the blame for it"; "it was a bum rap" [syn: blame] 2: a gentle blow [syn: strike, tap] 3: the sound made by a gentle blow [syn: pat, tap] 4: (informal) voluble conversation 5: genre of African-American music of the 1980s and 1990s in which rhyming lyrics are chanted to a musical accompaniment; several forms of rap have emerged [syn: rap music] 6: the act of hitting vigorously; "he gave the table a whack" [syn: knock, belt, whack, whang] 7: not being concerned; "I don't give a rap."

v 1: strike sharply; "rap him on the knuckles" [syn: knap] 2: make light, repeated taps on a surface; "he was tapping his fingers on the table impatiently" [syn: tap, knock, pink] 3: perform rap music 4: talk volubly

wrap
n 1: cloak that is folded or wrapped around a person [syn: wrapper] 2: the covering (usually paper or cellophane) in which something is wrapped [syn: wrapping, wrapper]

v 1: arrange or fold as a cover or protection; "wrap the baby before taking her out"; "Wrap the present" [syn: wrap up] [ant: unwrap] 2: wrap or coil around; "roll your hair around your finger"; "Twine the thread around the spool" [syn: wind, roll, twine] [ant: unwind] 3: enclose or enfold completely with or as if with a covering; "Fog enveloped the house" [syn: envelop, enfold, enwrap, enclose]

rapped, rapt, wrapped /ɹæpt/
rapped
v : (past of rap) (see rap)

rapt
adj 1: deeply moved; "sat completely still, enraptured by the music"; "listened with rapt admiration"; "rapt in reverie" [syn: enraptured, captive] 2: wholly absorbed as in thought; "deep in thought"; "that engrossed look or rapt delight"; "the book

I-162

HOMOPHONES

had her totally engrossed"; "enwrapped in dreams"; "so intent on this fantastic... narrative that she hardly stirred"- Walter de la Mare; "rapt with wonder"; "wrapped in thought" [syn: absorbed, engrossed, enwrapped, intent, wrapped]

wrapped

adj 1: covered with or as if with clothes or a wrap or cloak; "leaf-clothed trees"; "fog-cloaked meadows"; "a beam draped with cobwebs"; "cloud-wrapped peaks" [syn: cloaked, clothed, draped, mantled] 2: enclosed securely in a covering of paper or the like; "gaily wrapped gifts" [ant: unwrapped]

v : (past of wrap) "They wrapped the Christmas gifts last week."

rational, rationale

rational /ˈɹæʃɪnəl/

adj 1: consistent with or based on or using reason; "rational behavior"; "a process of rational inference"; "rational thought" [ant: irrational]   2: of or associated with or requiring the use of the mind; "intellectual problems"; "the triumph of the rational over the animal side of man" [syn: intellectual]   3: (math) capable of being expressed as a quotient of integers; "rational numbers" [ant: irrational]   4: having its source in or being guided by the intellect (distinguished from experience or emotion); "a rational analysis"

rationale /ɹæʃɪˈnæl/

n : an explanation of the working of some device in terms of laws of nature; "the principles of internal-combustion engines" [syn: principle]

ray, re /ɹeɪ/

ray

n 1: a column of light (as from a beacon) [syn: beam, beam of light, light beam, ray of light, shaft, shaft of light]   2: a branch of an umbel or an umbelliform inflorescence   3: (mathematics) a straight line extending from a point   4: a group of nearly parallel lines of electromagnetic radiation [syn: beam, electron beam]   5: any of the stiff bony rods in the fin of a fish   6: cartilaginous fishes having horizontally flattened bodies and enlarged wing-like pectoral fins with gills on the underside; most swim by moving the pectoral fins

v 1: emit as rays; "That tower rays a laser beam for miles across the sky." 2: extend or spread outward from a center or focus or inward towards a center; "spokes radiate from the hub of the wheel"; "This plants radiates spines in all directions" [syn: radiate]   3: expose to radiation; "irradiated food" [syn: irradiate]   4: send out real or metaphoric rays; "She radiates happiness" [syn: radiate]

re

n: the syllable naming the second (supertonic) note of any major scale in solmization

reactance, reactants

/ɹiˈæktənts/

reactance

n : opposition to the flow of electric current resulting from inductance and capacitance (rather than resistance)

reactants

n : chemical substances that are present at the start of chemical reactions

read, red, redd /ɹɛd/

read

adj : having been read; often used in combination; "a widely read newspaper" [ant: unread]

n : something that is read; "the article was very interesting"

v : (past of read (riːd) (see next entry)

red

adj 1: having any of numerous bright or strong colors reminiscent of the color of blood or cherries or tomatoes or rubies [syn: reddish, ruddy, blood-red, carmine, cerise, cherry, cherry-red, crimson, ruby, ruby-red, scarlet] 2: (used of hair or fur) of a reddish brown color; "red deer"; reddish hair" [syn: reddish]   3: characterized by violence or bloodshed; "writes of crimson deeds and barbaric days"- Andrea Parke; "fann'd by Conquest's crimson wing"- Thomas Gray; "convulsed with red rage"- Hudson Strode [syn: crimson, violent]   4: (especially of the face) reddened or suffused with or as if with blood from emotion or exertion; "crimson with fury"; "turned red from exertion"; "with puffy reddened eyes"; "red-faced and violent"; "flushed (or crimson) with embarrassment" [syn: aflame, crimson, reddened, red-faced, flushed]   5: red with or characterized by blood; "waving our red weapons o'er our heads"- Shakespeare; "The Red Badge of Courage"; "the red rules of tooth and claw"- P.B.Sears   6: (of wine) deep reddish in color; "a red wine such as a claret or burgundy"; "a pinot noir is a red burgundy" [ant: white]

n 1: the quality or state of the chromatic color resembling the hue of blood [syn: redness]   2: emotionally charged terms used to refer to extreme radicals or revolutionaries, especially communists [syn: Bolshevik, Marxist, pinko, bolshie)

redd

n : the spawning ground or nest of various fishes

read, rede, reed /ɹid/

read

n : something that is read; "the article was a very good read"

I-163

HOMOPHONES

v 1: interpret something that is written or printed; "read the advertisement" 2: have or contain a certain wording or form; "The passage reads as follows"; "What does the law say?" [syn: say] 3: look at, interpret, and say out loud something that is written or printed; "The King will read the proclamation at noon" 4: obtain data from various media; "This computer can read data from magnetic disks and tapes" [syn: scan] 5: interpret the significance of, as of palms, tea leaves, intestines, the sky, etc.; also of human behavior; "She can read the sky and predict rain"; "I can't read his strange behavior" 6: interpret something in a certain way; convey a particular meaning or impression; "I will read this address as a satire"; "How should I take this message?" 7: indicate a certain reading; of gauges and instruments; "The thermometer shows thirteen degrees below zero"; "The gauge reads `empty'" [syn: register, show, record] 8: be a student of a certain subject; "She is reading for the bar exam" [syn: learn, study, take] 9: audition for a stage role by reading parts of a role; "He is auditioning for Julius Cesar at Stratford this year" 10: to hear and understand; "I read you loud and clear!" 11: make sense of a language; "She understands French"; "Can you read Greek?" [syn: understand, interpret, translate]

rede

n: advice or counsel given by one person to another; "what is your rede?"

v: 1. advise (someone); "therefore, my son, I rede thee stay at home" 2. interpret (a riddle or dream).

reed

adj : operated by a read; "clarinet is a reed instrument"

n 1: tall woody perennial grasses with hollow slender stems especially of the genera Arundo and Phragmites 2: mechanical device consisting of a thin strip of stiff material that is fitted into the mouthpiece of woodwind instruments and that vibrates to produce a tone when air streams over it 3: a musical instrument that sounds by means of a reed [syn: beating-reed instrument]

real, reel /ɹil/

real

adj 1: being or occurring in fact or actuality; having verified existence; not illusory; "real objects"; "real people; not ghosts"; "a film based on real life"; "a real illness"; "real humility"; "Life is real! Life is earnest!"- Longfellow [syn: existent] [ant: unreal] 2: no less than what is stated; worthy of the name; "the real reason"; "real war"; "a real friend"; "a real woman"; "meat and potatoes--I call that a real meal"; "it's time he had a real job"; "it's no penny-ante job--he's making real money" [ant: unreal] 3: being or reflecting the essential or genuine character of something; "her actual motive"; "a literal solitude like a desert"- G.K.Chesterton; "a genuine dilemma" [syn: actual, genuine, literal] 4: not synthetic or spurious; of real or natural origin; "real mink"; "true gold" [syn: true] 5: not to be taken lightly; "statistics demonstrate that poverty and unemployment are very real problems"; "to the man sleeping regularly in doorways homelessness is real" 6: possible to be treated as fact; "tangible evidence"; "his brief time as Prime Minister brought few real benefits to the poor" [syn: tangible] 7: (economics) being value measured in terms of purchasing power; "real prices"; "real income"; "real wages" [ant: nominal] 8: having substance or capable of being treated as fact; not imaginary; "the substantial world"; "a mere dream, neither substantial nor practical"; "most ponderous and substantial things"- Shakespeare [syn: substantial, material] [ant: insubstantial] 9: (of property) fixed or immovable; "real property consists of land and buildings; real estate" 10: coinciding with reality; "perceptual error... has a surprising resemblance to veridical perception"- F.A.Olafson [syn: veridical] 11: founded on practical matters; "a recent graduate experiencing the real world for the first time"

n 1: any rational or irrational number [syn: real number] 2: an old small silver Spanish coin

adv : intensifiers; "she was very gifted"; "he played very well"; "a really enjoyable evening"; (`real' is sometimes used informally for `really' as in "I'm real sorry about it"; `rattling' is informal as in "a rattling good yarn") [syn: very, really, rattling]

reel

n 1: a roll of photographic film holding a series of frames to be projected by a movie projector 2: music composed for dancing a reel 3: winder consisting of a revolving spool with a handle; attached to a fishing rod 4: a winder around which thread or tape or film or other flexible materials can be wound [syn: bobbin, spool] 5: a lively dance of Scottish highlanders; marked by circular moves and gliding steps [syn: Scottish reel] 6: an American country dance which starts with the couples facing each other in two lines [syn: Virginia reel] v 1: walk as if unable to control one's movements [syn: stagger, keel, lurch, swag, careen] 2: revolve quickly and repeatedly around one's own axis; "The

HOMOPHONES

dervishes whirl around and around without getting dizzy" [syn: spin, spin around, whirl, gyrate] 3: move unsteadily or with a weaving or rolling motion [syn: wamble, waggle] 4: wind onto or off a reel

rebait, rebate /'ɹibɛɪt/

rebait
v : bait again or anew; "This time, rebait the fish hook with worms."

rebate
n 1: a refund of some fraction of the amount paid [syn: discount] 2: a rectangular groove made to hold two pieces together [syn: rabbet]
v 1: give a rebate 2: as of timber or stone [syn: cut a rebate in] 3: join with a rebate, as of pieces of timber or stone

recede, reseed /ɹi'sid/

recede
v 1: pull back or move away or backward; "The enemy withdrew"; "The limo pulled away from the curb" [syn: withdraw, retreat, pull away, draw back, pull back, retire, move back] 2: move back and away from; "The enemy fell back" [syn: fall back, retire] [ant: advance] 3: retreat [syn: fall back, lose, drop off, fall behind] [ant: gain] 4: become faint or more distant; "the unhappy memories of her childhood receded as she grew older"

reseed
v 1: seed again or anew 2: maintain by self-seeding; "Some plants reseed themselves indefinitely"

receipt, reseat /ɹi'sit/

receipt (also ri 'si:t)
n 1: the act of receiving [syn: reception] 2: an acknowledgment (usually tangible) that payment has been made
v 1: acknowledge the receipt of [syn: acknowledge] 2: mark or stamp as paid

reseat
v 1: provide with a new seat, as of a chair 2: provide with new seats, as of a hall 3: show to a different seat; "The usher insisted on reseating us"

recite, resite /ɹi'saɪt/

recite
v 1: recite in elocution [syn: declaim] 2: repeat aloud from memory; "she recited a poem"; "The pupil recited his lesson for the day" 3: render verbally, "recite a poem"; "retell a story" [syn: retell] 4: narrate or give a detailed account of; "Tell what happened"; "The father told a story to his child" [syn: tell, narrate, recount] 5: specify individually; "She enumerated the many obstacles she had encountered"; "The doctor recited the list of possible side effects of the drug" [syn: enumerate, itemize]

resite
v: to relocate to another site; "Plans are to

resite the stadium next to the river."

reck, wreck /ɹɛk/

reck
v : worry, care

wreck
n 1: something or someone that has suffered ruin or dilapidation; "the house was a wreck when they bought it"; "thanks to that quack I am a human wreck" 2: an accident that destroys a ship at sea [syn: shipwreck] 3: a serious accident (usually involving one or more vehicles); "they are still investigating the crash of the TWA plane" [syn: crash] 4: a ship that has been destroyed at sea
v : smash or break forcefully; "The kid busted up the car" [syn: bust up, wrack]

reek, wreak /ɹik/

reek
n : a distinctive odor that is offensively unpleasant [syn: malodor, stench, stink, fetor]
v 1: have an element suggestive (of something); "his speeches smacked of racism" [syn: smack] 2: smell to heaven [syn: stink] 3: be wet with sweat or blood, as of one's face [syn: fume] 4: give off smoke, fumes, warm vapor, steam, etc.; "Marshes reeking in the sun"

wreak
v : cause to happen or to occur as a consequence; "I cannot work a miracle" "wreak havoc"; "bring comments"; "play a joke"; "The rain brought relief to the drought-stricken area" [syn: bring, work, play, make for]

reference, referents /'ɹɛfəɹɛnts/

reference
n 1: a remark that calls attention to something or someone; "she made frequent mention of her promotion"; "there was no mention of it"; "the speaker made several references to his wife" [syn: mention] 2: a short note acknowledging a source of information or quoting a passage; "the student's essay failed to list several important citations"; "the article includes mention of similar clinical cases" [syn: citation, credit, mention, quotation] 3: an indicator that orients you generally; "it is used as a reference for comparing the heating and the electrical energy involved" [syn: reference point, point of reference] 4: a book to which you can refer for authoritative facts; "he contributed articles to the basic reference work on that topic" [syn: reference book, reference work, book of facts] 5: a formal recommendation by a former employer to a potential future employer describing the person's qualifications and dependability; "requests for character references are

HOMOPHONES

all to often answered evasively" [syn: character, character reference] 6: the class of objects that an expression refers to; "the extension of `satellite of Mars' is the set containing only Demos and Phobos" [syn: denotation, extension] 7: the act of referring; "reference to an encyclopedia produced the answer" [syn: consultation] 8: a publication (or a passage from a publication) that is referred to; "he carried an armful of references back to his desk"; "he spent hours looking for the source of that quotation" [syn: source] 9: the relation between a word or phrase and the object or idea it refers to; "he argued that reference is a consequence of conditioned reflexes"

v : refer to [syn: cite]

referents

n : (plu of referent) 1: something referred to; the object of a reference 2: the first term in a proposition; the term to which other terms relate 3: something that refers; a term that refers to another term

remark, remarque /ɹiˈmɑɹk/
remark

n 1: a statement that expresses a personal opinion or belief; "from time to time she contributed a personal comment on his account" [syn: comment] 2: explicit notice; "it passed without remark" [syn: observation]

v 1: make mention of; "She observed that his presentation took up too much time"; "They noted that it was a fine day to go sailing" [syn: note, observe, mention] 2: make or write comment to make a comment on [syn: comment, notice, point out]

remarque

n 1: a small design etched on the margin of a plate and supposed to be removed after the earliest proofs have been taken 2: any feature distinguishing a particular stage of the plate; print or proof so distinguished [syn: Remarque proof]

rends, wrens /ɹɛnz/
rends

v : (3rd pers sing) : tear or be torn violently; "The curtain ripped from top to bottom"; "pull the cooked chicken into strips" [syn: rips, rives, pulls]

wrens

n : (plu of wren) : several small active brown birds of the northern hemisphere with short upright tails; they feed on insects [syn: jenny wren]

residence, residents
/ˈɹɛzɪdɛnts/
residence

n 1: the address where a person lives; "it is his legal place of residence" [syn: abode] 2: the official house or establishment of an important person (as a sovereign or president); "he refused to live in the governor's residence" 3: the act of dwelling in a place [syn: residency, abidance] 4: a large and imposing house [syn: mansion, mansion house, manse, hall]

residents

n : (plu of resident) 1: people who live at a particular place for a prolonged period or who were born there [syn: occupants, occupiers] 2: physicians (especially interns) who live in a hospital and care for hospitalized patients under the supervision of the medical staff of the hospital [syn: house physicians, resident physicians]

rest, wrest /ɹɛst/
rest

n 1: something left after other parts have been taken away; "there was no remainder"; "he threw away the rest" [syn: remainder, residual, residue, residuum] 2: freedom from activity (work or strain or responsibility); "took his repose by the swimming pool" [syn: ease, repose, relaxation] 3: a pause for relaxation; "people actually accomplish more when they take time for short rests" [syn: respite, relief, rest period] 4: a state of inaction; "a body will continue in a state of rest until acted upon" 5: euphemisms for death (based on an analogy between lying in a bed and in a tomb); "she was laid to rest beside her husband"; "they had to put their family pet to sleep" [syn: eternal rest, sleep, eternal sleep, quietus] 6: a support on which things can be put; "the gun was steadied on a special rest" 7: a musical notation indicating a silence of a specified duration

v 1: not move; be in a resting position 2: take a short breath [syn: breathe, catch one's breath, take a breather] 3: give a rest to; "He rested his bad leg"; "Rest the dogs for a moment" 4: have a place in relation to something else: "The fate of Bosnia lies in the hands of the West"; "The responsibility rests with the Allies" [syn: lie] 5: be at rest [syn: repose] [ant: be active] 6: stay the same; remain in a certain state; "The dress remained wet after repeated attempts to dry it"; "rest assured"; "stay alone"; "He remained unmoved by her tears"; "The bad weather continued for another week" [syn: stay, remain] [ant: change] 7: be inherent or innate in; [syn: reside, repose] 8: put something in a resting position, as for support or steadying; "Rest your head on my shoulder" 9: sit, as on a branch; "The birds perched high in the tree" [syn: perch, roost] 10: rest on or as if on a pillow, of one's head [syn: pillow] 11: be inactive, refrain from acting on something

HOMOPHONES

wrest
v : obtain by seizing forcibly or violently, also metaphorically; "wrest the knife from his hands"; "wrest a meaning from the old text"; "wrest power from the old government"

retch, wretch /ɹɛtʃ/
retch
n : an involuntary spasm of ineffectual vomiting; "a bad case of the heaves" [syn: heave]

v 1: eject the contents of the stomach through the mouth; "After drinking too much, the students vomited" [syn: vomit, vomit up, cast, sick, cat, regurgitate, be sick, disgorge, puke, barf, spew, chuck, upchuck, honk, throw up] [ant: keep down] 2: make an unsuccessful effort to vomit; strain to vomit [syn: gag, heave]
wretch
n 1: person performs some wicked deed 2: someone you feel sorry for [syn: poor devil]

review, revue /ɹɪˈvuə/
review
n 1: a new appraisal or evaluation [syn: reappraisal, revaluation, reassessment] 2: an essay or article that gives a critical evaluation (as of a book or play) [syn: critique, critical review, review article] 3: a second (or subsequent) examination [syn: follow-up, reexamination] 4: (accounting) an accounting service (less exhaustive than an audit) that provides some assurance to interested parties as to the reliability of financial data [syn: limited review] 5: a variety show with topical sketches and songs and dancing and comedians [syn: revue] 6: a periodical that publishes critical essays on current affairs or literature or art 7: a summary that repeats the substance of a longer discussion [syn: recapitulation, recap] 8: (law) a judicial reexamination of the proceedings of a court (especially by an appellate court) 9: practice intended to polish performance or refresh the memory [syn: brush up] 10: a formal or official examination; "the platoon stood ready for inspection" [syn: inspection]

v 1: look at again; examine again [syn: reexamine] 2: appraise critically; "She reviews books for the New York Times"; "Please critique this performance" [syn: critique] 3: hold a review (of troops) [syn: go over, survey] 4: refresh one's memory [syn: brush up, refresh] 5: look back upon (a period of time, sequence of events, etc.); remember; "she reviewed her achievements with pride" [syn: look back, retrospect] 6: study anew, as for a test
revue
n : a variety show with topical sketches and songs and dancing and comedians

rex, wrecks /ɹɛks/
rex
n: animal showing a genetic recessive variation in which the guard hairs are shorter than the undercoat or are entirely lacking
wrecks
n : (plu of wreck) (see wreck)
v : (3rd pers sing of wreck) (see wreck)

rheum, room /ɹum/
rheum
n 1: a watery or thin mucous discharge from the eyes or nose 2: rhubarb [syn: Rheum, genus Rheum]
room
n 1: an area within a building enclosed by walls and floor and ceiling; "the rooms were very small but they had a nice view" 2: space for movement; "room to pass"; "make way for": "hardly enough elbow room to turn around" [syn: way, elbow, elbow room] 3: opportunity for; "room for improvement" 4: the people who are present in a room; "the whole room was cheering"
v : live and take one's meals (in a certain place) [syn: board]

rheumy, roomie, roomy /ˈɹumi/
rheumy
adj : of or pertaining to rheum (watery discharge from the eyes or nose); abounding in, or causing, rheum; affected with rheum
roomie
n : one of two or more persons sharing the same room or living quarters [syn: roommate]
roomy
adj : (of buildings and rooms) having ample space; "a roomy but sparsely furnished apartment"; "a spacious ballroom" [syn: spacious]

rho, roe, row /ɹoʊ/
rho
n : the 17th letter of the Greek alphabet
roe
n 1: fish eggs or egg-filled ovary; having a grainy texture [syn: hard roe] 2: eggs of female fish 3: the egg mass or spawn of certain crustaceans such as the lobster 4: the eggs or egg-laden ovary of a fish
row
n 1: an arrangement of objects or people side by side in a line: "a row of chairs" 2: a long continuous strip (usually running horizontally); "a mackerel sky filled with rows of clouds"; "rows of barbed wire protected the trenches" 3: a layer of masonry; "a course of bricks" [syn: course] 4: a linear array of numbers side by side 5: a continuous chronological succession without an interruption; "they

HOMOPHONES

won the championship three years in a row" 6: the act of rowing as a sport [syn: rowing]

v : propel with oars; "row the boat"; down the lake"

rhos, roes, rose, rows /ɹoʊz/

rhos
n : (plu of rho)

roes
n : (plu of roe)

rose
adj : having a dusty purplish pink color; "the roseate glow of dawn" [syn: roseate, rosaceous]

n 1: any of many plants of the genus Rosa 2: pinkish table wine from red grapes whose skins were removed after fermentation began [syn: blush wine, pink wine, rose wine] 3: a dusty pink color

v : (past of rise) : "The balloon rose to the ceiling."

rows
n : (plu of row) (see rho); "They set fifty rows of chairs in the auditorium.";

rhumb, rum /ɹʌm/

rhumb
n : a line on a sphere that cuts all meridians at the same angle; the path taken by a ship or plane that maintains a constant compass direction [syn: rhumb line, loxodrome]

rum
adj : beyond or deviating from the usual or expected; "a curious hybrid accent"; "her speech has a funny twang"; "they have some funny ideas about war"; "had an odd name"; "the peculiar aromatic odor of cloves"; "something definitely queer about this town"; "what a rum fellow"; "singular behavior" [syn: curious, funny, odd, peculiar, queer, rummy, singular]

n 1: liquor distilled from fermented molasses 2: a card game based on collecting sets and sequences; the winner is the first to meld all their cards [syn: rummy]

rhyme, rime /ɹaɪm/

rhyme
n 1: correspondence in the sounds of two or more lines (especially final sounds) [syn: rime] 2: a piece of poetry [syn: verse]

v 1: compose rhymes [syn: rime] 2: be similar in sound, especially with respect to the last syllable; "hat and cat rhyme" [syn: rime]

rime
v : (var of rhyme)

n 1: ice crystals forming a white deposit (especially on objects outside) [syn: frost, hoar, hoarfrost] 2: var of rhyme

rigger, rigor /ˈɹɪgɹ/

rigger
n 1: someone who rigs; "he is an oil rigger"

2: a long slender pointed sable brush used by artists [syn: rigger brush]

rigor
n 1: something hard to endure; "the asperity of northern winters" [syn: asperity, grimness, hardship, severity, rigorousness] 2: the quality of being logically valid [syn: cogency, validity] 3: excessive sternness; "severity of character"; "the harshness of his punishment was inhuman"; "the rigors of boot camp" [syn: severity, harshness, inclemency, hardness, stiffness]

right, rite, wright, write /ɹaɪt/

right
adj 1: free from error; especially conforming to fact or truth; "the correct answer"; "the correct version"; "the right answer"; "took the right road"; "the right decision" [syn: correct] [ant: incorrect, incorrect] 2: being or located on or directed toward the side of the body to the east when facing north; "my right hand"; "right center field"; "a right-hand turn"; on the right when facing downstream; "the right bank of the river" [ant: left] 3: socially right or correct; "it isn't right to leave the party without saying goodbye"; "correct behavior" [syn: correct] 4: in conformance with justice or law or morality; "do the right thing and confess" [ant: wrong] 5: correct in opinion or judgment; "time proved him right" [syn: correct] [ant: wrong] 6: appropriate for a condition or occasion; "everything in its proper place"; "the right man for the job"; "she is not suitable for the position" [syn: proper, suitable] 7: of or belonging to the political or intellectual right [ant: left, center] 8: on the right-hand side of a vessel or aircraft when facing forward; "the starboard side" [syn: starboard] [ant: port] 9: in or into a satisfactory condition; "things are right again now"; "put things right" 10: intended for the right hand; "a right-hand glove" [syn: right, right-hand] 11: in accord with accepted standards of usage or procedure; "what's the right word for this?"; "the right way to open oysters" [syn: correct] 12: (geometry) having the axis perpendicular to the base; "a right angle" 13: of the side of cloth or clothing intended to face outward; "the right side of the cloth showed the pattern"; "be sure your shirt is right side out" 14: most suitable or right for a particular purpose; "a good time to plant tomatoes"; "the right time to act"; "the time is ripe for great sociological changes" [syn: good, ripe]

n 1: an abstract idea of that which is due to a person or governmental body by law or tradition or nature: "they are endowed by their Creator with certain unalienable Rights"; "Certain rights can never be

I-168

HOMOPHONES

granted to the government but must be kept in the hands of the people"-Eleanor Roosevelt; "a right is not something that somebody gives you; it is something that nobody can take away" 2: (frequently plural) the interest possessed by law or custom in some intangible thing: "mineral rights"; "film rights" 3: location near or direction toward the right side; i.e. the side to the south when a person or object faces east: "he stood on the right" [ant: left] 4: a turn to the right; "take a right at the corner" 5: the conservative faction of a political party [syn: wing] 6: anything in accord with principles of justice; "he feels he is in the right"; "the rightfulness of his claim" [syn: rightfulness] [ant: wrong] 7: the hand that is on the right side of the body; "he writes with his right hand but pitches with his left"; "hit him with quick rights to the body" [syn: right hand] 8: the piece of ground in the outfield on the catcher's right [syn: right field]

adv 1: precisely, exactly; "stand right here!" 2: immediately; "she called right after dinner" 3: (informal) exactly; "he fell flop on his face" [syn: flop] 4: toward or on the right; "he looked right and left"; also figuratively; "the party has moved right" [ant: left] 5: in the right manner; "please do your job properly!" "can't you carry me decent?" [syn: properly, decently, decent, in good order, the right way] [ant: improperly] 6: an interjection expressing agreement [syn: right on] 7: completely; "she felt right at home"; "he fell right into the trap" 8: (Southern regional intensive) very; "the baby is mighty cute"; "he's mighty tired"; "it is powerful humid"; "that boy is powerful big now"; "they have a right nice place" [syn: mighty, powerful] 9: in accordance with moral or social standards; "that serves him right"; "do right by him" [syn: justly] 10: in a correct manner; "he guessed right" [syn: correctly, aright] [ant: incorrectly]

v 1: make reparations or amends for; "right a wrong" [syn: compensate, redress, correct] [ant: wrong] 2: put in or restore to an upright position; "They righted the sailboat that had capsized" 3: regain an upright or proper position; "The capsized boat righted again" 4: make right or correct; "Correct the mistakes" [syn: correct] [ant: falsify]

rite
n 1: an established ceremony prescribed by a religion; "the rite of baptism" [syn: religious rite] 2: any customary observance or practice [syn: ritual]

wright
n: someone who makes or repairs something (usually used in combination;

e.g., wainwright -- someone who makes wagons)

write
v 1: produce a literary work; "She composed a poem"; "He wrote four novels" [syn: compose, pen, indite] 2: communicate or express by writing; "Please write to me every week" 3: have (one's written work) issued for publication; "How many books did Georges Simenon write?" 'She published 25 books during her long career" [syn: publish] 4: communicate (with) in writing; "Write her soon, please!" [syn: drop a line] 5: communicate by letter; "He wrote that he would be coming soon" 6: write music; "Beethoven composed nine symphonies" [syn: compose] 7: mark or trace on a surface; "The artist wrote Chinese characters on a big piece of white paper" 8: record data on a computer; "boot-up instructions are written on the hard disk" 9: write or name the letters that comprise the conventionally accepted form of (a word or part of a word); "He spelled the word wrong in this letter" [syn: spell]

righting, writing /ˈɹaɪtɪŋ/
righting
v 1: to bring or restore to the proper or natural position; to set upright; to make right or straight (that which has been wrong or crooked); to correct 2: To do justice to; to relieve from wrong; to restore rights to; to assert or regain the rights of; as, to right the oppressed; to right one's self; also, to vindicate 3: o right a vessel (nautical), "to restore her to an upright position after careening" 4: to right the helm (nautical), to place it in line with the keel.

writing
n 1: the act of creating written works; "writing was a form of therapy for him"; "it was a matter of disputed authorship" [syn: authorship, composition, penning] 2: the work of a writer; anything expressed in letters of the alphabet (especially when considered from the point of view of style and effect); "the writing in her novels is excellent"; "that editorial was a fine piece of writing" [syn: written material, piece of writing] 3: (usually plural) the collected work of an author; "the idea occurs with increasing frequency in Hemingway's writings" 4: letters or symbols written or imprinted on a surface to represent the sounds or words of a language; "he turned the paper over so the writing wouldn't show"; "the doctor's writing was illegible" 5: the activity of putting something in written form: "she did the thinking while he did the writing" [syn: committal to writing]

v : (progressive of write); "She is writing

rime, rhyme /ɹaɪm/

rime

n 1: ice crystals forming a white deposit (especially on objects outside) [syn: frost, hoar, hoarfrost]

rhyme

n 1: correspondence in the sounds of two or more lines (especially final sounds) 2: a piece of poetry [syn: verse]

v 1: compose rhymes 2: be similar in sound, esp. with respect to the last syllable; "hat and cat rhyme"

ring, wring /ɹiŋ/

ring

n 1: a characteristic sound; "it has the ring of sincerity" 2: a toroidal shape; "a ring of ships in the harbor"; "a halo of smoke" [syn: halo, annulus, doughnut, anchor ring] 3: a rigid circular band of metal or wood or other material used for holding or fastening or hanging or pulling; "there was still a rusty iron hoop for tying a horse" [syn: hoop] 4: (chemistry) a chain of atoms in a molecule that forms a closed loop [syn: closed chain] [ant: open chain] 5: an association of criminals; "police tried to break up the gang"; "a pack of thieves" [syn: gang, pack, mob] 6: the sound of a bell ringing; "the distinctive ring of the church bell"; "the ringing of the telephone"; "the tintinnabulation that so voluminously swells from the ringing and the dinging of the bells"--E. A. Poe [syn: ringing, tintinnabulation] 7: a square platform marked off by ropes in which contestants box or wrestle 8: jewelry consisting of a circular band of a precious metal worn on the finger; "she had rings on every finger" [syn: band]

v 1: make a ringing sound [syn: peal] 2: ring or echo with sound; "the hall resounded with laughter" [syn: resound, echo, reverberate] 3: make (bells) ring, often for the purposes of musical edification; "Ring the bells"; "My uncle rings every Sunday at the local church" [syn: knell] 4: be around; "Developments surround the town"; "The river encircles the village" [syn: surround, environ, encircle, circle, round] 5: get or try to get into communication (with someone) by telephone; "I tried to call you all night"; "Take two aspirin and call me in the morning" [syn: call, telephone, call up, phone] 6: attach a ring to; "ring birds"

wring

n : a twisting squeeze; "gave the wet cloth a wring" [syn: squeeze]

v 1: twist and press out of shape [syn: contort, deform, distort] 2: twist and compress, as if in pain or anguish; "Wring one's hand" [syn: wrench] 3: obtain by coercion or intimidation; "They extorted money from the executive by threatening to reveal his past to the company boss" [syn: extort, rack, gouge] 4: twist, squeeze, or compress in order to extract liquid; "wring the towels"

rise, ryes /ɹaɪz/

rise

n 1: a growth in strength or number or importance [ant: fall] 2: the act of changing location in an upward direction [syn: ascent, ascension, ascending] 3: an upward slope or grade (as in a road); "the car couldn't make the grade" [syn: ascent, acclivity, raise, climb, upgrade] [ant: descent] 4: a movement upward; "they cheered the rise of the hot-air balloon" [syn: rising, ascent, ascension] [ant: fall] 5: the amount a salary is increased; "he got a 3% raise"; "he got a wage hike" [syn: raise, wage hike, hike, wage increase, salary increase] 6: the property possessed by a slope or surface that rises [syn: upgrade, rising slope] 7: a wave that lifts the surface of the water or ground [syn: lift] 8: an increase in cost; "they asked for a 10% rise in rates" [syn: boost, hike, cost increase] 9: increase in price or value: "the news caused a general advance on the stock market" [syn: advance]

v 1: move upward; "The fog lifted"; "The smoke arose from the forest fire" [syn: lift, arise, move up, go up, come up] [ant: descend] 2: increase in value or to a higher point; "prices climbed steeply"; "the value of our house rose sharply last year" [syn: go up, climb] 3: rise to one's feet; "The audience got up and applauded" [syn: arise, get up, stand up] [ant: sit down, lie down] 4: rise up; "The building rose before them" [syn: lift, rear] 5: come to the surface [syn: surface, come up, rise up] 6: become more extreme; "The tension heightened" [syn: heighten] 7: come into existence; take on form or shape; "A new religious movement originated in that country" "a love that sprang up from friendship"; "the idea for the book grew out of a short story"; "An interesting phenomenon uprose" [syn: originate, arise, develop, spring up, grow] 8: be promoted, move to a better position [syn: move up] 9: go up or advance; "Sales were climbing after prices were lowered" [syn: wax, mount, climb] [ant: wane] 10: get up and out of bed; "I get up at 7 A.M. every day"; "They rose early"; "He uprose at night" [syn: get up, turn out, arise] [ant: go to bed, go to bed] 11: rise in rank or status; "Her new novel jumped high on the bestseller list" [syn: jump, climb up] 12: increase in volume; of dough [syn: prove] 13: become heartened or elated; "Her spirits rose when she heard the good news"

HOMOPHONES

14: exert oneself to meet a challenge; "rise to a challenge"; "rise to the occasion" 15: take part in a rebellion; renounce a former allegiance [syn: rebel, arise, rise up] 16: grow in volume, as under the influence of heat or fermentation; of substances 17: come up, of celestial bodies; "The sun also rises" [syn: come up, ascend] [ant: set] 18: get up from a sitting or lying position; "The audience rose when then conductor entered the orchestra pit"; "Rise from your chair" [syn: straighten] [ant: sink] 19: return from the dead; "Christ is risen!" "The dead are to rise up"

ryes

n : (plu of rye) (see rye)

ritz, writs /ɹɪts/

ritz

n 1: ostentatious display of elegance; "they put on the ritz" 2: (informal) an ostentatiously elegant hotel [syn: Ritz]

writs

n : (plu of writ) : legal documents issued by a court or judicial officer [syn: judicial writs]

road, rode, rowed /ɹoʊd/

road

adj 1: taking place over public roads; "road racing" [ant: cross-country] 2: working for a short time in different places; "itinerant laborers"; "a road show"; "traveling salesman"; "touring company" [syn: itinerant, touring, traveling]

n 1: an open way (generally public) for travel or transportation [syn: route] 2: a way or means to achieve something; "the road to fame"

rode

v : (past of ride) : "He rode his bike to school every day."

rowed

v : (past of row) : "propelled with oars" "They rowed their boat across the lake."

roan, rown /ɹoʊn/

roan

adj : (used of especially horses) having a brownish coat thickly sprinkled with white or gray; "a roan horse"

n 1: a soft sheepskin leather that is colored and finished to resemble morocco; used in bookbinding 2: horse having a roan coat

rown

adj : impelled by oars

róc, rock /ɹɑk/

roc

n : mythical bird of prey having enormous size and strength

rock

n 1: a lump of hard consolidated mineral matter; "he threw a rock at me" [syn: stone] 2: material consisting of the aggregate of minerals like those making up the Earth's crust [syn: stone] 3: hard

stick bright-colored stick candy typically peppermint flavored [syn: rock candy] 4: a genre of popular music originating in the 1950s; a blend of Black rhythm-and-blues with White country-and-western; "rock is a generic term for the range of styles that evolved out of rock'n'roll." [syn: rock 'n' roll, rock-and-roll, rock music] 5: pitching dangerously to one side [syn: careen, sway, tilt]

v 1: move back and forth in an unstable manner; "the ship was rocking"; "the tall building swayed"; "the tree shook in the wind" [syn: sway, shake] 2: rock or place in or as if in a cradle; "He cradled the infant in his arms" [syn: cradle]

roil, royal /'ɹɔɪ(ə)l/

roil

v 1: be agitated; of liquids [syn: churn, boil, moil] 2: make turbid by stirring up the sediments of [syn: rile]

royal

adj 1: of or relating to or indicative of or issued or performed by a king or queen or other monarch; "the royal party"; "the royal crest"; "by royal decree"; "a royal visit" 2: established or chartered or authorized by royalty; "the Royal Society" 3: being of the rank of a monarch; "of royal ancestry"; "princes of the blood royal" 4: belonging to or befitting a supreme ruler; "golden age of imperial splendor"; "purple tyrant"; "regal attire"; "treated with royal acclaim"; "the royal carriage of a stag's head" [syn: imperial, majestic, purple, regal] 5: invested with royal power as symbolized by a crown; "the royal (or crowned) heads of Europe"

n 1: a sail set next above the topgallant on a royal mast 2: stag with antlers of 12 or more branches [syn: royal stag]

role, roll /ɹoʊl/

role

n 1: the actions and activities assigned to or required or expected of a person or group: "the function of a teacher"; "the government must do its part"; "play its role" [syn: function, office, part] 2: an actor's portrayal of someone in a play; "she played the part of Desdemona" [syn: character, theatrical role, part, persona] 3: what something is used for; "the function of an auger is to bore holes"; "ballet is beautiful but what use is it?" [syn: function, purpose, use] 4: normal or customary activity of a person in a particular social setting; "what is your role on the team?"

roll

n 1: rotary motion of an object around its own axis; "wheels in axial rotation" [syn: axial rotation, axial motion] 2: a list of names; "his name was struck off the rolls" [syn: roster] 3: a long heavy sea wave as it advances towards the shore [syn: roller, rolling wave] 4: photographic film rolled up inside a container to protect it from light 5: a round shape formed by a series of concentric circles [syn: coil, whorl, curl, curlicue, ringlet, gyre, scroll] 6: a roll of currency notes (often taken as the resources of a person or business etc.); "he shot his roll on a bob-tailed nag" [syn: bankroll] 7: small rounded bread either plain or sweet [syn: bun] 8: a deep prolonged sound (as of thunder or large bells) [syn: peal, pealing, rolling] 9: the sound of a drum (especially a snare drum) beaten rapidly and continuously [syn: paradiddle, drum roll] 10: a document that can be rolled up (as for storage) [syn: scroll] 11: anything rolled up in cylindrical form 12: the act of throwing dice [syn: cast] 13: walking with a rolling gait 14: a flight maneuver; aircraft rotates about its longitudinal axis without changing direction or losing altitude 15: the act of rolling something (as the ball in bowling)

v 1: to rotate or cause to rotate: "The child rolled down the hill"; "She rolled the ball"; "They rolled their eyes at his words"; "turn over to your left side" [syn: revolve, turn over] 2: move along on or as if on wheels or a wheeled vehicle; "The President's convoy rolled past the crowds" [syn: wheel] 3: occur in soft rounded shapes; "The hills rolled past" [syn: undulate] 4: flatten or spread with a roller; "roll out the paper" [syn: roll out] 5: emit, produce, or utter with a deep prolonged reverberating sound; "The thunder rolled"; "rolling drums" 6: wrap or coil around; "roll your hair around your finger"; "Twine the thread around the spool" [syn: wind, wrap, twine] [ant: unwind] 7: begin operating or running; "The cameras were rolling"; "The presses are already rolling" 8: shape by rolling; "roll a cigarette" 9: execute a roll, in tumbling; "The gymnasts rolled and jumped" 10: sell something to or obtain something from by energetic and esp. underhanded activity [syn: hustle, pluck] 11: pronounce with a roll, of the phoneme /ɹ/ "She rolls her r's". 12: boil vigorously; "The liquid was seething" [syn: seethe]

rood, rude, rued /ɹud/

rood

n : representation of the cross on which Jesus died [syn: crucifix, rood-tree]

rude

adj 1: socially incorrect in behavior; "resentment flared at such an unmannered intrusion" [syn: ill-mannered, unmannered, unmannerly] 2: (of persons) lacking in refinement or grace [syn: ill-bred, bounderish, lowbred, underbred,

yokelish] 3: lacking civility or good manners; "want nothing from you but to get away from your uncivil tongue"-Willa Cather [syn: uncivil] [ant: civil] 4: (used especially of commodities) in the natural unprocessed condition; "natural yogurt"; "natural produce"; "raw wool"; "raw sugar"; "bales of rude cotton" [syn: natural, raw] 5: belonging to an early stage of technical development; characterized by simplicity and (often) crudeness; "the crude weapons and rude agricultural implements of early man"; "primitive movies of the 1890s"; "primitive living conditions in the Appalachian mountains" [syn: crude, primitive]

rued

v : (past of rue) : felt remorse for; felt sorry for; having been contrite about [syn: repented, regretted]

roomer, rumor /'ɹumɚ/

roomer

n : a tenant in someone's house [syn: lodger, boarder]

rumor

n : gossip (usually a mixture of truth and untruth) passed around by word of mouth [syn: hearsay]

v : tell or spread rumors; "It was rumored that the next president would be a woman" [syn: bruit]

root, route /ɹut/

root

adj : arising from or going to the root; "a radical flaw in the plan" [syn: radical]

n 1: the usually underground organ that lacks buds or leaves or nodes; absorbs water and mineral salts; usually it anchors the plant to the ground 2: (linguistics) the form of a word after all affixes are removed; "thematic vowels are part of the stem" [syn: root word, base, stem, theme, radical] 3: the place where something begins, where it springs into being; "the Italian beginning of the Renaissance"; "Jupiter was the origin of the radiation"; "Pittsburgh is the source of the Ohio River"; "communism's Russian root" [syn: beginning, origin, source] 4: a number that when multiplied by itself some number of times equals a given number 5: the set of values that give a true statement when substituted into an equation [syn: solution] 6: someone from whom you are descended (but usually more remote that a grandparent) [syn: ancestor, ascendant, antecedent] [ant: descendant] 7: a simple form inferred as the common basis from which related words in several languages can be derived by linguistic processes [syn: etymon] 8: the part of a tooth that is embedded in the jaw and serves as support [syn: tooth root]

HOMOPHONES

v 1: take root; begin to grow; of plants 2: come into existence, originate 3: plant by the roots 4: dig with the snout; "the pig was rooting for truffles" [syn: root, rootle] 5: take sides with; align oneself with; show strong sympathy for; "We all rooted for the home team"; "I'm pulling for the underdog"; "Are you siding with the defender of the title?" [syn: side, pull] 6: become settled or established and stable in one's residence or life style; "He finally settled down" [syn: settle, take root, steady down, settle down] 7: cause to take roots

route (also /ɹaʊt/)

n 1: an established line of travel or access [syn: path, itinerary] 2: an open way (generally public) for travel or transportation [syn: road]

v 1: send documents or materials to appropriate destinations 2: send via a specific route 3: divert in a specified direction: "divert the low voltage to the engine cylinders" 4: send by a particular route, as of mail for postal delivery

rote, wrote /ɹoʊt/

rote

n : memorization by repetition [syn: rote learning]

wrote

v : (past of write) (see right); "The students wrote essays for the final exam."

rough, ruff /ɹʌf/

rough

adj 1: having or caused by an irregular surface; "trees with rough bark"; "rough ground"; "a rough ride"; "rough skin"; "rough blankets"; "his unsmooth face"; "unsmooth writing" [syn: unsmooth] [ant: smooth] 2: (of persons or behavior) lacking refinement or finesse; "she was a diamond in the rough"; "rough manners" 3: not quite exact or correct; "the approximate time was 10 o'clock"; "a rough guess"; "a ballpark estimate" [syn: approximate, ballpark] 4: full of hardship or trials; "the rocky road to success"; "they were having a rough time" [syn: rocky] 5: violently agitated and turbulent; "boisterous winds and waves"; "the fierce thunders roar me their music"- Ezra Pound; "rough weather"; "rough seas" [syn: boisterous, fierce] 6: unpleasantly harsh or grating in sound; "a gravelly voice" [syn: grating, gravel, gravelly, rasping, raspy] 7: ready and able to resort to force or violence; "pugnacious spirits...lamented that there was so little prospect of an exhilarating disturbance"- Herman Melville; "they were rough and determined fighting men" [syn: pugnacious] 8: (botany) of the margin of a leaf shape; having the edge cut or fringed or scalloped [ant: smooth] 9: not shaped by cutting or trimming;

"an uncut diamond"; "rough gemstones" [syn: uncut] [ant: cut] 10: not carefully or expertly made; "managed to make a crude splint"; "a crude cabin of logs with bark still on them"; "rough carpentry" [syn: crude] 11: not perfected; "a rough draft"; "a few rough sketches" 12: unpleasantly stern; "wild and harsh country full of hot sand and cactus"; "the nomad life is rough and hazardous" [syn: harsh]

n : the part of a golf course bordering the fairway where the grass is not cut short

adv 1: with roughness or violence; "he was pushed roughly aside"; (`rough' is informal as in "they treated him rough") [syn: roughly] 2: with rough motion as over a rough surface; "ride rough" [syn: roughly]

v 1: prepare in preliminary or sketchy form [syn: rough in, rough out] 2: draw up an outline or sketch for something; "draft a speech" [syn: draft, outline]

ruff

n 1: a high tight collar [syn: choker, ruffle, neck ruff] 2: common Eurasian sandpiper; male has an erectile ruff in breeding season [syn: Philomachus pugnax] 3: (cards) the act of taking a trick with a trump when unable to follow suit [syn: trumping]

v : play a trump, in card games [syn: trump]

rouse, rows /ɹaʊz/

rouse

v 1: become active: "He finally bestirred himself" [syn: bestir] 2: force or drive out; "The police routed them out of bed at 2 A.M." [syn: rout out, drive out, force out] 3: cause to be agitated, excited, or roused; "The speaker charged up the crowd with his inflammatory remarks" [syn: agitate, turn on, charge, commove, excite, charge up] [ant: calm] 4: cause to become awake or conscious; "He was roused by the drunken men in the street"; "Please wake me at 6 AM." [syn: awaken, wake, waken, wake up, arouse] [ant: cause to sleep]

rows

n : (plu of row) : angry disputes; "they had constant rows about money"; "they had quarrels"; "they had words" [syn: quarrels, wrangles, words, run-ins, dustups]

rout, route /ɹaʊt/

rout

n 1: a disorderly crowd of people [syn: mob, rabble] 2: an overwhelming defeat

v 1: cause to flee [syn: rout out, expel] 2: dig with the snout; "the pig was rooting for truffles" [syn: root, rootle] 3: make a groove in [syn: gouge, groove] 4: defeat disastrously [syn: spread-eagle]

route (also /ɹut/)

n 1: an established line of travel or access [syn: path, itinerary] 2: an open

way (generally public) for travel or transportation [syn: road]
v 1: send documents or materials to appropriate destinations 2: send via a specific route 3: divert in a specified direction; "divert the low voltage to the engine cylinders"

roux, rue /ɹu/

roux
n : a mixture of fat and flour heated and used as a basis for sauces

rue
n 1: European strong-scented perennial herb with gray-green bitter-tasting leaves; an irritant similar to poison ivy [syn: herb of grace, Ruta graveolens] 2: leaves sometimes used for flavoring fruit or claret cup but should be used with great caution: can cause irritation like poison ivy 3: sadness associated with some wrong done or some disappointment; " to his rue, the error cost him the game" [syn: sorrow, regret, ruefulness] 4: (French) a street or road in France
v : feel remorse for; feel sorry for; be contrite about [syn: repent, regret]

rues, ruse /ɹuz/

rues
v : (3rd per sing for rue): (see roux)

ruse
n : a deceptive maneuver (especially to avoid capture) [syn: artifice]

rung, wrong, wrung

rung /ɹʌŋ/
n 1: a crosspiece between the legs of a chair [syn: round, stave] 2: one of the crosspieces that form the steps of a ladder [syn: rundle, spoke]
v : (past of ring) : "He had rung the bell five times."

wrong /ɹɔŋ/
adj 1: not correct; not in conformity with fact or truth; "an incorrect calculation"; "the report in the paper is wrong"; "your information is wrong"; "the clock showed the wrong time"; "found themselves on the wrong road"; "based on the wrong assumptions" [syn: incorrect] [ant: correct, correct] 2: contrary to conscience or morality or law; "it is wrong for the rich to take advantage of the poor"; "cheating is wrong"; "it is wrong to lie" [ant: right] 3: not appropriate for a purpose or occasion; "unsuitable attire for the office"; "said all the wrong things" [syn: unsuitable, improper] 4: not functioning properly; "something is amiss"; "has gone completely haywire"; "the telephone is out of order"; "what's the matter with your vacuum cleaner?"; "something is wrong with the engine" [syn: amiss, awry, haywire, out of order, the matter] 5: not according with the facts; "unfortunately the statement was simply untrue"; "the facts as reported were wrong" [syn: untrue] 6: based on or acting or judging in error; "it is wrong to think that way" [ant: right] 7: not in accord with established usage or procedure; "the wrong medicine"; "the wrong way to shuck clams" 8: not conforming with accepted standards of propriety or taste; undesirable; "incorrect behavior"; "she was seen in all the wrong places"; "He thought it was wrong for her to go out to work" [syn: inappropriate, incorrect] 9: used of the side of cloth or clothing intended to face inward; "socks worn wrong side out" 10: badly timed; "an ill-timed intervention"; "you think my intrusion unseasonable"; "an untimely remark"; "it was the wrong moment for a joke" [syn: ill-timed, ill timed, unseasonable, untimely]
n 1: that which is contrary to the principles of justice or law; "he feels that you are in the wrong" [syn: wrongfulness] [ant: right] 2: a legal injury is any damage resulting from a violation of a legal right [syn: legal injury, damage]
adv : in an incorrect manner; "she guessed wrong" [syn: incorrectly, wrongly] [ant: correctly, correctly]
v : treat unjustly; do wrong to [ant: right]

wrung /ɹʌŋ/
v : (past of wring) : "She wrung the water out of the towels."

rye, wry /ɹaɪ/

rye
n 1: the seed of the cereal grass 2: hardy annual cereal grass widely cultivated in northern Europe where its grain is the chief ingredient of black bread and in North America for forage and soil improvement [syn: Secale cereale] 3: distilled from rye or rye and malt [syn: rye whiskey, rye whisky]

wry
adj 1: humorously sarcastic or mocking; "dry humor"; "an ironic remark often conveys an intended meaning obliquely"; "an ironic novel"; "an ironical smile"; "with a wry Scottish wit" [syn: dry, ironic, ironical] 2: bent to one side; "a wry neck" 3: disdainfully or ironically humorous; scornful and mocking [syn: sardonic]

HOMOPHONES

-S-

sac, sack /sæk/

sac

n 1: an enclosed space [syn: pouch, sack, pocket] 2: a case or sheath especially a pollen sac or moss capsule [syn: theca] 3: a structure resembling a bag in an animal

sack

n 1: a bag made of paper or plastic for holding customer's purchases [syn: poke, paper bag, carrier bag] 2: an enclosed space [syn: pouch, sac, pocket] 3: the quantity contained in a sack [syn: sackful] 4: any of various light dry strong white wine from Spain and Canary Islands (including sherry) 5: a woman's full loose hiplength jacket [syn: sacque] 6: a hanging bed of canvas or rope netting (usually suspended between two trees); swing easily [syn: hammock] 7: a loose-fitting dress hanging straight from the shoulders without a waist [syn: chemise, shift] 8: the termination of someone's employment (leaving them free to depart) [syn: dismissal, discharge, firing, liberation, release, sacking] 5: (slang) bed; "I'm going to hit the sack."

v 1: plunder after capture, as of a town [syn: plunder] 2: terminate the employment of; "The boss fired his secretary today" [syn: fire, give notice, can, dismiss, give the axe, send away, force out, terminate] [ant: hire] 3: make as a net profit; "The company cleared $1 million" [syn: net, sack up, clear] 4: put in a sack; "The grocer sacked the onions"

saccharin, saccharine /'sækəɹɪn/

saccharin

n : a crystalline substance 500 times sweeter than sugar; used as a calorie-free sweetener [syn: $C_7H_5NO_3S$]

saccharine

adj 1: overly sweet; cloying, syrupy] 2: ingratiatingly or affectedly agreeable or friendly 3: overly sentimental

sachet, sashay /sæ'ʃeɪ/

sachet

n : a small soft bag containing perfumed powder; used to perfume items in a drawer or chest

sashay

n 1: a square dance figure; partners circle each other taking sideways steps 2: (ballet) quick gliding steps with one foot always leading [syn: chasse] 3: a journey taken for pleasure; "many summer excursions to the shore"; "it was merely a pleasure trip"; "after cautious sashays into the field" [syn: excursion, jaunt, outing, junket, pleasure trip, expedition]

v 1: move sideways [syn: sidle] 2: to walk with a lofty proud gait, often in an attempt to impress others: "He strut around like a rooster in a hen house." [syn: swagger, ruffle, prance, strut, cock]

sacs, sacks, sacques, sax /sæks/

sacs

n : (plu of sac) (see sac)

sacks

n : (plu of sack)

v : (3rd pers sing of sack) (see sack)

sacques

n : infant short jackets that fasten at the neck

sax

n : a single-reed woodwind with a conical bore [syn: saxophone]

sail, sale /seɪl/

sail

n 1: a large piece of fabric (as canvas) by means of which wind is used to propel a sailing vessel [syn: canvas, sheet] 2: an ocean trip taken for pleasure [syn: cruise]

v 1: traverse or travel by ship on (a body of water); "We sailed the Atlantic"; "He sailed the Pacific all alone" 2: move with sweeping, effortless, gliding motions; "The diva swept into the room"; "Shreds of paper sailed through the air"; "The searchlights swept across the sky" [syn: sweep] 3: travel in a boat propelled by wind; "I love sailing, especially on the open sea" 4: travel by boat on a boat propelled by wind or by other means; "The QE2 will sail to Southampton tomorrow" [syn: voyage, navigate]

sale

n 1: the general activity of selling; "they tried to boost sales"; "laws limit the sale of handguns" 2: a particular instance of selling; "he has just made his first sale"; "they had to complete the sale before the banks closed" 3: the state of being purchasable; offered or exhibited for selling; "vitamin C is on sale at most pharmacies"; "the new line of cars will soon be on sale" 4: an occasion (usually brief) for buying at specially reduced prices; "they held a sale to reduce their inventory"; "I got some great bargains at their annual sale" [syn: cut-rate sale, sales event] 5: an agreement (or contract) in which property is transferred from the seller (vendor) to the buyer (vendee) for a fixed price in money (paid or agreed to be paid by the buyer); "the salesman faxed the sales agreement to his home office" [syn: sales agreement]

sailer, sailor /'seɪləɹ/

sailer

n : ship or boat having specified sailing qualities

sailor

n 1: any member of a ship's crew [syn: crewman] 2: a serviceman in the navy [syn: bluejacket, navy man, sailor boy] 3: a stiff straw hat with a flat crown [syn: boater, leghorn, Panama, Panama hat, skimmer, straw hat]

salter (see Psalter)

salver, salvor /'sælvə.ɪ/

salver

n : a tray (or large plate) for serving food or drinks; usually made of silver

salvor

n : person who salvages [syn: salvager]

sandhi, sandy /'sɛəndi/

sandhi

n : modification of the pronunciation of a morpheme according to its context; examples are '-ed' pronounced as /d/ in amazed and as /t/ in raced

sandy

adj 1: composed of or covered with relatively large particles; "granular sugar"; "gritty sand" [syn: farinaceous, coarse-grained, grainy, granular, granulose, gritty, mealy] 2: (used of soil) loose and large-grained in consistency; "light sandy soil" [syn: friable, light] 3: of hair color; pale yellowish to yellowish brown; "flaxen locks" [syn: flaxen] 4: resembling or containing sand; or growing in sandy areas; "arenaceous limestone"; "arenaceous grasses" [syn: arenaceous, sand-like] [ant: argillaceous] 5: abounding in sand; "Florida's sandy beaches"

sane, seine /sɛɪn/

sane

adj 1: mentally healthy; free from mental disorder; "appears to be completely sane" [ant: insane] 2: marked by sound judgment; "sane nuclear policy" [syn: reasonable]

seine

n : a large fishnet that hangs vertically, with floats at the top and weights at the bottom
v : fish with a seine; catch fish with a seine

sari, sorry /'saɹi/

sari

n : a dress worn primarily by Hindu women; consists of several yards of light material that is draped around the body

sorry

adj 1: keenly sorry or regretful; "felt bad about letting the team down"; "was sorry that she had treated him so badly"; "felt bad about breaking the vase" [syn: bad] 2: feeling or expressing sorrow or pity; "a pitying observer threw his coat around her shoulders" [syn: pitying, sorry for] 3: having regret or sorrow or a sense of loss over something done or undone; "felt regretful over his vanished youth"; "regretful over mistakes she had made"

[syn: regretful] [ant: unregretful] 4: feeling or expressing pain or sorrow for sins or offenses [syn: contrite, remorseful, rueful, ruthful] 5: bad; unfortunate; "my finances were in a deplorable state"; "a lamentable decision"; "her clothes were in sad shape"; "a sorry state of affairs" [syn: deplorable, distressing, lamentable, pitiful, sad] 6: depressing in character or appearance; "drove through dingy streets"; "drab old buildings"; "a dreary mining town"; "gloomy tenements"; [syn: dingy, dismal, drab, drear, dreary, gloomy] 7: without merit; "a sorry horse"; "a sorry excuse"; "a lazy no-count, good-for-nothing goldbrick"; "the car was a no-good piece of junk" [syn: good-for-nothing, good-for-naught, merit-less, no-account, no-count, no-good]

satiric, satyric /sæ'tɪɹɪk/

satiric

adj : of, relating to, or constituting satire; exposing human folly to ridicule; "a persistent campaign of mockery by the satirical fortnightly magazine" [syn: satirical]

satyric

adj : of or relating to or having the characteristics of a satyr; "his satyric old man pursues young girls" [syn: satyrical]

sault, sue /su/

sault

n : a rapid in some rivers; as, the Sault Sainte Marie in the U.S.

sue

v : institute legal proceedings against; file a suit against; "He was warned that the patient would sue him" [syn: litigate, process]

saurel, sorrel /'sɔɹəl/

saurel

n 1: large elongated compressed food fish of the Atlantic waters of Europe [syn: horse mackerel, Trachurus trachurus] 2: a California food fish [syn: horse mackerel, jack mackerel, Spanish mackerel, Trachurus symmetricus]

sorrel

adj : of a light brownish color [syn: brownish-orange]
n 1: any plant or flower of the genus Oxalis [syn: oxalis, wood sorrel] 2: any of certain coarse weedy plants with long taproots, sometimes used as table greens or in folk medicine [syn: dock, sour grass] 3: East Indian sparsely prickly annual herb or perennial sub-shrub widely cultivated for its fleshy calyxes used in tarts and jelly and for its bast fiber [syn: roselle, red sorrel, Jamaica sorrel, Hibiscus sabdariffa] 4: large sour-tasting arrowhead-shaped leaves used in salads and sauces [syn: common sorrel] 5: a horse of a brownish

HOMOPHONES

orange to light brown color

saver, savor /ˈseɪvəʳ/

saver

n 1: someone who saves something from danger or violence [syn: rescuer, recoverer] 2: someone who saves (especially money)

savor

n : the taste experience when a savory condiment is taken into the mouth [syn: relish, flavor, sapidity,, smack, tang]

v 1: derive or receive pleasure from; get enjoyment from; take pleasure in; "She relished her fame and basked in her glory" [syn: enjoy, bask, relish] 2: have flavor; taste of something [syn: taste] 3: taste appreciatively 4: give taste to)

scalar, scaler /ˈskeɪləʳ/

scalar

adj : of or relating to a directionless magnitude; "mass is a scalar value"

n : a variable quantity that cannot be resolved into components; "mass is a scalar"

scaler

n : 1: a dental instrument for removing tartar from teeth 2: an electronic device that operates a recorder or produces an output pulse after a specified number of input impulses 3: person who removes scales

scoot, scute /skut/

scoot

v : run or move very quickly or hastily; "She scooted into the yard" [syn: dart, dash, scud, flash, shoot]

scute

n : large bony or horny plate as on an armadillo or turtle

scend, send /sɛnd/

scend

n 1: upward movement of a pitching ship 2: lift of a wave

v : rise or heave upward under the influence of a natural force, as on a wave [syn: surge]

send

v 1: cause to go somewhere; "The explosion sent the car flying into the air"; "She sent her children to camp"; "He directed all his energies into his dissertation" [syn: direct] 2: to cause or order to be taken, directed, or transmitted to another place: "He had sent the dispatches downtown to the proper people and had slept." [syn: send out] 3: cause to be directed or transmitted to another place; "send me your latest results"; "I'll mail you the paper when it's written" [syn: mail, post] 4: transport commercially [syn: transport, ship] 5: assign to a station [syn: station, post, base, place] 6: transfer; "The spy sent the classified information off to Russia" [syn: get off, send off] 7: cause to be admitted; of persons to an institution:

"After the second episode, she had to be committed"; "he was committed to prison" [syn: commit, institutionalize, charge] 8: broadcast over the airwaves, as in radio or television; "We cannot air this X-rated song" [syn: air, broadcast, beam, transmit]

scene, seen /sin/

scene

n 1: the place where some action occurs; "the police returned to the scene of the crime" 2: an incident (real or imaginary) "their parting was a sad scene" 3: the visual percept of a region; "the most desirable feature of the park are the beautiful views" [syn: view, aspect, prospect, vista, panorama] 4: a consecutive series of pictures that constitutes a unit of action in a film [syn: shot] 5: a situation treated as an observable object; "the political picture is favorable" or "the religious scene in England has changed in the last century" [syn: picture] 6: a subdivision of an act of a play; "the first act has three scenes" 7: a display of bad temper; "he had a fit"; "she threw a tantrum"; "he made a scene" [syn: fit, tantrum, conniption] 8: graphic art consisting of the graphic or photographic representation of a visual percept; "he painted scenes from everyday life"; "figure 2 shows photographic and schematic views of the equipment" [syn: view] 9: the context and environment in which something is set: "the perfect setting for a ghost story" [syn: setting] 10: the painted structures of a stage set that are intended to suggest a particular locale; "they worked all night painting the scenery" [syn: scenery]

seen

adj : witnessed at first hand [syn: observed]

v : (past of see) "They had seen the movie twice."

scent (see cent)

scents (see cense)

scion, sion /ˈsaɪən/

scion

n : a descendent or heir; "a scion of royal stock"

sion

n: an imaginary place considered to be perfect or ideal [syn: utopia]

scissile, sisal /ˈsɪsɪl/

scissile

adj : capable of being cut smoothly or split easily

sisal

n 1: a plant fiber used for making rope [syn: sisal hemp] 2: Mexican or West Indian plant with large fleshy leaves yielding a stiff fiber used in e.g. rope [syn: Agave sisalana]

HOMOPHONES

scull, skull /skʌl/

scull

n 1: a long-handled oar mounted at the stern of a boat and moved left and right to propel the boat forward 2: one of a pair of short-handled oars 3: a racing shell propelled by one or two oarsmen pulling two oars

v : propel (a boat) with sculls

skull

n : the bony skeleton of the head of vertebrates

sea (see C)
seal (see ceil)
sealing (see ceiling)

seam, seem /sim/

seam

n 1: joint consisting of a line formed by joining two pieces 2: a slight depression in the smoothness of a surface; "his face has many lines"; "ironing gets rid of most wrinkles" [syn: wrinkle, furrow, crease, crinkle, line] 3: a stratum of ore or coal thick enough to be mined with profit; "he worked in the coal beds" [syn: bed]

v 1: put together with a seam; "seam a dress" 2: join with a seam

seem

v 1: give a certain impression or have a certain outward aspect; "She seems to be sleeping"; "This appears to be a very difficult problem"; "This project looks fishy"; "They appeared like people who had not eaten or slept for a long time" [syn: look, appear] 2: seem to be true, probable, or apparent; "It seems that he is very gifted"; "It appears that the weather in California is very bad" [syn: appear] 3: appear to exist; "There seems no reason to go ahead with the project now" 4: appear to one's own mind or opinion; "I seem to be misunderstood by everyone"; "I can't seem to learn these Chinese characters"

seamen, semen /'simɪn/

seamen

n : (plu of seaman) : men who serve as sailors [syn: mariners, tars, Jack-tars, old salts, seafarers, gobs, sea dogs]

semen

n : the thick white fluid containing spermatozoa that is ejaculated by the male genital tract [syn: seed, seminal fluid, ejaculate, cum]

sear (see cere)
seal (see ceil)
sealing (see ceiling)
sear (see cere)
seas (see C's)

season, seisin /'sizɪn/

season

n 1: a period of the year marked by special events or activities in some field; "he celebrated his 10th season with the ballet company" or "she always looked forward to the avocado season" 2: one of the natural periods into which the year is divided by the equinoxes and solstices or atmospheric conditions (Spring, Summer, Autumn and Winter); "the regular sequence of the seasons" [syn: time of year] 3: a recurrent time marked by major holidays; "it was the Christmas season"

v 1: lend flavor to; "Season the chicken breast after roasting it" [syn: flavor] 2: make fit; "This trip will season even the hardiest traveler" [syn: harden] 3: make more temperate, acceptable, or suitable by adding something else; moderate; "she tempered her criticism" [syn: temper]

seisin

n: possession of an estate of freehold; may be either in deed or in law; the former when there is actual possession, the latter when there is a right to such possession by construction of law; in parts of the U.S. seisin means merely ownership [syn: seizin]

sects, sex

sects /sɛkts/

n : (plu of sect) 1: subdivisions of a larger religious group [syn: religious sects, religious orders] 2: dissenting clique [syn: factions]

sex /sɛks/

n 1: activities associated with sexual intercourse; "they had sex in the back seat" [syn: sexual activity, sexual practice, sex activity] 2: either of the two categories (male or female) into which most organisms are divided; "the war between the sexes" 3: all of the feelings resulting from the urge to gratify sexual impulses; "he wanted a better sex life"; "the film contained no sex or violence" [syn: sexual urge] 4: the properties that distinguish organisms on the basis of their reproductive roles; "she didn't want to know the sex of the fetus" [syn: gender, sexuality]

v 1: stimulate sexually; "This movie usually arouses the male audience" [syn: arouse, excite, turn on, wind up] 2: tell the sex (of young chickens)

see (see C)
seed (see cede)
seeder (see cedar)
seel (see ceil)
seer (see cere)
sees (see C's)

seidel, sidle /'saɪdᵊl/

seidel

n : a glass for beer

sidle

v 1: move unobtrusively or furtively; "The young man began to sidle near the pretty girl sitting on the log" 2: move sideways

HOMOPHONES

[syn: sashay]
seize (see C's)
sell (see cel)
seller (cellar)
senate, sennet, sennit /'sɛnɪt/

senate

n 1: assembly possessing high legislative powers 2: the upper house of the United States Congress [syn: United States Senate, US Senate]

sennet

n : a signal call on a trumpet or cornet for entrance or exit on the stage

sennit

n : flat braided cordage that is used on ships

sense (see cense)
senses (see census)
sensor (see censer)
sent (see scent)
seraph, serif /'sɛɹɪf/

seraph

n : an angel of the first order; usually portrayed as the winged head of a child

serif

n : a short line at the end of the main strokes of a character

sere (see cere)
serene, serine /sɛ'ɹin/

serene

adj 1: characterized by absence of emotional agitation; "calm acceptance of the inevitable"; "remained serene in the midst of turbulence"; "a serene expression on her face"; "she became more tranquil"; "tranquil life in the country" [syn: calm, tranquil] 2: completely clear and fine; "serene skies and a bright blue sea"

serine

n : a sweetish crystalline amino acid involved in the synthesis by the body of cysteine

serial (see cereal)
serf, surf /sɜɹf/

serf

n : (medieval Europe) a person who is bound to the land and owned by the feudal lord [syn: helot, villein]

surf

n : waves breaking on the shore [syn: breaker, breakers]
v 1: ride the waves of the sea with a surfboard; "Californians love to surf" 2: look around casually and randomly, without seeking anything in particular; "browse a computer directory"; "surf the internet or the World Wide Web" [syn: browse] 3: switch channels, on television [syn: channel-surf]

serge, surge /sɜɹdʒ/

serge

n : a twilled woolen fabric

surge

n 1: a sudden forceful flow [syn: rush, spate, upsurge] 2: a sudden or abrupt strong increase: "stimulated a surge of speculation"; "an upsurge of emotion"; "an upsurge in violent crime" [syn: upsurge] 3: a large sea wave [syn: billow]
v 1: rise and move, as in waves or billows; "The army surged forward" [syn: billow, heave] 2: rise rapidly, as of a current or voltage [syn: soar, soar up, soar upwards, zoom] 3: rise in waves [syn: tide] [ant: ebb] 4: rise or heave upward under the influence of a natural force, as on a wave [syn: scend]

serous (see cerous)
serrate (see cerate)
session (see cession)
set, sett /sɛt/

set

adj 1: (usually followed by 'to' or 'for') on the point of or strongly disposed; "in no fit state to continue"; "fit to drop"; "laughing fit to burst"; "she was fit to scream"; "primed for a fight"; "we are set to go at any time" [syn: fit, primed] 2: fixed and unmoving; "with eyes set in a fixed glassy stare"; "his bearded face already has a set hollow look"- Connor Cruise O'Brien; "a face rigid with pain" [syn: fixed, rigid] 3: situated in a particular spot or position; "valuable centrally located urban land"; "strategically placed artillery"; "a house set on a hilltop"; "nicely situated on a quiet riverbank" [syn: located, placed, situated] 4: set down according to a plan: "a carefully laid table with places set for four people"; "stones laid in a pattern" [syn: laid] 5: being below the horizon; "the moon is set" 6: determined or decided upon as by an authority; "date and place are already determined"; "the dictated terms of surrender"; "the time set for the launching" [syn: determined, dictated] 7: converted to solid form (as concrete) [syn: hardened]

n 1: a group of things of the same kind that belong together and are so used: "a set of books"; "a set of golf clubs"; "a set of teeth" 2: (mathematics) an abstract collection of numbers or symbols; "the set of prime numbers is infinite" 3: several exercises intended to be done in series; "he did four sets of the incline bench press" [syn: exercise set] 4: representation consisting of the scenery and other properties used to identify the location of a dramatic production; "the sets were meticulously authentic" [syn: stage set] 5: an unofficial association of people or groups; "the smart set goes there"; "they were an angry lot" [syn: circle, band, lot] 6: a relatively permanent inclination to react in a particular way; "the set of his mind was obvious" [syn: bent] 7: the act of putting something in position; "he gave a final set to his hat" 8: a unit of play in tennis or squash; "they played two sets of tennis after dinner" 9: the process of becoming hard or solid by cooling or drying or crystallization; "the hardening of concrete"; "he tested the set of the glue" [syn: hardening, solidifying, solidification] 10: the descent of a heavenly body below the horizon; "before the set of sun" 11: (psychology) a temporary readiness to respond in a particular way; "the subjects' set led them to solve problems the familiar way and to overlook the simpler solution"; "his instructions deliberately gave them the wrong set" [syn: readiness] 11: any electronic equipment that receives or transmits radio or TV signals; "the early sets ran on storage batteries"

v 1: put into a certain place or abstract location; "Put your things here"; "Set the tray down"; "Set the dogs on the scent of the missing children"; "Place emphasis on a certain point" [syn: put, place, pose, position, lay] 2: fix conclusively or authoritatively; "set the rules" [syn: determine] 3: decide upon, as of variables in math [syn: specify, determine, fix] 4: establish as the highest level or best performance; "set a record" [syn: mark] 5: put into a certain state; cause to be in a certain state; "set the house afire" 6: fix in a border, as of precious stones 7: make ready or suitable in advance for a particular purpose or for some use, event, etc; "Get the children ready for school!"; "prepare for war" [syn: prepare, set up, ready, gear up] 8: set to a certain position; "set clocks or instruments" 9: locate; "The film is set in Africa" [syn: localize, place] 10: disappear beyond the horizon; of celestial bodies such as the sun and the moon [syn: go down, go under] [ant: rise] 11: adapt for performance in a different way; "set this poem to music" [syn: arrange] 12: put or set (seeds or seedlings) into the ground; "Let's plant flowers in the garden" [syn: plant] 13: apply or start; "set fire to a building" 14: become gelatinous; "the liquid jelled after we added the enzyme" [syn: jell, congeal] 15: put into a position that will restore a normal state; "set a broken bone" 16: insert (a nail or screw below the surface, as into a countersink) [syn: countersink] 17: give a fine, sharp edge to a knife or razor [syn: sic] 19: urge a dog to attack someone [syn: sic] 19: estimate: "We put the time of arrival at 8 P.M." [syn: place, put] 20: equip with sails, masts, etc.; of ships [syn: rig, set up] 21: get ready for a particular purpose or event; "set up an experiment"; "set the table"; "lay out the tools for the surgery" [syn: set up, lay out] 22: alter slightly, esp. to achieve accuracy; regulate; "Adjust the clock, please" [syn: adjust] 23: bear fruit, of plants [syn: fructify] 24: arrange attractively; "dress my hair for the wedding" [syn: dress, arrange, do, coif, coiffure]

sett

n 1: rectangular paving stone with curved top; once used to make roads [syn: cobble, cobblestone]

setaceous (see cetaceous)

settler, settlor /'sɛtlᵊ/
settler

n 1: a person who settles in a new colony or moves into new country [syn: colonist] 2: a negotiator who settles disputes 3: a clerk in a betting shop who calculates the winnings

settlor

n : person who makes a settlement or creates a trust of property

sew, so, sow /soʊ/
sew

v 1: fasten by sewing; do needlework [syn: run up, sew together, stitch] 2: create (clothes) with cloth; "Can the seamstress sew me a suit by next week?" [syn: tailor, tailor-make]

so

adj 1: conforming to truth; "I wouldn't have told you this if it weren't so"; "a truthful statement" [syn: truthful] 2: marked by system; in good order; "everything is in order"; "his books are always just so"; "things must be exactly so" [syn: in order]

n : the syllable naming the fifth (dominant) note of any musical scale in solmization [syn: sol]

adv 1: (intensifier) to a very great extent or degree; "the idea is so obvious"; "never been so happy"; "I love you so"; "my head aches so!" 2: in order that; "he stooped down so he could pick up his hat" 3: in such a condition or manner, especially as expressed or implied; "They're happy and I hope they will remain so"; "so live your life that old age will bring no regrets" 4: to a certain unspecified extent or degree; "I can only go so far with this student"; "can do only so much in a day" 5: in they same way; also; "I was offended and so was he"; "worked hard and so did she" 6: in the way indicated; "hold the brush so"; "set up the pieces thus"; ('thusly' is a nonstandard variant) [syn: thus, thusly] 7: (usually followed by 'that') to an extent or degree as expressed; "he was so tired he could hardly stand"; "so dirty that it smells" 8: subsequently or soon afterward (often used as sentence connectors); "then he left"; "go left first, then right"; "first came lightning, then thunder"; "we watched the late movie and then went to bed"; "and so home and to bed" [syn: then, and so, and then] 9: in truth (often tends to intensify); "they said the car would break down and indeed it did"; "it is very cold indeed"; "was indeed grateful"; "indeed, the rain may still come"; "he did so do it!" [syn: indeed]

sow

v 1: place (seeds) in the ground for future growth; "She sowed sunflower seeds" [syn: sough, seed] 2: introduce into an environment; "sow suspicion or beliefs" [syn: sough] 3: place seeds in (the ground); "sow the ground with sunflower seeds" [syn: inseminate, sow in]

sewer, sower /'souwəɹ/
sewer

n: someone who sews; "a sewer of fine gowns"

sower

n : someone who sows

sewer, suer /'suwəɹ/
sewer

n : a waste pipe that carries away sewage or surface water [syn: sewerage, cloaca]

suer

n 1: a man who courts a woman; "a suer for the hand of the princess" [syn: suitor, wooer] 2: someone who petitions a court for redress of a grievance or recovery of a right [syn: petitioner]

sewn, sown /soun/
sewn

adj : fastened with stitches [syn: sewed, stitched]

sown

adj : sprinkled with seed; "a seeded lawn" [syn: seeded]

shake, sheik /ʃɛik/
shake

n 1: building material used as siding or roofing [syn: shingle] 2: frothy drink of milk and flavoring and sometimes fruit or ice cream [syn: milkshake, milk shake] 3: a note that alternates rapidly with another note a semitone above it [syn: trill] 4: grasping and shaking a person's hand (as to acknowledge an introduction or to agree on a contract) [syn: handshake, handshaking, handclasp] 5: reflex shaking caused by cold or fear or excitement [syn: tremble, shiver] 6: causing to move repeatedly from side to side [syn: wag, waggle]

v 1: move or cause to move quickly back and forth; "The chemist shook the flask vigorously"; "My hands were shaking" [syn: agitate] 2: move with or as if with a tremor; "his hands shook"; "My legs trembled when I went onstage" [syn: tremble, didder] 3: (British) shake or (American) shake down

vibrate rapidly and intensively; "The old engine was juddering" [syn: judder] 4: move back and forth in an unstable manner; "the ship was rocking"; "the tall building swayed"; "the tree shook in the wind" [syn: rock, sway] 5: undermine or cause to waver; "my faith has been shaken"; "The bad news shook her hopes" 6: stir the feelings or emotions of; "These stories shook the community" [syn: stimulate, shake up, excite, stir] 7: get rid of; "I couldn't shake the car that was following me" [syn: shake off, throw off, escape from] 8: bring to a specified condition by or as if by shaking; "He was shaken from his dreams"; "shake the salt out of the salt shaker" 9: shake (a body part) to communicate a greeting, feeling, or cognitive state; "shake one's head"; "She shook her finger at the naughty students"; "The old enemies shook hands"; "Don't shake your fist at me!"

sheik (also /ʃik/)

n 1: the leader of an Arab village or family [syn: sheikh, Arab chief] 2: a man who is much concerned with his dress and appearance [syn: dandy, dude, fop, gallant, beau, swell, fashion plate, clotheshorse]

shays (see chaise)

shear, sheer /ʃiɹ/
shear

n 1: (physics) a deformation of an object in which parallel planes remain parallel but are shifted in a direction parallel to themselves; "the shear changed the quadrilateral into a parallelogram" 2: edge tool that cuts sheet metal by passing a blade through it

v 1: cut with shears, as of hedges 2: shear the wool from; "shear sheep" [syn: fleece] 3: cut or cut through with shears

sheer

adj 1: complete and without restriction or qualification; sometimes used informally as intensifiers; "absolute freedom"; "an absolute dimwit"; "a downright lie"; "out-and-out mayhem"; "an out-and-out lie"; "a rank outsider"; "many right-down vices"; "got the job through sheer persistence"; "sheer stupidity" [syn: absolute, downright, out-and-out, rank, right-down] 2: not mixed with extraneous elements; "plain water"; "sheer wine"; "not an unmixed blessing" [syn: plain, unmingled, unmixed] 3: very steep; having a prominent and almost vertical front; "a bluff headland"; "where the bold chalk cliffs of England rise"; "a sheer descent of rock" [syn: bluff, bold] 4: so thin as to transmit light; "a hat with a diaphanous veil"; "filmy wings of a moth"; "gauzy clouds of dandelion down"; "gossamer cobwebs"; "sheer silk stockings"; "transparent chiffon"; "vaporous silks" [syn: diaphanous, filmy, gauzy, gossamer, see-through, transparent, vaporous, cobwebby]

adv 1: straight up or down without a break [syn: perpendicularly] 2: directly; "he fell sheer into the water"

v 1: turn sharply; change direction abruptly; "The car cut to the left at the intersection"; "The motorbike veered to the right" [syn: swerve, curve, trend, veer, slue, slew, cut] 2: cause to sheer: "She sheered her car around the obstacle"

sheik (see chic)

shew, shoe, shoo /ʃu/

shew

v : establish the validity of something; "This behavior shows his true nature" [syn: prove, demonstrate, establish, show] [ant: disprove]

shoe

n 1: footwear shaped to fit the foot (below the ankle) with a flexible upper of leather or plastic and a sole and heel of heavier material 2: (card games) a case from which playing cards are dealt one at a time 3: nailed to underside of horse's hoof [syn: horseshoe, U-shaped plate] 4: restraint provided when the linings of the brake shoes are moved hydraulically against the brake drum to stop its rotation [syn: brake shoe]

v : furnish with shoes

shoo

v : drive away by crying "shoo!" [syn: shoo off, shoo away]

shier, shire /ˈʃaɪʲɹ/

shier

adj (comparative of shy): "She is shier than her best friend." [syn: shyer, more shy]

shire

n 1: (British) a former administrative district of England; equivalent to a county 2: British breed of large heavy draft horse [syn: shire horse]

shoed, shooed /ʃud/

shoed

adj : wearing footgear [syn: shod] [ant: unshod]

shooed

v : (past of shoo) : scared, driven, or sent away by crying or shouting shoo

shone, shown /ʃoʊn/

shone

v : (past of shine): "The sun shone all day."

shown

v : (past of show): "They were shown to their seats." [syn: showed]

shoot (see chute)

sic, sick /sɪk/

sic

adv : intentionally so written (used after a printed word or phrase)

v : urge a dog to attack someone [syn: set]

sick

adj 1: not in good physical or mental health; "ill from the monotony of his suffering" [syn: ill] [ant: well] 2: feeling nausea; feeling about to vomit [syn: nauseated, queasy, sickish] 3: affected with madness or insanity; "a man who had gone mad" [syn: brainsick, crazy, demented, distracted, disturbed, mad, unbalanced, unhinged] 4: having a strong distaste from surfeit; "grew more and more disgusted"; "fed up with their complaints"; "sick of it all"; "sick to death of flattery"; "gossip that makes one sick"; "tired of the noise and smoke" [syn: disgusted, fed up, sick of, tired of]

n : people who are sick; "they devote their lives to caring for the sick"

sics, six /sɪks/

sics

v : (3rd pers sing of sic) (see sic)

six

adj : denoting a quantity consisting of six items or units [syn: 6, vi, half dozen, half a dozen]

n : the cardinal number that is the sum of five and one [syn: 6, VI, sixer, sise, Captain Hicks, half a dozen, sextet, sestet, sextuplet, hexad]

side, sighed /saɪd/

side

adj 1: located on a side; "side fences"; "the side porch" [ant: top, bottom] 2: minor or subordinate; 'by' is often used in combination; "a side interest"; "a by (or bye) effect"; "only a by comment"; "by-election"; "bye-election"; "a by-product"; "by-play" [syn: by, bye] 3: added as a consequence or supplement; "a side benefit"

n 1: a place within a region identified relative to a center or reference location; "they always sat on the right side of the church"; "he never left my side" 2: one of two or more contesting groups (in games or war or politics); "the Confederate side was prepared to attack" 3: either the left or right half of a body (human or animal); "he had a pain in his side" 4: an extended outer surface of an object; "he turned the box over to examine the bottom side"; "they painted all four sides of the house" 5: a surface forming part of the outside of an object; "he examined all sides of the crystal"; "dew dripped from the face of the leaf" [syn: face] 6: a line segment forming part of the perimeter of a plane figure; "the hypotenuse of a right triangle is always the longest side" 7: an aspect of something (as contrasted with some other implied aspect); "he was on the heavy side"; "he is on the purchasing side of the business";

"it brought out his better side" 8: a family line of descent; "he gets his brains from his father's side" 9: a lengthwise dressed half of an animal's carcass used for food [syn: side of meat] 10: an opinion that is held in opposition to another in an argument or dispute; "there are two sides to every question" [syn: position] 11: an elevated geological formation; "he climbed the steep slope"; "the house was built on the side of the mountain" [syn: slope, incline] 12: (sports) the spin given to a ball by striking it on one side or releasing it with a sharp twist [syn: English]

v 1: take sides with; align oneself with; show strong sympathy for; "We all rooted for the home team"; "I'm pulling for the underdog"; "Are you siding with the defender of the title?" [syn: pull, root] 2: take the side of; be on the side of; "Whose side are you on?" "Why are you taking sides with the accused?" [syn: go with] [ant: straddle]

sighed
v : (past of sigh) : heaved or uttered a sigh; breathed deeply and heavily; "She sighed sadly."

sigh (see psi)
sigher, sire /ˈsaɪjᵊɹ/
sigher
n : person who sighs

sire
n 1: a title of address formerly used for a man of rank and authority 2: the founder of a family; "keep the faith of our forefathers" [syn: forefather, father] 3: male parent of an animal especially a domestic animal such as a horse
v : make children; "Abraham begot Isaac"; "Men often sire children but don't recognize them" [syn: beget, get, engender, father, generate, bring forth]

sighs (see psis)
sight (see cite)
sign, sine /saɪn/
sign
adj : used of the language of the deaf [syn: gestural, signed, sign-language]
n 1: a perceptible indication of something not immediately apparent (as a visible clue that something has happened); "he showed signs of strain"; "they welcomed the signs of spring" [syn: mark] 2: a public display of a (usually written) message; "he posted signs in all the shop windows" 3: any communication that encodes a message; "signals from the boat suddenly stopped" [syn: signal, signaling] 4: structure displaying a board on which advertisements can be posted; "the highway was lined with signboards" [syn: signboard] 5: one of 12 equal areas into which the zodiac is divided [syn: sign of the zodiac, mansion,

house, planetary house] 6: (medical) any objective evidence of the presence of a disorder or disease; "there were no signs of asphyxiation" 7: having an indicated pole (as the distinction between positive and negative electric charges); "he got the polarity of the battery reversed"; "charges of opposite sign" [syn: polarity] 8: an event that is experienced as indicating important things to come; "he hoped it was an augury"; "it was a sign from God" [syn: augury] 9: a gesture that is part of a sign language 10: (linguistics) a fundamental linguistic unit linking a signifier to that which is signified; "The bond between the signifier and the signified is arbitrary"-- de Saussure 11: a character indicating a relation between quantities; "don't forget the minus sign"

v 1: mark with one's signature; write one's name (on); "She signed the letter and sent it off"; "Please sign here" [syn: subscribe] 2: write one's name in token of assent, responsibility, or obligation; "All parties signed the peace treaty"; "Have you signed your contract yet?" [syn: ratify] 3: be engaged by a written agreement; "He signed to play the casino on Dec. 18"; "The soprano signed to sing the new opera" 4: engage by written agreement; "They signed two new pitchers for the next season" [syn: fee, contract, sign on, sign up] 5: communicate silently and non-verbally by signals or signs; "He signed his disapproval with a dismissive hand gesture"; "The diner signaled the waiters to bring the menu" [syn: signal, signalize] 6: place signs, as along a road; "sign an intersection"; "This road has been signed" 7: communicate in sign language; "I don't know how to sign, so I could not communicate with my deaf cousin" 8: make the sign of the cross over someone in order to call on God for protection; consecrate [syn: bless]

sine
n : ratio of the opposite side to the hypotenuse [syn: sin]
signet (see cygnet)
silicon, silicone
silicon /ˈsɪlɪkən/
n : a tetravalent nonmetallic element; next to oxygen it is the most abundant element in the earth's crust; occurs in clay and feldspar and granite and quartz and sand; used as a semiconductor in transistors [syn: Si, atomic number 14]
silicone /ˈsɪlɪkoʊn/
n : any of a large class of siloxanes that are unusually stable over a wide range of temperatures; used in lubricants, adhesives, coatings, synthetic rubber, electrical insulation and breast implants

HOMOPHONES

[syn: silicone polymer]

sink (see cinque)

site (see cite)

size (see psis)

slay, sleigh /sleɪ/

slay

v 1: kill intentionally and with premeditation; "The mafia boss ordered his enemies murdered" [syn: murder, hit, dispatch, bump off, polish off, remove] 2: cause extreme laughter; "His jokes slay me!"

sleigh

n : a vehicle mounted on runners and pulled by horses or dogs; for transportation over snow; "Eight reindeer pull Santa's sleigh." [syn: sled, sledge]

v : ride (on) a sled [syn: sled]

sleave, sleeve /sliv/

sleave

n (archaic) fine thread or skein of thread

sleeve

n 1: the part of a garment that is attached at armhole and provides a cloth covering for the arm [syn: arm] 2: small case into which an object fits

sleight, slight /slaɪt/

sleight

n : adroitness in using the hands [syn: dexterity, manual dexterity]

slight

adj 1: almost no or (with 'a') at least some; very little; "there's slight chance that it will work"; "there's a slight chance it will work" 2: having little substance or significance; "a flimsy excuse"; "slight evidence"; "a tenuous argument"; "a thin plot" [syn: flimsy, tenuous, thin] 3: being of delicate or slender build; "she was slender as a willow shoot is slender"-Frank Norris; "a slim girl with straight blonde hair"; "watched her slight figure cross the street" [syn: slender, slim]

n : a deliberate discourteous act (usually as an expression of anger or disapproval) [syn: rebuff]

v : pay no attention to, disrespect; "She cold-shouldered her ex-fiancé" [syn: cold-shoulder]

slew, slough, slue /slu/

slew

n : (often followed by `of') a large number or amount or extent: "a batch of letters"; "a deal of trouble"; "a lot of money"; "he made a mint on the stock market"; "it must have cost plenty" [syn: batch, deal, flock, good deal, great deal, hatful, heap, lot, mass, mess, mint, peck, pile, plenty, pot, quite a little, raft, sight, spate, stack, tidy sum, wad, whole lot, whole slew]

v 1: turn sharply; change direction abruptly; "The car cut to the left at the intersection"; "The motorbike veered to the right" [syn: swerve, sheer, curve, trend, veer, slue, cut] 2: move obliquely or sideways, usually in an uncontrolled manner; "the wheels skidded against the sidewalk" [syn: skid, slip, slue, slide] 3: (past of slay) (see slay) [syn: slayed]

slough

n : a stagnant swamp (especially as part of a bayou); a marshy pond

slue

v : (var slew)(see slew)

sloe, slough, slow /sloʊ/

sloe

n 1: wild plum of northeastern United States having dark purple fruits with yellow flesh [syn: Allegheny plum, Alleghany plum, Prunus alleghaniensis] 2: a thorny Eurasian bush with plum-like fruits [syn: blackthorn, Prunus spinosa] 3: small sour dark purple fruit of especially the Allegheny plum bush

slough

n : a hole filled with mud

slow

adj 1: not moving quickly; taking a comparatively long time; "a slow walker"; "the slow lane of traffic"; "her steps were slow"; "he was slow in reacting to the news"; "slow but steady growth" [ant: fast] 2: (music) at a slow tempo; "the band played a slow waltz" [ant: fast] 3: slow to learn or understand; lacking intellectual acuity; "so dense he never understands anything I say to him"; "never met anyone quite so dim"; "although dull at classical learning, at mathematics he was uncommonly quick"; "dumb officials make some really dumb decisions"; "he was either normally stupid or being deliberately obtuse"; "worked with the slow students" [syn: dense, dim, dull, dumb, obtuse] 4: (used of timepieces) indicating a time earlier than the correct time; "the clock is slow" [ant: fast] 5: so lacking in interest as to cause mental weariness; "a boring evening with uninteresting people"; "the deadening effect of some routine tasks"; "a dull play"; "his competent but dull performance"; "a ho-hum speaker who couldn't capture their attention"; "what an irksome task the writing of long letters is"- Edmund Burke; "tedious days on the train"; "the tiresome chirping of a cricket"; "other people's dreams are dreadfully wearisome" [syn: boring, deadening, dull, ho-hum, irksome, tedious, tiresome, wearisome] 6: (of business) not active or brisk; "business is dull (or slow)"; "a sluggish market" [syn: dull, sluggish]

adv 1: without speed; "he spoke slowly"; "go easy here--the road is slippery"; "glaciers move tardily"; (`slow' is sometimes used informally for `slowly'

HOMOPHONES

as in "please go slow; I want to see the sights") [syn: slowly, easy, tardily] [ant: quickly]   2: of timepieces; "the clock is almost an hour slow"; "my watch is running behind" [syn: behind]

v 1: lose velocity; move more slowly; "The car decelerated" [syn: decelerate, slow down, slow up, retard] [ant: accelerate]   2: become slow or slower; "Production slowed" [syn: slow down, slow up, slack, slacken]   3: cause to proceed more slowly; "The illness slowed him down" [syn: slow down, slow up]

soar, sore /sɔɹ/

soar

n : the act of rising upward into the air [syn: zoom]

v 1: rise rapidly, as of a current or voltage [syn: soar up, soar upwards, surge, zoom]   2: fly by means of a hang glider [syn: hang glide]   3: fly upwards or high in the sky   4: go or move upward; "The stock market soared after the cease-fire was announced"   5: fly a plane without an engine [syn: sailplane]

sore

adj 1: hurting; "the tender spot on his jaw" [syn: sensitive, tender]   2: causing misery or pain or distress; "it was a sore trial to him"; "the painful process of growing up" [syn: afflictive, painful]   3: (informal) roused to anger; "stayed huffy a good while"-Mark Twain; "she gets mad when you wake her up so early"; "mad at his friend"; "sore over a remark" [syn: huffy, mad]   4: inflamed and painful; "his throat was raw"; "had a sore throat" [syn: raw]

n : an open skin infection

soared, sword /sɔɹd/

soared

v : (past of soar): "Her spirits soared after she passed the exam."

sword

n : a cutting or thrusting weapon with a long blade [syn: blade, brand, steel]

sol, sole, soul /soʊl/

sol

n 1: a colloid that has a continuous liquid phase in which a solid is suspended in a liquid [syn: colloidal solution, colloidal suspension]   2: the syllable naming the fifth (dominant) note of any musical scale in solmization [syn: soh, so]

sole

adj 1: being the only one; single and isolated from others; "the lone doctor in the entire county"; "a lonesome pine"; "an only child"; "the sole heir"; "the sole example"; "a solitary instance of cowardice"; "a solitary speck in the sky" [syn: lone, lonesome, only, solitary]   2: not divided or shared with others; "they have exclusive use of the machine"; "sole rights

of publication" [syn: exclusive]

n 1: the underside of footwear or a golf club   2: lean flesh of any of several flatfish [syn: fillet of sole]   3: the underside of the foot   4: right-eyed flatfish; many are valued as food; most common in warm seas especially European

v : put a new sole on; "sole the shoes" [syn: resole]

soul

n 1: the immaterial part of a person; the actuating cause of an individual life [syn: psyche]   2: a human being; "there was too much for one person to do" [syn: person, individual, someone, somebody, mortal, human]   3: deep feeling or emotion [syn: soulfulness]   4: the human embodiment of something; "the soul of honor"   5: a secular form of gospel that was a major Black musical genre in the 1960s and 1970s; "soul was politically significant during the Civil Rights movement

sold, soled, souled /soʊld/

sold

adj : disposed of to a purchaser; "this merchandise is sold" [ant: unsold]

v : (past of sell) "They sold 25 computers last week."

soled

adj : having a sole or soles especially as specified; used in combination; "half-soled"; "rubber-soled" [ant: soleless]

v : (past of sole) (see sole); "These shoes were newly soled last month."

souled

adj : having a soul; possessing soul and feeling

some, sum /sʌm/

some

adj 1: quantifier; used with either mass nouns or plural count nouns to indicate an unspecified number or quantity; "have some milk"; "some roses were still blooming"; "having some friends over"; "some apples"; "some paper" [ant: no, all]   2: unknown or unspecified; "some lunatic drove into my car"; "some man telephoned while you were out"; "some day my prince will come"; "some enchanted evening"   3: relatively much but unspecified in amount or extent; "we talked for some time"; "he was still some distance away"   4: relatively many but unspecified in number; "they were here for some weeks"; "we did not meet again for some years"   5: (informal; slang) remarkable; "that was some party"; "she is some skier"

adv : (of quantities) imprecise but fairly close to correct; "lasted approximately an hour"; "in just about a minute"; "he's about 30 years old"; "I've had about all I can stand"; "we meet about once a month"; "some forty people came"; "weighs around a hundred pounds"; "roughly $3,000"; "holds 3 gallons, more or less"; "20 or so people were at the party" [syn: approximately, about, close to, just about, roughly, more or less, around, or so]

sum

n 1: a quantity of money; "he borrowed a large sum"; "the amount he had in cash was insufficient" [syn: sum of money, amount, amount of money] 2: a quantity obtained by addition [syn: amount, total] 3: the final aggregate; "the sum of all our troubles did not equal the misery they suffered" [syn: sum total] 4: the choicest or most essential or most vital part of some idea or experience: "the gist of the prosecutor's argument"; "the heart and soul of the Republican Party"; "the nub of the story" [syn: kernel, substance, core, center, essence, gist, heart, heart and soul, inwardness, marrow, meat, nub, pith, nitty-gritty] 5: the whole amount [syn: total, totality, aggregate] 6: a set containing all and only the members of two or more given sets; "let C be the union of the sets A and B" [syn: union, join]

v : determine the sum of; "Add all the people in this town to those of the neighboring town" [syn: total, tot, tot up, sum up, summate, tote up, add, add together, tally, add up]

son, sun /sʌn/

son

n : a male human offspring; "their son became a famous judge"; "his boy is taller than he is" [syn: boy] [ant: daughter]

sun

n 1: a typical star that is the source of light and heat for the planets in the solar system; "the sun contains 99.85% of the mass in the solar system" 2: the rays of the sun; "the shingles were weathered by the sun and wind" [syn: sunlight, sunshine] 3: a person considered as a source of warmth or energy or glory, etc 4: any star around which a planetary system evolves

v 1: expose one's body to the sun [syn: sunbathe] 2: expose to as if to sun rays

sonny, sunny /'sʌni/

sonny

n : a male child (a familiar term of address to a boy) [syn: cub, lad, laddie, sonny boy]

sunny

adj 1: abounding with sunlight; "a bright sunny day"; "one shining morning"- John Muir; "when it is warm and shiny" [syn: bright, shining, shiny, sunshiny] 2: bright and pleasant; promoting a feeling of cheer; "a cheery hello"; "a gay sunny room"; "a sunny smile" [syn: cheery, gay]

sordid, sorted

sordid /'sɔːdɪd/

adj 1: morally degraded; "a seedy district";

"the seamy side of life"; "sleazy characters hanging around casinos"; "the sordid details of his orgies stank under his very nostrils"- James Joyce; "the squalid atmosphere of intrigue and betrayal" [syn: seamy, seedy, sleazy, squalid] 2: unethical or dishonest; "dirty police officers"; "a sordid political campaign" [syn: dirty] 3: foul and run-down and repulsive; "a flyblown bar on the edge of town"; "a squalid overcrowded apartment in the poorest part of town"; "squalid living conditions"; "sordid shantytowns" [syn: flyblown, squalid] 4: meanly avaricious and mercenary; "sordid avarice"; "sordid material interests"

sorted /'sɔːtɪd/

adj 1: arranged according to size 2: arranged into groups [syn: grouped]

v : (past of sort) "They sorted the apples according to size."

sough, sow /saʊ/

sough

n : a moaning or groaning sound

v : indicate pain, discomfort, or displeasure; "The students groaned when the professor got out the exam booklets"; "The ancient door soughed when opened" [syn: groan, moan]

sow

n : an adult female hog

spade, spayed /speɪd/

spade

n 1: a playing card in the major suit of spades 2: a sturdy hand shovel that can be pushed into the earth with the foot 3: (ethnic slur) offensive name for a black person

v : dig (up) with a spade; "I spade compost into the flower beds"

spayed

adj : (of a female animal) having the ovaries removed

v : (past of spay) removed the ovaries; "The vet spayed my kitten last week."

spec, speck /spɛk/

spec

n : a detailed description of design criteria for a piece of work [syn: specification]

speck

n 1: a very small spot; "the plane was just a speck in the sky" [syn: pinpoint] 2: (non-technical usage) a tiny piece of anything [syn: atom, molecule, particle, mote] 3: a small but appreciable amount; "this dish could use a touch of garlic" [syn: touch, hint, mite, pinch, jot, soupcon]

v : produce specks in or on

spier, spire /spaɪɹ/

spier

n: spy

spire

n: a tall tower that forms the superstructure

HOMOPHONES

of a building (usually a church or temple) and that tapers to a point at the top) [syn: steeple]

spinner, spinor /'spɪnᵊɹ/

spinner

n 1: someone who spins (who twists fibers into threads) [syn: spinster, thread maker] 2: board game equipment that consists of a dial and an arrow that is spun to determine the next move in the game 3: fisherman's lure; revolves when drawn through the water

spinor

n : vector whose components are complex numbers in a two-dimensional or four-dimensional space and which is used especially in the mathematics of the theory of relativity

stabile, stable /'steɪbᵊl/

stabile

adj 1: (chemistry, physics, biology) resistant to change 2: not able or intended to be moved; "the immovable hills" [syn: immovable, immoveable, unmovable]
n : a sculpture having fixed units (usually constructed of sheet metal) and attached to a fixed support [ant: mobile]

stable

adj 1: resistant to change of position or condition; "a stable ladder"; "a stable peace"; "a stable relationship"; "stable prices" [ant: unstable] 2: firm and dependable; subject to little fluctuation; "the economy is stable" 3: not taking part readily in chemical change 4: maintaining equilibrium 5: showing little if any change; "a static population" [syn: static, unchanging]
n : a farm building for housing horses or other livestock [syn: stalls, horse barn]
v : shelter in a stable; "stable horses"

staff, staph /stæf/ or /stɛəf/

staff

n 1: personnel who assist their superior in carrying out an assigned task; "the hospital has an excellent nursing staff"; "the general relied on his staff to make routine decisions" 2: the body of teachers and administrators at a school; "the dean addressed the letter to the entire staff of the university" [syn: faculty] 3: a strong rod or stick with a specialized utilitarian purpose; "he walked with the help of a wooden staff" 4: a rod carried as a symbol 5: (music) the system of five horizontal lines on which the musical notes are written [syn: stave]
v : provide with staff; "We need to staff the school with more math teachers."

staph

n : spherical gram-positive parasitic bacteria that tend to form irregular colonies; some cause boils or septicemia

or infections [syn: staphylococcus, staphylococci]

staid, stayed /steɪd/

staid

adj : characterized by dignity and propriety [syn: sedate]

stayed

v : (past of stay) 1: stayed the same; remained in a certain state; "The dress remained wet after repeated attempts to dry it"; "rested assured"; "stayed alone"; "He remained unmoved by her tears"; "The bad weather continued for another week" [syn: remained, rested, continued] [ant: changed] 2: stayed put (in a certain place); "We stayed in Detroit; we are not moving to Cincinnati" [syn: stuck, stuck around, stayed put] [ant: moved] 3: dwelled (archaic); "He stayed with me while he was in town" [syn: bided, abided] 4: continued in a place, position, or situation: "After graduation, she stayed on in Cambridge as a student adviser"; "despite student protests, he remained Dean for another year"; "She continued as deputy mayor for another year" [syn: stayed on, continued, remained] 5: remained behind; "I stayed at home and watched the children" [ant: departed] 6: stop or halt; "They stayed the bloodshed" [syn: detained, delayed] 7: stayed behind; "The smell stayed in the room"; "The hostility remained long after they made up" [syn: persisted, remained] 8: a trial of endurance; "ride out the storm" [syn: lasted out, rode out, outrode] 9: stop a judicial process; "The judge stayed the execution order" 10: fastened with stays 11: overcame or allay; "quelled my hunger" [syn: quelled, appeased]

stair, stare /stɛəɹ/

stair

n : support consisting of a place to rest the foot while ascending or descending a stairway; "he paused on the bottom step" [syn: step]

stare

n : a fixed look with eyes open wide
v 1: look at with fixed eyes; "The students stared at the teacher with amazement" [syn: gaze] 2: fixate one's eyes; look at with a fixed gaze, as of a sculpture or a painting; "The ancestor in the painting stared down at us menacingly"

stake, steak /steɪk/

stake

n 1: a right or legal share of something; a financial involvement with something; "they have interests all over the world"; "a stake in the company's future" [syn: interest] 2: a pole or stake set up to mark something (as the start or end of a race track) [syn: post] 3: instrument of execution consisting of a vertical post

I-187

HOMOPHONES

that a victim is tied to for burning 4: the money risked on a gamble [syn: stakes, bet, wager]

v 1: put at risk; "I will stake my good reputation for this" [syn: venture, hazard, adventure, jeopardize] 2: place a bet on; "Which horse are you backing?" "I'm betting on the new horse" [syn: bet on, back, gage, game, punt] 3: mark with a stake; "stake out the path" [syn: post] 4: tie or fasten to a stake; "stake your goat" 5: kill by piercing with a spear or sharp pole; "the enemies were impaled and left to die" [syn: impale]

steak

n : a slice of meat cut from the fleshy part of an animal or large fish

statice, status /'stætɪs/ or /'stædɪs/

statice

n : any of various plants of the genus Limonium of temperate salt marshes having spikes of whit or mauve flowers [syn: sea lavender, marsh rosemary]

status

n 1: the relative position or standing of things or especially persons in a society: "he had the status of a minor"; "the novel attained the status of a classic"; "atheists do not enjoy a favorable position in American life" [syn: position] 2: a condition or state at a particular time: "a condition (or state) of disrepair"; "the current status of the arms negotiations" [syn: condition]

stationary, stationery /'steɪʃɪnɛɹi/

stationary

adj 1: standing still; "the car remained stationary with the engine running" 2: not capable of being moved; "stationary machinery"

stationery

n : paper cut to an appropriate size for writing letters; usually with matching envelopes [syn: letter paper, notepaper]

steal, steel, stele /stil/

steal

n : an advantageous purchase; "she got a bargain at the auction"; "the stock was a real steal at that price" [syn: bargain, buy]

v 1: take without the owner's consent; "Someone stole my wallet on the train"; "This author stole entire paragraphs from my dissertation" 2: move stealthily; "The ship slipped away in the darkness" [syn: slip] 3: steal a base, in baseball 4: to go stealthily or furtively; "..stead of sneaking around spying on the neighbor's house" [syn: sneak, mouse, creep, pussyfoot]

steel

n 1: an alloy of iron with small amounts of carbon; widely used in construction; mechanical properties can be varied over

a wide range 2: a cutting or thrusting weapon with a long blade [syn: sword, blade, brand] 3: knife sharpener consisting of a ridged steel rod

v : get ready for something difficult or unpleasant; " need to steel myself for this competition." [syn: nerve]

stele

n 1: the usually cylindrical central vascular portion of the axis of a vascular plant 2: an ancient upright stone slab bearing markings [syn: stela]

step, steppe /stɛp/

step

n 1: any maneuver made as part of progress toward a goal; "the situation called for strong measures"; "the police took steps to reduce crime" [syn: measure] 2: the distance covered by a step; [syn: footstep, pace, stride] 3: the act of changing location by raising the foot and setting it down; "he walked with unsteady steps" 4: support consisting of a place to rest the foot while ascending or descending a stairway; "he paused on the bottom step" [syn: stair] 5: relative position in a graded series: "always a step behind"; "subtle gradations in color"; "keep in step with the fashions" [syn: gradation] 6: a short distance; "it's only a step to the drugstore" [syn: stone's throw] 7: the sound of a step of someone walking; "he heard footsteps on the porch" [syn: footfall, footstep] 8: a musical interval of two semitones [syn: tone, whole tone, whole step] 9: a mark of a foot or shoe on a surface; a clue that someone was present; "the police made casts of the footprints in the soft earth outside the window" [syn: footprint, footmark] 10: a sequence of foot movements that make up a particular dance; "he taught them the waltz step" [syn: dance step]

v 1: take a step 2: put down the foot, place the foot; "Please step to the stage to receive your diplomas."; "For fools rush in where angels fear to tread" [syn: tread]

steppe

n : extensive plain without trees (associated with eastern Russia and Siberia)

stile, style /staɪl/

stile

n : an upright that is a member in a door or window frame

style

n 1: a particular kind (as to appearance); "this style of shoe is in demand" 2: a manner of performance; "a manner of living"; "in the characteristic New York style"; "a way of life" [syn: manner, mode, way, fashion] 3: a way of expressing something (in language or art or music etc.) that is characteristic of a particular person or group of people or period; "all the reporters were expected to adopt the style of the newspaper" [syn: expressive style] 4: distinctive and stylish elegance; "he wooed her with the confident dash of a cavalry officer" [syn: dash, elan, flair, panache] 5: the popular taste at a given time; "leather is the latest vogue"; "he followed current trends"; "the 1920s had a style of their own" [syn: vogue, trend] 6: the narrow elongated part of the pistil between the ovary and the stigma 7: editorial directions to be followed in spelling and punctuation and capitalization and typographical display 8: a pointed tool for writing or drawing or engraving; "he drew the design on the stencil with a steel stylus" [syn: stylus] 9: a slender bristle-like or tubular process: "a cartilaginous style"

v 1: designate by an identifying term; "They styled their nation `The Confederate States'" 2: make stylish; in fashion or hairdressing 3: style and tailor in a certain fashion; "cut a dress"; "style a wedding dress" [syn: cut, tailor]

stolen, stolon /'stouləⁿn/
stolen
adj 1: taken dishonestly; "the purloined letter" [syn: purloined] 2: baseball technique; "a stolen base"

stolon
n : a horizontal branch from the base of plant that produces new plants from buds at its tips [syn: runner, offset]

stoop, stoup /stup/
stoop
n 1: an inclination of the top half of the body forward and downward 2: small porch or set of steps at the front entrance of a house

v 1: bend one's back forward from the waist on down; "he crouched down"; "She bowed before the Queen"; "The young man stooped to pick up the girl's purse" [syn: crouch, bend, bow] 2: debase oneself morally, act in an undignified, unworthy, or dishonorable way; "I won't stoop to reading other people's mail" [syn: condescend, lower oneself] 3: descend swiftly, as if on prey; "The eagle stooped on the mice in the field" 4: sag, bend, bend over or down; "the rocks stooped down over the hiking path" 5: carry oneself, often habitually, with head, shoulders, and upper back bent forward; "The old man was stooping but he could walk around without a cane"

stoup
n 1: an archaic drinking vessel 2: basin for holy water

straight, strait /stɹeɪt/
straight
adj 1: successive (without a break); "sick

for five straight days" [syn: consecutive] 2: having no deviations; "straight lines"; "straight roads across the desert"; "straight teeth"; "straight shoulders" [ant: crooked] 3: (of hair) having no waves or curls; "her naturally straight hair hung long and silky" [ant: curly] 4: erect in posture; "behind him sat old man Arthur; he was straight with something angry in his attitude"; "stood defiantly with unbowed back" [syn: unbent, unbowed, upright] 5: right; in keeping with the facts; "set the record straight"; "made sure the facts were straight in the report" 6: honest and morally upright; "I just want a straight answer to the question"; "straight dealing" [ant: crooked] 7: no longer coiled [syn: uncoiled] [ant: coiled] 8: without curves [ant: curved] 9: neatly arranged; not disorderly; "the room is straight now" 10: characterized by honesty and fairness; "a square deal"; "wanted to do the square thing" [syn: square] 11: (informal) not homosexual 12: accurately fitted; level; "the window frame isn't quite true" [syn: true] 13: without water; "took his whiskey neat" [syn: neat, full-strength] 14: reliable in matters of fact; "he was always straight with me" 15: following a correct or logical method; "straight reasoning" 16: (slang) rigidly conventional or old-fashioned [syn: square] 17: being heterosexual

n 1: a heterosexual person; someone having a sexual orientation to persons of the opposite sex [syn: heterosexual, heterosexual person, straight person] 2: a poker hand with 5 consecutive cards (regardless of suit) 3: a straight segment of a roadway or racecourse [syn: straightaway]

adv 1: without deviation; "the path leads directly to the lake"; "went direct to the office" [syn: directly, direct] 2: in a forthright manner; candidly or frankly; "he didn't answer directly"; "told me straight out"; "came out flat for less work and more pay" [syn: directly, flat] [ant: indirectly] 3: in a straight line; in a direct course; "the road runs straight"

strait
adj : (archaic) strict and severe; "strait is the gate"

n 1: a narrow channel of the sea joining two larger bodies of water 2: a bad or difficult situation or state of affairs [syn: pass, straits]

straighten, straiten /'stɹeɪtəⁿn/
straighten
v 1: straighten up or out; make straight [syn: unbend] [ant: bend] 2: make straight [syn: straighten out] 3: get up from a sitting or slouching position; "The students straightened when the teacher entered" 4:

HOMOPHONES

put (things or places) in order; "Straighten out your room!" [syn: tidy, tidy up, clean up, neaten, straighten out, square away] 5: straighten by unrolling; "roll out the big map" [syn: roll out] 6: make straight or straighter; "Straighten this post"; "straighten hair"

straiten

v : squeeze together

strider, stridor /'stɹaɪdəɹ/

strider

n : a person who walks rapidly with long steps; "he was such a strider that she couldn't keep up without running"

stridor

n : a whistling sound when breathing (usually heard on inspiration); indicates obstruction of the trachea or larynx

subtler, sutler /'sʌtləɹ/

subtler

adj (compar of subtle) 1: be more difficult to detect or grasp by the mind; "his whole attitude had undergone subtler changes"; "a subtle difference"; "that elusive thing the soul" [syn: more elusive] 2: more faint and more difficult to analyze; "subtler aromas" 3: able to make finer distinctions; "a subtler mind" 4: working or spreading in a hidden and usually more injurious way; "glaucoma is a more insidious disease than gingivitis "; "a subtle poison" [syn: more insidious, more pernicious]

sutler

n : a supplier of victuals or supplies to an army [syn: provisioner]

succor, sucker /'sʌkəɹ/

succor

n : assistance in time of difficulty; "the contributions provided some relief for the victims" [syn: relief, ministration]

v : help in a difficult situation

sucker

n 1: a person who is gullible and easy to take advantage of [syn: chump, fool, gull, mark, patsy, fall guy, schlemiel, soft touch, mug] 2: a shoot arising from a plant's roots 3: a drinker who sucks (as at a nipple or through a straw) 4: flesh of any of numerous North American food fishes with toothless jaws 5: hard candy on a stick [syn: lollipop, all-day sucker] 6: an organ specialized for sucking nourishment or for adhering to objects by suction 7: mostly North American freshwater fishes with a thick-lipped mouth for feeding by suction; related to carps

suede, swayed /sweɪd/

suede

n 1: leather with a napped surface 2: a fabric made to resemble suede leather [syn: suede cloth]

swayed

adj : being persuaded; "I am swayed by the facts."

v : (past of sway) 1: move back and forth in an unstable manner; "the ship was rocking"; "the tall building swayed"; "the tree shook in the wind" [syn: rocked, shook] 2: move or walk in a swinging or swaying manner; "He swung back" [syn: swung] 3: win approval or support for; "Carry all before one" [syn: carried, persuaded] 4: move sideways or in an unsteady way, as of a ship or a vehicle out of control [syn: careened, wobbled, shifted, tilted] 5: sway gently back and forth, as of flowers or tress in the wind [syn: nodded]

suite, sweet /swit/

suite

n 1: a musical composition of several movements only loosely connected 2: apartment consisting of a series of connected rooms used as a living unit (as in a hotel) [syn: rooms] 3: the group following and attending to some important person [syn: cortege, retinue, entourage] 4: a matching set of furniture (often pronounced su: for this meaning)

sweet

adj 1: having a pleasant taste (as of sugar) [ant: sour] 2: having a sweet nature befitting an angel or cherub; "an angelic smile"; "a cherubic face"; "looking so seraphic when he slept"; "a sweet disposition" [syn: angelic, angelical, cherubic, seraphic] 3: pleasing to the ear; "the dulcet tones of the cello" [syn: dulcet, honeyed, mellifluous, mellisonant] 4: one of the four basic taste sensations; very pleasant; like the taste of sugar or honey 5: pleasing to the senses; "the sweet song of the lark"; "the sweet face of a child" 6: pleasing to the mind or feeling; "sweet revenge" [syn: gratifying] 7: having a natural fragrance; "odoriferous spices"; "the odorous air of the orchard"; "the perfumed air of June"; "scented flowers" [syn: odoriferous, odorous, perfumed, scented, sweet-scented, sweet-smelling] 8: (used of wines) having a sweet taste [ant: dry] 9: not having undergone fermentation; "sweet cider" [syn: unfermented] 10: not soured or preserved; "sweet milk" [syn: fresh] 11: with sweetening added [syn: sugared, sweetened] 12: not having a salty taste; "sweet water" [syn: unsalted]

n 1: a sweet served as the last course of a meal [syn: dessert] 2: a food rich in sugar [syn: confection, confectionery] 3: the taste experience when sugar dissolves in the mouth [syn: sweetness, sugariness] 4: the property of containing sugar [syn: sweetness]

adv : in an affectionate or loving manner; "Susan Hayward plays the wife sharply

HOMOPHONES

and sweetly"; (`sweet` is a poetic or informal variant for `sweetly` as in "how sweet the moonlight sleeps upon this bank"- Shakespeare; "talking sweet to each other") [syn: sweetly]

summary, summery /'sʌmᵊɹi/
summary
adj 1: performed speedily and without formality; "a summary execution"; "summary justice" [syn: drumhead] 2: briefly giving the gist of something; "a short and compendious book"; "a compact style is brief and pithy"; "succinct comparisons"; "a summary formulation of a wide-ranging subject" [syn: compendious, compact, succinct]
n : brief account that presents the main points in a concise form [syn: summarization]
summery
adj : belonging to or characteristic of or occurring in summer; "summery weather"; "summery dresses" [ant: autumnal, wintry, vernal]

sundae, Sunday /'sʌndɛɪ/
sundae
n : ice cream served with a topping [syn: ice-cream sundae]
Sunday
adj : used of clothing; "my good clothes"; "her Sunday-go-to-meeting clothes" [syn: good, go-to-meeting, Sunday, Sunday-go-to-meeting]
n : first day of the week; observed as a day of rest and worship by most Christians [syn: Lord's Day, Sun]
v : spend Sunday; "We sundayed in the country"

surplice, surplus /'səɹplᵊs,'/
surplice
adj : having a diagonally overlapping neckline or closing
n : a loose-fitting white ecclesiastical vestment with wide sleeves
surplus
adj : more than is needed, desired, or required; "trying to lose excess weight"; "found some extra change lying on the dresser"; "yet another book on heraldry might be thought redundant"; "skills made redundant by technological advance"; "sleeping in the spare room"; "supernumerary ornamentation"; "it was supererogatory of her to gloat"; "delete superfluous (or unnecessary) words"; "extra ribs as well as other supernumerary internal parts"; "surplus cheese distributed to the needy" [syn: excess, extra, redundant, spare, supererogatory, superfluous, supernumerary]
n : a quantity much larger than is needed [syn: excess]

swat, swot /swat/
swat
n : a sharp blow
v : hit swiftly with a violent blow; "swat flies"
swot
n : a student who studies excessively [syn: grind, nerd, wonk]
v : study intensively, as before an exam; "I had to bone up on my Latin verbs before the final exam" [syn: cram, grind away, drum, bone up, get up, mug up, swot up, bone]

sycosis (see psychosis)
symbol (see cymbal)
sync (see cinque)

HOMOPHONES

-T-

T, tea, tee, ti /ti/

T
n: the 20th letter of the Roman alphabet [syn: t]

tea
n 1: a beverage made by steeping tea leaves in water; "iced tea is a cooling drink" 2: (British) a light mid-afternoon meal of tea and sandwiches or cakes; "an Englishman would interrupt a war to have his afternoon tea" [syn: afternoon tea, teatime] 3: dried leaves of the tea shrub; used to make tea; "the store shelves held many different kinds of tea"; "they threw the tea into Boston harbor" [syn: tea leaf] 4: a reception or party at which tea is served; "we met at the Dean's tea for newcomers" 5: a tropical evergreen shrub or small tree extensively cultivated in e.g. China and Japan and India; source of tea leaves; "tea has fragrant white flowers" [syn: Camellia sinensis]

tee
n 1: the starting place for each hole on a golf course; "they were waiting on the first tee" [syn: teeing ground] 2: support holding a football on end and above the ground preparatory to the kickoff [syn: football tee] 3: a short peg put into the ground to hold a golf ball off the ground [syn: golf tee]
v 1: place on a tee; "tee golf balls" [syn: tee up] 2: connect with a tee, as of pipes

ti
n 1: the syllable naming the seventh (subtonic) note of any musical scale in solmization 2: shrub with terminal tufts of elongated leaves used locally for thatching and clothing; thick sweet roots are used as food; tropical southeastern Asia, Australia and Hawaii [syn: Cordyline terminalis]

T's, teas, tease, tees, tis /tiz/

T's
n: more than one letter T

teas
n : (plu of tea)

tease
n 1: someone given to teasing (as by mocking or stirring curiosity) [syn: teaser, annoyer, vexer] 2: a seductive woman who uses her sex appeal to exploit men [syn: coquette, flirt, vamp, vamper, minx, prickteaser] 3: the act of harassing someone playfully or maliciously (especially by ridicule); provoking someone with persistent annoyances; "he ignored their teases"; "his ribbing was gentle but persistent" [syn: teasing, ribbing]

v 1: annoy persistently; "The children teased the boy because of his stammer" [syn: badger, pester, bug, beleaguer] 2: harass with persistent criticism or carping; "The children teased the new teacher"; "Don't ride me so hard over my failure"; "His fellow workers razzed him when he wore a jacket and tie" [syn: razz, rag, cod, tantalize, bait, taunt, twit, rally, ride] 3: to arouse hope, desire, or curiosity without satisfying them; "The advertisement is intended to tease the customers"; "She has a way of teasing men with her flirtatious behavior" 4: tear into pieces; "tease tissue for microscopic examinations" 5: raise the nap of (fabrics) 6: disentangle and raise the fibers of; "tease wool" [syn: tease apart, loosen] 7: separate the fibers of; "tease wool" [syn: card] 8: mock or make fun of playfully; "the flirting man teased the young woman" 9: ruffle (one's) hair by combing towards the ends towards the scalp, for a full effect [syn: fluff]

tees
n : (plu of tee)

tis
n: (plu of ti)

tacet, tacit /'tæsɪt/

tacet
n : a direction for a vocal or instrumental part to be silent during a whole movement

tacit
adj : indicated by necessary connotation though not expressed directly; "gave silent consent"; "a tacit agreement"; "the understood provisos of a custody agreement" [syn: implied, silent, understood]

tacked, tact /tækt/

tacked
adj : fastened with a tack
v : (past of tack) 1: fastened with tacks; "tacked the notice on the board" 2: turn into the wind; "The sailors tacked the boat."

tact
n : consideration in dealing with others and avoid being offensive [syn: tactfulness] [ant: tactlessness]

tachs, tacks, tax /tæks/

tachs
n : (plu of tach) : measuring instruments for indicating speed of rotation [syn: tachometers]

tacks
n : (plu of tack) 1: short nails with a sharp point and a large head 2: lines (ropes or chains) that regulate the angle at which sails are set in relation to the wind
v : (3rd pers sing for tack) : 1: fastens with tacks; "he tacks the notice on the board" 2: turns into the wind; "The sailor tacks the boat when the wind changes direction."

HOMOPHONES

tax

n : charge against a citizen's person or property or activity for the support of government [syn: taxation, revenue enhancement]

v 1: levy a tax on 2: determine the court costs of; in court actions [syn: assess] 3: use to the limit; "you tax my patience" [syn: task]

tael, tail, tale /teɪl/

tael

n : a unit of weight used in east Asia approximately equal to 1.3 ounces

tail

adj : (aeronautical) pertaining to the tail section of a plane

n 1: the posterior part of the body of a vertebrate especially when elongated and extending beyond the trunk or main part of the body 2: the time of the last part of something; "the fag end of this crisis-ridden century"; "the tail of the storm" [syn: fag end, tail end] 3: any projection that resembles the tail of an animal [syn: tail end] 4: the fleshy part of the human body that you sit on [syn: buttocks, nates, arse, butt, backside, bum, buns, can, fundament, hindquarters, hind end, keister, posterior, prat, rear, rear end, rump, stern, seat, tail end, tushie, tush, bottom, behind, derriere, fanny, ass] 5: a spy employed to follow someone and report their movements [syn: shadow, shadower] 6: (usually plural) the reverse side of a coin that does not bear the representation of a person's head [ant: head] 7: the rear part of an aircraft [syn: tail assembly, empennage] 8: the rear part of a ship [syn: tail, after part, quarter, poop] 9: female sex partner; "get some tail"

v 1: go after with the intent to catch [syn: chase, chase after, trail, tag, dog, go after, track] 2: remove or shorten the tail of an animal [syn: dock, bob] 3: remove the stalk of fruits or berries

tale

n 1: an account describing incidents or events; "a farfetched narrative"; "after dinner he told the children stories of his adventures" [syn: narration, narrative, story, recital, yarn] 2: a trivial lie; "he told a fib about eating his spinach"; "how can I stop my child from telling tales?" [syn: fib, story]

talesman, talisman /ˈtælɪsmᵊn/

talesman

n 1: a person called to make up a deficiency in the number of jurors 2: a member of a large pool of persons called for jury duty from which jurors are selected

talisman

n : a trinket or piece of jewelry thought to be a protection against evil [syn: amulet]

tao (see dhow)

taper, tapir /ˈteɪpᵊɹ/

taper

n 1: a convex shape that narrows toward a point 2: the property possessed by a shape that narrows toward a point (as a wedge or cone) 3: a loosely woven cord (in a candle or oil lamp) that draws fuel by capillary action up into the flame [syn: wick] 4: stick of wax with a wick in the middle [syn: candle, wax light]

v 1: diminish gradually; "Interested tapered off" 2: give a point to; "The candles are tapered" [syn: sharpen, point]

tapir

n : large inoffensive chiefly nocturnal ungulate of tropical America and southeast Asia having a heavy body and fleshy snout

tare, tear /tɛəɹ/

tare

n 1: any of several weedy vetches grown for forage 2: weedy annual grass often occurs in grain fields and other cultivated land; seeds sometimes considered poisonous [syn: darnel, bearded darnel, cheat, Lolium temulentum] 3: counterweight consisting of an empty container that is used as a counterbalance to obtain net weight

tear

n 1: an opening made forcibly as by pulling apart; "there was a rip in his pants" [syn: rip, rent, split] 2: an occasion for excessive eating or drinking; "they went on a bust that lasted three days" [syn: bust, binge, bout] 3: the act of tearing; "he took the manuscript in both hands and gave it a mighty tear"

v 1: separate or cause to separate abruptly; "The rope snapped"; "tear the paper" [syn: rupture, snap, bust] 2: to separate or be separated by force; "planks were in danger of being torn from the crossbars." 3: move quickly and violently; "The car tore down the street"; "He came charging into my office" [syn: shoot, shoot down, charge, buck] 4: strip of feathers; "pull a chicken"; "pluck the capon" [syn: pluck, pull, deplume] 5: move precipitously or violently; "The tornado ripped along the coast" [syn: rip]

taro, tarot /ˈtæɹoʊ/

taro

n 1: edible starchy tuberous root of taro plants [syn: cocoyam, dasheen, eddo] 2: herb of the Pacific islands grown throughout the tropics for its edible root and in temperate areas as an ornamental for its large glossy leaves [syn: taro plant, dalo, dasheen, Colocasia esculenta] 3: tropical starchy tuberous root [syn: taro root, cocoyam, dasheen, edda]

HOMOPHONES

tarot
n : any of a set of (usually 72) cards that include 22 cards representing virtues and vices and death and fortune etc.; used by fortunetellers [syn: tarot card]

tarry, terry
tarry /'tæɹi/
v 1: be about; "The high school students like to tarry in the Central Square"; "Who is this man that is hanging around the department?" [syn: loiter, lounge, lollygag, loaf, hang around, mess about, linger, lurk, mill about, mill around] 2: leave slowly and hesitantly [syn: linger]

terry /'tɛɹi/
n : a pile fabric (usually cotton) with uncut loops on both sides; used to make bath towels and bath robes [syn: terrycloth]

tartar, tarter /'taɹtəɹ/
tartar
n 1: a salt used especially in baking powder [syn: cream of tartar, potassium hydrogen tartrate] 2: a fiercely vigilant and unpleasant woman [syn: dragon] 3: (usually Tartar) a member of the Mongolian people of central Asia who invaded Russia in the 13th century [syn: Tatar, Mongol Tatar] 4: an incrustation that forms on the teeth and gums [syn: calculus, tophus]

tarter
adj 1: more tart 2: tasting more sour than a lemon [syn: more lemony, more tangy] 3: harsher; "sharper criticism"; "a tarter remark" [syn: sharper, sharper-worded]

taught, taut /tɔt/
taught
v : (past of teach) 1: imparted skills or knowledge to; "I taught them French"; "He instructed me in building a boat" [syn: instructed] 2: accustomed gradually to some action or attitude; "The child is taught to obey her parents"

taut
adj 1: pulled or drawn tight; "taut sails"; "a tight drumhead"; "a tight rope" [syn: tight] 2: subjected to great tension; stretched tight; "the skin of his face looked drawn and tight"; "her nerves were taut as the strings of a bow" [syn: drawn]

taupe, tope /toup/
taupe
adj : having a dusky brownish gray color [syn: fuscous]
n : a grayish brown

tope
v : drink excessive amounts of alcohol; be an alcoholic; "The husband drinks and beats his wife" [syn: drink]

team, teem /tim/
team
n 1: a cooperative unit [syn: squad] 2: two or more draft animals that work together to pull a vehicle
v : form a team; "Let's team up for this new project" [syn: team up]

teem
v : be teeming, be abuzz [syn: swarm]

tear, tier /tiɹ/
tear
n : a drop of the clear salty saline solution secreted by the lachrymal glands; "his story brought tears to her eyes" [syn: teardrop]
v: fill with tears or shed tears; "My eyes tear when I peel onions.'"

tier
n 1: a relative position or degree of value in a graded group: "lumber of the highest grade" [syn: grade, level] 2: any one of two or more competitors who tie one another 3: a worker who ties something [syn: tier up] 4: something that is used for tying; "the sail is fastened to the yard with tiers" 5: one of two or more layers one atop another: "tier upon tier of huge casks"; "a three-tier wedding cake"

tearer, terror
tearer /'tɛəɹəɹ/
n : a person who tears

terror /'tɛɹəɹ/
n 1: an overwhelming feeling of fear and anxiety [syn: panic] 2: a person who inspires fear or dread; "he was the terror of the neighborhood" [syn: scourge, threat] 3: a very troublesome child [syn: brat, little terror, holy terror]

teas, tease, tees /tiz/
teas
n : (plu of tea) (see T) "New professors are invited to many social teas."

tease
n 1: someone given to teasing (as by mocking or stirring curiosity) [syn: teaser, annoyer, vexer] 2: a seductive woman who uses her sex appeal to exploit men [syn: coquette, flirt, vamp, minx, prickteaser, cockteaser] 3: the act of harassing someone playfully or maliciously (especially by ridicule); provoking someone with persistent annoyances; "he ignored their teases"; "his ribbing was gentle but persistent" [syn: teasing, ribbing]
v 1: annoy persistently; "The children teased the boy because of his stammer" [syn: badger, harass, pester, bug, beleaguer] 2: harass with persistent criticism or carping; "The children teased the new teacher"; "Don't ride me so hard over my failure"; "His fellow workers razzed him when he wore a jacket and tie" [syn: razz, rag, cod, tantalize, bait, taunt, twit, rally, ride] 3: offer and withdraw 4: tear into pieces; "tease tissue for microscopic examinations" 5: raise the nap of (fabrics)

HOMOPHONES

6: disentangle and raise the fibers of; "tease wool" [syn: tease apart, loosen] 7: separate the fibers of [syn: card] 8: ruffle by combing towards the ends towards the scalp, for a full effect; of hair [syn: fluff]

tees

n : (plu of tee) (see T)

v : (3ʳᵈ pers sing of tee) (see T); "The first round tees off at eight in the morning."

tec, tech /tɛk/

tec

n : a police officer who investigates crimes [syn: detective, investigator, police detective]

tech

n 1: a school teaching mechanical and industrial arts and the applied sciences [syn: technical school] 2: a technician

tends, tens /tɛnz/

tends

v : (3ʳᵈ pers sing of tend) 1: have tendencies or dispositions to do or be something; be inclined; "She tends to be nervous before her lectures"; "This style runs small"; "He inclines to corpulence" [syn: is given, leans, inclines, runs] 2: has care of or looks after; "She tends to the children" 3: manages or runs; "tends a store"

tens

n : (plu of ten) (slang) extremely attractive women; "The actresses on 'Charlie's Angels' are all tens." [syn: hotties, foxes, babes]

tenner, tenor /'tɛnɹ/

tenner

n : the cardinal number that is the sum of nine and one; the base of the decimal system [syn: ten, 10, X, decade]

tenor

adj 1: (of a musical instrument) intermediate between alto and baritone or bass; "a tenor sax" 2: of or close in range to the highest natural adult male voice; "tenor voice"

n 1: the adult male singing voice above baritone [syn: tenor voice] 2: the pitch range of the highest male voice 3: an adult male with a tenor voice 4: pervading note of an utterance; "I could follow the general tenor of his argument" [syn: strain]

tense, tents /tɛnts/

tense

adj 1: in or of a state of physical or nervous tension [ant: relaxed] 2: (phonetics) pronounced with relatively tense tongue muscles (e.g., the vowel sound in `beat') [ant: lax] 3: taut or rigid; stretched tight; "tense piano strings" [ant: lax]

n : a grammatical category of verbs used to express distinctions of time

v 1: stretch or force to the limit; "strain the rope" [syn: strain] 2: increase the tension on; "tense a rope" 3: become tense or

tenser; "He tensed up when he saw his opponent enter the room" [syn: tense up] [ant: relax] 4: make tense [syn: strain, tense up] [ant: relax]

tents

n : (plu of tent) : portable shelters (usually of canvas stretched over supporting poles and fastened to the ground with ropes and pegs); "they pitched their tents near the creek" [syn: collapsible shelters]

tenser, tensor /'tɛnsɹ/

tenser

adj (compar of tense) : "We became tenser as the competition progressed." (syn: more tense]

tensor

n 1: a generalization of the concept of a vector 2: any of several muscles that cause an attached structure to become tense or firm

teras, terrace /'tɛɹɪs/

teras

n : (medicine) a grossly malformed and usually nonviable fetus [syn: monster]

terrace

n 1: usually paved outdoor area adjoining a residence [syn: patio] 2: a level shelf of land interrupting a declivity (with steep slopes above and below) [syn: bench] 3: a row of houses built in a similar style and having common dividing walls (or the street on which they face); "Grosvenor Terrace"

v 1: provide (a house) with a terrace; "We terrassed the country house" 2: make into terraces as for cultivation; "The Incas terraced their mountainous land"

tern, terne, turn /tɜɹn/

tern

n : small slender gull having narrow wings and a forked tail

terne

n: an alloy of lead and tin (typically 4:1 ratio) used as a coating to produce terneplate

turn

n 1: a circular segment of a curve: "a bend in the road"; "a crook in the path" [syn: bend, crook] 2: the act of changing or reversing the direction of the course; "he took a turn to the right" [syn: turning] 3: the activity of doing something in an agreed succession; "it is my turn"; "it is still my play" [syn: play] 4: an unforeseen development; "events suddenly took an awkward turn" [syn: turn of events, twist] 5: a movement in a new direction; "the turning of the wind" [syn: turning] 6: turning away or in the opposite direction: "he made an abrupt turn away from her" 7: turning or twisting around (in place); "with a quick twist of his head he surveyed the room" [syn: twist] 8: a time for working

I-195

HOMOPHONES

(after which you will be relieved by someone else); "it's my go"; "a spell of work" [syn: go, spell, tour] 9: (in sports) a period of play during which one team is on the offensive [syn: bout, round] 10: a short theatrical performance that is part of a longer program; "he did his act three times every evening"; "she had a catchy little routine"; "it was one of the best numbers he ever did" [syn: act, routine, number, bit] 11: a favor for someone; "he did me a good turn" [syn: good turn] 12: taking a short walk out and back; "we took a turn in the park"

v 1: change orientation or direction, also in the abstract sense; "Turn towards me"; "The mugger turned and fled before I could see his face"; "She turned from herself and learned to listen to others' needs" 2: undergo a change or development: "The water turned into ice"; "Her former friend became her worst enemy"; "He turned traitor" [syn: become] 3: undergo a transformation or a change of position or action; "We turned from Socialism to Capitalism"; "The people turned against the President when he stole the election" [syn: change state] 4: cause to move around or rotate; "turn a key" 5: pass into a condition gradually, take on a specific property or attribute; become; "The weather turned nasty"; "She grew angry"; "The teacher became impatient" [syn: grow] 6: to send or let go; "They turned away the crowd at the gate of the governor's mansion" 7: pass to the other side of; "turn the corner"; "move around the obstacle" [syn: move around] 8: move around an axis or a center; "The wheels are turning" 9: cause to move around a center so as to show another side of; "turn a page of a book" [syn: turn over] 10: change to the contrary; "The trend was reversed"; "the tides turned against him"; "public opinion turned when it was revealed that the president had an affair with a White House intern" [syn: change by reversal, reverse] 11: to break and turn over earth esp. with a plow; "Farmer Jones plowed his east field last week"; "turn the earth in the Spring" [syn: plow, plough] 12: change color, as of leaves in the Fall; "In Vermont, the leaves turn early" 13: cause to change or turn into something different; assume new characteristics; "The princess turned the frog into a prince by kissing him"; "The alchemists tried to turn lead into gold" 14: let (something) fall or spill a container; "turn the flour onto a plate" [syn: release] 15: twist suddenly so as to sprain; "wrench one's ankle"; "The wrestler twisted his shoulder"; "the hikers sprained their ankles when they fell"; "I turned my ankle and couldn't walk for several days" [syn: twist, sprain, wrench] 16: shape by rotating on a lathe or cutting device or a wheel; "turn the legs of the table"; "turn the clay on the wheel" 17: go sour or spoil; "The milk has soured"; "The wine worked"; "The cream has turned--we have to throw it out" [syn: sour, ferment, work] 18: accomplish by rotating; "turn a somersault"; "turn cartwheels" 19: get by buying and selling; "the company turned a good profit after a year" 20: cause to move along an axis or into a new direction; "turn your face to the wall"; "turn the car around"; "turn your dance partner around" 21: channel one's attention, interest, thought, or attention toward or away from something; "The pedophile turned to boys for satisfaction"; "people turn to mysticism at the turn of a millennium" 22: cause to assume a crooked or angular form; "bend the rod"; "twist the dough into a braid"; "the strong man could turn an iron bar" [syn: bend, deform, twist] [ant: unbend] 23: alter the functioning or setting of; "turn the dial to 10"; "turn the heat down" 24: direct at someone; "She turned a smile on me"; "They turned their flashlights on the car" 25: have recourse to or make an appeal or request for help or information to; "She called on her Representative to help her"; "She turned to her relatives for help" [syn: call on] 26: become officially one year older; "She is turning 50 this year"

ternary, ternery, turnery
/'tɜɹnᵊɹi/
ternary
adj : having three units or components or elements; "a ternary operation"; "a treble row of red beads"; "overcrowding made triple sessions necessary"; "triple time has three beats per measure"; "triplex windows" [syn: treble, triple, triplex]
n : the cardinal number that is the sum of one and one and one [syn: three, 3, III, trio, threesome, tierce, leash, troika, triad, trine, trinity, ternion, triplet, tercet, terzetto, trey, deuce-ace]
ternery
n : breeding place for flocks of terns
turnery
n 1: workshop where objects are made on a lathe 2: products made on a lathe

terse, tierce /tɜɹs/
terse
adj : brief and to the point; effectively cut short; "a crisp retort"; "a response so curt as to be almost rude"; "the laconic reply; `yes'"; "short and terse and easy to understand" [syn: crisp, curt, laconic]
tierce
n 1: the third canonical hour; about 9 a.m.

I-196

HOMOPHONES

[syn: terce] 2: the cardinal number that is the sum of one and one and one [syn: three, 3, III, trio, threesome, leash, troika, triad, trine, trinity, ternary, ternion, triplet, tercet, terzetto, trey, deuce-ace] 3: one of three equal parts of a divisible whole; "it contains approximately a third of the minimum daily requirement" [syn: one-third, third]

testees, testes /ˈtɛstiz/
testees
n : persons who are tested (as by an intelligence test or an academic examination) [syn: examinees]

testes
n : the two male reproductive glands that produce spermatozoa and secrete androgens; "she kicked him in the balls and got away" [syn: testicles, balls, nuts, eggs] (Note: singular form is testis /ˈtɛstɪs/)

than, then
than /ðæn/
conj 1: indicates the second member or the member taken as the point of departure in a comparison expressive of inequality; used with comparative adjectives and comparative adverbs "older than I am" "easier said than done" 2: indicates difference of kind, manner, or identity; used especially with some adjectives and adverbs that express diversity "anywhere else than at home" 3: preference indicator; "rather than" "other than"

prep : in comparison with; "you are younger than her"

then /ðɛn/
adj : at a specific prior time; "the then president"
n : that time; that moment; "we will arrive before then"; "we were friends from then on"
adv 1: subsequently or soon afterward (often used as sentence connectors); "then he left"; "go left first, then right"; "first came lightning, then thunder"; "we watched the late movie and then went to bed"; "and so home and to bed" [syn: so, and so, and then] 2: in that case or as a consequence; "if he didn't take it, then who did?"; "keep it then if you want to"; "the case, then, is closed"; "you've made up your mind then?"; "then you'll be rich" 3: at that time; "I was young then"; "prices were lower back then"; "science as it was then taught"

the, thee /ði/
the
definite article: (NOTE: The most common pronunciation is /ðʌ/. This pronunciation is provided here because it is sometimes used to give emphasis to what is being spoken about.) 'The' was originally a

demonstrative pronoun, being a weakened form of that. When placed before adjectives and participles, it converts them into abstract nouns; as, the sublime and the beautiful.. 'The' is used regularly before many proper names, as of rivers, oceans, ships, etc.; as, the Nile, the Atlantic, the Great Eastern, the West Indies, The Hague. 'The' with an epithet or ordinal number often follows a proper name; as, Alexander the Great; Napoleon the Third. 'The' may be employed to individualize a particular kind or species; as, the grasshopper shall be a burden.

thee
(2nd pers pron) : "This sword hath ended him; so shall it thee, Unless thou yield thee as my prisoner." –Shakespeare; 'Thee' and 'thou' are Old English forms of you; 'thou' being the subjective case and 'thee' the objective case.

their, there, they're /ðɛɹ/
their
pron : 3rd person plural to indicate possession; "Their house is very large."

there
n : a location other than here; that place; "you can take it from there" [ant: here]
adv 1: in or at that place; "they have lived there for years"; "it's not there"; "that man there" [syn: at that place, in that location] [ant: here] 2: in that matter; "I agree with you there" [syn: in that respect, on that point] 3: to or toward that place; away from the speaker; "go there around noon!" [syn: thither] [ant: here]

they're (also /ˈðɛɪjəʳ/)
contr : they are

theirs, there's /ðɛɹz/
theirs
pron : 3rd person plural to indicate possession when the noun to which it refers is not expressed, but implied or understood; "I will do my job, if everyone else does theirs."

there's
contr : there is

therefor, therefore /ˈðɛɹfɔɹ/
therefor
adv : (in formal usage; especially legal usage) for that or it; "ordering goods and enclosing payment therefor"; "a refund therefor"

therefore
adv 1: (used to introduce a logical conclusion) from that fact or reason or as a result; "therefore X must be true"; "the eggs were fresh and hence satisfactory"; "we were young and thence optimistic"; "it is late and thus we must go"; "the witness is biased and so cannot be trusted" [syn: hence, thence, thus] 2: as a consequence; "he had good reason to be grateful for

the opportunities which they had made available to him and which consequently led to the good position he now held" [syn: consequently]

threw, through /θɹu/

threw

v : (past of throw) 1: projected through the air; "threw a Frisbee" 2: moved violently, energetically, or carelessly; "She threw herself forwards" 3: got rid of; "he shed his image as a pushy boss" [syn: shed, cast, cast off, shook off, threw off, threw away, dropped] 4: placed with great energy; "She threw the blanket around the child" 5: conveyed or communicated; of a smile, a look, a physical gesture; "Threw a glance"; "She gave me a dirty look" [syn: gave] 6: caused to go on or t be engaged; set in operation; "switched on the light"; "threw the lever" [syn: flipped, switched] 7: put or sent forth; "She threw the flashlight beam into the corner"; "The setting sun threw long shadows"; "cast a spell"; "cast a warm light" [syn: projected, cast, contrived] 8: to put into a state or activity hastily, suddenly, or carelessly; "Jane threw dinner together", threw the car into reverse" 9: caused to be confused emotionally [syn: bewildered, bemused, discombobulated] 10: uttered with force; uttered vehemently; "hurled insults"; "threw accusations at someone" [syn: hurled] 11: organized or been responsible for; "held a reception," "had, threw, or made a party", "gave a course", etc. [syn: held, had, made, gave] 12: made on a potter's wheel; of pottery 13: caused to fall off; "The horse threw its inexperienced rider" 14: threw out onto a flat surface, as of die; "Threw a six" 15: been confusing or perplexing to; caused to be unable to think clearly: "These questions confused even the experts"; "This question completely threw me"; "This question befuddled even the teacher" [syn: confused, foxed, befuddled, fuddled, bedeviled, confounded, discombobulated]

through

adj 1: having finished or arrived at completion; "certain to make history before he's done"; "it's a done deed"; "after the treatment, the patient is through except for follow-up"; "almost through with his studies" [syn: done, through with] 2: of a route or journey etc.; continuing without requiring stops or changes; "a through street"; "a through bus"; "through traffic" [syn: through]
adv 1: from one end or side to the other; "jealousy pierced her through" 2: from beginning to end; "read this book through" 3: over the whole distance; "this bus goes through to New York" 4: to completion;

"think this through very carefully!" 5: in diameter; "this cylinder measures 15 inches through" 6: throughout the entire extent; "got soaked through in the rain"; "I'm frozen through"; "a letter shot through with the writer's personality"; "knew him through and through"; "boards rotten through and through" [syn: through and through]
prep : indicates movement into one side and out an other; "He went through the open door."

throes, throws /θɹouz/

throes   (The singular form, throe, is rarely used)

n 1: severe spasms of pain: "the throes of dying"; "the throes of childbirth" 2: hard or painful trouble or struggle: "a country in the throes of economic collapse"

throws

v : (3rd pers sing of throw) (see threw); "He throws a ball with great accuracy."

throne, thrown /θɹoun/

throne

n 1: the chair of state of a monarch, bishop, etc.; "the king sat on his throne" 2: a plumbing fixture for defecation and urination [syn: toilet, can, commode, crapper, pot, potty, stool] 3: the position and power of one who occupies a throne
v 1: sit on the throne as a ruler 2: put a monarch on the throne; "The Queen was enthroned more than 50 years ago" [syn: enthrone] [ant: dethrone]

thrown

adj 1: caused to fall to the ground; "the thrown rider got back on his horse"; "a thrown wrestler"; "a ball player thrown for a loss" 2: (archaic) twisted together; as of filaments spun into a thread; "thrown silk is raw silk that has been twisted and doubled into yarn" [syn: thrown and twisted]
v : (past of throw) (see threw); "He was thrown to the ground."

thyme, time /taɪm/

thyme

n 1: any of various mints of the genus Thymus 2: leaves can be used as seasoning for almost any meat and stews and stuffing and vegetables

time

n 1: an instance or single occasion for some event; "This time he succeeded"; "He called four times"; "he could do ten at a clip" [syn: clip] 2: an indefinite period (usually marked by specific attributes or activities); "he waited a long time"; "the time of year for planting"; "he was a great actor is his time" 3: a period of time considered as a resource under your control and sufficient to accomplish something; "take time to smell the roses";

HOMOPHONES

"I didn't have time to finish"; "it took more than half my time" 4: a suitable moment; "it is time to go" 5: the continuum of experience in which events pass from the future through the present to the past 6: the time as given by a clock; "do you know what time it is?"; "the time is 10 o'clock" [syn: clock time] 7: the fourth coordinate that is required (along with three spatial dimensions) to specify a physical event [syn: fourth dimension] 8: a person's experience on a particular occasion; "he had a time holding back the tears" or "they had a good time together" 9: rhythm as given by division into parts of equal time [syn: meter] 10: the period of time a prisoner is imprisoned; "he served a prison term of 15 months"; "his sentence was 5 to 10 years"; "he is doing time in the county jail" [syn: prison term, sentence]

v 1: measure the time or duration of an event or action or the person who performs an action in a certain period of time; "he clocked the runners" [syn: clock] 2: assign a time for an activity or event 3: set the speed, duration, or execution of 4: regulate or set the time of, as of a clock or watch

tic, tick /tɪk/

tic

n : a local and habitual twitching especially in the face

tick

n 1: a metallic tapping sound; "he counted the ticks of the clock" [syn: ticking] 2: any of two families of small parasitic arachnids with barbed proboscis; feed on blood of warm-blooded animals 3: a light mattress

v 1: make a clicking or ticking sound; "The clock ticked away" [syn: click] 2: make a sound like a clock or a timer; "the clocks were ticking"; "the grandfather clock beat midnight" [syn: tick tock, ticktack, beat] 3: sew, as of mattresses; "tick a mattress" [syn: retick]

tide, tied /taɪd/

tide

n 1: the periodic rise and fall of the sea level under the gravitational pull of the moon 2: something that may increase or decrease (like the tides of the sea); "a rising tide of popular interest" 3: there are usually two high and two low tides each day [syn: lunar time period]

v 1: rise in waves [syn: surge] [ant: ebb] 2: cause to float with the tide 3: be carried with the tide

tied

adj 1: bound or secured closely; "the guard was found trussed up with his arms and legs securely tied"; "a trussed chicken" [syn: trussed] 2: bound together by or as if by a strong rope; especially as by a

bond of affection; "people tied by blood or marriage" 3: fastened with strings or cords; "a neatly tied bundle" [syn: fastened] [ant: untied] 4: closed with a lace; "snugly laced shoes" [syn: laced] [ant: unlaced] 5: of the score in a contest; "the score is even" [syn: even]

v : (past of tie) 1: To fastened or secured with a rope, string, or cord; "They tied their victim to the chair" [syn: bound] [ant: untied] 2: finished a game with an equal number of points, goals, etc.; "The teams drew a tie" [syn: drew] 3: limited or restricted to; "I am tied to UNIX"; "These big jets are tied to large airports" 4: connected, fastened, or put together two or more pieces; "Can you connect the two loudspeakers?" "Tie the ropes together"; "Linked arms" [syn: connected, linked, linked up] [ant: disconnected] 5: formed a knot or bow in; "tied a necktie" 6: created social or emotional ties [syn: bound, bonded] 7: performed a marriage ceremony; "The minister married us on Saturday"; "We tied the knot the following week"; "The couple got spliced on Hawaii" [syn: marry, wed, splice, tied the knot] 8: made by tying pieces together: "The fishermen tied their flies" 9: united musical notes by a tie

tier, tire /ˈtaɪɚ/

tier

n 1: any one of two or more competitors who tie one another 2: a worker who ties something 3: something that is used for tying; "the sail is fastened to the yard with tiers"

tire

n 1: hoop that covers a wheel; "automobile tires are usually made of rubber and filled with compressed air" [syn: tyre]

v 1: get tired of something or somebody [syn: pall, weary, fatigue, jade] 2: exhaust or get tired through overuse or great strain or stress; "We wore ourselves out on this hike" [syn: wear upon, tire out, wear, weary, jade, wear out, outwear, wear down, fag out, fag, fatigue] 3: deplete; "exhaust one's savings"; "We quickly played out our strength" [syn: run down, exhaust, play out, sap] 4: cause to be bored [syn: bore]

tighten, titan /ˈtaɪtⁿn/

tighten

v 1: make tight or tighter; "Tighten the wire" [syn: fasten] [ant: loosen] 2: become tight or tighter; "The rope tightened" 3: restrict; "Tighten the rules"; "stiffen the regulations" [syn: stiffen, tighten up, constrain] 4: narrow or limit; "reduce the influx of foreigners" [syn: reduce]

titan

n 1: a person of exceptional importance and reputation [syn: colossus, behemoth,

HOMOPHONES

giant, heavyweight]

tighter, titer /taɪtᵊɹ/

tighter

adj (compar of tight) 1: more constrained or more constricted or more constricting; "tighter skirts"; "he hated tight starched collars"; "fingers closed in a tight fist"; "a tight feeling in his chest" [ant: looser] 2: pulled or drawn tight; "taut sails"; "a tight drumhead"; "a tight rope" [syn: taut] 3: set so close together as to be invulnerable to penetration; "in tight formation"; "a tight blockade" 4: pressed tightly together; "with lips compressed" [syn: compressed] 5: used of persons or behavior; characterized by or indicative of lack of generosity; "a mean person"; "he left a miserly tip" [syn: mean, miserly] 6: affected by scarcity and expensive to borrow; "tight money"; "a tight market" 7: of such close construction as to be impermeable; "a tight roof"; "warm in our tight little house" [ant: leaky] 8: of textiles; "a close weave"; "smooth percale with a very tight weave" [syn: close] 9: securely or solidly fixed in place; rigid; "the bolts are tight" 10: (of a contest or contestants) evenly matched; "a close contest"; "a close election"; "a tight game" [syn: close] 11: very drunk [syn: besotted, blind drunk, blotto, crocked, cockeyed, fuddled, loaded, pie-eyed, pissed, pixilated, plastered, potty, slopped, sloshed, smashed, soaked, soused, sozzled, stiff, tiddly, tipsy, wet] 12: exasperatingly difficult to handle or circumvent; "a nasty problem"; "a good man to have on your side in a tight situation" [syn: nasty] 13: demanding strict attention to rules and procedures; "rigorous discipline"; "tight security"; "stringent
safety measures" [syn: rigorous, stringent] 14: packed closely together; "the stood in a tight little group"; "hair in tight curls"; "the pub was packed tight"

adv 1: firmly or tightly; "held fast to the rope"; "her foot was stuck fast"; "held tighter" [syn: fast] 2: in an attentive manner; "he remained close on his guard" [syn: close, closely]

titer

n : the concentration of a solution as determined by titration

'til, till /tɪl/

'til

contr : until

till

n 1: unstratified soil deposited by a glacier; consists of sand and clay and gravel and boulders mixed together [syn: boulder clay] 2: a treasury for government funds [syn: public treasury, trough] 3: a strongbox for holding cash [syn: cashbox,

money box]

v : work land as by plowing, harrowing, and manuring, in order to make it ready for cultivation; "till the soil"

timber, timbre /'tɪmbᵊɹ/

timber

n 1: the wood of trees cut and prepared for use as building material [syn: lumber] 2: a beam made of wood 3: a post made of wood 4: land that is covered with trees and shrubs [syn: forest, woodland, timberland]

timbre

n : the distinctive property of a complex sound (a voice or noise or musical sound); "the timbre of her soprano was rich and lovely"; "the muffled tones of the broken bell summoned them to meet" [syn: quality, tone]

to, too, two /tu/

to

prep : 1: in a direction toward so as to reach "went to the city"; 2: towards "turned to me"; 3: reaching as far as "The ocean water was clear all the way to the bottom"; 4:to the extent or degree of "loved him to distraction"; 5:with the resultant condition of "nursed her back to health" 6: toward a given state "helping minority women to economic equality" 7: in contact with "against: their faces pressed to the windows" 8: in front of "stood face to face" 9: used to indicate appropriation or possession "looked for the top to the jar" 10: concerning; regarding "waiting for an answer to my letter" 11: in a particular relationship with "The brook runs parallel to the road." 12: as an accompaniment or a complement of "danced to the tune" 13 composing; constituting "two cups to a pin" 14: in accord with "job responsibilities suited to her abilities" 15: as compared with "a book superior to his other" 16: before: "The time is ten to five." 17: up till; until "worked from nine to five" 18: for the purpose of "went out to lunch" 19: in honor of "a toast to the queen" 20: used before a verb to indicate the infinitive "I'd like to go." 21: used alone when the infinitive is understood "Go if you want to." 22: used to indicate the relationship of a verb with its complement "refer to a dictionary"; "refer me to a dictionary" 23: used with a reflexive pronoun to indicate exclusivity or separateness "had the plane to ourselves"

adv 1: in one direction; toward a person or thing ""She came to me." 2: into a shut or closed position "pushed the door to" 3: into a state of consciousness "The patient came to." 4: into a state of action or attentiveness "sat down for lunch and fell to"; 5:(nautical) "into the wind"

HOMOPHONES

too
adv 1: to an excessive degree; "too big" [syn: excessively, overly] 2: in addition; "he has a Mercedes, too" [syn: besides, also, likewise, as well]

two
adj : being one more than one; "he received two messages" [syn: 2, ii]
n : the cardinal number that is the sum of one and one or a numeral representing this number [syn: 2, II, deuce]

toad, toed, towed /toʊd/

toad
n : any of various tailless stout-bodied amphibians with long hind limbs for leaping; semiaquatic and terrestrial species [syn: frog, toadfrog, anuran, batrachian, salientian]

toed
adj : having a toe or toes of a specified kind; often used in combination; "long-toed"; "five-toed" [syn: toe] [ant: toeless]
v : (past of toe) (see toe)

towed
adj : something being dragged; "Barges are towed flat-bottomed boats."
v : (past of tow) (see toe); "Horses towed barges along the canal."

toady, tody /'toʊdi/

toady
n : a person who tries to please someone in order to gain a personal advantage [syn: sycophant, crawler, lackey]
v : try to gain favor by cringing or flattering; "He is always kowtowing to his boss" [syn: fawn, truckle, bootlick, kowtow, suck up]

tody
n : tiny insectivorous West Indian bird having red-and-green plumage and a long straight bill

tocsin, toxin /'taksɪn/

tocsin
n 1: the sound of an alarm (usually a bell) [syn: alarm bell] 2: a bell used to sound an alarm [syn: warning bell]

toxin
n : a poisonous substance produced during the metabolism and growth of certain microorganisms and some higher plant and animal species

toe, tow /toʊ/

toe
adj : having a toe or toes of a specified kind; often used in combination; "long-toed"; "five-toed" [syn: toed] [ant: toeless]
n 1: one of the digits of the foot 2: the part of footwear that provides a covering for the toes 3: forepart of a hoof
v 1: walk so that the toes assume an indicated position or direction; "She toes inwards" 2: drive obliquely; "toe a nail" 3: hit the ball with the toe of the club, in golf 4: touch with the toe

tow
n : the act of hauling something (as a vehicle) by means of a hitch or rope; "the truck gave him a tow to the garage" [syn: towage]
v : drag behind; "Horses used to tow barges along the canal"

toke, toque /toʊk/

toke
n : a puff of a marijuana or hashish cigarette: "the boys took a few tokes on a joint"

toque
n : a small round woman's hat [syn: pillbox, turban]

told, tolled /toʊld/

tell
v : (past of tell) 1: expressed an idea, etc. in words; "He told me that he wanted to marry her"; "he told me what is bothering you"; "stated your opinion" [syn: stated, said] 2: let something be known; "I told them that you will be late" 3: narrated or gave a detailed account of; "told what happened"; "The father told a story to his child" [syn: narrated, recounted, spun, recited] 4: gave instructions to or directed somebody to do something; "I said to him to go home"; "She ordered him to do the shopping"; "The mother told the child to get dressed" [syn: ordered, enjoin, said] 5: informed positively and with certainty and confidence; "I told you that that man is a crook!" [syn: assured] 6: gave evidence; "he told on all his former colleagues" [syn: evidenced]

tolled
v : (past of toll) 1: ring slowly, of bells; "The bells tolled 4 o'clock." 2: rang recurrently; of bells [syn: pealed]

tole, toll /toʊl/

tole
n : lacquered or enameled metalware, usually gilded and elaborately painted

toll
n 1: a fee levied for the use of roads or bridges (used for maintenance) 2: value measured by what must be given or done or undergone to obtain something: "the cost in human life was enormous"; "the price of success is hard work"; "what price glory?" [syn: price, cost]
v 1: ring slowly, of bells; "For whom the bell tolls" 2: ring recurrently; of bells [syn: peal]

ton, tonne, tun /tʌn/

ton
n 1: a United States unit of weight equivalent to 2000 pounds [syn: short ton, net ton] 2: a British unit of weight equivalent to 2240 pounds [syn: long ton, gross ton]

HOMOPHONES

tonne

n : a unit of weight equivalent to 1000 kilograms [syn: metric ton, MT, t]

tun

n : a large cask especially one holding a volume equivalent to 2 butts or 252 gals

tongue, tung /tʌŋ/

tongue

n 1: a mobile mass of muscular tissue covered with mucous membrane and located in the oral cavity [syn: lingua, glossa, clapper] 2: a human written or spoken language used by a community; opposed to e.g. a computer language [syn: natural language] [ant: artificial language] 3: any long thin projection that is transient; "tongues of flame licked at the walls"; "rifles exploded quick knives of fire into the dark" [syn: knife] 4: a manner of speaking; "he spoke with a thick tongue"; "she has a glib tongue" 5: a narrow strip of land that juts out into the sea [syn: spit] 6: the tongue of certain animals used as meat 7: the flap of material under the laces of a shoe or boot 8: metal striker that hangs inside a bell and makes a sound by hitting the side [syn: clapper]

v 1: articulate by tonguing, as on wind instruments 2: lick or explore with the tongue

tung

n : Chinese tree bearing seeds that yield tung oil [syn: tung tree, tung-oil tree, Aleurites fordii]

tool, tulle /tul/

tool

n 1: an implement used in the practice of a vocation 2: the means whereby some act is accomplished; "my greed was the instrument of my destruction"; "science has given us new tools to fight disease" [syn: instrument] 3: a person who is used to perform unpleasant or dishonest tasks for someone else [syn: creature, puppet] 4: obscene terms for penis [syn: cock, prick, dick, shaft, pecker, peter]

v 1: informal: drive (a vehicle); "The convertible tooled down the street" 2: ride in a car with no particular goal and just for the pleasure of it [syn: joyride, tool around] 3: furnish with tools 4: work with a tool

tulle

n : a fine (often starched) net used for veils or tutus or gowns

toon, tune /tun/

toon

n : (slang) 1: cartoon 2: animated movie

tune

n 1: a succession of notes forming a distinctive sequence; "she was humming an air from Beethoven" [syn: melody, air, strain, melodic line, line, melodic phrase] 2: the property of producing accurately a note of a given pitch; "he cannot sing in tune"; "the clarinet was out of tune" 3: the adjustment of a radio receiver or other circuit to a required frequency

v 1: adjust for (better) functioning; "tune the engine" [syn: tune up] 2: of musical instruments; "My piano needs to be tuned" [syn: tune up] [ant: detune]

tooter, tutor /'tutɚ/

tooter

n : one who toots; one who plays upon a pipe or horn

tutor

n : a person who gives private instruction (as in singing or acting) [syn: coach, private instructor]

v 1: be a tutor to someone; give individual instruction; "Can you tutor me in Spanish?" 2: as a guardian to someone

topee, topi /'toupi/

topee

n : a light-weight hat worn in tropical countries for protection from the sun [syn: pith hat, pith helmet, sun helmet, topi]

topi

n 1: a large South African antelope; considered the swiftest hoofed mammal [syn: sassaby, Damaliscus lunatus] 2: var of topee

tor, tore, torr /tɔɹ/

tor

n 1: a prominent rock or pile of rocks on a hill 2: a high rocky hill

tore

n : commonly the lowest molding at the base of a column [syn: torus]

v : (past of tear) (see tare); "I tore my shirt."

torr

n : a unit of pressure equal to 0.001316 atmosphere; named after Torricelli [syn: millimeter of mercury, mm Hg]

tort, torte /tɔɹt/

tort

n : any wrongdoing for which an action for damages may be brought [syn: civil wrong]

torte

n : rich cake usually covered with cream and fruit or nuts; originated in Austria

tough, tuff /tʌf/

tough

adj 1: not given to gentleness or sentimentality; "a tough character" [ant: tender] 2: very difficult; severely testing stamina or resolution; "a rugged competitive examination"; "the rugged conditions of frontier life"; "the competition was tough"; "it's a tough life"; "it was a tough job" [syn: rugged] 3: physically toughened; "the tough bottoms of his feet" [syn: toughened] [ant: tender]

HOMOPHONES

4: substantially made or constructed; "sturdy steel shelves"; "sturdy canvas"; "a tough all-weather fabric"; "some plastics are as tough as metal" [syn: sturdy] 5: violent and lawless; "the more ruffianly element"; "tough street gangs" [syn: ruffianly] 6: feeling physical discomfort or pain ('tough' is occasionally used colloquially for 'bad'); "my throat feels bad"; "she felt bad all over"; "he was feeling tough after a restless night" [syn: bad] 7: tough to cut or chew [ant: tender] 8: unfortunate or hard to bear; "had hard luck"; "a tough break" [syn: hard]

n 1: someone who learned to fight in the streets rather than being formally trained in the sport of boxing [syn: street fighter] 2: an aggressive and violent young criminal [syn: hood, hoodlum, goon, punk, thug, toughie, strong-armer] 3: a cruel and brutal fellow [syn: bully, hooligan, ruffian, roughneck, rowdy]

tuff

n : hard volcanic rock composed of compacted volcanic ash [syn: tufa]

toughed, tuft /tʌft/
toughed

Idiom (slang) (past of / tough it out) : got through despite hardship; endured; "It was hard to run the marathon, but they toughed it out."

tuft

n 1: a bunch of hair or feathers or growing grass [syn: tussock] 2: a bunch of feathers, fur or hair

tracked, tract /tɹækt/
tracked

adj : having tracks; "new snow tracked by rabbits"; "tracked vehicles" [ant: trackless]
v : (past of track) 1: carried (as mud) on the feet and deposit 2: observed or plotted the moving path of something (e.g., a target or missile) 3: went after with the intent to catch [syn: chased, chased after, trailed, tailed, tagged, dogged, went after] 4: traveled across or passed over; "The caravan covered almost 100 miles each day" [syn: traversed, covered, crossed, passed over, got over, got across, cut through, cut across] 5: made tracks upon

tract

n 1: an extended area of land [syn: piece of land, piece of ground, parcel of land, parcel] 2: a system of body parts that together serve some particular purpose 3: a brief treatise on a subject of interest; published in the form of a booklet [syn: pamphlet] 4: a bundle of nerve fibers following a path through the brain [syn: nerve pathway, nerve tract, pathway]

trader, traitor
trader /ˈtɹeɪdɚ/

n : someone who purchases and maintains an inventory of goods to be sold [syn: bargainer, dealer, monger]

traitor /ˈtɹeɪtɚ/

n 1: someone who betrays his country by committing treason 2: a person who says one thing and does another [syn: double-crosser, double-dealer, two-timer, betrayer]

tray, trey /tɹeɪ/
tray

n : an open receptacle for holding or displaying or serving articles or food

trey

n 1: the cardinal number that is the sum of one and one and one [syn: three, 3, III, trio, threesome, tierce, leash, troika, triad, trine, trinity, ternary, ternion, triplet, tercet, terzetto, deuce-ace] 2: one of four playing cards in a deck having three pips

trews, trues /tɹuz/
trews

n : tight-fitting trousers; usually of tartan

trues

v : (3rd pers sing of true): makes level, squares, balances, or concentrics; "trues up the cylinder of an engine" [syn: trues up]

triptik, triptych /ˈtɹɪptɪk/
triptik

n : a bound series of road maps delineating a particular source to destination route

triptych

n 1: art consisting of a painting or carving (especially an altarpiece) on three panels (usually hinged together) 2: an ancient Roman writing tablet with three waxed leaves hinged together

troche, trochee /ˈtɹoʊki/
troche

n : a medicated lozenge used to soothe the throat [syn: cough drop, pastille]

trochee

n : metrical unit with one long syllable followed by one short syllable or of one stressed syllable followed by one unstressed syllable (as in apple)

troop, troupe /tɹup/
troop

n 1: a group of soldiers 2: a cavalry unit corresponding to an infantry company 3: a unit of girl or boy scouts [syn: scout troop, scout group] 4: an orderly crowd; "a troop of children" [syn: flock]
v 1: march in a procession [syn: parade, promenade] 2: move or march as if in a crowd; "The children trooped into the room"

troupe

n : organization of performers and associated personnel (especially theatrical); "the traveling company all stayed at the same hotel" [syn: company]

HOMOPHONES

trooper, trouper /ˈtɹuupˀɹ/

trooper

n 1: a soldier in a motorized army unit [syn: cavalryman] 2: a mounted policeman 3: a state police officer [syn: state trooper] 4: a soldier mounted on horseback; "a cavalryman always takes good care of his mount" [syn: cavalryman]

trouper

n : an actor who travels around the country presenting plays [syn: barnstormer, play actor]

trussed, trust /tɹʌst/

trussed

adj : bound or secured closely; "the guard was found trussed up with his arms and legs securely tied"; "a trussed chicken" [syn: tied]

v : (past of truss) : 1: tied the wings and legs of a bird before cooking 2: secured with or as if with ropes; "tied down the prisoners" [syn: tied down, tied up, bound] 3: supported structurally, of roofs or bridges

trust

n 1: something (as property) held by one party (the trustee) for the benefit of another (the beneficiary); "he is the beneficiary of a generous trust set up by his father" 2: certainty based on past experience; "he wrote the paper with considerable reliance on the work of other scientists"; "he put more trust in his own two legs than in the gun" [syn: reliance] 3: the trait of trusting; of believing in the honesty and reliability of others; "the experience destroyed his trust and personal dignity" [syn: trustfulness] [ant: distrust] 4: a consortium of companies formed to limit competition; "they set up the trust in the hope of gaining a monopoly" [syn: corporate trust, combine, cartel] 5: complete confidence in a person or plan etc; "he cherished the faith of a good woman"; "the doctor-patient relationship is based on trust" [syn: faith] 6: a trustful relationship; "he took me into his confidence"; "he betrayed their trust" [syn: confidence]

v 1: have confidence or faith in; "We can trust in God"; "Rely on your friends"; "bank on your good education"; "I swear by my grandmother's recipes" [syn: swear, rely, bank] [ant: distrust, distrust] 2: allow without fear 3: be confident about something; "I believe that he will come back from the war" [syn: believe] 4: expect with desire; "I trust you will behave better from now on"; "I hope she understands that she cannot expect a raise" [syn: hope, desire] 5: To confer a trust upon; "The messenger was entrusted with the general's secret"; "I commit my soul to God" [syn: entrust, confide, commit] 6: extend credit to

tucks, tux /tʌks/

tucks

n : (plu of tuck) : narrow flattened pleats or folds that are stitched in place

v : (3ʳᵈ pers sing of tuck) 1: fits snugly into [syn: inserts] 2: pulls up or draws into a fold; "tucks the sheets" 3: makes a tuck or several folds in; "tucks the fabric" 4: draws fabric together and sews it tightly [syn: gathers, puckers]

tux

n : semiformal evening dress for men [syn: dinner jacket, tuxedo, black tie]

twill, 'twill /twɪl/

twill

adj : of textiles; having parallel raised lines [syn: corded, pique, twilled]

n 1: a weave used to produce the effect of parallel diagonal ribs [syn: twill weave] 2: a cloth with parallel diagonal lines or ribs

v : weave diagonal lines into; of textiles

'twill

contr : it will; " 'twill be cold in the morning"

HOMOPHONES

-U-

U (see ewe)
udder, utter

udder /'ʌdəɹ/
n : mammary gland of bovids (cows and sheep and goats) [syn: bag]

utter /'ʌtᵊɹ/
adj 1: without qualification; used informally as (often pejorative) intensifiers; "an arrant fool"; "a complete coward"; "a consummate fool"; "a double-dyed villain"; "gross negligence"; "a perfect idiot"; "pure folly"; "what a sodding mess"; "stark staring mad"; "a thoroughgoing villain"; "utter nonsense" [syn: arrant, complete, consummate, double-dyed, everlasting, gross, perfect, pure, sodding, stark, staring, thoroughgoing, utter] 2: total; "dead silence"; "utter seriousness" [syn: dead, utter]
v 1: articulate; either verbally or with a cry, shout, or noise; "She expressed her anger"; "He uttered a curse" [syn: express, give tongue to] 2: express audibly; utter sounds (not necessarily words); "She let out a big heavy sigh"; "He uttered strange sounds that nobody could understand" [syn: emit, let out, let loose] 3: express in speech; "She talks a lot of nonsense" [syn: talk, speak, mouth, verbalize] 4: put into circulation; of counterfeit currency

undo, undue /ʌn'du/
undo
v 1: cancel, annul, or reverse an action or its effect; "I wish I could undo my actions" 2: deprive of certain characteristics [syn: unmake] [ant: do] 3: cause the ruin or downfall of; "A single mistake undid the President and he had to resign" 4: cause to become loose; "undo the shoelace"; "untie the knot"; "loosen the necktie" [syn: untie, loosen] 5: remove the outer cover or wrapping of; "Let's unwrap the gifts!"; "undo the parcel" [syn: unwrap] [ant: wrap]
undue
adj 1: not yet payable; "an undue loan" [syn: not due] [ant: due] 2: not appropriate or proper (or even legal) in the circumstances; "undue influence"; "I didn't want to show undue excitement"; "accused of using undue force" [ant: due] 3: lacking justification or authorization; "unreasonable searches and seizures"; "desire for undue private profit"; "unwarranted limitations of personal freedom" [syn: unjustified, unwarranted] 4: beyond normal limits; "excessive charges"; "a book of inordinate length";

"his dress stops just short of undue elegance"; "unreasonable demands" [syn: excessive, inordinate, unreasonable]

urn (see earn)

use (see ewes)

HOMOPHONES

-V-

vail, vale, veil /vɛɪl/

vail

v : to yield or recede; to give place; to show respect by yielding, uncovering, or the like

vale

n : a long depression in the surface of the land that usually contains a river [syn: valley]

veil

n 1: a garment that covers the head and face [syn: head covering] 2: the inner embryonic membrane of higher vertebrates (especially when covering the head at birth) [syn: caul, embryonic membrane] 3: a vestment worn by a priest at High Mass in the Roman Catholic Church; a silk shawl [syn: humeral veil]

v : to obscure, or conceal with or as if with a veil; "a conspiracy of silence veiling it" [ant; unveil]

vain, vane, vein /vɛɪn/

vain

adj 1: characteristic of false pride; having an exaggerated sense of self-importance; "a conceited fool"; "an attitude of self-conceited arrogance"; "an egotistical disregard of others"; "so swollen by victory that he was unfit for normal duty"; "growing ever more swollen-headed and arbitrary"; "vain about her clothes" [syn: conceited, egotistic, egotistical, self-conceited, swollen, swollen-headed] 2: unproductive of success; "a fruitless search"; "futile years after her artistic peak"; "a sleeveless errand"; "a vain attempt" [syn: bootless, fruitless, futile, sleeveless]

vane

n 1: flat surface that rotates and pushes against air or water [syn: blade] 2: mechanical device attached to an elevated structure; rotates freely to show the direction of the wind [syn: weathervane, weather vane, wind vane] 3: the flattened web-like part of a feather consisting of a series of barbs on either side of the shaft [syn: web]

vein

n 1: a blood vessel that carries blood from the capillaries toward the heart; all veins except the pulmonary carry unaerated blood [syn: vena] 2: a distinctive style or manner; "he continued in this vein for several minutes" 3: one of the vascular bundles or ribs that form the branching framework of conducting and supporting tissues in a leaf or other plant organ [syn: nervure] 4: a layer of ore between layers of rock [syn: mineral vein] 5: one of the horny ribs that stiffen and support the wing of an insect [syn: nervure]

v : make a vein-like pattern

valance, valence

valance /'vælɛnts/

n : a decorative framework to conceal curtain fixtures at the top of a window casing [syn: cornice, valance board, pelmet]

valence /'vɛɪlɪnts/

n 1: (biology) a relative capacity to unite or react or interact as with antigens or a biological substrate [syn: valency] 2: (chemistry) a property of atoms or radicals; their combining power given in terms of the number of hydrogen atoms (or the equivalent) [syn: valency]

valiance, valiants /'vælɪnts/

valiance

n : the qualities of a hero or heroine; exceptional or heroic courage when facing danger (especially in battle); "he showed great heroism in battle"; "he received a medal for valor" [syn: heroism, gallantry, valor, valorousness, valiancy]

valiants

n : persons who exhibit valiance

variance, variants /'vɛəɹɪents/

variance

n 1: an event that departs from expectations [syn: discrepancy, variant] 2: discord that splits a group [syn: division] 3: the second moment around the mean; the expected value of the square of the deviations of a random variable from its mean value 4: a difference between conflicting facts or claims or opinions; "a growing divergence of opinion" [syn: discrepancy, disagreement, divergence] 5: the quality of being subject to variation [syn: variability, variableness] [ant: invariability, invariability] 6: an activity that varies from a norm or standard; "any variation in his routine was immediately reported" [syn: variation]

variants

n : (plu of variant) 1: events that depart from expectations [syn: discrepancies, variances] 2: (biology) groups of organisms within a species that differ in trivial ways from similar groups; " new strains of microorganisms" [syn: forms, strains] 3: variable quantities that are random [syn: random variable, variates, stochastic variables, chance variables] 4: some things a little different from others of the same type; " experimental versions of the night fighter " [syn: versions, variations]

vary, very

vary /'væɹɪ/

v 1: make or become different in some

I-206

particular way, without permanently losing one's or its former characteristics or essence; "her mood changes in accordance with the weather"; "The supermarket's selection of vegetables varies according to the season" [syn: change, alter] 2: be at variance with; be out of line with [syn: deviate, diverge, depart] [ant: conform] 3: be subject to change: "Prices vary" 4: make something more diverse and varied; "Vary the menu" [syn: variegate, motley]

very /'vɛɹi/

adj 1: precisely as stated; "the very center of town" 2: being the exact same one; not any other.; "this is the identical room we stayed in before"; "the themes of his stories are one and the same"; "saw the selfsame quotation in two newspapers"; "on this very spot"; "the very thing he said yesterday"; "the very man I want to see" [syn: identical, one and the same [syn: selfsame] 3: used to give emphasis to the relevance of the thing modified; "his very name struck terror"; "caught in the very act" 4: used to give emphasis: "the very essence of artistic expression is invention"- Irving R. Kaufman; "the very back of the room"

adv 1: intensifiers; "she was very gifted"; "he played very well"; "a really enjoyable evening"; (`real' is sometimes used informally for `really' as in "I'm real sorry about it"; `rattling' is informal as in "a rattling good yarn") [syn: really, real, rattling] 2: precisely so; "on the very next page"; "he expected the very opposite"

vellum, velum /'vɛlᵊm/

vellum

n 1: a heavy creamy-colored paper resembling parchment 2: fine parchment prepared from the skin of a young animal e.g. a calf or lamb

velum

n 1: membrane of the young sporophore of various mushrooms extending from the margin of the cap to the stem and is ruptured by growth; represented in mature mushroom by an annulus around the stem and sometimes a cortina on the margin of the cap [syn: partial veil] 2: membrane initially completely investing the young sporophore of various mushrooms that is ruptured by growth; represented in the mature mushroom by a volva around lower part of stem and scales on upper surface of the cap [syn: universal veil] 3: a muscular flap that closes off the nasopharynx during swallowing or speaking [syn: soft palate]

veracious, voracious

veracious /vɛ'ɹɛɪʃᵊs/

adj 1: habitually speaking the truth; "an honest man"; "a veracious witness" [syn: honest] 2: precisely accurate; "a veracious

account"

voracious /vɔ'ɹɛɪʃᵊs/

adj 1: excessively greedy and grasping; "a rapacious divorcee on the prowl"; "ravening creditors"; "paying taxes to voracious governments" [syn: rapacious, ravening] 2: devouring or craving food in great quantities; "edacious vultures"; "a rapacious appetite"; "ravenous as wolves"; "voracious sharks" [syn: edacious, esurient, rapacious, ravening, ravenous, wolfish]

verdure, verger /'vᵊdʒrɛˑ/

verdure

n 1: green foliage [syn: greenery] 2: lush greenness of flourishing vegetation [syn: greenness, verdancy]

verger

n : a church officer who takes care of the interior of the building and acts as an attendant (carries the verge) during ceremonies

verses, versus /'vᵊsɪs/ or /'vᵊsɪz/)

verses

n : (plu of verse) 1: literature in metrical form [syn: poetry, poesy] 2: pieces of poetry [syn: rhymes] 3: lines of metrical text [syn: verse lines]

v : (3ʳᵈ pers sing of verse) : composes verses; puts into verse [syn: versifies, poetizes]

versus

prep : against; (legal) "John Doe versus Richard Roe"; (sports) "Yankees vs. Angels"; (political) "United States v. Iraq" [syn: v., vs.]

vial, vile, viol

vial /vaɪl/

n : a small bottle that contains a drug (especially a sealed sterile container for injection by needle) [syn: phial, ampule, ampoule]

vile /vaɪl/

adj 1: morally reprehensible; "would do something as despicable as murder"; "ugly crimes"; "the vile development of slavery appalled them" [syn: despicable, ugly, unworthy] 2: (informal) thoroughly unpleasant; "filthy (or foul or nasty or vile) weather we're having" [syn: filthy, foul, nasty] 3: causing or able to cause nausea; "a nauseating smell"; "nauseous offal"; "a sickening stench" [syn: nauseating, nauseous, noisome, loathsome, offensive, sickening]

viol /'vaɪʲl/

n : any of a family of bowed stringed instruments that preceded the violin family

vice, vise /vaɪs/

vice

adj : pertaining to illegal sexual and gambling activities; "the police have an

HOMOPHONES

active vice squad"

n 1: moral weakness [syn: frailty] 2: a specific form of evildoing; "vice offends the moral

standards of the community"

prep : in the place of; "I'll have rice vice potatoes."

vise

n : a holding device attached to a workbench; has two jaws to hold a work piece firmly in place [syn: bench vise]

villain, villein /ˈvɪlɪn/

villain

n 1: a wicked or evil person [syn: scoundrel] 2: the principle bad character in a work of fiction

villein

n : (medieval Europe) a person who is bound to the land and owned by the feudal lord [syn: serf, helot]

viscous, viscus /ˈvɪskᵊs/

viscous

adj 1: having a relatively high resistance to flow [syn: syrupy] 2: having the properties of glue [syn: gluey, glutinous, gummy, mucilaginous, pasty, sticky, viscid]

viscus

n : a main organ that is situated inside the body [syn: internal organ]

-W-

wack, WAC, whack /wæk/

adj : very bad; "walked out of a really wack movie"

n : a person regarded as eccentric

WAC

n : a member of the Women's Army Corps (World War II)

whack

n : the act of hitting vigorously; "he gave the table a whack" [syn: knock, belt, rap, whang]

v : hit hard; "The teacher whacked the boy" [syn: wham, whop, wallop]

wacks, WACs, wax, whacks /wæks/

wacks

n : (plu of wack) (see wack)

WACs

n : (plu of Wac) (see wack)

wax

n : any of various substances of either mineral origin or plant or animal origin; they are solid at normal temperatures and insoluble in water

v 1: cover with wax; "wax the car" 2: go up or advance; "Sales were climbing after prices were lowered" [syn: mount, climb, rise] [ant: wane] 3: increase in phase; "the moon is waxing" [syn: full] [ant: wane]

whacks

n : (plu of whack) (see wack)

v : (3ʳᵈ pers sing of whack) (see wack)

waddle, wattle, what'll

waddle /ˈwadᵊl/

n : walking with a waddling gait; walking with short steps and the weight shifting from one foot to the other

v : walk unsteadily; "small children toddle" [syn: toddle, coggle, totter, dodder, paddle]

wattle /ˈwatᵊl/

n 1: a fleshy wrinkled and often brightly colored fold of skin hanging from the neck or throat of certain birds (chickens and turkeys) or lizards [syn: lappet] 2: framework consisting of stakes interwoven with branches to form a fence

v 1: build of or with wattle 2: interlace to form wattle

what'll /ˈwatᵊl/

contr : what will; "What'll I do when you are far away?"

wade, weighed /weɪd/

wade

v : walk (through relatively shallow water); "Can we wade across the river to the other side?"; "Wade the pond"

weighed

v : (past of weigh) (see way)

HOMOPHONES

wail, wale, whale /weɪl/

wail
n 1: a cry of sorrow and grief; "their pitiful laments could be heard throughout the ward" [syn: lament, lamentation, plaint]
v 1: emit long loud cries; "wail in self-pity", "howl with sorrow" [syn: howl, ululate, roar, yawl] 2: cry weakly or softly; "she wailed with pain" [syn: whimper, mewl]

wale
n 1: a raised mark on the skin (as produced by the blow of a whip); characteristic of many allergic reactions [syn: welt, weal, wheal] 2: thick plank forming a ridge along the side of a wooden ship [syn: strake]

whale
n 1: a very large person; impressive in size or qualities [syn: giant, hulk, heavyweight] 2: any of the larger cetacean mammals having a streamlined body and breathing through a blowhole on the head
v : hunt for whales

wailer, whaler /'weɪlɚ/

wailer
n : a mourner who utters long loud high-pitched cries

whaler
n 1: a seaman who works on a ship that hunts whales 2: a ship engaged in whale fishing [syn: whaling ship]

wain, wane /weɪn/

wain
n : large open farm wagon

wane
n : a gradual decline (in size or strength or power or number) [syn: ebb, ebbing]
v 1: grow smaller; "Interest in the project waned" [syn: decline, go down] 2: become smaller; "Interest in his novels waned" [ant: wax] 3: decrease in phase; "the moon is waning" [ant: wax]

waist, waste /weɪst/

waist
n 1: the narrowing of the body between the ribs and hips [syn: waistline] 2: the narrow part of the shoe connecting the heel and the wide part of the sole [syn: shank]

waste
adj 1: disposed of as useless; "waste paper" [syn: cast-off, discarded, junked, scrap] 2: located in a dismal or remote area; desolate; "a desert island"; "a godforsaken wilderness crossroads"; "a wild stretch of land"; "waste places" [syn: desert, godforsaken, wild]
n 1: any materials unused and rejected as worthless or unwanted; "they collect the waste once a week"; "much of the waste material is carried off in the sewers" [syn: waste material, waste matter, waste product] 2: useless or profitless activity; using or expending or consuming thoughtlessly or carelessly; "if the effort brings no compensating gain it is a waste"; "mindless dissipation of natural resources" [syn: wastefulness, dissipation] 3: the trait of wasting resources; "a life characterized by thriftlessness and waste"; "the wastefulness of missed opportunities" [syn: thriftlessness, wastefulness] 4: an uninhabited wilderness that is worthless for cultivation; "the barrens of central Africa"; "the trackless wastes of the desert" [syn: barren, wasteland] 5: (law) reduction in the value of an estate caused by act or neglect [syn: permissive waste]
v 1: spend thoughtlessly; throw away; "He wasted his inheritance on his insincere friends" [syn: blow, squander] [ant: conserve] 2: use inefficiently or inappropriately; "waste heat"; "waste a joke on an unappreciative audience" 3: get rid of; "We waste the dirty water by channeling it into the sewer" 4: run off as waste: "The water wastes back into the ocean" [syn: run off] 5: get rid of; kill; "The mafia liquidated the informer" [syn: liquidate, knock off, do in] 6: spend extravagantly; "waste not, want not" [syn: consume, squander, ware] 7: lose vigor, health, or flesh, as through grief; "After her husband died, she just pined away" [syn: pine away, languish] 8: cause to grow thin or weak; "The treatment emaciated him" [syn: emaciate, macerate] 9: devastate or ravage; "The enemy lay waste to the countryside after the invasion" [syn: lay waste to, devastate, desolate, ravage] 10: waste away; "Political prisoners are wasting away in many prisons all over the world" [syn: rot]

wait, weight /weɪt/

wait
n 1: time during which some action is awaited; "instant replay caused too long a delay"; "he ordered a hold in the action" [syn: delay, hold, time lag, postponement] 2: the act of waiting (remaining inactive in one place while expecting something); "the wait was an ordeal for him" [syn: waiting]
v 1: stay in one place and anticipate or expect something; "I had to wait on line for an hour to get the tickets" 2: wait before acting [syn: hold off, hold back] 3: look forward to the probably occurrence of: "We were expecting a visit from our relatives"; "She is looking to a promotion"; "he is waiting to be drafted" [syn: expect, look, await] 4: wait on tables; serve as a waiter; in restaurants "I'm waiting on tables at Maxim's"

weight
n 1: the vertical force exerted by a mass

as a result of gravity 2: equipment used in callisthenic exercises and weightlifting [syn: exercising weight] 3: the relative importance granted to something; "his opinion carries great weight" 4: an artifact that is heavy 5: an oppressive feeling of heavy force; "bowed down by the weight of responsibility" 6: a system of units used to express the weight of something [syn: system of weights] 7: a unit used to measure weight; "he placed two weights in the scale pan" [syn: weight unit] 8: (statistics) a coefficient assigned to elements of a frequency distribution in order to represent their relative importance [syn: weighting]

v 1: weight down with a load [syn: burden, burthen, weight down] [ant: unburden] 2: present with a bias [syn: slant, angle]

waive, wave /weɪv/

waive

v 1: do without; "We are dispensing with formalities" [syn: relinquish, forgo, foreswear, dispense with] 2: lose or lose the right to by some error, offense, or crime [syn: forfeit, give up, throw overboard, forgo] [ant: claim]

wave

n 1: one of a series of ridges that moves across the surface of a liquid (especially across a large body of water) [syn: moving ridge] 2: a movement like that of an ocean wave; "a wave of settlers"; "troops advancing in waves" 3: (physics) a progressive disturbance propagated without displacement of the medium itself [syn: undulation] 4: something that rises rapidly and dies away; "a wave of emotion swept over him"; "there was a sudden wave of buying before the market closed" 5: the act of signaling by a movement of the hand [syn: waving, wafture] 6: a hairdo that creates undulations in the hair 7: an undulating curve

v 1: signal with the hands or nod; "She waved to her friends"; "He waved his hand hospitably" [syn: beckon] 2: move or swing back and forth; "She waved her gun." [syn: brandish, flourish] 3: move in a wavy pattern, as of curtains [syn: undulate, flap] 4: twist or roll into coils or ringlets; "curl my hair, please" [syn: curl] 5: set waves in; of hair

waiver, waver /ˈweɪvəʳ/

waiver

n : a formal written statement of relinquishment [syn: release, discharge]

waver

n 1: someone who communicates by waving 2: the act of pausing uncertainly; "there was a hesitation in his speech" [syn: hesitation, falter, faltering] 3: the act of moving back and forth [syn: flutter, flicker]

v 1: pause or hold back in uncertainty or unwillingness: "Authorities hesitate to quote exact figures." [syn: hesitate, waffle] 2: be unsure or weak; "Their enthusiasm is faltering" [syn: falter] 3: move hesitatingly, as if about to give way [syn: falter] 4: move in an unstable manner [syn: fluctuate, vacillate] 5: move back and forth very rapidly, as of a candle [syn: flicker, flitter, flutter, quiver] 6: sway to and fro [syn: weave] 7: give off unsteady sounds, alternating in amplitude or frequency [syn: quaver]

walk, wok

walk /wɔk/

n 1: the act of traveling by foot; "walking is a healthy form of exercise" [syn: walking] 2: (baseball) an advance to first base by a batter who receives four balls; "he worked the pitcher for a base on balls" [syn: base on balls, pass] 3: manner of walking; "he had a funny walk" [syn: manner of walking] 4: the act of walking somewhere; "he took a walk after lunch" 5: a path set aside for walking; "after the blizzard he shoveled the front walk" [syn: walkway] 6: a slow gait of a horse in which two feet are always on the ground 7: careers in general; "it happens in all walks of life" [syn: walk of life]

v 1: use one's feet to advance; advance by steps; "Walk, don't run!"; "We walked instead of driving"; "She walks with a slight limp"; "The patient cannot walk yet"; "Walk over to the cabinet" [ant: ride] 2: traverse or cover by walking; "Walk the tightrope"; "Paul walked the streets of Damascus"; "She walks 3 miles every day" 3: accompany or escort; "I'll walk you to your car" 4: obtain a base on balls, in baseball 5: live or behave in a specified manner; "walk in sadness" 6: take a walk; go for a walk; walk for pleasure; "The lovers held hands while walking"; "We like to walk every Sunday" [syn: take the air] 7: give a base on balls to; in baseball 8: be or act in association with; "We must walk with our dispossessed brothers and sisters"; "Walk with God" 9: make walk; "He walks the horse up the mountain"; "Walk the dog twice a day" 10: walk at a pace

wok /wak/

n : pan with a convex bottom; used for frying in Chinese cooking

wand, wanned /wand/

wand

n 1: a baton used by a magician or water diviner 2: a ceremonial or emblematic staff [syn: scepter, verge]

wanned

v : (past of wan) : became pale and sickly

HOMOPHONES

want, wont /wɒnt/

want

n 1: a state of extreme poverty [syn: privation, deprivation]   2: the state of needing something that is absent or unavailable; "there is a serious lack of insight into the problem"; "water is the critical deficiency in desert regions"; "for want of a nail the shoe was lost" [syn: lack, deficiency]

3: anything that is necessary but lacking; "he had sufficient means to meet his simple needs"; "I tried to supply his wants" [syn: need]   4: a specific feeling of desire; "he got his wish"; "he was above all wishing and desire" [syn: wish, wishing]

v 1: feel or have a desire for; want strongly; "I want to go home now; "I want my own room" [syn: desire]   2: have need of: "This piano wants the attention of a competent tuner" [syn: need, require]   3: wish or demand the presence of; "I want you here at noon!"   4: hunt or look for; want for a particular reason: "Your former neighbor is wanted by the FBI"; "Uncle Sam wants you"   5: be without, lack; be deficient in; "want courtesy"; "want the strength to go on living"; "flood victims wanting food and shelter" [syn: lack]

wont

n 1: an established custom; "it was their habit to dine at 7 every evening" [syn: habit]   2: a pattern of behavior acquired through frequent repetition; "she was wont to twirl the ends of her hair"; "long use had hardened him to it" [syn: habit, use]

wants (see once)

war, wore /wɔɹ/

war

n 1: the waging of armed conflict against an enemy; "thousands of people were killed in the war" [syn: warfare]   2: a legal state created by a declaration of war and ended by official declaration during which the international rules of war apply; "war was declared in November but actual fighting did not begin until the following spring" [syn: state of war] [ant: peace]   3: an active struggle between competing entities; "a price war"; "a war of wits"; "diplomatic warfare" [syn: warfare]   4: a concerted campaign to end something that is injurious; "the war on poverty"; "the war against crime"

v : make or wage war [ant: make peace]

wore

v : (past of wear) (see ware) : "She wore the same dress two days in a row."

ward, warred /wɔɹd/

ward

n 1: a person who is under the protection or in the custody of another   2: a district into which a city or town is divided for the

purpose of administration and elections   3: block forming a division of a hospital (or a suite of rooms) shared by patients who need a similar kind of care; "they put her in a 4-bed ward" [syn: hospital ward][syn: cellblock]

v : watch over or shield from danger or harm; protect; "guard my possessions while I'm away" [syn: guard]

warred

v : (past of war) (see war) "The United States and Iraq warred in 2003."

ware, wear, weir, where / wеəɹ/

ware

n : articles of the same kind or material; usually used in combination: silverware; software

v : spend extravagantly; "waste not, want not" [syn: consume, squander, waste]

wear

n 1: impairment resulting from long use; "the tires showed uneven wear"   2: covering designed to be worn on a person's body [syn: clothing, clothes, apparel, vesture, wearing apparel, article

of clothing]   3: the act of having on your person as a covering or adornment; "she bought it for everyday wear" [syn: wearing]

v 1: be dressed in; "She was wearing yellow that day" [syn: have on]   2: have on one's person; "He wore a red ribbon"; "bear a scar" [syn: bear]   3: have in one's aspect; wear an expression of one's attitude or personality; "He always wears a smile"

4: deteriorate through use or stress; "The constant friction wore out the cloth" [syn: wear off, wear out, wear thin]   5: have or show an appearance of; "wear one's hair in a certain way"   6: last and be usable; "This dress wore well for almost ten years" [syn: hold out, endure]   7: go to pieces; "The lawn mower finally broke"; "The gears wore out"; "The old chair finally fell apart completely" [syn: break, wear out, bust, fall apart]   8: exhaust or tire though overuse or great strain or stress; "We wore ourselves out on this hike" [syn: tire, wear upon, tire out, weary, jade, wear out, outwear, wear down, fag out, fag, fatigue] [ant: refresh]   9: put clothing on one's body; "What should I wear today?"; "He put on his best suit for the wedding"; "The princess donned a long blue dress"; "The queen assumed the stately robes"; "He got into his jeans" [syn: put on, get into, don, assume]

weir (also /wɪɹ/)

n 1: a low dam built across a stream to raise its level or divert its flow   2: a fence or wattle built across a stream to catch or retain fish

HOMOPHONES

where

adv 1: at or in what place; "Where is the calculator?" 2: in what situation or position: "Where would we be without a place to get water?" 3:from what place or source; "Where did you get this book?" 4: to what place; toward what end; "Where is this road leading?"

conj 1: at what or which place; "He moved to the country, where it's quiet." 2: In a place in which: "He works where the atmosphere is friendly." 3: in any place or situation in which; wherever; "Where there's smoke, there's fire". 4: to a place in which; "You should go where it's warmer." 5: to a place or situation in which; "I will go where I can be warm."

n 1:The place or occasion; "We know the ins but not the outs of it." 2: what place, source, or cause; "Where are they from?"

warn, worn /wɔɹn/

warn

v 1: notify of danger, potential harm, or risk; "The director warned him that he might be fired"; "you will get hungry if you don't eat," he warned; "The doctor warned me about the dangers of smoking" 2: admonish or counsel in terms of someone's behavior; "I warned him not to go too far"; "I warn you against false assumptions"; "She warned him to be quiet" [syn: discourage, admonish, monish] 3: ask to go away; "The old man warned the children off his property" 4: notify, usually in advance; "I warned you that I would ask some difficult questions"

worn

adj 1: affected by wear; damaged by long use; "worn threads on the screw"; "a worn suit"; "the worn pockets on the jacket" [ant: unworn] 2: showing the wearing effects of overwork or care or suffering; "looking careworn as she bent over her mending"; "her face was drawn and haggard from sleeplessness"; "that raddled but still noble face"; "shocked to see the worn look of his handsome young face"- Charles Dickens [syn: careworn, drawn, haggard, raddled]

v : (past of wear) (see ware); "He has worn out his welcome."

wart, wort /wɔɹt/

wart

n 1: any small rounded protuberance (as on certain plants or animals) 2: (pathology) a firm abnormal elevated blemish on the skin; caused by a virus [syn: verruca]

wort

n 1: usually used in combination: `liverwort'; `milkwort'; `whorlywort' 2: unfermented or fermenting malt

wary, wherry /'wæɹi/ or /'wɛəɹi/

wary

adj 1: marked by keen caution and watchful prudence; "they were wary in their movements"; "a wary glance at the black clouds"; "taught to be wary of strangers [ant: unwary] 2: openly distrustful and unwilling to confide [syn: leery, mistrustful, suspicious, untrusting]

wherry

n 1: sailing barge used especially in East Anglia [syn: Norfolk wherry] 2: light rowboat for use in racing or for transporting goods and passengers in inland waters and harbors

watt, what, wot /wat/

watt

n 1: a unit of power equal to 1 joule per second; the power dissipated by a current of 1 ampere flowing across a resistance of 1 ohm [syn: W, EI, I²R]

what

pron 1: which thing or which particular one of many; "What are they having for lunch? What did he want?" 2: which kind, character, or designation; "What are these things?" 3: one of how much value or significance; "What is the meaning of life?" 4: that which; "Listen to what she offers." 5: whatever thing that; "come what may" 6: (informal) something: I'll tell you what. 6: (nonstandard) which, who, or that: It's the poor what gets the blame.

adj 1: which one or ones of several or many; "What university are you attending?" "You should know what musical that song is from." 2: whatever; "They soon repaired what damage had been done." 3: how great; how astonishing; "What a fool!"

adv : how much; in what respect; how; "What does it matter?"

conj : that: "I don't know but what I'll go."

interj : used to express surprise, incredulity, or other strong and sudden excitement.

wot

v : (1st and 3rd pers sing of wit) 1: to be or become aware of; learn 2: to know.

wattle, what'll /'watᵊl/

wattle

n 1: a fleshy wrinkled and often brightly colored fold of skin hanging from the neck or throat of certain birds (chickens and turkeys) or lizards [syn: lappet] 2: framework consisting of stakes interwoven with branches to form a fence

v 1: build of or with wattle 2: interlace to form wattle

what'll

contr : what will; "What'll you take to the party?"

HOMOPHONES

watts, what's /wats/

watts

n : (plu of watt); "The toaster uses 1,500 watts."

what's

contr : what is; "What's going on here?"

way, weigh, whey /weɪ/

way

n 1: a manner of performance; "a manner of living"; "in the characteristic New York style"; "a way of life" [syn: manner, mode, style, fashion] 2: how a result is obtained or an end is achieved; "a means of control"; "an example is the best agency of instruction"; "the true way to success" [syn: means, agency] 3: a journey or passage; "they are on the way" 4: the condition of things generally; "that's the way it is" or "I felt the same way" 5: a course of conduct; "the path of virtue"; "we went our separate ways"; "our paths in life led us apart"; "genius usually follows a revolutionary path" [syn: path, way of life] 6: any artifact consisting of a road or path affording passage from one place to another; "he said he was looking for the way out" 7: a line leading to a place or point: "he looked the other direction"; "didn't know the way home" [syn: direction] 8: the property of distance in general; "it's a long way to Moscow"; (colloquial) "he went a long ways" [syn: ways] 9: doing as one pleases or chooses: "if I had my way" 10: a general category of things; used in the expression "in the way of": "they didn't have much in the way of clothing" 11: space for movement; "room to pass"; "make way for": "hardly enough elbow room to turn around" [syn: room, elbow room] 12: a portion of something divided into shares: "the split the loot three ways"

adv : (informal) to a great degree or by a great distance; very much; "way over budget"; "way off base"; "right smart" is regional (US S and midland) as in "the other side of the hill is right smart steeper than the side we are on" [syn: right smart]

weigh

v 1: have a certain weight 2: show consideration for; take into account; "You must consider her age"; "The judge considered the offender's youth and was lenient" [syn: consider, count] 3: determine the weight of; "The butcher weighed the chicken" 4: have weight; have import, carry weight; "It does not matter much" [syn: count, matter] 5: to be oppressive or burdensome; "weigh heavily on the mind", "Something pressed on his mind" [syn: press]

whey

n 1: the serum or watery part of milk that is separated from the curd in making cheese [syn: milk whey] 2: watery part of milk produced when raw milk sours and coagulates: "Little Miss Muffet sat on a tuffet eating some curds and whey"

we, wee, whee /wi/

we

pron (3rd pers plu) : "We went to the movies last night."

wee

adj 1: (used informally) very small; "a wee tot" [syn: bitty, teensy, teeny, weeny, weensy, teensy-weensy, teeny-weeny, itty-bitty, itsy-bitsy] 2: very early; "the wee hours of the morning"

n : (Scottish) a short time; "bide a wee"

v : eliminate urine; "Again, the cat had made on the expensive rug" [syn: make, urinate, piddle, puddle, micturate, piss, pee, pee-pee, make water, relieve oneself, take a leak, spend a penny, wee-wee, pass water]

whee

interj : expression of delight or exuberance

weak, week /wik/

weak

adj 1: having little physical or spiritual strength; "a weak radio signal"; "a weak link" [ant: strong] 2: overly diluted; thin and insipid; "washy coffee"; "watery milk"; "weak tea" [syn: watery, washy] 3: lacking power [syn: powerless] [ant: powerful] 4: used of vowels or syllables; pronounced with little or no stress; "a syllable that ends in a short vowel is a light syllable"; "a weak stress on the second syllable" [syn: unaccented, light] 5: having the attributes of man as opposed to e.g. divine beings; "I'm only human"; "frail humanity" [syn: fallible, frail, imperfect] 6: lacking force; feeble; "a forceless argument" [syn: forceless] 7: lacking physical strength or vitality; "a feeble old woman"; "her body looked sapless" [syn: decrepit, feeble, infirm, sapless, weakly] 8: (grammar) used of verbs having standard (or regular) inflection 9: lacking physical strength or vigor 10: characterized by excessive softness or self-indulgence; "an effeminate civilization" [syn: effeminate]

week

n 1: any period of seven consecutive days; "it rained for a week" [syn: hebdomad] 2: a period of seven consecutive days starting on Sunday [syn: calendar week] 3: hours or days of work in a calendar week; "they worked a 40-hour week" [syn: workweek]

weal, we'll, wheal, wheel /wil/

weal

n : a raised mark on the skin (as produced

HOMOPHONES

by the blow of a hip); characteristic of many allergic reactions [syn: wale, welt, wheal]

we'll

contr : we will; "We'll go to Florida next month."

wheal

n : (alt weal)

wheel

n 1: a simple machine consisting of a circular frame with spokes (or a solid disc) that can rotate on a shaft or axle (as in vehicles or other machines) 2: a handwheel that is used for steering [syn: steering wheel] 3: a circular helm to control the rudder of a vessel 4: game equipment consisting of a rotating wheel with slots that is used for gambling; players bet on which slot the roulette ball will stop in [syn: roulette wheel] 5: an instrument of torture that stretches or disjoints or mutilates victims [syn: rack] 6: a cycle that has two wheels; moved by foot pedals [syn: bicycle, bike]

v 1: change directions as of revolving on a pivot; "They wheeled their horses around and left" [syn: wheel around] 2: wheel somebody or something [syn: wheel around] 3: move along on or as if on wheels or a wheeled vehicle; "The President's convoy rolled past the crowds" [syn: roll] 4: ride a bicycle [syn: bicycle, cycle, bike, pedal]

weald, wheeled, wield /wild/

weald

n : (British) an area of open or forested country

wheeled

adj : having wheels; often used in combination [ant: wheelless]

v : (past of wheel) (see weal); "They wheeled their horses around and left."

wield

v 1: of power or authority [syn: exert, maintain] 2: handle effectively; "The burglar wielded an axe" [syn: handle]

wean, ween /win/

wean

v 1: deprive (infants) of mother's milk 2: detach the affections of

ween

v : (archaic); to think; suppose

weather, wether, whether /ˈwɛðəɹ/

weather

adj : towards the side exposed to wind [syn: upwind]

n : the meteorological conditions: temperature and wind and clouds and precipitation; "they were hoping for good weather"; "every day we have weather conditions and yesterday was no exception" [syn: weather condition,

atmospheric condition]

v 1: face or endure with courage; "She braved the elements" [syn: endure, brave, brave out] 2: cause to slope 3: sail to the windward of 4: change under the action or influence of the weather; "The cold, wet climate will quickly weather the old hut"

wether

n : male sheep especially a castrated one

whether

conj 1: used in indirect questions to introduce one alternative; "You should find out whether the store is open." 2: used to introduce alternative possibilities; "Whether she wins or whether she loses, this is her last tournament." 3: either; "He passed the test, whether by skill or luck."

weave, we've /wiv/

weave

n : pattern of weaving or structure of a fabric

v 1: interlace as if weaving [syn: interweave] [ant: unweave] 2: of textiles; create a piece of cloth by interlacing strands of fabric, such as wool or cotton [syn: tissue] 3: sway to and fro [syn: waver] 4: to move or cause to move in a sinuous, spiral, or circular course; "the river winds through the hills"; "the path meanders through the vineyards"; "sometimes, the gout wanders through the entire body" [syn: wind, thread, meander, wander]

we've

contr : we have; "We've searched the whole house."

we'd, weed /wid/

we'd

contr : we would; We'd help you if we had the time."

weed

n 1: any plant that crowds out cultivated plants [ant: cultivated plant] 2: a strong-smelling plant from whose dried leaves a number of euphoriant and hallucinogenic drugs are prepared (see gage) 3: a soft drug consisting of the dried leaves of the hemp plant (see gage); smoked or chewed for euphoric effect

v : clear of weeds; "weed the garden"

wedding, wetting, whetting /ˈwɛdɪŋ/

wedding

n 1: marriage ceremony usually with its accompanying festivities [syn: nuptials] 2: an act, process, or instance of joining in close association 3: a wedding anniversary or its celebration; usually used in combination "golden wedding"

wetting

v 1: causing to become wet; "Wetting your face" [ant: drying] 2: making one's bed or clothes wet by urinating; "This eight year old boy is still wetting his bed"

whetting

v 1: making keen or more acute; "whetting my appetite" [syn: quickening]   2: sharpening by rubbing, as on a whetstone

wees, wheeze /wiz/

wees

v : (3rd pers sing of wee) : "The cat wees in the litter box."

wheeze

n 1: breathing with a husky or whistling sound 2: a humorous anecdote or remark [syn: joke, gag, laugh, jest, jape, yak]
v : breathe with difficulty

weld, welled /wɛld/

weld

n 1: European mignonette cultivated as a source of yellow dye; naturalized in North America [syn: dyer's rocket, dyer's mignonette, Reseda luteola] 2: a metal joint formed by softening with heat and fusing or hammering together 1: join together by heating, as of metals2: unite closely or intimately; "Her gratitude welded her to him"

welled

v : (past of well) : came up, as of liquids: "Tears welled in her eyes" [syn: swelled]

wen, when /wɛn/

wen

n : a common cyst of the skin; filled with fatty matter (sebum) that is secreted by a sebaceous gland that has been blocked [syn: sebaceous cyst, pilar cyst, steatocystoma]

when

adv : as soon as; "once we are home, we can rest" [syn: once]

wends, wens, when's /wɛnz/

wends

v : (3rd pers sing of wend) : direct one's course or way; "he wends his way through the crowds"

wens

n : (plu of wen)

when's

contr : when is ; "When's supper going to be ready?"

we're, weir /wiɹ/

we're

contr : we are; "We're happy that you could visit us."

weir (also /wɛəɹ/)

n 1: a low dam built across a stream to raise its level or divert its flow 2: a fence or wattle built across a stream to catch or retain fish

were, whir /wəɹ/

were

v : (past plu of be) ; "We were happy to finally arrive."

whir

n : sound of something in rapid motion:

"whir of a bird's wings"; "the whir of the propellers" [syn: whirr, whirring, birr]
v : make a soft swishing sound, as of a motor working or wings flapping [syn: whizz, whiz, whirr, birr, purr]

wet, whet /wɛt/

wet

adj 1: covered or soaked with a liquid such as water; "a wet bathing suit"; "wet sidewalks"; "wet paint"; "wet weather" [ant: dry]   2: supporting or permitting the legal production and sale of alcoholic beverages; "a wet candidate running on a wet platform"; "a wet county" [ant: dry] 3: producing or secreting milk; "a wet nurse"; "a wet cow"; "lactating cows" [syn: lactating] [ant: dry] 4: consisting of or trading in alcoholic liquor; "a wet cargo"; "a wet canteen"   5: slang for 'drunk' [syn: besotted, blind drunk, blotto, crocked, fuddled, loaded, pie-eyed, pissed, pixilated, plastered, potty, slopped, sloshed, smashed, soaked, soused, stiff, tight, tipsy]
n : wetness caused by water; "drops of wet gleamed on the window" [syn: moisture]
v 1: cause to become wet; "Wet your face" [ant: dry] 2: make one's bed or clothes wet by urinating; "This eight year old boy still wets his bed"

whet

v 1: make keen or more acute; "whet my appetite" [syn: quicken] 2: sharpen by rubbing, as on a whetstone

whew (see hew)

which, witch /wɪtʃ/

which

pron 1: what particular one or ones; "Which of these is yours?" 2: The one or ones previously mentioned or implied, specifically 3: used as a relative pronoun in a clause that provides additional information about the antecedent; "my house, which is small and old" 4: used as a relative pronoun preceded by that or a preposition in a clause that defines or restricts the antecedent; "that which he needed"; "the subject on which she spoke" 5: used instead of 'that' as a relative pronoun in a clause that defines or restricts the antecedent; "The movie which was shown later was better." 6: any of the things, events, or people designated or implied; whichever; "Choose which you like best." 7: a thing or circumstance that; "He left early, which was wise."
adj 1: what particular one or ones of a number of things or people; "Which part of town do you mean?" 2: any one or any number of; whichever; "Use which door you please." 3: being the one or ones previously mentioned or implied; "It started to rain, at which point we ran."

HOMOPHONES

witch

n 1: a female sorcerer or magician [syn: enchantress] 2: a being (usually female) imagined to have special powers derived from the devil 3: an ugly evil-looking old woman [syn: hag, beldam, beldame, crone] 4: a despised or hated woman

v : cast a spell over someone or something; put a hex on someone or something [syn: **hex**, bewitch, glamour, enchant, jinx]

Whig, wig /wɪg/

Whig

n 1: person who urged social reform in 19th century England 2: supporter of the American Revolution 3: a member of the Whig Party in the United States in pre-Civil-War times

wig

n 1: hairpiece covering the head and made of human or synthetic hair 2: British slang for a scolding [syn: wigging]

while, wile /waɪl/

while

n : a period of indeterminate length (usually short) marked by some action or condition; "he was here for a little while"; "I need to rest for a piece"; "a spell of good weather" [syn: piece, spell]

conj : during the time that; "Watch TV while I cook dinner."

v : pass idle time without being bored; "while away the time"

wile

n : the use of tricks to deceive someone (usually to extract money from them) [syn: trickery, chicanery, guile, shenanigan]

whiled, wild /waɪld/

whiled

v : (past of while) : "They whiled away the time watching TV."

wild

adj 1: marked by extreme lack of restraint or control; "wild ideas"; "wild talk"; "wild originality"; "wild parties" [ant: tame] 2: in a natural state; not tamed or domesticated or cultivated; "wild geese"; "edible wild plants" [syn: untamed] [ant: tame] 3: in a state of extreme emotion; "wild with anger"; "wild with grief" 4: deviating widely from an intended course; "a wild bullet"; "a wild pitch" 5: (of colors or sounds) intensely vivid or loud; "a violent clash of colors"; "her dress was a violent red"; "a violent noise"; "wild colors"; "wild shouts" [syn: violent] 6: not subjected to control or restraint; "a violin played with a wild exuberance" 7: talking or behaving irrationally; "a raving lunatic" [syn: raving, raving mad] 8: produced without being planted or without human labor; "wild strawberries" [syn: spontaneous] 9: located in a dismal or remote area; desolate; "a desert island";

"a godforsaken wilderness crossroads"; "a wild stretch of land"; "waste places" [syn: desert, godforsaken, waste] 10: without civilizing influences; "barbarian invaders"; "barbaric practices"; "a savage people"; "fighting is crude and uncivilized especially if the weapons are efficient"-Margaret Meade; "wild tribes" [syn: barbarian, barbaric, savage, uncivilized] 11: (of the elements) as if showing violent anger; "angry clouds on the horizon"; "furious winds"; "the raging sea" [syn: angry, furious, raging, tempestuous]

n 1: a wild primitive state untouched by civilization; "he lived in the wild" [syn: natural state, state of nature] 2: a wild and uninhabited area [syn: wilderness]adv 1: in an uncontrolled and rampant manner; "weeds grew rampantly around here" [syn: rampantly] 2: in a wild or undomesticated manner; "growing wild"; "roaming wild"

whin, win /wɪn/

whin

n 1: very spiny and dense evergreen shrub with fragrant golden-yellow flowers; common throughout western Europe [syn: gorse, furze, Irish gorse, Ulex europaeus] 2: small Eurasian shrub having clusters of yellow flowers that yield a dye; common as weed in England and United States; sometimes grown as an ornamental [syn: woodwaxen, dyer's greenweed, dyer's-broom, dyeweed, greenweed, woadwaxen, Genista tinctoria]

win

n 1: a victory (as in a race or other competition); "he was happy to get the win" 2: something won (especially money) [syn: winnings, profits] [ant: losses]

v 1: be the winner in a contest or competition; be victorious; "He won the Gold Medal in skating"; "Our home team won"; "Win the game" [ant: lose] 2: win something through one's efforts [syn: gain] [ant: lose] 3: obtain advantages, such as points, etc.; "The home team was gaining ground"; "After defeating the Knicks, the Blazers pulled ahead of the Lakers in the battle for the number-one playoff berth in the Western Conference" [syn: gain, advance, pull ahead, make headway, get ahead, gain ground] [ant: fall back]

whine, wine /waɪn/

whine

n : a complaint uttered in a plaintive whining way [syn: whimper]

v 1: move with a whining sound; "The bullets were whining past us" 2: talk in a tearful manner [syn: snivel] 3: complain whiningly [syn: grizzle, yammer, yawp]

wine

n 1: fermented juice (of grapes especially)

HOMOPHONES

[syn: vino] 2: a red as dark as red wine [syn: wine-colored]

v 1: drink wine 2: treat to wine; "Our relatives in Italy wined and dined us for a week"

whined, wind, wined, wynd
/waɪnd/

whined

v : (past of whined) (see whine): "She whined after losing the tennis match."

wind

n: the act of winding or twisting; "he put the key in the old clock and gave it a good wind" [syn: winding, twist]

v 1: to move or cause to move in a sinuous, spiral, or circular course; "the river winds through the hills"; "the path meanders through the vineyards"; "sometimes, the gout wanders through the entire body" [syn: weave, thread, meander, wander] 2: extend in curves and turns; "The road winds around the lake" [syn: curve] 3: wrap or coil around; "roll your hair around your finger"; "Twine the thread around the spool" [syn: wrap, roll, twine] [ant: unwind] 4: catch the scent of; get wind of; "The dog nosed out the drugs" [syn: scent, nose] 5: of springs [syn: wind up] 6: form into a wreath [syn: wreathe] 7: raise or haul up with or as if with mechanical help; "hoist the bicycle onto the roof of the car" [syn: hoist, lift] 8: tighten the spring of (a mechanisms); wind up the toy" [syn: wind up]

wined

v : (past of wine) (see whine)

wynd

n : a narrow lane

whines, winds, wines
/waɪnz/

whines

n : (plu of whine) : complaints uttered in a plaintive whining way [syn: whimpers]

v : (3rd pers sing of whine) 1: moves with a whining sound; "The bullets were whining past us" 2: talks in a tearful manner [syn: snivels] 3: complains whiningly [syn: grizzles, yammers, yawps]

winds

v : (3rd pers sing of wind) 1: moves or causes to move in a sinuous, spiral, or circular course; "the river winds through the hills"; "the path meanders through the vineyards"; "sometimes, the gout wanders through the entire body" [syn: weaves, threads, meanders, wanders] 2: extends in curves and turns; "The road winds around the lake" [syn: curves] 3: wraps or coils around; "roll your hair around your finger"; "Twines the thread around the spool" [syn: wraps, rolls, twines] [ant: unwinds] 4: catches the scent of; gets wind of; "The dog nosed out the drugs"

[syn: scents, noses] 5: coils the spring of (some mechanical device) by turning a stem; "wind your watch" [syn: winds up] 6: forms into a wreath [syn: wreathes] 7: raises or hauls up with or as if mechanical help; "hoists the bicycle onto the roof of the car" [syn: hoists, lifts]

wines

n : (plu of wine) 1: fermented juices (of grapes especially); "California wines are excellent."

v : (3rd pers sing of wine) 1: drinks wine 2: treats to wine; "He wines and dines his family."

whirl, whorl /wɜːl/

whirl

n 1: confused movement; "he was caught up in a whirl of work"; "a commotion of people fought for the exits" [syn: commotion] 2: the shape of something rotating rapidly [syn: swirl, vortex, convolution] 3: a usually brief attempt; "he took a crack at it"; "I gave it a whirl" [syn: crack, fling, go, pass, offer] 4: the act of rotating rapidly; "he gave the crank a spin"; "it broke off after much twisting" [syn: spin, twirl, twist, twisting]

v 1: turn in a twisting or spinning motion; "The leaves swirled in the autumn wind" [syn: twirl, swirl, twiddle] 2: cause to spin; "spin a coin" [syn: birl, spin, twirl] 3: flow in a circular current, of liquids [syn: eddy, purl, whirlpool, swirl] 4: revolve quickly and repeatedly around one's own axis; "The dervishes whirl around and around without getting dizzy" [syn: spin, spin around, reel, gyrate] 5: fly around, as of paper on the sidewalk, or clothes in a dryer, or rising smoke in the wind [syn: skirl, tumble, whirl around]

whorl

n 1: a round shape formed by a series of concentric circles [syn: coil, roll, curl, curlicue, ringlet, gyre, scroll] 2: a strand or cluster of hair [syn: lock, curl, ringlet] 3: a structure consisting of something wound in a continuous series of loops; "a coil of rope" [syn: coil, spiral, volute, helix]

whirled, whorled, world
/wɜːld/

whirled

v : (past of whirl)

whorled

adj 1: like the pattern basic to the human fingerprint [syn: looped] 2: in the shape of a coil [syn: coiling, helical, spiral, spiraling, volute, voluted, turbinate] 3: forming one or more whorls (especially a whorl of leaves around a stem) [syn: verticillate, verticillated]

world

adj : involving the entire earth; not limited or provincial in scope; "global

war"; "global monetary policy"; "neither national nor continental but planetary"; "a world crisis"; "of worldwide significance" [syn: global, planetary, worldwide]
n 1: all of the inhabitants of the earth; "all the world loves a lover" [syn: human race, humanity, humankind, human beings, humans, mankind, man] 2: everything that exists anywhere; "they study the evolution of the universe"; "the biggest tree in existence" [syn: universe, existence, creation, cosmos, macrocosm] 3: all of your experiences that determine how things appear to you; "his world was shattered"; "we live in different worlds"; "for them demons were as much a part of reality as trees were" [syn: reality] 4: people in general; especially a distinctive group of people with some shared interest; "the Western world" [syn: domain] 5: the 3rd planet from the sun; the planet on which we live; "the Earth moves around the sun"; "he sailed around the world" [syn: Earth, globe] 6: the concerns of the world as distinguished from heaven and the afterlife; "they consider the church to be independent of the world" [syn: worldly concern, earthly concern, earth] 7: a part of the earth that can be considered separately; "the outdoor world"; "the world of insects" 8: people in general considered as a whole; "he is a hero in the eyes of the public" [syn: populace, public]

whirred, word /wɜɹd/
whirred
v : (past of whir) (see were)
word
n 1: a unit of language that native speakers can identify; "words are the blocks from which sentences are made"; "he hardly said ten words all morning" 2: a brief statement; "he didn't say a word about it" 3: new information about specific and timely events; "they awaited news of the outcome" [syn: news, intelligence, tidings] 4: a promise; "he gave his word" [syn: parole, word of honor] 5: a secret word or phrase known only to a restricted group; "he forgot the password" [syn: password, watchword, parole, countersign] 6: an exchange of views on some topic; "we had a good discussion"; "we had a word or two about it" [syn: discussion, give-and-take] 7: a verbal command for action; "when I give the word, charge!" 8: a word is a string of bits stored in computer memory; "large computers use words up to 64 bits long"
v : put into words or an expression; "He formulated his concerns to the board of trustees" [syn: formulate, phrase, articulate]

whish, wish /wɪʃ/
whish
v 1: make a sibilant sound 2: move with a whishing sound; "The car whished past her"
wish
n 1: a specific feeling of desire; "he got his wish"; "he was above all wishing and desire" [syn: wishing, want] 2: an expression of some desire or inclination; "I could tell that it was his wish that the guests leave"; "his crying was an indirect request for attention" [syn: indirect request] 3: (usually plural) a polite expression of desire for someone's welfare; "give him my kind regards"; "my best wishes" [syn: regard, compliments] 4: the particular preference that you have; "it was his last wish"; "they should respect the wishes of the people"
v 1: hope for; have a wish; "I wish I could go home now" 2: prefer or wish to do something; "Do you care to try this dish?"; "Would you like to come along to the movies?" [syn: care, like] 3: have in mind; "I will take the exam tomorrow" [syn: will] 4: make or express a wish; "I wish that Christmas were over" 5: feel or express a desire or hope concerning the future or fortune of [syn: wish well] [ant: begrudge] 6: order politely; express a wish for 7: invoke upon; "wish you a nice evening"; "bid farewell" [syn: bid]

whist, wist /wɪst/
whist
n : a card game for four players who form two partnerships; a pack of 52 cards is dealt and each side scores one point for each trick it takes in excess of six [syn: long whist, short whist]
wist
v : (archaic): know

whit, wit /wɪt/
whit
n : a tiny or scarcely detectable amount [syn: shred, scintilla, iota, smidgen]
wit
n 1: a message whose ingenuity or verbal skill or incongruity has the power to evoke laughter [syn: humor, witticism, wittiness] 2: mental ability; "he's got plenty of brains but no common sense" [syn: brain, brainpower, learning ability, mental capacity, mentality] 3: (informal) a witty amusing person who makes jokes [syn: wag, card]

white, wight, wite /waɪt/
white
adj 1: being of the achromatic color of maximum lightness; having little or no hue owing to reflection of almost all incident light; "as white as fresh snow"; "a bride's white dress" [syn: achromatic]

HOMOPHONES

[ant: black] 2: of or belonging to a racial group having light skin coloration; "voting patterns within the white population" [ant: black] 3: (of wine) almost colorless; "white wines such as chardonnays or Rieslings"; "a white burgundy"; "white Italian wines" [ant: red] 4: free from moral blemish or impurity; unsullied; "in shining white armor" 5: marked by the presence of snow; "a white Christmas"; "the white hills of a northern winter" [syn: snowy] 6: restricted to whites only; "under segregation there were even white restrooms and white drinking fountains"; "a lily-white movement which would expel Negroes from the organization" [syn: lily-white] 7: glowing white with heat; "white flames"; a white-hot center of the fire" [syn: white-hot] 8: benevolent; without malicious intent; "white magic"; "a white lie"; "that's white of you" 9: of a surface; not written or printed on; "blank pages"; "fill in the blank spaces"; "a clean page"; "wide white margins" [syn: blank, clean] 10: (of coffee) having cream or milk added 11: dressed (or especially habited) in white; "white nuns" 12: (of hair) having lost its color; "the white hairs of old age" [syn: whitened] 13: ash-colored or anemic looking from illness or emotion; "a face turned ashen"; "the invalid's blanched cheeks"; "tried to speak with bloodless lips"; "a face livid with shock"; "lips... livid with the hue of death"- Mary W. Shelley; "lips white with terror"; "a face white with rage" [syn: ashen, blanched, bloodless, livid] 14: of summer nights in northern latitudes where the sun barely sets; "white nights"
n 1: a member of the Caucasoid race [syn: White, white person, Caucasian] 2: the quality or state of the achromatic color of greatest lightness (bearing the least resemblance to black) [syn: whiteness] [ant: black] 3: (chess or checkers) the lighter pieces 4: (usually in the plural) trousers [syn: flannel, gabardine, tweed]

wight
n : a human being [syn: creature]

wite
n : punishment [syn: blame, responsibility]

whither, wither /ˈwɪðɚ/
whither
adv 1: to what place; "Whither will he go?" 2: to what position, degree, situation or end; "Wither will his studies take him?"
wither
v 1: wither, esp. with a loss of moisture; "The fruit dried and shriveled" [syn: shrivel, shrivel up, shrink] 2: lose freshness, vigor, or vitality; "Her bloom was fading" [syn: fade]

whoa, woe /woʊ/
whoa
v : a command to stand still
woe
n 1: misery resulting from affliction [syn: suffering] 2: intense mournfulness [syn: woefulness]

whole (see hole)
wholly (see holey)
whoop (see hoop)
whore (see hoar)
whored (see hoard)
who's, whose /huz/
who's
contr : who is; "Who's going to work today?"
pron : possessive case of who or which; "Whose book is this?"

why, wye, Y /waɪ/
why
n : the cause or intention underlying an action or situation especially in the phrase "the whys and wherefores" [syn: wherefore]
adv : question word; what is the reason; "why are you here?"; (`how come' is a nonstandard variant as in "how come he got an ice cream cone but I didn't?") [syn: how come]
wye
adj : as in the shape of a Y; "The three-phase field coils are wound in a wye configuration."
n 1: the letter Y 2: an object shaped like a Y
Y
n: the 25th letter of the Roman alphabet [syn: y]

whys, wise /waɪz/
whys
n : (plu of why) (see why)
wise
adj 1: having or prompted by wisdom or discernment; "a wise leader"; "a wise and perceptive comment" [ant: foolish] 2: marked by the exercise of good judgment or common sense in practical matters; "judicious use of one's money"; "a sensible manager"; "a wise decision" [syn: judicious, sensible] 3: evidencing the possession of inside information [syn: knowing, wise to] 4: able to take a broad view of negotiations between states [syn: diplomatic] 5: carefully considered; "a considered opinion" [syn: considered]
n 1: a way of doing or being: "in no wise"; "in this wise" [syn: method]

windlass, windless /ˈwɪndlɪs/
windlass
n : lifting device consisting of a horizontal cylinder turned by a crank, engine or motor on which a cable or rope winds [syn: winch]

HOMOPHONES

windless

adj : without or almost without wind; "he prefers windless days for playing golf" [syn: calm]

winds, wins, winze /wɪnz/
winds

n 1: air moving (also with considerable force) from an area of high pressure to an area of low pressure; "trees bent under the fierce winds"; "when there is no wind, row" 2: a tendency or force that influences events; "the winds of change" 3: musical instruments in which the sound is produced by an enclosed column of air that is moved by the breath [syn: wind instruments]

wins

v : (3rd pers sing of win) (see whin) : "He wins at ping-pong most of the time."

winze

n : steeply inclined passageway in a mine

won (see one)

wonts (see once)

wood, would /wʊd/
wood

adj 1: concerning or dwelling or situated in a wood; "a wood nymph"; "woods animals" [syn: woods] 2: made or consisting of (entirely or in part) or employing wood; "a wooden box"; "an ancient cart with wooden wheels"; "wood houses"; "a wood fire" [syn: wooden]

n 1: the hard fibrous lignified substance under the bark of trees 2: the trees and other plants in a large densely wooded area [syn: forest, woods] 3: any wind instrument other than the brass instruments [syn: woodwind, woodwind instrument] 4: a golf club with a long shaft used to hit long shots; originally made with a wooden head; metal woods are now available

would

v : expresses conditionality or possibility; "I would accept the offer if you upped the salary a bit."

worst, wurst /wɜːst/
worst

adj : (superlative of `bad') most wanting in quality or value or condition; "the worst player on the team"; "the worst weather of the year" [ant: best]

n 1: the least favorable outcome; "the worst that could happen" 2: the greatest damage or wickedness of which one is capable: "the invaders did their worst"; "so pure of heart that his worst is another man's best" 3: the weakest effort or poorest achievement one is capable of: "it was the worst he had ever done on a test" [ant: best]

adv : to the highest degree of inferiority or badness; "She suffered worst of all"; "schools were the worst hit by government spending cuts"; "the worst dressed person

present"

wurst

n : sausage

wrap (see rap)
wrapped (see rapped)
wreak (see reek)
wreck (see reck)
wrecks (see rex)
wrens (see rends)
wrest (see rest)
wretch (see retch)
wright (see right)
wring (see ring)
write (see right)
writing (see righting)
writs (see ritz)
wrong (see rung)
wrung (see rung)
wrote (see rote)
wry (see rye)

-X-

xenia, zinnia /'zɪnɪə/
xenia

n : effect of genes introduced by pollen especially on endosperm and embryo development

zinnia

n : any of various plants of the genus Zinnia cultivated for their variously and brightly colored flower heads [syn: old maid, old maid flower]

xi (see psi)
xis (see psis)

-Y-

yew (see ewe)
yews (see ewes)
yoke, yolk /joʊk/

yoke

n 1: fabric comprising a fitted part at the top of a garment 2: two items of the same kind [syn: couple, doubleton, pair, twosome, twain, brace, span, couplet, distich, duo, duet, dyad] 3: support consisting of a wooden frame across the shoulders that enables a person to carry buckets hanging from each end 4: connection between two things so they move together [syn: coupling] 5: stable gear that joins two draft animals at the neck so they can work together

v 1: become joined or linked together 2: link with or as with a yoke; "yoke the oxen together" [syn: link] 3: put a yoke on; join with a yoke; of draft animals; "Yoke the draft horses together" [ant: unyoke]

yolk

n : nutritive material of an ovum stored for the nutrition of an embryo (especially the yellow mass of a bird or reptile egg) [syn: vitellus]

yore, your, you're
yore /jɔɹ/

n : the time that has elapsed; "forget the past"; "in days of yore" [syn: past, past times, yesteryear] [ant: future]

your /jɔɹ/

adj : relating to you, yourself or yourselves indicating possession; "Is this your book?"

you're /ʊəɹ/

contr : you are; "You're a real sweetheart!"

you (see ewe)

you'll, Yule /ʊəl/

you'll

contr : you will; "You'll enjoy this movie.:

Yule

n : period extending from Dec. 24 to Jan. 6 [syn: Christmas, Christmastide, Christmastime, Yuletide, Noel]

you're (see ewer)

-Z-

zinnia (see xenia)

HETERONYMS

abstract
abuse
addict
address
advocate
affect
aged
aggregate
alternate
alum
animate
annex
appropriate
approximate
are
articulate
associate
attribute
axes
ay
bass
beloved
blessed
bow
bowed
buffet
bustier
close
closer
coax
combat
combine
commune
compact
complex
compound
compress
concert
concord
conduct
confederate
confines
conflict

congregate
conjugate
conscript
console
consort
construct
consummate
content
contest
contract
contrast
converse
convert
convict
coordinate
crooked
cursed
decline
decrease
defect
defense
degenerate
delegate
deliberate
desert
diffuse
digest
dingy
display
do
does
dogged
dove
drawer
duplicate
elaborate
entrance
escort
estimate
evening
excise
excuse
exploit

export
extract
fine
forte
graduate
house
impact
implant
import
imprint
incarnate
incense
incline
initiate
insert
insult
intern
intimate
invalid
invite
laminate
lather
lead
leading
learned
lineage
live
minute
moderate
moped
mouth
mow
multiply
number
nun
object
offense
overlook
pasty
pate
patent
peaked
perfect

HETERONYMS

periodic
permit
pervert
prayer
precedent
precipitate
predicate
predominate
present
primer
proceeds
process
produce
progress
project
proportionate
protest
pussy
putting
ragged
raven
read
rebel
rebound
recall

recess
recoil
record
recount
recreation
redress
refill
reflex
refund
refuse
regress
reject
rejoin
relay
rerun
resent
reside
resign
resume
retard
retort
retread
rewrite
row
rugged

sake
separate
sewer
shower
skied
slaver
slough
sow
stingy
subject
subordinate
survey
suspect
tarry
tear
toots
tower
transport
transplant
upset
use
viola
wicked
wind
wound

HETERONYMS

Each heteronym is **bold** followed by its /ˈpɹoʊnʌnsieɪʃᵊn/.

abstract
/ˈæbstɹækt/
adj 1: existing only in the mind; separated from embodiment; "abstract words like `truth' and `justice'" [ant: concrete] 2: not representing or imitating external reality or the objects of nature; "a large abstract painting" [syn: abstractionist, nonfigurative, nonobjective] 3: based on specialized theory; "a theoretical analysis" [syn: theoretical] 4: dealing with a subject in the abstract without practical purpose or intention; "abstract reasoning"; "abstract science"
n 1: a concept or idea not associated with any specific instance; "he loved her only in the abstract--not in person" [syn: abstraction] 2: a sketchy summary of the main points of an argument or theory [syn: outline, synopsis, adumbration]
/əbˈstɹækt/
v 1: consider a concept without thinking of a specific example; consider abstractly or theoretically 2: make off with belongings of others [syn: pilfer, cabbage, purloin, pinch, snarf, swipe, hook, sneak, filch, nobble, lift] 3: consider apart from a particular case or instance; "Let's abstract away from this particular example" 4: give an abstract (of)

abuse
/əˈbuəs/
n 1: cruel or inhumane treatment [syn: maltreatment, ill-treatment, ill-usage] 2: a rude expression intended to offend or hurt; "when a student made a stupid mistake he spared them no abuse"; "they yelled insults at the visiting team" [syn: insult, revilement, contumely] 3: improper or excessive use [syn: misuse]
/əˈbuəz/
v 1: treat badly; "This boss abuses his workers" [syn: mistreat, maltreat, ill-use, ill-treat] 2: change the inherent purpose or function of something; "Don't abuse the system"; "The director of the factory misused the funds intended for the health care of his workers" [syn: pervert, misuse] 3: use foul or abusive language towards; "The actress abused the policeman who gave her a parking ticket"; "The angry mother shouted at the teacher" [syn: clapperclaw, blackguard, shout]

addict
/ˈædɪkt/
n 1: someone who is so ardently devoted to something that it resembles an addiction; "a golf addict"; "a car nut"; "a control freak" [syn: nut, freak] 2: someone who is physiologically dependent on a substance; abrupt deprivation of the substance produces withdrawal symptoms
/əˈdɪkt/
v : to cause (someone or oneself) to become dependent (on something, esp. a narcotic drug) [syn: hook]

address
/ˈædɹɛs/
n 1: (computer science) the code that identifies where a piece of information is stored [syn: computer address] 2: the place where a person or organization can be found or communicated with 3: a formal spoken communication delivered to an audience; "he listened to an address on minor Roman poets" [syn: speech] 4: the manner of speaking to another individual; "he failed in his manner of address to the captain" 5: a sign in front of a house or business carrying the conventional form by which its location is described 6: written directions for finding some location; written on letters or packages that are to be delivered to that location [syn: destination, name and address] 7: social skill [syn: savoir-faire]
/əˈdɹɛs/
v 1: speak to; "He addressed the crowd outside the window" [syn: turn to] 2: give a speech to; "The chairman addressed the board of trustees" [syn: speak] 3: put an address on (an envelope, for example) [syn: direct] 4: direct a question at someone 5: address or apply oneself to something, direct one's efforts towards something, such as a question 6: greet, as with a prescribed form, title, or name; "He always addresses me with `Sir'"; "Call me Mister"; "She calls him by first name" [syn: call] 7: deal with verbally or in some form of artistic expression; "This book deals with incest"; "The course covered all of Western Civilization"; "The new book treats the history of China" [syn: cover, treat, handle, plow, deal] 8: speak to someone [syn: accost, come up to]

advocate
/ˈædvᵊkɪt/
n 1: a person who pleads for a cause or propounds an idea [syn: advocator, proponent, exponent] 2: a lawyer who pleads cases in court [syn: counsel, counselor, counselor-at-law, pleader]
/ˈædvᵊkeɪt/
v 1: push for something; "The travel agent recommended strongly that we not travel on Thanksgiving Day" [syn: recommend, urge] 2: speak, plead, or argue in favour of; "The doctor advocated a smoking ban in the entire house" [syn: preach]

HETERONYMS

affect
/ˈəfɛkt/
v 1: have an effect upon; "Will the new rules affect me?" [syn: impact, bear upon, bear on, touch on, touch] 2: act physically on; have an effect upon 3: connect closely and often incriminatingly; "This new ruling affects your business" [syn: involve, regard] 4: make believe; "He feigned that he was ill"; "He shammed a headache" [syn: feign, sham, pretend, dissemble] 5: have an emotional or cognitive impact upon; "This child impressed me as unusually mature"; "This behavior struck me as odd" [syn: impress, move, strike]
/əˈfɛkt/
n : the conscious subjective aspect of feeling or emotion

aged
/ˈɛɪdʒd/
adj 1: advanced in years; (`aged' is pronounced as two syllables); "aged members of the society"; "elderly residents could remember the construction of the first skyscraper"; "senior citizen" [syn: elderly, older, senior] 2: at an advanced stage of erosion (pronounced as one syllable); "aged rocks"
3: having attained a specific age; (`aged' is pronounced as one syllable); "aged ten"; "ten years of age" of age] 4: of wines, fruit, cheeses; having reached a desired or final condition; (`aged' pronounced as one syllable); "mature well-aged cheeses" [syn: ripened] 5: (used of tobacco) aging as a preservative process (`aged' is pronounced as one syllable) [syn: cured]
v : (past of age) 1: became old 2: manifested traits associated with old age 3: developed a certain quality of ripeness; became mature; e.g., wine and cheese
/ˈɛɪˈdʒɪd/
n : people who are old; "special arrangements were available for the aged" [ant: young]

aggregate
/ˈægɹəgɪt/
adj 1: gathered or tending to gather into a mass or whole; "the aggregate amount of indebtedness" [syn: aggregative, mass] 2: (botany) formed of separate units in a cluster; "raspberries are aggregate fruits"
n 1: a sum total of many heterogenous things taken together [syn: congeries, conglomeration] 2: the whole amount [syn: sum, total, totality] 3: mineral materials, such as sand or stone, used in making concrete
/ˈægɹəgɛɪt/
v 1: amount in the aggregate to 2: gather in a mass, sum, or whole [syn: combine]

alternate
/ˈɔltəɹnɪt/
n : someone who takes the place of another person [syn: surrogate, replacement]
/ˈɔltəɹnɛɪt/
v 1: go back and forth; swing back and forth between two states or conditions [syn: jump] 2: exchange people temporarily to fulfill certain jobs and functions 3: be an understudy or alternate for a role [syn: understudy] 4: reverse, as of direction or attitude [syn: interchange, switch, flip, flip-flop] 5: do something in turns; "We take turns on the night shift" [syn: take turns]

alum
/ˈæləm/
n 1: a white crystalline double sulfate of aluminum: the ammonium double sulfate of aluminum [syn: ammonia alum, ammonium alum] 2: a white crystalline double sulfate of aluminum: the potassium double sulfate of aluminum [syn: potassium alum, potash alum] 3: a double sulphate of aluminum and potassium that is used as an astringent (among other things)
/æˈləm/
n: a person who has received a degree from a school (high school or college or university) [syn: alumnus, alumna, graduate, grad]

animate
/ˈænəmɪt/
adj 1: (linguistics) belonging to the class of nouns that denote living beings; "the word `dog' is animate" [ant: inanimate] 2: relating to animal life as distinct from plant life; "animate life" 3: endowed with animal life as distinguished from plant life; "we are animate beings" [ant: inanimate] 4: endowed with feeling and unstructured consciousness; "the living knew themselves just sentient puppets on God's stage"- T.E.Lawrence [syn: sentient] [ant: insentient]
/ˈænəmɛɪt/
v 1: heighten or intensify; "These paintings exalt the imagination" [syn: inspire, invigorate, enliven, exalt] 2: give life-like qualities to; "animated cartoons" [syn: animize] 3: make lively; "let's liven up this room a bit" [syn: enliven, liven, liven up, invigorate] [ant: deaden] 4: make lively or spirited [syn: enliven] 5: give new life or energy to; "A hot soup will revive me" [syn: recreate, reanimate, revive, quicken, vivify, revivify]

annex
/ˈænɛks/
n : an addition that extends a main building [syn: extension, wing]
/æˈnɛks/
v 1: take illegally, as of territory 2: take

HETERONYMS

by conquest; as of territory [syn: take over] 3: attach to

appropriate
/ə'pɹoupɹiɪt/

adj 1: suitable for a particular person or place or condition etc; "a book not appropriate for children"; "a funeral conducted the appropriate solemnity"; "it seems that an apology is appropriate" [ant: inappropriate] 2: appropriate for achieving a particular end; implies a lack of concern for fairness [syn: advantageous] 3: meant or adapted for an occasion or use; "a tractor suitable (or fit) for heavy duty"; "not an appropriate (or fit) time for flippancy" [syn: suitable, suited] 4: suitable and fitting; "the tailored clothes were harmonious with her military bearing" [syn: harmonious] 5: being of striking appropriateness and pertinence; "the successful copywriter is a master of apposite and evocative verbal images"; "an apt reply" [syn: apposite, apt, pertinent]

/ə'pɹoupɹieɪt/

v 1: give or assign a share of money or time to a particular person or cause; "I will earmark this money for your research" [syn: allow, earmark, set aside, reserve] 2: take possession of without permission or take with force, as after a conquest or invasion; "the invaders seized the land and property of the inhabitants"; "The army seized the town"; "The militia captured the castle" [syn: capture, seize, conquer, take over]

approximate
/'əpɹaksəmɪt/

adj 1: not quite exact or correct; "the approximate time was 10 o'clock"; "a rough guess"; "a ballpark estimate" [syn: approximative, rough, ballpark] 2: very close in resemblance; "sketched in an approximate likeness"; "a near likeness" [syn: near] 3: located close together; "with heads close together"; "approximate leaves grow together but are not united" [syn: close together]

/ə'pɹaksəmeɪt/

v 1: be close or similar; "Her results approximate my own" [syn: come close] 2: form an opinion about; judge tentatively; form an estimate of, esp. quantities or time; "I estimate this chicken to weigh at three pounds" [syn: estimate, gauge, guess, judge]

are
/aɹ/

v : plu present tense of 'to be'

/ɛəɹ/

n : a unit of surface area equal to 100 square meters

articulate
/'aɹtɪkʊəlɪt/

adj 1: expressing yourself easily or characterized by clear expressive language; "articulate speech"; "an articulate orator"; "articulate beings" [ant: inarticulate] 2: consisting of segments held together by joints [syn: articulated] [ant: unarticulated]

/aɹ'tɪkʊəleɪt/

v 1: provide with a joint, as of two pieces of wood [syn: joint] 2: put into words or an expression; "He formulated his concerns to the board of trustees" [syn: formulate, word, phrase] 3: speak, pronounce, or utter in a certain way; "She pronounces French words in a funny way"; "I cannot say `zip wire'"; "Can the child sound out this complicated word?" [syn: pronounce, enounce, sound out, enunciate, say] 4: express or state clearly [syn: enunciate, vocalize]

associate
/ə'souʃiɪt/

adj : having partial rights and privileges or subordinate status; "an associate member"; "an associate professor"

n 1: a person who joins with others in some activity; "he had to consult his associate before continuing" 2: a person who is frequently in the company of another; "drinking companions"; "comrades in arms" [syn: companion, comrade, fellow, familiar] 3: any event that usually accompanies or is closely connected with another; "first was the lightning and then its thunderous associate" 4: a degree granted by a two-year college on successful completion of the undergraduates course of studies [syn: associate degree]

/ə'souʃieɪt/

v 1: make a logical or causal connection; "I cannot connect these two pieces of evidence in my mind" [syn: tie in, relate, link, link up, connect] [ant: dissociate] 2: keep company with; hang out with; "He associates with strange people"; "She affiliates with her colleagues" [syn: consort, affiliate, assort] 3: bring or come into friendly association; "The churches consociated to fight their dissolution" [syn: consociate]

attribute
/'ætɹɪbuət/

n 1: a construct whereby objects or individuals can be distinguished; "self-confidence is not an endearing property" [syn: property, dimension] 2: an abstraction belonging to or characteristic of an entity

/æ'tɹɪbuət/

v 1: attribute to a source or cause; "We attributed this quotation to Shakespeare" [syn: impute, ascribe, assign] 2: decide as

HETERONYMS

to where something belongs in a scheme; "The biologist assigned the mushroom to the proper class" [syn: assign]

axes
/'æksɪz/

n : (plu of axe) : edge tools with a heavy bladed head mounted across a handle

v : (3rd pers sing for axe) 1): chops or splits with an ax, as of wood 2): terminates, as of a project or a program; "She axes research programs when funding stops."

/'æksɪz/

n : (plu for axis) 1): straight lines through a body or figure that satisfies certain conditions 2): the centers around which things rotate [syn: axeis of rotation] 3): the main stems or central parts about which plant organs or plant parts such as branches are arranged 4): groups of countries in special alliance [syn: blocs] 5): the 2nd cervical vertebrae; serves as a pivot for turning the head [syn: axis vertebrae]

ay
/ɛɪ/

n (var of aye): an affirmative vote or voter; "The ays outnumber the nays on this issue."

adv : (var of aye): yes, yea; "voted ay on this issue"

/aɪ/

interj : used before 'me' to express distress or regret

adv : (var of aye) : always, ever; "pledged their love for ay"

bass
/beɪs/

adj : having or denoting a low vocal or instrumental range; "a deep voice"; "a bass voice is lower than a baritone voice"; "a bass clarinet" [syn: deep]

n 1): the lowest part of the musical range 2): the lowest part in polyphonic music [syn: bass part] 3): an adult male singer with the lowest voice [syn: basso] 4): the lowest adult male singing voice [syn: bass voice, basso] 5): the member with the lowest range of a family of musical instruments

/bæs/

n 1): the lean flesh of a saltwater fish of the family Serranidae [syn: sea bass] 2): any of various North American freshwater fish with lean flesh (especially of the genus Micropterus) [syn: freshwater bass] 3): non-technical name for any of numerous edible marine and freshwater spiny-finned fishes

beloved
/bɪ'lʌvd/

adj : dearly loved [syn: darling, dear]

/bɪ'lʌvɪd/

n : a beloved person; used as terms of endearment [syn: dear, dearest, loved one, honey, love]

blessed
/blɛst/

v : (past of bless) 1): made holy by religious rite [syn: sanctified] 2): made the sign of the cross over so as to sanctify 3): invoked divine favor upon 4): honored as holy; [syn: glorified] 5): conferred well-being or prosperity on 6): endowed, as with talent

/'blɛsɪd/

adj 1): highly favored or fortunate (as e.g. by divine grace); "our blessed land"; "the blessed assurance of a steady income" [syn: blest] [ant: cursed] 2): worthy of worship; "the Blessed Trinity" [syn: Blessed] 3): expletives used informally as intensifiers; "he's a blasted idiot"; "it's a blamed shame"; "a blame cold winter"; "not a blessed dime"; "I'll be damned (or blessed or darned or goddamned) if I'll do any such thing"; "he's a damn (or goddam or goddamned) fool"; "a deuced idiot"; "tired or his everlasting whimpering"; "an infernal nuisance" [syn: blasted, blame, blamed, damn, damned, darned, deuced, everlasting, goddam, goddamn, goddamned, infernal] 4): Roman Catholic; proclaimed one of the blessed and thus worthy of veneration [syn: beatified] 5): enjoying the bliss of heaven 6): characterized by happiness and good fortune; "a blessed time" 7): having good fortune bestowed or conferred upon; sometimes used as in combination; "blessed with a strong healthy body"; "a nation blessed with peace"; "a peace-blessed era" [syn: blessed with, endued with]

bow
/baʊ/

adj : pertaining to the forward part of a vessel

n : an appearance by actors or performers at the end of the concert or play in order to acknowledge the applause of the audience [syn: curtain call]

v 1): bend one's knee or body, or lower one's head; "He bowed before the King"; "She bowed her head in shame" [syn: bow down] 2): submit or yield to another's wish or opinion; "The government bowed to the military pressure" [syn: submit, defer, accede, give in] 3): bend the head or the upper part of the body in a gesture of respect or greeting; "He bowed before the King" 4): bend one's back forward from the waist on down; "he crouched down"; "She bowed before the Queen"; "The young man stooped to pick up the girl's purse" [syn: crouch, stoop, bend]

/boʊ/

n 1): a knot with two loops and loose ends; used to tie shoelaces [syn: bowknot] 2):

HETERONYMS

a slightly curved piece of resilient wood with taut horsehair strands, used in playing certain stringed instrument 3: front part of a vessel or aircraft; "he pointed the bow of the boat toward the finish line" [syn: fore, prow, stem] 4: curved piece of resilient wood with taut cord to propel arrows 5: something curved in shape [syn: arc] 6: bending the head or body or knee as a sign of reverence or submission or shame [syn: bowing, obeisance] 7: a decorative interlacing of ribbons 9: a stroke with a curved piece of wood with taut horsehair strands that is used in playing stringed instruments: play on a string instrument

bowed
/baʊd/
adj: showing an excessively deferential manner [syn: bowing]
v : (past of bow) "He bowed before the king."
/boʊd/
adj 1: used especially of the head or upper back; "a bent head and sloping shoulders" [syn: bent, inclined] 2: (music) of a stringed instrument; sounded by stroking with a bow [ant: plucked] 3: (architecture) forming or resembling an arch; "an arched ceiling" [syn: arced, arched, arching,] 4: have legs that curve outward at the knees [syn: bandy, bandy-legged, bowleg, bowlegged]

buffet
/ˈbʌfɪt/
v 1: strike against forcefully; "Winds buffeted the tent" [syn: knock about, batter] 2: strike, beat repeatedly; "The wind buffeted him"
/buˈfɛr/
n 1: a piece of furniture that stands at the side of a dining room; has shelves and drawers [syn: counter, sideboard] 2: a meal set out on a buffet at which guests help themselves 3: usually inexpensive bar [syn: snack bar, snack counter]

bustier
/ˈbʌstjɛr/
n : a formfitting sleeveless and usually strapless woman's top, worn as lingerie and often as evening attire
/ˈbʌstiᵊr/
adj (superlative of busty) : most full-busomed; "Pamela Anderson was the bustiest of all."

closer
/ˈkloʊsᵊr/
adj : (compar of 'close') indicating the one of two that is the shorter distance away; "take the near street and ten turn right" [syn: near]
adv : (compar of `near' or `close') within a shorter distance; "come closer, my dear!"; "they drew nearer"; "getting nearer to the true explanation" [syn: nearer, nigher]
/ˈkloʊzᵊr/
n 1: person who closes: "The closer of the shop has to lock up." 2: (baseball) a relief pitcher called upon to protect a lead late in a game 3: person who closes a business deal; loan closer

coax
/koʊks/
v : influence or urge by gentle urging, caressing, or flattering; "He palavered her into going along" [syn: wheedle, cajole, palaver, blarney, sweet-talk, inveigle]
/ˈkoʊæks/
n : a transmission line for high-frequency signals [syn: coaxial cable, coax cable]

close
/kloʊz/
n 1: the temporal end; the concluding time; "the stopping point of each round was signaled by a bell"; "the market was up at the finish"; "they were playing better at the close of the season" [syn: stopping point, finale, finis, finish, last, conclusion] 2: the last section of a communication; "in conclusion I want to say..." [syn: conclusion, end, closing, ending] 3: the concluding part of any performance [syn: finale, closing curtain, finis]
v 1: cease to operate or cause to cease operating; "The owners decided to move and to close the factory"; "My business closes every night at 8 P.M. [syn: fold, shut down, close down] [ant: open] 2: complete a business deal, negotiation, or an agreement; "We will close on the house on Friday"; "They closed the deal on the building" 3: move so that an opening or passage is obstructed; make shut; "Close the door"; "shut the window" [syn: shut] [ant: open] 4: bar access to; "Due to the accident, the road had to be closed for several hours" 5: finish or terminate; of meetings, speeches, etc. "The meeting was closed with a charge by the chairman of the board" [ant: open] 6: draw near: "The probe closed with the space station" 7: come to a close; "The concert closed with a nocturne by Chopin" 8: become closed; "The windows closed with a loud bang" [syn: shut] [ant: open] 9: come together, as if in an embrace; "Her arms closed around her long lost relative" [syn: come together] 10: unite or bring into contact or bring together the edges of; "close the circuit"; "close a wound" 11: bring together all the elements or parts of: "Management closed ranks" 12: engage at close quarters; "close with the enemy" 13: cause a window or an application to disappear on a computer desktop [ant: open] 14: fill or stop up; "Can you close the cracks with caulking?" [syn: fill, fill up]

/kloʊs/
adj 1: at or within a short distance in space or time or having elements near each other; "close to noon"; "how close are we to town?"; "a close formation of ships" [ant: distant] 2: close in relevance or relationship; "a close family"; "we are all...in close sympathy with..."; "close kin"; "a close resemblance" [ant: distant] 3: not far distant in time or space or degree or circumstances; "near neighbors"; "in the near future"; "they are near equals"; "his nearest approach to success"; "a very near thing"; "a near hit by the bomb"; "she was near tears"; "she was close to tears"; "had a close call" [syn: near] [ant: far] 4: rigorously attentive; strict and thorough; "close supervision"; "paid close attention"; "a close study"; "kept a close watch on expenditures" 5: marked by fidelity to an original; "a close translation"; "a faithful copy of the portrait"; "a faithful rendering of the observed facts" [syn: faithful] 6: (of a contest or contestants) evenly matched; "a close contest"; "a close election"; "a tight game" [syn: tight] 7: crowded; "close quarters" [syn: confining] 8: lacking fresh air; "a dusty airless attic"; "the dreadfully close atmosphere"; "hot and stuffy and the air was blue with smoke" [syn: airless, stuffy, unaired] 9: of textiles; "a close weave"; "smooth percale with a very tight weave" [syn: tight] 10: strictly confined or guarded; "kept under close custody" 11: confined to specific persons; "a close secret" 12: fitting closely but comfortably; "a close fit" [syn: snug, close-fitting] 13: used of hair or haircuts; "a close military haircut" 14: giving or spending with reluctance; "our cheeseparing administration"; "very close (or near) with his money"; "a penny-pinching miserly old man" [syn: cheeseparing, near, penny-pinching] 15: inclined to secrecy or reticence about divulging information; "although they knew her whereabouts her friends kept close about it" [syn: closemouthed, secretive, tightlipped]

combat
/ˈkʌmbæt/
n 1: an engagement fought between two military forces [syn: armed combat] 2: the act of fighting; any contest or struggle; "a fight broke out at the hockey game"; "there was fighting in the streets" [syn: fight, fighting]
/kəmˈbæt/
v : battle or contend against in or as if in a battle; "The Kurds are combat Iraqi troops in Nothern Iraq"; "We must combat the prejudices against other races"; "they battled over the budget" [syn: battle]

combine
/ˈkɑmbaɪn/
n 1: harvester that heads and threshes and cleans grain while moving across the field 2: a consortium of companies formed to limit competition; "they set up the trust in the hope of gaining a monopoly" [syn: trust, corporate trust, cartel] 3: an occurrence that results in things being combined [syn: combination, combining]
v : to harvest with a combine
/kəmˈbaɪn/
v 1: put or add together; "combine resources" [syn: compound] 2: have or possess in combination; "she unites charm with a good business sense" [syn: unite] 3: combine so as to form a whole; mix; "compound the ingredients" [syn: compound] 4: add together, as of resources [syn: pool] 5: join for a common purpose or in a common action; "These forces combined with others" 6: gather in a mass, sum, or whole [syn: aggregate] 7: mix together different elements; "The ingredients combine well [syn: blend, flux, mix, conflate, commingle, immix, fuse, coalesce, meld, merge]

commune
/ˈkɑmuən/
n 1: the smallest administrative district of several European countries (Belgium and France and Italy and Switzerland) 2: a body of people or families living together and sharing everything
/kəˈmuən/
v 1: communicate intimately with; be in a state of heightened, intimate receptivity; "He seemed to commune with nature" 2: receive Communion, in the Catholic church [syn: communicate]

compact
/ˈkɑmpækt/
adj 1: closely and firmly united or packed together; "compact soil"; "compact clusters of flowers" [ant: loose] 2: closely crowded together; "a compact shopping center"; "a dense population"; "thick crowds" [syn: dense, thick] 3: heavy and compact in form or stature; "a wrestler of compact build"; "he was tall and heavyset"; "stocky legs"; "a thick middle-aged man"; "a thickset young man" [syn: heavyset, stocky, thick, thickset] 4: briefly giving the gist of something; "a short and compendious book"; "a compact style is brief and pithy"; "succinct comparisons"; "a summary formulation of a wide-ranging subject" [syn: compendious, succinct, summary]
n 1: a small cosmetics case with a mirror; to be carried in a woman's purse [syn: powder compact] 2: a signed written agreement between two or more parties

(nations) to perform some action [syn: covenant, concordat]   3: a small and economical car [syn: compact car]
/kəm'pækt/

v 1: compress into a wad; "wad paper into the box" [syn: pack, bundle, wad] 2: make more compact by or as if by pressing; "compress the data" [syn: compress, pack together]   3: squeeze or press together; "she compressed her lips" [syn: compress, constrict, squeeze, contract, press]

complex
/kəm'plɛks/

adj 1: complicated in structure; consisting of interconnected parts; "a complex set of variations based on a simple folk melody"; "a complex mass of diverse laws and customs" [ant: simple]

/'kamplɛks/

n 1: a conceptual whole made up of complicated and related parts [syn: composite]   2: a compound described in terms of the central atom to which other atoms are bound or coordinated [syn: coordination compound]   3: (psychoanalysis) a combination of emotions and impulses that have been rejected from awareness but still influence a person's behavior 4: a whole structure (as a building) made up of interconnected or related structures [syn: building complex]

compound
/'kampaʊnd/

adj 1: (botany) of leaf shapes; of leaves composed of several similar parts or lobes [ant: simple]   2: consisting of two or more substances or ingredients or elements or parts; "soap is a compound substance"; "housetop is a compound word"; "a blackberry is a compound fruit"   3: (zoology) composed of many distinct individuals united to form a whole or colony; "coral is a colonial organism" [syn: colonial]

n 1: (chemistry) a substance formed by chemical union of two or more elements or ingredients in definite proportion by weight [syn: chemical compound]   2: a whole formed by a union of two or more elements or parts   3: an enclosure of residences and other building (especially in the Orient)

/kam'paʊnd/

v 1: make more intense, stronger, or more marked; "The efforts were intensified", "Her rudeness intensified his dislike for her", "Pot smokers claim it heightens their awareness"; "This event only deepened my convictions" [syn: intensify, heighten, deepen] 2: put or add together; "combine resources" [syn: combine]   3: calculate principal and interest 4: create by mixing

or combining 5: combine so as to form a whole; mix; "compound the ingredients" [syn: combine]

compress
/'kamprɛs/

n : a cloth pad or dressing (with or without medication) applied firmly to some part of the body (to relieve discomfort or reduce fever)

/kəm'prɛs/

v 1: make more compact by or as if by pressing; "compress the data" [syn: compact, pack together]   2: squeeze or press together; "she compressed her lips" [syn: constrict, squeeze, compact, contract, press]

concert
/'kansət/

n : a performance of music by players or singers not involving theatrical staging
/kən'sət/

v 1: contrive by mutual agreement, as of a plan 2: settle by agreement; "concert one's differences"

concord
/'kankəd/

n 1: a harmonious state of things and their properties (as of colors and sounds); congruity of parts with one another and with the whole [syn: harmony, accord, concordance]   2: the determination of grammatical inflection on the basis of word relations [syn: agreement] 3: agreement of opinions [syn: harmony, concordance]

/kan'kɔd/

v 1: go together; "The colors don't harmonize"; "Their ideas concorded" [syn: harmonize, consort, accord, fit in, agree]   2: arrange by concord or agreement; "Concord the conditions for the marriage of the Prince of Wales with a commoner" 3: arrange the words of a text so as to create a concordance; "The team concorded several thousand nouns, verbs, and adjectives" 4: be in accord; be in agreement; "We agreed on the terms of the settlement"; "I can't agree with you!"; "I hold with those you say life is sacred"; "Both philosophers concord on this point" [syn: agree, hold, concur] [ant: disagree]

conduct
/'kandʌkt/

n 1: manner of acting or conducting yourself [syn: behavior, doings]   2: behavioral attributes [syn: demeanor, behavior, deportment]

/kan'dʌkt/

v 1: direct the course of; manage or control; "You cannot conduct business like this" [syn: carry on, deal] 2: lead, as in the performance of a musical composition; "conduct an orchestra; Bairenboim conducted the Chicago symphony for years" [syn: lead, direct] 3: behave in a certain manner; "She carried herself well"; "he bore himself with dignity"; "They conducted themselves well during these difficult times" [syn: behave, acquit, bear, deport, comport, carry] 4: transmit or serve as the medium for transmission, as of sounds or images; "Sound carries well over water"; "The airwaves carry the sound"; "Many metals conduct heat" [syn: transmit, convey, carry, channel] 5: take somebody somewhere; "We lead him to our chief"; "can you take me to the main entrance?"; "He conducted us to the palace" [syn: lead, take, direct, guide]

confederate

/'kənfɛdᵊɹɪt/

adj: united in a confederacy or league [syn: allied, confederative]

n 1: someone who assists in a plot [syn: collaborator, henchman, partner in crime] 2: a person who joins with another in carrying out some plan (especially an unethical or illegal plan) [syn: accomplice]

/kən'fɛdᵊɹeɪt/

v 1: form a group or unite; "The groups banded together" [syn: band together] 2: form a confederation with; of nations

confines

/'kanfaɪnz/

n : a bounded scope; "he stayed with the confines of the city"

/kən'faɪnz/

v : (3ʳᵈ pers sing of confine) 1: restricts , as to area, extent, time, etc. [syn: limits, circumscribes] 2: place limits on; "restricts the use of this parking lot" [syn: restricts, restrains, trammels, limits, bounds, throttles] 3: prevents from leaving or from being removed 4: closes in or confines [syn: encloses, holds in] 5: deprives of freedom; takes into confinement [syn: detains] [ant: frees] 6: to close within bounds, limit or hold back from movement; "This holds the local until the express passengers change trains"; "About a dozen animals were confined inside the stockade"; "The illegal immigrants were held at a detention center"; "The terrorists held the journalists for ransom" [syn: restrains, holds]

conflict

/kᵊn'flɪkt/

v 1: be in conflict; "The two proposals conflict!": go against, as of rules and laws; "He ran afoul of thelaw"; "This behavior conflicts with our rules" [syn: run afoul, infringe, contravene]

/'kanflɪkt/

n 1: an open clash between two opposing groups (or individuals); "the harder the conflict the more glorious the triumph"--Thomas Paine; "police tried to control

the battle between the pro- and anti-abortion mobs" [syn: struggle, battle] 2: opposition between two simultaneous but incompatible feelings; "he was immobilized by conflict and indecision" 3: a hostile meeting of opposing military forces in the course of a war; "Grant won a decisive victory in the battle of Chickamauga"; "he lost his romantic ideas about war when he got into a real engagement" [syn: battle, fight, engagement] 4: a state of opposition between persons or ideas or interests; "his conflict of interest made him ineligible for the post"; "a conflict of loyalties" 5: an incompatibility of dates or events; "he noticed a conflict in the dates of the two meetings" 6: opposition in a work of drama or fiction between characters or forces (especially an opposition that motivates the development of the plot); "this form of conflict is essential to Mann's writing" 7: a disagreement or argument about something important; "he had a dispute with his wife"; "there were irreconcilable differences"; "the familiar conflict between Republicans and Democrats" [syn: dispute, difference, difference of opinion]

congregate

/'kaŋɹᵊgɪt/

adj : brought together into a group or crowd; "the accumulated letters in my office" [syn: accumulated, amassed, assembled, collected, massed]

/'kaŋɹᵊgeɪt/

v : move together [syn: gather, collect]

conjugate

/'kandʒᵊgɪt/

adj 1: joined together especially in a pair or pairs [syn: conjugated, coupled] 2: of a pinnate leaflet; having only one pair of leaflets 3: (chemistry) formed by the union of two compounds; "a conjugated protein" [syn: conjugated] 4: (chemistry) of an organic compound; containing two or more double bonds each separated from the other by a single bond [syn: conjugated]

n : a mixture of two partially miscible liquids A and B produces

two conjugate solutions: one of A in B and another of B in A [syn: conjugate solution]

/'kandʒᵊgeɪt/

v 1: unite chemically so that the product is easily broken down into the original compounds 2: of verbs (change form according to usage and tense)

conscript

/'kanskɹɪpt/

n : a serviceman who is drafted [syn: draftee] [ant: volunteer]

HETERONYMS

/kən'skɹɪpt/
v : enroll into service compulsorily; "The men were conscripted"

console
/'kansoʊl/
n 1: a small table fixed to a wall or designed to stand against a wall [syn: console table] 2: a scientific instrument consisting of displays and an input device that an operator can use to monitor and control a system (especially a computer system) 3: an ornamental scroll-shaped bracket (especially one used to support a wall fixture); "the bust of Napoleon stood on a console" 4: housing for electronic instruments, as radio or television [syn: cabinet]
/kən'soʊl/
v : give moral or emotional strength to [syn: comfort, soothe, solace]

consort
/'kansɔɹt/
n 1: the husband or wife of a reigning monarch 2: a family of similar musical instrument playing together [syn: choir]
/kən'sɔɹt/
v 1: keep company with; hang out with; "He associates with strange people"; "She affiliates with her colleagues" [syn: associate, affiliate, assort] 2: go together; "The colors don't harmonize"; "Their ideas concorded" [syn: harmonize, accord, concord, fit in, agree] 3: keep company; of male animals [syn: run]

construct
/'kanstɹəkt/
n : an abstract or general idea inferred or derived from specific instances [syn: concept, conception] [ant: misconception]
/kən'stɹəkt/
v 1: make by combining materials and parts: "this little pig made his house out of straw"; "Some eccentric constructed an electric brassiere warmer" [syn: build, make] 2: put together out of components or parts; "Ford makes cars"; "They manufacture small toys" [syn: manufacture, fabricate] 3: draw with suitable instruments and under specified conditions, of geometrical figures 4: of past events [syn: reconstruct, retrace]

consummate
/'kansəmɪt/
adj 1: having or revealing supreme mastery or skill; "a consummate artist"; "consummate skill"; "a masterful speaker"; "masterful technique"; "a masterly performance of the sonata"; "a virtuoso performance" [syn: masterful, masterly, virtuoso] 2: perfect and complete in every respect; having all necessary qualities; "a complete gentleman";

"consummate happiness"; "a consummate performance" [syn: complete] 3: without qualification; used informally as (often pejorative) intensifiers; "an arrant fool"; "a complete coward"; "a consummate fool"; "a double-dyed villain"; "gross negligence"; "a perfect idiot"; "pure folly"; "what a sodding mess"; "stark staring mad"; "a thoroughgoing villain"; "utter nonsense" [syn: arrant, complete, consummate, double-dyed, everlasting, gross, perfect, pure, sodding, stark, staring, thoroughgoing, utter]
/'kansəmeɪt/
v 1: of marriages (perform first sexual intercourse after being married) 2: make perfect; bring to perfection [syn: perfect]

content
/'kantɛnt/
n 1: everything that is included in a collection; "he emptied the contents of his pockets"; "the two groups were similar in content" 2: what a communication that is about something is about [syn: message, subject matter, substance] 3: the proportion of a substance that is contained in a mixture or alloy etc. 4: the amount that can be contained; "the gas tank has a capacity of 12 gallons" [syn: capacity] 5: the sum or range of what has been perceived, discovered, or learned [syn: cognitive content, mental object] 6: the state of being contented with your situation in life; "he relaxed in sleepy contentedness"; "they could read to their heart's content" [syn: contentedness] 7: something (a person or object or scene) selected by an artist or photographer for graphic representation; "a moving picture of a train is more dramatic than a still picture of the same subject" [syn: subject, depicted object]
/kʌn'tɛnt/
adj 1: satisfied or showing satisfaction with things as they are; "a contented smile" [syn: contented] [ant: discontented] 2: satisfied; enjoying well-being and contentment; "felt content with her lot"; "quite happy to let things go on as they are" [syn: happy] v 1: satisfy in a limited way; "He limited himself to three glasses of beer last night" 2: make content; "I am contented" [ant: discontent]

contest
/kən'tɛst/
v : to make the subject of dispute, contention, or litigation; "They contested the outcome of the race" [syn: contend, repugn]
/'kantɛst/
n 1: an occasion on which a winner is selected from among two or more contestants [syn: competition]

HETERONYMS

contract
/ˈkɑntɹækt/

n 1: a binding agreement between two or more persons that is enforceable by law 2: (bridge) the highest bid becomes the contract setting the number of tricks that the bidder must make 3: a variety of bridge in which the bidder receives points toward game only for the number of tricks he bid [syn: contract bridge]

/kənˈtɹækt/

v 1: enter into a contractual arrangement [syn: undertake] 2: engage by written agreement; "They signed two new pitchers for the next season" [syn: sign, fee, sign on, sign up] 3: squeeze or press together; "she compressed her lips" [syn: compress, constrict, squeeze, compact, press] 4: draw together; "The fabric shrank" [syn: shrink] [ant: stretch] 5: be stricken by an illness, fall victim to an illness; "He got AIDS"; "She came down with pneumonia"; "She took a chill" [syn: take, get] 6: make smaller; "The garment contracted in the dryer"; "The heat contracted the woolen garment" 7: compress or concentrate; "Congress condensed the three-year plan into a six-month plan" [syn: condense, concentrate] 8: make or become more narrow or restricted; "The selection was narrowed"; "The road narrowed" [syn: narrow] [ant: widen] 9: reduce in scope while retaining essential elements; "The manuscript must be shortened" [syn: abridge, foreshorten, abbreviate, shorten, cut, reduce]

contrast
/ˈkɑntɹæst/

n 1: the opposition or dissimilarity of things that are compared; "in contrast to", "by contrast" [syn: direct contrast] 2: the act of distinguishing by comparing differences 3: a conceptual separation or demarcation: "there is a narrow line between sanity and insanity" [syn: line, dividing line, demarcation] 4: the perceptual effect of the juxtaposition of very different colors

/kənˈtɹæst/

v 1: put in contrast 2: to show differences when compared; be different [syn: counterpoint] 3: put in contrast

converse
/ˈkɑnvɝs/

adj 1: of words so related that one reverses the relation denoted by the other; "'parental' and 'filial' are converse terms" 2: turned about in order or relation; "transposed letters" [syn: reversed, transposed]

n : (logic) a proposition obtained by conversion

/kənˈvɝs/

v : carry on a conversation [syn: discourse]

convert
/kənˈvɝt/

v 1: change the nature, purpose, or function of something; "convert lead into gold"; "convert hotels into jails; "convert slaves to laborers" 2: change from one system to another or to a new plan or policy; "We converted from 220 to 110 Volt" [syn: change over] 3: change religious beliefs, or adopt a religious belief; "She converted to Buddhism" 4: exchange or replace with another, usually of the same kind or category; "Could you convert my dollars into pounds?" "He changed his name"; "convert centimeters into inches"; "convert holdings into shares" [syn: change, exchange, commute] 5: cause to adopt a new or different faith; "The missionaries converted the Indian population" 6: make (someone) agree, understand, or realize the truth or validity of something; "He had finally convinced several customers of the advantages of his product" [syn: win over, convince] 7: exchange a penalty for a less severe one [syn: commute, exchange] 8: change in nature, purpose, or function; esp. undergo a chemical change; "The substance converts to an acid"

/ˈkɑnvɝt/

n : one who has been converted to another religious or political belief

convict
/kənˈvɪkt/

v : find or declare guilty [ant: acquit]

/ˈkɑnvɪkt/

n 1: a person serving a prison sentence [syn: con, inmate, jailbird] 2: a person convicted of a criminal offence

coordinate
/ˈkoʊɑɹdɪnɪt/

adj : of equal importance, rank, or degree

n : a number that identifies a position relative to an axis [syn: co-ordinate]

/koʊˈɑɹdɪneɪt/

v 1: bring order and organization to; "Can you help me organize my files?" [syn: organize] 2: bring into common action, movement, or condition; "coordinate the painters, masons, and plumbers"; "coordinate his actions with that of his colleagues"; "coordinate our efforts" 3: be co-ordinated; "These activities co-ordinate well" 4: bring (components or parts) into proper or desirable coordination correlation; "align the wheels of my car" [syn: align]

crooked
/kɹʊkt/

v : (past of crook) : "He crooked his neck so he could see." [syn: bent]

/ˈkɹʊkɪd/

adj 1: having or marked by bends or angles; not straight or aligned; "crooked country roads"; "crooked teeth" [ant: straight] 2: not straight; dishonest or immoral or evasive [syn: corrupt] [ant: straight] 3: irregular in shape or outline; "asymmetrical features"; "a dress with an crooked hemline" [syn: asymmetrical] 4: having the back and shoulders rounded; not erect; "a little oldish misshapen stooping woman" [syn: hunched, round-backed, round-shouldered, stooped, stooping]

cursed
/'kəɹsɪd/

adj 1: deserving a curse; sometimes used as an intensifier; "villagers shun the area believing it to be cursed"; "cursed with four daughter"; "not a cursed drop"; "his cursed stupidity"; "I'll be cursed if I can see your reasoning" [syn: curst] [ant: blessed] 2: (Christianity) in danger of the eternal punishment of hell; "poor damned souls" [syn: damned, doomed, unredeemed, unsaved]

/kəɹst/

v : (past of curse) 1: invoked evil or misfortune upon [syn: damned] 2: swore at 3: brought evil upon; "was cursed with crippling arthritis" [syn: afflict] 4. (ecclesiastical) to put under a ban or an anathema; excommunicate

decline
/'diklaɪn/

n 1: change toward something smaller or lower [syn: diminution] 2: a condition inferior to an earlier condition [ant: improvement] 3: a gradual decrease; as of stored charge or current [syn: decay] 4: a downward slope [syn: descent, declivity, fall, declension, downslope] [ant: ascent]

/di'klaɪn/

v 1: grow worse; "Conditions in the slum worsened" [syn: worsen] [ant: better] 2: refuse to accept; "He refused my offer of hospitality" [syn: refuse, reject, pass up, turn down] [ant: accept] 3: show unwillingness towards [syn: refuse] [ant: accept] 4: grow smaller; "Interest in the project waned" [syn: go down, wane] 5: go down 6: of nouns, pronouns, and adjectives

decrease
/'dikɹis/

n 1: a change downward; "there was a sharp drop-off in sales" [syn: lessening, drop-off] [ant: increase] 2: a process of becoming smaller [syn: decrement] [ant: increase, increase] 3: the amount by which something decreases [syn: decrement] [ant: increase] 4: the act of decreasing or reducing something [syn: diminution, reduction, step-down] [ant: increase]

/dɪ'kɹis/

v 1: decrease in size, extent, or range; "The amount of homework decreased towards

the end of the semester"; "The cabin pressure fell dramatically"; "her weight fall to under a hundred pounds"; "his voice fell to a whisper" [syn: diminish, lessen, fall] [ant: increase] 2: make smaller; "He decreased his staff" [syn: lessen, minify] [ant: increase]

defect
/'difɛkt/

n 1: an imperfection in a bodily system; "visual defects"; "this device permits detection of defects in the lungs" 2: a failing or deficiency; "that interpretation is an unfortunate defect of our lack of information" [syn: shortcoming] 3: an imperfection in a device or machine; "if there are any defects you should send it back to the manufacturer" [syn: fault, flaw] 4: a mark or flaw that spoils the appearance of something (especially on a person's body); "a facial blemish" [syn: blemish]

/dɪ'fɛkt/

v : desert (a cause, a country or an army), often in order to join the opposing cause, country, or army; "If soldiers deserted Hitler's army, they were shot" [syn: desert]

defense
/dɪ'fɛnts/

n 1: military action or resources protecting a country against potential enemies; "they died in the defense of Stalingrad"; "they were developed for the defense program" [syn: defensive measure] 2: the defendant and his legal advisors collectively; "the defense called for a mistrial" [syn: defense team, defense lawyers] [ant: prosecution] 3: protection from harm; "sanitation is the best defense against disease" 4: a structure used for defense; "the artillery battered down the defenses" [syn: defensive structure] 5: the speech act of answering an attack on your assertions; "his refutation of the charges was short and persuasive"; "in defense he said the other man started it" [syn: refutation] 6: the justification for some act or belief; "he offered a persuasive defense of the theory" [syn: vindication] 7: a defendant's answer or plea denying the truth of the charges against him; "he gave evidence for the defense" [syn: denial, demurrer] [ant: prosecution] 8: an organization of defenders that provides resistance against attack; "he joined the defense against invasion" [syn:, defense force] 9: (psychiatry) an unconscious process that tries to reduce the anxiety associated with instinctive desires [syn: defense mechanism, defense reaction]

/dɪ'fɛnts/

n : the team that is trying to prevent the other team from scoring; "his teams are always good on defense" [syn: defending team] [ant: offense]

HETERONYMS

degenerate

/'dɪdʒɛnəɹɪt/

adj : unrestrained by convention or morality; "Congreve draws a debauched aristocratic society"; "deplorably dissipated and degraded"; "riotous living"; "fast women" [syn: debauched, degraded, dissipated, dissolute, libertine, profligate, riotous, fast]

n : a person whose behavior deviates from what is acceptable especially in sexual behavior [syn: pervert, deviant, deviate]

/di'dʒɛnəɹeɪt/

v 1: become worse or disintegrate; "His mind deteriorated" [syn: deteriorate] 2: grow worse; "Her condition deteriorated" [syn: deteriorate, drop] [ant: recuperate]

delegate

/'dɛləgɪt/

n : a person appointed or elected to represent others

/'dɛləgeɪt/

v 1: transfer power to someone [syn: depute] 2: give an assignment to (a person) to a post, or assign a task to (a person) [syn: designate, depute, assign]

deliberate

/dɪ'lɪbəɹɪt/

adj 1: by conscious design or purpose; "intentional damage"; "a knowing attempt to defraud"; "a willful waste of time" [syn: intentional, knowing, willful] 2: with care and dignity; "walking at the same measured pace"; "with all deliberate speed" [syn: careful, measured] 3: produced or marked by conscious design or premeditation; "a studied smile" [syn: studied] [ant: unstudied] 4: marked by careful consideration or reflection; "a deliberate decision" 5: carefully thought out in advance; "a calculated insult"; "with measured irony" [syn: calculated, measured]

/dɪlɪ'bəɹeɪt/

v 1: think about carefully; weigh; "They considered the possibility of a strike"; "Turn the proposal over in your mind" [syn: consider, debate, moot, turn over] 2: discuss the pros and cons of an issue [syn: debate] 3: consider carefully and deeply; reflect upon; turn over in one's mind [syn: cogitate]

desert

/dɪ'zɜɹt/

v 1: leave someone who needs or counts on you; leave in the lurch; "The mother deserted her children" [syn: abandon, forsake, desolate] 2: desert (a cause, country or an army), often in order to join the opposing cause, country, or army; "If soldiers deserted Hitler's army, they were shot" [syn: defect]

/'dɛzəɹt/

adj : located in a dismal or remote area; desolate; "a desert island"; "a godforsaken wilderness crossroads"; "a wild stretch of land"; "waste places" [syn: godforsaken, waste, wild]

n : an arid region with little or no vegetation

diffuse

/dɪ'fuəs/

adj 1: spread out; not concentrated in one place; "a large diffuse organization" 2: lacking conciseness; "a diffuse historical novel"

/dɪ'fuəz/

v 1: move outward; "The soldiers fanned out" [syn: spread, spread out, fan out] 2: spread or diffuse through; "An atmosphere of distrust has permeated this administration" [syn: permeate, pervade, imbue] 3: cause to become widely known; "spread information"; "circulate a rumor"; "broadcast the news" [syn: circulate, circularize, distribute, disseminate, propagate, broadcast, spread, disperse, pass around, promulgate]

digest

/'daɪdʒɛst/

n 1: a periodical that summarizes the news 2: something that is compiled (as into a single book or file) [syn: compilation]

/dɪ'dʒɛst/

v 1: convert food into absorbable substances; "I cannot digest milk products" 2: arrange and integrate in the mind; "I cannot digest all this information"

dingy

/'dɪndʒi/

adj 1: thickly covered with ingrained dirt or soot; "a miner's begrimed face"; "dingy linen"; "grimy hands"; "grubby little fingers"; "a grungy kitchen" [syn: begrimed, grimy, grubby, grungy, raunchy] 2: (of color) discolored by impurities; not bright and clear; "dirty" is often used in combination; "a dirty (or dingy) white"; "the muddied gray of the sea"; "muddy colors"; "dirty-green walls"; "dirty-blonde hair" [syn: dirty, muddied, muddy] 3: depressing in character or appearance; "drove through dingy streets"; "drab old buildings"; "a dreary mining town"; "gloomy tenements" [syn: gloomy, sorry]

/'dɪngi/

adj : (slang) crazy, insane

display

/'dɪspleɪ/

n 1: something intended to communicate a particular impression; "made a display of strength"; "a show of impatience"; "a good show of looking interested" [syn: show] 2: something shown to the public; "the museum had many exhibits of oriental art" [syn: exhibit, showing] 3: an electronic

HETERONYMS

device that represents information in visual form 4: a visual representation of something [syn: presentation] 5: behavior that makes your feelings public; "a display of emotion" 6: exhibiting openly in public view; "a display of courage"

/dɪsˈplɛɪ/

v 1: to show, make visible or apparent: "The Metropolitan Museum is exhibiting Goya's works this month"; "Why don't you show your nice legs and wear shorter skirts?" "National leaders will have to display the highest skills of statesmanship.." [syn: expose, exhibit] 2: make clear and visible; "The article revealed the policies of the government" [syn: reveal, show] 3: attract attention by displaying some body part or posing; of animals

do
/du/

n 1: an uproarious party [syn: bash, brawl] v 1: engage in: "make love, not war"; "make an effort"; "do research"; "do nothing"; "make revolution" [syn: make] 2: to act or perform an action; "John did the painting, the weeding, and he cleaned out the gutters" [syn: perform, execute] 3: get (something) done; "I did my job" [syn: perform] 4: proceed or get along; "How is she doing in her new job?" "How are you making out in graduate school?" "He's come a long way" [syn: fare, make out, come, get along] 5: give rise to; cause to happen or occur, not always intentionally; "cause a commotion"; "make a stir"; "cause an accident" [syn: cause, make] 6: carry out or practice; as of jobs and professions: "practice law" [syn: practice, exercise] 7: be sufficient; be adequate, either in quality or quantity; "A few words would answer"; "This car suits my purpose well"; "Will $100 do?"; "A "B" grade doesn't suffice to get me into medical school"; "Nothing else will serve" [syn: suffice, answer, serve] 8: create or design, often in a certain way; "Do my room in blue"; "I did this piece in wood to express my love for the forest" [syn: make] [ant: unmake] 9: behave in a certain manner; show a certain behavior; conduct or comport oneself; "You should act like an adult"; "Don't behave like a fool"; "What makes her do this way?"; "She played the servant her husband's master" [syn: act, behave] 10: spend time in prison or in a labor camp; "He did six years for embezzlement" [syn: serve] 11: carry on or manage; "We could do with a little more help around here" [syn: manage] 12: arrange attractively; "dress my hair for the wedding" [syn: dress, arrange, set, coif, coiffure] 13: travel or traverse (a distance) "This car does 150 miles per hour"; "We

did 6 miles on our hike every day" 14: (slang) sexual intercourse; "he'll want to do her on their first date"

/doʊ/

n: the syllable naming the first (tonic) note of any major scale in solmization

does
/dʌz/

v : (3rd pers sing of do) (see do)

/doʊz/

n (plu of doe) : mature females of mammals of which the males are called 'bucks'

dogged
/ˈdɔgɪd/

adj : stubbornly unyielding; "dogged persistence"; "dour determination"; "the most vocal and pertinacious of all the critics"; "a mind not gifted to discover truth but tenacious to hold it"- T.S.Eliot; "men tenacious of opinion" [syn: bulldog, dour, pertinacious, tenacious, unyielding, obstinate]

/dɔgd/

v : (past of dog) 1: went after with the intent to catch [syn: chased, chased after, trailed, tailed, tagged, went after, tracked] 2 : held or fastened with a mechanical device: "Watertight doors and hatches were dropped into place and dogged down to give the ship full watertight integrity" - Tom Clancy

dove
/dʌv/

n 1: any of numerous small pigeons 2: someone who prefers negotiations to armed conflict in the conduct of foreign relations [syn: peacenik] [ant: hawk] 3: flesh of a pigeon suitable for roasting or braising; flesh of a dove (young squab) may be broiled [syn: squab] 4: an emblem of peace

/doʊv/

v : (past of dive) 1: dropped steeply; "the stock market plunged" [syn: plunged, plunked] 2: plunged into water; "She dove from the board into the pool" 3: swam under water; "the children enjoyed diving and looking for shells"

drawer
/dʒɔɹ/

n 1: a boxlike container in a piece of furniture; made so as to slide in and out

/ˈdɔˠɹ/

n 1: the person who writes a check or draft instructing the drawee to pay someone else 2: an artist skilled at drawing [syn: draftsman]

duplicate
/ˈduplɪkɪt/

adj 1: identically copied from an original; "a duplicate key" 2: being two identical [syn: matching, twin, twinned]n 1: something additional of the same kind;

HETERONYMS

" he always carried extras in case of an emergency" [syn: extra] 2: a copy that corresponds to an original exactly; "he made a duplicate for the files" [syn: duplication]

/'duplɪkeɪt/

v 1: make or do or perform again; "He could never replicate his brilliant performance of the magic trick" [syn: reduplicate, double, repeat, replicate] 2: duplicate or match; "The polished surface twinned his face and chest in reverse" [syn: twin, parallel] 3: make a duplicate or duplicates of; "Could you please duplicate this letter for me?" 4: increase twofold; "The population doubled within 50 years" [syn: double]

elaborate

/ɪ'læbᵊʌɪt/

adj 1: marked by complexity and richness of detail; "an elaborate lace pattern" [syn: luxuriant] 2: developed or executed with care and in minute detail; "a detailed plan"; "the elaborate register of the inhabitants prevented tax evasion"- John Buchan; "the carefully elaborated theme" [syn: detailed, elaborated]

/i'læbᵊʌeɪt/

v 1: add details, as to an account or idea; clarify the meaning of; "She elaborated on the main ideas in her dissertation" [syn: expatiate, exposit, enlarge, flesh out, expand, expound, dilate] 2: produce from basic elements or sources; change into a more developed product; "The bee elaborates honey" 3: make more complex, intricate, or richer; "refine a design or pattern" [syn: complicate, refine, rarify] 4: work out in detail; "elaborate a plan" [syn: work out]

entrance

/'entɪɪnts/

n 1: something that allows access (entry or exit); "they waited at the entrance to the garden"; "beggars waited just outside the entryway to the cathedral" [syn: entranceway, entryway, entry, entree] 2: a movement into or inward [syn: entering] 3: the act of entering; "she made a grand entrance" [syn: entering, entry, ingress, incoming]

/ɛn'tɹeɐnts/

v 1: attract; cause to be enamored; "She captured all the men's hearts" [syn: capture, enamor, trance, catch, becharm, enamor, captivate, beguile, charm, fascinate, bewitch, enchant] 2: put into a trance [syn: spellbind]

escort

/'ɛskɔɹt/

n 1: someone who escorts and protects a prominent person [syn: bodyguard] 2: the act of accompanying someone or something in order to protect them [syn:

accompaniment] 3: an attendant who is employed to accompany someone 4: a participant in a date; "his date never stopped talking" [syn: date]

/ɛs'kɔɹt/

v 1: accompany as an escort [syn: esquire] 2: accompany or escort: "I'll see you to the door" [syn: see]

estimate

/'ɛstɪmɪt/

n 1: an approximate calculation of quantity or degree or worth; "an estimate of what it would cost"; "a rough idea how long it would take" [syn: estimation, approximation, idea] 2: a judgment of the qualities of something or somebody; "many factors are involved in any estimate of human life"; "in my estimation the boy is innocent" [syn: estimation] 3: a document appraising the value of something (as for insurance or taxation) [syn: appraisal, estimation] 4: a statement indicating the likely cost of some job; "he got an estimate from the car repair shop" 5: the respect with which a person is held; "they had a high estimation of his ability" [syn: estimation]

/'ɛstɪmeɪt/

v 1: form an opinion about; judge tentatively; form an estimate of, esp. quantities or time; "I estimate this chicken to weigh at three pounds" [syn: gauge, approximate, guess, judge] 2: judge to be probable [syn: calculate, reckon, count on, figure, forecast]

evening

/'ivᵊnɪŋ/

n 1: the latter part of the day (the period of decreasing daylight from late afternoon until nightfall); "he enjoyed the evening light across the lake" [syn: eve, eventide] 2: a later concluding time period; "it was the evening of the Roman Empire" 3: the early part of night (from dinner until bedtime) spent in a special way; "an evening at the opera"

/'ivɛnɪŋ/

v : (progressive of even) 1: making level or straightening; "leveling the ground" [syn: leveling, evening out] 2: becoming even or more even; "evening out the surface" [syn: evening out] 3: making even or more even [syn: evening out]

excise

/'ɛksaɪz/

n : a tax that is measured by the amount of business done (not on property or income from real estate) [syn: excise tax]

/ɛk'saɪz/

v 1: remove by erasing or crossing out; "Please strike this remark from the record" [syn: strike, expunge] 2: levy an excise tax on 3: remove by cutting; "The surgeon excised the tumor"

excuse

/ɛk'skuəz/

v 1: accept an excuse for; "Please excuse my dirty hands" [syn: pardon] 2: grant exemption or release to; "Please excuse me from this class [syn: relieve, let off, exempt] 3: serve as an excuse for [syn: explain] 4: defend, explain, clear away, or make excuses for by reasoning; "rationalize the child's seemingly crazy behavior"; "he rationalized his lack of success" [syn: apologize, justify, rationalize] 5: ask for permission to be released from an engagement [syn: beg off] 6: excuse or make allowances for; be lenient with; "excuse someone's behavior" [syn: condone]

/ɛk'skuəs/

n 1: a defense of some offensive behavior or some failure to keep a promise etc.; "he kept finding excuses to stay"; "every day he had a new excuse for not getting a job"; "his transparent self-justification was unacceptable" [syn: alibi, self-justification] 2: a poor example; "it was an apology for a meal"; "a poor excuse for an automobile" [syn: apology]

exploit

/'ɛksplɔɪt/

n : a notable achievement: "he performed a great deed"; "the book was her finest effort" [syn: deed, feat, effort]

/ɛk'splɔɪt/

v 1: use to one's advantage; "He exploit the new taxation system"; "She knows how to work the system"; "he works his parents for sympathy" [syn: work] 2: draw from; make good use of (resources) [syn: tap] 3: work excessively hard [syn: overwork]

export

/'ɛkspɔɹt/

n : commodities (goods or services) sold to a foreign country [ant: import]

/ɛk'spɔɹt/

v : sell or transfer abroad [ant: import]

extract

/'ɛkstɹækt/

n 1: a solution obtained by steeping or soaking a substance (usually in water) [syn: infusion] 2: a passage selected from a larger work; "he presented excerpts from William James' philosophical writings" [syn: excerpt, selection]

/ɛk'stɹækt/

v 1: draw or pull out, usually with some force or effort; also used in an abstract sense; "pull weeds"; "extract a bad tooth"; "take out a splinter"; "extract information from the telegram" [syn: pull out, pull, pull up, take out, draw out] 2: get despite difficulties or obstacles: "I extracted a promise from the Dean for

two ne positions" 3: deduce (a principle) or construe (a meaning); "We drew out some interesting linguistic data from the native informant" [syn: educe, evoke, elicit, draw out] 4: extract by distillation, make by distillation [syn: distill] 5: separate (a metal) from an ore 6: obtain from a substance, as by mechanical action; "Italians express coffee rather than filter it" [syn: press out, express] 7: take out of a literary work in order to cite or copy [syn: excerpt, take out] 8: calculate the root of a number

fine

/faɪn/

adj 1: superior to the average; "in fine spirits"; "a fine student"; "made good grades"; "morale was good"; "had good weather for the parade" [syn: good] 2: (informal) being satisfactory or in satisfactory condition; "an all-right movie"; "the passengers were shaken up but are all right"; "is everything all right?"; "everything's fine"; "things are okay"; "dinner and the movies had been fine"; "another minute I'd have been fine" [syn: all right, ok, o.k., okay, hunky-dory] 3: minutely precise especially in differences in meaning; "a fine distinction" 4: of texture; being small-grained or smooth to the touch or having fine particles; "wood with a fine grain"; "fine powdery snow"; "fine rain"; "batiste is a cotton fabric with a fine weave"; "covered with a fine film of dust" [ant: coarse] 5: being in good health; "he's feeling all right again"; "I'm fine, how are you?" [syn: all right] 6: thin in thickness or diameter; "a fine film of oil"; "fine hairs"; "read the fine print" 7: characterized by elegance or refinement or accomplishment; "fine wine"; "looking fine in her Easter suit"; "a fine gentleman"; "fine china and crystal"; "a fine violinist"; "the fine hand of a master" 8: (metallurgy) free or impurities; having a high or specified degree of purity; "gold 21 carats fine" [syn: f.] 9: (of weather) pleasant; not raining, perhaps with the sun shining; "a fine summer evening"

n : money extracted as a penalty [syn: mulct, amercement]

adv 1: sentence-initial expression of agreement [syn: very well, alright, all right, OK] 2: in a delicate manner; "finely shaped features"; "her fine drawn body" [syn: finely, delicately, exquisitely] 3: in a superior and skilled manner; "the soldiers were fighting finely" [syn: finely]

v 1: impose a fine on [syn: mulct] 2: issue a ticket or a fine to; "I was fined for parking on the wrong side of the street"; "Move your car or else you will be ticketed!" [syn: ticket]

HETERONYMS

/'finɛɪ/
n : the end

forte
/fɔɹt/
n (NOTE: Correct pronunciation for these meanings, even though this is common usage, is /fɔɹ'teɪ/.); 1: an asset of special worth or utility; "cooking is his forte" [syn: strong suit, long suit, metier, specialty, strong point, strength] [ant: weak point] 2: the stronger part of a sword blade between the hilt and the foible

/fɔɹ'teɪ/
adj : used chiefly as a direction or description in music; "the forte passages in the composition" [syn: loud] [ant: piano]
adv : used as a direction in music; to be played relatively loudly [syn: loudly] [ant: piano]
n : (music) with great loudness [syn: fortissimo]

graduate
/'ɡɹædʒuɪt/
adj : of or relating to studies beyond a bachelor's degree; "graduate courses" [syn: postgraduate]
n 1: a person who has received a degree from a school (high school or college or university) [syn: alumnus, alumna, alum, grad] 2: a measuring instrument for measuring fluid volume; a glass container (cup or cylinder or flask) whose sides are marked with or divided into amounts

/'ɡɹædʒueɪt/
v 1: receive an academic degree upon completion of one's studies; "She graduated in 1990" 2: confer an academic degree upon; 'This school graduates 2,000 students each year" 3: make fine adjustments for optimal functioning "calibrate an instrument" [syn: calibrate, fine-tune]

house
/haʊs/
n 1: a dwelling that serves as living quarters for one or more families; "he has a house on Cape Cod"; "she felt she had to get out of the house" 2: an official assembly having legislative powers; "the legislature has two houses" 3: a building in which something is sheltered or located; "they had a large carriage house" 4: a social unit living together; "he moved his family to Virginia"; "It was a good Christian household"; "I waited until the whole house was asleep"; "the teacher asked how many people made up his home" [syn: family, household, home, ménage] 5: a building where theatrical performances or motion-picture shows can be presented; "the house was full" [syn: theater] 6: members of a business organization; "he worked for a brokerage house" [syn: firm,

business firm] 7: aristocratic family line; "the House of York" 8: the members of a religious community living together 9: the audience gathered together in a theatre or cinema; "the house applauded"; "he counted the house" 10: play in which children take the roles of father or mother or children and pretend to interact like adults; "the children were playing house" 11: one of 12 equal areas into which the zodiac is divided [syn: sign of the zodiac, sign, mansion, planetary house] 12: the management of a gambling house or casino; "the house gets a percentage of every bet"

/haʊz/
v 1: contain or cover; "This box houses the gears" 2: provide housing for [syn: put up]

impact
/'ɪmpækt/
n 1: the striking of one body against another 2: a forceful consequence; "the book had an important impact on my thinking" 3: influencing strongly; "they resented the impingement of American values on European culture" [syn: impingement, encroachment] 4: the violent interaction of individuals or groups entering into combat [syn: shock]

/ɪm'pækt/
v 1: press or wedge together; pack together 2: have an effect upon; "Will the new rules affect me?" [syn: affect, bear upon, bear on, touch on, touch]

implant
/'ɪmplænt/
n : a prosthesis placed permanently in tissue

/ɪm'plænt/
v 1: to fix or set securely or deeply: "Kneeling, Cobb planted a sturdy knee in the small of his back," [syn: engraft, embed, imbed, plant] 2: put firmly in the mind; "Plant a thought in the students' minds" [syn: plant]

import
/'ɪmpɔɹt/
n 1: commodities (goods or services) bought from a foreign country [ant: export] 2: an imported person brought from a foreign country; "the lead role was played by an import from Sweden"; "they are descendants of indentured importees" [syn: importee] 3: the message that is intended or expressed [syn: meaning, significance, signification] 4: a meaning that is not expressly stated but can be inferred; "the significance of his remark became clear only later"; "the expectation was spread both by word and by implication" [syn: significance, implication] 5: having important effects or influence; "decisions of great consequence are made by the

president himself"; "virtue is of more moment that security" [syn: consequence, moment] [ant: inconsequence]

/ɪmˈpɔɹt/

v 1: bring in from abroad [ant: export] 2: indicate or signify; "I'm afraid this spells trouble!" [syn: spell]

imprint

/ˈɪmpɹɪnt/

n 1: a distinctive influence; "English still bears the imprint of the Norman invasion" 2: a concavity in a surface produced by pressing; "he left the impression of his fingers in the soft mud" [syn: depression, impression] 3: an impression produced by pressure or printing [syn: embossment] 4: a device produced by pressure on a surface

/ɪmˈpɹɪnt/

v 1: establish or impress firmly in the mind; "We imprint our ideas onto our children" [syn: form] 2: mark or stamp with or as if with pressure; "To make a batik, you impress a design with wax" [syn: impress]

incarnate

/ɪnˈkɑɹnət/

adj 1: possessing or existing in bodily form; "what seemed corporal melted as breath into the wind"- Shakespeare; "an incarnate spirit"; "'corporate' is an archaic term" [syn: bodied, corporal, corporate, embodied] 2: invested with a bodily form especially of a human body; "a monarch... regarded as a god incarnate"

/ɪnˈkɑɹneɪt/

v 1: make concrete and real [ant: disincarnate] 2: represent in bodily form; "He embodies all that is evil wrong with the system" [syn: body forth, embody]

incense

/ˈɪnsɛnts/

n 1: a substance that produces a fragrant odor when burned 2: the pleasing scent produced when incense is burned; "incense filled the room"

/ɪnˈsɛnts/

v 1: perfume esp. with a censer [syn: cense, thurify] 2: make furious [syn: outrage, infuriate, exasperate]

incline

/ˈɪnklaɪn/

n 1: an elevated geological formation; "he climbed the steep slope"; "the house was built on the side of the mountain" [syn: slope, side] 2: an inclined surface or roadway that moves traffic from one level to another [syn: ramp]

/ɪnˈklaɪn/

v 1: have a tendency or disposition to do or be something; be inclined; "She tends to be nervous before her lectures"; "These dresses run small"; "He inclined to corpulence" [syn: tend, be given, lean, run] 2: bend or turn (one's ear) towards

a speaker in order to listen well; "He inclined his ear to the wise old man" 3: lower or bend (the head or upper body), as in a nod or bow; "She inclined her head to the student" 4: be at an angle; "The terrain sloped down" [syn: slope, pitch] 5: make receptive or willing towards an action or attitude or belief; "Their language inclines us to believe them" [syn: dispose] [ant: indispose]

initiate

/ɪˈnɪʃiɪt/

adj : having been introduced to something new [syn: initiated]

n 1: someone new to a field or activity [syn: novice, beginner, tyro] 2: someone who has been admitted to membership in a scholarly field [syn: learned person, pundit, savant] 3: people who have been introduced to the mysteries of some field or activity; "it is very familiar to the initiate" [syn: enlightened] [ant: uninitiate]

/ɪˈnɪʃieɪt/

v 1: bring into being; "He initiated a new program"; "Start a foundation" [syn: originate, start] 2: take the lead or initiative in; participate in the development of; "This South African surgeon pioneered heart transplants" [syn: pioneer] 3: accept young people into society, usually with some rite; "African men are initiated when they reach puberty" [syn: induct] 4: bring up a topic for discussion [syn: broach] 5: prepare the way for; "Hitler's attack on Poland led up to World War Two" [syn: lead up]

insert

/ˈɪnsəɹt/

n 1: a folded section placed between the leaves of another publication 2: an artifact that is inserted or is to be inserted [syn: inset] 3: (film) a still inserted and interrupting the action; (broadcasting) a local announcement inserted into a network broadcast [syn: cut-in]

/ɪnˈsəɹt/

v 1: put or introduce into something; "insert a picture into the text" [syn: infix, enter, introduce] 2: introduce; "Insert your ticket here" [syn: enclose, enclose, stick in, put in, introduce] 3: fit snugly into [syn: tuck] 4: insert casually; "She slipped in a reference to her own work" [syn: slip in, stick in, sneak in]

insult

/ˈɪnsəlt/

n 1: a rude expression intended to offend or hurt; "when a student made a stupid mistake he spared them no abuse"; "they yelled insults at the visiting team" [syn: abuse, revilement, contumely] 2: a deliberately offensive act or something producing the effect of an affront; "turning his back on me was a deliberate insult" [syn: affront]

/ɪnˈsʌlt/

v : treat, mention, or speak to rudely; "He insulted her with his rude remarks" [syn: affront]

intern

/ˈɪntɜɹn/

n : an advanced student or graduate in medicine gaining supervised practical experience ('houseman' is a British term) [syn: houseman, medical intern]

/ɪnˈtɜɹn/

v 1: work as an intern; "She interned at Florida Hospital." 2: to confine or impound; "intern enemy combatants"

intimate

/ˈɪntɪmɪt/

adj 1: very close in friendship or affection; "a bosom buddy"; "an intimate friendship" [syn: bosom] 2: showing profound and detailed knowledge and understanding as from long study; "an intimate knowledge of criminal law" 3: indicating knowledge of personal details that only a close confidant could have; "an intimate biography"; "intimate details of their relationship" 4: having or fostering a warm or friendly atmosphere; especially through smallness and informality; "had a cozy chat"; "a relaxed informal manner"; "an intimate cocktail lounge"; "the small room was cozy and intimate" [syn: cozy, informal] 5: closely interconnected or interrelated; "the intimate relations...between economics, politics, and legal principles"-V.L.Parrington 6: having mutual interests or affections; of established friendship; "on familiar terms"; "pretending she is on an intimate footing with those she slanders" [syn: familiar] 7: involved in a sexual relationship; "the intimate (or sexual) relations between husband and wife"; "she had been intimate with many men" [syn: sexual] 8: innermost or essential; "the inner logic of Cubism"; "the internal contradictions of the theory"; "the intimate structure of matter" [syn: inner, internal] 9: thoroughly acquainted with through study or experience; "this girl, so intimate with nature"-W.H.Hudson; "knowledgeable about the technique of painting"- Herbert Read [syn: intimate with, knowledgeable, knowledgeable about]

n : someone to whom private matters are confided [syn: confidant]

/ˈɪntɪmeɪt/

v 1: give to understand [syn: adumbrate, insinuate] 2: imply as a possibility; "The evidence suggests a need for more clarification" [syn: suggest]

invalid

/ɪnˈvælɪd/

adj 1: having no cogency or legal force; "invalid reasoning"; "an invalid driver's license" [ant: valid] 2: no longer valid; "the license is invalid"

/ˈɪnvᵊlɪd/

n : someone who is incapacitated by a chronic illness or injury [syn: shut-in]

v 1: force to retire, remove from active duty, as of firemen 2: injure permanently; "He was disabled in a car accident" [syn: disable, incapacitate, handicap]

invite

/ˈɪnvaɪt/

n : a colloquial expression for invitation; "he didn't get no invite to the party"

/ɪnˈvaɪt/

v 1: increase the likelihood of; "ask for trouble"; "invite criticism" [syn: ask for] 2: invite someone to one's house; "Can I invite you for dinner on Sunday night?" [syn: ask over, ask round] 3: give rise to a desire [syn: tempt] 4: ask someone in a friendly way to do something [syn: bid] 5: have as a guest; "I invited them to a restaurant" [syn: pay for] 6: ask to enter; "We invited the neighbors in for a cup of coffee" [syn: ask in] 7: request the participation or presence of; "The organizers invite submissions of papers for the conference" [syn: call for] 8: express willingness to have in one's home or environs; "The community warmly received the refugees" [syn: receive, take in]

laminate

/ˈlæmɪnɛt/

v 1: create laminate by putting together several thin sheets of a material 2: press or beat (metals) into thin sheets 3: cover with a thin sheet; "laminate the table"

/ˈlæmᵊnɪt/ or /ˈlæmᵊneɪt/

n : sheet of material made by bonding two or more sheets or layers

lather

/ˈlæðᵊ/

n 1: the froth produced by soaps or detergents [syn: soapsuds, suds] 2: agitation resulting from active worry; "don't get in a stew"; "he's in a sweat about exams" [syn: fret, stew, sweat, swither] 3: the foam resulting from excessive sweating (as on a horse)

v 1: cover with soap [syn: soap] 2: beat severely with a whip or rod; "The teacher often flogged the students"; "The children were severely trounced" [syn: flog, welt, whip, lash, slash, strap, trounce] 3: form a lather; "The shaving cream lathered" 4: rub soap all over, usually with the purpose of cleaning [syn: soap]

HETERONYMS

/ˈlæθɚ/

n: a workman who puts up laths

lead

/lid/

n 1: an advantage held by a competitor in a race: "he took the lead at the last turn" 2: evidence pointing to a possible solution; "the police are following a promising lead"; "the trail led straight to the perpetrator" [syn: track, trail] 3: a position of leadership (especially in the phrase `take the lead'); "he takes the lead in any group"; "we were just waiting for someone to take the lead"; "they didn't follow our lead" 4: the angle between the direction a gun is aimed and the position of a moving target (correcting for the flight time of the missile) 5: the introductory section of a story; "it was an amusing lead-in to a very serious matter" [syn: lead-in] 6: an actor who plays a principal role [syn: star, principal] 7: (baseball) the position taken by a base runner preparing to advance to the next base; "he took a long lead off first" 8: an indication of potential opportunity; "he got a tip on the stock market"; "a good lead for a job" [syn: tip, steer, confidential information, wind, hint] 9: a news story of major importance [syn: lead story] 10: the timing of ignition relative to the position of the piston in an internal-combustion engine [syn: spark advance] 11: restraint consisting of a rope (or light chain) used to restrain an animal [syn: leash, tether] 12: thin strip of metal used to separate lines of type in printing [syn: leading] 13: mixture of graphite with clay in different degrees of hardness; the marking substance in a pencil [syn: pencil lead] 14: a jumper that consists of a short piece of wire; "it was a tangle of jumper cables and clip leads" [syn: jumper cable, jumper lead] 15: the playing of a card to start a trick in bridge; "the lead was in the dummy"

v 1: take somebody somewhere; "We lead him to our chief"; "can you take me to the main entrance?"; "He conducted us to the palace" [syn: take, direct, conduct, guide] 2: result in; "The water left a mark on the silk dress"; "Her blood left a stain on the napkin" [syn: leave, result] 3: tend to or result in; "This remark lead to further arguments among the guests" 4: travel in front of; go in advance of others; "The procession was headed by John" [syn: head] 5: cause to undertake a certain action; "Her greed led her to forge the checks" 6: stretch out over a distance, space, time, or scope; run or extend between two points or beyond a certain point; "Service runs all the way to Cranbury"; "His knowledge doesn't go very far"; "My memory extends back to

my fourth year of life"; "The facts extend beyond a consideration of her personal assets" [syn: run, go, pass, extend] 7: be in charge of; "Who is heading this project?" [syn: head] 8: be ahead of others; be at the top; be the first 9: be conducive to; "The use of computers in the classroom lead to better writing" [syn: contribute, conduce] 10: lead, as in the performance of a musical composition; "conduct an orchestra; Bairenboim conducted the Chicago symphony for years" [syn: conduct, direct] 11: pass or spend; "lead a good life" 12: lead. extend, or afford access; "This door goes to the basement"; "The road runs South" [syn: go] 13: move ahead (of others) in time or space [syn: precede] [ant: follow] 14: cause something to pass or lead somewhere; "Run the wire behind the cabinet" [syn: run] 15: preside over; "John moderated the discussion" [syn: moderate, chair]

n : a soft heavy toxic malleable metallic element; bluish white when freshly cut but tarnishes readily to dull gray; "the children were playing with lead soldiers" [syn: Pb, atomic number 82]

leading

/ˈlidɪŋ/

adj 1: chief; principal; most important; foremost "a leading computer manufacturer" 2: coming in advance of others; first "We rode in the leading car" 3: [syn: directing, guiding]

n: the act of a person or thing that leads.

/ˈlɛdɪŋ/

n 1: thin strip of metal used to increase the space between lines of type in printing 2: a covering or framing of lead "the leading of a stained-glass window"

learned

/ˈlɚnɪd/

adj 1: having or showing profound knowledge; "a learned jurist"; "an erudite professor" [syn: erudite] 2: highly educated; having extensive information or understanding; "an enlightened public"; "knowing instructors"; "a knowledgeable critic"; "a knowledgeable audience" [syn: enlightened, knowing, knowledgeable, lettered, well-educated, well-read] 3: (psychology) established by conditioning or learning; "a conditioned response" [syn: conditioned] [ant: unconditioned] 4: acquired by learning; "learned skills"

/lɚnd/

v : (past of learn) 1: acquire or gain knowledge or skills; "She learned dancing from her sister"; "I learned Sanskrit" [syn: larned] 2: get to know or become aware of, usually accidentally; "I learned that she has two grown-up children"; "I

HETERONYMS

see that you have been promoted" [syn: heard, got word, got wind, picked up, found out, got a line, discovered, saw] 3: commit to memory; learn by heart [syn: memorized] 4: be a student of a certain subject; "She is reading for the bar exam" [syn: studied, read, took] 5: impart skills or knowledge to; "I taught them French"; "He instructed me in building a boat" [syn: taught, instructed] 6: find out, learn, or determine with certainty, usually by making an inquiry or other effort; "I want to see whether she speaks French"; "See whether it works"; "find out if he speaks Russian"; "Check whether the train leaves on time" [syn: determined, checked, found out, saw, ascertained, watched]

lineage
/ˈlɪnɪɪdʒ/
n 1: the descendants of one individual; "his entire lineage has been warriors" [syn: line, line of descent, descent, bloodline, blood line, blood, pedigree, ancestry, origin, parentage, stock] 2: the kinship relation between an individual and the individual's progenitors [syn: descent, line of descent, filiation] 3: inherited properties shared with others of your bloodline [syn: ancestry, derivation, filiation]

/ˈlaɪnɪdʒ/
n 1: a rate of payment for written material that is measured according to the number of lines submitted [syn: linage] 2: the number of lines in a piece of printed material [syn: linage]

live
/laɪv/
adj 1: actually being performed (or--for the audience--present) at the time of viewing; "a live television program"; "brought to you live from Lincoln Center"; "live entertainment" involves performers actually in the physical presence of a "live audience" [syn: unrecorded] (ant: recorded] 2: having life; "a live canary"; "hit a live nerve"; "famous living painters"; "living tissue"; "living plants and animals" [syn: living] 3: showing characteristics of life; exerting force or containing energy; "live coals"; "tossed a live cigarette out the window"; "got a shock from a live wire"; "live ore is unmined ore"; "a live bomb"; "a live ball is one in play" [ant: dead] 4: highly reverberant; "a live concert hall" 5: charged with an explosive; "live ammunition"; "a live bomb" 6: rebounds readily; "clean bouncy hair"; "a lively tennis ball"; "as resilient as seasoned hickory"; "springy turf" [syn: bouncy, lively, resilient, springy, whippy] 7: (informal) abounding with life and energy; "the club members are a really live bunch" 8: (printing) in current use or ready for

use; "live copy is ready to be set in type or already set but not yet proofread" 9: of current relevance; "a live issue"; "still a live option" 10: (electricity) charged or energized with electricity; "a hot wire"; "a live wire" [syn: hot] 11: capable of erupting; "a live volcano"; "the volcano is very much alive" [syn: alive]adv : not recorded; "the opera was broadcast live :
/lɪv/
v 1: make one's home or live in; "There are only 250,000 people in Iceland"; "I live in a 200-year old house"; "These people inhabited all the islands that are now deserted"; "The plains are sparsely populated" [syn: dwell, shack, reside, inhabit, people, populate] 2: lead a certain kind of life; live in a certain style; "we had to live frugally after the war" 3: continue to live; endure or last; "We went without water and food for 3 days"; "The legend of Elvis lives on"; "These superstitions survive in the backwaters of America"; "The racecar driver lived through several very serious accidents" [syn: survive, last, live on, go, endure, hold up, hold out] 4: support oneself; "he could barely exist on such a low wage"; "Can you live on $2000 a month in New York City?"; "Many people in the world have to subsist on $1 a day" [syn: exist, survive, subsist] 5: have life, be alive; "Our great leader is no more"; "My grandfather lived until the end of war" [syn: be] 6: have firsthand knowledge of states, situations, emotions, or sensations; "I know the feeling!" "have you ever known hunger?"; "I have lived a kind of hell when I was a drug addict"; "The holocaust survivors have lived a nightmare"; "I lived through two divorces" [syn: know, experience] 7: pursue a positive and satisfying existence; "You must accept yourself and others if you really want to live"

minute
/ˈmɪnɪt/
n 1: a unit of time equal to 60 seconds or 1/60th of an hour; "he ran a 4 minute mile" [syn: min] 2: an indefinitely short time; "wait just a moment"; "it only takes a minute"; "in just a bit" [syn: moment, second, bit] 3: a particular point in time; "the moment he arrived the party began" [syn: moment, second, instant] 4: a unit of angular distance equal to a 60th of a degree [syn: arc-minute, minute of arc] 5: a short note; "the secretary keeps the minutes of the meeting" 6: distance measured by the time taken to cover it; "we live an hour from the airport"; "its just 10 minutes away" [syn: hour]
/maɪˈnuət/
adj 1: infinitely or immeasurably small;

HETERONYMS

"two minute whip-like threads of protoplasm"; "reduced to a microscopic scale" [syn: infinitesimal, microscopic] 2: immeasurably small [syn: atomic, atom-like] 3: characterized by painstaking care and detailed examination; "a minute inspection of the grounds"; "a narrow scrutiny"; "an exact and minute report" [syn: narrow]

moderate
/'mɑdᵊɹɪt/

adj 1: being within reasonable or average limits; not excessive or extreme; "moderate prices"; "a moderate income"; "a moderate fine"; "moderate demands"; "a moderate estimate"; "a moderate eater"; "moderate success"; "a kitchen of moderate size"; "the X-ray showed moderate enlargement of the heart" [ant: immoderate] 2: not extreme; "a moderate penalty"; "temperate in his response to criticism" [syn: temperate] 3: marked by avoidance of extravagance or extremes; "moderate in his demands"; "restrained in his response" [syn: restrained]n : a person who takes a position in the political center [syn: centrist, middle of the roader, moderationist]
/'mɑdᵊɪeɪt/

v 1: preside over; "John moderated the discussion" [syn: chair, lead] 2: make less fast or intense; "moderate your speed" 3: lessen the intensity of; temper; hold in restraint; hold or keep within limits; "moderate your alcohol intake" "hold your tongue"; "hold your temper"; "control your anger" [syn: control, hold in, hold, contain, check, curb] 4: make less severe or harsh; "He moderated his tone when the students burst out in tears" [syn: mince, soften] 5: make less strong or intense; soften; "Tone down that aggressive letter"; "The author finally tamed some of his potentially offensive statements" [syn: tone down, tame] 6: restrain or temper [syn: chasten, temper] 7: make less severe or harsh [syn: mitigate]

moped
/moʊpt/

v : (past of mope) 1: moved around slowly and aimlessly [syn: moped around] 2: be apathetic, gloomy, or dazed [syn: mooned around, mooned about]
/'moʊpɛd/

n : a motorbike that can be pedaled or driven by a low-powered gasoline engine

mouth
/maʊθ/

n 1: the opening through which food is taken in and vocalizations emerge; "he stuffed his mouth with candy" [syn: oral cavity, oral fissure, rima oris] 2: the externally visible part of the oral cavity on the face and the system of organs surrounding the opening; "she wiped lipstick from her mouth" 3: an opening that resembles a mouth (as of a cave or a gorge); "he rode into the mouth of the canyon"; "they built a fire at the mouth of the cave" 4: the point where a stream issues into a larger body of water; "New York is at the mouth of the Hudson" 5: a person conceived as a consumer of food; "he has four mouths to feed" 6: (informal) a spokesperson (as a lawyer) [syn: mouthpiece] 7: an impudent or insolent rejoinder; "don't give me any of your sass" [syn: sass, sassing, backtalk, back talk, lip] 8: the opening of a jar or bottle; "the jar had a wide mouth"
/maʊð/

v 1: express in speech; "She talks a lot of nonsense" [syn: talk, speak, utter, verbalize] 2: articulate silently; form words with the lips only; "She mouthed a swear word" 3: touch with the mouth

mow
/moʊ/

v 1: cut with a blade or mower; "mow the grass" [syn: cut down] 2: make a sad face; "mop and mow" [syn: pout, mop]
/maʊ/

n : a loft for storing hay [syn: hayloft]

multiply
/'mʌltɪplaɪ/

v 1: combine by multiplication; "multiply 10 by 15" [ant: divide] 2: combine or increase by multiplication; "He managed to multiply his profits" [syn: manifold] 3: have young; used of animals; derogatory when used for people [syn: breed] 4: have offspring or young [syn: reproduce, procreate]
/'mʌltɪpli/

adv : in several ways; in a multiple manner; "they were multiply checked for errors" [ant: singly]

number
/'nʌmbᵊɹ/

n 1: the property possessed by a sum or total or indefinite quantity of units or individuals; "he had a number of chores to do"; "the number of parameters is small"; "the figure was about a thousand" [syn: figure] 2: a concept of quantity derived from zero and units; "every number has a unique position in the sequence" 3: a short theatrical performance that is part of a longer program; "he did his act three times every evening"; "she had a catchy little routine"; "it was one of the best numbers he ever did" [syn: act, routine, turn, bit] 4: a numeral or string of numerals that is used for identification; "she refused to give them her Social Security number" [syn: identification number] 5: the number

HETERONYMS

is used in calling a particular telephone; "he has an unlisted number" [syn: phone number, telephone number] 6: a symbol used to represent a number; "he learned to write the numerals before he went to school" [syn: numeral] 7: one of a series published periodically; "she found an old issue of the magazine in her dentist's waiting room" [syn: issue]

8: a select company of people; "I hope to become one of their number before I die" 9: (linguistics) the grammatical category for the forms of nouns and pronouns and verbs that are used depending on the number of entities involved (singular or dual or plural); "in English the subject and the verb must agree in number" 10: an item of merchandise offered for sale; "she preferred the black nylon number"; "this sweater is an all-wool number" 11: (informal) a clothing measurement: "a number 13 shoe"

v 1: add up in number or quantity; "The bills amounted to $2,000"; "The bill came to $2,000" [syn: total, add up, come, amount] 2: give numbers to; "You should number the pages of the thesis" 3: enumerate; "We must number the names of the great mathematicians" [syn: list] 4: put into a group; "The academy counts several Nobel Prize winners among its members" [syn: count] 5: determine the number or amount of; "Can you count the books on your shelf?"; "Count your change" [syn: count, enumerate] 6: place a limit on the number of [syn: keep down]

/'nʌm³ɹ/

adj (compar of numb) : more numb

nun

/nʌn/

n 1: a woman in a religious order 2: a buoy resembling a cone [syn: conical buoy, nun buoy]

/nʊn/

n: the 14th letter of the Hebrew alphabet

object

/əb'dʒɛkt/

v : express or raise an objection or protest; express dissent; "She never objected to the amount of work her boss charged her with"

/'abdʒɛkt/

n 1: a tangible and visible entity; an entity that can cast a shadow; "it was full of rackets, balls and other objects" [syn: physical object] 2: the goal intended to be attained (and which is believed to be attainable); "the sole object of her trip was to see her children" [syn: aim, objective, target] 3: a grammatical constituent that is acted upon; "the object of the verb" 4: the focus of cognitions or feelings; "objects of thought"; "the object of my affection"

offense

/'ɔfɛnts/

n 1: the team that has the ball (or puck) and is trying to score [syn: offence] [ant: defense] 2: the action of attacking the enemy [syn: offence, offensive]

/ɔ'fɛnts/

n 1: a lack of politeness; a failure to show regard for others; wounding the feelings or others [syn: discourtesy, offence, offensive activity] 2: a feeling of anger caused by being offended; "he took offence at my question" [syn: umbrage, offence] 3: a crime less serious than a felony [syn: misdemeanor, infraction, offence, violation, infringement]

overlook

/'ouvəɹluk/

n : a high place affording a good view

/ouvəɹ'luk/

v 1: look past, fail to notice 2: be oriented in a certain direction; "The house looks out on a tennis court"; "The apartment overlooks the Hudson" [syn: look out on, look out over, look across] 3: leave undone or leave out; "How could I miss that typo?"; "The workers on the conveyor belt miss one out of ten" [syn: neglect, omit, drop, miss, leave out, overlap] [ant: attend to] 4: look down on; "The villa dominates the town" [syn: dominate, command, overtop] 5: watch over

palsy

/'pɔlzi/

n 1: loss of the ability to move a body part [syn: paralysis] 2: a condition marked by uncontrollable tremor 3: a fit of strong emotion marked by the inability to act

v : affect with palsy

/'pælzi/

adj : very friendly; "He's become very palsy with her." [syn: palsy-walsy]

pasty

/'pɛɪsti/

adj 1: resembling paste in color; pallid; "the looked pasty and red-eyed"; "a complexion that had been paste-like was now chalky white" [syn: paste-like] 2: having the properties of glue [syn: gluey, glutinous, gummy, mucilaginous, sticky, viscid, viscous]

/'pæsti/

n 1: small meat pie or turnover 2: small areola covering used by exotic dancers (usually /'pɛɪsti/)

pate

/pɛɪt/

n: the top of the head [syn: poll, crown]

/'patɛɪ/ (actually spelled *pâté*)

n 1: liver or meat or fowl finely minced or ground and variously seasoned

/pɑt/ (actually spelled *pâte*)

n : a porcelain paste

II-24

HETERONYMS

patent
/ˈpætⁿnt/
n 1: a document granting an inventor sole rights to an invention 2: an official document granting a right or privilege [syn: letters patent]
v 1: obtain a patent for; "Should I patent this invention?" 2: grant rights to; grant a patent for 3: make open to sight or notice; "His behavior has patented an embarrassing fact about him"
/ˈpɛrtɛnt/
adj 1: (of a bodily tube or passageway) open; affording free passage; "patent ductus arteriosus" 2: clearly apparent or obvious to the mind or senses; "the effects of the drought are apparent to anyone who sees the parched fields"; "evident hostility"; "manifest disapproval"; "patent advantages"; "made his meaning plain"; "it is plain that he is no reactionary"; "in plain view" [syn: apparent, evident, manifest, plain]

peaked
/pikt/
v : (past of peak) : to reach the highest point; attain maximum intensity, activity; "That wild, speculative spirit peaked in 1929." [syn: reached a peak]
/ˈpikɪd/
adj 1: somewhat ill or prone to illness; "my poor ailing grandmother"; "feeling a bit indisposed today"; "you look a little peaked"; "feeling poorly"; "a sickly child"; "is unwell and can't come to work" [syn: ailing, indisposed, poorly, sickly, unwell] 2: having or rising to a peak; "the peaked ceiling"; "the island's peaked hills"

perfect
/ˈpəɹfɛkt/
adj 1: being complete of its kind and without defect or blemish; "a perfect circle"; "a perfect reproduction"; "perfect happiness"; "perfect manners"; "a perfect specimen"; "a perfect day" [ant: imperfect] 2: without qualification; used informally as (often pejorative) intensifiers; "an arrant fool"; "a complete coward"; "a consummate fool"; "a double-dyed villain"; "gross negligence"; "a perfect idiot"; "pure folly"; "what a sodding mess"; "stark staring mad"; "a thoroughgoing villain"; "utter nonsense" [syn: arrant, complete, consummate, double-dyed, everlasting, gross, pure, sodding, stark, staring, thoroughgoing, utter] 3: precisely accurate or exact; "perfect timing"
n : a tense of verbs used in describing action that has been completed (sometimes regarded as perfective aspect) [syn: perfective, perfective tense, perfect tense]

/pəˈfɛkt/
v 1: make perfect or complete; "perfect your French in Paris!" [syn: hone] 2: make perfect; bring to perfection [syn: consummate]

periodic
/ˈpɹiɑdɪk/
adj 1: happening or recurring at regular intervals [syn: periodical] [ant: aperiodic] 2: recurring at regular intervals 3: recurring or reappearing from time to time; "periodic feelings of anxiety"
/ˈpəɹaɪɑdɪk/
adj : pertaining to a strong oxidizing iodine acid [syn: periodic acid]

permit
/pəˈmɪt/
v 1: give permission; "She permitted her son to visit her estranged husband"; "I won't let the police search her basement"; "I cannot allow you to see your exam" [syn: allow, let, countenance] [ant: forbid] 2: make it possible through a specific action or lack of action for something to happen; "This permits the water to rush in"; "This sealed door won't allow the water come into the basement"; "This will permit the rain to run off" [syn: let, allow] [ant: prevent] 3: allow the presence of; "We don't allow dogs here"; "Children are not permitted beyond this point" [syn: allow]
/ˈpəɹmɪt/
n 1: a legal document giving official permission to do something [syn: license] 2: the act of giving a formal (usually written) authorization [syn: license, permission] 3: large game fish; found in waters of the West Indies [syn: Trachinotus falcatus]

pervert
/ˈpəɹvəɹt/
n : a person whose behavior deviates from what is acceptable especially in sexual behavior [syn: deviant, deviate, degenerate]
/pəˈvəɹt/
v 1: corrupt morally or by intemperance or sensuality; "debauch the young people with wine and women" [syn: corrupt, demoralize, demoralise, debauch, debase, profane, vitiate, deprave, misdirect] 2: change the meaning of [syn: twist, twist around, convolute, sophisticate] 3: change the inherent purpose or function of something; "Don't abuse the system"; "The director of the factory misused the funds intended for the health care of his workers" [syn: misuse, abuse]

prayer
/pɹeəɹ/
n 1: the act of communicating with a deity (especially as a petition or in adoration

or contrition or thanksgiving) [syn: supplication] 2: reverent petition to a deity [syn: communion, petition, orison] 3: earnest or urgent request; "an entreaty to stop the fighting"; "an appeal for help"; "an appeal to the public to keep calm" [syn: entreaty, appeal] 4: a fixed text used in praying

/'pɹeɪˀɹ/
n: someone who prays to God [syn: supplicant]

precedent

/'pɹɛsɪdɛnt/
n 1: an example that is used to justify similar occurrences at a later time [syn: case in point] 2: (civil law) a law established by following earlier judicial decisions [syn: case law, common law] 3: a subject mentioned earlier (preceding in time)

/pɹɪ'sidɛnt/
adj : preceding in time, order, or significance

precipitate

/pɹɛ'sɪpɪtɪt/
adj : done with very great haste and without due deliberation; "wondered whether they had been rather precipitate in deposing the king" [syn: hasty, overhasty, precipitant]

/pɹɛ'sɪpɪteɪt/
n : a precipitated solid substance in suspension or after settling or filtering
v 1: separate as a fine suspension of solid particles 2: bring about abruptly: "The crisis precipitated by Russia's revolution" 3: fall from clouds; "rain, snow and sleet were falling"; "Vesuvius precipitated its fiery, destructive rage on Herculaneum." [syn: come down, fall] 4: fall vertically, sharply, or headlong; "Our economy precipitated into complete ruin" 5: hurl or throw violently; "The bridge broke and precipitated the train into the river below"

predicate

/'pɹɛdɪkɪt/
adj : (grammar) of adjectives; relating to or occurring within the predicate of a sentence; "'red' is a predicative adjective in 'the apple is red'" [syn: predicative] [ant: attributive]
n 1: (logic) what is predicated of the subject of a proposition; the second term in a proposition is predicated of the first term by means of the copula; "'Socrates is a man' predicates manhood of Socrates" 2: (linguistics) one of the two main constituents of a sentence, the predicate contains the verb and its complements [syn: verb phrase]

/'pɹɛdɪkeɪt/
v 1: make the (grammatical) predicate in a proposition; "The predicate 'dog' is predicated of the subject 'Fido' in

the sentence 'Fido is a dog'" 2: affirm or declare as an attribute or quality of; "The speech predicated the fitness of the candidate to be President" [syn: proclaim] 3: involve as a necessary condition of consequence; as in logic; "solving the problem is predicated on understanding it well" [syn: connote]

predominate

/'pɹɪdamɪnɪt/
adj : having superior power and influence; "the predominant mood among policy-makers is optimism" [syn: overriding, paramount, predominant, preponderant]

/'pɹɪdamɪneɪt/
v : be larger in number, quantity, or importance; "Money reigns supreme here"; "Hispanics predominate in this neighborhood" [syn: dominate, rule, reign, prevail]

present

/'pɹɛzɪnt/
adj 1: temporal sense; intermediate between past and future; now existing or happening or in consideration; "the present leader"; "articles for present use"; "the present topic"; "the present system"; "present observations" [ant: future, past] 2: spatial sense; being or existing in a specified place; "the murderer is present in this room"; "present at the wedding"; "present at the creation" [ant: absent] 3: (grammar) a verb tense or other construction referring to events or states that exist at the moment
n 1: the period of time that is happening now; any continuous stretch of time including the moment of speech; "that is enough for the present"; "he lives in the present with no thought of tomorrow" [syn: nowadays] 2: something presented as a gift; "his tie was a present from his wife" 3: a verb tense that expresses actions or states at the time of speaking [syn: present tense]

/pɹɪ'zɛnt/
v 1: show or demonstrate something to an interested audience; "She shows her dogs frequently"; "We will demo the new software in Washington" [syn: show, demo, exhibit, demonstrate] 2: bring forward; "We presented the arguments to him" [syn: lay out] 3: perform (a play), esp. on a stage; "we are going to stage 'Othello'" [syn: stage] 4: hand over formally [syn: submit] 5: introduce; "This poses an interesting question" [syn: pose] 6: give, esp. as a reward; "bestow honors and prizes at graduation" [syn: award] 7: give as a present; make a gift of; "What will you give her for her birthday?" [syn: give, gift] 8: deliver (a speech, oration, or idea); "The commencement speaker

presented a forceful speech that impressed the students" [syn: deliver] 9: cause to come to know personally; "permit me to acquaint you with my son"; "introduce the new neighbors to the community" [syn: introduce, acquaint] 10: represent in a painting, drawing, sculpture, or verbally; "The father is portrayed as a coward in this play" [syn: portray] 11: present somebody with something, usually to accuse or criticize; ""We confronted him with the evidence"; "He was faced with all the evidence and could no longer deny his actions"; An enormous dilemma faces us" [syn: confront, face] 12: formally present a debutante, a representative of a country, etc. 13: assume a position; in the military [syn: salute]

primer
/ˈpɹaɪmᵊɹ/

n 1: any igniter by which an explosive charge is ignited [syn: fuse, fuze, fusee, fuzee, priming] 2: the first or preliminary coat of paint or size applied to a surface [syn: flat coat, ground, priming, primer coat, priming coat, undercoat]

/ˈpɹɪmᵊɹ/

n 1: an introductory textbook

proceeds
/ˈpɹousidz/

n : the income arising from land or other property; "the average return was about 5%" [syn: return, issue, take, takings, yield, payoff]

/pɹouˈsidz/

v : (3rd pers sing for proceed) 1: continues with one's activities; "I know it's hard," he continued, "but there is no choice"; "carry on--pretend we are not in the room" [syn: continues, goes on, carries on] 2: moves ahead; travels onward; "We proceeded towards Washington"; "She continued in the direction of the hills"; can also be used in the temporal sense: "We are moving ahead in time now" [syn: goes forward, continues] 3: follows a procedure or takes a course; "We should go further in this matter"; "She went through a lot of trouble"; "goes about the world in a certain manner"; "Messages must go through diplomatic channels" [syn: goes, moves] 4: follow a certain course; "The inauguration proceeds well"; "how did your interview go?" [syn: goes] 5: continues a certain state, condition, or activity; "Keep on working!"; "We continued to work into the night"; "Keep smiling"; "We went on working until well past midnight" [syn: continues, goes on, goes along, keeps on] [ant: discontinues]

process
/ˈpɹɑses/

n 1: a particular course of action intended to achieve a results; "the procedure of obtaining a driver's license"; "it was a process of trial and error" [syn: procedure] 2: a sustained phenomenon or one marked by gradual changes through a series of states; "events now in process"; "the process of calcification begins later for boys than for girls" 3: the performance of some composite cognitive activity; an operation that affects mental contents; "the process of thinking"; "the act of remembering" [syn: cognitive process, operation, cognitive operation, act] 4: a writ issued by authority of law; usually compels the defendant's attendance in a civil suit; failure to appear results in a default judgment against the defendant [syn: summons] 5: a mental process that you are not directly aware of; "the process of denial" [syn: unconscious process] 6: a natural prolongation or projection from a part of an organism either animal or plant; "a bony process" [syn: outgrowth, appendage]v 1: deal with in a routine way; "I'll handle that one"; "process a loan"; "process the applicants" 2: subject to a process or treatment, with the aim of readying for some purpose, improving, or remedying a condition; "process cheese"; "process hair"; "treat the water so it can be drunk"; "treat the lawn with chemicals" ; "treat an oil spill" [syn: treat] 3: perform mathematical and logical operations on (data) according to programmed instructions in order to obtain the required information; "The results of the elections were still being processed when he gave his acceptance speech" 4: institute legal proceedings against; file a suit against; "He was warned that the district attorney would process him" [syn: sue, litigate] 5: shape, form, or improve a material; "work stone into tools"; "process iron"; "work the metal" [syn: work, work on] 6: deliver a warrant or summons to someone; "He was processed by the sheriff" [syn: serve, swear out]

/pɹəˈses/

v: march in a procession; "They processed into the dining room" [syn: march]

produce
/ˈpɹoudus/ (also /ˈpɹouduəs/)

n : fresh fruits and vegetable grown for the market [syn: green goods, green groceries, garden truck]

/pɹouˈdus/

v 1: bring forth or yield: "The tree would not produce fruit" [syn: bring forth] 2: create or manufacture a man-made product: "We produce more cars than we can sell"; "The company has been making toys for two centuries" [syn: make, create] 3: cause to occur or exist: "This procedure produces a curious effect"; "The new law gave rise to many complaints"; "These chemicals produce a noxious vapor" [syn: bring about, give rise] 4: bring out for display: "The proud father produced many pictures of his baby"; "The accused brought forth a letter in court that he claims exonerates him" [syn: bring forth] 5: bring onto the market or release, as of an intellectual creation: "produce a movie"; "bring out a book"; "produce a new play" [syn: bring on, bring out] 6: cultivate by growing; often involves improvements by means of agricultural techniques: "The Bordeaux region produces great red wines"; "They produce good ham in Parma"; "We grow wheat here"; "We raise hogs here" [syn: grow, raise, farm] 7: come to have or undergo a change of (physical features and attributes); "He grew a beard"; The patient developed abdominal pains"; I got funny spots all over my body"; "Well-developed breasts" [syn: grow, develop, get, acquire]

progress
/ˈpɹɑgɹɛs/

n 1: gradual improvement or growth or development: "advancement of knowledge"; "great progress in the arts"; "their research and development gave them an advantage" [syn: advancement] 2: the act of moving forward toward a goal [syn: progression, advance, advancement, forward motion, onward motion] 3: a movement forward; "he listened for the progress of the troops" [syn: progression, advance]

/pɹɑˈgɹɛs/

v 1: develop in a positive way; "He progressed well in school"; "My plants are coming along"; "Plans are shaping up" [syn: come on, come along, advance, get on, get along, shape up] [ant: regress] 2: move forward, also in the metaphorical sense: "Time marches on" [syn: advance, pass on, move on, march on, go on] [ant: recede] 3: form steadily; "Resistance to the manager's plan built up quickly" [syn: build up, work up, build]

project
/pɹoʊˈdʒɛkt/

v 1: communicate vividly; "He projected his feelings" 2: extend out or project in space; "His sharp nose jutted out"; "A single rock stick out from the cliff" [syn: stick out, protrude, jut out, jut] 3: transfer from one domain into another, as of ideas and principles 4: project on a screen; "The images are projected onto the screen" 5: cause to be heard; "His voice projects well" 6: draw a projection of 7: make or work out a plan for; devise; "They contrived to murder their boss"; design a new sales strategy"; "plan an attack"

[syn: plan, contrive, design] 8: present for consideration [syn: propose] 9: imagine; conceive of; see in one's mind; "I can't see him on horseback!" "I can see what will happen"; "I can see a risk in this strategy" [syn: visualize, envision, fancy, see, figure, picture, image] 10: put or send forth; "She threw the flashlight beam into the corner"; "The setting sun threw long shadows"; "cast a spell"; "cast a warm light" [syn: cast, contrive, throw] 11: throw, send, or cast forward; "project a missile" [syn: send off] 12: regard as objective; in psychology [syn: externalize]

/ˈpɹɑdʒɛkt/

n 1: any piece of work that is undertaken or attempted; "he prepared for great undertakings" [syn: undertaking, task, labor] 2: a planned undertaking [syn: projection] 3: a school task requiring considerable effort [syn: classroom project]

proportionate
/pɹəˈpɔɹʃˀnɪt/

adj 1: being in due proportion [ant: disproportionate] 2: agreeing in amount, magnitude, or degree; "the figures are large but the corresponding totals next year will be larger" [syn: corresponding, in proportion to] 3: exhibiting equivalence or correspondence among constituents of an entity or between different entities [syn: harmonious, symmetrical]

/pɹəˈpɔɹʃəneɪt/

v : make proportionate

protest
/ˈpɹoʊtɛst/

n 1: a formal and solemn declaration of objection; "they finished the game under protest to the league president"; "the senator rose to register his protest"; "the many protestations did not stay the execution" [syn: protestation] 2: the act of protesting; a public (often organized) manifestation of dissent [syn: objection, dissent] 3: the act of making a strong public expression of disagreement and disapproval; "he shouted his protests at the umpire"; "a shower of protest was heard from the rear of the hall"

/pɹoʊˈtɛst/

v 1: utter words of protest 2: fight back, also metaphorically: "His body protested against the harsh training" [syn: resist, dissent] 3: affirm or avow formally or solemnly; "The suspect protested his innocence"

pussy
/ˈpʌsi/

adj : having undergone infection; having pus; "festering sores"; "an infected wound" [syn: festering, infected, purulent, putrid]

HETERONYMS

/ˈpʊsi/

n 1: slang term for female genitals [syn: cunt, puss, slit, snatch, twat] 2: informal term for a cat [syn: kitty, kitty-cat, puss, pussycat]

putting
/ˈpʊtɪŋ/

v : (progressive of put) 1) : put into a certain place or abstract location; "Put your things here"; "Set the tray down"; "Set the dogs on the scent of the missing children"; "Place emphasis on a certain point" [syn: setting, placing, posing, positioning, laying] 2: cause to be in a certain state; cause to be in a certain relation; "That song put me in awful good humor." 3: formulate in a particular style or language; "I wouldn't put it that way"; "She cast her request in very polite language" [syn: framing, redacting, casting, couching] 4: putting something on or into (abstractly) assign; ; "She put much emphasis on her last statement"; "He put all his efforts into this job"; "The teacher put an interesting twist to the interpretation of the story" [syn: assigning] 5: make an investment; "Put money into bonds" [syn: investing, committing, placing] [ant: divesting] 6: estimating; "We put the time of arrival at 8 P.M." [syn: placing, setting] 7: causing (someone) to undergo something; "He put her to the torture" 8: adapting; "put these words to music" 9: arranging thoughts, ideas, temporal events, etc.; "arrange my schedule;" "set up one's life"; "I put these memories with those of bygone times" [syn: arranging, setting up, ordering]

/ˈpʌtɪŋ/

n : hitting a golf ball on the putting surface with a putter; "his putting let him down today" [syn: putt]

v : (progressive of putt) 1: striking (a golf ball) lightly, with a putter; "he's putting the ball several feet past the hole" 2: (golf): hitting a putt; "he lost because he putted so poorly"

ragged
/ˈɹæɡɪd/

adj 1: being or dressed in clothes that are worn or torn; "clothes as ragged as a scarecrow's"; "a ragged tramp" 2: worn out from stress or strain; "run ragged" 3: having an irregular outline; "text set with ragged right margins"; "herded the class into a ragged line"

/ˈɹæɡd/

v : (past of rag) 1: to composed or played (a piece) in ragtime 2: teased or taunted [syn: bantered] 3: (slang) berate; scold 4: (ice hockey) maintained possession of (the puck) by outmaneuvering opposing players, especially so as to kill a penalty

raven
/ˈɹeɪvɪn/

n : large black bird with a straight bill and long wedge-shaped tail [syn: Corvus corax]

/ˈɹævɪn/

v 1: obtain or seize by violence 2: prey on or hunt for [syn: prey] 3: eat greedily [syn: devour, gulp, guttle, pig] 4: feed greedily

read
/ɹid/

n : something that is read; "the article has a very good read"

v 1: interpret something that is written or printed; "read the advertisement"; "Have you read Salman Rushdie?" 2: have or contain a certain wording or form; "The passage reads as follows"; "What does the law say?" [syn: say] 3: look at, interpret, and say out loud something that is written or printed; "The King will read the proclamation at noon" 4: obtain data from magnetic tapes; "This dictionary can be read by the computer" [syn: scan] 5: interpret the significance of, as of palms, tea leaves, intestines, the sky, etc.; also of human behavior; "She read the sky and predicted rain"; "I can't read his strange behavior" 6: interpret something in a certain way; convey a particular meaning or impression; "I read this address as a satire"; "How should I take this message?"; You can't take credit for this!" [syn: take] 7: indicate a certain reading; of gauges and instruments; "The thermometer showed thirteen degrees below zero"; "The gauge read `empty'" [syn: register, show, record] 8: be a student of a certain subject; "She is reading for the bar exam" [syn: learn, study, take] 9: audition for a stage role by reading parts of a role; "He is auditioning for Julius Cesar at Stratford this year" 10: to hear and understand; "I read you loud and clear!" 11: make sense of a language; "She understands French"; "Can you read Greek?" [syn: understand, interpret, translate]

/ɹɛd/

adj : having been read; often used in combination; "a widely read newspaper" [ant: unread]

v : (past of read)

rebel
/ˈɹɛbəl/

adj : used by northerners of Confederate soldiers; "the rebel yell"

n 1: (informal) `johnny' was applied as a nickname for Confederate soldiers by the Federal soldiers in the American Civil War; `grayback' derived from their gray Confederate uniforms [syn: Rebel, Reb, Johnny Reb, Johnny, grayback] 2: a person who takes part in an armed rebellion against the constituted authority (especially in the hope of improving conditions) [syn: insurgent, insurrectionist, freedom fighter] 3: someone who exhibits great independence in thought and action [syn: maverick]

/ɹɪ'bɛl/

adj: participating in organized resistance to a constituted government; "the rebelling confederacy" [syn: rebelling, rebellious]

v 1: take part in a rebellion; renounce a former allegiance [syn: arise, rise, rise up] 2: break with established customs [syn: renegade]

rebound

/'ɹibaʊnd/

n 1: a movement back from an impact [syn: recoil, repercussion, backlash] 2: a reaction to a crisis or setback or frustration; "he is still on the rebound from his wife's death" 3: the act of securing possession of the rebounding basketball after a missed shot

/ɹɪ'baʊnd/

v 1: spring back; spring away from an impact; "The rubber ball bounced"; "These particles do not resile but they unite after they collide" [syn: bounce, resile, take a hop, spring, bound, recoil, ricochet] 2: return to a former condition; "The jilted lover soon rallied and found new friends"; "The stock market rallied" [syn: rally]

recall

/'ɹikɔl/

n 1: the process of remembering (especially the process of recovering information by mental effort) [syn: recollection, reminiscence] 2: the act of removing an official by petition

/ɹɪ'kɔl/

v 1: recall knowledge from memory; have a recollection; "I can't remember saying any such thing"; "I can't think what her last name was"; "can you remember her phone number?" "Do you remember that he once loved you?"; "call up memories" [syn: remember, retrieve, call back, call up, recollect, remind, think] [ant: forget] 2: go back to something earlier; "This harks back to a previous remark of his" [syn: hark back, return, come back] 3: call to mind; "His words echoed John F. Kennedy" [syn: echo] 4: summon to return; "The ambassador was recalled to his country" 5: cause one's (or someone else's) thoughts or attention to return from a reverie or digression; "She was recalled by a loud laugh" 6: make unavailable; bar from sale or distribution; "The company recalled the product when it was found to be faulty" [ant: issue] 7: cause to be returned; "recall the defective auto tires"; The manufacturer tried to call back the

spoilt yogurt" [syn: call in, call back, withdraw]

recess

/'ɹisɛs/

n 1: a state of abeyance or suspended business [syn: deferral] 2: a small concavity [syn: recession, niche, corner] 3: an arm off of a larger body of water (often between rocky headlands) [syn: inlet] 4: an enclosure that is set back or indented [syn: niche] 5: a pause from doing something (as work); "we took a 10-minute break"; "he took time out to recuperate" [syn: respite, break, time out]

/ɹɪ'sɛs/

v 1: put into a recess; "recess lights" 2: make a recess in; "recess the piece of wood" 3: close at the end of a session; "The court adjourned" [syn: adjourn, break up]

recoil

/'ɹikɔɪl/

n 1: the backward jerk of a gun when it is fired [syn: kick] 2: a movement back from an impact [syn: repercussion, rebound, backlash]

/ɹɪ'kɔɪl/

v 1: draw back, as with fear [syn: flinch, squinch, funk, cringe, shrink, wince, quail] 2: spring back; spring away from an impact; "The rubber ball bounced"; "These particles do not resile but they unite after they collide" [syn: bounce, resile, take a hop, spring, bound, rebound, ricochet] 3: spring back, as from a forceful thrust; "The gun kicked back into my shoulder" [syn: kick back, kick]

record

/'ɹɛkᵊɹd/

adj : best of its kind on record; "in record time"

n 1: anything (such as a document or a phonograph record or a photograph) providing permanent evidence of or information about past events; "the film provided a valuable record of stage techniques" 2: the number of wins versus losses and ties a team has had; "at 9-0 they have the best record in their league" 3: an extreme attainment; the best (or worst) performance ever attested (as in a sport); "he tied the Olympic record"; "coffee production last year broke all previous records"; "Chicago set the homicide record" 4: sound recording consisting of a disc with continuous grooves; formerly used to reproduce music by rotating while a phonograph needle tracked in the grooves [syn: phonograph record, phonograph recording, disk, disc, platter] 5: the sum of recognized accomplishments; "the lawyer has a good record" [syn: track record] 6: a list of crimes for which an accused person

HETERONYMS

has been previously convicted; "he ruled that the criminal record of the defendant could not be disclosed to the court"; "the prostitute had a record a mile long" [syn: criminal record] 7: a compilation of the known facts regarding something or someone; "Al Smith used to say, 'Let's look at the record'"; "his name is in all the record books" [syn: record book, book] 8: a document that can serve as legal evidence of a transaction; "they could find no record of the purchase"

/ɹɪˈkɔɹd/

v 1: make a record of; set down in permanent form [syn: enter, put down] 2: register electronically [syn: tape] [ant: erase] 3: indicate a certain reading; of gauges and instruments; "The thermometer showed thirteen degrees below zero"; "The gauge read 'empty'" [syn: read, register, show] 4: be aware of [syn: register] 5: be a memorial to a person or an event; "This sculpture commemorates the victims of the concentration camps" [syn: commemorate, memorialize, immortalize]

recount
/ˈɹikaʊnt/

n : an additional (usually a second) count; especially of the votes in a close election

/ɹiˈkaʊnt/

v 1: narrate or give a detailed account of; "Tell what happened"; "The father told a story to his child" [syn: tell, narrate, spin, recite] 2: count again; "We had to recount all the votes after an accusation of fraud was made"

recreation
/ˌɹɛkɹiˈeɪʃɪn/

n : an activity that diverts or amuses or stimulates [syn: diversion]

/ˈɹikɹieɪʃɪn/

n : the act of creating again [syn: re-creation]

redress
/ˈɹidɹɛs/

n 1: a sum of money paid in compensation for loss or injury [syn: damages, amends, indemnity, indemnification, restitution] 2: act of correcting an error or a fault or an evil [syn: remedy, remediation]

/ɹiˈdɹɛs/

v : make reparations or amends for; "right a wrong" [syn: right, compensate, correct] [ant: wrong]

refill
/ˈɹifɪl/

n 1: a prescription drug that is provided again; "he got a refill of his prescription"; "the prescription specified only one refill" 2: a commercial product that refills a container with its appropriate contents; "he got a refill for his ball-point pen"; "he got a refill for his notebook"

/ɹiˈfɪl/

v : fill something that had previously been emptied; "refill my glass, please" [syn: replenish, fill again]

reflex
/ˈɹiflɛks/

adj : (physiology) without volition or conscious control; "the automatic shrinking of the pupils of the eye in strong light"; "a reflex knee jerk"; "sneezing is reflexive" [syn: automatic, reflexive]

n : an automatic instinctive unlearned reaction to a stimulus [syn: instinctive reflex, innate reflex, inborn reflex, unconditioned reflex, physiological reaction]

v 1: To bend, turn back, or reflect 2: cause to undergo a reflex process

refund
/ˈɹifʌnd/

n 1: money returned to a payer 2: the act of returning money received previously [syn: repayment]

/ɹɪˈfʌnd/

v : pay back; "Please refund me my money" [syn: return, repay, give back]

refuse
/ɹɪˈfuəz/ or /ɹɪˈfuəs/

v 1: show unwillingness towards [syn: decline] [ant: accept] 2: refuse to accept; "He refused my offer of hospitality" [syn: reject, pass up, turn down, decline] [ant: accept] 3: elude, esp. in a baffling way; "This behavior defies explanation" [syn: defy, resist] [ant: lend oneself] 4: refuse to let have; "She denies me every pleasure"; "he denies her weekly allowance" [syn: deny] [ant: allow] 5: refuse entrance or membership; "They turned away hundreds of fans"; "Black people were often rejected by country clubs" [syn: reject, turn down, turn away] [ant: admit]

/ˈɹɛfuəz/ or /ɹɛˈfuəs/

n : food that is discarded (as from a kitchen) [syn: garbage, food waste, scraps]

regress
/ˈɹigɹɛs/

n 1: the reasoning involved when you assume the conclusion is true and reason backward to the evidence [syn: reasoning backward] 2: returning to a former state [syn: regression, reversion, retrogression, retroversion]

/ɹiˈgɹɛs/

v 1: go back to a statistical means 2: go back to a previous state; "We reverted to the old rules" [syn: revert, return, retrovert, turn back] 3: get worse; fall back to a previous or worse condition [syn: retrograde, retrogress] [ant: progress] 4: go back to bad behavior; "Those who recidivate are often minor criminals" [syn:

HETERONYMS

relapse, lapse, recidivate, retrogress, fall back]

reject
/'ɹidʒɛkt/

n : the person or thing rejected or set aside as inferior in quality [syn: cull]

/ɹi'dʒɛkt/

v 1: refuse to accept or acknowledge; "I reject the idea of starting a war"; "The journal rejected the student's paper" [ant: accept] 2: refuse to accept; "He refused my offer of hospitality" [syn: refuse, pass up, turn down, decline] [ant: accept] 3: refuse to approve; "I disapprove of her child rearing methods" [syn: disapprove] [ant: approve] 4: reject with contempt; "She spurned his advances" [syn: spurn, freeze off, scorn, pooh-pooh, disdain, turn down] 5: refuse entrance or membership; "They turned away hundreds of fans"; "Black people were often rejected by country clubs" [syn: turn down, turn away, refuse] [ant: admit] 6: dismiss from consideration; "John was ruled out as a possible suspect because he had a strong alibi"; "This possibility can be eliminated from our consideration" [syn: rule out, eliminate]

rejoin
/ɹi'dʒɔɪn/

v 1: join again; "I'll rejoin the party later."

/ɹi'dʒɔɪn/

v : answer back; "You should rejoin his nasty remark." [syn: retort, come back, repay, return, riposte]

relay
/ɹi'leɪ/

v: to put down again; such as carpeting [syn: re-install]

/'ɹileɪ/

n 1: the act of relaying something 2: electrical device such that current flowing through it in one circuit can switch on and off a current in a second circuit [syn: electrical relay] 3: a team race

/ɹɪ'leɪ/

v 1: pass along; "Please relay the news to the villagers" 2: control or operate by relay

rerun
/ɹi'ɹʌn/

v 1: repeat a film or a TV show [syn: rebroadcast] 2: rerun a performance of a play, for example 3: run again for office: "The governor wants to rerun in 2004" 4: cause to perform again; "We have to rerun the subjects--they misunderstood the instructions"

/'ɹiɹʌn/

n : a program that is broadcast again; "she like to watch `I love Lucy' reruns"

resent
/ɹi'zɛnt/

v 1: feel bitter or indignant about; "She resents being paid less than her co-workers" 2: wish ill or allow unwillingly [syn: begrudge] [ant: wish]

/'ɹisɛnt/

v : (past of resent) : sent again; "The package was resent after being returned for insufficient postage."

reside
/ɹi'zaɪd/

v 1: make one's home or live in; "There are only 250,000 people in Iceland"; "I live in a 200-year old house"; "These people inhabited all the islands that are now deserted"; "The plains are sparsely populated" [syn: dwell, shack, live, inhabit, people, populate] 2: live (in a certain place) [syn: occupy, lodge in] 3: be inherent or innate in; [syn: rest, repose]

/'ɹisaɪd/

v : replace siding on a building

resign
/ɹi'zaɪn/

v 1: leave voluntarily; of a job, post or position; "She vacated the position when she got pregnant" [syn: vacate, renounce, give up] 2: accept as inevitable; "He resigned himself to his fate" [syn: reconcile, submit]

/ɹi'saɪn/

v : sign again; "You need to resign the modified contract." [syn: re-sign]

resume
/ɹi'zum/

v 1: take up or begin anew; "We resumed the negotiations" [syn: restart] 2: return to a previous location or condition: "The painting resumed its old condition when we restored it" [syn: take up] 3: assume anew; "resume a title"; "resume an office"; "resume one's duties" 4: give a summary (of); "he summed up his results" [syn: sum up, summarize, reiterate]

/ˈɹɛzumeɪ/ (actually spelled resumé)

n 1: short descriptive summary (of events) [syn: sketch, survey] 2: a summary of your academic and work history [syn: résumé, resumé, curriculum vitae, CV]

retard
/'ɹitaɹd/

n : (condescending) a person of subnormal intelligence [syn: idiot, imbecile, cretin, moron, changeling, half-wit]

/ɹɪ'taɪd/

v 1: slow the growth or development of [syn: check] 2: cause to move more slowly or operate at a slower rate; "This drug will retard your heart rate" 3: lose velocity; move more slowly; "The car decelerated" [syn: decelerate, slow, slow down, slow up] [ant: accelerate]

HETERONYMS

retort
/'ɪtɔɪt/

n 1: a quick reply to a question or remark (especially a witty or critical one); "it brought a sharp rejoinder from the teacher" [syn: rejoinder, return, riposte, comeback] 2: a vessel where substances are distilled or decomposed by heat

/ʌɪ'tɔɪt/

v : answer back [syn: come back, repay, return, riposte, rejoin]

retread
/'ɹitɹɛd/

n : a used automobile tire that has been remolded to give it new treads [syn: recap]

/ɹi'tɹɛd/

v 1: use again in altered form; "retread an old plot" [syn: rework, make over] 2: give new treads to (a tire) [syn: remold]

rewrite
/'ɹiɹaɪt/

n : something that has been written again; "the rewrite was much better" [syn: revision, rescript]

/ri: 'rait/

v 1: write differently; alter the writing of; "The student rewrote his thesis" 2: rewrite so as to make fit to suit a new or different purpose; "re-write a play for use in schools"

row
/ɹoʊ/

n 1: an arrangement of objects or people side by side in a line: "a row of chairs" 2: a long continuous strip (usually running horizontally); "a mackerel sky filled with rows of clouds"; "rows of barbed wire protected the trenches" 3: a layer of masonry; "a course of bricks" [syn: course] 4: a linear array of numbers side by side 5: a continuous chronological succession without an interruption; "they won the championship three years in a row" 6: the act of rowing as a sport [syn: rowing]

v : propel with oars; "row the boat"; down the lake"

/ɹaʊ/

n: an angry dispute; "they had a quarrel"; "they had words" [syn: quarrel, wrangle, words, run-in, dustup]

rugged
/'ʌɡɪdə/

adj 1: sturdy and strong in constitution or construction; enduring; "a rugged trapper who spent months in the wilderness"; "those that survive are stalwart rugged men"; "with a house full of boys you have to have rugged furniture" [ant: delicate] 2: topographically very uneven; "broken terrain"; "rugged ground" [syn: broken] 3: rocky and steep [syn: craggy] 4: very difficult; severely testing stamina or resolution; "a rugged competitive examination"; "the rugged conditions of frontier life"; "the competition was tough"; "it's a tough life"; "it was a tough job" [syn: tough]

/ʌgd/

adj : being covered with a rug [syn: carpeted]

sake
/seɪk/

n 1: a reason for wanting something done; "for your sake"; "died for the sake of his country"; "in the interest of safety"; "in the common interest" [syn: interest] 2: the purpose of achieving or obtaining; "for the sake of argument"

/'saki/

n : Japanese beverage from fermented rice usually served hot [syn: saki]

separate
/'sɛpəɹeɪt/

v 1: act as a barrier between; stand between; "The mountain range divides the two countries" [syn: divide] 2: force, take, or pull apart; "He separated the fighting children" [syn: disunite, divide, part] 3: mark as different; "We distinguish several kinds of maple" [syn: distinguish, differentiate, secern, secernate, severalize, tell, tell apart] 4: separate into parts or portions; "divide the cake into three equal parts"; "The British carved up the Ottoman Empire after World War I" [syn: divide, split, split up, disserver, carve up] [ant: unite] 5: come apart; "The two pieces that we had glued separated" [syn: divide, part] 6: divide into components or constituents; "Separate the wheat from the chaff" 7: arrange or order by classes or categories; "How would you classify these pottery shards--are they prehistoric?" [syn: classify, class, sort, assort, sort out] 8: become separated into pieces or fragments; "The figurine broke"; "The freshly baked loaf fell apart" [syn: break, split up, fall apart, come apart] 9: make a division or separation [syn: divide] 10: discontinue an association or relation; go different ways; "The business partners broke over a tax question"; "The couple separated after 25 years of marriage"; "My friend and I split up" [syn: part, split up, split, break, break up] 11: go one's own away; move apart; "The friends separated after the party" [syn: part, split] 12: treat differently on the basis of sex or race [syn: discriminate, single out] 13: divide into two or more branches; "The road forks" [syn: branch, ramify, fork]

/'sɛpəɹɪt/

adj 1: independent; not united or joint; "a problem consisting of two separate issues"; "they went their separate ways";

"formed a separate church" [ant: joint] 2: individual and distinct; "pegged down each separate branch to the earth"; "a gift for every single child" [syn: single] 3: standing apart; not attached to or supported by anything; "a freestanding bell tower"; "a house with a separate garage" [syn: freestanding] 4: not living together as man and wife; "decided to live apart"; "maintaining separate households"; "they are separated" [syn: apart, separated] 5: characteristic of or meant for a single person or thing; "an individual serving"; "separate rooms"; "single occupancy"; "a single bed" [syn: individual, single] 6: separated according to race, sex, class, or religion; "separate but equal"; "girls and boys in separate classes" 7: have the connection undone; having become separate [syn: disjoined]

n 1: a separately printed article that originally appeared in a larger publication [syn: offprint, reprint] 2: a garment that can be purchased separately and worn in combinations with other garments

sewer
/'soʊʷ.ɹ/
n: someone who sews; "a sewer of fine gowns"
/'suːɹ/
n : a waste pipe that carries away sewage or surface water [syn: sewerage, cloaca]

shower
/'ʃaʊwʷ.ɹ/
n 1: a plumbing fixture that sprays water over you; "they installed a shower in the bathroom" 2: washing yourself in a shower; you stand upright under water sprayed from a nozzle; "he took a shower after the game" [syn: shower bath] 3: a brief period of precipitation; "the game was interrupted by a brief shower" [syn: rain shower] 4: a sudden downpour (as of tears or sparks etc) likened to a rain shower; "a little shower of rose petals" 5: a party of friends assembled to present gifts (usually of a specified kind) to a person; "her friends organized a baby shower for her when she was expecting"
v 1: expend profusely; also used with abstract nouns: "He was showered with praise" [syn: lavish] 2: spray or sprinkle with; "The guests showered rice on the couple" 3: take a shower; wash one's body in the shower; "You should shower after vigorous exercise" 4: rain abundantly; "Meteors showered down over half of Australia." [syn: shower down] 5: provide abundantly with; "He showered her with presents"
/'ʃoʊwʷ.ɹ/
n : someone who organizes an exhibit for others to see [syn: exhibitor, exhibitioner]

skied
/skiːd/
v : (past of ski) : "He successfully skied down the beginner's slope."
/skaɪd/
adj : "It was a darkly skied night as the thunder rumbled in the distance."
v : (past of sky) 1: hit or threw (a ball, for example) high in the air 2: hung (a painting, for example) high up on the wall, above the line of vision

slaver
/'sleɪv.ɹ/
n 1: a person (or ship) engaged in slave trade [syn: slave dealer, slave trader] 2: someone who owns slaves [syn: slaveholder, slave owner]
/'slav.ɹ/
v : let saliva drivel from the mouth; "The baby drooled" [syn: drivel, drool, slobber, dribble]

slough
/slʌf/
n 1: necrotic tissue; a mortified or gangrenous part or mass [syn: gangrene, sphacelus] 2: any outer covering that can be shed or cast off (such as the cast-off skin of a snake)
v 1: cast off hair, skin, horn, or feathers; of animals [syn: discard, shed, molt, exuviate] 2: plod through as through snow or mud
/slaʊ/
n 1: a hollow filled with mud 2: a state of moral degradation or spiritual dejection
/sluː/
n : a stagnant swamp (especially as part of a bayou)

sow
/saʊ/
n : an adult female hog
/soʊ/
v 1: place (seeds) in the ground for future growth; "She sowed sunflower seeds" [syn: sough, seed] 2: introduce into an environment; "sow suspicion or beliefs" [syn: sough] 3: place seeds in (the ground); "sow the ground with sunflower seeds" [syn: inseminate, sow in]

subject
/'sʌbdʒɛkt/
adj 1: not exempt from tax; "the gift will be subject to taxation" 2: being under the power or sovereignty of another or others; "subject peoples"; "a dependent prince" [syn: dependent]
n 1: the material of a conversation or discussion; "he didn't want to discuss that subject"; "it was a very sensitive topic"; "his letters were always on the theme of love" [syn: topic, theme] 2: some situation or event that is thought about; "he kept drifting off the topic";

HETERONYMS

"he had been thinking about the subject for several years"; "it is a matter for the police" [syn: topic, issue, matter]   3: a branch of knowledge; "in what discipline is his doctorate?"; "teachers should be well trained in their subject"; "anthropology is the study of human beings" [syn: discipline, subject area, subject field, field, field of study, study, bailiwick, branch of knowledge]   4: something (a person or object or scene) selected by an artist or photographer for graphic representation; "a moving picture of a train is more dramatic than a still picture of the same subject" [syn: content, depicted object]   5: a person who is subjected to experimental or other observational procedures; someone who is an object of investigation; "the subjects for this investigation were selected randomly"; "the cases that we studied were drawn from two different communities" [syn: case, guinea pig]   6: a person who owes allegiance to that nation; "a monarch has a duty to his subjects" [syn: national]   7: (linguistics) one of the two main constituents of a sentence; the grammatical constituent about which something is predicated   8: (logic) the first term of a proposition
/səbˈdʒɛkt/
v 1: cause to experience or suffer; "He subjected me to his awful poetry"; "The sergeant subjected the new recruits to many drills"   2: make accountable for; "He did not want to subject himself to the judgments of his superiors"   3: make vulnerable or liable to; "People in Chernobyl were subjected to radiation"   4: make liable; "This action may subject you to certain penalties"   5: make subservient; force to submit [syn: subjugate]

subordinate
/səˈbɔːdɪnɪt/
adj 1: lower in rank or importance [syn: low-level] [ant: dominant]   2: subject or submissive to authority or the control of another; "a subordinate kingdom" [ant: insubordinate]   3: (grammar) of a clause; unable to stand alone syntactically as a complete sentence; "a subordinate (or dependent) clause functions as a noun or adjective or adverb within a sentence" [syn: dependent] [ant: independent]   4: inferior in rank or status; "the junior faculty"; "a lowly corporal"; "petty officialdom"; "a subordinate functionary" [syn: junior-grade, inferior, lower, lower-ranking, lowly, petty, secondary, subaltern]
n 1: someone subject to the authority or control of another [syn: subsidiary, underling]   2: a word that is more specific than a given word [syn: hyponym, subordinate word]

/ˈsʌbɔːdɪnɛɪt/
v : rank as less important

survey
/ˈsəɹvɛɪ/
n 1: a detailed critical inspection [syn: study]   2: short descriptive summary (of events) [syn: sketch, resume]   3: the act of looking or seeing or observing; "he tried to get a better view of it"; "his survey of the battlefield was limited" [syn: view, sight]
/səˈɹvɛɪ/
v 1: consider in a comprehensive way; "He appraised the situation carefully before acting" [syn: appraise]   2: look over in a comprehensively, inspect; "He surveyed his new classmates"   3: keep under surveillance; "The police had been following him for weeks but they could not prove his involvement in the bombing" [syn: follow]   4: hold a review (of troops) [syn: review, go over]   5: make a survey of; for statistical purposes   6: plot a map of (land)

suspect
/ˈsʌspɛkt/
adj : (informal) not as expected; "there was something fishy about the accident"; "up to some funny business"; "some definitely queer goings-on"; "a shady deal"; "her motives were suspect"; "suspicious behavior" [syn: fishy, funny, queer, shady, suspicious]
n 1: someone who is under suspicion   2: a person or institution against whom an action is brought in a court of law; the person being sued or accused [syn: defendant] [ant: plaintiff]
/sʌˈspɛkt/
v 1: imagine to be true or to be the case; "I suspect that there is more to the story"   2: imagine to be true; "I suspect he is a fugitive" [syn: surmise]   3: regard as untrustworthy; regard with suspicion; have no faith or confidence in [syn: distrust, mistrust] [ant: trust, trust]   4: hold in suspicion; believe to be guilty   5: suspect to be false; "I distrust that man" [syn: distrust, doubt]   6: believe guilty

tarry
/ˈtɑɹi/
adj : having the characteristics of pitch or tar [syn: pitchy, resinous, resiny]
/ˈtæɹi/
v 1: be about; "The high school students like to loiter in the Central Square"; "Who is this man that is hanging around the department?" [syn: loiter, lounge, lollygag, loaf, hang around, mess about, linger, lurk, mill about, mill around]   2: leave slowly and hesitantly [syn: linger]

tear
/tiɹ/
n: a drop of the clear salty saline solution

secreted by the lachrymal glands; "his story brought tears to her eyes" [syn: teardrop]

v: fill with tears or shed tears; "Her eyes were tearing"

/tɛəɹ/

n 1: an opening made forcibly as by pulling apart; "there was a rip in his pants" [syn: rip, rent, split] 2: an occasion for excessive eating or drinking; "they went on a bust that lasted three days" [syn: bust, binge, bout] 3: the act of tearing; "he took the manuscript in both hands and gave it a mighty tear"

v 1: separate or cause to separate abruptly; "The rope snapped"; "tear the paper" [syn: rupture, snap, bust] 2: to separate or be separated by force; "planks were in danger of being torn from the crossbars." 3: move quickly and violently; "The car tore down the street"; "He came charging into my office" [syn: shoot, shoot down, charge, buck] 4: strip of feathers; "pull a chicken"; "pluck the capon" [syn: pluck, pull, deplume, deplumate, displume] 5: move precipitously or violently; "The tornado ripped along the coast" [syn: rip]

toots

/tuts/

n : (plu of toot) : blasts of a horn

v : (3rd pers sing of toot) : makes a loud noise; "The horns of the taxis blared" [syn: honks, blares, beeps, claxons]

/tʊts/

n : (slang) babe; sweetie

tower

/'taʊwəɹ/

n 1: a structure taller than its diameter; can stand alone or be attached to a larger building 2: anything tall and thin approximating the shape of a column or tower; "the test tube held a column of white powder"; "a tower of dust rose above the horizon"; "a thin pillar of smoke betrayed their campsite" [syn: column, pillar]

v : appear very large [syn: loom, hulk]

/'toʊwəɹ/

n : a powerful small boat designed to pull or push larger ships [syn: tugboat, tug, towboat]

transplant

/'tɹænspleənt/

n 1: (surgery) tissue or organ transplanted from a donor to a recipient; in some cases the patient can be both donor and recipient [syn: graft] 2: an operation moving an organ from one organism (the donor) to another (the recipient); "he had a kidney transplant" [syn: transplantation, organ transplant] 3: the act of uprooting and moving a plant to a new location; "the transplant was successful"; "too frequent transplanting is not good for plants" [syn: transplanting, transplantation]

/tɹɛəns'plɛənt/

v 1: lift and reset in another soil or situation; "Transplant the young rice plants" [syn: transfer] 2: be transplantable; "These delicate plants do not transplant easily" 3: place the organ of a donor into the body of a recipient [syn: graft] 4: transfer from one place or period to another; "The ancient Greek story was transplanted into Modern America" [syn: transfer, transpose]

transport

/'tɹænspɔɹt/

n 1: something that serves as a means of transportation [syn: conveyance] 2: an exchange of molecules (and their kinetic energy and momentum) across the boundary between adjacent layers of a fluid or across cell membranes 3: the commercial enterprise of transporting goods and materials [syn: transportation, shipping] 4: a state of being carried away by overwhelming emotion: "listening to sweet music in a perfect rapture"- Charles Dickens [syn: ecstasy, rapture, exaltation, raptus] 5: a mechanism that transport magnetic tape across the read/write heads of a tape playback/recorder [syn: tape drive, tape transport]

/tɹæn'spɔɹt/

v 1: move something or somebody around; usually over long distances 2: move while supporting, either in a vehicle or in one's hands or on one's body; "You must carry your camping gear"; "carry the suitcases to the car"; "This train is carrying nuclear waste"; "These pipes carry waste water into the river" [syn: carry] 3: hold spellbound [syn: enchant, enrapture, enthrall, ravish, enthral, delight] [ant: disenchant] 4: transport commercially [syn: send, ship] 5: send from one person or place to another; "transmit a message" [syn: transmit, transfer, channel, channelize]

upset

/'ʌpsɛt/

adj 1: afflicted with or marked by anxious uneasiness or trouble or grief; "too upset to say anything"; "spent many disquieted moments"; "distressed about her son's leaving home"; "lapsed into disturbed sleep"; "worried parents"; "a worried frown"; "one last worried check of the sleeping children" [syn: disquieted, distressed, disturbed, worried] 2: thrown into a state of disarray or confusion; "troops fleeing in broken ranks"; "a confused mass of papers on the desk"; "the small disordered room"; "with everything so upset" [syn: broken, confused, disordered] 3: used of an unexpected defeat of a team favored to win; "the Bills' upset victory over the Houston Oilers" 4: mildly physically distressed; "an upset stomach" 5: having been turned so that the bottom is no longer the bottom; "an overturned car"; "the upset pitcher of milk"; "sat on an upturned bucket" [syn: overturned, upturned]

n 1: an unhappy and worried mental state; "there was too much anger and disturbance"; "she didn't realize the upset she caused me" [syn: disturbance, perturbation] 2: the act of disturbing the mind or body; "his carelessness could have caused an ecological upset"; "she was unprepared for this sudden overthrow of their normal way of living" [syn: derangement, overthrow] 3: condition in which there is a disturbance of normal functioning; "the doctor prescribed some medicine for the disorder"; "everyone gets stomach upsets from time to time" [syn: disorder] 4: the act of upsetting something; "he was badly bruised by the upset of his sled at a high speed" [syn: overturn, turnover] 5: an improbable and unexpected victory; "the biggest upset since David beat Goliath" [syn: overturn]

/ʌp'sɛt/

v 1: disturb the balance or stability of; "The hostile talks upset the peaceful relations between the two countries" 2: cause to lose one's composure [syn: discompose, disconcert, discomfit] 3: move deeply; "This book upset me"; "A troubling thought" [syn: disturb, trouble] 4: cause to overturn from an upright or normal position; "The cat knocked over the flower vase"; "the clumsy customer turned over the vase" [syn: overturn, tip over, turn over, knock over, bowl over] 5: form metals with a swage [syn: swage] 6: defeat suddenly and unexpectedly; "The foreign team upset the local team"

use

/ʊəs/

n 1: the act of using; "the steps were worn from years of use" [syn: usage, utilization, employment, exercise] 2: a particular service; "he put his knowledge to good use"; "patrons have their uses" 3: what something is used for; "the function of an auger is to bore holes"; "ballet is beautiful but what use is it?" [syn: function, purpose, role] 4: (economics) the utilization of economic goods to satisfy needs or in manufacturing; "the consumption of energy has increased steadily" [syn: consumption, economic consumption, usance, use of goods and services] 5: a pattern of behavior acquired through frequent repetition; "she had a habit

twirling the ends of her hair"; "long use had hardened him to it" [syn: habit, wont] 6: (law) the exercise of the legal right to enjoy the benefits of owning property; "we were given the use of his boat" [syn: enjoyment] 7: exerting shrewd or devious influence especially for one's own advantage; "his manipulation of his friends was scandalous" [syn: manipulation]

/ʊəz/

v 1: put into service; make work or employ (something) for a particular purpose or for its inherent or natural purpose: "use your head!"; "we only use Spanish at home"; "I can't make use of this tool"; "Apply a magnetic field here"; "This thinking was applied to many projects"; "How do you utilize this tool?"; "I apply this rule to get good results"; "use the plastic bags to store the food"; "He doesn't know how to use a computer" [syn: utilize, apply, employ] 2: take or consume (regularly); "She uses drugs rarely" 3: seek or achieve an end by using to one's advantage; "She uses her influential friends to get jobs"; "The president's wife used her good connections" 4: use up, consume fully; " The legislature expended its time on school questions." [syn: expend] 5: avail oneself to; "apply a principle"; "practice a religion"; "use care when going down the stairs"; "use your common sense"; "practice non-violent resistance" [syn: practice, apply] 6: habitually do something (use only in the past tense); "She used to call her mother every week but now she calls only occasionally"; "I used to get sick when I ate in that dining hall"; "They used to vacation in the Bahamas"

viola

/'vioʊlə/

n: a bowed stringed instrument slightly larger than a violin, tuned a fifth lower

/'vaɪoʊlə/

n 1: any of the numerous plants of the genus Viola 2: large genus of flowering herbs of temperate regions [syn: Viola, genus Viola]

wicked

/'wɪkɛd/

adj 1: morally bad in principle or practice [ant: virtuous] 2: having committed unrighteous acts; "a sinful person" [syn: sinful, unholy] 3: intensely or extremely bad or unpleasant in degree or quality; "severe pain"; "a severe case of flu"; "a terrible cough"; "under wicked fire from the enemy's guns"; "a wicked cough" [syn: severe, terrible] 4: morally bad or wrong; "evil purposes"; "an evil influence"; "evil deeds" [syn: evil] [ant: good] 5: highly offensive; arousing aversion or disgust; "a

HETERONYMS

disgusting smell"; "distasteful language"; "a loathsome disease"; "the idea of eating meat is repellent to me"; "revolting food"; "a wicked stench" [syn: disgusting, disgustful, distasteful, foul, loathly, loathsome, repellent, repellant, repelling, revolting, yucky]

ww/wɪkt/

v : (past of wick) conveyed by capillary action: water gradually wicked up through the bricks

wind
/waɪnd/

v 1: to move or cause to move in a sinuous, spiral, or circular course; "the river winds through the hills"; "the path meanders through the vineyards"; "sometimes, the gout wanders through the entire body" [syn: weave, thread, meander, wander] 2: extend in curves and turns; "The road winds around the lake" [syn: curve] 3: wrap or coil around; "roll your hair around your finger"; "Twine the thread around the spool" [syn: wrap, roll, twine] [ant: unwind] 4: catch the scent of; get wind of; "The dog nosed out the drugs" [syn: scent, nose] 5: of springs [syn: wind up] 6: form into a wreath [syn: wreathe] 7: raise or haul up with or as if with mechanical help; "hoist the bicycle onto the roof of the car" [syn: hoist, lift] 8: tighten the spring of (a mechanisms); wind up the toy" [syn: wind up]

/wɪnd/

n 1: air moving (sometimes with considerable force) from an area of high pressure to an area of low pressure; "trees bent under the fierce winds"; "when there is no wind, row" 2: a tendency or force that influences events; "the winds of change" 3: breath; "the collision knocked the wind out of him" 4: empty rhetoric or insincere or exaggerated talk; that's a lot of wind"; "don't give me any of that jazz" [syn: idle words, jazz, nothingness] 5: an indication of potential opportunity; "he got a tip on the stock market"; "a good lead for a job" [syn: tip, lead, steer, confidential information, hint] 6: a musical instrument in which the sound is produced by an enclosed column of air that is moved by the breath [syn: wind instrument] 7: a reflex that expels intestinal gas through the anus [syn: fart, farting, flatus, breaking wind] 8: the act of winding or twisting; "he put the key in the old clock and gave it a good wind" [syn: winding, twist]

wound
/wund/

n 1: any break in the skin or an organ caused by violence or surgical incision [syn: lesion] 2: a casualty to military personnel resulting from combat [syn: injury, combat injury] 3: the act of inflicting a wound [syn: wounding]

v 1: cause injuries or bodily harm to [syn: injure] 2: hurt the feelings of; "She hurt me when she did not include me among her guests"; "This remark really bruised me ego" [syn: hurt, injure, bruise, offend, spite]

/waʊnd/

adj : put in a coil; coiled up

v : (past of wind) "He wound the rope around the post."

www.ingramcontent.com/pod-product-compliance
Lightning Source LLC
Chambersburg PA
CBHW060614290326
41930CB00051B/1661